What the Bible teaches

JOSHUA JUDGES and RUTH

RITCHIE OLD TESTAMENT COMMENTARIES

What the Bible teaches

JOSHUA

S. Grant

EDITOR **D. E. WEST**

JUDGES

C. T. Lacey

EDITOR **D. E. WEST**

RUTH

J. M. Flanigan

EDITOR **W. S. STEVELY**

ISBN-13: 978 1 904064 86 2
ISBN-10: 1 904064 86 8

WHAT THE BIBLE TEACHES

40 Beansburn, Kilmarnock, Scotland

www.ritchiechristianmedia.co.uk

Typeset by John Ritchie Ltd.
Printed by Bell & Bain Ltd., Glasgow.

PREFACE

The publishers have commissioned this Old Testament series of commentaries to complement the completed set of New Testament commentaries issued under the general title "What the Bible Teaches". Together they seek to provide an accessible and useful tool for the study of, and meditation on, Scripture.

While there is no shortage of commentaries currently available on the various books of the Old Testament it was felt that there was no complete series that sought simply to apply the message of Genesis through to Malachi to the concerns of believers today.

The authors of these volumes are not scholars of the original languages and rely on others for guidance on the best modern views of word meanings and similar matters. However, all the authors share the conviction that the Bible in its entirety is the Word of God. They believe it to be reliable, accurate, and intended "for our learning" (Rom 15.4). This view has been explained further by Mr Stevely in a short series of articles that appeared in "The Believer's Magazine", also published by John Ritchie Ltd., in 1999.

The two Testaments fit together so that principles and illustrations from the Old are brought to bear on issues that arise on nearly every page of the New. Knowledge of the Old is therefore an indispensable aid to the proper understanding of the New. In particular the Lord Jesus can be seen in prophecy and picture again and again. He, Himself, as described in the Gospels, is an exemplar of this approach to the Old Testament through His constant reference to people and incidents whose histories are recorded for us, and to those prophetic statements that applied to Him.

Given this understanding of the nature and purpose of the Scriptures, the main lessons of the books are considered and applied to our circumstances today by authors experienced in preaching and teaching the Word of God.

Since no attempt is being made to produce an academic series the technical apparatus has been kept to a minimum. Where authors have judged it of value attention is drawn to linguistic and other issues. Transliteration, where appropriate, is accompanied by reference to the numerical system devised by Strong to allow the reader without knowledge of the original languages to gain access to the various lexical aids which have adopted this system. For clarity, numerical references to New Testament words only are given in italics, following the practice used in Strong's Concordance.

The system of transliteration generally used is that adopted by the *Theological Wordbook of the Old Testament* (TWOT), edited by Harris, Archer and Waltke, and published by Moody Press, Chicago, 1980. However, there are occasions when account has been taken of the commonly recognised English spelling of some Hebrew words.

References to Scripture without attribution are taken from the Authorised (King James) Version. Where other translations are quoted the source is indicated.

Biblical measurements are usually given in cubits. For ease of calculation the general assumption has been adopted that 1 cubit = 18 inches/46cms.

Since the commentaries do not necessarily follow a verse-by-verse approach, and to save space and cost, the text of Scripture is not included. It is assumed that all readers have available a copy of the Bible.

The complete Old Testament is expected to be covered in around fifteen to eighteen volumes. These will not appear in the order in which they are found in the Scriptures but simply in order of completion by the authors commissioned for the series.

W.S. STEVELY
D.E. WEST

CONTRIBUTORS

STEPHEN GRANT – Joshua

Stephen Grant was saved early in life, and as a teenager was baptised and received into assembly fellowship. At school, as a student at Dundee University and later while working as a solicitor he was active in the work of his local assembly and in the study of the Scriptures. Increasingly busy in serving the Lord in teaching and preaching around Scotland he left his secular employment in 1998 to give himself full-time to the Lord's work. Stephen has been much used of the Lord around the United Kingdom. While his ministry has proved highly acceptable to all ages he has, as a young man himself, a particularly valuable rapport with young people and has been an able communicator of 'sound doctrine' to many of them. He has contributed to the Believer's Magazine but this is his first major written work.

COLIN LACEY – Judges

Colin Lacey was born into a christian home in Sussex, saved at the age of fifteen, baptised, and received into fellowship in the assembly at Haywards Heath. He was head teacher of a large secondary school in the West Midlands for fourteen years and currently works part-time, training and assessing aspiring head teachers for the National Headship Qualification. He is an elder in the assembly at Stourbridge, and travels widely throughout the UK teaching the Word of God. He has a particular interest in working with and encouraging young people. He acknowledges his indebtedness to the faithful support of his wife, Alison, in the writing of this commentary and in the other aspects of his ministry.

JIM M. FLANIGAN – Ruth

Jim Flanigan had the great privilege of being raised in a Christian home in Northern Ireland. He was saved as a young man and received into the Parkgate Assembly, Belfast in 1946. In 1972 he resigned from full-time employment in response to the call of God to give more of his time to the work of the Lord. Most of this has been in ministering the Word of God, bringing before the Lord's people the unique glories of the Person of Christ. This ministry has resulted in him travelling widely in the British Isles, the USA, Canada, Australia and Israel, in the last of which he maintains a special interest. Jim has brought to his growing written ministry his own delightful style which is orderly, accurate, and Christ-centred. This latest work continues to express these features.

ABBREVIATIONS

ASV	American Standard Version (the American variant of the RV)
AV	Authorised Version (known in USA as King James Version)
JFB	Jamieson, Fausset and Brown's *Commentary on the Whole Bible*
JND	New Translation by J.N. Darby
JPS	Jerusalem Publication Society Old Testament
NAS	New American Standard Version
NIV	New International Version
NKJV	New King James Version
RSV	Revised Standard Version (Revision of the ASV)
RV	Revised Version, 1885 (published in England, Revision of the AV)
Septuagint	The ancient translation of the AV into Greek. Often quoted in the New Testament
TWOT	*Theological Wordbook of the Old Testament*, edited by Harris, Archer and Waltke
YLT	Young's Literal Translation

JOSHUA

S. Grant

CONTENTS

BIBLIOGRAPHY

Gaebelein, Arno C. *The Annotated Bible Volume 2 – Joshua.* New Jersey: Loizeaux Brothers, 1979.
A very readable, if somewhat brief, commentary.

Gill, John. *Expositor*: The modernised version of Gill's Expositor is copyrighted by Larry Pierce, 1994-1995.
The electronic version of John Gill's Expositor is included in most Bible software programs, including the widely used Online Bible. The language has been updated for readability since the original work was published in 1809.

Henry, Matthew. *Commentary on the Whole Bible, Complete and Unabridged, Volume 2 – Joshua*. Hendrickson Publishers, 1991.
Informative but written in the early 18th Century and requires application and patience.

Howard, David M. Jnr. *The New American Commentary, Volume 5 – Joshua*. Nashville, Tennessee: Broadman & Holman Publishers, 1998.
A helpful commentary which is based on the NIV text and contains extensive thematic excursi.

Huffman, John. *Mastering the Old Testament, Volume 6 – Joshua.* USA: Word Publishing, 1986.
Some interesting practical applications.

Jamieson, Fausset and Brown. *A Commentary on the Whole Bible*. USA: Zondervan Publishing House, 1871.
A valuable section of this complete commentary on the Bible which provides reliable comment.

Keil, C. F. & Delitzsch, F. *Commentary on the Old Testament, Volume 2 - Joshua*. Massachusetts: Hendrickson Publishers, Inc., 1996.
This book forms part of an excellent series which would assist any serious study of the Old Testament. It provides detailed information and comment on geography and language, together with exposition of the text. The only difficulty is that Hebrew words are presented in Hebrew text, which can cause difficulty for the reader.

MacDonald, William. *Believer's Bible Commentary, Old Testament.* USA: Thomas Nelson Publishers, 1992.
A very brief overview of Joshua.

MacLear, G. F. *The Cambridge Bible for Schools and Colleges, The Book of Joshua*. London: C. J. Clay and Sons, 1888.
A small and sometimes technical work which is useful as an additional geographical and reference source.

Pink A. W. *Gleanings in Joshua*. Chicago: Moody Press, 1964.
Although it requires to be studied with care, this book makes extensive applications of the text which are well worth reading.

Woudstra, Martin H. *New International Commentary on the Old Testament – Book of Joshua.* Grand Rapids, Michigan: Wm. B. Eerdmans Publishing Co., 1981.
Some readers may find this book too academic in its approach. It sets out sound arguments for conservative dating and authorship.

INTRODUCTION

Introductory Remarks

From Sunday School days, Joshua's name is linked with the spectacular fall of Jericho's walls. It was not the first, nor would it be the last, occasion that God intervened in a miraculous way under Joshua's leadership to bring victory to the children of Israel. The book of Joshua also records the crossing of the River Jordan, and the sun brought to a standstill at the battle of Gibeon. The children of Israel experienced wonderful times of blessing and victory under the leadership of Joshua.

It would be a mistake to assume that the book consists entirely of exciting battles and tales of conquest. In fact, there is very little detail given of the battles which Israel fought. The emphasis in the narrative is on their dependence upon God and His interventions which brought victory.

The book opens with the issue of leadership. Moses had died and the Lord instructed Joshua to take his place and lead the people. In obedience to the Lord, they crossed the River Jordan and began many years of conquest. Events which took place at the River Jordan, Jericho, Ai, and Gibeon, are commented upon at length, whereas others, such as the military campaigns in the south and north of the land, are not. When it is borne in mind that the book is not a detailed, chronological account of Israel's conquest of Canaan, the spiritual significance of the incorporation of certain events and details, at the expense of others, becomes clearer. Themes such as leadership, obedience, faithfulness, and complacency, are strongly developed throughout the book.

The overall impression of the book is one of success. Obstacles are overcome, battles are won, nations are defeated and land is occupied. There were failures along the way, with Ai perhaps being the most notable. Notwithstanding the failures, Joshua carried out his task in leading the nation into the land and, with God's help, subdued it.

The most difficult chapters of the book to read, and from which to gain spiritual benefit, are those dealing with the distribution of land among the tribes of Israel. There is a repetitive style of narrative and concentration of geographical detail which is not easy for the reader. When commenting upon these sections, an effort has been made to bring practical lessons from the detail. Some of the city lists and boundaries are not commented upon for fear of imposing forced applications upon the text. It must be remembered that these sections of the book, which may seem tedious to the Christian, were of great significance to the Israelite; they were the title deeds to his inheritance. The detail is recorded to mark the accurate fulfilment of the Lord's promises to Israel.

The Pentateuch looked forward to Israel's occupation of the promised land. The book of Judges is a sad record of failure and defeat within the land. The book of Joshua links the themes of promise and failure. In the success of victory and the enjoyment of the Lord's promise there were the seeds of failure and defeat. As the book comes to an end the progress of conquest stopped and the people were content to dwell among the ungodly nations which dwelt in Canaan, thus sowing the seeds of defeat which were reaped during the times of the judges.

Authorship and Date of Writing

The author of the book is not revealed in Scripture and therefore cannot be stated with any certainty. An examination of the book reveals a possible combination of authors. Parts of the book are directly attributed to Joshua (8.32; 24.26) and there are what reads like eyewitness accounts, especially in chs. 5-6, with the use of "we" and "us" (5.1, 6). The latter parts of the Book appear to have been written by a contemporary of Joshua. Rahab was still alive (6.25); the Jebusites occupied Jerusalem (15.8); the temple had not been built (9.27); the relocation of Dan (19.40) and death of Joshua (24.29-32) are recorded. Woudstra comments, "Could not the view of history developed in Joshua have been the product of the days in which Israel, according to the book's own testimony, 'served the Lord' (24.31), i.e., in the days of Joshua himself and of the elders who outlived him? The spirit of joyful optimism which pervades the book by and large could perhaps be accounted for best by that assumption".

OUTLINE OF THE BOOK

CHAPTERS 1-5

Ch.1.1-9:	Joshua charged as Moses' successor
Ch.1.10-18:	Preparation for crossing Jordan
Ch.2:	Spies in Canaan
Chs.3-4:	Crossing Jordan
Ch.5:	Pre-conquest preparations.

CHAPTERS 6-12

Ch.6:	Jericho destroyed
Ch.7:	Failure at Ai
Ch.8.1-29:	The capture of Ai
Ch.8.30-35:	The covenant reaffirmed
Ch.9:	The Gibeonites
Ch.10:	Southern Campaign
Ch.11.1-15:	Northern Campaign
Ch.11.16-23:	Summary of Joshua's conquest of the land
Ch.12:	List of conquered kings.

CHAPTERS 13-24

Ch.13.1-8a:	Command to divide the land
Ch.13.8b-33:	Distribution of land by Moses affirmed by Joshua
Ch.14.1-5:	Introduction to the division of land, West of Jordan
Ch.14.6-15.63:	Judah's inheritance
Chs.16-17:	Joseph's inheritance
Chs.18-19:	The other tribes' inheritance
Ch.20:	Cities of refuge
Ch.21:	Levitical cities
Ch.22:	Departure of trans-Jordan tribes
Ch.23:	Joshua's first farewell discourse
Ch.24.1-28:	Joshua's second farewell discourse
Ch.24.29-33:	Three burials.

JOSHUA 1

Verses 1-9: Joshua Charged as Moses' Successor

Verses 1-2: The Lord Commands Joshua

After the death of Moses (v.1)

Moses was dead. His death was as remarkable as his life and for thirty days Israel mourned (Deut 34.8). From the early days in Egypt and throughout the forty years of the wilderness journey, he had led the nation through times of rejoicing and rebellion, triumph and disaster, to the borders of the promised land. Like Enoch and Elijah, his body would remain undiscovered following his ascent of Mount Nebo and subsequent burial by God in the land of Moab (Deut 34.6).

There would never be another prophet like Moses. He is described as "the servant of the Lord" in v.1, a title which is used of him for the first time in Deuteronomy 34.5 and then thirteen times in this book. Apart from David (Ps 18.1; 36.1, where the title appears in the superscription of these Psalms), Joshua is the only other person in the Old Testament to have this title (24.29; Judg 2.8). Deuteronomy 34.10-12 sets out the uniqueness of Moses in his relationship with the Lord, together with his power before men and his authority as the leader of the nation of Israel. In speaking to the Lord face to face, in the great signs and miracles which he performed before Pharaoh and in the authority by which he led the nation of Israel for forty years through the wilderness, he was unique and Israel mourned his death.

The life and death of Moses were remarkable. However, the Spirit of God commences the book by setting the scene as being "after the death of Moses" (v.1). This in itself should be instructive for any generation in the service of God. Men and women are raised up by God to serve Him, and in due course that service comes to an end. Their influence and presence are missed, yet the work of God must go on. There is always an "*after*" to any servant of God. God's purpose and promises would not be thwarted by the failure of Moses, for, although he could not take Israel into the promised land, another man had been prepared by God for this task.

Joshua is introduced (v.1)

"The Lord spake unto Joshua the son of Nun, Moses' minister". Joshua was in a difficult position, with the shadow of Moses behind him and the conquest of Canaan before him. His name means "Jehovah saves" or "Jehovah delivers" (3091). It was changed by Moses from Oshea (Num 13.16), which means "salvation" or "deliverance" (1954). The addition of the title of Jehovah to his name is significant as this was the title of the Lord that was revealed to Moses at the burning bush (Ex 3.11-15), and is often associated with God's faithfulness and eternal existence. As the change of a name in the Bible usually indicates a change in the character of the person e.g. Jacob to Israel, Simon to Cephas, Saul to Paul, the maturing of Joshua is seen in this change of name. It is a sign of maturity not only to appreciate salvation but also to appreciate the God who saves. When he is mentioned in the New Testament his name is rendered "Jesus" (Acts 7.45; Heb 4.8), which is the same form as the name of the Lord Jesus.

The succession to Moses as the leader of the nation of Israel was not a contentious issue, with the only candidate being Joshua, the son of Nun. He is described as "Moses' minister" (8334), a description which is rendered as "Moses' attendant" (JND), or "assistant" (NKJV). When the relationship between Moses and the Lord is described, a slightly different word is employed by the Spirit of God to distinguish it from the relationship of Moses and Joshua. Moses was the "servant (5650) of the Lord" and although there is an overlap in the usage of the two words in the Old Testament, Moses was the bondservant of the Lord as opposed to Joshua who was Moses' minister. He had been well prepared for this day over a period of years and through many circumstances. He had gained the education and maturity, which were required for the task, as he served Moses and assisted him in the leadership of the nation through the wilderness years.

It is instructive to trace the references to Joshua in the Old Testament, prior to the death of Moses. The variety of circumstances and the lessons that he learned through them, mainly at the side of Moses, were vital for his development and preparation for this day. He had battled with Amalek in Rephidim (Ex 17.8-10) as one of Moses' young men, leading the army in the valley as Moses stood on the hill with the rod of God in his hand. As the servant of Moses he had stood at an altar and learned the meaning of the name "Jehovah-nissi" (3071), the Lord is my banner, "because the Lord hath sworn that the Lord will have war with Amalek from generation to generation" (Ex 17.16). He had risen up and accompanied Moses to Mount Sinai for the giving of the law (Ex 24.13) and when descending the mount had mistaken the sound of idolatry for the sound of war among the people (Ex 32.17). He had witnessed the dealings of Moses in the light of the nation's sin and his intercession in the tabernacle before the Lord, on behalf of the people (Ex 33.11). He also had searched the land and had had his report rejected by the people (Num 14). All of these lessons were learned over a period of time and through the difficulties of the wilderness and they remain important for any who seek to lead the people of God. These experiences helped to shape Joshua into the man that the Lord used in a mighty way. The lessons of subduing the flesh, valuing the Word of God, judging sin, interceding for a sinful people and coping with rejection are still vital for any leader to learn.

The choice of Joshua to succeed Moses and lead the nation into the promised land did not originate with Moses. It was not nepotism on the part of Moses and never should be when men and women of God are considering the future. When the Lord spoke to Moses and told him that he would not lead the nation into the promised land, he asked the Lord to appoint a man for the task (Num 27.15-23), that the nation be not "as sheep which have no shepherd" (v.17). In response, the Lord identified Joshua as the man that Moses had requested for the nation. He was set before Eleazar the priest and the congregation of Israel and Moses publicly identified him as his successor.

He had been called by the Lord to the task and identified by Moses in front of the nation as the man to lead (Deut 31). The people heard the words of Moses as he spoke to Joshua and assured him of the presence of the Lord. He had spent years as the servant of Moses and learned much about leadership. It is hardly surprising that when the time of mourning for Moses was past the people recognised Joshua as their leader as they "hearkened unto him, and did as the Lord commanded Moses" (Deut 34.9). Yet like many others, when the time came, it was only when the Lord spoke to Joshua that he moved into his sphere of service. Education in the service of God is important, as is maturity and acceptance among the people of God; however, it must be remembered that it is the word of God that is most important. God's word was that rock upon which Joshua could rest when difficulties arose. He would recall the day when the Lord had spoken to him and called him to the task, assuring him of His presence, power and victory. God's word remains the rock which any servant of God should value as being of the utmost importance if any service is to be undertaken for Him.

Joshua is instructed (v.2)

"Go over this Jordan". Joshua had been into Canaan before and the memories of that incursion must have been at the forefront of his mind. It had been a time of deep disappointment for Joshua as he and Caleb had brought back their report of the land after searching it for forty days. They had seen a land "flowing with milk and honey" yet occupied by fierce tribes, including the dreaded giants, the sons of Anak. With confidence in the Lord they had advised the people to commence the conquest, yet the people had listened to the ten spies who gave an evil report and dissuaded them from going into the land. Almost forty years had passed with Joshua and Caleb alone remaining of the men who turned back from Canaan. The promise of the Lord to them had been kept and they were finally to enjoy the promised land. It was a mark of the character of these men that when the nation had rebelled against the Lord and turned back from the land, they had followed them into the wilderness for forty years of discipline at the hand of the Lord. This example is consistent with the instruction of the Lord Jesus to the Christians in the seven assemblies of Revelation 2-3. Despite the evident sin and waywardness of some of the assemblies, the Lord did not instruct the believers who were faithful to Him to leave these assemblies but rather to remain and be overcomers in the circumstances. From Ephesus to Laodicea, the message was the same: to the overcomer there would be appropriate reward. Joshua, together with Caleb, had followed this course and now they were to enter into their reward.

"The land which I do give to them, even to the children of Israel." As the Lord commanded Joshua to lead the children of Israel in conquest over the Jordan and into the land, there was to be no doubt that the land was the gift of the Lord to the nation. They could not earn it in battle, neither were they inheriting it from their forefathers, it was the Lord who would give it to them as the fulfilment of the promise that He had first made to Abraham in Genesis 15 and then down through the generations of Israel's history. In this respect, Canaan is a picture of the heavenlies where, upon conversion, every spiritual blessing is received by every Christian (Eph 1.3).

The final point to notice in this opening section is that, although the leadership of the nation had changed following the death of Moses, the purpose of God for His people had not. It had been the purpose of God that Israel would come into Canaan (Ex 3.8). As a result of their disobedience, the people had wandered in the wilderness for forty years (Josh 14.10), but now they stood on the border of the land. The sin of the people, and even that of Moses which prevented him from leading the people into the land, could not disannul the promise of the Lord to His people and thwart His purpose. The blessings that God has given to every believer are in keeping with the example of His gift of Canaan to Israel, "for the gifts and calling of God are without repentance" (Rom 11.29). However, like Israel, a Christian can live without the enjoyment and full benefit of the blessings and promises, which were received upon conversion.

Verses 3-5: The Lord Encourages Joshua

When the Lord instructed Joshua to commence the conquest of Canaan, He reminded him that Caanan was a gift. However, He also brought to his attention the responsibility of the nation to go in and possess what they had been given. There is a parallel passage (Deut 11.24-25) where the same theme of responsibility and subsequent blessing is set out. This is still the way that God gives His blessings. They are given as a gift, yet they can only be enjoyed in the measure in which they are possessed. It is the principle of title and possession in operation. The Lord gave the title to the land to the nation, yet Israel would only gain the benefit and enjoyment of the land when they took occupation. If a person purchases a house, he receives title to the property. The enjoyment of the property is only experienced when he enters and takes possession. This is also true of the spiritual blessings which every believer received upon conversion (Eph 1.3). Christians have the blessings as a gift, yet do not gain the enjoyment and full benefit of these blessings unless they take possession of them and live them out in practice.

The two perspectives of the giving of the land to Israel can be seen in the verb forms employed by the Spirit of God, throughout the book. On occasions the "perfect" form of the verb "to give" occurs (1.3,14,15; 2.24; 13.8; 14.3; 18.3,7; 22.4,7; 23.13,15,16), indicating that the land had already been given to Israel. On other occasions the participle form of the verb is employed which does not indicate a specific time frame, but does denote an ongoing process (1.2,11,15), indicating that the giving of the land was yet to be accomplished.

Progressive occupation of the land (v.3)

"Every place that the sole of your foot shall tread upon". The Lord was giving Joshua the instruction to possess what He had given them, to take it and enjoy it. The possession of the land was to be a progressive occupation, which was in keeping with the promise of the Lord (Ex 23.29-30). The people of the land would not be driven out in one year as the land would become desolate and the beasts of the field would multiply against them. The gradual occupation would allow the children of Israel to multiply and be able to cultivate the land and preserve it from desolation.

No Christian can become spiritually mature overnight. As the children of Israel would occupy the land progressively, and in a manner which would allow them to take settled possession of what they were conquering, so the Christian's growth into spiritual maturity is a process which is gradual and likened to the development of a child into adulthood. Too much growth too soon for the believer usually leads to the problem of sustaining the growth that has taken place. It is better to conquer and consolidate for long-term gain.

The boundaries of the land (v.4)

"From the wilderness and this Lebanon even unto the great river, the river Euphrates, all the land of the Hittites, and unto the great sea toward the going down of the sun shall be your coast". The boundaries of the land to be conquered are given in this passage in an abbreviated form and are found in more detail in Numbers 34.3-12. This short description is also contained in the parallel passage of Deuteronomy 11.24 with a small difference in description as Keil & Delitzsch point out in their commentary on v.4: "The boundaries of the land are given as in Deuteronomy 11.24, with the simple difference in form, that the boundary line from the desert (of Arabia) and Lebanon, i.e. from the southern and northern extremity, is drawn first of all towards the east to the great river, the Euphrates, and then towards the west to 'the great sea, toward the going down of the sun,' i.e. the Mediterranean; and then between these two *termini ad quem* the more precise definition is inserted, 'all the land of the Hittites'; whereas in Deuteronomy the southern, northern, and eastern boundaries are placed in antithesis to the western boundary, and the more precise definition of the country to be taken is given by an enumeration of the different tribes that were to be destroyed by the Israelites (Deut 11.23)". It was only during the reigns of David and Solomon that the land came close to resembling this description.

Threefold encouragement for Joshua (v.5)
With the great responsibility of leadership resting upon his shoulders, the Lord encouraged Joshua. The promise of the Lord to the whole nation in the parallel passage of Deuteronomy 11.24-25, was now being given personally to Joshua. His need for encouragement would be no different from that of any other leader who feels the weight and magnitude of his responsibility before the Lord. It is one thing to anticipate serving God and sometimes another matter altogether when the reality of service is experienced. The weight of leadership rested upon Joshua and at this moment he heard the word of the Lord bringing encouragement and assurance. Leadership can be a lonely role in the service of God and great value should be placed upon the encouragement and assurance that the Word of God brings to those who serve as leaders among His people. Perhaps the saints of God would do well to learn the lesson that leaders require encouragement as well as those that are led by them.

"There shall not any man be able to stand before thee all the days of thy life". This first part of divine promise relates to the conflict that would form such an important part of the service into which the Lord had called Joshua. The promise of lifelong success in the conflict must have been of tremendous encouragement to him. It did not matter which tribe or nation would stand against the armies of Israel, they would not prevail. In this, as in so many other ways, Joshua is a picture of the Lord Jesus. As he stood on the banks of the Jordan with the conquest of Canaan before him, he was assured of complete success in the venture. No foe would be able to stand against him to thwart divine purpose. It was said of the Lord Jesus prophetically, "He shall not fail nor be discouraged" (Is 42.4); as the Servant of the Lord, He would not be diverted from fulfilling the divine purpose. The hostility or praise of men, the attacks of Satan and awfulness of Golgotha did not turn Him aside or cause Him to fail. With the determination of the bullock "he stedfastly set his face to go to Jerusalem" (Lk 9.51). He said, "The cup which my Father hath given me, shall I not drink it?" (Jn 18.11). With the complete assurance of fully accomplishing the purpose of God He approached Jerusalem: "The hour is come, that the Son of man should be glorified" (Jn 12.23). So it is that "this man, after he had offered one sacrifice for sins for ever, sat down on the right hand of God; from henceforth expecting till his enemies be made his footstool" (Heb 10.12-13).

"As I was with Moses, so I will be with thee". The Lord also gave Joshua the promise of His presence. As Joshua had companied with Moses in all the years of the wilderness journey, he had seen how the Lord had been with Moses and had manifested His power, compassion and wisdom that had been of such help to Moses as he led the people. Now the Lord was promising that, in the same way, He would be with Joshua, even although Joshua was not Moses and would never attain to the uniqueness of Moses (Deut 34.10-12). God is faithful to His servants and makes available the same resources of heaven to all who serve Him. There is no partiality with God in His service. It is the same Spirit who is the source of each spiritual gift. It is the same Lord whom each servant serves, no matter which gift is being exercised and it is the same God who brings the result from the exercise of the gift (1 Cor 12.4-6). In addition to spiritual gift, the vast, limitless riches of His grace and glory are freely available to the servant of God. A throne of grace, the indwelling Spirit of God and the Word of God are all available to all His servants. If failure does occur, it is not because of a lack of God-given resources.

"I will not fail thee, nor forsake thee". Joshua also received the assurance from the Lord that He would not abandon him, as he pursued the conquest of Canaan. The promise of the Lord's presence and help is also contained in the New Testament: "Let your conversation be without covetousness; and be content with such things as ye have: for he hath said, I will never leave thee, nor forsake thee" (Heb 13.5). The language is similar and gives wonderful encouragement to the Christian. In the context, the writer to the Hebrews is exhorting the believer to be content with such things as he has and gives the assurance of the presence and help of the Lord that will enable him to fulfil the exhortation regarding contentment. The Lord understood the need of His disciples to have His presence with them as they would go out into the world with the gospel. In the upper room, only a matter of hours before His suffering, He took the time to comfort them with the news that when He went to heaven another Comforter would come and abide with them for ever (Jn 14.16), and that, in this way, He would not leave them but would come to them (Jn 14.18). In the days after His resurrection, the Lord reassured the disciples of His continuing presence and extended it to all who would follow Him, to the end of the age (Mt 28.20).

Verses 6-9: The Lord Exhorts Joshua

In the previous section of the chapter, it was the Lord who was giving promises to Joshua, promises that had been given to the whole of Israel by Moses and were now made personal to Joshua by the Lord. However, these promises were not an invitation to Joshua to be complacent as he contemplated the service that lay before him, but rather would serve as an incentive to fulfil the obligations that the Lord now laid upon His servant. The intimacy and unique relationship that Moses had with the Lord had not annulled the obligations upon him, and so he died on the borders of Canaan because of his sin at Meribah-Kadesh (Deut 32.51-52). As the Lord had been with Moses, so He would be with Joshua and it was a stark lesson for the servant of God to learn, as obligation now followed promise.

This theme of promise and obligation is a common one throughout the Bible. Many of the New Testament epistles are structured with promises and blessings set out prior to obligation and exhortation. An appreciation of the blessings and promises of the Lord to the Christian brings encouragement and enables him to live out the obligations and exhortations set out in Scripture. One example of this structure is the Epistle to the Romans where for eleven chapters the apostle Paul gives an exposition of the gospel. On the basis of these eleven chapters he brings in the exhortation: "I beseech you therefore, brethren, by the mercies of God, that ye present your bodies a living sacrifice, holy, acceptable unto God, which is your reasonable service" (Rom 12.1). The mercies of God, as described in chs.1-11, provide a compelling incentive to implement this exhortation.

Strength and courage (v.6a)

Joshua was exhorted by the Lord to "be strong and of a good courage". Both of these attributes would be essential for the days ahead with battles to be fought, land and cities to be distributed and the administration of a nation to be faced. The exhortation occurs three times in this section (vv.6,7,9), as it does in the parallel section in Deuteronomy 31.6,7,23. Strength and courage in the face of the most intimidating circumstances will be drawn from the well of divine promise, which is why the exhortation follows the promises of vv.3-5.

The link between strength and courage is not isolated to this section of the Word of God. It also appears in Scripture when David charges Solomon with the task of building the temple (1 Chr 28.20), and by Hezekiah when the Assyrians were besieging Jerusalem (2 Chr 32.7). Strength should never be confused with aggression, as Paul explained to the Corinthians, "I take pleasure in infirmities, in reproaches, in necessities, in persecutions, in distresses for Christ's sake: for when I am weak, then am I strong" (2 Cor 12.10). Joshua would derive his strength from the Lord and His promises and it should be the same for a Christian: "Finally, my brethren, be strong in the Lord, and in the power of his might" (Eph 6.10); "Thou therefore, my son, be strong in the grace that is in Christ Jesus" (2 Tim 2.1). Paul exhorted the Corinthians in his first epistle, "Watch ye, stand fast in the faith, quit you like men, be strong" (1 Cor 16.13), and in the next verse balanced the exhortation, "Let all your things be done with charity" (1 Cor 16.14).

Here, the Lord Jesus is the supreme example for the Christian, as He is in every aspect of Christian living. His strength and courage were wonderfully blended with love and gentleness; when He faced the devil in the wilderness (Lk 4.1-13), or when He stood up in the synagogue in Nazareth declaring Himself to be the fulfilment of Isaiah 61.1-2 (Lk 4.16-30), and throughout His public ministry, until finally, with the shadow of Golgotha over His path, Gethsemane and Gabbatha were experienced to their full extent.

Three resources available to Joshua (vv.6b-9)

a) Promise to the fathers (v.6b)

Here the Lord reminds Joshua of His promise to the fathers of Israel. The immediate fathers of the present generation that stood on the banks of the Jordan had received a promise from the Lord, that "Joshua the son of Nun, which standeth before thee, he shall go in thither: encourage him. for he shall cause Israel to inherit it. Moreover your little ones, which ye said should be a prey, and your children, which in that day had no knowledge between good and evil, they shall go in thither, and unto them will I give it, and they shall possess it" (Deut 1.38-39). The children, who had stood on the borders of Canaan, were now the men and women of Israel, ready to go into the land. Joshua should take courage and draw strength from the inevitability of the divine promise being fulfilled, as any Christian should: "Whereby are given unto us exceeding great and precious promises" (2 Pet 1.4). The promises of the Lord are too numerous to outline in this context. They have been the source of strength and courage for Christians over generations of time, when facing mighty tasks for God and the difficulties of serving God in an ungodly world: "For all the promises of God in him are yea, and in him Amen, unto the glory of God by us" (2 Cor 1.20).

b) Precepts of the law (vv.7-8)

It is interesting that Joshua would be the first man to serve God with the written word of God as his guide and therefore it is instructive to observe the prominence that the Lord gives to the word of God in His directions to Joshua. The obligation laid upon Joshua is regarding "all the law". His observance was not to be partial. The familiar expression, "turn not from it to the right hand or to the left" (Deut 2.27; 5.32; 17.11,20; 28.14), is given here as the extent of the obedience expected of Joshua and, indeed, of all Israel under the Law.

In addition to complete obedience, the need for meditation was brought before Joshua. It was not the obedience of unintelligent habit that the Lord demanded, but rather the intelligent obedience of devotion. Vivid expressions are used by the Lord to convey the point – "this book of the law shall not depart out of thy mouth"; it was to be the constant source and subject of conversation and also of thought – "thou shalt meditate therein day and night". His external obedience to the Law was to flow from an appreciation and love for the Law that would come from daily meditation and constant conversation. When the way was hard and decisions had to be made, he would have the familiar resource of the Law available and would be able to respond in a manner that was in keeping with the Law. Lest any think that the Word of God is only for leaders among the people of God, it is important to understand that the same obligation of meditation and obedience of the Law had been brought before the whole nation of Israel by Moses (Deut 6.6-7; 11.18-19).

"Then thou shalt make thy way prosperous, and then thou shalt have good success". The promise of the Lord to Joshua was not that of material success and prosperity. In the Old Testament, prosperity and success are both linked with accomplishing the purpose of God, with the help of God (Ezra 6.14; Neh 2.20; Dan 3.30) and obedience to the word of God (1Kings 2.3; 2 Kings 18.6-7; 1 Chr 22.13). Here, these words are linked together for the only time in the Bible and serve as a reminder that setting the word of God in its rightful place, and responding to it, is vital for the accomplishment of the purpose of God.

During her coronation, Queen Elizabeth II was handed a Bible and had the following repeated to her: "Our gracious Queen, to keep your majesty ever mindful of the law and the gospel of God as the rule for the whole life and government of Christian princes, we present you with this book, the most valuable thing that this world affords. Here is wisdom; this is the royal law; these are the lively oracles of God". It is a great pity that the leaders of nations do not take these words to heart and place the Word of God in its rightful place, as Joshua was instructed by the Lord.

The presence of the Lord (v.9)

This promise had already been given to Joshua in slightly different words (v.5). The emphasis here is that, "the Lord thy God is with thee whithersoever thou goest". This expression mirrors that used in v.7 to speak of the prosperity that Joshua would know if he obeyed the Law. Thus obedience to the Law and the presence of the Lord are linked, and not without significance. The presence of the Lord would be that enablement that Joshua would require if he was going to obey the Law. Without the presence of the Lord, Joshua would be doomed to failure in respect of the obligation to observe it.

Verses 10-18: Preparation for Crossing Jordan

Joshua now took action and moved to fulfil the command of the Lord to take the nation over the Jordan and commence the conquest of Canaan. Before he did so, he dealt with issues that required attention before the Jordan could be crossed and the conquest begin. It was in this period between the Lord speaking in 1.1-9 and again in 3.7-8 that Joshua began to exercise his authority among the people of God.

Initial Mobilisation (vv.10-11)

Joshua had the monumental task of mobilising the nation to cross the river Jordan, which was a natural barrier to progress into Canaan. In order to accomplish this, he utilised the system of administration which had become part of the nation from their days of captivity in Egypt. "The officers of the people" were not priests or of the family of Levi, and do not appear to have had a role in any way related to the ark or tabernacle. They are first mentioned as being appointed by the taskmasters in Egypt (Ex 5.14). The expression is then used of some of the men chosen by Moses in the group of seventy who received the Spirit of the Lord (Num 11.16). As the books of Numbers and Deuteronomy progress, it is evident that these officers were men who fulfilled various administrative roles in the nation and functioned as the equivalent to a modern civil service. It is interesting to note that they had the task of assessing whether a man was to be excused military service (Deut 20.5-9) and therefore were the appropriate men to be used for the mobilisation of the nation.

The instruction from Joshua was, "Prepare you victuals; for within three days ye shall pass over this Jordan". There are two issues that arise from this command to the people. Firstly, there is no record of the Lord instructing either Moses or Joshua that the Jordan would be dried up in order for the nation to cross. Secondly, there does appear, on a cursory reading of the events that unfolded, to be a problem with the chronology of events from this point, until the Jordan was crossed.

How to cross Jordan?

In v.2 the Lord had commanded Joshua to "arise, go over this Jordan, thou, and all this people", but there was no explanation as to how this was to be achieved. The Lord had given Joshua the assurance that He would be with him as He was with Moses and would repeat it when He gave Joshua the command to bring the ark of the covenant into Jordan and stand still (3.7). In the circumstances, with the barrier of water in front of them, Joshua must have remembered the Red Sea and the intervention of the Lord. There is no record here of Joshua resisting the command of the Lord, nor questioning the logistical problems he would encounter, unlike the people when faced with the Red Sea. It would appear that he was content to leave the matter with the Lord and allow Him to provide the solution.

Three days?

Confusion with regard to the chronology of events arises with the mention of three days in 1.11; 2.22; 3.2. If "three days" in these chapters refer to the same period of time, the sequence of events does not make sense. In 1.11 Joshua gave the nation a period of three days in order to make ready for crossing Jordan; victuals had to be prepared and the people organised. As Joshua instructed the officers to mobilise the nation, he also sent spies into Canaan, who were gone for at least a period of three or four days (2.22-23). It would appear from 3.1 that, having received the news from the spies, Joshua brought the nation down from Shittim to the banks of the Jordan, and remained there for a further three days, before the officers moved through the people and prepared them for the crossing. The confusion arises when the three day period of 3.2 is equated with the three-day period of 1.11. From the initial steps of mobilisation that took place in v.11, it is likely that over a week passed before the nation commenced the crossing of Jordan. This delay was due to the events in Jericho that caused the spies to delay their return, and had not been anticipated by Joshua when the initial command was given. Many commentators view the three days in 1.11 and 3.2 as referring to the same period of time, and see the mission of the spies in ch.2 as having taken place prior to 1.10, with ch.2 forming a parenthesis, which is not in chronological order. This cannot be easily discounted. However, the flow of the text strongly indicates that Joshua issued the command to mobilise after the Lord had spoken to him in 1.1-9, as there is no indication of any delay on his part. To place the events of ch. 2 into a period of time between the Lord speaking to Joshua and then Joshua speaking to the nation would require the mission of the spies as recorded in ch. 2 to take place between 1.9 and 1.10, which seems unlikely.

Transjordan Tribes' Loyalty (vv.12-18)
Background

Following the preparation of the nation for the crossing of Jordan, Joshua had to address a matter of the utmost importance before battle could be commenced. As the nation had approached the borders of Caanan there had been a serious problem that Moses had been compelled to deal with. The tribes of Reuben, Gad and half of the tribe of Manasseh had approached Moses and requested that they be allowed to remain on the east side of the Jordan and not be forced to enter the land of Caanan with the rest of the nation. In addition, they requested that they receive their inheritance of land on the east side of Jordan (Num 32). The issue was resolved when they gave Moses an undertaking that they would not abandon the nation in their warfare but would go armed with the children of Israel (Num 32.16-19). They would leave their families on the east of Jordan and would not return until the nation had entered into their inheritance.

The desire of these tribes to settle on the east of Jordan was a serious error of judgment. The desire arose when they saw that land as being good for cattle and they had, "a very great multitude of cattle"(Num 32.1). They were demonstrating that they were happy to be redeemed out of the bondage of Egypt but did not want to dwell in the land that the Lord had given them. As has already been noted, Canaan is a picture of the spiritual blessings received upon salvation (Eph 1.3), and for reasons that are very often similar those given by these tribes, some Christians choose not to live in the good of the blessings they have been given. They are happy to have been saved and redeemed out of bondage but have more concern for the possessions of this world than the enjoyment of their salvation.

Having made their choice, Moses did not force them to settle in Canaan. The opportunity was there for them and they had every encouragement to go in with the rest of the nation. This is an important lesson to consider when young Christians are setting the direction of life. The Lord has given believers every encouragement to go in for the blessings attendant upon salvation, to investigate and experience them day by day. However, if a decision is made to reject that direction of life in favour of another, the Lord will not force the Christian down a pathway of obedience; it is a matter of choice.

The consequences of their action became evident with the passage of time. With Canaan settled and the inheritance divided, the tribes passed back over the Jordan (22.1-9). Civil war almost broke out when they erected an altar by Jordan in order to maintain some kind of link with the rest of the nation on the west of Jordan, for the benefit of their children (22.10-34). In spite of this feeble effort at maintaining links with the other tribes of Israel, they drifted apart from the tribes dwelling on the west of Jordan. The song of Deborah lamented the absence of the tribe of Reuben and the tribes that inhabited Gilead (Judg 5.15-17). Having once fought for a land in which they had no interest, they were not going to do it again and did not respond to the call to arms in the days of the judges. This division had its ultimate consequence when they are mentioned as being the first of the tribes to be taken into captivity by the Assyrians, never to return to Gilead (1 Chr 5.26).

The experience of these tribes should be a lesson to every believer. Drifting away from the people of God, together with a decision to live in a different way, with different priorities from the teaching of Scripture, is a serious mistake. It leaves the Christian vulnerable to attack from the devil, the flesh and the world and can be the root cause of an unfulfilled life at best, or even a destroyed testimony.

Tribes reminded of their obligation (vv.12-15)

"Remember the word which Moses the servant of the Lord commanded you". Moses had clearly set out the obligations which these tribes were under and which they had unreservedly accepted (Num 32.20-32; Deut 3.18-20). Now that Moses was dead and the tribes had their inheritance on the west of Jordan, with their cities under construction and their families settled, this was a critical point for Joshua. Would the tribes fulfil their promise to cross the Jordan and fight with the other tribes? Joshua had the same problem that Moses faced, as there was the possibility of discouragement in the nation if some of the tribes turned back from the land and disturbed the unity of the nation (Num 32.7). It was for this reason he reminded them of their undertaking, and the word of Moses, which allowed them to stay in the region of Gilead, on the condition that they fought in Canaan. He also brought before them the position that Moses held as the servant of the Lord. It was a timely reminder that it was the Lord, whom Moses served, whom they would answer to, in respect of their obligation.

"The Lord your God hath given you rest, and hath given you this land". The words of Moses in Deuteronomy 3.18-20, where he reiterated the message of Numbers 32.20-24, are taken up by Joshua and repeated with some interesting differences. In Deuteronomy 3.12-17 Moses detailed the land that he had given to these tribes on the west of Jordan. It was known as Gilead and had been taken in battle when Sihon and Og, the kings of the Amorites, were defeated (Num 21.21-35). Having received the land of Gilead, the tribes had entered into the rest that the Lord had given them. "Rest" in this context was the cessation of hostilities that allowed the people to enjoy the land. The tribes on the west of Jordan had entered into their rest, since the kings of the Amorites had been defeated and their families inhabited the cities and strongholds of the region. The other tribes would have to wage three major military campaigns before they could enter into their rest and cease from war (Josh 21.44; 22.4; 23.1). Even after these campaigns, the rest that they entered into was temporary, as hostilities would commence again. The writer to the Hebrews comments on this when he speaks of a future rest that awaits the people of God, explaining that the rest into which Joshua brought the people was not complete or else he would not have spoken of another day (Heb 4.8).

Moses had commanded them to leave their wives, little ones and livestock on the west of Jordan while the armed men went over Jordan to fight. It would appear that not all of the men capable of war went, with the majority remaining behind to protect their families and livestock. Around 40,000 men went from these tribes (4.13), whereas the record of the men above the age of twenty capable of going to war was over one hundred and ten thousand, allowance being made for the half tribe of Manasseh which came over Jordan (Num 26.7,18,34). Joshua did not want the whole of the fighting force that these tribes could muster, since that would have left them vulnerable at home and caused them anxiety as they were away fighting with Joshua. He requested the best of the men, those "mighty men of valour", and having chosen out 40,000 allowed the remaining 70,000 or more to remain behind. They are described in this section as "armed" (2571), which has the meaning of harnessed, or ranked in divisions of five and, as such, marshalled for war (Ex 13.18; Judg 7.11).

Response from the tribes (vv.16-18)

It is not clear from the text whether the "they answered" (v.16) refers to the tribes addressed in vv.12-15, or to the whole nation, who had been specifically addressed in vv.10-11 through the officers of the people. Notwithstanding this uncertainty, the answer must have been a tremendous relief and comfort to Joshua. In responding as they did, they gave him the assurance that the nation would be united as they entered Canaan for conquest. They offered a threefold assurance and an acceptance of the penalty that the Law of Moses carried for rebellion in the family circle. These assurances were comprehensive and put the people firmly under the authority of Joshua. They were undertaking to do what he commanded, to go where he directed, and to obey Joshua as they had done in the case of Moses. The response of the tribes has a formulaic structure that can be seen in the usage of the word "only". The three undertakings of the tribes are completed with a statement to encourage Joshua, which begins with "only" (v.17). This pattern is repeated when the penalty for failure in these matters is stated, and is completed with further encouragement to Joshua, which again begins with the word "only". These exhortations to Joshua are in themselves a summary of the promises and obligations that the Lord had given to Joshua earlier in the chapter. Despite the background of their determination not to settle in the land that the Lord had given them in Canaan, they did appreciate the importance of their leader having the Lord with him and being strong and courageous. They understood that the man to whom they had committed themselves as leader would have to be in touch with God and possess certain qualities. It is perhaps a mark of selfishness to appreciate some of the things of God and then take decisions that will have the effect of denying another generation the same opportunity. This is effectively what these tribes did when they returned over the Jordan.

"Whosoever he be that doth rebel against thy commandment, and will not hearken unto thy words in all that thou commandest him, he shall be put to death" (v.18). Throughout the wilderness journey the nation had been marked by rebellion and had even been called "rebels" by Moses (Num 20.10). They had rebelled at Horeb, Kadesh-barnea, Taberah, Massah, Kibroth-hattaavah, and, in fact, Moses brought the accusation before the nation that from the day they had left Egypt they had been rebellious against the Lord (Deut 9.7). Having seen the judgment of God and heard the Law of God in relation to rebellion, they understood that death was the appropriate penalty for such. With Joshua making such a statement, the tribes recognised that the past problem of the nation was usually that of rebellion, and acknowledged that it would be dealt with in accordance with the Law.

Thus the opening chapter comes to an end. Joshua is at this point confirmed as leader of Israel and commissioned to enter Canaan. With the assurance of the Lord's promises and the burden of obligation placed upon him, he has begun to take command. The order for the initial mobilisation of the army has gone out and the unity of the nation has been assured for the battles that lie ahead. United and empowered they wait at Shittim for the order to advance down to the banks of the Jordan where Joshua must depend upon the Lord for the second great crossing of water that the nation would experience. There are times like this in the lives of Christians when it is progress and success all the way. There does not appear to be a cloud on the horizon, as the wilderness of divine discipline is left behind and progress recommences. No obstacle seems too big and no task too great. It is significant that, in the experience of Joshua, these conditions always prevailed when the people were united and the word of God was given its rightful place among the people of God.

JOSHUA 2

Spies in Canaan

The story of the salvation of Rahab and her family from the destruction of Jericho is remarkable. The New Testament refers to it as an example of faith (Heb 11.31), and of justification by works (James 2.25). Rahab herself is brought into the genealogy of the Lord Jesus, as the mother of Boaz, the great-grandfather of David (Mt 1.5). The focus of the narrative now changes from Shittim to Jericho and from the leader of Israel to a Gentile harlot in Jericho.

Verse 1: Spies Sent into Canaan

As part of the mobilisation (1.10-12), or perhaps as a pre-cursor to it, Joshua sent two men into Canaan "to spy secretly, saying, Go view the land, even Jericho". The Scriptures do not reveal why Joshua sent these spies into the land but, as events unfold, it becomes evident that they went to Jericho to meet a woman called Rahab. The absence of a recorded command from the Lord to Joshua to send the spies does not mean that no such command was given. When Moses sent the twelve spies into Canaan, the record in Deuteronomy 1.22 attributes this to the people, yet in Numbers 13.1-2 it is the Lord who gave Moses the command to send the spies.

Throughout the conquest of Canaan Joshua displayed the characteristics of a good general. He is introduced in Scripture as a soldier fighting against Amalek in Rephidim (Ex 17), and, as a leader of the nation, he led them into many battles. The decision to send the spies into Canaan in advance of the nation made good military sense. The information that Joshua had from his own survey of the land was forty years old and could have been out-of-date. He had a fair idea of what lay before them, as he directed the spies to not only "view the land" but, in particular, gain information about Jericho. Good intelligence is often viewed as one of the most important aspects of winning a battle and Joshua does what the Lord had commissioned him to do, taking steps to lead the nation according to the best of the ability and the experience that the Lord had given him.

When the spies came into the land they made their way into Jericho and "came into an harlot's house, named Rahab, and lodged there". The summary of the spies' journey in Caanan is brief; however, the language used is carefully chosen by the Spirit of God to give no impression of sexual misconduct on their part. These spies were young men (6.23), and a careless reading of the chapter could give the wrong impression of them. When Samson visited a harlot for sexual reasons, the language is different from that employed here: "Then went Samson to Gaza, and saw there an harlot, and went in unto her" (Judg 16.1). The emphasis is upon the harlot, rather than her house. This careful use of language is maintained when the behaviour of the spies is described. They "lodged" in Rahab's house, with the word indicating that they "rested or lay down" (7901). This word is also used of sexual relations, but only when accompanied by the preposition "with" and the name or designation of another person. The inference that could be drawn from the youth of these men, and their presence in a harlot's house, is avoided by this discreet use of language.

The imagination could provide various scenarios that might have led these men to the house of Rahab the harlot, all of which would only be conjecture at the best. Scripture is silent as to why they made the decision to turn into that house, of all the houses in Jericho. Although the reason for their decision is not revealed, it is wonderful to see the hand of the Lord in the whole episode. It was a day that changed the lives of Rahab and her family, the day when the Lord sent two men into her home to bring her salvation from the judgment that would fall upon the city, and bring her into contact with the God of Israel about whom she had heard. The purpose of God is seen in this episode, as she was to be included in the genealogy of the Lord Jesus as the great-grandmother of king David. She was plucked from the obscurity of Jericho, a city that would be destroyed and cursed, and brought into a wonderful sphere of blessing. In this she is a picture of the work of the Lord in saving Gentile sinners, as Paul says: "That at that time ye were without Christ, being aliens from the commonwealth of Israel, and strangers from the covenants of promise, having no hope, and without God in the world" (Eph 2.12). Yet in His grace and mercy, the Lord has brought the gospel to the ears of Gentile sinners throughout the world and "hath delivered us from the power of darkness, and hath translated us into the kingdom of his dear Son" (Col 1.13).

Verses 2-3: King of Jericho Informed

"And it was told the king of Jericho" (v.2). His name is not revealed, neither is the source of his information. It was not only Joshua who gathered intelligence by the use of spies, for the king of Jericho had a system whereby he could gain information about the goings on within his city; it was not only the presence of the spies that had been noted, but also their purpose for being in Jericho. Whether they had been asking questions about the land and were indiscreet in their inquiries is not revealed in Scripture. The information that was passed to the king was detailed and accurate. They had been compromised in a manner, and by persons not known, and as a result found themselves in mortal danger.

"And the king of Jericho sent unto Rahab" (v.3). Having received the information concerning the spies, the king sent a demand to Rahab to bring the men out of her house. The demand put her in the position of choosing between the king of Jericho and the men of Israel. If she did not co-operate with the king, she would be turning her back on Jericho and placing her life and future in the hands of the men of Israel. The situation had developed into a crisis which was not of her making, yet would bring her to a point of decision which assured her safety and provided her with a future in Israel and with the God of Israel. The narrative of Scripture does not reveal whether she knew the identity of the men when they sought lodgings in her house, or whether it was the events that unfolded, and culminated in the message of the king, that brought this revelation to her. What is clear from Scripture is that she now had a decision to make in a moment of crisis.

Verses 4-8: Spies Hidden by Rahab

"The woman took the two men, and hid them" (v.4). Some translations place the action of Rahab as being before the king's men arrived at her door, e.g. "and the woman had taken and concealed the two men" (JND); this would indicate that the identity of the spies was known to Rahab before she received the king's demand. By hiding the spies, Rahab started on a pathway of blessing. She was doing a commendable thing, as she risked her life for the spies.

Having done the right thing by hiding the spies, she then did the wrong thing by beginning a series of lies to deceive the king's men. "There came men unto me, but I wist not whence they were" (v.4). The NKJV translates as, "I did not know where they were from". This could not be true, although it is not specifically stated that when she received and subsequently hid the spies, she did so knowing that they were from Israel. It is plain from the narrative that this must have been the reason why she hid them and was now lying for them. As she converses with the spies later in the narrative, she does reveal that she knew much concerning the children of Israel.

In v.5 her lies continued as she weaved a fanciful tale. "And it came to pass about the time of shutting of the gate, when it was dark, that the men went out: whither the men went I wot not: pursue after them quickly; for ye shall overtake them". It was a cunning lie as it removed her and the spies from any immediate danger, and took the search outside of the city, giving the spies an opportunity to escape. It also proved to be an effective lie, since the soldiers responded and set off from the city in search of the spies.

It is interesting that in the New Testament there is no mention of the lies that Rahab told when she is held out as an example of faith (Heb 11.31) and of justification by works (James 2.25). Scripture does not commend her for her lies; this is a reminder that an example taken from the Old Testament, to illustrate an aspect of truth in the New Testament, should not be taken beyond the point made in the New Testament. After all, the people of the Old Testament were only men and women with all the faults of fallen humanity and cannot be expected to be the perfect illustration of truth.

It is a mistake to admire the outcome of Rahab's lies, and from that point work back to her conduct, and view it as being acceptable to the

Lord. Her motive in deceiving the soldiers, however noble, was misplaced as it put her wisdom and deceit in place of the overruling hand of the Lord. This can be a temptation for any servant of the Lord facing a situation that is seemingly impossible. Surely the Lord would understand and allow a servant to lie, if it is to work out the purpose of the Lord? To adopt this view is to forget the character of God. The Lord hates "a lying tongue" (Prov 6.17) and "lying lips are abomination to the Lord" (Prov 12.22). The end does not justify the means when it comes to the service of God, and all that Rahab's lies did was to deprive her of seeing how the Lord would deliver the spies out of the hand of the king.

Rahab's fallibility should not diminish the importance of her role in securing their escape from Jericho. This is emphasised by the mention of the gates of the city being closed after the soldiers went out in search of the spies. The only way for them to get out of the city before the soldiers returned had been closed to them. They were now dependent on Rahab for their escape. She held their lives in her hands and at any moment could have delivered them to the king. The soldiers, "pursued after them the way to Jordan unto the fords" (v.7). There are indications in Scripture that the Jordan could be forded at certain times and in certain places (Judg 3.28; 12.5-6). However, this does not mean that the nation of Israel could have forded the river without the intervention of the Lord, since the sheer scale of the crossing would have made that impossible, especially at that time of the year (3.15).

When the soldiers had gone out of the city, Rahab spoke to the spies on the roof of the house where she had hidden them. There is no doubt that she was a resourceful and courageous woman, using the flax stalks on the roof to conceal the men. Keil & Delitzsch point out in their commentary on this section of the chapter that these stalks of flax would "grow to the height of three or four feet in Egypt, and attain the thickness of a reed, and would probably be quite as large in the plain of Jericho, the climate of which resembles that of Egypt, and would form a very good hiding-place for the spies if they were piled up upon the roof to dry in the sun".

Verses 9-13: Rahab's Confession

In the first eight verses of the chapter there has been no indication of why Rahab would risk her life for these spies. In this section she opens her heart and Scripture records one of the longest uninterrupted statements of a woman in the Bible, as she explains to the spies her motive in hiding them and her hopes and fears for the future.

As the verses unfold in the narrative, it becomes clear why the writer to the Hebrews included Rahab in the catalogue of men and women of faith, spoken of as a cloud of witnesses (Heb 12.1). "By faith the harlot Rahab perished not with them that believed not, when she had received the spies with peace" (Heb 11.31). Her motive in hiding the spies, and even in her misplaced deception of the soldiers, is revealed; she had believed in the

God of Israel. This is remarkable when her status is considered as a Gentile woman, living an immoral life, with her house on the wall of Jericho. In the most unlikely place, was this most unlikely woman, who had heard of and trusted in the God she had never seen. In this she is an example of faith for, "faith cometh by hearing, and hearing by the word of God" (Rom 10.17).

Three things Rahab knew about Israel (v.9)

1. "*I know that the Lord hath given you the land*". She knew what Joshua had been told on seven occasions in ch.1 that the Lord had given the land to Israel. It is interesting that she expresses this as an established fact, despite the barriers of Jordan and Jericho standing between the nation of Israel and the land. Her conviction about the land was not something that her eyes supported, nor even her natural mind; it went against all reason.

2. "*And that your terror is fallen upon us*". This should not have been a surprise to the spies as Moses and the children of Israel had spoken of this when they had come over the Red Sea and sung the song of deliverance (Ex 15.16). The Lord had also promised that this would happen to the nations (Deut 2.25; 11.25) and now the whole of the land, not just Jericho, had experienced this terror.

3. "*And that all the inhabitants of the land faint because of you*". The third aspect of Rahab's testimony to the spies referred to the effect that this terror was having on the inhabitants of the land. All of this information was exactly what the spies had been looking for, since it confirmed two things: firstly, the people of Canaan were demoralised and, secondly, the Lord had kept His promises and had been working among the inhabitants of the land to discourage them. They had lost heart as the song had prophesied that "all the inhabitants of Canaan shall melt away" (Ex 15.15). The information that Rahab gave the spies meant that they could return to Joshua with a picture of the land from a woman who had proved herself trustworthy and committed to the cause of Israel.

What she knew had caused her to hide the spies. Her knowledge had caused her to act, which is an essential element of faith. In the New Testament, a sinner receives salvation on the principle of faith (Eph 2.8). This is not a passive reception without the involvement of the sinner, for it is his responsibility to make the decision to trust the Lord Jesus as Saviour. It was when Rahab received the spies in peace that she was saved from perishing. There have been many souls who have known the gospel but have never acted upon what they knew and trusted the Saviour. Rahab was different and staked her all with the men of Israel and with the God whom they represented.

Basis of Rahab's faith (v.10)

Rahab's faith was based upon what she had heard and not upon what she had seen. Her eyes would have told her that the barriers facing Israel were too great for them to overcome: Jordan, Jericho and the combined might of the Canaanitish kings. The wisdom of this world is based upon what is seen. It is the tangible and physical being accepted as the complete picture, which leads to humanistic thinking. Men will only believe in what they see and will not accept a God they cannot see or a spiritual dimension to life that is not tangible. The Christian has a different perspective, as faith is based upon hearing and not seeing (Rom 10.17); "While we look not at the things which are seen, but at the things which are not seen: for the things which are seen are temporal; but the things which are not seen are eternal" (2 Cor 4.18); "Now faith is the substance of things hoped for, the evidence of things not seen" (Heb 11.1). Rahab had heard and believed in the God of Israel and took the decision to receive the spies in peace, which brought her salvation when the judgment of God fell on Jericho. She is like those spoken of by the Lord: "blessed are they that have not seen, and yet have believed" (Jn 20.29).

Her faith was based upon two events that she had heard about in the experience of the nation of Israel. One took place forty years before, and the other was of more recent times, encompassing the whole of their wilderness journey. In addition to being great demonstrations of the power of the Lord, the two events served as a warning to any people who would oppose the nation of Israel.

1. *"For we have heard how the Lord dried up the water of the Red sea for you, when ye came out of Egypt"*. Rahab had learned her history well. She accepted the story of the Red Sea as being true and attributed it to the work of the Lord. Forty years had passed since the event had occurred, but such was its magnitude it had remained in the minds of the inhabitants of Caanan and caused them fear and trepidation. If the Lord could take them through the Red Sea then the Jordan was not such a barrier to their progress after all.

2. *"And what ye did unto the two kings of the Amorites, that were on the other side Jordan, Sihon and Og, whom ye utterly destroyed"*. The destruction of the kings of the Amorites was a more recent event and also had its effect upon the people of Canaan. Og was the last of the giants to occupy the land on the east of Jordan (Deut 3.11) and both he and Sihon were systematically defeated, as the Lord delivered them into the hands of the children of Israel (Num 21.21-35). The expression "utterly destroyed" (2763) is also used by Moses when rehearsing the victories in the hearing of the children of Israel (Deut 2.34; 3.6), and giving instruction for the conquest of Canaan (Deut 7.2-6). There was to be no mercy and utter destruction was to be the order of the day. This does seem a brutal way to wage war, with the women and children destroyed as well as the armies. Moses explained that this was to prevent the children of Israel from making covenants with the tribes of Canaan and being taught their idolatrous practices. It was, in essence, to preserve the children of Israel from being

drawn into sinning against God. There was to be no accommodation of the Canaanite tribes and no compromise on the part of Israel. The necessity for these instructions to Israel and the need to wage war in this fashion is seen in the subsequent history of Israel when they failed to obey the word of the Lord and utterly destroy the tribes of Canaan. The result of this failure was that the tribes of Canaan led them into sin and idolatry.

Conclusion of Rahab's faith (v.11)

It is interesting that Rahab testified to the spies that others had heard of these great events involving Israel. However, she was the only person who responded in faith. The effect upon the whole population was one of fear: "as soon as we had heard these things, our hearts did melt, neither did there remain any more courage in any man, because of you". The fear of the Lord is a good thing, but never brings salvation. James wrote of the fear of God: "Thou believest that there is one God; thou doest well. the devils also believe, and tremble" (James 2.19). This was also the experience of Felix when he heard the gospel; he trembled and yet there is no record of him trusting the Lord Jesus as Saviour (Acts 24.25).

Like Nebuchadnezzar when he brought out the three Hebrew children from the furnace (Dan 3.29), Rahab confessed that the God of Israel is the true God. Her words are similar to those of Moses (Deut 4.39) when he speaks to the children of Israel and recalls the mighty miracles of the Lord in their redemption from Egypt and in their wilderness journey. It is a measure of Rahab's faith that she came to this conclusion only through hearing of these things and not being present to witness them. She came to the conclusion that the God of Israel is "God in heaven above, and in earth beneath".

Request for salvation (vv.12-13)

The next stage of Rahab's confession took the form of a request for salvation from the coming judgment which she knew would fall upon her city. Firstly, she began by saying, "Now therefore, I pray you". This form of words drew attention to all that she had said in her confession to the spies. She then reminded them that "I have shewed you kindness". These two reasons were a compelling argument since they refer to her confession, and her actions, which demonstrated the reality of what she had said. She asked the spies to reciprocate her kindness by showing kindness to her and her family; since she had given them shelter from danger, she requested that they reciprocate that act of kindness by giving her and her family shelter.

It is interesting that her request carried moral weight. Joseph was able to do the same when he had interpreted the dreams of the butler and baker in the prison and had given the good news to the butler: "Think on me when it shall be well with thee, and shew kindness, I pray thee, unto me, and make mention of me unto Pharaoh, and bring me out of this house" (Gen 40.14). David was careful to reciprocate kindness when he, "sent messengers unto the men of Jabesh-gilead, and said unto them, Blessed be ye of the Lord, that ye have shewed this kindness unto your lord, even unto Saul, and have buried him. And now the Lord shew kindness and truth unto you. and I also will requite you this kindness, because ye have done this thing" (2 Sam 2.5-6). A response to a request for kindness is more likely when kindness has first of all been shown. However, the expression that Rahab used for "showing kindness" (Gen 24.12; Ex 20.6; Judg 8.35 – 6213, 2617), has a meaning that took her request beyond that of "one good deed deserves another". She was not asking them to be kindly disposed to them, but was asking them to preserve their lives and families for future generations. The Hebrew word is "hard to translate by one English equivalent. The word principally means that one is loyal to a covenant relationship, but it also contains the notions of mercy and kindness" (*New International Commentary on the Old Testament*, p73 Note 24). The word is used when the house of Joseph went up against Bethel and saw a man come out of the city. They asked him to show them the way into the city and in return they undertook to spare the man and his family (Judg 1.22-26).

"Swear unto me by the Lord". By pressing the spies to take an oath of the Lord, she wanted a guarantee that, to her mind, would be binding. Whether this was altogether necessary is a different matter. It could be that with her background of paganism, the taking of an oath was a common form of sealing an agreement or making a secure promise. To her there was no higher authority than the Lord as she had already confessed that "the Lord your God, he is God in heaven above, and in earth beneath" (v.11), and therefore it would be the greatest security that she could have. "Give me a true token". This refers to the oath that she asked of the spies, which to her was a sign of truth.

Verses 14-21: Undertaking of the Spies

The chronology of events in this section is not altogether clear. A conversation commenced in Rahab's house and finished with the spies out of the window, conversing with her from outside the city walls. The verse that changed the location of the spies is v.15, which records them making their exit from the city through the window of the house and being let down the wall by a scarlet cord. It does appear a little odd that a conversation, which was crucial to the covenant that they made, would commence in the house and be continued after they had been let out of the city. It may well be that the order of events is not recorded chronologically and that the escape of the men through the window is mentioned in v.15 to give an explanation and meaning of the instruction of the spies regarding the scarlet cord (v.18). However unlikely though it may seem, bearing in mind the emphasis in Scripture of the formidable walls of the city, the content of the conversation does support the chronology of events as unfolded in the narrative. In v.18 the spies speak to Rahab and mention the scarlet cord that had been used to let them down. This part of the conversation must have taken place after they were out of the window as it refers to the action as having taken place. Therefore the conversation, which runs from v.15, must have transpired after they had been let down from the window.

It is worth noting that on the face of it the spies were breaking the command of the Lord to make no covenant with the Canaanite (Deut 7.2). The instruction of the Lord was that the Canaanite tribes were to be utterly destroyed, yet the spies were giving assurances that some of the city would not be destroyed. In order to understand why the command of the Lord was for the utter destruction of the cities of Canaan, the context of such a command must be examined and contrasted with the context of the undertaking that the spies gave to Rahab. It has already been noted that it was for the preservation of the holiness of Israel and protection from the temptation to sin that these tribes were to be destroyed. In addition, the cities of Canaan were places where idolatry and sin abounded and the invasion of the land was in itself an exercise of divine judgment upon these people. With Rahab it was different. She had already confessed her commitment to the God and people of Israel and in so doing had cast off idolatry. She was able to rely upon the provision that the Lord had made for the stranger throughout the Law, for the stranger was to be welcomed and accommodated among the children of Israel as long as they were willing to adhere to the conditions that the Law imposed upon them.

Three elements of the covenant between the spies and Rahab (v.14)

1. "*Our life for yours*". Rahab had already risked her life for theirs and so the undertaking was a reciprocation of her kindness to them. By making this statement they placed their lives as forfeit should anything befall her in the conquest of Canaan. They would protect her, as she had protected them.

2. "*If ye utter not this our business*". The covenant was conditional upon Rahab continuing her protection of the spies, which was necessary for them not only to get out of the city, but to escape over Jordan.

3. "*And it shall be, when the Lord hath given us the land, that we will deal kindly and truly with thee*". This third element of the covenant gave her the timescale of her deliverance and entrance into the fold of the children of Israel. She asked for kindness and a true token and the spies now undertake to give her both when they come in conquest.

Response of Rahab (vv.15-16)

Having received the promise from the spies, Rahab took action. She had already shown her faith in God by receiving the spies in peace and hiding them when the king had sent men to her house in search of them, a fact which is commented on by the writer to the Hebrews (Heb 11.31).

When James is illustrating justification by works, he cites two contrasting people, Abraham and Rahab. Both are examples of faith and proved the reality of their faith by their works. For Abraham it was the offering up of Isaac (James 2.21-23) and for Rahab it was "when she had received the messengers, and had sent them out another way" (James 2.25). Her works demonstrated her faith as seen by her reception of the spies, and then by her actions as described in vv.14-15, when she sent them out of the city by her window. In a scene that is almost replicated by Paul escaping from Damascus in a basket from the wall (2 Cor 11.32-33), the spies got out of the city of Jericho. With the open country before them she gave them instruction to "Get you to the mountain, lest the pursuers meet you; and hide yourselves there three days, until the pursuers be returned. and afterward may ye go your way". Thus she had overcome the two obstacles that hindered the spies escaping, viz. the shut gate and the search party from the king.

Conditions of the covenant expanded (vv.17-20)

According to v.14, the spies had agreed to guarantee Rahab's safety when the city was destroyed on the understanding that she fulfilled her part of the agreement by continuing to protect them as they made their escape over Jordan. As they stand outside of the city walls, the spies now give Rahab detailed instructions for the salvation of her and her family. What had been agreed in principle is now explained in detail. There are instructions which Rahab had to fulfil:

1. "Bind this line of scarlet thread in the window which thou didst let us down by".
2. "Thou shalt bring thy father, and thy mother, and thy brethren, and all thy father's household, home unto thee. And it shall be, that whosoever shall go out of the doors of thy house into the street, his blood shall be upon his head, and we will be guiltless. and whosoever shall be with thee in the house, his blood shall be on our head, if any hand be upon him".
3. "If thou utter this our business, then we will be quit of thine oath which thou hast made us to swear".

There has been much written and preached about the scarlet thread mentioned by the spies. It was used by Rahab to let the spies down from the window and was to be retained by her and displayed in the window of her house. Some have thought that it is a fitting picture of the death of the Lord Jesus, in a similar way to the application of blood from the lamb of the household, to the door posts and lintel in Egypt, prior to the passover night (Ex 12.7). There may well be that typology within the narrative, however, it is not something that the New Testament supports and therefore cannot be pressed. The salvation of Rahab in the New Testament is a picture of faith and works and not of sheltering under the blood of Christ. It is a mistake to read more into the narrative than is supported by the New Testament simply based on the colour of the cord.

The three conditions meant that the spies wanted her house to be easily identifiable to them when the carnage began in the city, with her family within the house, to guarantee their safety. These were very practical and sensible arrangements to put into place before the attack began. It would be a measure of her faith whether she would keep the cord in the window and retain her family in her house. In addition, the spies reiterated the need for her to keep their presence in the land a secret. If she failed to do this, they would be discharged from the oath.

The conversation between them comes to an end in v.21 with Rahab agreeing to the conditions and demonstrating this as "she bound the scarlet line in the window".

Verses 22-24: The Return of the Spies

The spies heeded the words of Rahab and stayed in the mountains for three days; this is seen as having been good advice with the search party from the king of Jericho returning from their fruitless search and in so doing leaving the way clear for the spies to cross over Jordan to the camp of Israel. The spies "came unto the mountain, and abode there three days". According to Keil & Delitzsch the mountains are most likely "the range on the northern side of Jericho, which afterwards received the name of *Quarantana* (Arab. *Kuruntul*), a wall of rock rising almost precipitously from the plain to the height of 1200 or 1500 feet [370/462m], and full of grottoes and caves on the eastern side. These mountains were well adapted for a place of concealment; moreover, they were the nearest to Jericho, as the western range recedes considerably to the south of Wady Kelt".

The chapter ends with the spies making their report to Joshua. They "told him all things that befell them", and in so doing must have spoken of Rahab and the covenant they had entered into with her. This must have received Joshua's approval as no censure of the spies is recorded and in fact Joshua is attributed with saving Rahab when Jericho fell (6.22-25). The report that they brought to Joshua was essentially that which they had received from Rahab and is again a demonstration of the confidence that the spies had in her.

JOSHUA 3

Crossing Jordan

Finally, the day had arrived. Forty years in the wilderness had passed and now the children of Israel were going into the land that the Lord had promised them. Chapters 3 and 4 are closely linked in the narrative, with the emphasis in ch.3 on the ark of the covenant, and in ch.4, on the memorial stones. The two chapters may be analysed according to the flow of instruction from the Lord to Joshua, and then the execution of the instructions by the people and priests. Thus:

3.1-6	Final preparations
3.7-8	Command of the Lord
3.9-13	Communication by Joshua
3.14-17	Execution by the People
4.1-3	Command of the Lord
4.4-7	Communication by Joshua
4.8-13	Execution by the People
4.14-16	Command of the Lord
4.17	Communication by Joshua
4.18-20	Execution by the People.

Final Preparations

Verse 1: Israel Moves Camp

With the spies now returned, there was no time to be lost and Joshua rose "early in the morning". Whenever there was business to be done for God, he rose early (6.12; 7.16; 8.10), and in this he is like the Lord Jesus, who was marked by such diligence (Mk 1.35; Lk 4.42). The people had been encamped at Shittim since the defeat of Og and Sihon (Num 22.1), and with no hint of delay Joshua began to move the nation into position in order to cross the Jordan.

Verses 2-4: Officers of the People

Three days' wait (v.2)

The issue of the chronology of events has already been dealt with (1.11). However, a comparison of the relevant verses provides further evidence that the two periods of three days (1.11; 3.3) are not the same. In this verse it is "after three days, that the officers went through the host", whereas in 1.11 the command is given by Joshua prior to the commencement of that three-day period. In addition, the instructions that the officers communicated were different. In 1.11 the officers speak to the people about victuals, but in 3.3 the subject is the ark, of which there is no mention in ch.1.

Three days of seeing the Jordan overflowing its banks (3.15; 4.18) must have had its effect upon the children of Israel; it impressed upon them the futility of attempting the crossing by themselves, and brought them to recognise that the Lord would have to take them over. The contemplation of a difficulty is very often the means that the Lord uses to bring the Christian to a realisation of his complete dependence upon Him. This had already been the experience of the children of Israel, when they had come out of Egypt. The barrier of the Red Sea had lain before them and the Egyptian army advanced from behind them (Ex 14.8-10). The psalmist speaks of a similar experience, "Hungry and thirsty, their soul fainted in them. Then they cried unto the Lord in their trouble, and he delivered them out of their distresses" (Ps 107.5-6).

The ark of the covenant of the Lord your God (v.3)

The "ark of the covenant" plays a significant role in the events that unfold, with it being mentioned ten times in ch.3 and on a further seven occasions in ch.4. Its function is central to the crossing of the Jordan, and to an understanding of the significance of the Jordan in the New Testament. The ark is given more than one title in these chapters and is referred to as the "ark of the covenant of the Lord your God" (v.3), "the ark of the covenant of the Lord of all the earth" (v.11), "the ark of the covenant" (v.14), and "the ark of the covenant of the Lord" (v.17). It was the most significant article within the tabernacle, signifying the presence of the Lord among His people and led to the tabernacle being called the "tabernacle of testimony" (Num 1.50,53). It was the meeting place of the Lord and His people (Ex 25.22) and was placed within the holiest of all. When it had to be moved, the ark was carried by staves which were not to be removed, and was borne by the sons of Kohath from the tribe of Levi (Num 4.15). During these journeys, it was not to be touched by those who carried it or be visible to the eyes of the people. Aaron and his sons had to wrap the ark in "the covering vail...and put thereon the covering of badgers' skins, and...spread over it a cloth wholly of blue" (Num 4.5-6).

The ark is a wonderful picture of the Lord Jesus. The materials used in its construction speak of Him: shittim wood, overlaid within and without with pure gold (Ex 25.10-22). With the incorruptible wood signifying the incorruptible humanity of the Lord Jesus, and the pure gold speaking of His undiminished deity, it is a delightful picture of "God ...manifest in the flesh"(1 Tim 3.16). Not God and man separated, but the wood and gold made into one object, and so it is with the Lord Jesus who not only became a man, but will remain a man throughout eternity. The mercy seat, staves, and crown of gold all point to the Lord Jesus, in the glory of His person. Within the ark there were three items that spoke of the relationship that the Lord had with the children of Israel: "the golden pot that had manna, and Aaron's rod that budded, and the tables of the covenant" (Heb 9.4). These items are also a picture of the relationship that the believer has with the Lord Jesus as He is in heaven and the believer is in the world. He is the bread of God of John's Gospel, the Great High Priest of the Epistle to the Hebrews, and the second man who has fulfilled the righteous requirements of the Law (1 Cor 15.47).

The significance of the ark being described as the "ark of the covenant", as the children of Israel were poised to enter the land, should not be overlooked. The covenant that is referred to was made at Sinai (Ex 19.1-6; 24.1-8), when the Lord gathered the children of Israel and brought to them the Law, which was to be the basis of their relationship with Himself. The Lord had made promises to Abraham and the children of Israel had responded by putting themselves under obligation, when they accepted the terms of the Law and undertook to obey it. The ten commandments are described as the "tables of testimony" (Ex 31.18) and were the record, from the finger of God, of the terms of the Law that formed the basis of the covenant (Ex 34.28). However, the sad history of Israel was that they did not keep the Law and therefore broke the covenant (Deut 4.13). A. W. Pink (*Gleanings in Joshua*) comments, "the evil conduct of Israel is summed up by the Psalmist in those solemn words, 'they kept not the covenant of God, and refused to walk in his law' (Ps 78.10). Their breaking of the covenant at once released the Lord from making good unto that perverse generation His declarations unto Abraham, and therefore He told them `your carcases they shall fall in this wilderness...after the number of the days in which ye searched the land, even forty days, each day for a year, shall ye bear your iniquities, even forty years, and ye shall know my breach of promise' (Num 14.32, 34)...The promises Jehovah made to Abraham and Moses would not be fulfilled unto that particular generation because of their unbelief and disobedience; but unto their descendants they should be made fully good".

The prominent place given to the ark of the covenant in the crossing of Jordan is therefore explained by the history of the children of Israel. The Lord was giving the land of Canaan to them as a fulfilment of the covenant promises and, in turn, they had obligations to fulfil in terms of the covenant. The ark was to remain in the vision of the people, and be seen to be central to their progress through the land, as a constant reminder of their covenant obligations.

The officers commanded the people, "When ye see the ark of the covenant of the Lord your God, and the priests the Levites bearing it, then ye shall remove from your place, and go after it". They were to wait for the ark to move and not go before nor lag behind it, but allow it to guide and lead them through the difficulty that faced them. This is a tremendous picture of serving God, not going beyond the guidance of the Lord or falling behind and losing sight of Him.

Distance between the people and the ark (v.4)

The instruction by the officers was qualified by the stipulation that there would be "a space between you and it, about two thousand cubits by measure. come not near unto it". This would not have been a surprise to the children of Israel as they knew that they did not have access to the ark, or indeed its immediate proximity, when it was in the tabernacle; the holiness of the presence of the Lord was such that, if an inappropriate approach was made, then death would result. This was seen when the ark was lost to the Philistines and caused them such trouble that they sent it back to Israel (1 Samuel 5-6); thereafter the men of Beth-shemesh looked into the ark with the result that the Lord slew 50,070 men (1 Sam 6.19). Even on the return of the ark to Jerusalem, the Lord moved in judgment when Uzzah steadied the ark on the cart by reaching out and touching it (2 Sam 6.6-7). The holiness of the Lord would have kept the people from touching the ark or looking at it directly, but the stipulation of 2,000 cubits had another purpose: "that ye may know the way by which ye must go. for ye have not passed this way heretofore". Some commentators have taken the view that this is speaking of the spiritual path that is mentioned as a manner of life in other Old Testament Scriptures (Gen18.19; Ex18.20; Deut 5.33). It does appear from the context that the literal distance of 2,000 cubits was principally for a very practical reason. By keeping at such a distance the vast multitude of the children of Israel would be able to see the ark, which would not have been the case had they crowded around it, and by so doing limited the vision of those at a distance from it. The children of Israel followed the ark when they departed from the mount of the Lord and sought out a resting place (Num 10.33), and this was to continue in the crossing of Jordan. It was new territory and the ark was going to be the guide for the children of Israel and central to the crossing of the Jordan.

When it is remembered that the ark is a picture of the Lord Jesus, the words of the New Testament from the Hebrew writer are pertinent: "Let us run with patience the race that is set before us, looking unto Jesus the author and finisher of our faith; who for the joy that was set before him endured the cross, despising the shame, and is set down at the right hand of the throne of God. For consider him that endured such contradiction of sinners against himself, lest ye be wearied and faint in your minds" (Heb 12.1-3). He is the inspiration for the Christian who is seeking to live for God in this world. Looking unto Him and considering His walk here below should encourage weary saints. The pathway of His life is the example for every saint of God to follow; as a Shepherd going before the flock (1 Pet 2.25), as a Great High Priest who has passed through all the valleys of temptation apart from sin (Heb 4.14-15), as a sufferer at the hands of men

(1 Pet 2.21-24), and in many other ways, He brought pleasure to the heart of God.

Verse 5: People

"Sanctify yourselves", was the command of Joshua to the people as preparation for crossing the Jordan. They were not asked to perform miracles or wonders, but their responsibility was to be holy. The word "sanctify"(6942) has the thought of separation from what is sinful, with the word, or its derivatives, often translated as "holy", "sacred" or "consecrate". The people at Mount Sinai were sanctified when the Law was given (Ex 19.10) and throughout the book of Leviticus, when the various aspects of the tabernacle and its service were instituted, the need for sanctification was repeatedly stressed. There is no record of Joshua, or the officers, instructing the people how to sanctify themselves. As they stood near Jordan, it is possible that they were to do what was commanded of the people at Mount Sinai, washing their clothes and abstaining from sexual relations (Ex 19.14-15). The important point to note is the purpose of the command rather than its implementation, which is not recorded. Holiness was the Lord's demand for His people since He was going to do wonders among them.

The need for the people of God to be sanctified is also a common theme in the New Testament, although the emphasis is not on the external ceremonial aspect of sanctification, as it is in the Old Testament. Separation from sin is as necessary for Christians, as it was for the children of Israel. "For this is the will of God, even your sanctification, that ye should abstain from fornication" (1 Thess 4.3). For a believer the external ceremony of sanctification in the Old Testament is a picture of the internal sanctification that is required today. The cleansing of the life by confession of sins (1 Jn 1.9), and avoidance of the immoral things of the world, are necessary for the believer to remain sanctified and in a fit condition for the Lord to do wonders. "Having therefore these promises, dearly beloved, let us cleanse ourselves from all filthiness of the flesh and spirit, perfecting holiness in the fear of God" (2 Cor 7.1).

"Tomorrow the Lord will do wonders among you." This had been the promise of the Lord to Moses when he was on Mount Sinai receiving the second tables of stone: "Behold, I make a covenant. before all thy people I will do marvels, such as have not been done in all the earth, nor in any nation" (Ex 34.10). This promise to do "wonders" (6381) was given in the context of the covenant and it is interesting that this had already been brought before the people, as the officers had spoken of the "ark of the covenant of the Lord your God" (3.3). The "wonders" spoken of by Joshua would be seen in the crossing of the Jordan, with the magnitude of the Lord's intervention underlined with the use of "wonders", which word is also employed to describe the signs wrought in Egypt in order to persuade Pharaoh to let the children of Israel go (Ex 3.20).

Verse 6: Priests

"And Joshua spake unto the priests, saying, Take up the ark of the covenant, and pass over before the people". This instruction to the priests must have been given after Joshua had spoken to the people and on the "tomorrow" that he had referred to (v.5). It is inserted at this point in the narrative to give a material, rather than chronological, order to the chapter. The verses that follow must have preceded this verse chronologically as they provide the fuller instruction that Joshua gave to the priests and people. They would have been uttered by Joshua before the ark was carried to the Jordan, as he instructed in this verse. This is in keeping with the form of narrative in chs. 3-4.

Verses 7-8: Command of the Lord

Verse 7 commences the textual structure consisting of the command to Joshua, the communication to the people and then the execution by the people. This pattern occurs three times, providing the structure of the remaining verses of the chapter, and is the key to the success of the children of Israel. Joshua listened to the Lord and then the people hearkened to Joshua, and finally, the people obeyed the word of the Lord.

Throughout Scripture the pattern is the same, with the Lord having spoken to patriarchs, prophets, kings and apostles. In turn, the people of God have the Word of God communicated to them by teachers, and have the responsibility to implement what God has said to them through His servants. In order for the blessing of the Lord to be known, the messenger has to listen to the Lord; this is a challenge for the Bible teacher of today. It can be a temptation for the teacher to listen more to the words of men than the word of the Lord, and spend more time reading the comments of men on the Bible, rather than the Bible itself. When the teacher hears the word of the Lord through study and meditation on the Word of God, he has a responsibility to accurately communicate what he has learned to the people of God. They, in turn, must be willing to submit to the authority of the Word of God. When any aspect of this pattern breaks down, problems arise.

Joshua magnified (v.7)

"This day will I begin to magnify thee in the sight of all Israel". At this point the Lord is recorded as having spoken to Joshua for the first time since He had encouraged and challenged him in 1.1-9. Having promised to be with Joshua as He was with Moses, the Lord was going to demonstrate this to the people by performing a great wonder, which would remind the children of Israel of the wonders He performed through Moses when they came out of Egypt and through the Red Sea. The leadership of Moses had been established by the Red Sea experience (Ex 14.31), and was only one of many such occasions when the Lord performed a wonder to demonstrate the authority and validity of Moses' leadership. It is important to note that it was not Joshua who magnified himself before the people, since that would have been self-exaltation. It was the Lord who magnified him, and did so in such a manner which left no room for doubt that He had done this thing.

This was just the beginning of the wonders that the Lord performed, which taught the people that He was with Joshua just as He had been with Moses. These wonders did have the desired effect upon them, since there is no rebellion against Joshua recorded in the book and, in fact, the effect of these wonders lived on after Joshua had died (24.31).

The significance of the promise of the Lord to Joshua cannot be missed when considering Joshua as a picture of the Lord Jesus Christ. It was at "Beth-abara beyond Jordan" (Jn 1.28), that John stood and made his declaration regarding the Lord Jesus as the Lamb of God, and bore testimony to the Spirit of God descending from heaven, testifying that "this is the Son of God" (Jn 1.34). It was also at this place that a voice from heaven testified, "This is my beloved Son, in whom I am well pleased" (Mt 3.17). At Beth-abara the Father who spoke from heaven, and the Holy Spirit who descended from heaven, magnified the Lord Jesus. Thayer gives the meaning of Beth-abara as "house of the ford" and comments that "This may correspond to Beth-barah (fords of Abarah), the ancient ford of the Jordan on the road to Gilead a place beyond Jordan". If this be the case, it was the same place where the Lord began to magnify Joshua in the sight of Israel.

Instruction to the priests (v.8)

"When ye are come to the brink of the water of Jordan, ye shall stand still in Jordan". The instruction that Joshua received for the priests defied all natural instincts as the Jordan was overflowing its banks at that time of year. When the children of Israel had crossed the Red Sea, they had seen it dried up before they stepped down into the sea bed (Ex 14.21-22).

Verses 9-13: Communication by Joshua

Having received his instructions from the Lord, Joshua then communicates them to the people. As he did in v.4, Joshua gives the people a reason for the command of the Lord. He now explains that they will cross the Jordan in a certain manner, and provides them with two reasons for so doing. There were other paths that led into Canaan, but none of them would bring them into the land with such an assurance of the presence of the Lord among them and the certainty of success. It is often the Lord's way to bring the people of God into situations which appear to be impossible in order to bless them with displays of His manifold attributes, not only dealing with the situation, but blessing the people of God in a manner which would never have been known, but for the difficulty. It was in the storm that the disciples learned of the power of the Lord Jesus over the elements (Mk 4.39) and His ability to walk on water

(Mt 14.25). It was when the multitude was hungry and there was no bread to be found, apart from the provision of a young lad, that the disciples saw bread and fish multiply in the hands of the Lord Jesus (Jn 6.5-14).

Twofold benefit in crossing the Jordan (v.10)

"Hereby ye shall know that the living God is among you". The assurance of the Lord's presence that Joshua received directly from the Lord (1.5,9), was going to be given to the people by way of a great wonder. They would know that the "living God" (2416) (410) was among them. This title of the Lord occurs, in this form, another three times in the Old Testament (Ps 42.2; 84.2; Hos 1.10), and serves to remind the children of Israel that the gods of the nations that faced them in Canaan were not like their God. He was living and they were dead. In addition to this, He was among them. It is one thing to worship a God that lives; it is another thing to have the presence of the living God among His people. The presence of the living God among them would be graphically symbolised by the role that the ark of the covenant would play in the crossing of the Jordan.

"He will without fail drive out from before you the Canaanites, and the Hittites, and the Hivites, and the Perizzites, and the Girgashites, and the Amorites, and the Jebusites". The wonder that was to be performed that day would give the children of Israel the assurance that the Lord would, without fail, drive out the seven nations listed as occupying Canaan. When the apostle Paul was preaching in the synagogue in Antioch, he narrated the history of Israel, and spoke of the conquest of Canaan: "And when he had destroyed seven nations in the land of Chanaan, he divided their land to them by lot" (Acts 13.19). Similiar lists occur twenty three times in the Old Testament and on five occasions in Joshua (3.10; 9.1; 11.3; 12.8; 24.11). When they are considered together, there is a total of twelve nations listed as occupying Canaan with the seven in this chapter being the core nations that occur most frequently, and whose territories covered the geographical extent of the land that the children of Israel would seek to conquer.

"Canaanites"

This is sometimes used as a title of all of the occupants of the land. However, when the name is included in a list such as this, it refers to a distinct group of people with their own identity. Canaan was the son of Ham (Gen 9.18) and was the father of Heth (Hittites) and ten others, which interestingly include the Girgashites, Jebusites, Amorites and Hivites (1 Chr 1.13). He appears to have been the head of all of these families, which were scattered throughout the region "from Sidon, as thou comest to Gerar, unto Gaza; as thou goest, unto Sodom, and Gomorrah, and Admah, and Zeboim, even unto Lasha" (Gen 10.19). From Canaan the land was occupied by the nations that descended from his family, with a group of them retaining the name of Canaan. They were evidently traders and merchants, since the name is used in this way later in the Old Testament

(Zeph 1.11), and they appeared to have dwelt around the coasts of the land. When the spies went into the land after the exodus from Egypt they reported “the Canaanites dwell by the sea, and by the coast of Jordan” (Num 13.29). This remained their situation as the later comment reveals, “all the kings of the Canaanites, which were by the sea” (5.1). It appears from these references, that they dwelt by the coasts of the land on the east, and to the west, beside Jordan.

“Hittites”

This name occurs forty-eight times in the Bible and twenty times in the lists of those tribes which occupied the land of Canaan. They dwelt in the hill country of the land and are mentioned as the people from whom Abraham bought the cave at Machpelah, near Hebron (Gen 23). They are also mentioned in relation to Bethel (Judg 1.22-26), Jerusalem (Ezek 16.3), and the mountains (11.3; Num 13.29). It was Hittite women that Esau took as wives and caused grief to his parents (Gen 26.34; 27.46), yet it was Uriah the Hittite who was a faithful, if ultimately wronged, servant of David (2 Sam 11).

“Hivities”

They are mentioned as living in the shadow of Mount Hermon (11.3) and Mount Lebanon (Judg 3.3). The word means “villagers” (2340), and little else is known about them as to their character or subsequent history as a nation. The Gibeonites, from one of the cities of the Hittites, feature in the account of the conquest of Canaan due to their subterfuge, and subsequent peace treaty, which they obtained from the children of Israel (ch. 9). The result of this pact was that the four cities of the Hittites were spared from destruction: “And the children of Israel journeyed, and came unto their cities on the third day. Now their cities were Gibeon, and Chephirah, and Beeroth, and Kirjath-jearim. And the children of Israel smote them not, because the princes of the congregation had sworn unto them by the Lord God of Israel” (9.17-18).

“Perizzites”

This is another of the nations mentioned that has obscure beginnings. They are first noted as being in the land, along with the Canaanites, when Abraham returned from Egypt (Gen 13.7). They are located with others as dwelling in the mountains (11.3), and in the forests: “...get thee up to the wood country, and cut down for thyself there in the land of the Perizzites” (17.15). The name means “belonging to a village” (6522).

“Girgashites”

They are referred to on seven occasions in the Old Testament, and only in these lists of nations. As a descendant of Canaan, the Girgasite appears as the fifth son (Gen 10.16). There is not much noted as to the location of the Girgashites in the Old Testament although in the New Testament some commentators make the connection with the area on the east side of the Sea of Galilee (Mt 8.28). Josephus (*Ant.* i. 6, 2) wrote that "we possess the name and nothing more; not even the more definite notices of position, or the slight glimpses of character, general or individual, with which we are favoured in the case of the Amorites, Jebusites, and some others of these ancient nations".

"Amorites"

The Amorites were another people who dwelt in the mountains (Num 13.29) and were located at Hazezon-tamar (Gen 14.7), which Easton's Bible Dictionary places on the heights west of the Jordan. They are also mentioned as being at Hebron (Gen 14.13), Gilead, Bashan (Deut 3.10), and Hermon (Deut 3.8; 4.48). Prior to the children of Israel crossing the Jordan they defeated Sihon, king of the Amorites, and Og king of Bashan, and occupied some of the land of the Amorites, which was east of the Jordan. This was the area of Gilead which the tribes of Reuben, Gad and half of the tribe of Manasseh desired for an inheritance. The Amorites also had land west of the Jordan, as the kings of the Amorites are noted as dwelling on the side of the Jordan westward (5.1).

"Jebusites"

The Jebusites are the last nation to appear on the list. They are linked with a city rather than an area of the country, and were the pre-Israelite occupants of the city that became known as Jerusalem (15.8; 18.28). The Jebusite was the third son of Canaan (Gen 10.16), and whether as an individual, or a nation, his name always occurs as a singular word in the original language of the Old Testament.

Verses 11-13: How the crossing would be accomplished.

When Joshua explained to the children of Israel how the Lord was going to perform this great wonder, he identified three elements that would have an essential role in its execution. The extent of the role that each of these elements would have is expanded in ch.4.

1. *"Behold, the ark of the covenant of the Lord of all the earth passeth over before you into Jordan"* (v.11). He drew their attention to the ark, which was to play the central role in the crossing. The significance of the names given to the ark has been considered already (v.3). On this occasion, Joshua refers to it as the "ark of the covenant of the Lord of all the earth", which in itself was a wonderful reminder of the sovereign power of their God. This title of the Lord is first used in Scripture in this chapter where it also occurs in v.13. In the original language of the Old Testament, it is found in four other Scriptures and translated as "the Lord of the whole earth" (Ps 97.5; Mic 4.13; Zech 4.14; 6.5). On this occasion, and the four others mentioned above, the word employed for "Lord" is "Adon" (113),

which has the meaning of sovereign Lord. The people were in covenant relationship with the sovereign Lord of the land they were about to enter, and indeed, of all lands.

2. *"Take you twelve men out of the tribes of Israel, out of every tribe a man"* (v.12). Without going into any further detail at this stage of the narrative, Joshua instructs the tribes to pick out the man who is going to represent his tribe during the crossing. It is interesting that the only qualification is that he has to belong to a tribe. The task that these men performed was very important, with more detail provided in ch. 4.

3. *"And it shall come to pass, as soon as the soles of the feet of the priests that bear the ark of the Lord, the Lord of all the earth, shall rest in the waters of Jordan, that the waters of Jordan shall be cut off from the waters that come down from above; and they shall stand upon an heap"* (v.13). The priests had the responsibility of carrying the ark and, as the Lord had commanded (v.8), they were to step into the waters of Jordan. It was at the point at which they carried the ark into the waters of the Jordan that the wonder would commence. The twofold description of the drying up of the river contained in this verse is expanded in vv.16-17.

The circumstances of the crossing of the Red Sea and Jordan seem, on the face of it, to be identical, yet there are significant differences which are worthy of note. By contrasting Ex 14.21-31 with this chapter, it is evident that the intervention of the Lord at the Red Sea and the Jordan had many distinctive elements:

a) When the children of Israel faced the Red Sea they had an army of Egyptians seeking their destruction, and from whom they were escaping. In contrast, the children of Israel crossed the Jordan to commence a campaign of conquest. The Red Sea would take the people out and away from danger, whereas the Jordan would take them in and toward conflict.

b) There was no preparation required among the people for the crossing of the Red Sea, other than to stand still and watch. Before the Jordan was crossed the instruction for the people was to sanctify themselves.

c) At the Red Sea Moses stretched out his rod to commence the wonder. At the Jordan it was the soles of the priests' feet entering Jordan that commenced the wonder.

d) God used a strong east wind to cause the Red Sea to go back, whereas at the Jordan there is no mention of any specific means employed by God.

e) The Red Sea was dried up during the night and the Jordan during the day.

f) The Red Sea is described as being divided, whereas the river Jordan was cut off and stood upon a heap.

g) After the crossings took place, there were the Egyptians dead upon the shores of the Red Sea, and the twelve stones on the banks of the Jordan.

Although there are other differences, these serve to illustrate that the circumstances of the two crossings were notably distinct; this is significant when the application of the crossings are made in the New Testament context.

Verses 14-17: Execution by the People

This section, which describes the crossing of the Jordan in some detail, brings the narrative to a walking pace, and has an unusual sentence structure in the original Hebrew language. The section begins with the expression "And it came to pass" (AV) which can be rendered "so it was" (NKJV). Each of the following clauses in vv.14-15 which detail the movements of the people and priests, are subordinate to this clause, which is the commencement of the main thought of the section and is continued in v.16. David M. Howard Jnr. in the *New American Commentary* on Joshua at pp.130-131 helpfully states that "when v.16 is finally reached, the language changes and in quick succession two verbs appear describing the water stoppage: they stood up and they rose up. A few words later, two more verbs occur, describing this from a different perspective: they were completely cut off (the Hebrew here literally reads, they completely, they were cut off). In the short space of one verse, then, we find four different verbs reflecting on what happened to the waters. The language piles up in a manner that reminds us of the waters themselves piling up". The structure of the section serves to focus the reader's attention on the miracle that enabled the crossing to be made, rather than on the crossing itself.

The people move toward Jordan (v.14)

The Lord had spoken to Joshua (vv.7-8) and Joshua had spoken to the people (vv.9-13), and now there is the test of obedience. By moving toward Jordan and obeying the commands given to them through Joshua, they put the word of the Lord to the test. The sight must have been awesome, with the priests carrying the ark 2,000 cubits ahead of the people, and then, in marching order, the people coming behind; a nation on the move toward an impassable natural barrier. While the tribes of Canaan were concerned about the fields and harvests, the people of God must have had their eyes fixed upon the ark and the Jordan, as the distance between them narrowed.

The priests enter Jordan with the ark (v.15)

The moment arrived when "they that bare the ark were come unto Jordan, and the feet of the priests that bare the ark were dipped in the brim of the water". This moment was what is often described as the "moment of truth". If the waters did not dry up, then the whole future of the people of God would be thrown into confusion. The leadership of Joshua would have been fatally undermined, and any confidence that the people had in God would have disappeared. It really was a moment of truth. Such moments are still experienced by the people of God, as faith puts the promises of God to the test, in obedience to the Word of God. It can be a difficult experience, yet it is the route to blessing. If the promises of God fail, then everything fails for the child of God. If even one of His promises fails, then everything fails. This is the reason for the seemingly unnecessary insertion of the section in the Roman Epistle dealing with Israel past, present and future (Rom chs.9-11). If the promises of God to Israel have not been kept, then why should the gospel, about which Paul has written eight chapters, be different? Paul shows that God has, and will, keep His promises to Israel, giving confidence to any who would rely on His promises in the gospel.

The insertion of the comment, "for Jordan overfloweth all his banks all the time of harvest", ensures that any possibility of underestimating the wonder is removed. In fact, to cross the Jordan at this time of year, without the miracle that the Lord performed, is later noted as an act of valour on the part of the Gadites (1 Chr 12.14-15). This was evidently a feat which was possible for a comparatively small group of men, but impossible for a nation.

Jordan cut off (v.16)

Comment on the geographical location of the crossing and the extent of the drying up of Jordan is contained in a note at the end of the chapter.

Israelites pass over Jordan (v.17)

"And the priests that bare the ark of the covenant of the Lord stood firm on dry ground in the midst of Jordan". The priests held the ark in the middle of the Jordan while the whole of the nation crossed. There is no timescale given for the crossing, which was accomplished without any assault by the armies of the Canaanites.

The typical significance of the ark remaining in the Jordan, while the nation crossed, is worthy of note. It has already been seen that the ark is a picture of the Lord Jesus (v.3) and that there are distinctions between the crossing of the Red Sea and the Jordan, which have typical significance (v.13).

When the nation crossed the Red Sea, it was to come out of Egypt and away from bondage. Escape was the priority for the people, as the armies of Egypt sought to return them to their former servitude. The Red Sea did two things: it separated them from Egypt and was the means of destroying the military power of Egypt, with the sea having drowned the flower of Pharaoh's army. This is a picture of the Lord Jesus in His death upon the cross, bringing deliverance to sinners from the bondage of sin. In the New Testament Paul explains that the Lord Jesus has "delivered us from the power of darkness, and hath translated us into the kingdom of his dear Son" (Col 1.13). The writer to the Hebrews comments that "Forasmuch then as the children are partakers of flesh and blood, he also himself likewise took part of the same; that through death he might destroy him that had the power of death, that is, the devil" (Heb 2.14). The Red Sea is all about the death, burial and resurrection of the Lord Jesus for the sinner.

When the typical significance of the Jordan is considered, the emphasis is on the death, burial and resurrection of the believer with the Lord Jesus. The nation was not escaping an enemy, but rather going in to face many enemies, as they crossed the Jordan: it took them into blessing, whereas the Red Sea took them out of bondage. As the ark entered the Jordan, it provided a picture of the death, burial and resurrection of the Lord Jesus and the entrance into blessing that this had for the sinner. If the Red Sea emphasised what the sinner was saved from, the Jordan emphasises the blessings that the sinner has been saved for. Canaan has already been noted as a picture of the spiritual blessings which the believer receives upon conversion (Eph 1.3). The Jordan is a picture of the means of bringing the believer into the good of these blessings. This identification of the believer with the Lord Jesus in His death is taken up by Paul: "Wherefore if ye be dead (have died, JND) with Christ from the rudiments of the world, why, as though living in the world, are ye subject to ordinances"(Col 2.20), as is the resurrection: "If ye then be risen (have been raised, JND) with Christ, seek those things which are above, where Christ sitteth on the right hand of God" (Col 3.1).

As the people walked past the ark, they were made aware that it was the presence of the ark in the Jordan that was bringing them into the realisation of the Lord's promises. It was important that they did not forget how they had crossed, and who had brought them into the sphere of their blessing. Thus, instructions are given in ch.4 for memorials to be constructed.

Notes

16 Richard Hess (Tyndale Old Testament Commentaries on Joshua p.105) helpfully comments, "Adam is a site in the Jordan valley, identified with Tell ed-Damiye, 18 miles north of Jericho. Zarethan also lies east of the Jordan. Archaeologists have identified it with Tell es-Sa `idiyeh, 12 miles north of Adam, or with Tell Umm Hamid, 3 miles north of Adam. The site of Adam, immediately south of the Jabbok river, is important as a convenient point for crossing the Jordan. South of Adam the river becomes more difficult to cross. The Sea of the Arabah (the Salt Sea) is the Dead Sea which lies 18 miles from Adam, although the meandering Jordan is several times longer. The flood affected 29% of the Jordan valley".

The description of the geographical extent of the miracle is commented on by Keil & Delitzsch. "It was necessary, therefore, that the Lord of the whole earth should make a road by a miracle of His omnipotence, which arrested the descending waters in their course, so that they stood still as a heap *'very far'*, sc., from the place of crossing, *'by the town of Adam which is by the side of Zarthan.'* The city of Adam, which is not mentioned anywhere else is not to be confounded with Adamah, in the tribe of Naphtali (19.36). The town of *Zarthan,* by the side of which Adam is situated, has also vanished. *Knobel* supposes that Adam was situated in the neighbourhood of the present ford *Damieh,* near to which the remains of a bridge belonging to the Roman era are still to be found (*Lynch*, Expedition).

The distance of Kurn Sartabeh from Jericho is a little more than fifteen miles, which tallies very well with the expression 'very far'. Through this heaping up of the waters coming down from above, those which flowed away into the Dead Sea (the sea of the plain, see Deut 4.49) were completely cut off and the people went over, probably in a straight line from Wady Hesbân to Jericho".

JOSHUA 4

Crossing Jordan (cont.)

With the children of Israel having crossed the Jordan, ch.4 focuses on the establishment of two memorials. It has already been noted that the narrative of chs.3 and 4 is not presented chronologically, but is set out in a manner which primarily concentrates on the miracle which made the crossing possible; this is the reason for the prominence of the ark in ch.3. As ch.4 unfolds, the emphasis in the narrative changes to focus on the responsibility of the people to remember what had been done by the Lord, hence the prominence of the memorial stones in ch.4. This style of narrative switches the reader's attention from one participant in the crossing to another and, in so doing, builds the sense of drama and excitement which must have been the experience of the people as they approached and crossed over the Jordan.

A common saying is that "the only lesson that is learned from history is that no lessons are learned from history". The children of Israel were not to make this mistake and throughout their history were instructed by the Lord to observe feasts, build altars, construct memorials and recite their history to their children, to the end that their experience with God would not be lost to subsequent generations. Chapter 4 is the account of the construction of memorials, which were to remind the people of what had happened on the day that they crossed the Jordan.

Verses 1-9: The Establishment of Memorials

Choice of twelve men (vv.1-3)

The chapter opens with the repetition of the last words of ch.3, "all the people were clean passed over Jordan". Verse 1 sets the subsequent instruction to Joshua in a time frame, which could be viewed as problematic if a chronological view of the two chapters were adopted. From ch.3 the reader has already noted that Joshua had instructed the people to choose twelve men, one man out of each tribe (v.12). Yet here in 3.1, the Lord gave the instruction to Joshua to do that very thing. Keil & Delitzsch address the issue and take the following view: "This makes it appear as though God did not give the command to Joshua until the people had all crossed over, whereas the twelve men had already been chosen for the purpose (3.12). But this appearance, and the discrepancy that seems to arise, vanish as soon as we take the different clauses...as follows. 'Then Joshua called the twelve men...as Jehovah had commanded him, saying, Take you twelve men out of the people...and said to them'".

There is no record of the Lord giving instruction to Joshua to take twelve men from the tribes prior to the crossing (3.12). This in itself should not preclude the reader from coming to the conclusion that Joshua had been instructed to do so by the Lord. The further instruction (4.2-3), giving the purpose of the twelve men, is recorded as being given to Joshua after the crossing of Jordan. Again, this should not be viewed as problematic, as it is not inconsistent with the pattern of repetition and addition in the narrative, and the progressive nature of the instructions that Joshua received from the Lord.

The Lord instructed Joshua to "take you twelve men out of the people, out of every tribe a man" (v.2). These men were representative of all the nation which had crossed the Jordan. This could not have been done if the two and a half tribes had remained on the east side of the Jordan and had not agreed to cross over and fight with the rest of the people. As a result of their obedience the nation was united in their crossing and this is symbolised in the twelve men, with one from each tribe. The unity of the nation was always a matter of importance and no more so than at this time of conquest. The people were strong when they were united, having a common purpose, focused on the land and enemies that had to be faced. Weakness among the people came with division. This is still true with unity being one of the aspects of the Lord's prayer for Christians in His absence (Jn 17.11, 21-23). The inability to unite around the Word of God and the Lord Jesus has arguably been the greatest weakness of Christian witness throughout the ages, leading to fragmented denominationalism.

Each man had to take a stone from "out of the midst of Jordan, out of the place where the priests' feet stood firm" (v.3). This was the place in the Jordan where the priests had held the ark until the entire nation had passed over. The stones were taken from that place and carried out of the Jordan river bed for the purpose of forming a memorial. It is interesting that the river that would divide the two and a half tribes in Gilead from the rest of the nation provided the stones for the memorial of the Lord's wonder for the whole nation. The stones were to be left in the place where the people would lodge for the night after the crossing, which was named Gilgal (v.19). No mention is made at this stage of the construction of the memorial, since that task fell to Joshua and is recorded later (v.20).

Meaning of the stones (vv.4-7)

The pattern of the narrative continues throughout this section of ch.4, as it did in the previous chapter. The Lord gave instruction to Joshua, he then communicated this to the people, and they are recorded as having executed his command. This pattern has produced a fair amount of repetition in the text with some additional comments, which are important to note.

Joshua "called the twelve men, whom he had prepared of the children of Israel, out of every tribe a man" (v.4). It is instructive to note that Joshua "called" men that he had "prepared". The word "prepared" (3559) comes from the same root Hebrew word which appears in the expressions which are translated, "prepare you victuals" (1.11), "stood firm" (4.3) and "be ye all ready" (8.4). It has the idea of preparations that have been fixed or determined. This reinforces the view that Joshua had already spoken to the tribes about the twelve men (3.12) and now calls them, having prepared them prior to the crossing.

The additional element to the repetition of the instruction of the Lord to Joshua from v.3, gives an idea of the size of the memorial that was established at Gilgal. Each man was instructed to take "a stone upon his shoulder" (v.5), which indicates that the stones were large, yet each of a size that could be borne by one man. Twelve such stones would make a memorial that was unassuming in its dimensions, perhaps no taller than a man. It would be a landmark that was durable, but not so impressive as to become a cause for worship and idolatry. The purpose of the memorial was to draw attention to the wonder that the Lord had performed, rather than to the memorial itself.

It is appropriate at this point to make comment on the New Testament memorial to the death and resurrection of the Lord Jesus, which is a weekly reminder of the wonder that the Jordan and the Red Sea typify. The Lord's Supper was instituted by the Lord Jesus on the Passover night before He died, "and he took bread, and gave thanks, and brake it, and gave unto them, saying, This is my body which is given for you. this do in remembrance of me. Likewise also the cup after supper, saying, This cup is the new testament in my blood, which is shed for you" (Lk 22.19-20). Paul expanded the instruction of the Lord Jesus, when he wrote to the Corinthians (1 Cor 11.23-26), explaining that "as often as ye eat this bread, and drink this cup, ye do shew the Lord's death till he come" (1 Cor 11.26). The believer has a reminder of the Lord Jesus in His death, as he partakes of the Lord's Supper on the first day of the week (Acts 20.7), being the day of the week on which He rose again. The Supper, in its simplicity and unassuming nature, serves as a weekly landmark drawing the attention of the believer to the Lord Jesus, just as the stones at Gilgal reminded the children of Israel of the miracle that the Lord performed to bring them into Canaan. Bearing in mind the above comments on the size of the memorial at Gilgal, it is important that this lesson is not lost when the Lord's Supper is considered. The purpose of the bread and cup, which are the essential elements of the Supper, is to draw attention to the body and blood of the Lord Jesus. They are not to be the centre of attention for the believer, nor should they be treated as holy objects in the way that items of the tabernacle were to be treated by the children of Israel. To attach a disproportionate significance to the bread and cup would be equivalent to the children of Israel venerating the memorial in Gilgal and forgetting its purpose, which was to bring the children of Israel to worship the Lord.

The purpose behind the removal of the twelve stones from the Jordan and the erection of a memorial in Gilgal is explained to the twelve men in vv.6-7. The stones and the memorial were to provoke the children to ask their fathers in days to come, "What mean ye by these stones?" (v.6). The question posed was personal and can be rendered, "What do these stones mean to you?" (NKJV). This was not a new concept to the children of Israel as they had already received similar instruction in connection with the Passover (Ex 12.26-27), the separation of the firstborn for the Lord (Ex 13.14-16) and "the testimonies, and the statutes, and the judgments" (Deut 6.20). They were not to be afraid of a generation rising up with questions and, in fact, these questions were to be provoked by the presence of the memorial stones. A new generation among the people of God was to be educated in the things of God by a generation who had experienced great blessing, through the intervention of the Lord on their behalf. This could remove the inevitable problems associated with a second and third generation. The impact of the wonder that the Lord performed would not be lost to children growing up, enjoying the benefit of what the Lord had accomplished, yet not being present when it took place.

This can be a problem for Christians who have been brought up by believing parents, and have never known the extent of sin, and the world, that their parents knew before they were saved. It also applies when saints who paid a great price for identifying themselves with a local assembly, turning their back on the denominational systems of the world, raise a family within the local assembly sphere, who do not appreciate the blessings which their parents paid a heavy price to enjoy. It is the problem of the second and third generation. One of the ways to counter this problem is to do what the Lord instructed the children of Israel to do: to encourage an attitude of enquiry among a new generation, that they might question the meaning and purpose behind the Christian life lived out before them; to place value upon an enquiring mind, which does not accept everything at face value in ignorance, but seeks rather to investigate and uncover the truth of God by asking an older generation.

"Then ye shall answer them" (v.7). The responsibility was laid upon them to answer the younger generation. Older Christians should not consider such questions as arising from impertinence or rebellion. A lack of patience, or intolerance of youth, can lead to some older Christians attempting to instruct the young in the ways of God by imposing rules, rather than explaining the truth.

The explanation that the people were instructed to give to their children had two elements to it. Firstly, "the waters of Jordan were cut off" (v.7), which is repeated in the verse and was the explanation of what had happened (3.13,16). Secondly, the "ark of the covenant of the Lord" is mentioned and provides the answer to the question that would inevitably follow, "How had the waters of the Jordan been cut off ?".

The stones were to be for "a memorial unto the children of Israel for ever". The Hebrew word which is translated as "memorial" appears only here in Joshua, but occurs on twenty-four occasions in the Old Testament, thirteen of which are in the books of Exodus, Leviticus and Numbers. It is employed to describe the Passover and exodus (Ex 12.14; 13.9), the defeat of the Amalekites (Ex 17.14), the high priest's ephod (Ex 28.12, 29; 39.7), the atonement money (Ex 30.16), the feast of trumpets (Lev 23.24; Num

10.10), a grain offering (Num 5.15,18), bronze censers (Num 16.40) and the offering of the gold from the captains of thousands and hundreds (Num 31.54). Therefore remembrance by way of a memorial was an intrinsic part of the nation's life. The establishment of these stones added to the permanent memorials that helped form the structure of national life for the children of Israel. The stones were to be a perpetual memorial and were not to be established as a temporary structure which would fall into disrepair and become a meaningless relic of a bygone age. It is worth reiterating the importance of education among the people of God in relation to the things of God. The truth of God must be passed down through the generations, as Paul instructed Timothy: "The things that thou hast heard of me among many witnesses, the same commit thou to faithful men, who shall be able to teach others also" (2 Tim 2.2). If this is not practised by older Christians, then exhortations like that of Paul, "Therefore, brethren, stand fast, and hold the traditions which ye have been taught, whether by word, or our epistle" (2 Thess 2.15), become meaningless to a younger generation of believers.

The two memorials (vv.8-9)

Verses 8 and 9 record the implementation of the command of Joshua by the people. They "did so as Joshua commanded, and took up twelve stones out of the midst of Jordan, as the Lord spake unto Joshua, according to the number of the tribes of the children of Israel". The twelve men who represented the twelve tribes took the stones, but the people are recognised as being obedient to the command of Joshua, which was in effect the command of the Lord. There were other occasions in the history of Israel when the Lord placed the responsibility for the actions of a few men upon the whole nation, either for good or for evil. This is seen in the experience of Achan who sinned, yet the Scriptures record that "the children of Israel committed a trespass in the accursed thing" (7.1).

The stones were placed on the west side of the Jordan in the place where the people lodged. It is not until later in the narrative that the location of the memorial is identified (v.20). The emphasis in this verse is upon the obedience of the people. The responsibility ultimately fell upon Joshua to construct the memorial, but here the memorial is not recorded as being built, only the material is gathered at the "place where they lodged" (v.8).

There have been some commentators who do not accept that there were two memorials, and take the view that v.9 is a record of the construction by Joshua of the memorial at Gilgal, which is then mentioned again in v.20. They would see v.9 as being parenthetical, and providing a description of the gathering up of stones in the Jordan when the priests were holding the ark in the river bed. However, the comments of Keil & Delitzsch are worthy of note in relation to the presence of a memorial in the river bed of Jordan: "There is nothing to warrant our calling this statement in question, or setting it aside as a probable gloss, either in the circumstance that nothing is said about any divine command to set up these stones, or in the opinion that such a memorial would have failed of its object, as it could not possibly have remained, but would very speedily have been washed away by the stream ... But it cannot be so absolutely affirmed that these stones would be carried away at once by the stream, so that they could never be seen any more. As the priests did not stand in the middle or deepest part of the river, but just in the bed of the river, and close to its eastern bank, and it was upon this spot that the stones were set up, and as we neither know their size nor the firmness with which they stood, we cannot pronounce any positive opinion as to the possibility of their remaining. It is not likely that they remained there for centuries; but they were intended rather as a memorial for the existing generation and their children, than for a later age, which would be perpetually reminded of the miraculous help of God by the monument erected in Gilgal".

The typical significance of the two memorials is also very important, since it is a reminder of the association which the believer has with the death and resurrection of the Lord Jesus. The stones in the Jordan speak of the death of the Lord Jesus and the stones in Gilgal of His resurrection.

The memorial which was established by Joshua in the Jordan was different from that built in Gilgal. It was said of the memorial in Gilgal that it was to be a "memorial ... for ever" (v.7). The stones within the Jordan were "set up" and "are there unto this day". The expression "unto this day", or, "until this day", appears frequently in the book of Joshua and is used in this book more than in any other book in the Old Testament. It is employed when an explanation of the background is given to places or people, which would have provoked interest among the children of Israel at the time that the book of Joshua was written, e.g. the name given to Gilgal (5.9), the presence of Rahab and her family in Israel (6.25), the name given to the valley of Achor after the death of Achan and his family (7.26), the heap of stones raised over the body of the king of Ai (8.29), and the presence of certain people in the land (9.27; 13.13; 14.14; 15.63; 16.10).

THE TYPICAL SIGNIFICANCE OF THE TWELVE STONES

In the New Testament the Lord would have believers remember His intervention in power on their behalf, which was altogether greater than the parting of the Jordan. The memorial stones which were established, in and out of the Jordan, have a symbolic significance for the Christian.

In order to understand the significance of the memorials in the context of the New Testament, it is important to place the Jordan in the context of the Epistle to the Colossians. In this epistle the two memorials established by Joshua can be seen typically. The apostle Paul teaches that the Christian has been identified with the Lord Jesus in His death, as typified by the ark entering the Jordan and being held in the centre of the river bed, with a memorial subsequently established at that point. Thus the apostle describes the believer as "buried with him in baptism" (Col 2.12), and also states, "if ye be dead (have died, JND) with Christ" (Col 2.20). He then proceeds to show that the believer is also identified with the Lord Jesus in His resurrection, as typified by the stones which were removed from the place where the priests had stood with the ark, and placed as a memorial at Gilgal (v.20). The apostle speaks of the believer in the following way, "ye are risen with him" (Col 2.12), "if ye then be risen with Christ (if then you were raised with Christ, NKJV)" (Col 3.1). Both of these aspects of the believer's identification with the Lord Jesus are summarised by the apostle: "for ye are dead, and your life is hid with Christ in God" (Col 3.3).

Paul emphasises the practical import of these aspects of truth in the Colossian Epistle. When the Red Sea deliverance is considered in the context of the New Testament, it brings before the believer an appreciation of salvation from sin and bondage, which the Lord Jesus brought about as a result of His death and resurrection. The emphasis is upon that from which the believer has been saved. The crossing of the Jordan and the establishment of the memorial stones, point to the place where the believer has been taken in his experience with God, having died and risen with Christ. With the issues of the wilderness past, the believer, by faith, grasps the significance of his union with Christ, not only in His death, but also in His resurrection, which takes him on to new ground in his experience with God. This is the truth upon which the apostle builds his exhortation in order to take the Colossian believers away from the rudiments of the world, which were associated with the flesh: "seek those things which are above, where Christ sitteth on the right hand of God. Set your affection on things above, not on things on the earth" (Col 3.1-2).

It is worthy of note that the epistle which takes the typology beyond the crossing of the Jordan is that to the Ephesians. The progression of typology in this connection can be traced from the Epistle to the Romans, which finds us in Egyptian conditions, under the bondage of sin, and brings us into the blessing of salvation through the death of Christ for sins, and His resurrection for the believer's justification (Rom 3.20-6.23). As we have seen, the Epistle to the Colossians brings the believer into death with Christ and then on to resurrection ground with Christ. However, there is no mention of heavenly places in Colossians. The Epistle to the Ephesians takes the believer from the Jordan into Canaan; He has "raised us up together, and made us sit together in heavenly places in Christ Jesus" (Eph 2.6).

Verses 10-18: The Completion of the Crossing

The crossing of the people (v.10)

Verse 10 provides a summary of the crossing of the people over the Jordan and emphasises their obedience to the word of the Lord. The crossing was completed by the people as "the priests which bare the ark stood in the midst of Jordan". This had already been stated (3.17) with the emphasis on the fact of their crossing. In this verse the complete obedience of the people, as they crossed over, is stressed. The priests remained standing in the Jordan "until every thing was finished that the Lord commanded Joshua to speak unto the people, according to all that Moses commanded Joshua". The command of the Lord had come directly to Joshua (1.2-9; 3.7-8; 4.2-3) and had been preceded by those given to him by Moses (Num 32.28-30; Deut 31.3, 7-8). It is interesting to observe that one of the specific areas of command Joshua received from Moses referred to the tribes which were settling in Gilead on the east of the Jordan. Joshua was instructed to make sure they passed over Jordan and were prepared to fight, in accordance with their undertaking to Moses.

The people did not delay in their crossing and made their way across the river bed in haste – "the people hasted and passed over". This is in contrast to the priests who stood and held the ark while the people crossed. The patient obedience of the priests caused them to remain still, while the ready obedience of the people caused them to hurry across. Both were obedient, yet one group stood still while the other moved quickly. This is the character of the service of God, which has diversity yet with unity of purpose. Both groups had their roles to fulfil which caused them to take different stances in the Jordan, yet the purpose was the same. There is an appropriate time for standing still in the service of God and for moving quickly. When it is time for one person to move in service for God, it may be that another must stand still. The priests were engaged in facilitating the crossing of the people and were as active in so doing as they bore the ark, as the people who moved across. Without the patient perseverance of the priests the people would not have crossed. Conversely, if the people delayed in their crossing then the strain on the priests as they bore the ark would have been great.

The crossing of the priests with the ark (v.11)

"All the people were clean passed over", is a phrase which has already been used to describe the crossing of the people (3.17; 4.1), with the structure of the phrase translated in a slightly different order in 3.17. The verb employed in the phrase is also used to describe the completion of the commands of Joshua (v.10). Thus the language indicates a full and complete response by the children of Israel. It was only when everything had been done and everyone was over the Jordan, that the priests moved from their position on the river bed of Jordan.

The record of the crossing by the priests is interesting, since it gives the impression that the ark passed over by itself and the priests followed on. This, of course, was not the case, but the narrative does give the place of prominence to the ark and not to the priests: "the ark of the Lord passed over, and the priests". The important point was that the ark remained in the Jordan until all the people had crossed over. The priests were secondary to the ark and this is why the narrative does not speak of the priests coming out of the Jordan with the ark.

As the ark passed over the Jordan and the priests came out, it was "in the presence of the people". The people had not only witnessed the ark in the Jordan as they passed over, they also witnessed the ark coming out of the Jordan. There were many who witnessed the death of the Lord Jesus, as typified by the ark remaining in the Jordan (Mt 27.54-61; Mk 15.39-41; Lk 23.47-52; Jn 19.32-42). Just as the ark came out of the Jordan, so Christ rose from the dead as He had said, "I lay down my life, that I might take it again. No man taketh it from me, but I lay it down of myself. I have power to lay it down, and I have power to take it again" (Jn 10.17-18). The picture continues as the people witnessed the ark coming out of the Jordan in the same way that the resurrection of the Lord Jesus was witnessed, as recorded by the apostle Paul (1 Cor 15.5-8).

Trans-Jordan tribes cross (vv.12-13)

The mention that the trans-Jordan tribes passed over the Jordan is significant, as it emphasises the unity in the nation at the time of the crossing. This had been the concern of Moses and Joshua when the tribes had asked Moses for their inheritance on the east of the Jordan. This has already been the subject of comment (1.12-18). The further detail that is given regarding their crossing is worthy of note.

They "passed over armed" (v.12) and "prepared for war" (v.13). In so doing they fulfilled the command of Joshua (1.14). They marched in battle array and were prepared for war. It has already been noted (1.14) that the word "armed" (2571), has the meaning of harnessed, or ranked in divisions of five and, as such, marshalled for war (Ex 13.18; Judg 7.11). The word "prepared" (2502), in the form in which it appears, has the meaning of being equipped. There was no doubt that these tribes were passing over to fight as they marched in battle order, fully equipped for war.

It is interesting that they are described as having passed over "before the children of Israel" (v.12), and "before the Lord" (v.13). The Hebrew word translated "before" (6440) is the same word which is translated "in the presence of" (v.11). The narrative has followed the pattern which is by now familiar to the reader, presenting the information in an order of thought rather than of time. The structure of the section in the chapter, which presents the trans-Jordan tribes crossing Jordan after the mention of the ark coming out of the Jordan, does not imply that these tribes were behind the ark. This was not possible, as the waters came together after the ark left the river bed (v.18). Nor does the use of the word "before" imply that these tribes passed over the Jordan as an advance party to provide a secure area on the west of the river, while the other tribes crossed over. Rather, the narrative is informing the reader that these tribes passed over in the presence of the other tribes and of the Lord. This was in accordance with the instruction of Moses (Num 32.20-22; Deut 3.18-20), which had been re-iterated by Joshua (1.12-15). Reference should be made to comments on (1.14) regarding the number of armed men from these tribes who crossed Jordan.

Completion of the crossing from the divine perspective (vv.14-18)
Emphasis on the Lord

As the account of the crossing of the Jordan is completed, the emphasis of the narrative returns to the Lord, with a symmetry in chs.3 and 4 which is worthy of note:

"And the Lord said unto Joshua, This day will I begin to magnify thee in the sight of all Israel, that they may know that, as I was with Moses, so I will be with thee" (3.7).

"On that day the Lord magnified Joshua in the sight of all Israel; and they feared him, as they feared Moses, all the days of his life" (4.14).

"And thou shalt command the priests that bear the ark of the covenant, saying, When ye are come to the brink of the water of Jordan, ye shall stand still in Jordan" (3.8).

"And the Lord spake unto Joshua, saying, Command the priests that bear the ark of the testimony, that they come up out of Jordan." (4.15-16).

In terms of chronology, the ark was already seen to be out of the Jordan (v.11), yet, as has been repeatedly noted in chs.3 and 4, the style of narrative presents the crossing of the Jordan in a manner which not only informs, but also instructs, the reader. Bearing this in mind, this section (vv.14-18) commences and closes with instruction from the Lord. By presenting the account in this way, the emphasis is placed upon the Lord rather than the miracle that He accomplished. He was in control and only when He gave instruction did the waters cease and only after He spoke did the waters return.

New perspective

The perspective has also changed from the previous verses, which informed the reader that the ark was out of the Jordan. Up until this point the ark "passed over" (v.11), but here the command to the priests was to "come up out of Jordan" (v.16). The perspective is now from the west of the Jordan rather than from the east. This is a significant change as the east of the Jordan was now past for the majority of the children of Israel and everything had changed. The crossing of the Jordan had altered their perspective and now they looked upon things from the west of the river. This is also true of believers in the New Testament context. It is only when the believer realises that he has died with Christ and risen with Him (see earlier comments on the typical significance of the twelve stones), that his perspective changes and everything is seen from a different viewpoint.

Waters returned

Verse 18 provides some detail regarding the return of the river Jordan to its former condition. It was at the precise moment "when the priests that bare the ark of the covenant of the Lord were come up out of the midst of Jordan, and the soles of the priests' feet were lifted up unto the dry land, that the waters of Jordan returned unto their place, and flowed over all his banks, as they did before". The people were left in no doubt that the presence of the ark in the Jordan had been instrumental in the waters drying up, and with its removal the river returned to its natural condition for that time of the year, with no adverse after effect.

Verses 19-24: The Memorial at Gilgal

The date of the crossing (v.19)

Until this point in the book, there is no indication of the date on which the children of Israel crossed the Jordan. The time of year had been broadly identified as harvest time, when the Jordan flooded (3.15). Now the reader is informed that "the people came up out of Jordan on the tenth day of the first month". This is another link with the crossing of the Red Sea. It has already been the subject of some comment that the typical significance of the Jordan and of the Red Sea centres on the death, burial and resurrection of the Lord Jesus, both for the believer and of the believer with the Lord Jesus. Now the Scriptures reveal that the crossings were undertaken at the same time of year, thus providing a further link between them.

The first month was named Abib (Ex 13.4; 23.15; 34.18; Deut 16.1). Easton, in his Bible Dictionary, gives the meaning of the word as, "an ear of corn, the month of newly-ripened grain, the first of the Jewish ecclesiastical year, and the seventh of the civil year. It began about the time of the vernal equinox, on 21 March. It was called Nisan, after the Captivity (Neh 2.1)".

It was on the tenth day of the first month, forty years previously, that the Lord had instructed the children of Israel to set apart a lamb for sacrifice (Ex 12.3). When the twelve spies had returned from Canaan and the people had been disobedient to the Lord, He had said that "your children shall wander in the wilderness forty years, and bear your whoredoms, until your carcases be wasted in the wilderness" (Num14.33). The tenth day of the first month meant that it was four days short of the forty year period when they entered the land. It was necessary for the people to come over Jordan at this time in order to prepare for the Passover which was to be observed in the land. The Passover lamb was killed on the fourteenth day of the first month (Ex 12.6,18; Josh 5.10), which gave them time to make the appropriate preparations.

More will be said later when the Passover is considered in ch.5; however, it is noteworthy at this point that the children of Israel began their journey out of Egypt with the establishment of the Passover. Their beginning as a nation was associated with that typical feast which speaks so eloquently of the death of the Lord Jesus (1 Cor 5.7). It is not without significance that the entrance of the nation into the land was also closely associated with the Passover. It is therefore good to remember that the liberation from the bondage of sin that salvation brings is a direct consequence of the sacrifice of the Lord Jesus at Calvary. It is also true that the blessings that are received by the believer, upon conversion, which have "raised us up together, and made us sit together in heavenly places in Christ Jesus" (Eph 2.6), are traced back to Calvary.

After crossing the Jordan the people "encamped in Gilgal, in the east border of Jericho". This is not the first mention of Gilgal in the Old Testament. When Moses was bringing a blessing and curse before the people (Deut 11.16-32), he spoke of mount Gerizim and mount Ebal as being situated "on the other side Jordan, by the way where the sun goeth down, in the land of the Canaanites, which dwell in the champaign over against Gilgal, beside the plains of Moreh" (Deut 11.30). This is unlikely to be the same place which is mentioned as the first encampment of the children of Israel in Canaan (see note at the end of the chapter). The "east border of Jericho" and "the plains of Jericho" (v.13) are the only geographical pointers provided in this chapter enabling the reader to locate Gilgal.

The memorial erected (v.20)

The stones for the memorial and the erection of them by Joshua provide two further points of illustration regarding the Lord's Supper of the New Testament. The memorial was a reminder of the unity of the nation, as they were brought into the sphere of blessing. One stone from each tribe formed the memorial and was a landmark to the dealings of the Lord among all the children of Israel. It is interesting that in the New Testament the apostle Paul refers to the Lord's Supper as the feature of the Lord's Table which is illustrative of fellowship. He speaks of the believer partaking of the bread and the cup as a declaration of "the communion of the blood of Christ" and "the body of Christ" (1Cor 10.16). He proceeds to state that "we being many are one bread, and one body. for we are all partakers of that one bread" (1 Cor 10.17). The weekly memorial to the death and resurrection of the Lord Jesus is also a declaration of the fellowship of the saints.

"Those twelve stones...did Joshua pitch in Gilgal". Joshua, and not the people who would be served by it, built the memorial. This is another point of comparison with the Lord's Supper which was instituted by the Lord Jesus, and not by the disciples.

The purpose of the memorial (vv.21-24)

The instructions of vv.6-7 are repeated in this closing part of the chapter. As is consistent with the style of narrative employed in the chapter, there are additions to the instructions which are noted, and are representative of the new perspective of the people (vv.14-18).

Perhaps the most significant addition is the first mention of the fact that "the Lord your God dried up the waters of Jordan from before you, until ye were passed over, as the Lord your God did to the Red sea, which he dried up from before us, until we were gone over"(v.23). Although the verb "dried up" does not appear in the Exodus account of the Red Sea crossing, Rahab uses it when she refers to the crossing of the Red Sea (2.10). The link between the two miracles is made explicitly, lest the reader miss the point and fail to make the comparison.

There was a twofold purpose in the memorial from the perspective of Canaan. Firstly, "That all the people of the earth might know the hand of the Lord, that it is mighty" (v.24). This had been the effect upon the people of the land when they had heard about the Red Sea and the defeat of the two kings of the Amorites on the east side of the Jordan (2.10-11). The strength and might of the Lord would now reverberate around Canaan, as a result of the Jordan having been crossed. Secondly, the miracle that the Lord performed in drying up the Jordan would also have an effect upon the people, "that ye might fear the Lord your God for ever" (v.24). When the Red Sea was crossed, there was also an effect upon the people, "And Israel saw that great work which the Lord did upon the Egyptians. and the people feared the Lord, and believed the Lord, and his servant Moses" (Ex 14.31). Thus the establishment of the memorial at Gilgal had a message for the people of Canaan, to remind them of the might of the Lord, and also for the children of Israel, to make them continually fear the Lord. It is interesting that this twofold purpose of the memorial in Gilgal has an echo in the words of the apostle Paul regarding the Lord's Supper. It is for the people of God: "this do in remembrance of me" (1 Cor 11.24), but it also has a message for those who are not believers: "ye do shew the Lord's death till he come" (1 Cor 11.26).

Notes

19 It is unlikely that the Gilgal of Deuteronomy 11.30 is the same place at which the people encamped for their first night in Canaan. They named the place Gilgal after they had re-introduced circumcision among the people. Keil & Delitzsch comment that this is "not the southern Gilgal between Jericho and the Jordan, which received its name for the first time in Josh 4.20 and Josh 5.9; but probably … is only about twelve and a half miles [20 kilometres] from Gerizim in a southern direction, and has been preserved in the large village of *Jiljilia* to the south-west of Sinjil … Judging from this description of the situation, Mount Gerizim must be visible from this Gilgal, so that Gerizim and Ebal might very well be described as over against Gilgal".

Smith's Revised Bible Dictionary (1999), also comments on the possibility of two Gilgals in Canaan and speaks of the Gilgal of Joshua in the following terms: "But this was certainly a distinct place from the Gilgal which is connected with the last scene in the life of Elijah, and with one of Elisha's miracles. The chief reason for believing this is the impossibility of making it fit into the notice of Elijah's translation. He and Elisha are said to 'go down' from Gilgal to Bethel (2 Kings 2.1), in opposition to the repeated expressions of the narratives in Joshua and 1 Samuel, in which the way from Gilgal to the neighbourhood of Bethel is always spoken of as an ascent, the fact being that the former is nearly 1,200 feet [370 metres] below the latter. Thus there must have been a second Gilgal at a higher level than Bethel, and it was probably that at which Elisha worked the miracle of healing on the poisonous pottage (2 Kings 4.38). Perhaps the expression of (2 Kings 2.1), coupled with the 'came again' of 2 Kings 4.38, may indicate that Elisha resided there".

JOSHUA 5

Pre-Conquest Preparations

One of the keys to success in any military campaign is momentum. This is where the military historian would find the behaviour of Joshua "the general" unusual, following the crossing of the Jordan. Having established a bridgehead, it might have been expected that Joshua would have sought to engage the enemy as soon as possible, to prevent the nations of Canaan attacking Israel when they were vulnerable. But Joshua did not advance and engage the enemy after the crossing of Jordan. In fact, he brought them to a halt and instructed them to conduct a ceremony which left them physically weakened and, as a result, seemingly defenceless.

Although the halt in the advance at Gilgal did not make military sense, it was vital for the children of Israel. It served to instruct them, yet again, that the conquest of Canaan would not be accomplished by military might or planning, but would be given to them by the Lord, if they obeyed His voice and carried out His commands. The strength of the children of Israel was not to be compared with that of the nations of Canaan and therefore to rely upon this for their victory would have been folly. This has been the pattern of spiritual conflict in which the people of God have been engaged throughout the ages of time. The forces of Satan and the might of his emissaries have always seemed stronger than the people of God. Victory for God's people cannot be achieved by their own strength. It was thus when the bondage of Egypt was left behind and the armies of the Egyptians were destroyed in the Red Sea, and it continued throughout the times of the judges, kings and the recovery from Babylon. When the history of the people of God is traced throughout the early years of the New Testament, the pattern remains that of overwhelming force on the side of Satan, yet victory known by the people of God as a result of obedience and devotion to the Lord.

It was a new beginning for the children of Israel, just as the crossing of the Red Sea had been for them. With this new beginning there had to be change, and time was required in order to make the adjustments which were necessary for their entrance into the land. The sojourn at Gilgal served a fourfold purpose. The rite of circumcision was re-introduced and the Passover celebrated once again, together with a change of diet and revelation of the Lord to Joshua. The chapter may be divided as follows:

v.1	Fear of the Nations of Canaan
vv.2-9	Circumcision
v.10	Passover
vv.11-12	Change of Diet
vv.13-15	Revelation of the Lord.

Verse 1: Fear of the Nations of Canaan

Before the chapter unfolds the details of what took place at Gilgal, there is mention of the effect that the crossing of the Jordan had upon the people of Canaan. This provides the explanation as to why the nations in Canaan did not attack the children of Israel as they waited at Gilgal. The description of the nations is abbreviated to "all the kings of the Amorites, which were on the side of Jordan westward, and all the kings of the Canaanites, which were by the sea". This description encapsulates the warlike tribes that dwelt in the mountains, as represented by the Amorites who were the strongest and most powerful of that group, and the trading tribes in the lowlands and by the sea, who were represented by the Canaanities. All of the tribes, notwithstanding their character or location within Canaan, were affected by the miracle which the Lord performed at the Jordan. The debilitating effect upon the tribes of Canaan had been prophesied in the song of Moses (Ex 15.14-16) forty years before and had been confirmed by Rahab (2.10-11) in her conversation with the spies. Without a single blow struck in battle, the tribes of Canaan had been rendered afraid and had had their resolve diminished as they faced the children of Israel; the Lord had demoralised them to such an extent "that their heart melted, neither was there spirit in them any more".

It is worth pointing out that the position of the people as they faced the conquest of Canaan was extremely advantageous. They had been brought over the Jordan in fulfilment of the Lord's promise, and in such a manner that the enemy's morale was low; they were paralysed by fear. In order to arrive at such a position the children of Israel had only to obey the word of the Lord, as they had done in the crossing. Samuel brought this very lesson to Saul: "Hath the Lord as great delight in burnt offerings and sacrifices, as in obeying the voice of the Lord? Behold, to obey is better than sacrifice, and to hearken than the fat of rams" (1 Sam 15.22). How often the importance of simple obedience to the Lord is forgotten in the schemes and plans of believers, as progress is sought in the spiritual sphere.

Verses 2-9: Circumcision

What was circumcision ?

When the Lord appeared to Abraham (Gen 17.1-9) and entered into a covenant with him, He also gave Abraham a sign of the covenant (Gen 17.10-14), which was to be borne by every male child from the age of eight days. The covenant promises of the Lord related to Abraham and his seed and their eventual occupation of Canaan, "And I will give unto thee, and to thy seed after thee, the land wherein thou art a stranger, all the land of Canaan, for an everlasting possession" (Gen 17.8).

The sign of the covenant that was given to Abraham was the circumcising of the foreskin of each male child. This was a surgical procedure which would mark the male child from eight days old until death. It was a sign that the children of Israel were in covenant relationship with the Lord and was a permanent and continual reminder to them. The word "circumcise" (4135) means to "cut off". The Lord made clear to Abraham the importance of circumcision, since any male child who was not circumcised was to be "cut off from his people; he hath broken my covenant" (Gen 17.14).

Instruction from the Lord (v.2)

"At that time", is an expression which occurs on three further occasions in the book (6.26; 11.10,21), introducing action from Joshua and in so doing setting it in a time frame for the reader. The phrase is used differently here since it is setting the scene for a command from the Lord, which Joshua subsequently communicates to the people. It not only gives the context in terms of time but also refers to the morale of the tribes, as noted in v.1. A. W. Pink comments on the significance of "that time": "first, when the Lord their God had so signally shown Himself strong on their behalf by performing a miracle of mercy for them. Second, when they had just passed through the river that spoke of death and judgment. Third, as soon as they had set foot within the borders of their promised inheritance. Fourth, four days before the Passover, as a necessary pre-requisite and qualification for them to participate in that feast. Fifth, ere they begin the real task of possessing their possessions – by vanquishing those who would seek to prevent their enjoyment of the same" (*Gleanings in Joshua,* p.122).

"Make thee sharp knives", was the first part of the instruction that the Lord gave Joshua. Other translations have "stone knives" (JND) and "flint knives" (NKJV). The Hebrew word translated as "sharp" in the AV occurs only twice in the Old Testament, with the other occurrence being the incident in which Zipporah circumcised Moses' child (Ex 4.25). It is unclear from the Old Testament whether these knives had any ceremonial value to the children of Israel, or were simply the most accessible and effective means of carrying out circumcision. As will be evident when the numbers of those circumcised is considered, there must have been the need for a very large number of these knives. Whatever form they took, the command of the Lord was not to "take" but to "make", which indicates that they did not possess the knives as part of their everyday life.

"Circumcise again the children of Israel the second time", was the second part of the instruction from the Lord. It is important that the language employed by the Lord is understood in the context in which it was spoken. The instruction was given to Joshua, but this was not a task that he could undertake personally since it would have been impossible to accomplish within the time limits which the approach of the Passover determined. This task had to be done within a three-day period. They had erected the memorial at Gilgal on the tenth day of the first month (4.19), and on the reasonable assumption that the memorial was erected on the day that the children of Israel came out of the Jordan, that gave them three days before the Passover on the fourteenth day of the same month.

The "second time" must also be understood in its context. It does not require a literal interpretation which would not make sense in light of the history of circumcision among the children of Israel. The expression is explained in the following verses (vv.4-9) and relates to the re-commencement of the rite of circumcision among them, after a lapse of almost forty years whilst they were in the wilderness. As far as the Old Testament is concerned, from the time when Abraham had received the command of the Lord to circumcise every man child (Gen 17.10-14), until the people had been disobedient in the wilderness (Num 14), circumcision had been practised. The wilderness experience marked the first recorded period of time during which the people had not circumcised their male offspring in accordance with the instruction of the Lord.

The people circumcised (v.3)

With the ready obedience that characterised him, Joshua implemented the instructions of the Lord. "And Joshua made him sharp knives, and circumcised the children of Israel at the hill of the foreskins". The narrative does give the impression that this was carried out by Joshua in person, yet a consideration of the logistics of the procedure would show that this was an impossibility. It is more likely that Joshua oversaw the execution of the Lord's command and in so doing was credited with having carried it out. The responsibility lay with him. As has already been noted, the circumcision had to be carried out within a three-day period and would have involved a considerable number as the following verses reveal.

The circumcision took place at "the hill of the foreskins" which is translated as "the hill of Araloth" (JND) and "Gibeath-haaraloth" (RSV). This is the only time in the Old Testament that this name is found, it is the other name of Gilgal which is used in every other reference to the place. It is unclear from the text whether the name was derived from a literal hill which existed at the location at which the circumcision took place or whether it is so described because of the very large number of foreskins which were disposed of as a result of the circumcision.

Explanation of the circumcision (vv.4-7)

There are two reasons given in the narrative for the necessity of the circumcision which took place at Gilgal:

1. "All the people that came out of Egypt, that were males, even all the men of war, died in the wilderness by the way, after they came out of Egypt" (v.4).

2. "Now all the people that came out were circumcised: all the people that were born in the wilderness by the way as they came forth out of Egypt, them they had not circumcised" (v.5).

Forty years earlier the children of Israel had arrived at the borders of Canaan and having received the report from the twelve spies, they rebelled against the Lord and refused to enter the land. The result was that the Lord decreed that "your carcases shall fall in this wilderness; and all that were numbered of you, according to your whole number, from twenty years old and upward, which have murmured against me, doubtless ye shall not come into the land, concerning which I sware to make you dwell therein, save Caleb the son of Jephunneh, and Joshua the son of Nun" (Num 14.29-30). The Lord had kept His word and every male from the age of twenty who had stood on the borders of Canaan that day had perished in the wilderness. It must be remembered that this did not mean that every person who had left Egypt died in the wilderness, as the Lord also spoke of those who were under the age of twenty and said that "your little ones, which ye said should be a prey, them will I bring in, and they shall know the land which ye have despised" (Num 14.31). Therefore the children and teenagers who were brought out of Egypt did cross over the Jordan and stood at Gilgal.

"All the people" (v.5) leaving Egypt and coming through the Red Sea were circumcised, but now there was a difference among the people. Those men who were under the age of twenty when they left Egypt, and were spared the judgment of the wilderness, were circumcised, but "all the people that were born in the wilderness" (v.5) were uncircumcised. This required to be addressed as the people were not united in a matter which was of vital significance to them in relation to the covenant promises of the Lord.

In order to gain an understanding of the reasons for the development of this situation, there is an explanation given in vv.6-7. Firstly, the death of the men of war in the wilderness is explained. "For the children of Israel walked forty years in the wilderness, till all the people that were men of war, which came out of Egypt, were consumed, because they obeyed not the voice of the Lord: unto whom the Lord sware that he would not shew them the land, which the Lord sware unto their fathers that he would give us, a land that floweth with milk and honey". This refers back to the rebellion of the children of Israel (Num 14) and has already been noted, and provides a summary of the judgment that the Lord pronounced (Num 14.29). Some commentators consider that it took the children of Israel forty-two years from the time that they left Egypt until they reached Canaan as they rebelled in the second year of the journey from Egypt to Canaan (Num 10.11-12). However, this is not inconsistent with the forty year wilderness sojourn decreed by the Lord, as other Scriptures specifically state it was in the fortieth year that they crossed the Jordan. Therefore the totality of time in the wilderness amounted to forty years from the time they passed through the Red Sea until they passed through the Jordan (Deut 1.3; Acts 7.36).

The cessation of the observance of the rite of circumcision among the children of Israel is not recorded in the historical accounts of their wilderness experience. It is unclear when they ceased to circumcise and the precise circumstances that brought it about. Scripture does not reveal whether the Lord forbade them or whether they were disobedient.

It is important to note the significance of the absence of circumcision in the wilderness. When the people were practising circumcision, they were testifying to their character as a people in covenant relationship with the Lord. This covenant related to their ultimate possession of Canaan and would have been fulfilled had they not accepted the report of the ten spies and subsequently rebelled against God. As a result, when they were in the wilderness under the judgment of the Lord, it was not appropriate to practise the rite of circumcision, on the basis that they had failed to keep their obligations under the covenant and were, in fact, in denial of their covenant relationship with the Lord.

It is for this reason that the explanatory note (v.6) refers to the "land that floweth with milk and honey" and the promise of the Lord to give the land to the people. Through their disobedience they did not enter the land and therefore did not experience the covenant promises. To circumcise in the wilderness would have been to deny the judgment of the Lord and claim the blessing of the covenant which was being denied them. The very point of circumcision was that the covenant was not automatic. A failure to circumcise excluded the individual from the covenant. Conversely, having been excluded, they should not circumcise.

Lest the accusation be made against the Lord that He had made covenant promises and failed to fulfil them, the narrative proceeds to demonstrate that the covenant was fulfilled, but not to the generation who had excluded themselves by their rebellion and disobedience. The Lord raised up a new generation, unaffected by past rebellion; "their children, whom he raised up in their stead, them Joshua circumcised: for they were uncircumcised, because they had not circumcised them by the way" (v.7).

Before the New Testament application of circumcision is considered, it is worth noting that there is a simple, yet profound lesson for Christians in the experience of the children of Israel, in relation to the absence of circumcision and the exclusion of the people of God from the blessings of God. The Lord did not break the promise which He had made to Abraham (Gen 17). However, the behaviour of this generation was such as to exclude them from the enjoyment of what the Lord had promised. Faith and obedience would have brought the people into the land without the experience of the wilderness which became the graveyard for a whole generation. How sobering to consider that faith and obedience are still required lest the people of God wander in a spiritual wilderness, outside the enjoyment of the blessings of the Lord. "Whose carcases fell in the wilderness" (Heb 3.17), could be the description of many believers who, as a result of disobedience and rebellion, failed to enter the enjoyment of what they received from the Lord at conversion.

New Testament circumcision

There is clear instruction in the New Testament that the rite of circumcision ceased to have a place amongst the people of God after the commencement of the church. It was appropriate in Old Testament times for the children of Israel to have a physical sign of a covenant between them and the Lord. In the New Testament, believers are not linked to the Lord by a covenant in the same way that the children of Israel were in the Old Testament. The distinctions between Israel and the Gentile nations do not exist in the New Testament context, which is made plain by the apostle Paul: "...there is neither Greek nor Jew, circumcision nor uncircumcision, Barbarian, Scythian, bond nor free" (Col 3.11), "In Christ Jesus neither circumcision availeth any thing, nor uncircumcision" (Gal 6.15).

Although circumcision as a physical rite ceased, Paul did write of a circumcision which was applicable to believers – "in whom also ye are (were, NKJV) circumcised with the circumcision made without hands, in putting off the body of the sins of the flesh by the circumcision of Christ" (Col 2.11). It is not appropriate to comment at length on this and other New Testament verses which provide the apostolic teaching regarding New Testament circumcision other than to note that when false teaching arose among the early assemblies regarding the requirement for circumcision for believers Paul taught them that they had no need of physical circumcision since they had received a far greater circumcision when they were saved. The "circumcision of Christ" is experienced by the believer at conversion and is spiritual. It brings about liberation from the bondage of the flesh, of which the physical rite of circumcision was a picture; "For he is not a Jew, which is one outwardly; neither is that circumcision, which is outward in the flesh. But he is a Jew, which is one inwardly; and circumcision is that of the heart, in the spirit, and not in the letter; whose praise is not of men, but of God" (Rom 2.28-29).

The practical application of the renewal of circumcision is taken up by Paul when he writes to the Colossians, "If ye then be risen with Christ... Mortify therefore your members which are upon the earth; fornication, uncleanness, inordinate affection, evil concupiscence, and covetousness, which is idolatry" (Col 3.1,5). The responsibility rests with the believer to take stock of the practical action required by him in order to enter the blessing of his position with Christ. There requires to be a decision by the Christian to "Put to death therefore your members which are upon the earth, fornication, uncleanness, vile passions, evil lust, and unbridled desire, which is idolatry" (Col 3.5, JND). Unless this is done, there will be no spiritual progress as he will be hindered by the sins that the flesh will crave.

The recovery of the people (v.8)

"And it came to pass, when they had done circumcising all the people", would confirm that the circumcision was not carried out by Joshua alone since it is attributed to "they", rather than "he". There is no timescale given for this, but many commentators take the view that it could have been accomplished within a day, e.g. "it has been calculated that the proportion between those already circumcised (under twenty when the doom was pronounced) and those to be circumcised, was one to four, and consequently the whole ceremony could easily have been performed in a day" (Jamieson, Faussett and Brown).

It is interesting that there is a record of the danger that circumcision brought to men who relied on physical strength for their safety. In the story of the defilement of Dinah, Hamor and Shechem circumcised their people and on the third day Simeon and Levi came upon them, and slaughtered them, with the Scripture recording that they attacked "on the third day, when they were sore" (Gen 34.25). Evidently, after circumcision took place there was a recovery period of at least three days before a man was fit for battle. During this period "they abode in their places in the camp, till they were whole". There was no more vulnerable period in the immediate history of the children of Israel, with the vast majority of the men of war not fit for battle.

Gilgal named (v.9)

With the people circumcised, "the Lord said unto Joshua, This day have I rolled away the reproach of Egypt from off you". This has been understood in a variety of ways by commentators. Some take the view that the "reproach of Egypt" was the shame of association with Egypt, which was removed once-and-for-all when the children of Israel finally entered the land, and in so doing came into the blessing of the covenant to which they testified in their circumcision. The reproach was the slavery and bondage with which they had been humiliated in Egypt. Others see the generation which came out of Egypt and subsequently perished in the wilderness, as the "reproach of Egypt". The reproach of this generation was removed when circumcision was renewed at Gilgal.

Although there may be merit in either of these views of the "reproach of Egypt", the more likely explanation is that the reproach came from Egypt. The children of Israel had cast off the yoke of bondage and escaped from the sphere of their slavery, with the purpose of entering Canaan in fulfilment of the promise of the Lord (Ex 6.7-8). However, for forty years they had been wandering in the wilderness and appeared to be proof to the Egyptians that they had left for nothing more than a nomadic life in the wilderness. As a result they were the object of Egypt's scorn and reproach. Moses was sensitive to what the Egyptians would say when the Lord threatened to punish the children of Israel for their idolatry with the golden calf: "Wherefore should the Egyptians speak, and say, For mischief did he bring them out, to slay them in the mountains, and to consume them from the face of the earth?" (Ex 32.12). In the same way, he interceded with the Lord after the sin of the people in refusing to enter Canaan: "And Moses said unto the Lord, Then the Egyptians shall hear it, (for thou broughtest up this people in thy might from among them;) And they will tell it to the inhabitants of this land...Because the Lord was not able to bring this people into the land which he sware unto them, therefore he hath slain them in the wilderness" (Num 14.13-14,16). In their uncircumcised condition they had been subject to the reproach of Egypt as they wandered in the wilderness, but that had been rolled away when they entered the land and confirmed their renewal as a covenant people by bearing the sign of the covenant on their bodies.

This was not the only time in the Old Testament that the children of Israel were subject to the reproach of other nations. The Old Testament speaks of the "reproach of the heathen our enemies" (Neh 5.9), the "reproach of the daughters of Syria" (Ezek 16.57) and the "reproach of Moab" (Zeph 2.8).

Reproach is a burden that the Lord Jesus had to bear unjustly. "I am a worm, and no man; a reproach of men, and despised of the people" (Ps 22.6). "Reproach hath broken my heart; and I am full of heaviness" (Ps 69.20). Unjust reproach was the portion of the Saviour in His life and is also the burden that a Christian is often called upon to bear. Paul wrote to Timothy, "For therefore we both labour and suffer reproach, because we trust in the living God, who is the Saviour of all men, specially of those that believe" (1 Tim 4.10). The writer to the Hebrews exhorted the believers, "Let us go forth therefore unto him without the camp, bearing his reproach" (Heb 13.13).

"Wherefore the name of the place is called Gilgal unto this day". The name of the place arose from the Lord's explanation of the significance of the events that had taken place there, with the name Gilgal (1537) coming from the Hebrew verbal root "to roll".

Verse 10: Passover

There is a progression of thought in the chapter which is significant when the practical application of these events is considered. It is no coincidence that the events of the chapter are set out in the order that they appear, with the circumcision of the people preceding the Passover, and thereafter the cessation of manna and the new diet of the people described, followed by the experience of Joshua as he received a revelation of the Lord. In order to get to his experience and make the application, the pathway through circumcision, Passover and diet must be followed. There are no short cuts in the chapter, and, equally, no "quick fixes" in the application to the spiritual experience of a believer in the New Testament context.

Significance of the Passover

The significance of the Passover in the national life of Israel has already been considered briefly (4.19). The Passover was instituted by Moses among the children of Israel in Egypt (Ex 12.1-14), and was thereafter one of the seven feasts which constituted the new calendar of Israel (Lev 23). It was the feast which marked the beginning of a new year for the children of Israel and reminded them of the day when the blood of the lamb, which they had slain for their household, preserved them from God's judgment on the firstborn (Ex 12.21-30). Paul leaves the reader of the New Testament in no doubt as to the significance of the Passover as an illustration of the death of the Lord Jesus: "Christ our passover is sacrificed for us" (1 Cor 5.7). The details of the chosen lamb, and the application of its blood, are a profitable meditation as a picture of the sacrifice of the Lord Jesus.

When the Passover feast was observed by the children of Israel, it was a memorial feast. It had relevance in Israel until the last Passover, which the Lord Jesus celebrated with His disciples in the upper room, prior to moving out to Gethsemane. The picture gave way to reality as the Lord Jesus sacrificially offered Himself upon the cross. It is interesting that, as one memorial feast finished, He instituted a remembrance Supper to the end that Christians would recall the sacrifice that brought about their redemption.

The feast was also a picture of the provision of the Lord for His people in the Person of Christ. They were strengthened as they feasted upon the lamb roast with fire, and the bitter herbs, eating with loins girded and staff in hand. It had given them strength for the journey out of Egypt and likewise prepared them for the entrance into Canaan. Thus it can be seen that the Passover is a picture of the fellowship that a believer enjoys with Christ which enables him to maintain his pilgrim character. The blood of the lamb sheltered them from judgment and their feasting upon the lamb strengthened them for the journey.

Where it took place

"And the children of Israel encamped in Gilgal". The children of Israel could not have enjoyed the Passover prior to their circumcision at Gilgal, since the Lord had stated that "no uncircumcised person shall eat thereof" (Ex 12.48). Therefore, one of the consequences of their failure to enter Canaan, and of their disobedience in being uncircumcised, was their inability to eat the Passover as a united nation, and so they could not eat it at all.

From the time that they had left Egypt they had eaten the Passover on one occasion, which was the first anniversary of their exodus (Num 9.10-14). After thirty-eight years without the Passover, with the sign of the covenant renewed, they obeyed the command that the Lord had given before Egypt had been left behind, "And ye shall observe this thing for an ordinance to thee and to thy sons for ever. And it shall come to pass, when ye be come to the land which the Lord will give you, according as he hath promised, that ye shall keep this service" (Ex 12.24-25).

In the same way as no uncircumcised souls could eat the Passover, in the New Testament the Lord's Supper is only for those who have experienced the circumcision of Christ. It is one of the problems that a believer has if he joins a denomination; he will find himself sharing "communion" with unbelievers. Another sad situation arises when a believer does not partake of the Lord's Supper, some for many years, and in some cases a whole lifetime without participating. The remembrance of the Lord Jesus in the way in which He requested is only for believers, but should be observed by all believers. How sad it is that many Christians fail to respond to such a simple request, living outside the fellowship of a local assembly and therefore unable to remember the Lord in accordance with New Testament instruction.

"At even in the plains of Jericho". It was within sight of the city, which was a barrier to their progress into Canaan and represented the strength and intransigence of their enemies' opposition to them, that they remembered a greater enemy and a more imposing obstacle that had held them captive. In the Passover they were remembering an intervention of the Lord on their behalf which had brought them out from the sphere of their slavery and through the impassable barrier of the Red Sea. What tremendous encouragement this must have been to the children of Israel as they contemplated Jericho.

It is a lesson for any believer to learn that a contemplation of the power and strength of the enemy of the people of God will only bring discouragement. However, to remember the power and strength of the Lord, who has already intervened in his experience in salvation, will serve to encourage the believer in the face of difficulties. It is good to take time to remember the sacrifice of Christ and the redeeming power of His precious blood.

When it took place

"On the fourteenth day of the month at even". This Passover has more links with the first Passover than the one which was celebrated in the wilderness (Num 9.1-5) or other ones of historical note (2 Chr 30. 15; Ezra 6.19-22; Lk 22.7-14). There are the mentions of the tenth day (Ex 12.3; Josh 4.19) and the "milk and honey" (Ex 13.5; Josh 5.6), which do not occur in any other of the instructions given by the Lord, or accounts of the celebration of the Passover.

There was evidently a desire to obey the Lord in the details of the observance of the Passover, for they were careful not only about the day, but also about the right time of day. The Lord had given instruction that "the whole assembly of the congregation of Israel shall kill it in the evening" (Ex 12.6).

Verses 11-12: Change of Diet

Throughout their wilderness journey, the children of Israel had eaten manna. It had been sent from heaven every day of the week, apart from the sabbath, and was collected and eaten by the people in accordance with specific instructions given by the Lord (Ex 16.1-31). The manner in which He provided food for His people was appropriate to their circumstances. There was nothing in the wilderness to sustain them and as a result they relied upon the Lord for their food and indeed for water, meat and clothing.

The wilderness is a picture of the world for a believer. There is nothing in the world which can sustain the believer spiritually. As a stranger and pilgrim the Christian relies upon the Lord for spiritual sustenance, as pictured in the manna and His other provision. The manna reminds the believer of the Lord Jesus in the "days of his flesh" (Heb 5.7), as "upon the face of the wilderness there lay a small round thing, as small as the hoar frost on the ground" (Ex 16.14). The characteristics of the manna and the circumstances surrounding its arrival and collection by the children of Israel all speak of the Lord Jesus in His life of holy perfection and humiliation. For the believer, it is meditation on and appropriation of the Lord Jesus that will give the necessary strength to live in the wilderness of the world. The Lord Jesus explained that "I am the living bread which came down from heaven … He that eateth my flesh, and drinketh my blood, dwelleth in me, and I in him" (Jn 6.51,56).

The wilderness had been left behind in the experience of the children of Israel and they had entered the land of Canaan. It was therefore appropriate that their diet changed in accordance with their different circumstances. "They did eat of the old corn of the land on the morrow after the Passover" (v.11). There is a beautiful balance within this statement. It is the complement of the obedience of the people and the fulfilment of the Lord's promise.

Obedience of the people

When the directions for the Passover were given by Moses to the people, they were instructed to observe a seven day feast (Ex 12.1-20; Lev 23.5-8). This feast of unleavened bread involved the people abstaining from leaven in their food and its removal from their dwelling places. It was an integral part of the Passover. It spoke of the demand for holiness and separation from sin that a participation in the Passover required. The apostle Paul took this picture and applied it to the Corinthians in the context of dealing with the problem of immorality within the assembly: "Purge out therefore the old leaven, that ye may be a new lump, as ye are unleavened. For even Christ our Passover is sacrificed for us. Therefore let us keep the feast, not with old leaven, neither with the leaven of malice and wickedness; but with the unleavened bread of sincerity and truth" (1 Cor 5.7-8).

The obedience of the people is seen as they ate of the old corn of the land. In accordance with the instructions regarding the Passover they ate "unleavened cakes, and parched corn" (v.11). The symbolism involved in their observance of the detail of the Passover and Feast of Unleavened Bread is significant. They were commencing their conquest of Canaan and their appropriation of the promises of the Lord with a display of accurate obedience to His command. This is the starting point of any progress that a believer may make in his life with God, an appreciation of the sacrifice of the Lord Jesus and the demand for that holy living that it makes.

Promise of the Lord

If the Feast of Unleavened Bread was to be observed, there was a logistical problem that the people faced. They carried no bread with them, as they had been fed on a daily basis with manna from heaven. They were not in possession of their land in Canaan and had neither sown nor reaped in order to make their bread. They did not have the necessary resources to carry out the Lord's command.

In some way that is not recorded in the narrative, they came into possession of the old corn of the land. Some have thought that when the people of Canaan heard of their approach they withdrew into the cities and left the granaries and crops to the children of Israel. The manner in which the people came into possession of the corn is irrelevant, since it was the fulfilment of the promise of the Lord, "And it shall be, when the Lord thy God shall have brought thee into the land which he sware unto thy fathers, to Abraham, to Isaac, and to Jacob, to give thee great and goodly cities, which thou buildedst not, and houses full of all good things, which thou filledst not, and wells digged, which thou diggedst not, vineyards and olive trees, which thou plantedst not; when thou shalt have eaten and be full" (Deut 6.10-11).

The land was cultivated before the people entered it and as a result they came into the good and blessing of a harvest they had neither sown nor reaped. This is in accord with the statement that the people crossed over the Jordan at "the time of harvest" (3.15). They feasted on the benefit of other men's labours. This was true of all the land that the children of Israel possessed and is a beautiful picture of the blessings of salvation which a believer comes into by faith. The blessings have been provided at great cost to the Lord, and the believer is required only to take possession of His provision.

The Lord had also promised the people that when they went up to Jerusalem three times a year to observe the feasts, they could leave their land since no man would "desire thy land" (Ex 34.24). As they observed the Passover and Feast of Unleavened Bread in the plains of Jordan, they received the first evidence of the Lord's protection. They were unmolested by the people of Jericho or the other cities nearby which, in itself, was evidence of the Lord fulfilling His promise.

Christ exalted

If the manna speaks of the Lord Jesus in His humiliation, the old corn of the land speaks of Him in His exaltation. It is where He is now as risen, ascended, exalted and glorified. It is a picture of the Lord in the heavenlies, where He has sat down at the right hand of God. The manna was suitable nourishment for the people in the wilderness. What is it that will sustain the Christian in the difficulties and trials of living for God in the world? It is a meditation on the life of the Lord Jesus as He lived here in this world. As has been noted before, the land of Canaan speaks of the believer as he has been placed with Christ in the heavenlies. This spiritual sphere of the believer's life requires something else from the Lord Jesus along with a contemplation of the days of His flesh. In heaven He is the Great High Priest with God and the Advocate with the Father, who will intercede for, and sustain, the believer.

Forty years completed

"And the manna ceased on the morrow after they had eaten of the old corn of the land; neither had the children of Israel manna any more; but they did eat of the fruit of the land of Canaan that year" (v.12). Moses had spoken of the manna being given to the children of Israel for the duration of the journey through the wilderness: "And the children of Israel did eat manna forty years, until they came to a land inhabited; they did eat manna, until they came unto the borders of the land of Canaan" (Ex 16.35). The narrative of the cessation of the manna is carefully dated. The Passover was observed on the fourteenth day of the first month, followed by the people eating the old corn of the land on the fifteenth day and thereafter the manna ceased on the sixteenth day. It was during their first year within Canaan that they began to enjoy the fruit of the land. It is a wonderful truth of salvation that a believer does not require to wait for a certain period of time before he can enjoy the blessings of salvation. They are immediately available to him and can be increasingly enjoyed as time goes on when the blessings are explored and possessed.

Verses 13-15: Revelation of the Lord

"And it came to pass, when Joshua was by Jericho, that he lifted up his eyes and looked, and, behold, there stood a man over against him with his sword drawn in his hand" (v.13). It was only after the people had known the re-institution of circumcision, the Passover, and the change of diet, that Joshua met this man. The revelation did not take place at the beginning of the chapter, as there was the necessity for obedience on the part of the people before the Lord would reveal Himself. It is also interesting to note that it was when Joshua was near the enemy and engaged in service for God that the Lord met and spoke with him.

These points are instructive when the experience of the Christian is considered. It is often the case that a believer seeks revelation from the Lord as a first step in spiritual experience without knowing anything of the mortification of the flesh and an appreciation of the sacrifice of the Lord Jesus. There are no shortcuts in the Christian life, so it is when the believer has considered the lessons of circumcision, Passover, and the old corn of the land that he will know progress in his experience with God. Jericho was the stronghold of the enemy and how encouraging it must have been for Joshua to have the Lord appear to him in the shadow of that great obstacle to progress.

The man who appeared to Joshua was the Lord. It was not the first or the last time that the Lord would appear to men, prior to His incarnation. Bible scholars describe these appearances as theophanic manifestations. Throughout the Old Testament the Lord appeared to men as an angel or a man, through visions or tangibly and for a variety of purposes: e.g., He appeared to Hagar as the angel of the Lord (Gen 16.7-13); to Abraham, as a man at the door of his tent (Gen 18.1-33); to Jacob, as the man who wrestled with him (Gen 32.24-30); and to Gideon, as the angel of the Lord (Judg 6.12-18). The reader is made aware of the identity of the man or angel in different ways. On some occasions the angel or man spoke and the Scripture recorded that the Lord spoke. Another method of identification is to note the response to the appearance of the angel or man. When an angel appeared to men and was worshipped, the angel rejected the worship as being inappropriate; however, when it was the Lord appearing as an angel the worship was accepted.

The appearance of the Lord to Joshua was both timely and fitting. The Lord knew His servant and at the appropriate moment gave him the encouragement that he required. It was just as the Lord had promised him before the Jordan was crossed – "as I was with Moses, so I will be with thee: I will not fail thee, nor forsake thee" (1.5). Joshua was about to lead an army into battle, having the Lord's promise of victory, and on the eve of the conflict he received a revelation of the Lord as the "captain of the host of the Lord" (v.14). It was the same with Moses when "the angel of the Lord appeared unto him in a flame of fire out of the midst of a bush" (Ex 3.2). Moses was commissioned to go in before Pharoah and perform miracles and the Lord revealed himself in the form of a miracle, as the bush burned with fire, but was not consumed. He is still able to bring appropriate encouragement to His people in the different circumstances of life and in the trials and tribulations which they experience. Whether it is an appreciation of the "God of all comfort" (2 Cor 1.3), the "great high priest" (Heb 4.14), the "God of truth" (Deut 32.4), or the many other titles and descriptions of the Lord, the believer can find encouragement in the Lord, as a revelation of Him is gained through the Scriptures. Joshua was granted a revelation of the Lord as the "captain" (commander, NKJV) of the armies of heaven. Some commentators take the view that the "host of the Lord" was the armies of Israel (Ex 7.4; 12.41); however, the Lord had given Joshua the role of their commander. It is more likely that the armies of heaven are in view, the same armies that Micaiah saw (1 Kings 22.19). What great encouragement for Joshua as the Lord who promised the victory in Canaan was revealed as the "captain of the host of the Lord".

The balance of the revelation to Joshua was a reminder of the holiness of the Lord. "And the captain of the Lord's host said unto Joshua, Loose thy shoe from off thy foot; for the place whereon thou standest is holy. And Joshua did so" (v.15). The promise of victory was bound up with the people's acknowledgement of the holiness of the Lord. It does not matter where the believer finds himself in his experience with the Lord, holiness must govern his life and service for Him. This lesson was stressed to Moses at the bush and Joshua was reminded of the same. Both Moses and Joshua were on the verge of doing great things for God but their service had to be based upon the acknowledgement of the holiness of the Lord in their lives. And so it is that the last recorded acts of Joshua, before the Lord gave instructions for the conquest of Jericho, are to obey and appreciate the holiness of the Lord. The exhortation of the Lord, as recorded by Peter, is the basic requirement for any believer - "as he which hath called you is holy, so be ye holy in all manner of conversation" (1 Pet 1.15).

JOSHUA 6

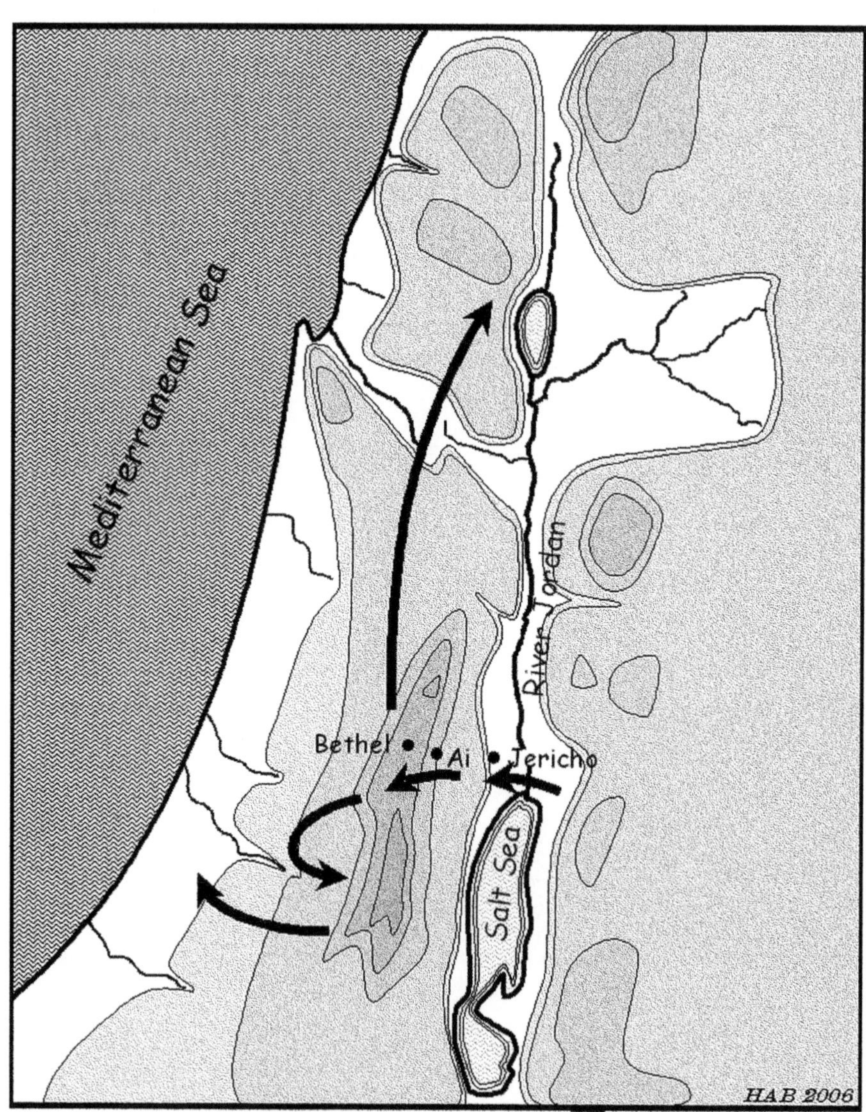

Schematic map of Israel, showing the main movements in its conquest by Joshua.

JOSHUA 6

Jericho Destroyed

Although the book of Joshua is essentially a record of the conquest of Canaan, it is interesting that there is no mention of conflict until ch.6. The middle section of the book, chs.6-12, records the battles of conquest whilst the rest of the book deals with the division and administration of the land. The structure points to the fact that preparation for conflict and consolidation following conquest were vital components for the progress of the children of Israel.

The description of the battle for Jericho is detailed and is similar to the account of the crossing of the Jordan (ch.3). The style of narrative is repetitive with small additional comments made as the chapter narrates the words of the Lord to Joshua, the subsequent communication of these instructions to the people and their implementation. The division between chs.5 and 6 is unfortunate as it disrupts the flow of the narrative, separating the Lord's appearance to Joshua from His instructions.

Verse 1: The Scene is Set

"Now Jericho was straitly shut up because of the children of Israel: none went out, and none came in" (v.1). The opening words of the chapter can be translated, "And Jericho shutteth itself up, and is shut up" (YLT). A. W. Pink comments, "It is an expressive emphasis in the Hebrew like …'in blessing I will bless thee' (Gen 22.17)". The language employed highlights the effectiveness and permanence of the fortifications of the city. The verse provides an explanatory note which emphasises the magnitude of the task that faced them.

There had been no change in the attitude of the people of Jericho from the time when the spies were in the city and Rahab had informed them that "I know that the Lord hath given you the land, and that your terror is fallen upon us, and that all the inhabitants of the land faint because of you" (2.9). The people had retreated behind the city walls in order to gain protection and preservation from the children of Israel. It seems to have been a sensible move since the walls were unassailable by conventional means and did provide security. The nomadic armies of Israel would have had to lay siege to the city and sit in a vulnerable position outside the walls of Jericho, eventually having to move to obtain food and other supplies. The people of Jericho were employing good military tactics and, after all, what had they done to deserve an assault and destruction at the hands of the invading army? At this point and without a consideration of the background, the sympathy of the reader is surely drawn to the men of Jericho as the victims, rather than to the children of Israel as the aggressors.

However, there were other factors that require to be considered as the scene is set for the battle of Jericho. The people of the land were guilty of abominations in the sight of God and were subject to the judgment of God for their deeds. The invasion of the land by the children of Israel and the overthrow of the existing inhabitants of the land was, in itself, an act of divine judgment: "When thou art come into the land which the Lord thy God giveth thee, thou shalt not learn to do after the abominations of those nations. There shall not be found among you any one that maketh his son or his daughter to pass through the fire, or that useth divination, or an observer of times, or an enchanter, or a witch, or a charmer, or a consulter with familiar spirits, or a wizard, or a necromancer. For all that do these things are an abomination unto the Lord: and because of these abominations the Lord thy God doth drive them out from before thee" (Deut 18.9-12). For this reason the children of Israel were instructed not to enter into any treaty or compromise with the people of the land as their abominations would have defiled and corrupted them (Deut 20.16-18).

The city of Jericho was also a military obstacle which had to be removed before the children of Israel could make progress in their conquest of Canaan. They could not afford to leave such a stronghold behind them, since it would have meant leaving soldiers to contain the city and to prevent the army of Jericho from attacking them and cutting off their lines of communication and supply. Such a formidable obstacle to progress for the children of Israel is a picture of seemingly immoveable obstacles to progress in the lives of believers. A Christian will find that he is not far into the land before he encounters his Jericho - a relationship, a family issue, something at work. These tests or trials cannot be by-passed, but require to be faced and overcome, if they are not to be a continual impediment and hindrance to him as he seeks to move on for God.

Verses 2-5: Battle orders

Assurance of victory (v.2)

Before the battle commenced and the army moved towards Jericho, the Lord spoke to Joshua and gave him the assurance of victory over the city and its inhabitants: "And the Lord said unto Joshua, See, I have given into thine hand Jericho, and the king thereof, and the mighty men of valour".

The Lord spoke of victory as an accomplished fact, although the battle had not commenced; this was a test of faith. The phrase "I have given" is in the perfect tense and indicates a completed action. He was instructed to "see" (7200) and, as he lifted his eyes, the sight did not match the assurance given by the Lord. The walls of the city were a compelling reason to reject the word of the Lord. The certainty of God's promise before its realisation is a common theme in the Bible, and is always a test of faith for the individual concerned. When the Lord appeared to Abraham He told him that "a father of many nations have I made thee" (Gen 17.5), yet Abraham was ninety years of age and Sarah was barren. The test for Joshua was the same as he had faced when he stood before the Jordan, when the evidence of his eyes ran counter to the assurance of the Lord. Faith accepts what the Lord has said, rather than relying on the evidence of the eyes. "For we walk by faith, not by sight" (2 Cor 5.7).

The second reason for the Lord's statement at this time was the reiteration of the truth that they had received the land from the Lord. They forgot this after Jericho was taken, and it led to the disaster at Ai (7.2-5). Military might or skill was not sufficient for the conquest of the land. This remains the pattern of spiritual conflict for the believer. It is a conflict in which faith is essential to lay hold of the promises of the Lord in spite of the evidence of the eye. The obstacles can be great and the enemies strong, but the believer can know victory and progress in spiritual experience when strength and succour are drawn from the Lord. When the apostle Paul wrote to the Ephesians about spiritual conflict, he encouraged the believers to "be strong in the Lord, and in the power of his might" (Eph 6.10).

Battle instructions (vv.3-5)

The assurance from the Lord that Jericho had already been given into the hand of Joshua did not mean that he could sit back and passively wait for it to happen. The Lord gave him precise instructions, which he had to carry out in order for Jericho to fall. This balance of sovereignty and responsibility occurs time and again in God's dealings with His people. It characterises the work of the gospel, as demonstrated by the labours of the apostle Paul in Corinth. The Lord informed Paul that "I have much people in this city" (Acts 18.10), and yet Paul reminds the Corinthians that "I delivered unto you first of all that which I also received" (1 Cor 15.3). He knew that many people in the city would be saved, but nevertheless he discharged his responsibility of preaching the gospel.

The battle instructions took the form of a ceremony rather than a military operation. They were strange indeed, and, instead of inspiring fear in the city, had the potential of making the armies of Israel a laughing stock. The approach of Israel and the methods employed were far removed from anything that the people of Jericho would have seen before. It was a radically different approach from conquering a stronghold. Likewise, the methods employed by the Christian to overcome obstacles in his life are not those that the world would understand. "For though we walk in the flesh, we do not war after the flesh: (For the weapons of our warfare are not carnal, but mighty through God to the pulling down of strong holds;) casting down imaginations, and every high thing that exalteth itself against the knowledge of God, and bringing into captivity every thought to the obedience of Christ" (2 Cor 10.3-5).

Men of war

"Ye shall compass the city, all ye men of war, and go round about the city once. Thus shalt thou do six days" (v.3).

The approach to Jericho did take the form of a ceremony but retained the threat of a military assault, as the procession that compassed the city for a week consisted of priests and men of war. At the end of the week, an assault would be made on the city when the Lord had removed the obstacle of the walls.

The believer should not forget that his spiritual experience will never lose the character of a conflict until he enters heaven.

Compass the city

For a period of six days the army of the children of Israel had to walk around the city of Jericho. No offensive action was to be undertaken and they had to parade before the walls of the city in close proximity to this obstacle to their progress into Canaan. By the end of the week they would be fully aware of the magnitude of the task that they faced as well as of their own helplessness. The Lord was ensuring that both of these lessons were not lost on the people.

If the believer is going to overcome obstacles in his life, he must be realistic in his approach. It is a mistake to underestimate the difficulties and overestimate his own ability to overcome them.

The ark

"And seven priests shall bear before the ark seven trumpets of rams' horns: and the seventh day ye shall compass the city seven times, and the priests shall blow with the trumpets" (v.4).

The unfolding of the instructions for the taking of Jericho must have reminded Joshua of the word of the Lord for the crossing of the Jordan. The ark was central to both of these great events and was symbolic of the place that the Lord had to have amongst His people in order for them to overcome the impossibilities that they faced. Much has been said in relation to the ark in connection with the crossing of the Jordan (3.3), yet it is worth reiterating the importance of the place that the ark occupied among the people, and in the procession that wound its way around the city. Having the ark in the midst of them, the people were stating their dependence on the Lord and their confidence in Him for victory. They had already seen the waters of Jordan dry up, when the priests stood in the river with the ark, and were familiar with the cloud by day and the pillar of fire by night, which had led them through the wilderness. There was another reason for the ark being taken around the walls of the city. The people of Jericho would have seen the importance of the ark to the children of Israel, since it occupied the central place in the procession. To them it was a display of the presence of the Lord which gave them the opportunity to open the gates and cast themselves upon His mercy, as the people of Nineveh did in the days of Jonah the prophet.

There is a lovely picture of the grace of God displayed in the gospel when the ark was taken around the city walls under the gaze of the ungodly. The righteous judgment of God was due to fall upon the city but, before it did so, they were exposed to that which pointed forward to the Lord Jesus Christ. This can be seen as a picture of the longsuffering of God in the gospel. His judgment is pending for a world of sinners and yet the Lord Jesus is presented to the world as the Saviour of sinners.

Seven days

The number seven(th) is mentioned four times in v.4. Seven priests, seven trumpets and seven times on the seventh day they were to compass the city. Some commentators have suggested that the seven-day period relates to the seven days following the Passover (5.10), which would have been the Feast of Unleavened Bread. This would also link with the period of time following the first Passover when the children of Israel came out of Egypt and witnessed the destruction of the Egyptian armies in the Red Sea (Ex 12-14), and the procession of the children of Israel from Mount Sinai into the wilderness following the second Passover (Num 9-10). There is no specific mention of the time period following the observance of the Passover in which the assault on Jericho commenced and therefore it cannot be stated with certainty that the seven-day period of compassing Jericho coincided with the Feast of Unleavened Bread.

Throughout Scripture the number seven is associated with completeness, beginning with the seven days of creation, and its repeated use in relation to the conquest of Jericho points to the complete victory that the Lord would give to the children of Israel.

Trumpets of rams' horns

Seven priests had to go before the ark bearing trumpets of rams' horns. With the people silent during the compassing of the city, the only sound to be heard was that of the seven trumpets being blown by the priests as they went before the ark. The trumpets ensured that the attention of the children of Israel and the people of Jericho was firmly fixed on the ark. There could be no doubt as to what was the central object of the procession, as it moved around the city.

The description of the trumpets in these verses is interesting since there are three different Hebrew words employed to describe them. Some translators give the literal rendering of "horns of jubilee", that is, the bent or crooked trumpets with which the jubilee was proclaimed. "Many interpreters understand it as signifying the complete liberty to which Israel was now brought, and the bringing of the land of Canaan into the hands of its just and rightful owners" (Matthew Henry). The sounding of the trumpets of jubilee was most appropriate for the entrance of the people into the land of Canaan. They had been promised the land as their inheritance and one of the aspects of the year of jubilee, with which the trumpets were associated, was the return of property which had been alienated through debt or other means (Lev 25). "Just as the trumpet blast heard by the people when the covenant was made at Sinai (Ex 19.16,19) was, as it were, a herald's call, announcing to the tribes of Israel the arrival of the Lord their God to complete His covenant...so the blowing of trumpets in connection with the round of feasts was intended partly ... at the end of every seven times seven years to announce on the great day of atonement, the coming of the great year of grace and freedom, which was to bring to the people of God deliverance from bondage, return to their possessions, and deliverance from the bitter labours of this earth, and to give them a foretaste of the blessed and glorious liberty to which the children of God would attain at the return of the Lord to perfect His kingdom" (Keil & Delitzsch).

The trumpets were unimpressive in themselves and were not the most musical of instruments available to the children of Israel. "No less than five times in this chapter are we told that those employed on this occasion were made of 'rams' horns' – a cruder or meaner material could scarcely be imagined. They were in striking contrast with the 'silver trumpets' which were normally used in the camp of Israel (Num 10.1-10). It was God pouring contempt on *the means used* – those which were despicable in the eyes of men – that Israel's pride might be stained and Himself glorified, for His strength is ever made perfect through weakness" (A. W. Pink, *Gleanings in Joshua*). When the application of the procession around Jericho is made to the presentation of the gospel, it can be seen that the heralds of the gospel are not to be centre of attention or impressive in themselves, but are to direct the attention of the people to the Lord Jesus. "God hath chosen the foolish things of the world to confound the wise; and God hath chosen the weak things of the world to confound the things which are mighty" (1 Cor 1.27).

"And it shall come to pass, that when they make a long blast with the ram's horn, and when ye hear the sound of the trumpet, all the people shall shout with a great shout; and the wall of the city shall fall down flat, and the people shall ascend up every man straight before him" (v.5).

Having compassed the city for six days and seven times on the seventh day, the Lord instructed Joshua that the assault on the city was to take place. There would be four aspects to the attack, with three of them coming from the people and the priests, and one of them from the Lord.

a) "The sound of the trumpet"

The sound of the seven rams' horns being blown by the priests would be familiar to the people within the city and to the children of Israel. For a week they had heard the blasts from the trumpets, but on this occasion, with the procession having compassed the city seven times on the seventh day, the sound was different. It was to be a "long blast". The difference in note is commented on by Keil & Delitzsch: "The jubilee trumpets ... gave a loud far-sounding tone (cf. Lev 23.24). 'Blow with the trumpets' (*lit.* strike the trumpets) is used in v.4, 'make a long blast' (draw with the horn, i.e., blow the horn with long-drawn notes), is used in v.5 (cf. Ex 19.13)".

The significance of the rams' horns being blown, announcing the liberation of the land, has been noted above. The second aspect to the blowing of trumpets was the announcement of judgment upon the inhabitants of Jericho. The overthrow of Jericho is a picture of the judgment of God upon an ungodly world and the blowing of trumpets has become associated with this throughout Scripture (Rev 8.6).

b) "A great shout"

The sound from the children of Israel outside the city walls was to be a combination of the priests blowing the trumpets and the people shouting with a "great shout". This combination occurred again when Gideon led his 300 men into battle against the Midianities (Judg 7.16-22), as they blew trumpets and cried with their voices. It will also feature when the Lord comes to the air in order to rapture Christians to glory, "For the Lord himself shall descend from heaven with a shout, with the voice of the archangel, and with the trump of God: and the dead in Christ shall rise first" (1 Thess 4.16). The shout is associated with victory and, although the walls of the city would not fall until the shout was heard, it was an expression of the people's confidence in the promise of the Lord (v.2) that victory was assured, and the city had already been given into the hand of Joshua. It was the shout of faith: "By faith the walls of Jericho fell down, after they were compassed about seven days" (Heb 11.30).

c) "The wall of the city shall fall down flat"

The Lord told Joshua that, when the sound of the trumpets was mingled with the voices of the people, the effect would be seen in the destruction of the wall of Jericho. It was not the sound that brought the wall down, it was the work of the Lord. There is, however, a lovely picture of the privilege that the Lord has granted to His people to have fellowship with Him in the gospel. Paul described himself and others as "workers together with him" (2 Cor 6.1) and "labourers together with God" (1 Cor 3.9). The priests, the people and the Lord were all involved in overcoming the wall. When the city of Jericho is seen as a picture of the difficulties and obstacles which hinder the progress of a believer, the lesson is the need for faith, and for fellowship with the Lord, to overcome such obstacles.

The expression "fall down (5307) flat (8478)" has caused some commentators to state that the Lord was informing Joshua that following the long blast of the trumpets and the shout of the people, the wall of the city would sink into the ground like an elevator and be swallowed up by the earth. The comments in the *Treasury of Scripture Knowledge* are interesting in this context: "The wall shall fall down from its very foundation; which was probably the case in every part, though large breaches in different places might have been amply sufficient first to admit the armed men, after whom the host might enter to destroy the city. There is no ground for the supposition that the walls sunk into the earth".

d) "The people shall ascend up every man straight before him"

In order for the people to enter the city, the wall had to come down in a manner that would not form a barrier of rubble preventing the people from achieving their goal of entering the city. The emphasis is that there was not a mountain of stone after the destruction of the wall, but rather a clear path over which the people entered. The wall would give way at the foundation so that every man could march into the city from the location he occupied outside the city. The implications of this were significant for Joshua. For the final assault on the city, he did not require to group his soldiers at specific locations to make a breach in the wall. The wall would come down and the assault would be made by every man from the position he occupied at that time, which would have the effect of a simultaneous entrance into the city by the children of Israel from all sides. Such an assault would be impossible to resist.

The Lord had already told Joshua, "I have given into thine hand Jericho, and the king thereof, and the mighty men of valour" (v.2). However, the children of Israel still had to take action. The Lord would do what they could not, but they were expected to do what they could. The same is true for a believer serving God today.

Verses 6-7: Orders Conveyed to the Priests and the People

Joshua communicated the instructions that the Lord had given him to the priests and the people. The pattern of the narrative means that there are details of the assault which are revealed in a progressive manner. In this section some of the order of the march is revealed: "Let him that is armed pass on before the ark of the Lord" (v.7). Evidently the "men of war" (v.3) were to be divided into two sections, with one forming an advance guard, going before the ark, and the rest forming the "rereward" (v.9) of the procession.

Verses 8-21: The assault on Jericho

Day 1 (vv.8-11)

The first day of the attack on Jericho began as the Lord had instructed Joshua as "the seven priests bearing the seven trumpets of rams' horns passed on before the Lord" (v.8). The ark occupied the most prominent position in the procession that began to compass Jericho. This is further emphasised by the variety of titles of the ark used in these verses. It is the "ark" (v.4), the "ark of the covenant" (v.6), the "ark of the Lord" (v.6), "the Lord" (v.8) and the "ark of the covenant of the Lord" (v.8). The presence of the Lord was synonymous with the ark and therefore as the priests walked past the ark, to them they were passing before the Lord Himself, and were conscious of His presence among them (4.13).

The entirety of the procession is detailed. "And the armed men went before the priests that blew with the trumpets, and the rereward came after the ark, the priests going on, and blowing with the trumpets" (v.9). The account of the assault on Jericho does not give the tribal division of the "men of war" (v.3). It may be the case that they formed the same order of march that had pertained in the wilderness (Num 10.14-28). There is, however, no specific mention of the position of the tribes in the march around Jericho. This is in itself instructive when the battle is considered. The role of the children of Israel in the conquest of Jericho is further reduced by the lack of detail regarding the position of the tribes and the order of march, whereas the ark is repeatedly mentioned and given various titles (v.8), thus continually drawing attention away from the soldiers of Israel to the Lord Himself.

If a man had stood on the wall of Jericho that first day, the most striking impression he would have gained would have been from the sound of the children of Israel. In the record of that first day, there is more said about sound than any other aspect of the events that occurred. The priests are mentioned as they "blew with the trumpets" (vv.8-9) and "going on, and blowing with the trumpets" (v.9). Equally striking would have been the silence of the rest of the men as they walked around the wall. Silence from an army in close proximity to an enemy must have been most unusual and, at the very least, spoke of tremendous discipline. The role of sound in the conquest of Jericho is interesting. There was the sound of the trumpets each day with the final long blast on the seventh day, the absence of any sound from the people for thirteen encirclings of the city, and the final shout, which preceded the destruction of the walls. The command of Joshua had been given before the commencement of the procession around the city and forbade the exultant shout of the battle or victory cry, "ye shall not shout" (v.10), the noise, frivolity or clamour of a people on the march, "nor make any noise with your voice" (v.10), or any conversation among the people, "neither shall any word proceed out of your mouth" (v.10). In other words, there was to be complete silence.

If the sounding of the trumpets of rams' horns is a fitting picture of the herald sounding out the gospel and drawing the attention of the ungodly to the Lord Jesus Christ, as typified by the ark, then the silence of the people is also important. When the gospel is declared, the attention of sinners should be centred on the Lord Jesus Christ, and any distraction from that is not welcome. It was a serious business at Jericho and the people had to conduct themselves in a fitting manner as they accompanied the ark around the wall. The commotion and general clamour of a people on the move was gone, with the hearts of the people focused on the trumpets sounding out the notes of warning. It was not only the ungodly whose attention was drawn to the ark.

As the first day drew to a close, the wall of the city remained intact and, to the eyes of those present, the effort had been in vain. No enemy had been engaged and no stone had fallen from the edifice. If anything, the people had been made to look foolish in the eyes of the ungodly as they silently, in obedience to the command of the Lord, made their way around the city. This is such a clear picture of the spread of the gospel in the day of the Saviour's rejection. In the eyes of the world it is not a highly esteemed task to make known the name of the Lord Jesus Christ in the gospel. Yet, what appeared as foolishness in the eyes of the world was wonderful obedience in God's eyes.

Days 2-6 (vv.12-14)

There is very little additional information given in the account of the following five days of marching round the city. The same procedure was followed each day. There are some lessons for believers to learn from this repetition by the people. The days that followed the first march around the city seem to have been tedious with not much "action" for a battle. Perhaps those men bearing arms wondered if they would get the opportunity to wield them. However, they continued to march and there is no record of discontent among them. It could have become a daily grind to rise and proceed in silence around the city, the same old routine with no visible effect or value.

The Bible places very little emphasis on the outcome of gospel service. Greater emphasis is placed upon the faithfulness of the servant discharging his duty to the Lord in the spread of the gospel. How quickly some believers weary in the work of the gospel, when no visible results are seen! How soon the methods of the Bible are questioned, and rejected as being ineffective, or even foolish! The lesson from the six days of marching around the city is that they kept at it with their attention focused on the ark and the command of the Lord, rather than on the ideas of men or the reproach of the world.

Day 7 (vv.15-21)

"On that day they compassed the city seven times" (vv.15-16). Having exposed themselves to the gaze of the ungodly for six days, they continued into the seventh day. Instead of the test diminishing, it increased, as "they rose early about the dawning of the day, and compassed the city after the same manner seven times" (v.15). It was only when they had demonstrated their faith, in obedience to the word of the Lord, that they received the promise of victory. Joshua had been told by the Lord that the land was already given into his hand (v.2), but it was not until the obedience of the people had been proved over the seven days that "Joshua said unto the people, Shout; for the Lord hath given you the city" (v.16). This balance of the Lord's promise and the people's responsibility can be seen in the timing of the events. In the New Testament some of the promises of God, which are often quoted out of context, are dependent on the Christian's obedience. For example, "But my God shall supply all your need according to his riches in glory by Christ Jesus" (Phil 4.19), is not a blank cheque for the believer, since the context reveals that Paul's confidence resulted from the giving of the Philippians – "I am full, having received of Epaphroditus the things which were sent from you, an odour of a sweet smell, a sacrifice acceptable, well-pleasing to God" (Phil 4.18).

"And the city shall be accursed" (vv.17-19)

Before the people had entered the land they had been instructed by Moses, "Of the cities of these people, which the Lord thy God doth give thee for an inheritance, thou shalt save alive nothing that breatheth. But thou shalt utterly destroy them; namely, the Hittites, and the Amorites, the Canaanites, and the Perizzites, the Hivites, and the Jebusites; as the Lord thy God hath commanded thee: that they teach you not to do after all their abominations, which they have done unto their gods; so should ye sin against the Lord your God" (Deut 20.16-18). This instruction, in all its severity, was repeated by Joshua as the people prepared to enter Jericho with the consequences of disobeying the command reinforced: "The city shall be accursed, even it, and all that are therein, to the Lord" (v.17).

"Accursed" (2764) is translated as "devoted to the Lord for destruction" (RSV) and is an important concept in the book of Joshua. The verb occurs fourteen times and the noun thirteen times. The meaning of the word can be seen in relation to an offering made to the Lord "notwithstanding no devoted thing, that a man shall devote unto the Lord of all that he hath, both of man and beast, and of the field of his possession, shall be sold or redeemed. every devoted thing is most holy unto the Lord" (Lev 27.28). When something or someone was devoted to the Lord, the person renounced any rights to that object or person and it became the Lord's possession. It has been described as "an irrevocable renunciation of any interest in the object 'devoted'...uncompromising consecration without possibility of recall or redemption" (J.P.U. Lilley, *Understanding the 'Herem'*).

The city of Jericho was devoted to the Lord and the consequences of this were made clear to the people before they entered. "Only Rahab the harlot shall live, she and all that are with her in the house, because she hid the messengers that we sent" (v.17). There would be no survivors in Jericho, apart from Rahab and the people within her house, in accordance with the covenant of the spies, since the people could not obtain servants from the city. "And ye, in any wise keep yourselves from the accursed thing, lest ye make yourselves accursed, when ye take of the accursed thing, and make the camp of Israel a curse, and trouble it" (v.18). Nothing from within the city was to be taken by the people as it all belonged to the Lord. If they did take the anything devoted to the Lord they would themselves become "accursed", i.e. liable to destruction, and this would also have its effect upon the whole camp. The camp would become a "curse" and they would "trouble it"; this will be discussed later in relation to Achan where the same word is employed (7.25). It is worth noting at this point that the people were informed that disobedience in this matter would have a devastating effect upon them and the whole camp. In addition to the destruction of the city and the people, Joshua informed the people that "all the silver, and gold, and vessels of brass and iron, are consecrated unto the Lord: they shall come into the treasury of the Lord" (v.19). The location of the "treasury of the Lord" is not clear. There was no temple and therefore it must be assumed that the treasure of Jericho would be stored with the ark and the tabernacle, which was probably not settled in one location at this point owing to the advance of the people.

The Lord took Jericho to Himself as the firstfruits of the land. The city was the first and greatest in Canaan and the spoils of it were offered to the Lord in accordance with the principles of firstfruits. However, the destruction of Jericho and the subsequent annihilation of Hazor (11.11-12) does raise the question as to why the Lord demanded the removal of the occupants of the land in such a manner. There are two basic reasons for this as set out in Scripture. Firstly, the people who occupied the land of Canaan were being judged for their sins. The catalogue of their conduct

(Gen 15.16; Lev 18.6-30; Deut 9.4-5) shows that they were committing grievous sins and had been doing so from the time of Abraham. Secondly, if the people of Canaan were left in the land, they would have caused the children of Israel to sin, and in fact, that is what happened owing to their failure to drive them out and fulfil the Lord's command.

The conquest of Jericho (vv.20-21)

In accordance with the instructions of the Lord, "the people shouted when the priests blew with the trumpets" and the "the wall fell down flat" (v20). The most remarkable aspect of the record of the destruction of Jericho is the limited detail and comment made upon it within the narrative. In contrast to the crossing of the Jordan and the ceremonial procession around the walls for the seven days, the conquest of the city is simply recorded as, "and they took the city" (v.20). This is in keeping with the general tenor of the book as the emphasis is not on the fighting of the Israelites, but rather the miraculous intervention of the Lord. The Lord gave the victory to the people and therefore the actual fighting that took place is not dwelt upon in the narrative.

The destruction of the city was rigorously enforced with the putting to death of "all that was in the city, both man and woman, young and old, and ox, and sheep, and ass, with the edge of the sword" (v.21).

Verses 22-27: The Aftermath of the Conquest

In the closing verses of the chapter, the narrative ties up the loose ends of the story with an explanation of the consequences for Rahab and her family, the city of Jericho and Joshua himself.

What happened to Rahab and her family?

It was fitting that Joshua had spoken to the two spies, prior to the crossing of the Jordan, and given them the responsibility to "Go into the harlot's house, and bring out thence the woman, and all that she hath, as ye sware unto her" (v.22). They fulfilled this task and brought out of the city "Rahab, and her father, and her mother, and her brethren, and all that she had; and they brought out all her kindred" (v.23). All her relations by birth or marriage, her brothers and sisters and all the persons belonging to her were brought out of the city alive. It is a testimony to the witness of Rahab's faith that all of these people had been brought into the shelter of her house, in dependence upon the promise she had received from the spies.

Having brought them out of the city, the spies "left them without the camp of Israel" (v.23). This was no doubt a temporary position as "she dwelleth in Israel even unto this day" (v.25), and is included in the genealogy of the Lord as the great - great - grandmother king David (Mt 1.5-6). The necessity for the initial exclusion of Rahab from the camp is perhaps explained by the need for ceremonial purification prior to her being allowed to become part of the camp. The people were instructed to carry out such a purification on captives and this could have applied to Rahab (Num 31.19).

What happened to Jericho?

"They burnt the city with fire and all that was therein" (v.24). In addition to the destruction of the city Joshua pronounced a curse on the city, "Cursed be the man before the Lord, that riseth up and buildeth this city Jericho: he shall lay the foundation thereof in his firstborn, and in his youngest son shall he set up the gates of it" (v.26). This was in accordance with the instructions of Moses in relation to that which was accursed (Deut 13.12-16). The word "buildeth" did not refer to the construction of dwelling houses on the site, as this did occur without the intervention of the Lord and the effect of the curse being implemented (Josh 18.21; 2 Sam 10.5). According to Keil & Delitzsch the idea is "the restoration of the town as a fortification, the word being frequently used to denote the fortification of a town (1 Kings 15.17; 2 Chr 11.6; 14.6)". However in the days of Ahab, "did Hiel the Bethelite build Jericho: he laid the foundation thereof in Abiram his firstborn, and set up the gates thereof in his youngest son Segub, according to the word of the Lord, which he spake by Joshua the son of Nun" (1 Kings 16.34).

What happened to Joshua?

"So the Lord was with Joshua; and his fame was noised throughout all the country" (v.27). In accordance with the promises that he had received from the Lord, Joshua had known the presence of the Lord throughout the momentous early days of his leadership of the children of Israel. They had crossed the Jordan and taken Jericho and the land lay open to them. The reputation of Joshua was spread abroad and it is at this very high point of his experience with God that the narrative of the conquest of Jericho closes.

JOSHUA 7

Failure at Ai

The immediate aftermath of the victory at Jericho is a sad account of Israel's failure, in contrast to the victory that the Lord had accomplished on their behalf. Following the triumph at Jericho, with the land open for conquest, the children of Israel experienced defeat at the hands of their enemy and the sanctifying judgment of God in their midst. The chapter is the solemn record of one man's sin, which affected a nation and resulted in severe public judgment upon him and his family. The contrast with Rahab's experience is startling. Achan was an Israelite who did not believe the word of the Lord and suffered the consequences with his family. Rahab was a Canaanite who exercised faith and she and her family were brought into blessing as strangers in the camp of Israel.

Verse 1: The Trespass of the Nation

The chapter commences with a word of contrast, "But", and in so doing sets the events of ch.7 in contrast with those described in ch.6, with the emphasis on the closing verse. Jericho had fallen and the news of the victory had enhanced Joshua's reputation throughout the land of Canaan. The people had participated in a resounding victory without any losses and, as far as the reader is aware, had obeyed the command of the Lord to destroy the city and its inhabitants, reserving the wealth for the Lord.

It is at the height of "spiritual success" that Christians can be susceptible to failure. The root cause of the disaster at Ai lay with the transgression of Achan; however, the people, Joshua and the spies also failed. Perhaps the spirit of Nebuchadnezzar had crept in among the people – "Is not this great Babylon, that I have built for the house of the kingdom by the might of my power, and for the honour of my majesty" (Dan 4.30). Sin had come in among them and they were oblivious to its defiling presence.

"The children of Israel committed a trespass in the accursed thing". It is instructive that the whole nation of Israel was deemed to be guilty of a trespass. Achan had committed the sin, yet all of the children of Israel were held responsible. This was consistent with the warning given by the Lord: "And ye, in any wise keep yourselves from the accursed thing, lest ye make yourselves accursed, when ye take of the accursed thing, and make the camp of Israel a curse, and trouble it" (6.18). A principle was established at the beginning of the occupation of Canaan; the sin of one man affected the whole camp. This principle remains true for Christians: "A little leaven leaveneth the whole lump" (1 Cor 5.6). In the same way that Achan's sin had consequences for the whole nation, so the sin of one believer has consequences for every member of the assembly. It is important to remember that Christians do not live in isolation, but as functioning members of a body, affecting each other for good or evil (1 Cor 12.14-27).

The sin of the children of Israel is described as a "trespass" (4604), which is defined by Strong as "an unfaithful or treacherous act". The word is used of a wife's adultery (Num 5.12-13) and is also employed in reference to the trans-Jordan tribes building an altar (ch.22). The thought is that such an act constitutes a breach of trust and this was the case with Achan. The Lord considered it a breach of the covenant into which they had entered before Jericho was taken, when they agreed to render to the Lord the spoils of the city (6.17).

The trespass of the nation was caused by "Achan, the son of Carmi, the son of Zabdi, the son of Zerah, of the tribe of Judah". His genealogy is given here and in 1 Chronicles 2.6-7 where his name is changed slightly, "the sons of Zerah; Zimri, and Ethan, and Heman, and Calcol, and Dara. five of them in all. And the sons of Carmi; Achar, the troubler of Israel, who transgressed in the thing accursed". The Lord had warned the people that He would "trouble"(6.18) the camp of Israel if they took of the accursed thing and Achan is described as the source of that trouble. His genealogy is important as he is identified as being the great-great-grandson of Judah from his relationship with Tamar, his daughter-in-law (Gen 38.30). A.W. Pink comments, "What a solemn example of the sins of the fathers being visited upon the children!".

Verses 2-5: Defeat at Ai

The failure of Joshua (v.2)

On a cursory reading of the chapter, it appears that Joshua adopted the same approach to Ai which had been so effective at Jericho. He "sent men from Jericho to Ai, which is beside Bethaven, on the east side of Bethel, and spake unto them, saying, Go up and view the country". The method was the same; send spies into the land to report on the strength and nature of the enemy. However, Joshua forgot the most important element of the preparation for taking Jericho. Prior to the scouting of the land and battle plans being implemented, the Lord had spoken to Joshua. It is significant that the Lord was silent as Joshua planned for the conquest of Ai. By failing to notice the silence of the Lord, he missed the sign that there was a problem in the camp.

Joshua had known success and had become complacent, falling back on the methods that had been successful and not listening for the word of the Lord for the new challenges that faced the people. How quickly believers can become insensitive to the silence of the Lord as they seek to serve Him, relying on routine and past help from God rather than seeking fresh help and direction in service.

The failure of the spies (v.3)

"And they returned to Joshua, and said unto him, Let not all the people go up; but let about two or three thousand men go up and smite Ai". The complacency that had marked Joshua is also evident in the report of the spies. They brought an inaccurate report, which seemed to be permeated by arrogance and over confidence. The glaring omission from their report was any mention of the Lord, in contrast to the report of the spies. When they came back from Jericho they said, "Truly the Lord hath delivered into our hands all the land" (2.24). The present report was flawed as it did not give a correct estimate of the strength of Ai, only that "they are but few", which proved to be wrong; a total of 12,000 were slain when the city fell (8.25). Their report was also inappropriate, containing advice that Joshua should have sought from the Lord, rather than from the spies. It was the Lord who had given the battle plans for Jericho, but on this occasion Joshua was content to implement the rather vague advice of the spies, which was based upon the incorrect prediction of the strength of the city, and the desire that Joshua "make not all the people to labour thither".

It may have seemed a good idea to send only a few thousand up to Ai, but it was not the word of the Lord. They should have remained where they were in light of the silence from heaven and sought the Lord's face to discover the reason for the lack of direction and communication. As it was, they had to suffer the pain of defeat at Ai before they were found in repentance before the Lord.

The failure of the soldiers (v.4)

"So there went up thither of the people about three thousand men. and they fled before the men of Ai". For the first time in battle, the full fighting strength of Israel was not employed. Throughout the victories over the kings of the Amorites on the east of the Jordan, and the conquest of Jericho, the people had fought as one army, with all of the men of war present. Now they experienced defeat and disgrace as they ran away from the enemy.

The fear of the people (v.5)

The small army of 3,000 men was routed as the men of Ai "chased them from before the gate even unto Shebarim, and smote them in the going down". They had stood at the gate of the city before being repulsed and driven to "Shebarim" (7671) ("quarries", RV margin), a place of uncertain location. The cause of the defeat, in military terms, is not included in the narrative since it is unimportant. The root cause was the absence of the Lord.

"And the men of Ai smote of them about thirty and six men". The number of casualties suffered by the force of 3,000 men was comparatively small, yet it was significant. On only one other occasion had the children of Israel known defeat in battle, and that was after they had accepted the report of the ten spies and attempted to enter the land when the Lord was not with them (Num 14.41-45). On that occasion the "ark of the covenant of the Lord, and Moses, departed not out of the camp" (Num 14.44). The loss of the thirty-six men was the cause of national distress, "wherefore the hearts of the people melted, and became as water". As a result of going into battle without the Lord, they became like the inhabitants of Jericho (2.11). Casualties were an accepted consequence of war, yet when the Lord was fighting for them there was no expectation of losing men in battle. Failure due to sin brought this about. This is also true of the spiritual conflict in which every believer is engaged. It is only when sin brings failure that there are casualties among the people of God. They are not inevitable, but are possible.

It became apparent to the people that something was seriously wrong when they failed to take Ai and thirty-six men died. The effect of defeat at the hands of the ungodly was great. All the bravado that preceded the battle of Ai had gone and was replaced by uncertainty and fear. It is a fearful thing for any Christian to realise that the Lord is at a distance and not helping him.

Verses 6-9: Grief of Joshua and the Elders

Mourning (v.6)

Rather than berate the soldiers who fled from the face of the enemy or seek to answer the problem by military means, "Joshua rent his clothes, and fell to the earth upon his face before the ark of the Lord until the eventide" (v.6). He sought the presence of the Lord and humbled himself in a posture which signified his grief and mourning. Throughout the Old Testament, physical postures and outward symbols of mourning signified an attitude of heart, in a manner than would not be common in the modern western world. Sackcloth was worn (Gen 37.34), fasting (2 Sam 3.35) and postures, such as lying down (2 Sam 12.16), were adopted.

The elders of Israel joined Joshua and they "put dust upon their heads" (v.6). The response of these leaders is a lesson for any believer who has known defeat in spiritual conflict. They were humbled in the presence of the Lord and mourned. It was not a passing moment, since they were there "until the eventide". Lingering before the ark of the Lord in an attitude of humility and grief was the right thing to do. They were acknowledging that the answer to their defeat would come from the Lord when they humbled themselves, losing the pride and complacency that had caused their defeat. The lesson is there for any who would try to rectify such a situation in their own experience, without spending time before the Lord mourning their defeat and seeking an answer from the Lord. The approach of Joshua and the elders of the children of Israel can be contrasted to the attitude of the assembly at Corinth, when sin was in the midst – "ye are puffed up, and have not rather mourned" (1 Cor 5.2). Such an attitude was condemned by Paul and should not be present in any assembly when sin is discovered among the saints.

Lament (vv.7-9)

A.W. Pink comments that "As is so often the case with us, especially when deeply perturbed, there was a strange mingling of the flesh and the spirit seen in the prayer which is now to engage our attention. While some of the expressions cannot be approved, yet it should be borne in mind that Joshua was not here murmuring against any direct dealing of the Lord with himself, but was venting his sore distress over what had just befallen his nation".

"Alas, O Lord God, wherefore hast thou at all brought this people over Jordan, to deliver us into the hand of the Amorites, to destroy us? would to God we had been content, and dwelt on the other side Jordan!" (v.7). The opening statement of Joshua's prayer is a sad reflection of the condition of his heart. The downward spiral had been rapid since the fall of Jericho and the comment, "So the Lord was with Joshua; and his fame was noised throughout all the country" (6.27). From the heights of that experience Joshua had failed to consult the Lord regarding the assault on Ai and had slighted the ark in not giving it its rightful place among the people as they went to battle. As Joshua prostrated himself before the Lord, he uttered an accusation, which others had expressed on previous occasions (Ex 16.3; 17.3; Num 11.4-6; 14.2-3), and which he had condemned (Num 14.6-9). His accusation was unreasonable and contradictory. He acknowledged the great miracle of the Jordan crossing and the sovereign control of the Lord in the affairs of the children of Israel, yet accused the Lord of seeking to destroy them in direct contradiction of His earlier promises. The words that Joshua uttered in the Lord's presence were the outpouring of his heart and reflected the confusion, disappointment and fear that he was experiencing following the dramatic reversal at Ai. They were not admirable, but did mark the beginning of Joshua's recovery. Elsewhere in the Bible men of God have poured out their hearts to Him in inappropriate language, and yet such an experience has marked the beginning of a spiritual recovery. In such circumstances the answer of the Lord was often a revelation of their sin.

"O Lord, what shall I say, when Israel turneth their backs before their enemies!" (v.8). As Joshua spoke to the Lord the tone of his remarks began to alter with the focus changing from accusations against the Lord for what He had done, to being at a loss for words to describe the shame of the defeat at Ai. The manner of their defeat exposed the children of Israel to the ridicule of the people of Canaan. They "turneth (2015) their backs (6203) before their enemies"- this can be rendered "Israel hath turned the neck before its enemies" (YLT). This is the only place in Old Testament where this expression is employed although a similar form of words is used in v.12. "Turneth" has the idea of turmoil and is often translated as "overturned" or "overthrown". The expression conveys the dramatic and shameful character of the defeat that took place at Ai.

"For the Canaanites and all the inhabitants of the land shall hear of it, and shall environ us round, and cut off our name from the earth: and what wilt thou do unto thy great name?" (v.9). The consequences of the manner in which they had been defeated were not lost on Joshua, and he expressed this before the Lord. He had a concern for two names, those of the children of Israel and the Lord. He understood that their enemies would take heart from this defeat and seek to surround them and destroy them in the same manner as they had destroyed Jericho. They would be wiped off the face of the earth without any trace of them left. If this occurred, then the name of the Lord would also be affected, for the children of Israel were His people and in covenant relationship with Him. If the covenant were broken and the people destroyed then the name of the Lord, that is, the character and reputation of the Lord, would be shamed in the land. This was an argument that had been used by Moses on previous occasions when the people had sinned and the judgment of God had been pending (Ex 32.11-14; Num 14.11-19; Deut 9.26-29).

Having known defeat, Joshua poured out his heart before the Lord. His prayer was honest and ranged from an accusation against the Lord to a confession of his fear of further defeat and the consequential shame brought on the name of the Lord. In his time of confusion and disappointment, Joshua prayed like Jeremiah in his lamentation and Job in his distress. Such prayers are the mark of men who are sincere in the presence of the Lord.

Verses 10-15: Answer of the Lord

The Lord's answer to Joshua can be divided into three paragraphs, consisting of His explanation of the defeat at Ai (vv.10-12), the requirement for sanctification (v.13), and the transgressor identified (vv.14-15).

Defeat at Ai explained (vv.10-12)

The Lord did not overlook the accusation of Joshua (v.7), and, as He answered, there was a rebuke contained in His words: "Get thee up; wherefore liest thou thus upon thy face?" (v.10). When considering the response of the Lord, it is important to remember the context of Joshua's lament. The Lord did not rebuke Joshua for his penitential posture on the ground; it was rather the inappropriate charge regarding His motives in bringing them over the Jordan. This placed an element of blame upon the Lord for the catastrophe at Ai and, instead of lying before the Lord with these thoughts, Joshua was instructed to get up and deal with the true cause of defeat.

At times in the Christian's experience, remorse and tearful lamenting over sin and spiritual defeat are necessary, yet this is, in itself, insufficient to deal with the issue and enable the believer to move on for the Lord. There is a point when he requires to get up from before the Lord and deal with the sin that brought defeat. An attitude of remorse has its place, but should not bring a person into a fixed condition of sorrowful paralysis.

The sin that caused the defeat is attributed to Israel and not to one man: "Israel hath sinned" (v.11). The significance of this corporate responsibility has been noted earlier (v.1). The seriousness of the sin was brought before Joshua with the use of six verbs within one verse, as the Lord identified the exact nature of what had taken place. It is a lesson as to the character of the Lord that the actions of one man, in doing what some would see as a simple and insignificant thing, had far reaching consequences and required detailed exposure and comprehensive judgment. Any Christian who sins, and considers it an insignificant thing not worthy of confession before the Lord, ought to take note, as the Lord has not changed and neither has His attitude to sin amongst His people.

1. *"Israel hath sinned (2398)"*
The general word for sin is employed.
2. *"they have also transgressed (5674) my covenant which I commanded them"*
They had stepped over the line of acceptable conduct. The Lord had entered into a covenant with the children of Israel in relation to the taking of Jericho and it was this covenant that Israel had transgressed.
3. *"for they have even taken (3947) of the accursed thing"*
The third clause of the verse completes the description of the sin as it related to God. It was a removal of property which belonged to the Lord.
4. *"and have also stolen (1589)"*
It was theft.
5. *"and dissembled also (3584)"*
There had been lies and deception.
6. *"they have put (7760) it even among their own stuff"*
The sin of removing these items had been compounded by the location where they had been stored. They had been placed among their own belongings for their own use.

The sin had a twofold effect: "The children of Israel could not stand before their enemies, but turned their backs before their enemies" (v.12). This explained the defeat at Ai. In addition, the future well-being of the children of Israel was under threat as the Lord stated that "neither will I be with you any more, except ye destroy the accursed from among you" (v.12). Such was the seriousness of the sin in the eyes of the Lord, that it not only had caused the defeat at Ai and the death of about thirty-six men, but it would continue to have an effect upon the children of Israel unless the cause of the sin was dealt with, in accordance with the Lord's instructions (6.18). The children of Israel had to learn that sin cannot be overlooked and the passing of time does not diminish its seriousness.

The requirement for sanctification (v.13)

"Up, sanctify the people" was the first step on the road to recovery. Prior to the crossing of the Jordan the instruction had been the same (3.5) but on that occasion it was the prelude to the Lord doing wonders. Holiness was the Lord's requirement when He would do wonders for them and was also necessary when He would reveal sin among them.

Although there is no mention in the narrative of the process required for the people to be sanctified, there does appear to be a ceremonial aspect to it. This was a necessary step toward self examination in preparation for the public exposure of sin amongst the people. The importance of this is stressed in the New Testament when the apostle Paul wrote to the Galatians and taught them that "if a man be overtaken in a fault, ye which are spiritual, restore such an one in the spirit of meekness; considering thyself, lest thou also be tempted" (Gal 6.1). The context of dealing with a fellow believer's sin demands self examination.

Instructions for identifying the transgressor (vv.14-15)

The Lord instructed Joshua to implement a systematic process of identification, which left no possibility of error and gradually increased the pressure on the individual; this in turn would have the effect of achieving a full confession. This approach was for the benefit of the children of Israel who observed the process. It had the effect of demonstrating the all-knowing and all-seeing character of their God and the righteousness of divine justice. The whole scene was solemn and dramatic and would have lived long in the memory of those present that day. Justice was done, and was seen to be done; such an approach is necessary when discipline has to be exercised among God's people. The message was sent out and no doubt received; sin is serious and brings its own consequences.

Joshua was instructed to begin the process by bringing the people "according to your tribes: and it shall be, that the tribe which the Lord taketh shall come according to the families thereof; and the family which the Lord shall take shall come by households; and the household which the Lord shall take shall come man by man" (v.14). The social structure of the children of Israel was revealed in the step-by-step investigation that Joshua was instructed to carry out. Most commentators conclude that not all of members of the tribes, families and households would have stood before Joshua that morning. It would be more likely that the head of each tribe, family or household would have represented them.

There are two general views as to the meaning of the expressions "which the Lord shall take" and "which the Lord taketh". It is not possible to be certain as to the meaning since there is no explanation provided in the narrative. Eleazar the priest could have used the Urim and Thummim to give Joshua advice. This means of determining the will of God was stated when Joshua took on the responsibility of leadership: "He shall stand before Eleazar the priest, who shall ask counsel for him after the judgment of Urim before the Lord: at his word shall they go out, and at his word they shall come in, both he, and all the children of Israel with him, even all the congregation" (Num 27.21). The actual process of using the Urim and

Thummim is not revealed in Scripture. Alternatively, lots may have been cast. Keil & Delitzsch note that "which the Lord taketh" is "the technical term employed, according to 1 Samuel 14.42, to denote the falling of the lot upon a person. Moreover, the lot was frequently resorted to in cases where a crime could not be brought home to a person by the testimony of eyewitnesses (1 Sam 14.41-42; Prov. 18.18; Jonah 1.7)".

The judgment pronounced by the Lord was severe: "he that is taken with the accursed thing shall be burnt with fire, he and all that he hath" (v.15). The burning of the body took place after stoning (v.25) and was a public expression of the severity and comprehensive nature of God's judgment upon the sin.

There were two reasons given for the severe punishment. Firstly, "he hath transgressed the covenant of the Lord" (v.15). This was the covenant that the Lord entered into with the children of Israel in relation to the conquest of Jericho. Secondly, "he hath wrought folly in Israel" (v.15). The expression "wrought folly" (6213) denotes something which was "disgraceful" (NKJV) or "wickedness" (JND). Keil & Delitzsch describe the actions of Achan as "a crime as was irreconcilable with the honour of Israel as the people of God".

Verses 16-26: Judgment Executed

Achan identified as the culprit (vv.16-18)

"So Joshua rose up early in the morning" (v.16). On four occasions in the book there is the record of Joshua rising early in the morning. The three other times are when the children of Israel approached Jordan (3.1), on the first day of the encirclement of Jericho (6.12), and when Ai was finally taken (8.10). Having received instruction from the Lord for these great tasks, Joshua did not delay.

The process began with the examination of the tribes, and "Judah was taken" (v.16). This was a shameful experience for that noble tribe. They had led the march of Israel across the wilderness (Num 10.14) and were given the largest inheritance in Canaan (Deut 34.2). Matthew Henry comments that "since Judah was to have the largest lot in Canaan, the more inexcusable is one of that tribe if, not content to wait for his own share, he break in upon God's property". The search was narrowed down to "the family of the Zarhites" (v.17). This family came from the son of Judah (Num 26.20) who was born to Tamar (Gen 38.30). Within that family "Zabdi was taken" (v.17) and the procedure continued until "Achan, the son of Carmi, the son of Zabdi, the son of Zerah, of the tribe of Judah, was taken" (v.18). It is amazing that up to this point Achan had not confessed his sin. As the search narrowed toward him, he allowed it to run its course until he was publicly identified. The inevitability of his identification did not cause him to stop the process. It may be that he held out hope that he would avoid detection even when his family and household were taken. The narrative does not explain his reasoning as he stood before Joshua that day, but the exposure of his sin does demonstrate that sin cannot be hidden from the Lord. Denial or silence may be effective in hiding sin from others, even the closest family members, but it is futile before the Lord.

Achan's confession (vv.19-21)

"And Joshua said unto Achan, My son..." (v.19). The manner in which Joshua spoke to Achan is striking. "By this example, judges are taught that, while they punish crimes, they ought so to temper their severity as not to lay aside the feelings of humanity, and, on the other hand, that they ought to be merciful without being reckless and remiss; that, in short, they ought to be as parents to those they condemn, without substituting undue mildness for the sternness of justice" (Calvin). The tension must have built up throughout the day, as Achan was being identified as the man who had brought defeat and death to the people. Yet it was at this point that Joshua demonstrated true leadership, obtaining a confession that was substantiated by the discovery of the goods in accordance with the detail of the confession, and by so doing, the righteousness of the judgment could not be gainsaid.

To obtain the confession, Joshua gave Achan four commands (v.19). Achan obeyed these commands in one expression of confession:

1. "*give, I pray thee, glory to the Lord God of Israel*"
2. "*and make confession unto him*"
3. "*and tell me now what thou hast done*"
4. "*hide it not from me*".

The first two commands related to the need for Achan to have dealings with God. Joshua was not commanding Achan to engage in two separate acts, but rather as he confessed his sin to God, he would be giving glory to Him. It is interesting that this form of words was used by the Pharisees when they spoke to the man who had been born blind and healed by the Lord Jesus (Jn 9.24). On that occasion the Pharisees believed they were doing what Joshua had done with Achan in exposing his sin.

Achan was in a position where he could bring glory to the Lord by making confession of his sin. This did not mean that the Lord was condoning his actions or that his sin could be overlooked as a result of his confession. However, he could acknowledge the attributes of God: righteousness, omniscience, holiness, and, in so doing, bring glory to Him. God is able to make even the sin of men work out to His glory, which can be seen in the work of Christ at Calvary, when He brought glory to God by dealing sacrificially with sin.

In addition to making his confession to the Lord, Achan was instructed to reveal the whole matter to Joshua, as the third and fourth commands demonstrate. In the New Testament there are sins which require to be confessed to the Lord and revealed to others. Not every sin falls into this category, but some do. The consequences of Achan's sin had involved the whole nation and as a result there was the requirement for a public exposure of that sin. There are occasions, especially in a moral context, where sin has consequences for others in the fellowship of an assembly and as a result must not only be confessed to the Lord but also revealed to others, most likely those who are elders among the saints. This exposure of sin is not for the punishment of sin, as in the Old Testament, but for repentance and righteousness to be displayed as publicly as the sin itself.

"Indeed I have sinned against the Lord God of Israel, and thus and thus have I done" (v.20). Achan confessed his sin in detail only after he was found out. At no point in the process did he confess voluntarily or display signs of repentance. In this way he was similar to Saul, who said, "I have sinned ...I have transgressed the commandment of the Lord" (1 Sam 15.24). If he had avoided detection, there is no evidence in the narrative to suggest that Achan would have confessed. As a result his confession could only bring glory to God and not salvation to him.

His confession is a lesson as to the detail that is required when acknowledging sin to God. There was a progression to his sin, which was similar to the recorded sins of Adam and David.

"When I saw among the spoils a goodly Babylonish garment, and two hundred shekels of silver, and a wedge of gold of fifty shekels weight" (v.21). It all began with a look. This is where it went wrong for Eve: "when the woman saw that the tree was good for food, and that it was pleasant to the eyes, and a tree to be desired to make one wise" (Gen 3.6), and for David: "from the roof he saw a woman washing herself; and the woman was very beautiful to look upon" (2 Sam 11.2). There are many warnings throughout the Scriptures regarding the eyes and what is seen; "Turn away mine eyes from beholding vanity; and quicken thou me in thy way" (Ps 119.37), "I made a covenant with mine eyes; why then should I think upon a maid?" (Job 31.1). Every believer must take care what he puts before his eyes, keeping the warning of the New Testament before him: "For all that is in the world, the lust of the flesh, and the lust of the eyes, and the pride of life, is not of the Father, but is of the world" (1 Jn 2.16).

The articles that Achan saw were of great value. The garment was "a Babylonish cloak (lit. a cloak of Shinar, or Babylon)... a costly cloak, artistically worked, such as were manufactured in Babylon, and distributed far and wide through the medium of commerce" (Keil & Delitzsch).

"Then I coveted them" (v.21). What Achan saw provoked sinful desires within him. It is interesting that this progression is also seen in the experience of Eve in the garden in Eden where the same Hebrew word is employed, and translated as "desired" (2530). Achan had broken the tenth commandment (Ex 20.17) when he desired the goods that belonged to the Lord. There are exhortations in the New Testament regarding covetousness (Col 3.5; Heb 13.5) which make it clear that every believer must guard against this sin within the heart, since it causes tremendous problems amongst saints.

"And took them" (v.21). What began with a look that stirred up sin within Achan's heart quickly translated into action. Thus it was with Eve, "she took of the fruit thereof, and did eat, and gave also unto her husband with her; and he did eat" (Gen 3.6). David also followed the same path, "and David sent messengers, and took her" (2 Sam 11.4).

"They are hid in the earth in the midst of my tent, and the silver under it" (v.21). Having sinned, Achan sought to conceal his sin by covering the evidence. Both Eve (Gen 3.7) and David (2 Sam 11.6-27) attempted to do the same thing and failed. How futile it is to attempt to hide sin from God. It may be possible to hide it from other believers but the Scripture does say, "Be sure your sin will find you out" (Num 32.23).

Stolen goods recovered (vv.22-23)

The narrative picks up pace again as it moves towards the climax of the episode. "So Joshua sent messengers, and they ran unto the tent; and, behold, it was hid in his tent, and the silver under it" (v.22). There was a sense of urgency as the messengers ran. With the goods recovered, they "laid them out before the Lord" (v.23). The expression "laid them out" (3332), is elsewhere translated as "poured out" (Lev 9.9). "The accursed things were not poured out 'unto the Lord' for His acceptance, but before Him for His destruction – they were never brought into His treasury for use in His service, but totally destroyed, as the sequel shows" (A. W. Pink).

Judgment effected (vv.24-26)

All of the items that had been recovered from Achan's tent, together with "his sons, and his daughters, and his oxen, and his asses, and his sheep, and his tent, and all that he had" (v.24), were taken away from the camp of Israel for destruction. The judgment was severe and comprehensive. Each thing and person associated with Achan was destroyed. It must be remembered that this was not the application of the Law in relation to the punishment of sins in the ordinary course of life, since the punishment of children for their fathers' sin was expressly prohibited under the Law (Deut 24.16). It was the application of the Law of the ban (Deut 13.16-17) and the express instruction of the Lord for this specific case.

By remaining silent about the stolen goods within their tent, Achan's family had all participated in his sin. Their punishment serve as a warning to the people. For the children of Israel to remember the events that had unfolded, "a great heap of stones" (v.26) was raised over the burned bodies, animals and goods. The stones erected at Gilgal reminded the people of the Lord's presence among them (4.7) and these stones in the "valley of Achor" (v.24) reminded them of the consequences of sin. The seriousness of sin and its consequences should never be forgotten. It requires only a look to Calvary to remember the cost of redemption and the cleansing that is available for believers from the defilement of sin.

After the sin had been exposed and the judgment effected, "the Lord turned from the fierceness of his anger" (v.26). Fellowship was restored and the valley of Achor became a place which was associated with putting things right with God (Is 65.10; Hos 2.15).

JOSHUA 8.1-29

The Capture of Ai

Defeat at Ai had been a traumatic experience for the children of Israel. Having tasted the sweet joy of victory at Jericho, they had now swallowed the bitterness of defeat and humiliation at Ai. With Achan and all that belonged to him destroyed, they were now a cleansed people and able to resume their progress into Canaan. Their sin had halted their advance into the land and diminished them in the eyes of the Canaanites. In order for them to continue they had to revisit the scene of their defeat and overcome what had overcome them. This is the pathway of progress in spiritual experience. There is no diversion around defeat. Abraham realised this when he returned from Egypt to the place of the altar between Bethel and Hai, "which he had made there at the first: and there Abram called on the name of the Lord" (Gen 13.4).

The account of the battle of Ai is the first and most detailed account of a battle in the book of Joshua. The conquest of Jericho was accomplished by direct intervention from the Lord and required no military strategy; at Ai the means were different but the help and presence of the Lord was equally essential. It was more difficult to take Ai at the second attempt than it would have been without the trespass of the people at Jericho. This is the cost of failure, since a road littered with diversions is a harder road to negotiate.

There are some difficulties with the numbers of men (vv.3,12) that are mentioned and the chronology of events in this chapter. This has been the subject of much debate amongst commentators and will be briefly mentioned below, without allowing it to distract from the lessons of the passage.

Chronology and numbers

On the face of the narrative, there appears to be a complicated and contradictory account of the ambush that Joshua put in place prior to the assault on Ai. The difficulty arises from Joshua sending out a force of 30,000 men (v.3), "and they went to lie in ambush, and abode between Bethel and Ai, on the west side of Ai" (v.9). He then sent out a force of 5,000 men to the same place (v.12) to lie in ambush. Were there two large groups of men lying in wait? What happened to the 30,000 men since there is no mention of them being involved in the battle?

There are two main schools of thought regarding this apparent textual problem. Some commentators take the view that there was one ambush force of either 30,000 or 5,000 men, with the more likely figure being 5,000. They attribute the different numbers to a copyist error, albeit "it is a drastic measure to postulate an emendation with no manuscript support, but it seems the best solution to a difficult problem" (David M. Howard Jnr., *The New American Commentary).* In contrast, other commentators take the view that there were two separate forces of 30,000 and 5,000 men. "The narrative makes it quite plain that they were a separate force which was now assigned to a different position. Joshua's design therein was evident, for his project served a twofold purpose: it cut off Bethel sending any reinforcements to Ai, and it prevented the forces of Ai escaping in that direction" (A. W. Pink).

The narrative is structured in a similar fashion to the account of the crossing of the river Jordan (ch.3), where the verses are not necessarily in chronological order, but are set out in a manner to emphasise certain aspects of the events that unfolded. There is repetition and gradual revelation within the structure of these verses.

Verses 1-2: Instructions for Assaulting Ai

It was clear from the aftermath of the first assault on Ai, that the city would not be taken by the children of Israel without the presence of the Lord among them, in fulfilment of His promise to Moses (Deut 1.21) and Joshua (Deut 31.8; Josh 1.9). It was vital that Joshua received the assurance of the presence and help of the Lord prior to commencing a further attack on Ai. "Fear not, neither be thou dismayed" (v.1), was the encouragement he received from the Lord. He had already been assured that the Lord's anger had been turned from the people, yet that fell short of restoring them to the position they occupied before the trespass at Jericho. They had been discouraged at Ai to the extent that "the hearts of the people melted, and became as water" (7.5), but now they were encouraged by the message of full restoration, the outcome of true repentance.

The directions of the Lord for taking Ai provide interesting contrasts with the first assault on Ai and similarities with the conquest of Jericho.

"Take all the people of war with thee" (v.1). The whole fighting force of Israel was involved in the battle, unlike the few thousand that advanced on the first occasion. When Jericho was taken all the men of war encircled the city (6.3). The people would know victory in their unity.

"See, I have given into thy hand the king of Ai, and his people, and his city, and his land" (v.1). This time the Lord gave Joshua the assurance of a completed victory, in the same way as He had when instructing him to take Jericho (6.2). His voice had been silent prior to the first attack on Ai.

"And thou shalt do to Ai and her king as thou didst unto Jericho and her king: only the spoil therof, and the cattle thereof, shall ye take for a prey unto yourselves" (v.2). Instructions for dealing with the inhabitants and plunder from the city had also been given at Jericho, but were transgressed. The voice of the Lord had been silent on this subject as the men of Israel made their way up to attack Ai. Utter destruction of the city and the death of the king was the order of the day, since that had been the instruction from the Lord prior to the taking of Jericho (6.21). The difference on this occasion was that the spoil was available to the people. If only Achan had waited!

"Lay thee an ambush for the city behind it" (v.2). Here were the battle orders for the successful attack on Ai. They were in sharp contrast to the previous silence of the Lord and the ceremonial character of the approach at Jericho. This was to be a battle fought with a military strategy that required discipline, which had been sadly lacking at Jericho and Ai.

Verses 3-13: Battle Orders

Thirty thousand men chosen (v.3)

"So Joshua arose, and all the people of war, to go up against Ai" (v.3). As a united people they moved toward the scene of their humiliation. Joshua then implemented the direction of the Lord and "chose out thirty thousand mighty men of valour, and sent them away by night" (v.3).

Instructions for the ambush (vv.4-8)

They were to "lie in wait against the city, even behind the city" (v.4) and were to "go not very far from the city" (v.4). "As the distance from Gilgal to Ai was about fifteen miles... the detachment sent forward might easily accomplish the distance in a night, so as to arrive on the western side of Ai before the break of day" (Keil & Delitzsch). In their position of ambush, they were to heed the instruction of Joshua, "be ye all ready" (v.4). Waiting is hard and can lead to complacency. They were to wait but maintain a state of readiness, so that when the moment for action arrived they would not be unprepared.

The strategy was simple. The main army would make a frontal approach to the city – "I, and all the people that are with me, will approach unto the city" (v.5). Joshua anticipated that as the men of Ai saw them draw near, they would assume that they were adopting similar tactics to the first time and come out to meet them: "when they come out against us, as at the first, that we will flee before them" (v.5). The men with Joshua would then withdraw and give the impression of an army in retreat. By so doing, they would encourage the men of Ai to leave their city and pursue them. "They will say, They flee before us, as at the first: therefore we will flee before them" (v.6). When the men of Ai pursued Joshua, the ambush force was instructed to "rise up from the ambush, and seize upon the city" (v.7). It was a classic military ruse, which by itself would not accomplish the task but would be used by the Lord to give them the city, as Joshua indicated to the men of the ambush party, "the Lord your God will deliver it into your hand" (v.7). When they had taken the city they were instructed by Joshua to "set the city on fire" (v.8). All of these instructions were then given added weight, "according to the commandment of the Lord shall ye do. See, I have commanded you" (v.8), which was most probably emphasised in light of the last foray against Ai. These plans were the Lord's and as such had to be adhered to in every detail.

Implicit in Joshua's instructions was the requirement for obedience.

Although it was a different strategy from that used against Jericho, there was still the need for discipline and adherence to the Lord's instructions. In addition, the knowledge of the enemy, which they had gained in their failure, was to be utilised. Obedience to the word of the Lord, knowledge of the enemy and dependence upon the Lord were necessary for success. When a believer revisits the scene of his failure and seeks to overcome the obstacle which blocks the pathway of progress in his walk for the Lord, it is necessary for him to obey the Word of God and also utilise his knowledge of the enemy Paul stated that "we are not ignorant of his devices" (2 Cor 2.11) and draw strength from the Lord for the conflict.

Men of war move into position (vv.9-13)

It is in this section that the difficulties regarding chronology and numbers are found. Without excluding the possibility of an alternative explanation, it would appear that vv.11-13 are a reiteration of some of the events already described and, as such, are a parenthesis in the chronology of the passage. This style of writing is by now familiar to the reader since it has already been encountered in the account of the crossing of the river Jordan (chs.3-4).

The ambush force obeyed Joshua's instructions and, as was stated earlier (v.3), left for their position by night. Joshua did not accompany them as he "lodged that night among the people" (v.9). His leadership is evident in his decision to remain with the majority of the men of war. He was not distant or in any way separated from the people. The crucial importance of the events that were to follow on the morning could not be underestimated. Having experienced defeat at the hands of the men of Ai, they could not afford to be defeated again since this would mean the end of their advance into the land. At a time of crisis and pressure among the people of God, a true leader will be found among them. It was the night before His suffering and the scattering of His disciples, that the Lord spent time with them in the upper room comforting and preparing them for the days that lay ahead.

The critical point of the battle would be the persuasion of the men of Ai to leave their city and pursue the children of Israel. In order to accomplish this, the discipline of the people was vital. It was not long since the "hearts of the people melted, and became as water" (7.5). Joshua's position as leader was at the head of the men as they advanced toward Ai: "Joshua rose up early in the morning, and numbered the people, and went up, he and the elders of Israel, before the people to Ai" (v.10). In the place of prominence at the head of the procession were the men who had "put dust on their heads" (7.6) and humbled themselves before the Lord. This is an example to those who would seek to lead the people of God. There are times when they will be in the forefront of the spiritual battle, in the place of prominence, and at other times humbled on their faces before the Lord.

As has already been noted, there is a parenthesis in the narrative, which, if removed, takes the reader from the end of v.10 to the beginning of v.14. In common with other restatements of events in the book, the parenthetical verses provide further detail, as well as emphasis, within the narrative.

Verse 11 provides details of the troop movements between v.3, when Joshua began the preparations, and v.10, when they moved on the following morning. The exact location of their camp is given as "the north side of Ai: now there was a valley between them and Ai" (v.11). The whole battlefield is described with the placement of the ambush force restated, "between Bethel and Ai, on the west side of the city" (v.12). On the north, the main force was placed across a valley from Ai. On the west, hidden from sight, the ambush force waited. The scene was set for the battle to commence. During the night when he lodged with the main battle force, across the valley from Ai, Joshua did something similar to what he had done at Jericho (5.13) and "went that night into the midst of the valley" (v.13). His leadership is seen again as he would not lead the people into ground where he had not stood. When the spiritual battle rages among believers, it is good to have leaders who lead the saints through ground where they themselves have stood. Personal experience of the battlefield is important for a leader in any conflict.

Verses 14-29: The Battle of Ai

1st stage (vv.14-15)

The narrative that preceded the parenthesis of vv.11-13 continues in v.14. In the morning the king of Ai saw the main body of men outside the city, with Joshua at their head. The battle commenced as Joshua had anticipated (v.5): "the men of the city went out against Israel to battle, he and all his people" (v.14). The geography of the battlefield is further described, "at a time appointed, before the plain" (v.14). The expression "at a time appointed" is translated "at an appointed place" (NKJV) and would indicate that they set the battle in motion at the same place where the first battle was fought. This is identified as "the steppe (Arabah, not the valley of the Jordan, but the steppe or desert of Bethaven; cf. 7.2)" (Keil & Delitzsch). The first stage of the battle concluded when "Joshua and all Israel made as if they were beaten before them, and fled by the way of the wilderness" (v.15).

2nd stage (vv.16-17)

The reaction of the men of Ai was exactly as Joshua had said. The ease of their previous victory no doubt lulled them into a false sense of security "and all the people that were in Ai were called together to pursue after them" (v.16). It is worth noting that not only was Ai emptied of men, but "there was not a man left in Ai or Bethel, that went not out after Israel" (v.17). This is interesting because the ambush force was situated between Bethel and Ai and if men had been sent from one city to the other it would have been discovered, since it consisted of five thousand or even thirty thousand men. It is more likely, although not stated, that the men of Bethel were in Ai prior to the commencement of the battle and perhaps as a result of Joshua's first attempt to take Ai. There is very little detail concerning Bethel in the record of the conquest of Canaan, other than the king of Bethel being one of the kings listed as slain by Joshua (12.16). Some commentators have speculated that a treaty of mutual support bound Bethel and Ai or that, owing to its size, Ai was a satellite city of Bethel. The end of the 2nd stage of the battle concluded with the city of Ai open and defenceless.

3rd stage (vv.18-19)

Under the instruction of the Lord, "Joshua stretched out the spear that he had in his hand toward the city" (v.18). Whether this had been a pre-arranged sign to the men of the ambush is not clear. It is interesting that the weapon raised by Joshua is not described by the usual word for a spear, but by a word which can be translated as "javelin" (RSV). In the same way as the Lord instructed Aaron to "stretch forth thine hand with thy rod" (Ex 8.5) and Moses to "lift thou up thy rod, and stretch out thine hand over the sea, and divide it" (Ex 14.16), Joshua was to stretch out the spear toward the city and remain in that position until the city was taken (v.26). There are similarities to the upheld arms of Moses, when he held the rod of God (Ex 17.9,12), as Joshua fought the Amalekites at Rephidim.

The locations of Joshua in the conflict are a foreshadowing of those of the Lord Jesus. The night before the battle, Joshua was "among the people" (v.9) as the Lord Jesus was in the upper room. Joshua was in the "midst of the valley" before the battle began, which is a picture of the loneliness of Gethsemane and the depths of sorrow and agony He endured. Joshua appeared to be defeated as he withdrew his forces in the face of the enemy (v.15), which is exactly what the world thought of the Lord Jesus when they saw Him crucified at Calvary. With victory assured (v.8) he directed the men of war to accomplish the victory and stood as a visible encouragement to them - a picture of the Lord Jesus in glory with His triumph accomplished.

4th stage (vv.20-23)

The ambush worked to perfection. "When the men of Ai looked behind them, they saw, and, behold, the smoke of the city ascended up to heaven, and they had no power to flee this way or that way. and the people that fled to the wilderness turned back upon the pursuers" (v.20). The men of Israel, who had been fleeing into the wilderness in seeming retreat, turned and fought against the men of Ai, "and when Joshua and all Israel saw that the ambush had taken the city, and that the smoke of the city ascended, then they turned again, and slew the men of Ai" (v.21), who were also attacked from their rear by the ambush party that had burned Ai. It was a classic military manoeuvre, which resulted in the men of Ai "in the midst of Israel, some on this side, and some on that side: and they smote them, so that they let none of them remain or escape" (v.22). The defeat of Ai was complete when "the king of Ai they took alive, and brought him to Joshua" (v.23).

5th stage (vv.24-29)

The ambush had resulted in the complete destruction of the men from Ai who had pursued the children of Israel out of the city. Following this "all the Israelites returned unto Ai, and smote it with the edge of the sword" (v.24). In accordance with the Lord's instruction, the children of Israel killed all the inhabitants of Ai, "And so it was, that all that fell that day, both of men and women, were twelve thousand, even all the men of Ai" (v.25). There were four things that Joshua had to do at Ai. Firstly, "Joshua drew not his hand back, wherewith he stretched out the spear, until he had utterly destroyed all the inhabitants of Ai" (v.26). Secondly, "the cattle and the spoil of that city Israel took for a prey unto themselves, according unto the word of the Lord which he commanded Joshua" (v.27). Thirdly, "Joshua burnt Ai, and made it an heap for ever, even a desolation unto this day" (v.28). Having had the city set on fire by the ambush force (v.19), Joshua completely destroyed it with fire. In addition to its destruction, he ensured that it would never be rebuilt and it was an "everlasting heap of desolation to this day" (JND). The picture is clear. Having been defeated at Ai on one occasion they would not be defeated there again, and to make sure, Joshua obliterated the city. This is the only way for the Christian to deal with the cause of defeat in his life. The utter destruction of the obstacle will ensure that it never troubles him again. This was the lesson that Jacob failed to learn when he was returning to Gilgal and dealt with the idols in his household. "Jacob hid them under the oak which was by Shechem" (Gen 35.4). It would have been better to grind them into dust as Josiah did (2 Chr 34.4). Buried idols can be resurrected into the Christian's life; those which are destroyed do not cause problems in the future. Fourthly, "the king of Ai he hanged on a tree until eventide: and as soon as the sun was down, Joshua commanded that they should take his carcase down from the tree, and cast it at the entering of the gate of the city, and raise thereon a great heap of stones, that remaineth unto this day" (v.29). The king of Ai was dealt with as the Lord had instructed Joshua. He had resisted and defeated the children of Israel and was dealt with in accordance with the Law of Moses (Deut 21.22-23). The place of defeat was now the location of a memorial to their ultimate victory. Cairns of stones sat at Gilgal, the valley of Achor and Ai lest they forgot the hard learned lessons of spiritual warfare.

JOSHUA 8.30-35

The Covenant Reaffirmed

Following the capture of Ai, the children of Israel repeated a course of action which would make no sense to the military mind. As was previously noted, momentum is a key element of any successful campaign of conquest, and Joshua willingly gave this up again, having already waited at Gilgal for the circumcision of the people. With the cities of Jericho and Ai destroyed, the gateway into Canaan was open, but he did not take the people through. It would appear that the lesson of Ai had been learned, although the events of ch.9 tend to negate that view. Nevertheless, there was no rash advance into Canaan with Joshua demonstrating obedience to the command of the Lord by taking the people to Mount Gerizim and Mount Ebal for the fulfilment of the Lord's command through Moses. Yet again the reader is reminded that the advance into Canaan was directed by the Lord and that, for success in such a conflict, obedience to the word of the Lord is the paramount consideration.

There is debate among scholars as to the correct location of these verses within the narrative. Some manuscripts place them between the record of the circumcision of the people and the observance of the Passover (5.9-10), or after the coalition of Canaanite nations (9.2). It is difficult to determine the chronology of the events that are recorded, with the language employed not providing a definite time frame for the events. "The account … is attached, it is true, to the conquest of Ai by the introduction, 'Then Joshua built'; but simply as an occurrence which had no logical connection with the conquest of Canaan and the defeat of its kings. The participle … is used, for example, in cases where the historian either wishes to introduce contemporaneous facts, that do not carry forward the main course of the history, or loses sight for the time of the strictly historical sequence and simply takes note of the occurrence of some particular event" (Keil & Delitzsch). The uncertainty among some commentators as to the chronology of these verses does not detract from the significance of the events or the lessons that can be learned from their insertion at this point in the narrative.

Verses 30-31: The Altar and the Offerings

The location (v.30)

"Then Joshua built an altar unto the Lord God of Israel in mount Ebal". The location of Mount Ebal was given to the people by Moses before they came into the land, "on the other side Jordan, by the way where the sun goeth down, in the land of the Canaanites, which dwell in the champaign over against Gilgal, beside the plains of Moreh" (Deut 11.30). Moses had set the Law before the people and instructed them to go to Mount Gerizim and Mount Ebal and "put the blessing upon mount Gerizim, and the curse upon mount Ebal" (Deut 11.29). He had set before the people the blessing of obedience to the Law and the curse of disobedience. They had to associate these mountains with the blessing and curse of the Law in order that they would never forget the character of the Law of God and its jurisdiction over all the land.

Moses also instructed the people to build an altar on Mount Ebal (Deut 27.4), when they crossed over the Jordan, and it was those instructions which Joshua carried out in these verses. His obedience and attention to detail is noteworthy as he again displayed the vital characteristic of submission to the Word of God. This is seen to be so important looking back at the events through the lens of the New Testament. Almost the whole of the land is visible from the top of Mount Ebal and therefore it was a most suitable place to build an altar for worship and to have the Law read and acknowledged as being the Law for the land that lay before them.

The altar constructed (v.31)

Moses had given precise instructions for the construction of the altar and its purpose (Deut 27.4-8). The altar was built, "as Moses the servant of the Lord commanded the children of Israel, as it is written in the book of the law of Moses". It seems strange that the altar, which would have offerings placed upon it speaking of worship and sacrifice, would be built upon the mount that was associated with the curse of the Law. Yet, when the altar is seen as a picture of the Lord Jesus, its location is appropriate. For "Christ hath redeemed us from the curse of the law, being made a curse for us: for it is written, Cursed is every one that hangeth on a tree" (Gal 3.13). Therefore on the mount where the curse of the Law was pronounced, the altar was constructed. It is important to remember that in the New Testament the Lord Jesus is seen in three aspects in relation to sacrifice: the altar, the offering and the offerer (Heb 9.14; 13.10).

"An altar of whole stones" was in accord with the general instructions of Moses regarding the construction of altars (Ex 20.25) and also his specific instructions regarding this altar (Deut 27.5-6). It was not to be finished by the tools of man and was to be of unhewn stone. This again speaks of the Lord Jesus who was not polished or adorned by men and, in fact, was not attractive to the men of His day: "he hath no form nor comeliness; and when we shall see him, there is no beauty that we should desire him" (Is 53.2). Yet to the eye of God He was perfect and required no tool to dress the stones; no improvement could be made, as He was complete.

Upon this altar, which speaks of Christ, "they offered thereon burnt offerings unto the Lord, and sacrificed peace offerings". The burnt offering was a voluntary offering which was consumed on the altar, producing a sweet savour and making atonement (Lev 1). It is a picture of the death of the Lord Jesus on the cross, which brought pleasure to the heart of God and atonement for man, so that every believer is "accepted in the beloved" (Eph 1.6). The peace offering was the only offering which provided a portion for God, the priest and the offerer (Lev 3.1-17; 7.11-21), with the sweet savour arising to heaven as a result of the sacrifice. It speaks of the enjoyment of fellowship between God and man, which is only possible as a result of the work of the Lord Jesus.

With the smoke of the offerings arising from the altar and the land spread out before the people, the scene was set for the fulfilment of the command of Moses. They were acknowledging their God in worship and sacrifice.

Verses 32-35: The Law and the People

The Law written (v.32)

"And he wrote there upon the stones a copy of the law of Moses, which he wrote in the presence of the children of Israel". There is little detail given concerning the inscription of the Law upon the stones of the altar. It is reasonable to assume that Joshua carried out the instructions of Moses as precisely as he did in going to the mountains and in the construction of the altar. If that is so, they were to cover stones with plaister and write the Law upon them (Deut 27.2-4). They were not to be touched by iron (Deut 27.5) and therefore if the Law was to be inscribed upon them, they would have to be covered with plaister for them to be inscribed without using iron.

The altar was a symbol to the people of the character of their God and their responsibilities to Him in terms of their covenant with Him. The nation was reminded that their covenant relationship with the Lord was based upon the Law and their observance of it. Their acceptance before the Lord and their fellowship with Him was dependent on their obedience; thus the offerings that were laid on the altar were burned on stones inscribed with the Law.

As a picture of the Lord Jesus, the inscription of the Law upon the stones made it complete. In the days of His flesh, He magnified the Law and made it honourable (Is 42.21). He is seen in the unhewn, complete stones with the Law written upon them and the burnt offerings and peace offerings laid on the altar. At the cross, the Lord Jesus in the untouched perfection of His manhood, offered Himself as a sacrifice to bring pleasure to the heart of God, atonement for man and fellowship between God and man. In so doing He offered a life which was in complete accord with the Law of God, and in giving Himself to the death of the cross, He fulfilled the righteous requirements of the Law in relation to sin.

Position of the people (v.33)

The importance of these events is seen by the gathering of the people in accordance with the previous instruction of Moses (Deut 27.11-13), with the whole nation gathered: "all Israel, and their elders, and officers, and their judges, stood on this side the ark and on that side before the priests the Levites, which bare the ark of the covenant of the Lord, as well the stranger, as he that was born among them". It is interesting that there was provision for the "stranger" (1616) among the children of Israel. "The stranger" was a description of residents in Israel who were permanently associated with the children of Israel, but were not Israelites by birth. They had to enter into a covenant relationship with the Lord (Deut 29.11-12) and enjoyed the blessings of the children of Israel as seen in their participation in the feasts of the Lord (Ex 12.43-49; 20.10; Deut 16.10-14; 26.10-11). It is important to note that the stranger was not a temporary visitor among them. He would have the same status as an Israelite (Lev 22.25; Deut 14.21). His presence with the people around the ark was important to establish his commitment to the God of Israel and acceptance of the Law with its blessings and curses.

The people were divided into two groups, in accordance with the instruction of Moses, "half of them over against mount Gerizim, and half of them over against mount Ebal; as Moses the servant of the Lord had commanded before, that they should bless the people of Israel".

The Law read (vv.34-35)

"And afterward he read all the words of the law, the blessings and cursings, according to all that is written in the book of the law. There was not a word of all that Moses commanded, which Joshua read not before all the congregation of Israel, with the women, and the little ones, and the strangers that were conversant among them". The nation had not gathered in this way for forty years, since they had been at Mount Sinai (Ex 24). On that occasion Moses had read the Law to the people and they had entered into a covenant with the Lord. The generation who had covenanted with the Lord had fallen in the wilderness and a new generation had entered the land. A restatement of the basis of their relationship with Him was required, together with their agreement to the terms of the covenant.

The people that had left Egypt had failed and had not entered into the land. They had fallen under the curse of the Law as a result of their disobedience and lack of faith in their God. Their failure did not mean that a new generation had to fail. They were given the same opportunity as their predecessors to affirm their covenant with the Lord as they entered into the land. The lesson for Christians is that failure among a past generation does not mean inevitable failure for the next. How good it is to see a new generation committing themselves to the Lord and seeking to live for Him, notwithstanding the failures of the past.

JOSHUA 9

The Gibeonites

Following the events at Ai, the nations within Canaan began to come together to oppose the advance of the children of Israel. Prior to Ai, fear of Israel had paralysed the inhabitants of the land (5.1), and as a result the children of Israel had been able to take the offensive and conquer Jericho and Ai without fear of attack.

Chapters 9, 10 and 11 begin with details of alliances that were formed with the common aim of destroying the Israelites. Israel no longer faced single cities, which could be dealt with in isolation, but were now engaged in a conflict with confederations of cities and nations. In addition, the children of Israel faced a new strategy of deceit by men from a "great city" (10.2) called Gibeon. Before the frontal assault by the confederation of nations, the people of God had to contend with a subtle and deceptive approach by one of their enemies. The story of their deception is another lesson to be learned by Christians engaged in spiritual warfare. Satan not only uses blatant, outward hostility to weaken believers, but he is the master of deception and subterfuge and defeats many saints by subtlety.

Verses 1-2: Confederation of Nations

The opening statement of this chapter is remarkably similar to the commencement of ch.5.

"And it came to pass, when all the kings which were on this side Jordan, in the hills, and in the valleys, and in all the coasts of the great sea over against Lebanon, the Hittite, and the Amorite, the Canaanite, the Perizzite, the Hivite, and the Jebusite, heard thereof" (v.1).

"And it came to pass, when all the kings of the Amorites, which were on the side of Jordan westward, and all the kings of the Canaanites, which were by the sea, heard" (5.1).

At the beginning of ch.5 the inhabitants of the land had heard of the crossing of the Red Sea and were affected by the display of divine power. However, by the time Ai had finally been taken they had heard a different story. The miracle of the Red Sea brought the enemies of the people God into a condition of fear and put them on the defensive, but when they heard of the defeat at Ai they were emboldened and began to form an alliance in order to take offensive action against the children of Israel. The consequences of the sin of the nation at Jericho and Ai were far reaching. Although the immediate judgment of the Lord had been removed from the people, their testimony had been damaged and their enemies took courage from the display of weakness. What does the world hear about the people of God today? Is it a story of sin and defeat, or is it the evidence of God's power at work amongst His people?

The record of the nations that formed the alliance is instructive, since it covers the geographic extent of the land: the coast, hills and valleys. Six nations are listed as leading the alliance against Israel. These nations are among the seven listed earlier (3.10), but are presented in a different order. They were identically listed when Moses addressed the people and gave them instruction about destroying the inhabitants of Canaan and not making peace with them (Deut 20.1-20); this is significant given the subsequent events within the chapter.

"They gathered themselves together, to fight with Joshua and with Israel, with one accord" (v.2). The alliance of nations was united in their opposition to the people of God. No matter how disparate a group of people or nations are, when faced with the Lord or His people they unite. The clearest illustration of this took place when the strange confederate of Sadducees, Pharisees, Herodians and Romans united to crucify the Lord Jesus. This unity, among previously opposing groups, was prophesied by the Psalmist (Ps 2.1-2), and referred to in prayer by the early Christians: "For of a truth against thy holy child Jesus, whom thou hast anointed, both Herod, and Pontius Pilate, with the Gentiles, and the people of Israel, were gathered together" (Acts 4.27). United opposition to the Lord and His people will continue until the final chapter in the world's history, when Satan gathers the nations together against Israel (Rev 20.8-9). Unity among the ungodly exists when they have a common enemy to oppose. Unity among saints should be different since it has its source from within. The apostle Paul describes it as the "unity of the Spirit" since "There is one body, and one Spirit, even as ye are called in one hope of your calling; one Lord, one faith, one baptism, one God and Father of all, who is above all, and through all, and in you all" (Eph 4.4-6).

Verses 3-13: The Gibeonites' Deceit

Preparation (vv.3-5)

Not all the nations in Canaan reacted in the same way to the news of Israel's conquest of Jericho and Ai. It is important to understand that Satan does not always attack the people of God in the same manner; he can use the subtle approach of the serpent (Gen 3.1) or the aggression of the lion (1 Pet 5.8). "In stirring up the kings of Canaan to fight with Joshua, Satan is relying upon the use of arms; but in moving the Gibeonites to cloak their character and pose to be what they were not, so that Israel might be deceived into making a league with them, we behold his craftiness, purposing to introduce his leaven into the meal" (A. W. Pink).

The Gibeonites were Hivites (11.19) and were a brave people (10.2), but on hearing of the exploits of Israel "they did work wilily (acted with craft JND)" (v.4). The response of the inhabitants in Canaan to the news of the children of Israel differed greatly. Rahab believed (Heb 11.31), the inhabitants of Jericho fainted (2.9), the hearts of the kings of the Amorites and all the kings of the Canaanites melted (5.1), the king of Jerusalem feared greatly (10.2). Some responded by craft and others by force, instructing the New Testament believer that there will be a variety of responses to the news of the work of the Lord in the gospel. The vast majority did not exercise faith and seek after God, but rather sought to oppose or compromise the people of God.

The Gibeonites sent men to Joshua in an elaborate disguise. They took great care over their appearance since it was an essential element in their deception. Their appearance gave credibility to their story.

There were two aspects to the disguise of the Gibeonites:

1. "made as if they had been ambassadors" (v.4).
2. "took old sacks upon their asses, and wine bottles, old, and rent, and bound up; and old shoes and clouted upon their feet, and old garments upon them; and all the bread of their provision was dry and mouldy" (vv.4-5).

Their disguise gave them the appearance of having travelled a distance, and were therefore not close neighbours, and not of the nations which Israel had to destroy. In addition, the ambassadorial appearance gave the impression that they had been sent as a delegation to enter into a treaty with the children of Israel. Thus, before they spoke, they had given the wrong impression.

This was a subtle and clever approach. Their appearance was calculated to cloud the judgment of Joshua and the leaders of the people, thus enhancing the impact of their deception. Appearances can be deceptive and must not be the sole basis of any judgment formed by the people of God. The New Testament has many warnings about the danger of false teachers who gain entrance among gullible Christians, who accept people at face value. "For such are false apostles, deceitful workers, transforming themselves into the apostles of Christ. And no marvel; for Satan himself is transformed into an angel of light. Therefore it is no great thing if his ministers also be transformed as the ministers of righteousness; whose end shall be according to their works" (2 Cor 11.13-15); "For there are certain men crept in unawares, who were before of old ordained to this condemnation, ungodly men, turning the grace of our God into lasciviousness, and denying the only Lord God, and our Lord Jesus Christ" (Jude v.4). Care must be taken when people, who are unknown to the saints, approach the assembly and seek fellowship. Reception into the fellowship of an assembly based on outward appearance can lead to havoc, with unbelievers or those with strange doctrines being received among the saints. "Beloved, believe not every spirit, but try the spirits whether they are of God. because many false prophets are gone out into the world" (1 Jn 4.1).

Initial approach (v.6)

"And they went to Joshua unto the camp at Gilgal". There is nothing in the narrative to indicate that this place is different from the Gilgal of chs.4

and 5, where circumcision, the erection of the twelve stones from the Jordan, Passover, and the revelation of the Lord to Joshua all took place. However, it is likely that the Gilgal described by Moses in relation to the location of the mountains Gerizim and Ebal, as being "beside the plains of Moreh" (Deut 11.30), is the place where the Gibeonites met with the children of Israel. This would put the journey of the children of Israel to Mounts Gerizim and Ebal chronologically at the end of ch.8. This Gilgal was near these mounts and therefore the people would not have had to travel back to the Gilgal beside the river Jordan for the chronology of the narrative to make sense.

"We be come from a far country: now therefore make ye a league with us". The approach of the Gibeonites exploited the instruction of the Lord concerning the treatment of cities that were not within the land. Moses had given the instruction, "When thou comest nigh unto a city to fight against it, then proclaim peace unto it. And it shall be, if it make thee answer of peace, and open unto thee, then it shall be, that all the people that is found therein shall be tributaries unto thee, and they shall serve thee" (Deut 20.10-11). This only applied to "the cities which are very far off from thee, which are not of the cities of these nations. But of the cities of these people, which the Lord thy God doth give thee for an inheritance, thou shalt save alive nothing that breatheth" (Deut 20.15-16). It is not clear whether the Gibeonites were aware of the instruction that Moses had given to the people.

This approach is an illustration of the subtlety of the devil. He uses the Word of God and seeks to bring the Christian into a position of compromise through the misapplication of its truth. The closer his approach is to the Word of God then the greater possibility there is of the deception working. This can be seen among Christians today where the misunderstanding of Bible doctrine, or the naïve, superficial application of its truth, has led many into relationships with unbelievers in business, marriage and so-called churches; this has led to compromise and weakness in the things of the Lord.

The desire of the Gibeonites was to enter a covenant with the children of Israel, which was expressly forbidden (Ex 34.12). Satan's plan to hinder the people of God through compromise has been employed by him in both the Old Testament and New Testament. In the days of Ezra, outright opposition was not the first approach of the enemy: "They came to Zerubbabel, and to the chief of the fathers, and said unto them, Let us build with you. for we seek your God, as ye do" (Ezra 4.2). In the New Testament when the gospel came to Philippi and before the preachers were imprisoned, they were followed around the city by the demon-possessed girl who associated herself with the gospel and thus compromised its distinctive message. (Acts 16.16-18).

Initial response of Israel (v.7)

"And the men of Israel said unto the Hivites...". The narrator identified the men of Gibeon as being a people that had to be destroyed and, by so doing at this point, leaves the reader in no doubt as to the correct course that Israel should have followed. If the men of Israel had uncovered their true identity, they would have been able to deal with the matter in accordance with the instruction of the Lord.

It is possible that the Hivites had learned the art of deception from their history: "The sons of Jacob answered Shechem and Hamor his father deceitfully" (Gen 34.13). Hamor was a Hivite (Gen 34.2) and he and his son, together with all the males of their city, were slain as a result of the deception. The descendants of people that suffered as a result of deceit employed the same tactics generations later. It is a pity if the ungodly learn such behaviour from the people of God.

"Peradventure ye dwell among us; and how shall we make a league with you ?". The initial response of the men of Israel demonstrated that they were aware of the importance of the prohibition on making a covenant with people who lived nearby. The problem did not arise out of ignorance of the word of the Lord. At this stage of the conversation, it appears that they had not been taken in by the Gibeonites' appearance and so they raised the issue of their identity.

Gibeonites' answer (v.8)

"And they said unto Joshua, We are thy servants". In response to the initial enquiry, the Gibeonites gave a vague answer. "We are at thy service, which, according to the obsequious language common in the East, was nothing more than a phrase intended to secure the favour of Joshua, and by no means implied a readiness on their part to submit to the Israelites... they wished for a friendly alliance, by which their territory and also full liberty would be secured to themselves" (Keil & Delitzsch).

Joshua's further response (v.8)

"And Joshua said unto them, Who are ye? and from whence come ye?" The men of Israel had answered the initial approach of the Gibeonites, but it was Joshua who asked the pertinent questions. He wanted to know who they were and whence they came. In his question he demonstrated that the Gibeonites' appearance was having the desired effect. The grammar of the verse is interesting. The word "come" (935) is in the imperfect tense and as such indicates that Joshua thought that the journey of the Gibeonites was not complete. This is in contrast to v.6 when the Gibeonites speak of their journey as completed by employing the same word in the perfect tense.

Gibeonites further answer (vv.9-13)

The answer of the Gibeonites to Joshua's direct question was designed to flatter and deceive. They said that they were come from a "very far country"(v.9) which was a further exaggeration of the lie they had told to the men of Israel, when they said they were come from a "far country" (v.6). They had come a long way just to make contact with the children of Israel, which was an indication of how important the children of Israel were!

They were come because of "the name of the Lord thy God: for we have heard the fame of him, and all that he did in Egypt, and all that he did to the two kings of the Amorites, that were beyond Jordan, to Sihon king of Heshbon, and to Og king of Bashan, which was at Ashtaroth" (vv.9-10). This was similar to what Rahab had said to the spies in Jericho and was again designed to flatter and deceive. There was no mention of the events at Jericho and Ai, which would give the impression that news of these events had not travelled the distance to the "very far country" from which they had travelled. The purpose of their coming and the cause of their approach to Joshua seemed plausible, and was substantiated by the condition of the men and their provisions, to which they were quick to draw Joshua's attention: "This our bread we took hot for our provision out of our houses on the day we came forth to go unto you; but now, behold, it is dry, and it is mouldy: And these bottles of wine, which we filled, were new; and, behold, they be rent: and these our garments and our shoes are become old by reason of the very long journey" (vv.12-13). What they did not say was more significant than what they did. They gave neither nationality nor place of residence and thus Joshua's question went unanswered. The answer they did give was a mixture of truth and falsehood, which distracted Joshua.

Verses 14-15: Treaty

Following the briefest investigation, "the men took of their victuals, and asked not counsel at the mouth of the Lord" (v.14); they entrusted the judgment of this matter to their senses of hearing, sight and taste. What they saw, heard and tasted deceived them since they did not seek the counsel of the Lord.

The children of Israel were caught by subtlety and their pride and complacency in not seeking counsel from the Lord. The Lord had given them instruction for situations where they required direct guidance: "And he shall stand before Eleazar the priest, who shall ask counsel for him after the judgment of Urim before the Lord" (Num 27.21). This was the same mistake that led to the defeat at Ai. Joshua had relied upon the strength of Israel and on this occasion he acted on the basis of his own wisdom, rather than the wisdom of the Lord. How easy it is to be deceived, yet the Lord has made provision for situations where wisdom and discernment are required. "If any of you lack wisdom, let him ask of God, that giveth to all men liberally, and upbraideth not; and it shall be given him" (James 1.5).

"And Joshua made peace with them, and made a league with them, to let them live. and the princes of the congregation sware unto them" (v.15).

Having been deceived, the treaty that Joshua and the princes of the congregation entered into compounded their error. The essence of the agreement was that Israel would let the Gibeonites live. This was the Gibeonites' core concern which had caused them to seek the treaty in the first place. Subsequent events demonstrated that obligations of mutual support and assistance during times of crisis were included. It had no time limit and the obligations were still binding in the days of Saul (2 Sam 21.1). By entering into a league with the Gibeonites they had compromised the integrity of the promised land and could not undo the wrong.

It is a solemn matter for any believer to enter an agreement with an unbeliever that binds them together, whether in business, marriage or any area of life. The warning note is sounded in the New Testament: "Be ye not unequally yoked together with unbelievers: for what fellowship hath righteousness with unrighteousness? and what communion hath light with darkness?" (2 Cor 6.14). On this occasion the agreement was entered into unwittingly, as a result of deception. It is a lesson to all believers to be on their guard, lest they be permanently weakened in their spiritual conflict with the devil, through a compromising agreement that cannot be undone.

Verses 16-27: Gibeonites' Relationship with Israel
Deception discovered (vv.16-18)

It was not long before the children of Israel realised their mistake. "And it came to pass at the end of three days after they had made a league with them, that they heard that they were their neighbours, and that they dwelt among them." (v.16). No details are given in the narrative that reveal how they discovered the truth, other than "they heard". It is ironic that the Gibeonites had come to the children of Israel because of what they had heard; it was now the turn of the children of Israel to approach the Gibeonites on the same basis. There must have been lines of communication across the land of Canaan, probably resulting from trade routes, which took the news from place to place. The crossing of the Red Sea and the battles on the east of Jordan had been known in Jericho. News had travelled to the cities of the Gibeonites and to the whole of the land, resulting in the confederacy at the commencement of the chapter.

Having made the blunder of entering into a covenant with their neighbours, the children of Israel did not delay in dealing with the situation. They displayed sensitivity to the seriousness of the situation, which perhaps was borne out of the memory of recent events which had followed the sin of Achan. It was right that they "journeyed, and came unto their cities on the third day" (v.17). They could not ignore this matter or hope that it would disappear. The Gibeonites dwelt in four cities, "Gibeon, and Chephirah, and Beeroth, and Kirjath-jearim" (v.17), that formed part of the inheritance given to the tribes of Benjamin (18.25-26) and Judah (18.14). The city of Kirjath-jearim was also known as Baalah (15.9), Kirjath-baal (15.60), and Baale of Judah (2 Sam 6.2) and although allotted to Judah, stood on the boundary between Judah and Benjamin (15.60; 18.15).

The situation was difficult for the children of Israel. When they arrived at the cities they did not act in haste and launch an assault in order to punish the Gibeonites. "The children of Israel smote them not, because the princes of the congregation had sworn unto them by the Lord God of Israel" (v.18). The seriousness of their league with the Gibeonites was underlined by the mention of the "Lord God of Israel" by whom they had sworn. If they attacked the Gibeonites, they would have invoked the displeasure of the Lord, since it was by His name they had sworn. It was bad enough to have entered into the treaty, but to break it would have compounded the error by bringing shame upon the name of the Lord. The dilemma which they faced was how to obey the Lord's commandment regarding the inhabitants of Canaan, without breaking their treaty with the Gibeonites.

"And all the congregation murmured against the princes" (v.18). The response of the congregation put pressure on the princes. For the first time since they had crossed the Jordan the people are recorded as murmuring. This had been a characteristic of their forefathers in the wilderness and had been the cause of the forty years of wilderness wanderings (Num 14.2). On this occasion the discontent was understandable. They had been bound to the inhabitants of the four cities by a treaty which their leaders had entered into without consulting either the Lord or them. Leaders among the people of God must take care when making decisions that affect the people for whom they are responsible to the Lord. The complacent folly of Joshua and the princes had the potential to cause serious division among the people and to sow the seeds of rebellion. It was a mark of the progress of that generation that the murmuring is not mentioned again in the chapter or in connection with the subsequent dealings with the Gibeonites. They were unhappy, but not rebellious.

The oath considered (vv.19-21)

In response to their murmuring, the princes of the congregation explained to the people why they had to refrain from slaying the Gibeonites and respect the treaty: "We have sworn unto them by the Lord God of Israel: now therefore we may not touch them" (v.19). The only course of action available to them was to honour the terms of their treaty and "let them live" (v.20), for the consequences of any other course of action was that "wrath be upon us, because of the oath which we sware unto them" (v.20). The nature of the Lord's response should the treaty be broken was seen years later when Saul attacked the Gibeonites and the Lord brought a famine into the land (2 Sam 21.1).

The swearing of an oath in the Old Testament was a serious step and had significant consequences. It was the unbreakable word of a person, which invoked the authority of the name by whom the oath was sworn. To swear an oath by the name of the Lord God was to swear by the greatest of all authority. All the authority and character of the Lord was invoked by the oath and the consequences of breaking it were accepted as coming from the Lord: "When God made promise to Abraham, because he could swear by no greater, he sware by himself" (Heb 6.13). In the Old Testament the Lord condemned those who swore falsely (Zech 5.3-4; Mal 3.5). In the New Testament James instructs the believer, "Swear not, neither by heaven, neither by the earth, neither by any other oath: but let your yea be yea; and your nay, nay; lest ye fall into condemnation" (James 5.12). The Christian should not have to call upon a greater authority to lend weight to his word. As a believer his word should be true.

The princes of the congregation could not allow the Gibeonites to cohabit with them in the land. The Lord had warned them that if they did allow the inhabitants of Canaan to remain in the land they would be troubled by the idolatry of these nations.

"The princes said unto them, Let them live; but let them be hewers of wood and drawers of water unto all the congregation; as the princes had promised them" (v.21). The princes' solution was in keeping with the instruction of the Lord for the type of people that they professed to be. When cities, which were not in the land, sought peace with the children of Israel, they did so on the basis "that all the people that is found therein shall be tributaries unto thee, and they shall serve thee" (Deut 20.11). The Gibeonites had sought peace, on the basis that they were from a very far country. Although they were found to be neighbours, they were spared but still had to become the servants of the whole congregation. The servitude put upon them was of the lowest in the camp of Israel.

Curse of perpetual servitude pronounced (vv.22-27)

a) Explanation demanded (v.22)

The princes of the congregation had explained to the people the reasons for not attacking the cities of the Gibeonites. When they themselves were told of their fate, it was Joshua who had that responsibility. The sphere of the princes' authority related to the administration of the people that they represented and not to what could be termed "diplomatic relations" with other nations. Joshua called the Gibeonites and demanded an explanation for their deceit. "Wherefore have ye beguiled us, saying, We are very far from you; when ye dwell among us?"(v.22). The ruse had entrapped the children of Israel into a treaty, but was not to be seen as a pattern for behaviour among God's people.

b) Curse pronounced (v.23)

Although there is a good deal of repetition in the narrative, there are additional details revealed by Joshua. Three new aspects of the solution are revealed in this verse.

"Now therefore ye are cursed". The servitude to which they were to be subjected was a curse, in line with the declaration of blessing and curse on the Mounts Gerizim and Ebal (8.34).

"There shall none of you be freed from being bondmen". The servitude was to be without end. It was not restricted to the generation that stood before Joshua that day. The curse of their servitude meant that they "belonged to an accursed posterity" (A.W. Pink). In this the Gibeonites, who were Hivites and descendants of Canaan, fulfilled the curse pronounced upon Canaan: "Cursed be Canaan; a servant of servants shall he be unto his brethren" (Gen 9.25).

"Hewers of wood and drawers of water for the house of my God". When the princes had spoken to the people they had informed them that the Gibeonites would be servants to the whole congregation. This was extended by Joshua to include the house of his God. They would do the menial manual tasks that were necessary for the functioning of the camp of Israel and the maintenance of the house of the God of Israel. At this point in the history of Israel this would be the tabernacle and then the house of the Lord that was present in Shiloh (18.1; 1 Sam 1.7) until Solomon established the temple in Jerusalem.

c) Explanation given (vv.24-25)

The Gibeonites' relief was evident as they offered no excuse for their conduct in deceiving the children of Israel and did not seek to justify themselves. They did offer an explanation as to why they had acted in the way they did. They had been told of the promise of the Lord to the children of Israel: "The Lord thy God commanded his servant Moses to give you all the land, and to destroy all the inhabitants of the land from before you" (v.24). The news of this promise had struck fear into the people of Jericho and had reached the ears of the Gibeonites. As a result they had taken action to preserve their lives: "We were sore afraid of our lives because of you, and have done this thing" (v.24). This was a fulfilment of the promise that the Lord had given to His people prior to their entrance into Canaan. "I will send my fear before thee, and will destroy all the people to whom thou shalt come, and I will make all thine enemies turn their backs unto thee" (Ex 23.27).

Having explained their actions, they stated to Joshua, "We are in thine hand: as it seemeth good and right unto thee to do unto us, do" (v.25), casting themselves upon his discretion.

d) Outcome (vv.26-27)

The Gibeonites were spared from death and became "hewers of wood and drawers of water for the congregation, and for the altar of the Lord, even unto this day, in the place which he should choose" (v.27). They combined the service of the congregation with the altar of the Lord, as directed by the Lord.

The whole incident with the Gibeonites is an instructive example of the dealings of God with the unintentional folly of His people. They were duped into making a treaty and sealing it with an oath. It would not have been the right course of action to break their agreement, even although it had been entered into on a false premise. They had to honour their word and implement a compromise, which the Lord recognised and approved. The inheritance of Benjamin and Judah did not suffer as they took possession of the four cities when they received their inheritance (18.14, 25-26). In addition, the result of the curse placed upon the Gibeonites was that the altar of the Lord was served by them. The Lord turned the cunning of men to help bring worship to His name. Compromise is sometimes the only solution to resolve a situation, where to get out of the difficulty would involve going back on one's word.

JOSHUA 10

Southern Campaign

The conquest of Canaan was accomplished by three military campaigns:

chs. 1-9 Central Campaign
ch. 10 Southern Campaign
ch. 11 Northern Campaign.

Joshua's strategy has been acknowledged as a classic example of how to deploy a numerically weaker army against a stronger enemy and accomplish victory by dividing the enemy and attacking each smaller section in turn. The destruction of Jericho and Ai, together with the treaty with Gibeon, had given the children of Israel control of the central part of the land, dividing the land and thus preventing the southern and northern cities from joining together.

Joshua did not instigate the southern and northern campaigns. On both occasions he responded to an attack by a coalition of kings and, having defeated the combined armies, went on to secure the territory which the Lord had given them. Having sought to defeat Israel by subterfuge in ch.9, Satan resorted to outright hostility in chs.10 and 11. These tactics were also employed in the days of Ezra when Zerubbabel refused the offer of assistance: "Then the people of the land weakened the hands of the people of Judah, and troubled them in building" (Ezra 4.4).

The Conquest of Gibeon

Verses 1-5: Southern Coalition

What Adoni-zedek heard (v.1)

The manner in which people responded to the children of Israel is often attributed to what they heard. Rahab believed (2.10). "The kings of the Amorites which were on the west side of the Jordan, and all the kings of the Canaanities which were by the sea" were paralysed by fear (5.1). "All the kings which were on this side Jordan, in the hills, and in the valleys, and in all the coasts of the great sea over against Lebanon, the Hittite, and the Amorite, the Canaanite, the Perizzite, the Hivite, and the Jebusite … gathered themselves together, to fight" (9.1-2). The Gibeonites sought a treaty by guile (9.4). In this instance, Adoni-zedek, king of Jerusalem "feared greatly" (10.2) and sought an alliance with other kings in the south of the country.

The name Adoni-zedek means "lord of righteousness" and, according to Keil & Delitzsch, "is synonymous with Melchizedek (king of righteousness), and was a title of the Jebusite kings, as Pharoah was of the Egyptian".

Jerusalem (3389) appears for the first time in Scripture with this name.

Strong gives its meaning as "teaching of peace", others, "the founding or possession of peace". The city was known as Salem in the time of Abraham (Gen 14.18) and later as Jebus (Judg 19.10; 1 Chr 11.4), from which the Jebusites took their name. It was finally taken from the Jebusites by David (2 Sam 5.6-9) and became the capital city of Israel.

Adoni-zedek heard of two matters which caused him to fear: firstly, "Joshua had taken Ai, and had utterly destroyed it; as he had done to Jericho and her king, so he had done to Ai and her king". It is interesting that the emphasis is upon the destruction of the cities and their kings. Not only had the cities fallen to the children of Israel, but the inhabitants, including the king, had been slain. Adoni-zedek was afraid for his life. Secondly, "the inhabitants of Gibeon had made peace with Israel, and were among them"; news had reached him that Gibeon had broken ranks with the cities which opposed Israel and could not be counted upon as an ally.

Importance of Gibeon (v.2)

The Gibeonites' approach to the children of Israel is seen in a different light from ch.9. Gibeon was a "great city, as one of the royal cities". As such it would have had a king and been independent of the other cities in the region. There were at least another thirty-one such cities in the land (12.7-24), of varying size and importance. It was the men of a "great city" who had sought an accommodation with Israel.

The Gibeonites could have caused the other nations in Canaan to lose heart and capitulate to the children of Israel. They were "mighty" (1368) and yet had chosen to become servants of the Israelites, rather than engage them in battle. Each city that had resisted had been defeated. Adoni-zedek decided that victory could only be accomplished if an alliance of cities stood together against Israel and their new ally.

Alliance formed (vv.3-4)

Adoni-zedek consequently sent a message to four kings whose cities lay southwest of Jerusalem: "Hoham king of Hebron, and unto Piram king of Jarmuth, and unto Japhia king of Lachish, and unto Debir king of Eglon" (v.3). Apart from Hebron, Scripture locates these cities in the lowlands of Judah (15.35,39). Evidently Hebron lay south of Jerusalem since it was one of the places where Caleb had walked (14.9) when he was spying the land from the south, and was given to him by Joshua as his inheritance (14.14-15). Keil & Delitzsch place it as "twenty-two Roman miles south of Jerusalem, in a deep and narrow valley upon the mountains of Judah".

"Come up unto me, and help me, that we may smite Gibeon: for it hath made peace with Joshua and with the children of Israel" (v.4). The appeal to the kings was to join forces to attack Gibeon and not the children of Israel. They felt threatened and joined together in hostility against the Gibeonites. Making peace with Israel had the effect of making enemies of the people of the land. Despite the history of the Gibeonites and the means employed by them to obtain their peace, they can be seen as a picture of sinners who have broken ranks with the world to seek after God. The response of the neighbouring cities illustrates the antagonism of the world towards those who enjoy peace with God. This is often the experience of a Christian who has recently been saved. Former friends and neighbours can become distant and, on occasions, hostile because they feel threatened by the change that is evident in a Christian: "Wherein they think it strange that ye run not with them to the same excess of riot, speaking evil of you" (1 Pet 4.4).

Gibeon attacked (v.5)

The confederation of southern cities "gathered themselves together, and went up, they and all their hosts, and encamped before Gibeon, and made war against it". It was an alliance of Amorites, the ancient enemy of the people of God, with self-preservation, and, no doubt, with Gibeon being a royal city, an eye for plunder, uniting them.

Verses 6-15: Battle of Gibeon

The account of the battle of Gibeon divides into two sections. Joshua's response to the plea from the Gibeonites, followed by the night march to Gibeon, the attack by the children of Israel and the intervention by the Lord with hailstones, form the first section. Thereafter, there is the account of the miraculous event in the heavens, when the Lord responded to Joshua's request and brought the sun to a halt. This extended the daylight hours, enabling the children of Israel to accomplish complete victory. The presentation of these events in this manner does not preclude them from having taken place concurrently.

Defeat of the Five Kings (vv.6-11)

a) Gibeonites' appeal (v.6)

The test came early for the Gibeonites. Having entered into a treaty with the children of Israel, they were now put to the test. They were faced with the option of renouncing the peace they had established with the Israelites or rely upon that treaty for their preservation. Did they trust the Israelites?

"And the men of Gibeon sent unto Joshua to the camp to Gilgal, saying, Slack not thy hand from thy servants; come up to us quickly, and save us, and help us: for all the kings of the Amorites that dwell in the mountains are gathered together against us".

The response of the Gibeonites was to seek help in terms of the treaty they had established with the children of Israel. They acknowledged their place as servants and sought urgent assistance.

b) Joshua's response (vv.7,9)

Joshua was also tested at this time. Just as the Gibeonites faced up to the test, so too did Joshua. There was no word of complaint, excuse or delay: "So Joshua ascended from Gilgal, he, and all the people of war with him, and all the mighty men of valour" (v.7). His response was the correct one and he moved to honour the terms of the treaty without delay. He mobilised the fighting strength of Israel, as he had done to attack Ai (8.3), demonstrating that the fulfilment of the treaty and salvation of the Gibeonites was just as important as the conquest of Ai.

It has already been noted that, on occasions, Joshua is an illustration of the Lord Jesus. In his response to the Gibeonites he is a faint picture of the Saviour who, without hesitation, moved in response to the need for salvation and left heaven to "seek and to save that which was lost" (Lk 19.10). In his ascent from Gilgal, with no messenger or emissary preceding him, the shadow of the Lord Jesus is seen again: "Once in the end of the world hath he appeared to put away sin by the sacrifice of himself" (Heb 9.26).

The urgency of the situation and Joshua's rapid response is evidenced by the night march and resultant surprise that was achieved. "Joshua therefore came unto them suddenly, and went up from Gilgal all night" (v.9).

c) The intervention of the Lord (vv.8,10-11)

The Lord intervened to encourage Joshua and accomplish the victory at Gibeon. The emphasis is on the Lord in this section, for although Joshua and the children of Israel were fighting, it was the Lord who was giving the victory.

"And the Lord said unto Joshua, Fear them not. for I have delivered them into thine hand; there shall not a man of them stand before thee" (v.8). Despite the failure of Joshua and the people at Jericho and Ai, the Lord was faithful. Encouragement and the assurance of victory were given again to Joshua, as they had been when he stood on the banks of the Jordan (1.5, 9) and prepared to attack Ai (8.1). It was a new challenge for Joshua. For the first time, he was encountering a confederation of nations in battle. It is supposition, yet very likely, that he faced an enemy that outnumbered him and were already engaged in battle against the Gibeonites. The Lord's words would have been a necessary encouragement to him in these circumstances.

"And the Lord discomfited them before Israel, and slew them with a great slaughter at Gibeon, and chased them along the way that goeth up to Beth-horon, and smote them to Azekah, and unto Makkedah" (v.10).

Three verbs are employed in this verse, with one being repeated, describing the comprehensive involvement of the Lord in the battle. Each verb is singular and this would indicate that it was the Lord alone who did these things:

• "Discomfited" (2000). Some translations render the word, "threw them into confusion", or "routed". There are occasions in Scripture where this word is used to describe the direct intervention of the Lord by means of thundering and lightning (1 Sam 7.10; Ps 18.14). In other places it is used of the effect of the Lord working through the sword wielded by soldiers (Judg 4.15). This was the fulfilment of the Lord's promise to Moses (Ex 23.27), though here the means He employed are not revealed.

• "Slew" (5221). The confusion brought about by the Lord led to a great slaughter of the Amorites. This was the work of the Lord, even though the weapons were in the hands of the children of Israel.

• "Chased" (7291). Even the pursuit of the enemy was attributed to the Lord. The extent of it is noted in the narrative. "The way that goeth up to Beth-horon" and "the going down to Beth-horon" (v.11), according to Keil & Delitzsch, refer to the pass between upper and lower Beth-horon which "leads downward from Gibeon toward the western plain, and was called sometime the ascent, or going up to Beth-Horon, and sometime the descent, or going down from it".

• "Smote" (5221). This is the same verb that was used earlier. It is employed again to describe the location of the slaughter rather than its extent. The pursuit must have taken them approximately twenty miles (32 kilometres) until they reached "Azekah and unto Makkedah", both of which are mentioned as neighbouring cities of the Amorite kings (15.35, 41). They were fleeing in a homeward direction, probably southwest from Gibeon.

"The Lord cast down great stones from heaven upon them unto Azekah, and they died: they were more which died with hailstones than they whom the children of Israel slew with the sword" (v.11). During the pursuit of the Amorites, the Lord slew more by the miraculous hailstones He sent down from heaven, than the Israelites accomplished by conventional military means. The hailstones were not a storm of stones, but were a deadly storm of hail. The Lord had done this before in Egypt (Ex 9.18-33). The children of Israel were preserved from the hailstones at Azekah as they had been in Goshen in the land of Egypt.

The sun and moon stand still (vv.12-15)

There are different views among commentators and scholars as to the origin and extent of the quotation from the Book of Jasher, which is included in this section of the narrative. In addition, some interpret the record of the sun and moon standing still during the defeat of the Amorites literally and others metaphorically. A short consideration of these views will follow, but the most important aspect of the section should not be missed when considering the detail of the events recorded. During the pursuit and destruction of the Amorites "the Lord hearkened unto the voice of a man" (v.14) in a way which is unique. Men had been involved in miracles before this occasion and these had affected the environment of the world and the laws of nature, e.g. the plagues in Egypt, the crossing of the Red Sea and of the Jordan. However, each of these miracles was instigated by the Lord. This time it was a man who sought the miracle and the Lord responded by altering the laws of nature. This is worthy of note when the character of God and the value of prayer are considered. It was one thing for Elijah to pray for the implementation of the word of the Lord in the withholding of rain (James 5.17-18), it was another matter altogether for Joshua to pray for the sun and moon to stand still, without any promise from the Lord. This was a remarkable demonstration of faith. Three miracles took place that day: hailstones came from heaven, the sun and moon stood still and the Lord hearkened to the voice of a man.

a) Joshua's prayer (v.12)

i) *when?* "In the day when the Lord delivered up the Amorites before the children of Israel". During the attack and subsequent rout of the Amorites, Joshua spoke to the Lord. Therefore the events recorded in this section happened on the same day as those in the previous verses.

ii) *where?* "And he said in the sight of Israel". There is the possibility within the text for this part of the verse to refer to the Lord, rather than Joshua. Some take this view and, on this basis, explain the direct communication with the sun and moon as coming from the Lord as Creator and Sovereign (Gen 1.14-17; Is 40.26). The more likely reading of the verse has Joshua speaking to the Lord and doing so before Israel. By making his request publicly, Joshua was demonstrating his confidence in the Lord and leaving the children of Israel in no doubt as to the reason for the unnatural extension of the day. Without an understanding of the cause of the miracle, it could have become a source of fear and alarm to the Israelites.

iii) *what?* "Sun, stand thou still upon Gibeon; and thou, Moon, in the valley of Ajalon". It is likely that the battle commenced early in the morning when the night march of the Israelites and the suddenness of their attack is considered (v.8). Taking this into account, in all probability Joshua's request was made sometime in the morning, and certainly before noon. This is the conclusion of Keil & Delitzsch when they comment on the location of Gibeon and Ajalon: "As Joshua smote the enemy at Gibeon, and they fled to the southwest, he was no doubt on the west of Gibeon when he commanded the sun and moon to stand still: and therefore from his point of view the sun would be in the east when it stood over Gibeon, and the moon in the far west when it stood over the valley of Ajalon. But that could only be the case before noon, a few hours after sunrise, when the moon had not yet set in the western sky".

It is not the purpose of this work to provide an analysis of the numerous explanations of these verses provided by scholars. There are two basic approaches: either the language is metaphorical or it is literal. If it is literal, then the means whereby the sun and moon stood still are not to be the subject of long debate, for they are not revealed in Scripture.

The metaphorical interpretation may have some merit. On other occasions within Scripture, poetical comment is provided on battles or events involving the people of God (Judg 5.20; Hab 3.11). It may be that this section has a similar structure to the song of Moses, which followed the account of the crossing of the Red Sea (Ex 15.1-18), and the song of Deborah, after the defeat of Sisera (Judg 5.1-31). Perhaps the quotation from the Book of Jasher is a poetical comment on the defeat of the Amorites.

The literal interpretation is to be preferred. The ability of the Lord to order the course of the solar system should be beyond doubt. He caused the sun to cease shining in Egypt for three days (Ex 10.22-23), and yet the children of Israel had light in their dwellings. He also changed the course of the sun in the days of Hezekiah when "the sun returned ten degrees, by which degrees it was gone down" (Is 38.8). In response to Joshua's request the Lord performed a miracle and, as such, it is beyond natural explanation. The location of the sun and moon are given to provide the geographic setting and to paint a word picture of the scene, thus strengthening the literal interpretation. Early in the day, Joshua made the request and the Lord answered his prayer by prolonging the day, enabling him to complete the battle and enter into the fulness of the Lord's promise of complete victory.

b) Joshua's prayer answered (v.13)

The miraculous extension of the day continued "until the people had avenged themselves upon their enemies ... it hasted not to go down about a whole day". Such was the impact of the victory and the miraculous intervention of the Lord, Joshua refers the reader to another book outside of the canon of Scripture: "Is not this written in the book of Jasher?". There is a reference to this book in David's lament over the death of Saul and Jonathan (2 Sam 1.18), with some scholars also pointing to the "book of the wars of the Lord" (Num 21.14) as being the same book. It would appear to be a historical record of the wars and conflicts of the children of Israel, and would have been known to the readers of the Old Testament books and available to them to read. "Jasher" (3474) means "righteous" or "upright". Strong describes the book as " a collection of songs in praise of the heroes of Israel". By referring to another book, the author of Joshua was citing a source to corroborate the account of the miracle.

Some commentators take the view that vv.12-15 are not a direct quotation from the Book of Jasher but are pointing the reader to an account within that book. However, the poetical structure of these verses in the original Hebrew, which is not apparent in the English language of the AV, would indicate that a direct quotation from the Book of Jasher is included, the extent of which is not readily identified. It is possible that the quotation commences in v.12 and concludes at the end of v.15.

c) Character of the Lord's response to Joshua (v.14)

The events of that day were notable for two reasons, neither of which includes the position of the sun and moon.

Firstly, "the Lord hearkened unto the voice of a man". The word "hearkened" (8085) is a strong word which is used in this way on only three occasions in the Old Testament where the Lord is the subject (Num 21.3; Josh 10.14; 1 Kings 17.22). On the other two occasions, the Lord responded to Israel by giving the Canaanites over to them, and to Elijah by bringing a young boy back to life. When the sun and moon stood still, for the first time, the Lord obeyed – for that is the strength of the word - the voice of a man. The occasion involving Elijah was recorded many years after the book of Joshua was written, hence the statement that "there was no day like that before it or after it".

Secondly, "the Lord fought for Israel". In v.13 the battle is described from the people's point of view as they took their revenge on their enemies. However, the intervention of the Lord in the hailstones and the prolongation of the day meant that on that day "The Lord fought for Israel". It is a tremendous encouragement for a Christian to know that he is not alone when the spiritual conflict rages. The Lord, who fought the greatest battle to secure salvation for the sinner, continues to intervene on behalf of the saint in the day of conflict. Temptations and struggles have to be faced, laughter and derision have to be endured, decisions and choices have to be made, but the Lord sustains and helps in the daily struggle. Paul appreciated the presence of the Lord in the day of trial: "Notwithstanding the Lord stood with me, and strengthened me" (2 Tim 4.17).

d) Back to Gilgal (v.15)

"And Joshua returned, and all Israel with him, unto the camp to Gilgal". There is little doubt that this verse appears out of place in the chronological order of the southern campaign. It is improbable that having defeated the kings at Gibeon, and pursued them to their utter destruction, that he would then march the children of Israel back to Gilgal, only to bring them back to capture the five kings in the cave at Makkedah. In addition, the children of Israel had endured a night's march, a prolonged day of fighting and the pursuit of the enemy. To march them back to Gilgal and then return them to Makeddah would have been physically punishing.

"The absence of the word 'then' at the beginning of the verse precludes the necessity of our understanding it to mean that they returned immediately unto the camp at Gilgal" (A. W. Pink). The repetition of the words at the end of the account of the southern campaign (v.43), gives credence to the view that v.15 is the end of the quotation from the Book of Jasher. From v.16 there is an account of events up until Joshua did return to Gilgal.

Verses 16-27: Pursuit of the Five Kings

The kings trapped (vv.16-18)

When the battle at Gibeon went against them, the "five kings fled, and hid themselves in a cave at Makkedah." (v.16). They had escaped the hailstones and swords of the children of Israel by taking refuge in a cave near to one of the royal cities of the Amorites (12.16). It is a lesson to all who would seek to escape the judgment of God, that "it was told Joshua, saying, The five kings are found hid in a cave at Makkedah" (v.17). To fight against Israel was to fight against the Lord and there is no hiding place from Him. Adam was found among the trees of the garden, Jonah ran from God and was found on the sea, Sisera perished in the tent of Jael, Adonijah and Joab were found clinging to the horns of the altar. How pointed is the challenge of the gospel for unsaved people, and seeking to shelter from the wrath and judgment of God, "How shall we escape, if we neglect so great salvation?" (Heb 2.3).

Having found the kings, Joshua gave instruction that they were to be trapped in the cave: "Roll great stones upon the mouth of the cave, and set men by it for to keep them" (v.18). This would allow the pursuit of their armies to continue and permit Joshua to deal with them at a time of his choosing. It has already been pointed that from time to time Joshua is a picture of the Lord Jesus. His actions in trapping the kings and keeping them for future judgment is a picture of the present condition of the souls of men who have passed into eternity without being saved. They are reserved in hell for the great white throne judgment (Rev 20.11-15). In the darkness of the cave, the kings must have understood that their fate was sealed and that there was no hope of release or rescue; this is also true of men in hell (Lk 16.19-31).

The battle concluded (vv.19-21)

The Amorite armies were without their kings and in full retreat toward their cities. Joshua commanded the children of Israel to "pursue after your enemies, and smite the hindmost of them; suffer them not to enter into their cities: for the Lord your God hath delivered them into your hand" (v.19). In this they were partly successful. The complete destruction of their enemies depended upon them being kept out of their cities. However, "when Joshua and the children of Israel had made an end of slaying them with a very great slaughter, till they were consumed, that the rest which remained of them entered into fenced cities" (v.20). The failure to keep them out of their cities necessitated further action against them (vv.31-37) and would be the explanation for people remaining in these five cities after this phase of the southern campaign came to a close.

"And all the people returned to the camp to Joshua at Makkedah in peace" (v.21). The outcome of obedience to the Lord was the enjoyment of peace by the children of Israel: "none moved his tongue against any of the children of Israel" (v.21). "The translation 'moved' (KJV; ASV; RSV) has little support either in the Hebrew or Akkadian usage. The expression literally means 'to sharpen the tongue' and evidently connotes speaking against another with hostility" (TWOT). Fear and awe came upon the inhabitants of Canaan and none sought to raise his voice against the people of God, never mind a sword.

The kings brought to Joshua (vv.22-26)

"Then said Joshua, Open the mouth of the cave, and bring out those five kings unto me out of the cave" (v.22). The scene that unfolds in these verses points forward, in type, to another day, when John records that "I saw the dead, small and great, stand before God … And the sea gave up the dead which were in it; and death and hell delivered up the dead which were in them. and they were judged every man according to their works" (Rev 20.12-13). Those who are reserved in hell will be brought out to stand before the Lord Jesus, as He sits on the great white throne of judgment. After the conflict, when the people of God had entered into rest, the judgment of those within the cave took place. The names of the kings are then listed – "the king of Jerusalem, the king of Hebron, the king of Jarmuth, the king of Lachish, and the king of Eglon" (v.23). This is a reminder that the judgment of a coming day will be personal.

When the kings were brought before Joshua he "called for all the men of Israel, and said unto the captains of the men of war which went with him, Come near, put your feet upon the necks of these kings. And they came near, and put their feet upon the necks of them" (v.24). This was symbolic. The kings were humbled before the children of Israel and, by placing their feet on their necks, the commanders were demonstrating their complete subjugation. This symbolism is employed to describe the complete victory of the Lord Jesus over His enemies (1 Cor 15.25-27).

The symbolic demonstration of victory served as an encouragement to the commanders of the children of Israel. If the Lord brought the five kings under their feet, then they ought to be encouraged for future battles. Without exception, the Lord would vanquish the enemies of Israel. Joshua also exhorted them with the words he had received from the Lord: "Fear not, nor be dismayed, be strong and of good courage: for thus shall the Lord do to all your enemies against whom ye fight"(v.25). It is instructive that encouragement for the people of God was required in times of victory as well as in defeat. It was after the debacle at Ai that the Lord had spoken to Joshua (8.1) and now, in the aftermath of victory, His words are the same. In times of victory and discouragement the Christian needs a word from the Lord.

The outcome for the five kings was inevitable. The enemies of the people of God are the enemies of God and there can be no victory for any man in that conflict. Ultimate destruction is the only prospect, and that without mercy. At the great white throne, the time for mercy will be past and the righteous judgment of God will be brought to bear upon the unforgiven sinner. "And afterward Joshua smote them, and slew them, and hanged them on five trees: and they were hanging upon the trees until the evening" (v.26). Each king bore the curse associated with hanging upon a tree, in accordance with the Law of Moses (Deut 21.22-23) and consistent with the treatment of the king of Ai (8.29).

The end of the day (v.27)

"And it came to pass at the time of the going down of the sun". It had been an extraordinary day in terms of its duration and its events. There is no indication as to how long the day lasted, but at its end the responsibilities of the children of Israel toward the Gibeonites had been fully discharged. It had been a day when the children of Israel had experienced the full benefit of complete obedience to the Lord: miracles in the heavens, victory without casualties, peace following conflict.

The bodies of the kings were not left to rot on the trees; they were buried: "And they took them down off the trees, and cast them into the cave wherein they had been hid, and laid great stones in the cave's mouth, which remain until this very day". The picture of future judgment reaches its conclusion. In a coming day at the great white throne, "whosoever was not found written in the book of life was cast into the lake of fire" (Rev 20.15). The bodies were put into the cave and its mouth was sealed, There they were until the day that the book of Joshua was written. What a picture of the place where those who die without salvation will endure the never-ending judgment of a holy God!

Verses 28-39: Southern Campaign Completed

The narrative gathers pace following the detailed description of the conquests of Jericho and Ai, and the battle at Gibeon. Seven cities in the south were subsequently taken. The presentation of these conquests has a symmetry that hinges on the account of the destruction of the king of Gezer (v.33):

Makkedah (v.28)		king, city, souls
Libnah (v.29)		king, city, souls
Lachish (v.32)		city, souls
	Horam, king of Gezer (v.33)	
Eglon (v.35)		city, souls
Hebron (v.37)		king, city, souls
Debir (v.39)		king, city, souls.

The description of the conquest of each of the seven cities is similar, yet sufficiently different to reinforce the historical authenticity of the narrative.

Makkedah (v.28)

The general pattern of conquest is established in the account of the victory at Makkedah. This was close to the place where the five kings had been found in a cave and where Joshua had made a camp (v.21). The fall of Makkedah to the children of Israel is recorded briefly: "And that day Joshua took Makkedah". No detail is given of a battle and there appears to have been little opposition.

Having taken Makeddah, Joshua prosecuted the instruction of the Lord. In relation to the city itself, he "smote it with the edge of the sword". The king of the city was "utterly destroyed" and dealt with as Joshua "did unto the king of Jericho"; "all the souls that were therein" were destroyed.

The conclusion at Makeddah was that of complete success with no battle or hold-up recorded. Nothing was left of the city, as the Lord had given commandment.

Libnah (vv.29-30)

After Makeddah, the same general pattern of narrative is followed with some notable exceptions. At Libnah there was fighting which involved all Israel: "Then Joshua passed from Makkedah, and all Israel with him, unto Libnah, and fought against Libnah" (v.29). The taking of the city was not as straightforward a matter as the previous one, however, the end result was the same – "and the Lord delivered it also" (v.30).

Lachish (vv.31-32)

From Libnah, Joshua moved Israel southwest to Lachish and "encamped against it, and fought against it" (v.31). There appears to be increasing difficulty in the campaign. Lachish was not overcome immediately or without fighting. The impression given is that by encamping at Lachish the children of Israel had to exercise patience and resolve until they "took it on the second day".

There is no mention of the king of Lachish since he had been one of the five kings slain by Joshua (v.36).

Horam, king of Gezer (v.33)

There is no record of the capture of the town of Gezer. It lay on the southern boundary of Ephraim, when the land was divided into the inheritances of the children of Israel (16.3), and was given to the "families of the children of Kohath, the Levites which remained of the children of Kohath" (21.20). Josephus (Ant. 7.4,1) described the city as the frontier of the territory of the Philistines, due to its location some distance northwest from Lachish. Joshua is never said to have taken Gezer, with the city remaining under occupation by the Canaanites (16.10; Judg 1.29).

He was involved in a two-day fight against Lachish, and then, "Horam king of Gezer came up to help Lachish". He, in turn, was defeated and destroyed.

Eglon (vv.34-35)

From Lachish they moved southeast to Eglon, a lowland city (15.39) and dealt with it in the same manner. The king is not mentioned as he was slain at Makeddah along with the king of Lachish.

Hebron (vv.36-37)

The king of Hebron had been killed at Makeddah and so there must have been another king who took the throne of Hebron following their defeat at Gibeon. Hebron was a city in the mountains and had towns which belonged to it, "and they took it, and smote it with the edge of the sword, and the king thereof, and all the cities thereof" (v.37).

Debir (vv.38-39)

The pattern continued as the Israelites moved south from Hebron to Debir. "As he had done to Hebron, so he did to Debir, and to the king thereof; as he had done also to Libnah, and to her king" (v.39).

While a number of the cities were taken in an identical manner, the conquest of some appears to have been more straightforward than others. The variation in these accounts serves to remind the reader that the enemies a believer will face in his spiritual warfare will not all be the same. Some will be overcome quickly and in a straightforward fashion, whereas others may require patience and perseverance. The circumstances that pertained when the children of Israel faced one city did not necessarily apply when they moved to the next one. The believer must always remain alert to the character of the foe that he faces at any particular time and adjust his approach accordingly.

Verses 40-43: Summary

The whole of the southern campaign is summarised in these verses. It must be borne in mind that they present a broad sweep of territory, borders and kings which were subjugated by the Israelites. As the reader progresses through the book of Joshua, it becomes evident that, although the armies of the southern region of the land were all defeated and the regions brought under the control of the Israelites, there remained opposition and some unconquered people in the south of the land. The campaign against the south was a long one (11.18) and was consistent with the promise of the Lord: "I will not drive them out from before thee in one year; lest the land become desolate, and the beast of the field multiply against thee. By little and little I will drive them out from before thee, until thou be increased, and inherit the land" (Ex 23.29-30).

Territory (v.40)

The central and southern regions of the land, apart from those of the coast, are described in terms of the "the country of the hills, and of the south, and of the vale, and of the springs". This covers "the mountains

(15.48), the Negeb (the south land, 15.21), the lowlands (15.33) and the slopes, i.e., the hill region (12.8)" (Keil & Delitzsch). The people of these regions were annihilated, the point being reinforced by the author – "he left none remaining, but utterly destroyed all that breathed, as the Lord God of Israel commanded".

Borders (v.41)

"From Kadesh-barnea even unto Gaza, and all the country of Goshen, even unto Gibeon". The southern regions conquered by Joshua are given their border on the west by a line running from Kadesh-barnea in the far south to Gaza, a city further north, which remained in Philistine control until the days of king David (13.3; Judg 16.21; 1 Kings 4.24, where the Hebrew name of Azzah is employed). On the east side of the land, the border is defined as running from south to north, from Goshen to Gibeon. Gibeon has been the subject of much comment in this chapter and Goshen was a city in the mountains of the south of the land (15.51).

Kings (v.42)

"All these kings and their land did Joshua take at one time, because the Lord God of Israel fought for Israel". The success of the southern campaign is attributed to the Lord God and presented as one complete campaign. The failure of the Israelites to drive out every enemy that they faced will be brought before the reader in later chapters and in different contexts. On this occasion the campaign is seen from the divine standpoint as a complete success. The Lord had kept His promise to Joshua and when the children of Israel met the armies of Canaan in the south of the land they knew only victory.

Return to Gilgal (v.43)

With the campaign completed "Joshua returned, and all Israel with him, unto the camp to Gilgal". It is important to see that after the exertions and the success they had experienced they returned to Gilgal. The name of the place reminds the reader of the lessons learned at another Gilgal (ch.4), and emphasises the need for spiritual renewal and the cutting away of the flesh in the service of the Lord. It is a mistake for any Christian to think that he does not need to constantly revisit the principles of Gilgal and examine his spiritual condition. The importance of fellowship with the Lord and the mortification of the flesh cannot be overemphasised. In fact, it is probably at times of great success that the believer is most vulnerable to sins of the flesh, such as pride and self sufficiency, and therefore it is essential to get back to Gilgal.

JOSHUA 11

The Northern Campaign

This chapter records the creation of a confederation of northern nations within Canaan and their defeat by the children of Israel. It is the last of the three military campaigns that Joshua fought in taking the land. The narrative follows a similar pattern to the description of the southern campaign in ch.10, concluding with the statement, "And the land rested from war" (v.23); this marks the end of the first half of the book. Following this statement the emphasis changes from the conquest of the land to the division of the land among the children of Israel.

Conquest of the North

Verses 1-5: Northern coalition

The formation of the coalition (vv.1-3)

In ch.10 Adoni-zedek, king of Jerusalem, instigated the formation of the southern alliance after he had heard of the events at Ai. It is interesting that history repeated itself: "When Jabin king of Hazor had heard those things" (v.1), that is, he heard of the defeat of the southern nations and he communicated with other kings and nations in various regions of the northern territories of the land. The aim was to form a third coalition, in order to defeat the Israelites in battle. It is surprising that the comprehensive destruction of the central and southern nations did not lead him to seek an accommodation, rather than a confrontation, with Israel.

As with Adoni-zedek in Jerusalem, Pharoah in Egpyt, and Ben-hadad in Syria, Jabin was the title given to the king of Hazor. This can be seen in the days of Deborah and Barak, who were raised up of God to defeat the army of "Jabin king of Canaan, that reigned in Hazor" (Judg 4.2). Jabin is recorded as having been defeated by Joshua and then subdued by God (Judg 4.23), until he is finally destroyed (Judg 4.24). In this he is a picture of Satan, who was defeated at Calvary (Heb 2.14), yet continues to oppose the people of God until he will be subdued (Rev 20.2) and then destroyed (Rev 20.10).

The kings with whom Jabin communicated are described in different ways. The name of the first is "Jobab king of Madon". The combination of the name of the king and the name of the city gives an interesting meaning. Strong provides the meaning of the names as "a desert" (3103) and "strife" (4068). This is the only city of the coalition which has the name of its king recorded. On this basis the meaning must have significance and, when it is combined with the meaning of Jabin, provides a word picture of the wisdom of this world, as personified by Jabin, bringing strife and barrenness among the people of God. The only other scriptural reference to Madon is in the later list of conquered kings (12.19).

Jabin also sent to "the king of Shimron, and to the king of Achshaph" (v.1). Shimron was later given to the tribe of Zebulun as part of its inheritance (19.15) and Achshaph to the tribe of Asher (19.25).

The narrative now changes from the names of the kings and their cities to the regions from which they came: "And to the kings that were on the north of the mountains, and of the plains south of Chinneroth, and in the valley, and in the borders of Dor on the west" (v.2). The northern confederacy covered an extensive geographical area.

- "north of the mountains"

In the description of the southern land conquered by Joshua (10.40) the word "hills" (2022) is employed; it is the same word as is translated "mountains" in this verse, and refers to the mountainous area of the south of Canaan which is later described in detail (15.48-60). The word is also used of the mountainous region in the north that was given to Naphtali (20.7), according to Keil & Delitzsch.

- "plains south of Chinneroth"

Chinneroth was the former name for Galilee (12.3; Num 34.11, spelt Chinnereth). The "plains south of Chinneroth" was the area of land between the Sea of Galilee and the Dead Sea.

- "in the valley"

"The valley" was a description of the lowlands, translated by some as "the western foothills" and "vale" (10.40). It was the northern region of that area, probably as far down as Joppa.

- "in the borders of Dor on the west"

Dor is mentioned on six occasions in the Old Testament (11.2; 12.23; 17.11; Judg 1.27; 1Kings 4.11; 1 Chr 7.29) and was a coastal region (12.23).

The description of the coalition changes again with the mention of six nations, "And to the Canaanite on the east and on the west, and to the Amorite, and the Hittite, and the Perizzite, and the Jebusite in the mountains, and to the Hivite under Hermon in the land of Mizpeh" (v.3). These nations are mentioned in the description of the confederation of nations which gathered together to fight Joshua after the victory at Ai (9.1). The order in which they are listed is different, but it is the same group of nations.

The strength of the coalition (v.4)

The northern coalition was militarily superior to the children of Israel. Firstly, they were stronger numerically. Drawn from many areas of the land and representing cities, regions and peoples they are described as "much people, even as the sand that is upon the sea shore in multitude". This description is not to be understood literally, since it is used on other occasions in Scripture as a proverbial expression to indicate a large number which was beyond the estimate of men (Gen 22.17; Judg 7.12; 1 Sam 13.5). Secondly, they had superior weaponry, "with horses and chariots very many". This set them apart from Israel who had been instructed by the

Lord not to develop horses for warfare (Deut 17.16). Thus overwhelming military force was being employed by the northern coalition in an attempt to destroy the people of God. It is interesting that after having conquered the central and southern regions of the land, the enemy that faced them was stronger than ever. The success of the Israelites increased the intensity of the opposition that they faced. This has been the experience of many Christians who have discovered that, when they overcome the evil one, he regroups and returns with renewed vigour to the conflict.

The encampment (v.5)

The striking thing about the gathering of the northern coalition is the emphasis upon their unity. They "met together" and they "pitched together". It has already been noted regarding other gatherings of nations who opposed Israel, that it would be unlikely that these people would have much in common other than their opposition to the people of God. Such was their determination to overcome the Israelites they were prepared to unite to accomplish their goal. Oftentimes the people of God are not marked by the same unity as those who oppose them. They made their encampment "at the waters of Merom", an area to the north of the Sea of Galilee.

Verses 6-9: Battle of Merom

The description of the battle, which took place at Merom, is brief and lacks the detail given in previous accounts of battles at Jericho, Ai and Gibeon.

"The Lord said unto Joshua" (v.6)

The encouragement that the Lord gave Joshua is a recurring theme (1.5,9; 8.1; 10.8). It is of comfort to a Christian today that a man who experienced the repeated intervention of the Lord in such miraculous ways, still required and received encouragement from the Lord. The Lord had three things to say to Joshua.

1. "Be not afraid because of them". It was the same word that he had received from the Lord when they had left Gilgal to rescue the Gibeonites (10.8). This was the fulfilment of a previous promise that the children of Israel had received through Moses: "When thou goest out to battle against thine enemies, and seest horses, and chariots, and a people more than thou, be not afraid of them...the Lord your God is he that goeth with you, to fight for you against your enemies" (Deut 20.1,4).

2. "For to morrow about this time will I deliver them up all slain before Israel". The exhortation to "be not afraid" was given added weight by a promise from the Lord. There would be no dramatic intervention from heaven, as when the children of Israel pursued the enemy from Gibeon (10.11-14). However, the promise of victory was given. The Lord would win the battle, although the children of Israel would do the

fighting. Here, the timescale of the victory was given to Joshua, thus giving him the necessary encouragement to commence the battle as soon as possible.

3. "Thou shalt hough their horses, and burn their chariots with fire". The Lord undertook to slay the men and instructed Joshua to deal with the weapons that they possessed, namely the chariots of war. In order to do this he had to burn the chariots and hamstring the horses. This was a practice which David later adopted (2 Sam 8.4).

"So Joshua came ..." (v.7)

"So Joshua came, and all the people of war with him, against them by the waters of Merom suddenly; and they fell upon them". The response of Joshua was immediate and the children of Israel attacked with the element of surprise with them, as it had been at Gibeon (10.9).

"And the Lord delivered..." (v.8)

The pattern is there to be observed. The word of the Lord followed by the obedience of His servant, and the fulfilment of the Lord's promise. It is a simple yet profound sequence that characterises God's dealings with His people throughout the ages.

The balance of promise and responsibility appears again in the description of the battle: "And the Lord delivered them into the hand of Israel", in accordance with His promise. However, it was the Israelites "who smote them, and chased them unto great Zidon, and unto Misrephoth-maim, and unto the valley of Mizpeh eastward; and they smote them, until they left them none remaining". The recognition of this perfect balance, between dependence upon God and diligence on the part of the people of God, is important in the sphere of gospel service. The Lord revealed to Paul that he had "much people" in Corinth (Acts 18.10), but the same man later testified, "woe is unto me, if I preach not the gospel!" (1 Cor 9.16).

The defeat of the enemy at Merom was absolute and had the same character as the victory at Gibeon. There was an initial victory followed by the pursuit of the enemy as they fled in the opposite direction. In this case, they chased them westward to Zidon, eastward to Mizpeh, and probably southwards to Misrephoth-maim. In other words, the enemy was scattered and pursued, until they were completely destroyed.

"And Joshua did..." (v.9)

Joshua obeyed the instruction of the Lord and destroyed the valuable weaponry which he had captured. There were three reasons for doing so:

- He had been instructed to do this by the Lord and, in light of their experience at Ai, the continued presence of the Lord and the consequent success was dependent upon their obedience.
- The destruction of the chariots and the hamstringing of the horses prevented the children of Israel from using them in future battles. Reliance

on chariots and horses would detract from their dependence on the Lord and therefore was not to be considered. It was Solomon who introduced chariots and horsemen to the army of Israel (1 Kings 4.26; 10.26) and by so doing changed the character of the army from foot soldiers helped by the Lord, to an army dependent on military strength. The warning of Isaiah is pertinent: "Woe to them that go down to Egypt for help; and stay on horses, and trust in chariots, because they are many; and in horsemen, because they are very strong; but they look not unto the Holy One of Israel, neither seek the Lord!" (Is 31.1).

• Joshua's actions also prevented these chariots and horses from being used against the children of Israel again. The destruction of their enemies' weapons would render them less able to trouble the people of God.

Joshua's obedience in this matter is a valuable lesson for the Christian today. There was purpose in the instruction of the Lord which would prevent them from straying from their dependence on Him and would affect the ability of their enemies from troubling them to the same extent again. In the spiritual conflict in which the Christian is engaged, the Lord's instructions have similar benefits which go beyond the value of simple obedience.

Verses 10-15: Subjugation of the Northern Coalition

Hazor (vv.10-11)

The chapter began with Jabin, king of Hazor, gathering a coalition against Israel and evidently being the focal point of the force that arrayed itself against them. Having defeated the armies of the north, Joshua turned his attention to the cities. He "took Hazor, and smote the king thereof with the sword: for Hazor beforetime was the head of all those kingdoms. And they smote all the souls that were therein with the edge of the sword, utterly destroying them: there was not any left to breathe: and he burnt Hazor with fire". In the three military campaigns that Joshua conducted in conquering the land, he is recorded as having burnt only three cities: Jericho, Ai, and Hazor (6.24; 8.19,28). The general pattern of conquest involved preserving the cities of the land, in order for the children of Israel to occupy them rather than inherit a wasteland (Deut 6.10-11). However, this did not apply to these three cities which were destroyed, albeit, in the case of Hazor, rebuilding evidently took place shortly thereafter, and it again became a stronghold for the enemies of Israel (Judg 4.2). There is no single reason given for the different approach to Jericho, Ai, and Hazor. Jericho was cursed (6.24) and therefore made uninhabitable. Ai had been the scene of the only military defeat that Joshua experienced in the land and the city was a reminder of that shame. The Lord was graciously removing the landmark of their defeat when Ai was burnt with fire. With regard to Hazor, the purpose may have been strategic since it had been the most strongly fortified city in the north of the land and the centre of the alliance of northern cities. To burn and destroy it removed a potential stronghold of resistance to the children of Israel.

Northern cities conquered (vv.12-15)

In this section the comprehensive conquest of the northern cities, from which the armies of the coalition had been drawn, is recorded. The cities which had their own kings are mentioned first: "all the cities of those kings, and all the kings of them, did Joshua take, and smote them with the edge of the sword, and he utterly destroyed them" (v.12). Further emphasis is given to the distinction made between the treatment of Hazor in contrast to that of the other cities: "But as for the cities that stood still in their strength, Israel burned none of them, save Hazor only; that did Joshua burn" (v.13). The expression "stood still in their strength" is translated elsewhere as, "stood still upon their hills" (JND.), and, "still standing upon their mound" (Rotherham). It may well be that the writer's reference is to the remaining presence of these cities in their original location at the time of writing. The cities remained, but the population was destroyed and "the spoil of these cities, and the cattle, the children of Israel took for a prey unto themselves" (v.14).

The account of the destruction of Hazor and the appropriation of the other cities, following the putting to death of their inhabitants, commences with the comment that it was done "as Moses the servant of the Lord commanded" (v.12), and concludes, "As the Lord commanded Moses his servant, so did Moses command Joshua, and so did Joshua; he left nothing undone of all that the Lord commanded Moses" (v.15). The reader is left in no doubt that this concluding battle, and the subsequent destruction of the population of the northern cities and regions, were completed in obedience to the word of the Lord, communicated to Moses, and thereafter to Joshua. It is a wonderful testimony to Joshua that he had not failed to discharge his responsibility of leadership. His service was not perfect, and in this he is like all other men who have rendered service to God, apart from the Lord Jesus. He alone could say, "I have glorified thee on the earth. I have finished the work which thou gavest me to do" (Jn 17.4). Yet Joshua accomplished what should be the ambition of all who serve the Lord, in that the tasks that were committed to him were completed.

Conquest of the Land

Verses 16-17: Geography of the Conquered Land

Regions (v.16)

"So Joshua took all that land". This is a remarkable statement in itself. He directed an army and had the Lord fighting his enemies, yet in the summary of the three military campaigns the victory is attributed to him. How gracious the Lord is when He assesses His servants!

The land that Joshua took is described in terms of seven regions: "the hills, and all the south country, and all the land of Goshen, and the valley, and the plain, and the mountain of Israel, and the valley of the same". The terminology is familiar since it has already been employed to summarise the southern (10.40-41) and northern campaigns (11.2).

Borders (v.17)

The conquered land went as far south as "the mount Halak, that goeth up to Seir". There is uncertainty as to the location of the mount, which is only mentioned here and in 12.7. Its name is translated as "the smooth mountain" (JND), with the word "Halak" (2510) being defined by Strong as "bald". Keil & Delitzsch state that it is "in all probability the northern edge of the Azazimeh mountain with its white and glistening masses of chalk". Seir was the name of the mountainous country occupied by the Edomites (Gen 14.6; 32.3; Deut 2.8).

In the north, the land extended to "Baal-gad in the valley of Lebanon under mount Hermon". Sometimes called Baal-hermon (Judg 3.3; 1 Chr 5.23), the city was a place where Baal was worshipped. The name also suggests that he was worshipped by his ancient name of Gad, which appears in Isaiah 65.11: "Ye who forsake Jehovah, who forget my holy mountain, who prepare a table for Gad, and fill up mixed wine unto Meni" (JND). Jamieson, Fausset and Brown in their commentary on Isaiah state that Gad was "the Babylonian god of fortune, the planet Jupiter, answering to Baal or Bel".

Verse 18: Duration of the Conquest

The summarising of the southern and northern campaigns may give the reader the impression that they were accomplished within a matter of weeks or even months. However, "Joshua made war a long time with all those kings". The conflict was protracted and required endurance and application on the part of Joshua and the children of Israel.

The expression, "a long time", is relative. A calculation can be made when the words of Moses and Caleb are examined. Moses spoke to the people at the end of their wilderness journey and summarised their experience as "the space in which we came from Kadesh-barnea, until we were come over the brook Zered, was thirty and eight years; until all the generation of the men of war were wasted out from among the host, as the Lord sware unto them" (Deut 2.14). When Caleb spoke to Joshua about his inheritance he said, "Forty years old was I when Moses the servant of the Lord sent me from Kadesh-barnea to espy out the land" (14.7), and then added, "Now, lo, I am this day fourscore and five years old" (14.10). Taking these figures together, they were thirty-eight years in the wilderness after departing from Kadesh-barnea and a further seven years passed until Caleb asked Joshua for his inheritance. Therefore, the conquest of the land must have taken approximately seven years.

The conquest of the land took a comparatively long time, lasting longer than World War II in the 20th century. This was in keeping with the stated purpose of God that the occupation of the land would be progressive and not immediate (Ex 23.29-30), and emphasises the need for endurance and commitment in the service of God. This is a recurring theme in the New Testament, with the Christian life seen as a marathon race rather than a sprint. Joshua kept at the job and did not allow the successes or failures he experienced to sidetrack him from his task. So much of Christian living is routine and requires discipline, and may lack the excitement that many seek. Success in the service of God is to continue, to go on for God when times are good and when times are bad. How much better to have the testimony of Jacob who, at the end of his life, "worshipped, leaning upon the top of his staff" (Heb 11.21) rather than that of Solomon, who started well, but ended badly (1 Kings 11.11).

Verses 19-20: Sovereignty of God

A description of anything that has been accomplished for God is incomplete if it does not acknowledge His sovereignty. Some might wonder why "there was not a city that made peace with the children of Israel, save the Hivites the inhabitants of Gibeon" (v.19), especially since the conflict was over a long period of time and the children of Israel always experienced victory, apart from at Ai. The explanation is given: "For it was of the Lord to harden their hearts" (v.20). The Lord did to the nations of Canaan what he had done to Pharoah in Egypt (Ex 4.21). God's purpose was that every nation within the land would be completely destroyed by Joshua, "as the Lord commanded Moses" (v.20). There was to be "no favour" (v.20).

Any attempt to rationalise the purpose of God into terminology that a man might view as fair or righteous is pointless. God is just and that is the starting point when considering His dealings with men. There is an indication within Scripture that the destruction of the Canaanite nations was the judgment of God upon them. It had been intimated in the time of Abraham (Gen 15.16), and was the outcome of their sin. It was not their resistance to Israel that caused them to be destroyed without mercy, but the fact that their iniquity was full. The sparing of the Gibeonites as a result of their covenant with Joshua and the leaders of Israel was the outcome of disobedience on the part of Israel. The mistake was not repeated.

Verses 21-22: Anakims

The summary of Joshua's conquest of the land is brought to a fitting conclusion with the record of the defeat of the Anakims. These were the people who had caused terror among the spies forty years previously: "And there we saw the giants, the sons of Anak, which come of the giants. and we were in our own sight as grasshoppers, and so we were in their sight" (Num 13.33). They had a fearsome reputation as warriors (Deut 1.28; 9.2), and in order for the children of Israel to dwell in the land in peace, they had to remove the cause of their fear by destroying the Anakims.

"And at that time came Joshua, and cut off the Anakims from the mountains, from Hebron, from Debir, from Anab, and from all the mountains of Judah, and from all the mountains of Israel: Joshua destroyed them utterly with their cities" (v.21). The destruction of the inhabitants from Hebron and Debir has already been recorded as part of the southern campaign (10.36-39). The distinction made between the mountains of Judah and Israel existed when the book of Joshua was written owing to the staggered nature of the occupation of the land by the different tribes. Judah had entered into their inheritance with the double tribe of Joseph (Ephraim and Manasseh) before any of the other tribes had moved from Gilgal. As a result, the mountains which formed part of the inheritance of Judah, are described as the "mountains of Judah" and all of the other mountains, where the rest of the children of Israel were gathered, were called the "mountains of Israel".

It is interesting that Scripture does not record the complete annihilation of the Anakims. They remained in "Gaza, in Gath, and in Ashdod" (v.22). These were cities of the Philistines in the southwest of the land along the coastal area and, although allotted to the tribe of Judah (15.47), were never taken as possessions by that tribe. From time to time in the history of Israel, the Philistines of these cities were subject to the Israelites (13.3), but were never removed from their cities. In later years, David fought a giant from Gath, named Goliath (1 Sam 17.4), a descendant of the Anakims who survived Joshua's conquest.

Verse 23: Final Summary

Three statements summarise the service of Joshua.

• "So Joshua took the whole land, according to all that the Lord said unto Moses".

Chapters 1-11 are summarised in this succinct statement. The use of the term "the whole land" does not indicate that every area of land, and settlement of people within the land, were occupied and destroyed by the children of Israel. The land as a whole was taken in accordance with the instruction that the Lord had given to Moses. The armies of the inhabitants of Canaan had been broken and the cities, which were the centres of opposition to the children of Israel, had been destroyed.

• "And Joshua gave it for an inheritance unto Israel according to their divisions by their tribes".

This is a summary of chs.12–24. Although the land had been taken, there was still much for each tribe to do in order to enter into the good of the inheritance that the Lord had given them. The land had been given, but it was the responsibility of the tribes to take possession of what they owned.

• "And the land rested from war".

In order for the division of the land to take place and the people of God to enjoy their inheritance, peace was required and not war. This is an important lesson for believers to learn. The full enjoyment of all that the

Lord has given in salvation can only be experienced in conditions of peace. There is nothing that disturbs the Christian's appreciation of salvation as much as conflict and strife. There are many injunctions in the New Testament regarding the importance of peace for Christians, e.g. "Be at peace among yourselves" (1 Thess 5.13); "Let us therefore follow after the things which make for peace" (Rom 14.19).

JOSHUA 12

List of Conquered Kings

The first main section (chs.1-11) ends with the land at rest from war (11.23). The second main section of the book (chs.13-24) records the division of the land by Joshua. The change from war to peace did not mean that Joshua's service was at an end. The Lord had further work for him to do, albeit in a different context. He had been Moses' minister (1.1) and then the military leader of the children of Israel. Times had changed, but Joshua was still able to serve the Lord. The lesson is simple; serving the Lord in one area of His work does not preclude the Lord from directing His servant into other spheres of labour.

This chapter provides an appendix to chs.1-11. These chapters give the historical accounts of the three military campaigns that Joshua fought to conquer the land. Details are given of some of the battles, whereas others are summarised within a verse or two (10.40; 11.17). It has already been noted that the conquest of the land must have taken approximately seven years (11.18) and involved many battles. This chapter provides the facts and figures of the long war. It is the "what" of the conquest, with chs.1-11 providing the "how".

The chapter is also an introduction to chs.13-24. The fighting had come to an end and the land had to be divided in order for the tribes of Israel to enter into their inheritance. The land had to be surveyed and divided, with the geographical boundaries of each portion clearly delineated.

The record of the thirty-three kings that were defeated, and the land which was gained as a result, is a reminder of the faithfulness of the Lord and His rich grace toward His people. It was a great inheritance that the children of Israel had been given and a wonderful experience that they had come through, as they had seen the hand of the Lord fighting for them during these seven years. There are times when a consideration of such an inventory of blessing and grace toward the people of God is of tremendous benefit to the believer. How often it has been sung, "Count your blessings, name them one by one, and it will surprise you what the Lord hath done".

Verses 1-6: Kings and Territory east of Jordan

It is interesting that the description of all the territory conquered by the children of Israel should begin with land on the east of Jordan. This was not part of the inheritance which had been promised to the children of Israel, but had been requested by the tribes of Reuben, Gad, and half of the tribe of Manasseh (1.12-15). The summary of the kings and their territory is presented in the chronological order of conquest, hence the trans-Jordan region is at the head of the list.

Geography (v.1)

The land that the children of Israel conquered on the east of the Jordan is described in terms of natural landmarks: "The other side Jordan toward the rising of the sun, from the river Arnon unto mount Hermon, and all the plain on the east". The Jordan formed a natural border on the west, with the conquered land extending from the River Arnon in the south, to Mount Hermon in the north. The territory does not have a definite border to the east, but is described as encompassing the eastern plain (Arabah), which Keil & Delitzsch define as "the valley of the Jordan on the eastern side of the river".

King Sihon (vv.2-3)

Moses and the children of Israel defeated two kings on the east of the Jordan. Sihon's territory was mainly in the south, "from Aroer, which is upon the bank of the river Arnon, and from the middle of the river, and from half Gilead, even unto the river Jabbok, which is the border of the children of Ammon" (v.2). His land also extended east "from the plain" and north "to the sea of Chinneroth on the east, and unto the sea of the plain, even the salt sea on the east, the way to Beth-jeshimoth; and from the south, under Ashdoth-pisgah" (v.3). The seat of Sihon's kingdom was at Heshbon, which subsequently became a Levitical city.

King Og (vv.4-5)

Og ruled the northern portion of the land on the east of Jordan and is given the title of "king of Bashan". His kingdom is described in almost identical terms as those employed by Moses when he recited the exploits of the children of Israel (Deut 3.10-11): "Mount Hermon, and in Salcah, and in all Bashan, unto the border of the Geshurites and the Maachathites, and half Gilead, the border of Sihon king of Heshbon" (v.5). He ruled his kingdom from the cities of Ashtaroth and Edrei.

Summary (v.6)

The conquest of these kings is summarised succinctly with the emphasis placed upon the obedience of Moses as the "servant of the Lord".

Verses 7-24: Kings and Territory west of Jordan

Geography (vv.7-8)

The territory taken by Joshua on the west of Jordan has already been described (11.17), and this further description does not add any new information but does reverse the order in which the northern and southern boundaries of the conquered land are presented. The geography of the western conquest is summarised by six areas of land and six groups of people: "In the mountains, and in the valleys, and in the plains, and in the springs, and in the wilderness, and in the south country; the Hittites, the Amorites, and the Canaanites, the Perizzites, the Hivites, and the Jebusites", all of which have been the subject of previous comment.

Kings (vv.9-24)

Joshua defeated thirty-one kings on the west side of Jordan. These kings ruled over cities, some of which are mentioned here for the first time, indicating that the military campaign extended beyond the seven cities of ch.10 and the geographical description of ch.11. The kings which have been mentioned previously in the narrative are set out in the order in which they were defeated, with those mentioned for the first time inserted within the chronology.

Kings from the centre of Canaan (v.9)

Jericho
Ai.

Kings from the south of Canaan (vv.10-16a)

Jerusalem
Hebron
Jarmuth
Lachish
Eglon
Gezer
Debir
Geder
Hormah
Arad
Libnah
Adullam
Makkedah.

This list includes four kings who are not mentioned in ch.10, viz. the kings of Geder, Hormah, Arad, and Adullam.

Further kings from the centre of Canaan (vv.16b-18)

It does appear from chs.6-7 that Jericho and Ai were the only cities in the centre of the land to be conquered. However, a further five kings and their cities from the centre of Canaan are included in the list of conquered kings.

Bethel
Tappuah
Hepher
Aphek
Lasharon.

Kings from the north of Canaan (vv.19-24)

Madon
Hazor
Shimron-meron
Achshaph
Taanach
Megiddo
Kedesh
Jokneam of Carmel
Dor in the coast of Dor
The nations of Gilgal
Tirzah.

JOSHUA 13

Introduction to Chapters 13-21

Purpose and Character of Land Lists

The free flowing narrative of chs.1-11 is brought to an end in ch.12. The list of defeated kings prepares the reader for the administrative nature of the chapters that follow, particularly chs.13-21. Following the detail of battles, miracles, victory, defeat, and diplomacy, the presentation of geographical boundaries and names of cities, towns and villages, many of which are of uncertain location, is a challenge to the reader, but a testimony to the faithfulness of the Lord and His interest in the detail of the inheritance which he had given to the children of Israel.

Every tribe received an inheritance, although the description of their possessions differ, with some containing a boundary list and others a list of cities, or both. Fourteen tribes are given an inheritance which takes into account the division of Joseph's inheritance between Ephraim and the divided tribe of Manasseh. A further complication exists with the territory of Simeon being placed within that of Judah (19.1,9).

Boundaries

Three of the tribes have no boundary description for their inheritance. Levi was given no land, only cities, since their inheritance was the Lord Himself (13.14,33; 18.7). Simeon was within Judah (19.1,9) and the people of Dan left their original grant of land (19.47).

The language employed in the boundary descriptions is full of verbs, giving the feel of the journey through the land which had been undertaken by the twenty-one surveyors sent out from Shiloh (18.4).

"Many different verbs are used to describe the way in which boundaries operate. H. V. Paranak has highlighted the nine for which the word 'boundary' is the grammatical subject: to go, walk; to go out along; to go down; to go around; to pass along; to go up; to pass by, touch; to turn back; to turn, bend...Along with directional indicators – prepositions and nouns such as, from; to; alongside; to the north; to the sea; to the east - as well as geographical nouns such as border; tongue; shoulder; valley; hill; sea – the verbs combine to generate interesting and precise boundary descriptions. The fact that many of the points described are not known today should not obscure the marvel and precision of the original lists" (*The New American Commentary,* David M. Howard Jnr.).

Cities

There are some anomalies within the lists of cities. The emphasis is on the cities on the west of Jordan with none mentioned for the tribes of Gad and Manasseh on the east, whilst Reuben's cities are incorporated only as part of the boundary description. The reason for this is that land on the east of Jordan was not within the original inheritance granted to the children of Israel. It is not possible to provide an explanation for the exclusion of cities on the west of the Jordan belonging to Ephraim and Manasseh. Some are mentioned within another tribe's territory, or feature as part of a boundary description.

The largest city list belongs to Judah, even although many of the cities do not appear in the Bible again. Their position as the most important tribe is emphasised by this list.

Narratives

In addition to lists of geographical boundaries and cities, there are five narratives of the grant of land resulting from special pleas to Joshua:

- Caleb (14.6-15)
- Caleb's daughter, Achsah (15.13-19)
- Daughters of Zelophehad (17.3-6)
- Joseph (17.14-18)
- Levites (21.1-3).

For the Israelite the chapters of seemingly inconsequential information regarding his inheritance had great significance. These chapters contain the title deeds to his land. The extent of the inheritance taught him the greatness of the God from whom it had been given. When the spiritual blessings of the New Testament are considered, it should be no surprise to the Christian to discover that great descriptions are given. This serves to educate the believer as to the fulness of the inheritance that he has received from the Lord. Reading the account of the division of the land would have similar significance to those who were entering into their inheritance in Canaan. Possessing the inheritance involves contemplating the character of God and appreciating the faithful fulfilment of His promises.

Command to Divide the Land

Verse 1: Instruction for an Aged Joshua

"Now Joshua was old and stricken in years; and the Lord said unto him, Thou art old and stricken in years". He was unlike Moses who retained his physical strength to the day of his death (Deut 34.7). As an old man, Joshua's work was not finished even though, in all probability, he had passed the age of 100. He was 110 when he died (24.29) and it is thought by many commentators that it took seven years to survey and divide the land. The service that the Lord now had for Joshua had changed. He was no longer able to do what he had done as a young man; however, his long years of serving the Lord had prepared him for this final task.

For most servants of the Lord, age does bring change. The physical limitations that accompany advancing years often mean that activity, which was previously carried out, is no longer possible. That does not mean that their service is finished. It does mean that it has changed. It is sad when a believer refuses to acknowledge the onset of age and will not allow others to take on his responsibilities. This was one of the problems in the days of Hosea when "gray hairs are here and there upon him, yet he knoweth not" (Hos 7.9). It is good when a brother is willing to accept a new sphere of service to which the Lord has directed him and for which his experience has fitted him.

"And there remaineth yet very much land to be possessed". This was not a rebuke or even an indication of failure on the part of Joshua. It was a statement of fact in relation to the inheritance that the Lord had promised the children of Israel. Joshua had done what had been required of him, yet the work of possessing the land was not finished. Joshua was being instructed to divide the land, even if parts of the territory to be allocated to certain tribes were not yet under their control.

They had come a long way from the slavery of Egypt, but they were not to be content with a partial inheritance. Before Joshua gave his farewell speeches to the nation, he was to maintain the focus of the people on the land that they had been given and which required to be possessed in its entirety.

Verses 2-6: Land still to be Possessed

The remaining land is succinctly described in geographical terms and separated into three areas; the south, an uncertain Canaanite region, and the north.

The south (vv.2-3)

"All the borders of the Philistines, and all Geshuri" (v.2). This is the first mention of the Philistines in the book. They were a people who are first mentioned in Genesis 10.14 (RV). In the time of Abraham and Isaac they inhabited the south-west of what was later called Judaea, Abimelech of Gerar being their king (Gen 21.32,34; 26.1). They are, however, not noted among the Canaanitish tribes mentioned in the Pentateuch, but are spoken of by Jeremiah (Jer 47.4,) and Amos (Amos 9.7), as coming from Caphtor, i.e. probably Crete, or, as some think, the Delta of Egypt. In the whole record from Exodus to Samuel they are represented as inhabiting the country which lay between Judaea and Egypt (Ex 13.17; 1 Sam 4.1). They became an enemy of the children of Israel and remained a thorn in their flesh until the days of king Hezekiah. Even when subdued, they remained in their land with all their old hostility (Ezek 25.13-17).

Geshuri is most likely the same territory which was later invaded by king David, "David and his men went up, and invaded the Geshurites, and the Gezrites, and the Amalekites: for those nations were of old the inhabitants of the land, as thou goest to Shur, even unto the land of Egypt" (1 Sam 27.8).

The land of the Philistines and Geshurites is described as extending from "Sihor, which is before Egypt, even unto the borders of Ekron northward, which is counted to the Canaanite" (v.3). Sihor means "black", or "dark" and "is probably 'the river of Egypt' (1Chr 13.5) which flows 'before Egypt', i.e. in a north-easterly direction from Egypt, and enters the sea about 50 miles (80 kilometres) south-west of Gaza" (Easton's Revised Bible Dictionary). Ekron was the most northerly of the Philistine cities. It was initially within the territory assigned to Judah (15.11,45) and subsequently was given to Dan (19.43).

The Philistines were a people who were ruled by "five lords of the Philistines; the Gazathites, and the Ashdothites, the Eshkalonites, the Gittites, and the Ekronites" (v.3) and whose territory included the "the Avites". There is little said about this last people other than "the Caphtorims, which came forth out of Caphtor, destroyed them, and dwelt in their stead" (Deut 2.23). They appear to have been swallowed up by the Philistines and are mentioned elsewhere only in relation to idolatry (2 Kings 17.31).

An uncertain Canaanite region (v.4)

"From the south, all the land of the Canaanites, and Mearah that is beside the Sidonians, unto Aphek, to the borders of the Amorites". There is some difficulty in determining the exact location of this territory. It would appear to be unconquered land lying between the southern lands of vv.3-4 and the northern portions described in v.5.

The north (v.5)

The northern territory that remained unconquered extended as far north as "the land of the Giblites", "their capital was Gebal or Bylbos (Greek), on the Mediterranean, 40 miles (64 kilometres) north of Sidon" (Ps 83.7; Ezek 27.9), (Jamieson, Faussett and Brown). Toward the east, "all Lebanon, toward the sunrising, from Baal-gad under mount Hermon unto the entering into Hamath" remained out of the control of the children of Israel. Baal-gad (11.17; 12.7) marked the southern point of the valley of Lebanon, and the entrance to Hamath (Num 13.21; 34.8), was at the northern end of the valley.

The Lord's promise and Joshua's charge (v.6)

"All the inhabitants of the hill country from Lebanon unto Misrephoth-maim, and all the Sidonians, them will I drive out from before the children of Israel: only divide thou it by lot unto the Israelites for an inheritance, as I have commanded thee". The Lord's promise to continue what He had commenced during Joshua's life is significant. The process of allocating unconquered territory to the children of Israel would have been a futile exercise if the Lord was not going to be with them following Joshua's death. After all, it was the Lord who was giving the children of Israel the victory over the inhabitants of the land. On the two recorded occasions when they had left the Lord out of their decision-making, at Ai and with the Gibeonites, they had known only defeat and compromise.

This promise of the Lord was not unconditional. It was a reiteration of an old promise that had been given, firstly to Moses, and then to Joshua. Although it is not mentioned, inherent in the Lord's promise was the necessity for faithfulness and diligence on the part of Israel. If they continued to serve the Lord, as they had done under the leadership of Joshua, then the Lord would continue to give them victory over their enemies.

Verses 7-8a: Land for the nine and a half Tribes

"Now therefore divide this land for an inheritance unto the nine tribes, and the half tribe of Manasseh, with whom the Reubenites and the Gadites have received their inheritance" (vv.7-8a). Although the land had been gained by military conquest, it was to be received as an inheritance from the Lord. Joshua had been reminded of this before the conquest began and now, following the end of hostilities, he is again reminded that the land was from the Lord and was to be accepted as such.

This had significance that went beyond the initial entrance into the land. As an inheritance they had the responsibility to pass it on to their children and never to sell or dispose of what they received from the Lord. It was an appreciation of this very point that prevented Naboth from selling his vineyard to Ahab (1 Kings 21.3).

The land was not to be divided according to the thoughts of Joshua or the desires of the people, but "by lot" (v.6). This ensured that the portion which each tribe received was what that the Lord had given them for their benefit and blessing. The gifts and blessings, which God gives to His people, are always for their good. This is not always obvious owing to the short-sightedness that is a feature of frail flesh.

Distribution of Land by Moses Affirmed by Joshua

Prior to dealing with the inheritance of the nine and a half tribes on the west of the Jordan, Joshua re-affirmed the distribution of land made by Moses prior to the crossing of the Jordan.

By including the trans-Jordan territory, Joshua was demonstrating to the children of Israel that they were to remain one nation, even though the Jordan would separate them geographically. Their inheritance was to have the same status as that which was granted to the nine and a half tribes on the west of Jordan. He also gave continuing authority to the words of Moses, which were not to be disregarded, thus ratifying the validity of the inheritance of the trans-Jordan tribes, and the landless state of the Levites.

Verses 8b-13: Overview of the Trans-Jordan Land

Introduction (v.8b)

In the introduction to the general survey of the land on the east of

Jordan there is a double reminder that this land was given by Moses: "...which Moses gave them, beyond Jordan eastward, even as Moses the servant of the Lord gave them" (v.8). This refers back to the original grant of the land and the subsequent occasion, prior to crossing Jordan, when Moses reminded the children of Israel of their history (Num 32.33-42; Deut 3.8-17). Joshua was bound by the past in relation to the land which the trans-Jordan tribes were entitled to occupy. Moses had been the servant of the Lord and had not acted on his own initiative.

Some within Israel could have argued that times had changed and circumstances had altered to such an extent that the words of Moses were out of date and irrelevant to a new generation. However, by publicly associating himself with his predecessor's decision Joshua did not allow for this and, by so doing, demonstrated the authority of God's word for successive generations. It is important to understand that the Word of God does not change. The philosophies and fashions of men may alter but the Word of God is immutable. Therefore, although the application of divine truth may differ with a new generation facing new challenges, the truth of God is the same in the twenty-first century as it was when the Scriptures were written. This ought to be especially borne in mind by younger Christians who perhaps identify certain aspects of truth with an older generation and feel that they have no relevance or application to them. It is good to remember that the teaching of the Word of God remains unaltered in relation to subjects such as the display of headship in gatherings of the local assembly, the importance of the priesthood of all believers, the scriptural context for expressing worship, the means of communicating the gospel, and other such issues which are increasingly determined without recourse to the Bible.

Survey of the land (vv.9-12)

The survey of the land does not require detailed comment, since it is not substantially different from the description in the previous chapter (12.1-6). It is interesting that the description ends with the statement, "For these did Moses smite, and cast them out" (v.12). When Moses had conquered the kingdoms of Sihon and Og by defeating the kings in battle, he took control of their land. This did not exempt the tribes of Reuben, Gad and the half of the tribe of Manasseh from possessing the extent of their inheritance, and, in order to do so, they needed to remove completely the occupants of the land.

Failure to drive out inhabitants (v.13)

When Joshua was instructed to divide the land (vv.6-7) there were substantial areas still unconquered. The situation presented here is different: "Nevertheless the children of Israel expelled not the Geshurites, nor the Maachathites. but the Geshurites and the Maachathites dwell among the Israelites until this day" (v.13). The Geshurites and Maachathites had been defeated by Moses (12.5-6), but were allowed to remain within their land and became a problem to the children of Israel in years to come. The children of Israel had not followed through the defeat that Moses had inflicted upon these peoples and, as a result, they remained within the inheritance given to the two and a half tribes. This is the commencement of a recurring theme throughout the historical books of the Old Testament. The seeds of many of the problems that afflicted Israel during their united occupation of the land can be traced to the early years of conquest. Their enemies were permitted to remain within the land and the children of Israel settled down among them and became idolaters; this ultimately led to their removal from their land in discipline.

It is worthy of note that the Geshurites troubled David, with their descendants providing a wife for Absalom (2 Sam 3.3) and refuge for him during his rebellion (2 Sam 13.37-38). The Maachathites joined in opposition to David when they supplied 1,000 men for the Ammonite army that fought against him (2 Sam 10.6,8). This should serve as a warning that disobedience can have repercussions for subsequent generations.

Verse 14: The Levites' Inheritance

"Only unto the tribe of Levi he gave none inheritance". No land was given to the tribe of Levi by Moses, and Joshua complied with that in the distribution of the inheritance. It was right and proper that this should be made clear before the detail of the other tribes' inheritance was announced. This avoided any misunderstanding that could have arisen when the other tribes received their portions while Levi had none.

Although the tribe of Levi received no land, they did obtain an inheritance that was unique: "The sacrifices of the Lord God of Israel made by fire are their inheritance". When Jacob gave his blessing to his sons he had pronounced that Levi would be divided in Jacob and scattered in Israel (Gen 49.7). Thereafter they redeemed themselves in the matter of the golden calf (Ex 32.26-28) and were blessed with the function of priesthood in Israel (Num 3.1-39). Their labour was to be centred on the tabernacle and, in order for them to be sustained, they were entitled to receive the tithes given to the Lord (Num 18.20-24). Their service meant that they would not be free to cultivate any land or tend flocks. This was compensated for by the Lord Himself, with their food and clothing coming from offerings given to the Lord at the altar. It is an interesting study to discover what a priest was entitled to from the various offerings and to find that, amongst other things, he received meat, wine, oil, fleece, and grain (Deut 18.1-8).

Paul used the inheritance of the Levites as an illustration of the right of a man to be partaker of his labour: "Do ye not know that they which minister about holy things live of the things of the temple? and they which wait at the altar are partakers with the altar?" (1 Cor 9.13). He demonstrated that his rights as an apostle to forbear working, and to be sustained by the believers among whom he laboured, were based on a principle well established in nature, the Law, and the words of the Lord Jesus. The principle extends beyond apostles and is applied by Paul to the work of an elder. If an elder is discharging his responsibilities, it may take up time that he could otherwise have spent earning money. The assembly has a responsibility to recognise this and make good such loss of income: "Let the elders that rule well be counted worthy of double honour, especially they who labour in the word and doctrine" (1 Tim 5.17).

Verses 15-23: Reuben's Inheritance

For the first time, there is given a detailed description of the land given to each of the trans-Jordan tribes. The territorial integrity of these tribes was as important as that of the nine and a half tribes on the west of Jordan.

Boundaries

Reuben's inheritance lay in the south of the land described earlier (vv.9-13). The description follows the boundary from south to north along the eastern border of that land. "And their coast was from Aroer, that is on the bank of the river Arnon, and the city that is in the midst of the river, and all the plain by Medeba; Heshbon, and all her cities that are in the plain" (vv.16-17a). This border is the same, word for word, as that outlined in v.9, with Heshbon, and her cities, marking the north-eastern limit of Reuben's territory. The western boundary "was Jordan, and the border thereof" (v.23).

Cities

"Dibon, and Bamoth-baal, and Beth-baal-meon, and Jahazah, and Kedemoth, and Mephaath, and Kirjathaim, and Sibmah, and Zareth-shahar in the mount of the valley, and Beth-peor, and Ashdoth-pisgah, and Beth-jeshimoth, and all the cities of the plain" (vv.17b-21a). Twelve named cities lay within Reuben's inheritance. Some of them have a place within the recorded history of Israel. Jahazah (Jahaz) was the place where Sihon was defeated in battle (Num 21.23-24) and which was later given to the tribe of Levi. Beth-peor was the place where Israel sinned in the matter of the Moabite women (Num 25.1-3; 31.16) and was also linked with Moses' burial (Deut 34.6).

Notable features

"And all the kingdom of Sihon king of the Amorites, which reigned in Heshbon" (v.21b). From a cursory reading it would appear that all of the region taken from Sihon was given to the tribe of Reuben. However, that is not consistent with the later description of the territory of Gad (v.27). Keil & Delitzsch comment: "All the kingdom of Sihon, so far as it extended over the plain. The limitations of the words are implied in the context". An alternative rendering is "which all had been the kingdom of Sihon", indicating that the cities mentioned lay within the territory of Sihon, but were not a description of the extent of his kingdom.

"Whom Moses smote with the princes of Midian, Evi, and Rekem, and Zur, and Hur, and Reba, which were dukes of Sihon, dwelling in the country" (v.21a). These five princes of Midian were vassals of Sihon, who had been defeated by the children of Israel on a separate occasion (Num 31). The Midianites are mentioned only here in the book, albeit they were a persistent foe of Israel. Their defeat by Phinehas (Num 31) did not remove them as a threat to the children of Israel. Midian is one of three nations which are a picture of the flesh, the others being Ammon and Amalek, and they were finally dealt with by Gideon (Judg 7), but only to the extent of being subdued and not destroyed. In this and many other ways they picture the kind of enemy that the flesh is to the believer. Even when defeated, it is never removed and can rise up again if given any encouragement.

"Balaam also the son of Beor, the soothsayer, did the children of Israel slay with the sword among them that were slain by them" (v.22). When the defeat of the five princes of Midian is first recorded, the death of Balaam is also mentioned (Num 31.8). His death was an important moment in the history of Israel and, together with his life, features throughout the Old Testament (Deut 23.4-5; Josh 24.9-10; Neh 13.2; Mic 6.5), serving as a warning to the children of Israel of the destructive influence of the love of money and a reminder of the Lord's intervention to turn a curse into a blessing.

Verses 24-28: Gad's Inheritance

Eastern boundary

"And their coast was Jazer, and all the cities of Gilead, and half the land of the children of Ammon, unto Aroer that is before Rabbah" (v.25). Lying north of Reuben's lot, the portion of Gilead referred to was that which belonged to Sihon and not the area stretching north into the territory of Og. Toward the east it encompassed the land which had belonged to the Ammonites situated between the Arnon and Jabbok rivers, which "the Amorites under Sihon had captured from the Ammonites, namely, the land on the east of Gilead, on the western side of the Upper Jabbok" (Deut 2.37; 3.16) (Keil & Delitszch). The other territory which belonged to the Ammonites when Moses conquered Sihon and Og, was left by the children of Israel since the Lord had given it to the children of Lot for a possession (Deut 2.19).

Northern and southern boundaries

"And from Heshbon unto Ramath-mizpeh, and Betonim; and from Mahanaim unto the border of Debir" (v.26). There appear to be two sections mentioned: Heshbon to Ramath-mizpeh and Betonim, marking the southern boundary to the middle of the portion of land, and then

Mahanaim to Debir, marking the middle to the north of the Gad's inheritance.

Mahanaim was the place where the angel appeared to Jacob before he crossed the ford of Jabbok (Gen 32.2,22), where Ish-bosheth was proclaimed king (2 Sam 2.8-9), and the city to which David fled during Absalom's rebellion, being sustained there by Barzillai the Gileadite (2 Sam 17.27; 19.32).

Western boundary

"And in the valley, Beth-aram, and Beth-nimrah, and Succoth, and Zaphon, the rest of the kingdom of Sihon king of Heshbon, Jordan and his border, even unto the edge of the sea of Chinnereth on the other side Jordan eastward" (v.27). The western border of Gad's inheritance extended along the Jordan from the Dead Sea as far as the Sea of Chinnereth (Galilee). The four cities mentioned lay within the Jordan valley which was effectively the western boundary. Succoth features, without distinction, in the story of Gideon (Judg 8.3-16). Matthew Henry also notes in his Commentary that "within the limits of this tribe lived those Gadarenes that loved their swine better than their Saviour, fitter to be called Girgashites than Israelites".

Verses 29-31: Manasseh's Inheritance

"Their coast was from Mahanaim, all Bashan, all the kingdom of Og king of Bashan, and all the towns of Jair, which are in Bashan, threescore cities" (v.30). The north of the land taken on the east of Jordan, was given to the half tribe of Manasseh. This was the territory of Og, king of Bashan, and it was by all accounts a rich and fertile land (Jer 50.19; Mic 7.14), which had sixty cities, indicating that it was heavily populated.

"And half Gilead, and Ashtaroth, and Edrei, cities of the kingdom of Og in Bashan, were pertaining unto the children of Machir the son of Manasseh, even to the one half of the children of Machir by their families" (v.31). The portion of Gilead which did not belong to Gad was given to Manasseh, along with the royal cities of Ashtaroth and Edrei (12.4; 13.12).

It is interesting that Machir is mentioned rather than Manasseh. He was Manasseh's eldest son and is often spoken of as the father of Gilead (Num 26.29-33; Josh 17.1; 1 Chr 7.14-15). His name is given to distinguish the descendants of Manasseh who had their inheritance on the west of Jordan, from those who had chosen to remain on the east (17.2).

Verses 32-33: Summary

Joshua's reaffirmation of the land grants given to the two and a half trans-Jordan tribes concludes with an expansion of the position into which the Levites had been brought. Their inheritance is described as "the Lord God of Israel" (v.33). This reminded the children of Israel of the close association that existed between the Lord and the altar.

JOSHUA 14

Introduction to the Division of Land West of Jordan

The Lord had already given Moses instructions for this day when the land of Canaan would be divided for the children of Israel (v.2). The men and methods employed were critical and stand as a testimony to the wisdom of God. There could be no possibility of bias or injustice in this matter; impartial righteousness was required. Each tribe had to see that the land which they received was given to them on an equitable basis from the Lord, otherwise the seeds of longstanding tribal conflict could be sown.

Verse 1: Men Involved

Eleazar the priest

In accordance with the instruction that the Lord had given to Moses (Num 34.17), Eleazar was involved in the division of the land. He was the son and successor of Aaron (Ex 6.25; Num 20.26-28) and, significantly, was associated with Joshua at his inauguration and in his leadership role. For Joshua to know the mind of the Lord when leading the children of Israel, Eleazar would "ask counsel for him after the judgment of Urim before the Lord: at his word shall they go out, and at his word they shall come in, both he, and all the children of Israel with him, even all the congregation" (Num 27.21).

Joshua the son of Nun

Joshua is referred to as the "son of Nun" at ten key points in the book (1.1; 2.1,23; 6.6; 14.1; 17.4; 19.49,51; 21.1; 24.29).

The heads of the fathers of the tribes of the children of Israel

The names of fathers of the tribes were given to Moses (Num 34.18-29). One man from each tribe was involved in order for the nation to be comprehensively represented in the process. The leadership, priesthood, and tribes all had their place. However, this was not democracy at work. In the Bible, the voice of the majority is rarely in accord with the mind of God and is not a reliable guide for making decisions about spiritual matters. The men were to serve as witnesses to the integrity of the land division and to oversee its implementation.

Verse 2: Method Employed

There is an interesting anomaly in the method employed by the Lord for the division of the land. There was a responsibility upon the men (v.1) to divide the land, yet "By lot was their inheritance, as the Lord commanded by the hand of Moses". The instruction of the Lord to Moses contained this two-fold idea of responsibility and sovereignty: "Divide the land by lot for an inheritance among your families: and to the more ye shall give the more inheritance, and to the fewer ye shall give the less inheritance: every man's inheritance shall be in the place where his lot falleth; according to the tribes of your fathers ye shall inherit" (Num 33.54). Moses was instructed to divide the land in order for each tribe to receive an inheritance that was consistent with its size, yet the division would be made by lot. This ensured that the principle of equity would be upheld. Human error or bias was taken out of the reckoning by the use of the lot, thus allowing Joshua, Eleazar and the fathers of the tribes to divide the land righteously. "This was the force of the lot: there were ten lots cast in such a manner as to decide that some were next to the Egyptians, some to have the sea coasts, some to occupy the higher ground, and some to settle in the valleys. When this was done, it remained for the heads of the nations to determine the boundaries of their different territories according to some equitable standard. It was their place, therefore, to ascertain how many thousand heads there were in each tribe, and then to adjudicate a larger or smaller space according to the size of the tribe" (Calvin). It will be the subject of comment later (18.1-7) that the approach of the people to the lot altered when they relocated to Shiloh.

It is not possible to be definite about the details of "the lot". Some commentators strongly advocate that it is a reference to the use of the Urim and Thummim, otherwise known as the "judgment of the Urim" (Num 27.21). Bringing the various scriptural references together, it is likely that these were two precious stones, which were held in the breastplate of the High Priest (Ex 28.30). Their purpose was to determine the mind of God in relation to matters of national importance, and the High Priest referred to them in an undisclosed manner. It may well be that the phrases, "came up", "came forth" and "came out", indicate the Urim and Thummim being taken from the breastplate.

The wisdom of the Lord is seen in the absence of detail in relation to the working of the lot. The tendency of many people towards superstition and religious idolatry is anticipated by the silence of Scripture on this matter. It is not important to know how the lot was cast. The mechanics of the process did not determine the outcome, it was simply a method that the Lord used to show the people His mind and provide guidance for the leadership of the nation: "The lot is cast into the lap; but the whole disposing thereof is of the Lord" (Prov 16.33). How easy it is to get caught up with the means whereby the Lord makes His will known to His people and forget that it is the Lord Himself who is important. This is a vital lesson for any believer to learn. Preaching, teaching, singing, witnessing, and praying all have their appropriate place; however, they are only a means to an end. When a person begins to focus on the means rather than the end he loses perspective and the means become the end, e.g. good singing can be a means of worship, but when the singing is worshipped rather than the Lord, the point of the singing has been lost.

Verses 3-5: Nine and a half Tribes Explained

Having stated that the land was to be divided as an inheritance among nine and a half tribes, on the west of Jordan, there is an explanatory note inserted: "For Moses had given the inheritance of two tribes and an half tribe on the other side Jordan: but unto the Levites he gave none inheritance among them" (v.3). For the reader who is doing his arithmetic, there is a problem. If the Levities received no inheritance of land and two and a half tribes were given their inheritance on the east of Jordan, there are only eight and a half tribes left. This problem is explained: "For the children of Joseph were two tribes, Manasseh and Ephraim" (v.4). The incorporation of two tribes out of Joseph finds its origin in the adoption of Joseph's sons by Jacob (Gen 48.5).

There is a little more information provided regarding the inheritance of the Levites. In ch.13 it had been described as "the sacrifices of the Lord God of Israel made by fire" (13.14), and "the Lord God of Israel" (13.33); it is now described as "cities to dwell in, with their suburbs for their cattle and for their substance" (v.4). These were to be given to them out of the inheritance of the other tribes (Num 35.1-8), the names of which are provided in ch.21. In addition to the cities, they were given the immediate land surrounding the cities for pasture for their cattle.

Chapter 14.6 – Chapter 15.63: Judah

The largest section of the narrative, dealing with the division of the land, relates to Judah. He was the recipient of a special blessing from Jacob (Gen 49.8-12) and had become the most important of all the tribes of Israel, not least because out of Judah the royal line of David would come, culminating in the birth of the Messiah.

"Judah and Joseph were the two sons of Jacob on whom Reuben's forfeited birth-right devolved. Judah had the dominion entailed on him, and Joseph the double portion, and therefore these two tribes were first seated, Judah in the southern part of the land of Canaan and Joseph in the northern part, and on them the other seven did attend, and had their respective lots as appurtenances to these two; the lots of Benjamin, Simeon, and Dan, were appendant to Judah, and those of Issachar and Zebulun, Naphtali and Asher, to Joseph. These two were first set up to be provided for, it should seem, before there was such an exact survey of the land as we find afterwards" (Matthew Henry).

Before the detail of Judah's inheritance is given, one of the five passages (14.6-15; 15.13-19; 17.3-6, 14-18; 21.1-3) dealing with the grant of land is presented. Caleb's story is broken into two sections, interrupting the description of the boundary and cities of Judah, with the latter section involving his daughter, Achsah.

Caleb

Verse 6: Caleb's Approach to Joshua

When the "the children of Judah came unto Joshua in Gilgal", Caleb, one of the heads of the tribe approached Joshua. He was named as the representative of the tribe in connection with the division of the land (Num 34.19) and sought out Joshua to speak to him about a personal matter. It is instructive to consider the manner of his approach to Joshua. He was the one man out of all of the spies who had stood with Joshua and given a good report of the land (Num 14.6-9), and with Joshua was the only other survivor of that generation. Although they shared so much history, he was willing to acknowledge the authority that had been vested in Joshua and seek his permission to proceed with the possessing of the land that he had been promised by the Lord, through Moses.

His lineage is mentioned in order that there should be no mistake as to his identity: "Caleb the son of Jephunneh the Kenezite". It should not be inferred from his name that he was a descendent of the Kenizzites (Gen 15.19), who were not of the children of Israel. The better explanation is that Kenaz was the father of Othniel, Caleb's brother (15.17), and therefore through his relationship with Kenaz, Caleb is known as the son of Jephunneh, who was related to Kenaz. He in turn was the grandson of Judah (1 Chr 2.5,18,25), and therefore Caleb was of the tribe of Judah (Num 13.6) and the son of Jephunneh the Kenezite.

Caleb's issue was well known to Joshua. Of all the men among the children of Israel, he was the only one to whom Caleb could say, "Thou knowest the thing that the Lord said unto Moses the man of God concerning me and thee in Kadesh-barnea". They were joined together by forty-five years of experience with God and His people. It had been some years since Moses had died; yet the memory of his life had remained with Caleb. What Moses had said was received by Caleb as from the Lord because Moses was the man of God. It is an indication of the deep impression that Moses left on Caleb that he should refer to him as "the man of God". Caleb took Joshua back to the days of crisis in the history of the nation when they had stood together, under tremendous pressure, and had received the blessing of the Lord for their whole-hearted obedience and faith in the Lord.

Caleb provided Joshua with reasons from the past, and from the present, for granting his request.

Verses 7-9: The Past

Caleb's integrity (v. 7)

"Forty years old was I when Moses the servant of the Lord sent me from Kadesh-barnea to espy out the land; and I brought him word again as it was in mine heart". These events, to which Caleb referred (Num 13-14), were a demonstration of his integrity. He followed his heart despite the pressure applied by the other spies (Num 13.27-29), and by the people themselves (Num 14.10).

Caleb's faithfulness (v.8)

"Nevertheless my brethren that went up with me made the heart of the people melt: but I wholly followed the Lord my God". In contrast with his integrity and steadfastness, the other spies caused fear and dissent among the people. Matthew Poole states in his commentary, "I spake my opinion sincerely, without flattery and fear, when the other spies were biased by their own fears, and the dread of the people, to speak otherwise than in their consciences they believed". Having emphasised his own integrity, Caleb then reminded Joshua of his faithfulness in discharging his service for the Lord.

Moses' oath (v.9)

"And Moses sware on that day, saying, Surely the land whereon thy feet have trodden shall be thine inheritance, and thy children's for ever, because thou hast wholly followed the Lord my God". The consequence of Caleb's integrity and faithfulness was a promise from the Lord, through His servant Moses, although it is interesting that the oath which Moses made does not appear in previous accounts of the events at Kadesh-barnea (Num 14.24; Deut 1.35-36). His oath did not refer to the whole land of Canaan but to that part through which Caleb had journeyed, the south of the land to Hebron. It was this area that was being referred to as his inheritance (Judg 1.20). Of the twelve spies, it was Caleb who spied out Hebron: "And they ascended by the south, and came unto Hebron; where Ahiman, Sheshai, and Talmai, the children of Anak, were. (Now Hebron was built seven years before Zoan in Egypt)" (Num 13.22). "In the original text it is, 'he came', Caleb, and he only, according to Jarchi and the Rabbins in Abendana; and certain it is that he was there, and he had this place on which his feet trod given him for an inheritance, and it is very probable that the spies did not go together, but perhaps singly, and at most but two together" (John Gill's Expositor).

Verses 10-12: The Present

The faithfulness of the Lord (v.10)

"And now, behold, the Lord hath kept me alive, as he said, these forty and five years, even since the Lord spake this word unto Moses". Caleb was building a compelling case for Joshua to give him his request. Throughout the dangers and demands of the wilderness journey and subsequent warfare in Canaan, Caleb had experienced the preserving care of the Lord. It was not his skill as a soldier, nor mere physical strength, that had brought him to this point in his life. He attributed his preservation to the Lord, and His fulfilment of a promise made forty-five years previously. He understood that the Lord had kept him alive for a purpose and, even at the age of eighty-five, he was determined to accomplish it.

Although Caleb had a special promise from the Lord, it is the Lord who sustains each life, and this ought to be a cause for gratitude. Paul reminded the Athenians of their reliance upon God, as creatures of His hand: "For in him we live, and move, and have our being" (Acts 17.28). The believer ought to have a greater understanding and appreciation of the sustaining grace of God. The Psalmist has said, "My times are in thy hand" (Ps 31.15).

Caleb's strength (v.11)

"As yet I am as strong his day as I was in the day that Moses sent me: as my strength was then, even so is my strength now, for war, both to go out, and to come in". Moses and Caleb had this in common. Not only were their lives preserved, but also their strength. "And Moses was an hundred and twenty years old when he died: his eye was not dim, nor his natural force abated" (Deut 34.7). Caleb insisted that he was strong enough to take possession of his inheritance, even though he was advanced in years. The spiritual application is clear: age is no barrier to possessing what the Lord has given to the believer in salvation. Rather than diminishing, Caleb's appetite for the inheritance remained as great as it had been, and he was determined to possess it. How encouraging it is to see an older saint living in the good of what he received from the Lord many years before. It is even better to see an older saint, having a desire to further explore his spiritual inheritance. Caleb had no thought of retirement in his service for the Lord, nor was he satisfied with his apprehension of spiritual matters, at the age of eighty-five!

Caleb's request (v.12)

"Now therefore give me this mountain, whereof the Lord spake in that day". Caleb was specific in his request. He sought the land that the Lord had promised to him, even although it was probably the most difficult portion of Canaan to possess. Caleb reminded Joshua of their journey into the land as spies and the report that they had heard from the people of the land relating to this area: "For thou heardest in that day how the Anakims were there, and that the cities were great and fenced". It was no easy option for Caleb, and he did not shrink from the task. His request is a wonderful statement of spiritual ambition, infused with certainty. It is inspiring to dwell upon the thought that this man, after a lifetime of faithful service, pushed ever onward and upward in his spiritual experience. What a challenge to every believer who is content with mediocrity and a life without spiritual goals!

The desire of Caleb to be given the mountain was founded on his confidence in his Lord. He had experienced His faithfulness in the preservation of his life for forty-five years and, with simple humility, was prepared to continue to rely upon Him for the complete fulfilment of His promise. This is the context for his statement: "if so be the Lord will be with me, then I shall be able to drive them out, as the Lord said". This was not a statement of doubt. It was a confession of his dependence on the Lord. He could not accomplish this task on his own, but if the Lord was with him, he would drive out the Anakims and possess the mountain. There is an echo of this confidence in the words of the three Hebrews before they were cast into the furnace, "If it be so, our God whom we serve is able to deliver us from the burning fiery furnace, and he will deliver us out of thine hand, O king" (Dan 3.17).

Verses 13-15: Caleb's Inheritance

"And Joshua blessed him, and gave unto Caleb the son of Jephunneh Hebron for an inheritance" (v.13). This is only the second time in the book where there is a record of a blessing being given, the previous occasion being at Mount Ebal (8.33). There was nothing that Joshua could give Caleb of himself that would prosper him or grant him his desire. By blessing him, Joshua was accepting the validity of his request and calling upon God to prosper him in the desire of his heart.

The whole subject of blessing in Scripture is interesting. God is the originator of every blessing. When a man blesses another man, he desires that God will prosper him. Therefore, the spiritual character of the man who blesses is important, since his blessing will have more significance if he has power with God; "without all contradiction the less is blessed of the better" (Heb 7.7). When a man blesses God, he is unable to prosper God. He is able, however, to ascribe worship and praise to Him; this is seen when Paul writes to the Christians at Ephesus, "Blessed be the God and Father of our Lord Jesus Christ, who hath blessed us with all spiritual blessings in heavenly places in Christ" (Eph 1.3).

"Hebron therefore became the inheritance of Caleb the son of Jephunneh the Kenezite unto this day, because that he wholly followed the Lord God of Israel" (v.14). Hebron (2275) means "fellowship", and provides a fitting inheritance for a man who wholly followed the Lord. It is remarkable that this man is seen as stretching out for fellowship with God at the age of eighty-five. It is also worthy of note that in order for an aged man to obtain this, and maintain it, he still has enemies to defeat. The intimacy of fellowship with God ought to be the ultimate aim of every believer. The apostle John sees it as the evidence of spiritual maturity (1 Jn 2.13-14). Abraham enjoyed wonderful communion with the Lord at this place (Gen 13.18) and perhaps that is why it was given the name of Hebron, having been known as "Kirjath-arba; which Arba was a great man among the Anakims" (v.15).

"And the land had rest from war". These words bring the chapter to a close. Despite the presence of the Anakims and other peoples within the land, the division of the inheritance was accomplished in general conditions of peace, and suffered no delay.

JOSHUA 15

Judah's Inheritance

Verses 1-12: Boundaries

The boundary description of Judah's inheritance is the most detailed of all the tribes. It is "painstaking and true to life in its presentation, describing, it seems, every twist and turn, every dip and rise, every right angle of the lines that marked off this tribe...nine different verbs are used a total of thirty-five times to describe the movement of the southern and northern boundary lines, as they move from east to west ... the word boundary occurs an astonishing twenty one times in these twelve verses, a remarkable proportion, since the word occurs a total of eighty-four times in the book" (*The New American Commentary*, David M. Howard, Jnr.). The attention to geographical detail further emphasises the importance of this tribe, and its territorial integrity, within the nation.

The south (vv.1-4)

The inheritance of Judah was in the south of the land, with their southern border forming the southern boundary of the land (Num 34.3-5). "This then was the lot of the tribe of the children of Judah by their families; even to the border of Edom the wilderness of Zin southward was the uttermost part of the south coast" (v.1). Edom lay south and east of the Dead Sea, with the wilderness of Zin an area of uncertain location, south of Canaan, which featured in the wilderness wanderings of the children of Israel (Num 13.21; 27.14; 33.36; 34.3).

The boundary description is vivid, passing westward from "the shore of the salt sea, from the bay that looketh southward. And it went out to the south side to Maaleh-acrabbim, and passed along to Zin, and ascended up on the south side unto Kadesh-barnea, and passed along to Hezron, and went up to Adar, and fetched a compass to Karkaa. From thence it passed toward Azmon, and went out unto the river of Egypt" (vv.2-4).

The east (v.5a)

The natural barrier of the Dead Sea formed the eastern boundary: "And the east border was the salt sea, even unto the end of Jordan".

The north (vv.5b-11)

Of all the boundaries, the north has the most detail. The starting point of the description is at the northern point of the eastern border: "And their border in the north quarter was from the bay of the sea at the uttermost part of Jordan" (v.5). The eastern border ran the full length of the Dead Sea to the point where the Jordan river joined. The northern border is described as moving in a generally westerly direction, as is the southern border. The tribe of Benjamin was granted the land on the other side of Judah's northern border and therefore the description of the border is repeated when the southern boundary of Benjamin is described (18.15-19).

Initially the border went north from the Dead Sea: "And the border went up to Beth-hogla, and passed along by the north of Beth-arabah; and the border went up to the stone of Bohan the son of Reuben" (v.6). It is interesting that this is the only mention of a son of Reuben called Bohan. There is no further information in Scripture about this man. However, there was a landmark associated with him and known to the children of Israel at that time. The border "went up" toward the stone of Bohan, indicating that it climbed up the mountains to the east of Jerusalem and the Mount of Olives. It continued on the high ground "toward Debir from the valley of Achor, and so northward, looking toward Gilgal, that is before the going up to Adummim, which is on the south side of the river: and the border passed toward the waters of En-shemesh, and the goings out thereof were at En-rogel" (v.7). Eventually, the border arrived at the city of Jerusalem, or, as it is described, "unto the south side of the Jebusite; the same is Jerusalem" (v.8). The boundary continued "up to the top of the mountain that lieth before the valley of Hinnom westward, which is at the end of the valley of the giants northward" (v.8). From the high point, north of Jerusalem, the border followed a north-westerly and then westerly direction toward the sea, passing landmarks of cities, springs of water and mountains (vv.9-11).

The west (v.12)

The description is as brief as that of the eastern border: "And the west border was to the great sea, and the coast thereof".

Verses 13-19: Caleb's Inheritance

The second paragraph dealing with Caleb and his inheritance focuses on the city of Debir. The narrative is similar to the section in Judges 1.12-15 and has also some overlap with the previous paragraph in 14.6-15, where Caleb made his request for his inheritance.

Hebron (vv.13-14)

From the information given in ch.14, the reader is aware of the desire and ambition of Caleb to possess the land that the Lord had promised him. This included the city of Hebron and the surrounding district. These verses add some detail to what has already been recorded.

Firstly, the granting of Caleb's inheritance is attributed, not only to a command that Moses received (14.6,9) but also "according to the commandment of the Lord to Joshua" (v.13). This is consistent with the pattern of the Lord's commands to Moses, which were communicated to Joshua and carried the same weight and authority.

Secondly, it is noted that Caleb "drove thence the three sons of Anak,

Sheshai, and Ahiman, and Talmai, the children of Anak" (v.14). These men were present when Caleb spied out the land (Num 13.22). In the account in Judges 1.10 the credit for driving out the Anakims is given to the tribe of Judah and not Caleb specifically. It must be remembered that Caleb was a leader of the tribe of Judah and therefore there is no inconsistency in attributing the victory both to the children of Judah and to him. Another matter to note is that this was not the first time that Hebron had been conquered and the Anakims driven out. Joshua had accomplished this some time before (11.21-22), but evidently they had returned into the area. "For that expulsion did not preclude the possibility of the Anakites and Canaanites returning to their former abodes, and taking possession of their towns again, when the Israelitish army had withdrawn and was engaged in the war with the Canaanites of the north; so that when the different tribes were about to settle in the towns and districts allotted to them, they were obliged to proceed once more to drive out or exterminate the Anakites and Canaanites who had forced their way in again" (Keil & Delitzsch).

Debir (vv.15-19)

a) Capture of Debir (vv.15-17)

"And he went up thence to the inhabitants of Debir: and the name of Debir before was Kirjath-sepher" (v.15). The former name of Debir was Kirjath-sepher, which means "city of the book". It was likely a place of learning and has been described as a type of university town. It was evidently a fortress of some renown and is thought to have been approximately 10 miles (16 kilometres) south of Hebron.

Caleb made an offer to any man who could capture the city: "And Caleb said, He that smiteth Kirjath-sepher, and taketh it, to him will I give Achsah my daughter to wife" (v.16). This is not the only occasion in Scripture where a father offered his daughter to the man who would accomplish some notable feat: King Saul offered his daughter to the man who could slay Goliath (1 Sam 17.25; 18.17). There was more to Caleb's offer than a desire to take the city of Debir. He had, after all, expressed his faith in the Lord and proved that he had the desire and courage to take the city himself. This was an opportunity for him to seek out a suitable husband for his daughter. The nature of the task ensured that the man who would succeed would be a man who trusted in the Lord, as Caleb did, and prove himself to be a worthy husband.Unlike Laban, who reneged on his promise to give Rachel to Jacob after seven years of labour, Caleb kept his word: "And Othniel the son of Kenaz, the brother of Caleb, took it: and he gave him Achsah his daughter to wife" (v.17). The designation of Othniel has led to some debate as to whether he was Caleb's younger brother or nephew. The expression, "the son of Kenaz" is equivalent to "the Kenezite" (14.6). It is difficult to be certain as to the relationship between Caleb and Othniel since there are not many other Scriptures which give help on the subject.

The references to Othniel in the book of Judges (1.13; 3.9) only give the further information that he was Caleb's younger brother. Commentators are divided on this matter; however, the present author prefers the view taken by Keil & Delitzsch that he was the younger brother of Caleb rather than his nephew.

Whether he was the nephew or brother does not change the significance of his actions in taking Debir and winning the hand of Achsah, Caleb's daughter. Marrying a niece or cousin was not forbidden by the Law and was perfectly acceptable. He proved himself a worthy husband for Achsah and continued to demonstrate that he was a man of spiritual worth. After the death of Joshua, he was the first man raised up by the Lord to deliver the children of Israel (Judg 3.9-11), leading them to victory over Chushan-rishathaim, king of Mesopotamia.

Concern about a suitable match for his daughter was wise and in keeping with the Caleb's character. It resulted in the capture of Debir for the tribe of Judah and also demonstrated the fitness of Othniel to marry Achsah. In accordance with the customs of the time, Caleb set an example for any father to follow. Traditions surrounding marriage may vary from place to place. However, in accordance with the practices of the land in which he lives, and in keeping with biblical teaching, a father ought to have a desire that his daughter marry a suitable husband, someone with an interest in the Word of God and the work of God. The means of working this out may differ, but prayer plays an essential role, no matter what the customs of the land may be.

b) Upper and nether springs (vv.18-19)

Achsah proved herself to be good match for Othniel. Her desire was for an inheritance in the land rather than personal wealth, jewels, or other adornments. When she became Othniel's wife, "she moved him to ask of her father a field" (v.18). She had already received land from her father, "thou hast given me a south land" (v.19), but she was not content to accept land without the means to make it fertile and productive. She made her request to her father who granted "the upper springs, and the nether springs" (v.19).

In this little cameo is seen the spirituality of Othniel's wife; they were perfectly matched. It is an excellent picture of a marriage of equals. How important it is for the husband and wife in a marriage to share spiritual ambition, to have the same desire to enjoy the inheritance they received when they were saved, and to be fruitful in the things of the Lord. Achsah was prepared to act in order to see her ambition realised. She did not wait for her husband to do for her what she could do for herself.

The upper and nether springs were necessary to make the land fertile and fruitful. Here is another picture of the importance of the Word of God in the life of a believer. The Psalmist said, "Blessed is the man that walketh not in the counsel of the ungodly, nor standeth in the way of sinners, nor sitteth in the seat of the scornful. But his delight is in the law of the Lord; and in his law doth he meditate day and night. And he shall be like a tree planted by the rivers of water, that bringeth forth his fruit in his season; his leaf also shall not wither; and whatsoever he doeth shall prosper" (Ps 1.1-3).

Caleb's generosity is seen in his granting his daughter's request and more beside. What father could refuse his daughter on the day that he gave her to her husband? If a father acted like this toward to his daughter whom he loved, how much more the Father in heaven? When responding to the disciples' request to be taught how to pray, the Lord Jesus said, "If ye then, being evil, know how to give good gifts unto your children: how much more shall your heavenly Father give the Holy Spirit to them that ask him?" (Lk 11.13). The character of God has not changed and He remains faithful and kind. The vast resources of heaven are available to the believer to draw upon.

Verse 20: Summary

"This is the inheritance of the tribe of the children of Judah according to their families". This refers to what has gone before and serves as a summary of the details of the land given to Judah. Similar wording occurs twelve times in Joshua, in relation to the inheritance of each tribe (13.23,28; 15.20; 16.8; 18.20,28; 19.8,16,23,31,39,48).

Verses 21-62: Cities

The list of the cities within the portion of Judah's inheritance is divided into four geographical areas. Of all the lists this is the longest. There is not much on which to comment, other than the obvious emphasis which is placed upon the extensive areas of population within Judah's land, marking out the important place that the tribe occupied in Israel.

South-land (vv.21-32)

"And the uttermost cities of the tribe of the children of Judah toward the coast of Edom southward were:

- Kabzeel, and Eder, and Jagur, and Kinah, and Dimonah, and Adadah, and Kedesh, and Hazor, and Ithnan (vv.21-23)
- Ziph, and Telem, and Bealoth, and Hazor, Hadattah, and Kerioth, and Hezron, which is Hazor (vv.24-25)
- Amam, and Shema, and Moladah, and Hazar-gaddah, and Heshmon, and Beth-palet, and Hazar-shual, and Beer-sheba, and Bizjothjah (vv.26-28)
- Baalah, and Iim, and Azem, and Eltolad, and Chesil, and Hormah, and Ziklag, and Madmannah, and Sansannah, and Lebaoth, and Shilhim, and Ain, and Rimmon (vv.29-32a)

all the cities are twenty and nine, with their villages" (v.32b).

The cities of the south-land are divided into four groups and are separated by the absence of the word "and". Thirty-eight cities are listed yet the final number is given as twenty-nine. Commentators are divided as to the reason for the discrepancy, with some attributing it to a copyist's error. Others rework the names and conclude that the removal of the word "Hazor", which means "settlement", assists in reconciling the numbers. Other explanations are that some of the places mentioned were not substantial enough to be included in the total number. The problem with the numbers should not detract from the point that the writer is making. There was a significant number of cities within Judah's territory, which was appropriate for the most important tribe in the land. Many of the cities mentioned in this section are not referred to again within Scripture and in themselves would appear to have no spiritual significance.

Lowland (vv.33-47)

"And in the valley:

• Eshtaol, and Zoreah, and Ashnah, and Zanoah, and En-gannim, Tappuah, and Enam, Jarmuth, and Adullam, Socoh, and Azekah, and Sharaim, and Adithaim, and Gederah, and Gederothaim; fourteen cities with their villages (vv.33-36)

• Zenan, and Hadashah, and Migdalgad, and Dilean, and Mizpeh, and Joktheel, Lachish, and Bozkath, and Eglon, and Cabbon, and Lahmam, and Kithlish, and Gederoth, Beth-dagon, and Naamah, and Makkedah; sixteen cities with their villages (vv.37-41)

• Libnah, and Ether, and Ashan, and Jiphtah, and Ashnah, and Nezib, and Keilah, and Achzib, and Mareshah; nine cities with their villages (vv.42-44)

• Ekron, with her towns and her villages (v.45)

• From Ekron even unto the sea, all that lay near Ashdod, with their villages (v.46)

• Ashdod with her towns and her villages, Gaza with her towns and her villages, unto the river of Egypt, and the great sea, and the border thereof (v.47).

The first three sub-groups of the low-land cities were south-west of Jerusalem. Ekron, Ashdod and Gaza were Philistine cities which were unconquered at the time of writing (13.3). More details are given about these cities than of any of the others that lay within Judah's territory. The explanation for this may be that they were not within the control of the children of Israel and therefore more information was required to identify them accurately.

Mountains (vv.48-60)

"And in the mountains:

• Shamir, and Jattir, and Socoh, and Dannah, and Kirjath-sannah, which is Debir, and Anab, and Eshtemoh, and Anim, and Goshen, and Holon, and Giloh; eleven cities with their villages (vv.48-51)

• Arab, and Dumah, and Eshean, and Janum, and Beth-tappuah, and Aphekah, and Humtah, and Kirjath-arba, which is Hebron, and Zior; nine cities with their villages (vv.52-54)

• Maon, Carmel, and Ziph, and Juttah, and Jezreel, and Jokdeam, and Zanoah, Cain, Gibeah, and Timnah; ten cities with their villages (vv.55-57)

• Halhul, Beth-zur, and Gedor, and Maarath, and Beth-anoth, and Eltekon; six cities with their villages (vv.58-59)

• Kirjath-baal, which is Kirjath-jearim, and Rabbah; two cities with their villages" (v.60).

These cities are listed in groups, commencing in the south of the mountain region which lay immediately north of the south-land (vv.21-32), and proceed northwards.

The wilderness (vv.61-62)

"In the wilderness: Beth-arabah, Middin, and Secacah, and Nibshan, and the city of Salt, and En-gedi; six cities with their villages" (vv.61-62).

Verse 63: Jerusalem

"As for the Jebusites the inhabitants of Jerusalem, the children of Judah could not drive them out: but the Jebusites dwell with the children of Judah at Jerusalem unto this day".

When the king of Jerusalem formed a coalition against Gibeon, Joshua defeated him and took all his land (10.26,42). Further information is provided in the book of Judges: "Now the children of Judah had fought against Jerusalem, and had taken it, and smitten it with the edge of the sword, and set the city on fire" (1.8). Evidently, the Jebusites retook the city and probably dwelt in the fort at the top of the mountain, while the children of Israel possessed the city, until the reign of king David (2 Sam 5.5-10). During the period of the Judges it was regarded as a foreign city (Judg 19.11-12).

Their failure to drive out the Jebusites was significant. Each victory accomplished by them was as a result of their dependence on the Lord and their desire to possess what they had been given as an inheritance; any defeat was a product of their lack in both these areas. No military reason is given for their inability to drive out the Jebusites; this points to the fact that it was a spiritual problem. No doubt, if the tribe of Judah had been asked why they had not taken possession of Jerusalem, they would have had many reasons. They may have spoken about the fortress on top of the mountain and the tenacity of the Jebusities. Any failure to live in the good of what the Lord has given to the believer is a spiritual problem. The reasons put forward, relating to circumstances, opposition, difficulties, etc., are excuses which mask the root problem of a lack of dependence on the Lord and an absence of desire on the part of the believer.

It does appear that the tribe of Judah settled down and tolerated the situation at Jerusalem, which pertained throughout the period of the Judges and the reign of king Saul. For generations the presence of the Jebusites was a daily reminder of defeat and failure for the tribe of Judah, yet the sad part is that they accepted this and lived with it. It is easy to become familiar with failure as a Christian and accept it as normal, rather than to view it as unacceptable and damaging to the full enjoyment and benefits of salvation.

JOSHUA 16

Joseph's Inheritance

The order in which Joshua apportioned the land was in harmony with the historical declaration made by Jacob on his deathbed (Gen 49.22-26). Judah was first in priority, followed by the tribes of Joseph. It has already been pointed out that these two allotments comprised the largest of the land portions and were given when the people were gathered at Gilgal (14.6), whereas the other tribes received their inheritance at Shiloh (18.1). The status of these two tribes within the nation is summarised in 1 Chronicles 5.1-2: "Now the sons of Reuben the firstborn of Israel, (for he was the firstborn; but, forasmuch as he defiled his father's bed, his birthright was given unto the sons of Joseph the son of Israel: and the genealogy is not to be reckoned after the birthright. For Judah prevailed above his brethren, and of him came the chief ruler; but the birthright was Joseph's)".

Although Joseph's two sons, Ephraim and Manasseh, are often dealt with as separate tribes, in relation to the lot they are brought together as one entity, which became the cause of a complaint to Joshua (17.14-18).

Verses 1-4: Southern Boundary

"And the lot of the children of Joseph fell from Jordan by Jericho" (v.1). The language employed to begin the description of Joseph's southern boundary is different from the other boundary descriptions, with the reference to Simeon being the closest. (19.1). Another translation of the phrase is, "And the lot for the sons of Joseph goeth out from Jordan by Jericho" (YLT), with the emphasis on the lot going out and not the boundary. Keil & Delitzsch provide the helpful paraphrase: "There came out the lot to the children of Joseph, namely, the inheritance, which goes out from, or whose boundary commences at, the Jordan by Jericho".

"And goeth out from Bethel to Luz, and passeth along unto the borders of Archi to Ataroth" (v.2). Elsewhere in Scripture the cities of Bethel and Luz are synonymous (Gen 28.19), with Luz being the name given to the city by the Canaanites. Some have suggested that Bethel, in this context, refers to the mountains which belonged to the city, rather than the city itself. However, the NIV translation renders the verse, "from Bethel (that is, Luz)", indicating that the one city was in view and it was given both names for the sake of clarity in identification. The border ran in a south-westerly direction from the Jordan, by Jericho, toward Ataroth, through the borders of Archi, whence came Hushai, one of David's advisors (2 Sam 15.32).

"And goeth down westward to the coast of Japhleti, unto the coast of Beth-horon the nether, and to Gezer. and the goings out thereof are at the sea" (v.3). From the Jordan in the east of the land, the border reached westward toward the sea. This direction took it through territory described as Japhleti. Two further landmarks are provided to identify the route that the southern boundary took: Beth-horon and Gezer. Both places have featured in the narrative prior to his point. Beth-horon was the place to which the Amorite kings fled when Joshua defeated them at Gibeon (10.10-11). The king of Gezer came to assist Lachish in their battle with Joshua and was defeated. His city is thought to have been approximately 15 miles (24 kilometres) from the sea. From Gezer the boundary went to the sea, with Keil & Delitszch assuming that it went "toward the north-west…to the north of Japho, which was assigned to the Danites, according to ch.19.46".

"So the children of Joseph, Manasseh and Ephraim, took their inheritance" (v.4). The description of Joseph's inheritance as one lot ends with this verse. Thereafter Manasseh and Ephraim have separate borders and cities allocated to them, within the territory given to Joseph. Some commentators suggest that the description of the one border separating the territory of Benjamin and Judah from that of Manasseh and Ephraim and the other more northerly tribes, was an indication that there was a north–south divide, even at the earliest period of the occupation of Canaan. This is reinforced by the absence of a description of Joseph's northern boundary, underlining the separation of Judah and Benjamin from the other ten tribes. The tribe of Dan did receive land which lay between Joseph and Judah (19.40-46), yet, as shall be commented upon later, they migrated under pressure from the Amorites (Judg 1.34) and settled on the northern borders of Naphtali and eastern Manasseh, at the northern extremity of Canaan.

Verses 5-9: Ephraim's Portion

The southern boundary of Ephraim's inheritance is described briefly, since it has already been detailed from the perspective of Joseph's lot (vv.1-4), being, in fact, the same boundary. "And the border of the children of Ephraim according to their families was thus: even the border of their inheritance on the east side was Ataroth-addar, unto Beth-horon the upper" (v.5).

The north of Ephraim's portion is described in two parts, commencing with the eastern section. "And the border went out toward the sea to Michmethah on the north side; and the border went about eastward unto Taanath-shiloh, and passed by it on the east to Janohah; and it went down from Janohah to Ataroth, and to Naarath, and came to Jericho, and went out at Jordan" (vv.6-7). Michmethah would appear to be a central point of reference, of uncertain location, from which the border ran eastward. The only other mention of the place occurs in the description of the same border from Manasseh's perspective (17.7), where it is located near to Shechem. The general direction of the boundary was eastward, and then south-easterly until it met with the commencement of the southern boundary at the Jordan. As a result, there is no eastern boundary for Ephraim, with the northern and southern boundaries having the same easterly starting point.

The western section of the northern boundary began at Tappuah, a short distance from the commencement of the eastern section at Michmethah. The boundary description of Manasseh, which describes the same border from the Manasseh point of view, fills in the descriptive gap (17.7-9). "The border went out from Tappuah westward unto the river Kanah; and the goings out thereof were at the sea. This is the inheritance of the tribe of the children of Ephraim by their families" (v.8).

The description of the inheritance that Ephraim received is completed by the mention of cities, all of which lay within the inheritance of Manasseh and included Tappuah (17.8). "And the separate cities for the children of Ephraim were among the inheritance of the children of Manasseh, all the cities with their villages" (v.9). There is no explanation provided for Ephraim gaining cities that lay beyond their borders, although it is worth pointing out that Manasseh was also granted cities that were not within its boundaries (17.11).

Verse 10: Ephraim's Failure

Judah was not alone in failing to fully occupy its inheritance; the Ephraimites "drave not out the Canaanites that dwelt in Gezer: but the Canaanites dwell among the Ephraimites unto this day". It is interesting that the situation here is different. It was said of Judah that they "could not drive them out" (15.63), indicating that some effort had been made to do so, resulting in failure and defeat and, ultimately, compromise. There does not appear to have been any compromise by the Jebusites in their relationship with Judah. However, there is no indication from the text that attempts were made by Ephraim to remove the Canaanites from Gezer; they simply did not do it. Instead they brought them into servitude.

Ephraim was able to subdue the Canaanites at Gezer and exercise authority over them. By contrast, the Jebusites never submitted to the control of Judah; in fact they are seen as having a relationship of equals. Notwithstanding the difference, both situations were not in keeping with the instruction of the Lord through His servants Moses and Joshua, and were a mark of failure on the part of the tribes (Deut 20.11,16-18). The Jebusites and Canaanites should have been driven out of Jerusalem and Gezer.

Judah could not. Ephraim would not. Judah tried to do what was right, but must have lacked faith, since the Lord had promised them victory. Ephraim could have done what was right, but chose to compromise and settle for second best. Failure among the people of God is a familiar story. Sometimes it is because of a lack of faith and dependence on the Lord and the resultant inability to do what should be possible. On other occasions it is a lack of desire to accomplish the will of the Lord and a willingness to go only so far and settle for what is considered to be an easier option. Both tribes discovered through the passage of time that failure, no matter its character and extent, has consequences that have to be faced.

JOSHUA 17

Joseph's Inheritance (cont.)

Verses 1-11: Manasseh's Portion

Their divided inheritance placed Manasseh in a unique position among the tribes of Israel. A reminder that this was not the only portion of land given to the tribe prefaces the description of the inheritance given to them on the west of the river Jordan.

The description of their lot on the west of Jordan also differs from that of the other tribes. It is divided into named family portions. This is related to the decision by Moses to grant a portion of their inheritance to the female descendants of one of the families, owing to the absence of a male heir, thus establishing an important legal precedent for the whole nation.

The uniqueness and privilege extended to Manasseh was based upon his position as firstborn of Joseph: "There was also a lot for the tribe of Manasseh; for he was the firstborn of Joseph" (v.1). Jacob, in his blessing of the children of Joseph, had declared that although Manasseh was the firstborn, Ephraim would be the greater of the two (Gen 48.19-20). However, Manasseh retained the status of the firstborn and as a result received an inheritance distinct from Ephraim; indeed it could be viewed as a double portion. "The sense is, though Ephraim was to be more potent and numerous, yet Manasseh was the first-born, and had the privilege of the first-born, which was translated to Joseph, to wit, a double portion; and therefore though this were but half the tribe of Manasseh, yet they are not made inmates to Ephraim, but have a distinct lot of their own, as their brethren or other half tribe had beyond Jordan" (Matthew Poole's *Commentary of the Bible*).

Machir (v.1)

"For Machir the firstborn of Manasseh, the father of Gilead: because he was a man of war, therefore he had Gilead and Bashan". Machir was the eldest, or perhaps only, son of Manasseh (Gen 50.23; Num 26.29; Josh 13.31; 1 Chr 7.14-15). He had a son called Gilead and he also became lord of the area known as Gilead. The reference here is not to his son, but to the land. Keil & Delitzsch point out that when the name of Gilead appears with the definite article, i.e., the Gilead, it refers to the land and when it appears without the article, it is the son of Machir that is in view. On this occasion the article is present, so the reference is to the land. Machir had become the lord, or possessor, of the land with his name being used on one occasion as a reference to the inheritance of Manasseh on the west side of the Jordan (Judg 5.14).

Machir's character is given as a reason for his possession of Gilead and Bashan. The reference may be to his warlike character and exploits. However, it is evident that his sons were raised in Egypt when Joseph was alive (Gen 50.23), and therefore he could not have fought in the conquest of the land. He must have died either in Egypt or in the wilderness. His descendants did fight in the battles with Sihon and Og on the east of the Jordan and throughout the campaigns in Canaan and evidently bore the character of their forefather.

Sons of Manasseh (v.2)

The portion of land given to Manasseh on the west of the Jordan was divided into ten portions, five of which were divided among the families of the male descendants of Manasseh through Machir and his son Gilead (Num 26.30-32). "There was also a lot for the rest of the children of Manasseh by their families; for the children of Abiezer, and for the children of Helek, and for the children of Asriel, and for the children of Shechem, and for the children of Hepher, and for the children of Shemida: these were the male children of Manasseh the son of Joseph by their families" (v.2). No detail is provided of the location or the extent of the land that was given to each of the families. The point is not that Manasseh was unique in the distribution of land by families; that was true of all of the tribes, but the names and individual portions of the families are mentioned only in relation to Manasseh.

Daughters of Zelophehad (vv.3-6)

During the wilderness journey of the children of Israel, "Zelophehad, the son of Hepher, the son of Gilead, the son of Machir, the son of Manasseh" (v.3) had died and left no sons. He did leave five daughters: "These are the names of his daughters, Mahlah, and Noah, Hoglah, Milcah, and Tirzah" (v.3). They were concerned about their father's inheritance which would be lost to the family as a result of the lack of a male heir.

They had brought their problem to Moses, Eleazar the priest, and the ten princes of the congregation and stated their case. They pointed out that their father had not joined the rebellion of the sons of Korah and had died without a son. They asserted that they would be the subject of an injustice if the inheritance of their father went to another family owing to the lack of a male heir (Num 27.1-11). They had their request granted and a statute of judgment was passed to apply the decision to the daughter of any man who had died leaving no son: "They came near before Eleazar the priest, and before Joshua the son of Nun, and before the princes, saying, The Lord commanded Moses to give us an inheritance among our brethren. Therefore according to the commandment of the Lord he gave them an inheritance among the brethren of their father" (v.4).

The insertion of the request by the daughters of Zelophehad has great significance with regard to the division of land and the establishment of clear borders. The right of a woman to inherit land from her father, if there was no male heir, was not universal under the various systems of land ownership at the time. It was important that this right was re-affirmed in what amounted to the title deeds of the land. The result of the application in this instance of the judgment passed down by Moses was that the inheritance of Manasseh on the west of the Jordan was sub-divided into ten portions, which included separate grants of land for each of the daughters. This gave them equal property status with the male descendants: "And there fell ten portions to Manasseh, beside the land of Gilead and Bashan, which were on the other side Jordan; because the daughters of Manasseh had an inheritance among his sons: and the rest of Manasseh's sons had the land of Gilead" (vv.5-6).

Manasseh's borders (vv.7-11)

The description of Manasseh's borders begins with the southern boundary, which was the northern border of Ephraim (16.6-8). The boundary is given from Manasseh's perspective commencing "from Asher to Michmethah, that lieth before Shechem; and the border went along on the right hand unto the inhabitants of En-tappuah" (v.7). Most commentators conclude that Asher is not a reference to the tribe bearing that name, but to a city: "Not from the border of the tribe of Asher...for that was at too great a distance; but a city of the tribe of Manasseh" (John Gill's Expositor). Others take the view that this is a description of the northern and southern extremes of Manasseh's territory from Asher in the north to Michmethah in the south (16.6). It is more likely that the former view is correct with Keil & Delitszch identifying the city of Asher as a "place on the high road from Neapolis to Scythopolis, fifteen Roman miles from the former".

The southern boundary "descended unto the river Kanah, southward of the river: these cities of Ephraim are among the cities of Manasseh: the coast of Manasseh also was on the north side of the river, and the outgoings of it were at the sea: southward it was Ephraim's, and northward it was Manasseh's, and the sea is his border" (vv.9-10). This coincides with the description of Ephraim's northern boundary. The river within the Kanah ravine was the boundary between Ephraim and Manasseh and was the last point of reference given before the border reached the sea.

The northern aspect of Manasseh's boundaries is simply given: "They met together in Asher on the north, and in Issachar on the east" (v.10).

It is interesting that "Manasseh had in Issachar and in Asher Beth-shean and her towns, and Ibleam and her towns, and the inhabitants of Dor and her towns, and the inhabitants of En-dor and her towns, and the inhabitants of Taanach and her towns, and the inhabitants of Megiddo and her towns, even three countries" (v.11). To the north and east of Manasseh's territory were cities belonging to them but lying within the borders of Asher and Issachar respectively. In the south they had the territory of En-tappuah, yet the city of Tappuah itself belonged to Ephraim (v.8). The reason for such satellite cities within the territory of another tribe is not given, however, the comments of Matthew Henry are worthy of consideration:

"Though every tribe had its peculiar inheritance, which might not be alienated from it, yet they should thus intermix one with another, to keep up mutual acquaintance and correspondence among the tribes, and to give occasion for the doing of good offices one to another, as became those who, though of different tribes, were all one Israel, and were bound to love as brethren".

Verses 12-13: Manasseh's Failure

It is disappointing to note that the first three tribes to receive their inheritance did not fully occupy their territory. Manasseh joined Judah and Ephraim in their failure to remove the existing inhabitants of the land.

"Yet the children of Manasseh could not drive out the inhabitants of those cities; but the Canaanites would dwell in that land" (v.12). The emphasis is upon the determination of the Canaanites to remain in the land, resisting any attempt to remove them. The NKJV provides the translation, "the Canaanites were determined to dwell in that land". This is another aspect to the problem of failing to take possession of the inheritance. When noting Judah and Ephraim's failure, the focus was upon their inability or lack of desire to remove the Canaanites. On this occasion, the Canaanites displayed a determination to occupy the land which was evidently missing from Manasseh. Despite their success in subduing the Canaanites, they could not expel them from the land and as a result followed the example of Ephraim in accepting a compromise of servitude from them: "Yet it came to pass, when the children of Israel were waxen strong, that they put the Canaanites to tribute; but did not utterly drive them out" (v.13). Such a compromise with those who dwelt in the land was forbidden for any tribe of Israel, but was acceptable with strangers from a distant land. (Deut 20.10-18). The believer should not underestimate the resolve of the enemy. The devil enjoys great success bringing about situations where there appears to be victory when, in fact, it is a compromise which may slowly erode the believer's separation and practical holiness. Compromise in the conflict with the world, the flesh and the devil is, in fact, latent defeat.

Verses 14-18: Joseph's Complaint

The tribe of Joseph had received their inheritance as a single lot (16.1-4), and then had it divided into two areas, one for Ephraim and the other for Manasseh (16.5-17.13). The tribe of Joseph united in their complaint to Joshua. Their complaint was unlike the conversations involving Caleb and the daughters of Zelophehad which were based upon existing promises that the Lord had made. Joseph was aggrieved at what he had received, not because he had been promised something more or different, but because the lot did not reflect his own estimation of his place within the nation. Two statements made by Joseph drew a response from Joshua.

"Why hast thou given me but one lot and one portion to inherit, seeing

I am a great people, forasmuch as the Lord hath blessed me hitherto?" (v.14).

The complaint was based on the large number of people in the tribe, which they attributed to the blessing of the Lord to that point in time: "I am a numerous people, since hitherto the Lord has blessed me" (RSV). When the figures given in Numbers 26 are considered, it is evident that there was no true foundation to their complaint: "Manasseh...fifty and two thousand and seven hundred; Ephraim...thirty and two thousand and five hundred" (Num 26.34,37), compared with Judah, Issachar, or Dan: "Judah...threescore and sixteen thousand and five hundred; Issachar...threescore and four thousand and three hundred; Dan...threescore and four thousand and four hundred" (Num 26.22, 25, 42-43). Only half of the tribe of Manasseh settled on the west of the Jordan, therefore the tribe of Joseph was less numerous than Judah, Dan, or Issachar.

What the tribe of Joseph did possess were pride and arrogance. They wanted more, even though they had not fully possessed what they had received. If they had felt that their lot was too small, they ought to have made more of a sustained effort to occupy the full extent of that territory. It is perhaps more likely that space was not the issue. Their position as the sons of Joseph was perhaps not being given the full recognition that they felt it deserved.

"And Joshua answered them, If thou be a great people, then get thee up to the wood country, and cut down for thyself there in the land of the Perizzites and of the giants, if mount Ephraim be too narrow for thee" (v.15). The answer of Joshua was straight to the point. If they felt restricted, they had the option of doing something about it themselves by clearing out land for habitation. Joshua directed them to the land of the Perizzites and giants. Since they were so great a people they should have no difficulty obtaining and clearing the land, even if it belonged to the war-like Perizzites and giants. In sporting phraseology, he put the ball back into their court.

Joshua's psychology in dealing with Joseph was effective. By giving them permission to extend their lot, he provided them with the means and opportunity of solving their own complaint. In assembly life it is easy to complain. It can be about dissatisfaction with the level of recognition or responsibility. It may be complaints about decisions made by elders, a lack of gospel activity, or the standard of Bible teaching. One way of dealing with such complaints is to adopt the approach of Joshua in this instance and challenge the complainer to provide an answer to the situation, and, in certain circumstances, providing the means and opportunity to do so.

"And the children of Joseph said, The hill is not enough for us: and all the Canaanites that dwell in the land of the valley have chariots of iron, both they who are of Beth-shean and her towns, and they who are of the valley of Jezreel" (v.16). The response of Joseph was pathetic. Here was a tribe whose people had a high opinion of themselves and claimed that the blessing of the Lord had made them great, yet they were afraid of the

Canaanites. Instead of taking on the challenge of Joshua and looking to the Lord for His help to extend their territory, they started to make excuses. The impression gained from their conversation with Joshua is that they were a negative people.

The first reason for their rejection of Joshua's answer was that the hill country was still insufficient for their needs. They added another aspect to their complaint about the lot given to them. The northern portion of their lot around the Jezreel valley and Beth-shean was, in their view, unreasonably dangerous for them, since it was occupied by Canaanites with military superiority represented by their chariots of iron.

Initially they did not like the lot because it was too small. When they were given an opportunity to extend it, they rejected the idea and then, suddenly, the might of the occupying Caananites was a problem. Evidently Joseph did not want to engage in conflict, either to occupy the lot or extend it. They demonstrated a lack of faith and a poor recollection of how they had come to be in possession of the land in the first place. They had become a whingeing, negative problem for Joshua. It is a sad fact of assembly life that some believers become malcontents. They are not happy, whatever the position within the assembly: not happy when they are not asked to do something and then not happy when they are, complaining about the lack of interest shown in them and then objecting to the intervention of elders. The assembly can work with them extensively to solve one problem and then another issue arises, sometimes before the first has been resolved. This is evidence of a self-centred attitude which would rather focus on perceived injustices rather than on the blessings and promises of the Lord.

"And Joshua spake unto the house of Joseph, even to Ephraim and to Manasseh, saying, Thou art a great people, and hast great power: thou shalt not have one lot only. But the mountain shall be thine; for it is a wood, and thou shalt cut it down: and the outgoings of it shall be thine: for thou shalt drive out the Canaanites, though they have iron chariots, and though they be strong" (vv.17-18). Joshua responded again with a straight answer. He did not pander to them. His answer could be paraphrased: "You have the capability, just get on with it !". If they chose to, they would be able to extend their land into the plains where they had the strength to drive out the Canaanites. It was up to them.

What a lesson for all believers to learn. God will not do for the believer what He has equipped him to do for himself. There was no easy answer for the tribe of Joseph, no shortcut. If they wanted more land, they should take it. If they wanted victory, they must needs fight. It is interesting that there is no more mention of the extension of the lot and no account of any campaign by Joseph to occupy land beyond their original lot. It would seem that when faced with a solution to their complaint which meant effort and courage on their part, they were no longer interested. It is a shame that such character marked the tribe which bore the name of Joseph.

JOSHUA 18

Verses 1-10: Introduction to the Remaining Seven Tribes

The short and uniform accounts of the division of the land to the remaining seven tribes are in contrast to the long and diverse descriptions given to the portions of land which Judah, Ephraim and Manasseh received; this is a reflection of the standing which each of these tribes had within the nation. Judah and Joseph (in particular Ephraim) quickly became the dominant tribes in the south and north of the land, to the extent that upon the partition of the nation into southern and northern kingdoms, they would be known as Judah and Ephraim on many occasions.

Gilgal to Shiloh (vv.1-2)

"And the whole congregation of the children of Israel assembled together at Shiloh" (v.1). Since the crossing of the Jordan, Israel had encamped at Gilgal. It was a place of great significance with the presence of the memorial of twelve stones being a simple, yet vivid, reminder of the miraculous crossing of the Jordan and the commencement of their campaigns of conquest. It must have been a solemn day when the congregation of the children of Israel moved from Gilgal to Shiloh. Although the camp of Israel had been at Gilgal over a period of approximately seven years, campaigns of conquest had periodically taken the fighting strength of the nation away (11.18), but their base of operations remained at Gilgal; this can be seen by their presence there following the various campaigns (9.6; 10.6,15,43; 14.6). The move from Gilgal to Shiloh involved the whole congregation and resulted in the establishment of a new location for the tabernacle, which was the focal point of the nation.

Shiloh (7887) means "place of rest" and the children of Israel "set up the tabernacle of the congregation there. And the land was subdued before them" (v.1). With the majority of the land under their control, it was appropriate that the dwelling place of the Lord be moved to a place, the name of which signified conditions which ought to have prevailed thereafter, "until Shiloh come; and unto him shall the gathering of the people be" (Gen 49.10). The ark of the covenant remained in this location for over 300 years until it was lost to the Philistines in the days of Eli (1 Sam 4.11). When the ark was removed, Shiloh lost its significance and entered into a period of decline, which culminated in its destruction (Ps 78.60-61; Jer 7.12-14; 26.6). The symbolism ought not to be overlooked. Shiloh, as a place, was nothing in itself. It was the presence of the Lord that gave the place significance. This is true of any dwelling place of the Lord. The temple became an empty shell of a building in spiritual terms when the glory of the Lord departed (Ezek 11.23), and a local assembly in the New Testament context can also become an empty place spiritually when the presence of the Lord is removed (Rev 2.5).

A. W. Pink takes the view that the move from Gilgal to Shiloh was "dictated by what the flesh terms prudential considerations – their own convenience". He cites the lack of recorded instructions from the Lord, the failure among the tribes to fully possess the land, and the title given to the tabernacle as the "tabernacle of the congregation", rather than the "house of the Lord" (6.24), or Lord's tabernacle" (22.19). However, there are significant indicators within the passage which point to the involvement of the Lord in the move from Gilgal to Shiloh: the presence of the tabernacle there (18.1; 19.51), without censure from the Lord; the presence of the Lord (18.6,8,10; 19.51), and the effective use of the lot, as a means of determining the mind of the Lord (18.6,10-11; 19.1,10,17,24,32,40,51). Israel had entered into the land which should have been the place of their promised rest, with the dwelling place of the Lord in the land situated at a location bearing a name which reflected this. He had stated that He would choose the place where His name would dwell (Deut 12.11). It was the subsequent sin of the people which meant that peace no longer marked the nation and, as a result, the Lord removed His presence from the place that symbolised rest.

"And there remained among the children of Israel seven tribes, which had not yet received their inheritance" (v.2). The business of dividing the land amongst the tribes was unfinished and, despite the move to Shiloh or, perhaps, as a result of that move, remained so for an undisclosed period of time. There is no indication of time within the passage, but the situation that prevailed moved Joshua to rebuke the tribes for their indolence. "Various causes led to a long delay in resuming it. The satisfaction of the people with their change to so pleasant and fertile a district, their preference of a nomad life, a love of ease, and reluctance to renew the war, seem to have made them indifferent to the possession of a settled inheritance. But Joshua was too much alive to the duty laid on him by the Lord to let matters continue in that state" (Jamieson, Fausset and Brown).

Rebuke (v.3)

"And Joshua said unto the children of Israel, How long are ye slack to go to possess the land, which the Lord God of your fathers hath given you?". Joshua seems a little harsh to rebuke the tribes for slackness in possession, when they had not been informed of the land which they had to possess. However, the rebuke which he gave them does indicate a lack of desire on their part to possess their inheritance. He did not charge them with failing to drive out the inhabitants of specific areas of the land. They were in a different situation from Judah, Ephraim and Manasseh who had settled into a compromise with the inhabitants of the land. The remaining seven tribes had shown no willingness even to commence the process of obtaining their inheritance. This was a more elementary problem.

Dwelling at Shiloh would have been a pleasant experience for the seven tribes. They were together and did not have the difficulties of possessing the territory of their foes or of transporting their people to new, and perhaps difficult, parts of the land. "The countries that remained to be divided lay at a distance, and some parts of them in the hands of the Canaanites. If they go to take possession of them, the cities must be rebuilt or repaired, they must drive their flocks and herds a great way, and carry their wives and children to strange places, and this will not be done without care and pains, and breaking through some hardships" (Matthew Henry).

It has already been the subject of comment that the lots given to Judah, Ephraim and Manasseh were not fully occupied by them. In each account there is an emphasis upon one particular aspect of their failure. Judah could not and Ephraim would not. As for Manasseh, they faced a foe displaying a determination which they themselves lacked. The seven tribes displayed indolence resulting in a failure to commence the process in the first place. The apostle Paul encountered the same attitude when he wrote to the assembly at Corinth. He upbraided them for their conduct and informed them that they had prematurely entered into rest when, in fact, they should have been involved in conflict: "Now ye are full, now ye are rich, ye have reigned as kings without us: and I would to God ye did reign, that we also might reign with you" (1 Cor 4.8).

Some believers wish to emulate the two and a half tribes that settled on the wrong side of the Jordan. They desire to go in for the things of the world whilst continuing to maintain some loose connection with the Lord's people. Others come up against an obstacle or an enemy, which they cannot overcome, and come to accept failure and live with it. Some believers feel that compromise is the best way forward and exploit what should be absent from their lives in order to enhance their quality of life. The tribes who took possession of their inheritance thus far in the narrative have provided illustrations of these problems. The remaining seven tribes point to a tendency among some Christians to be content with a shallow, superficial life of spiritual neutrality. They do not wish to go into the world and live a sinful life, yet display no desire to go in for the things of the Lord. Such inertia is displeasing to the Lord and carries great risk to a believer's spiritual well-being. It is the equivalent to standing still in no-man's-land.

Joshua's instructions (vv.4-7)

In order for the land to be divided among the remaining seven tribes, Joshua instructed them to carry out a survey of the land: "Give out from among you three men for each tribe: and I will send them, and they shall rise, and go through the land, and describe it according to the inheritance of them; and they shall come again to me" (v.4). In any service for the Lord there is a balance between the servant's responsibility to take action and the Lord's sovereignty in the commissioning and controlling of the servant. Thus the tribes were given the responsibility of choosing the men to conduct the survey, but these men derived their authority for their mission from Joshua, and were instructed to report to him when they returned. They were not only sent by Joshua but were accountable to him for their service. Paul taught Timothy that it was his responsibility to "stir up the gift of God which is in thee" (2 Tim 1.6). He also reminded the Corinthians that the spiritual gifts which they had been given to enable them to serve the Lord, were to be used under the control of the Lord (1 Cor 12.5-6).

The Lord's answer to the tribes' indolence was activity. The solution to this problem was not a period of contemplation or prayer. The time for that was past and it required action on their part to move the process forward. In the service of the Lord there are times when prayer and waiting upon Him are necessary and then there are other times when hard work has to be undertaken. The disciples experienced such a variety of experiences when they walked with the Lord Jesus. He often prayed and sought times of isolation from the crowds, but not to the detriment of His work which was marked by diligent activity. Laziness has no place in the service of the Lord, not even when disguised by piety.

The task given to the men from each tribe was specific. They were to travel throughout the land and "describe" (3789) it in the context of it being the inheritance of the tribes. The word employed has the meaning of "writing down" and indicates that they were to provide Joshua with a written record of the land, with particular emphasis upon the cities (v.9). In this section of the chapter the instruction to "describe" is recorded twice (vv.4,6), emphasising the importance of the written record for later generations.

"And they shall divide it into seven parts: Judah shall abide in their coast on the south, and the house of Joseph shall abide in their coasts on the north. Ye shall therefore describe the land into seven parts, and bring the description hither to me, that I may cast lots for you here before the Lord our God" (vv.5-6). The second part of the task involved the division of the inheritance into seven portions. This did not go as far as the assignation of portions to the various tribes, since that remained in the hand of the Lord through the use of the lot. The men were reminded that areas of the land had already been distributed to Judah and the house of Joseph and therefore would not form part of the survey.

It is further evidence of the God's grace that He allowed men from each tribe to be involved in determining their inheritance. Joshua and Caleb had already surveyed the land a long time ago, but now the tribes had their own representatives travel throughout the land. This would also serve to avoid any accusations of bias against Joshua in the distribution of the land. He brought before the Lord their description of the land and, through the lot, the Lord assigned portions to each of the remaining seven tribes. There could be no argument against Joshua; if any complaint was to be made they could only look to their representatives, whom they had chosen, or even to the Lord who had used the lot to communicate His mind.

Fourteen land grants were made in total and all are recorded here. Judah, the house of Joseph (v.5), the seven remaining tribes (v.6), the Levites (v.7), and the trans-Jordan tribes of Gad, Reuben, and half of Manasseh (v.7).

It has already been noted that the tribe of Levi had no inheritance of land within Canaan (13.14). Their inheritance was described as "the sacrifices of the Lord God of Israel made by fire" (13.14), and "the Lord God of Israel" (13.33). A third description is now given as "the priesthood of the Lord" (v.7). The Levites had no land to cultivate, but had their portion from the sacrifices brought to the Lord. The source of their sustenance was not the people who gave the sacrifices but rather the Lord to whom the sacrifices had been offered. In addition it can be seen that although their inheritance was given to them in the same way that the land was given to the other tribes, Levi had to work as the priesthood of the Lord in order to gain any benefit from their inheritance. In this they did not differ from the other tribes who had to occupy and cultivate the land they had been given in order to gain any profit from it.

Execution of Joshua's commands (vv.8-9)

"And the men arose, and went away: and Joshua charged them that went to describe the land, saying, Go and walk through the land, and describe it, and come again to me, that I may here cast lots for you before the Lord in Shiloh. And the men went and passed through the land, and described it by cities into seven parts in a book, and came again to Joshua to the host at Shiloh". The details of the execution of Joshua's command does not add much to the previous verses. The messengers made a written record of the land by cities, which does indicate that the populated areas were of most interest and formed the content of the written account passed to Joshua. This makes sense since the survey was for the purpose of dividing the land for habitation and not for wildlife or conservation.

Completion of the division of the land (v.10)

"And Joshua cast lots for them in Shiloh before the Lord: and there Joshua divided the land unto the children of Israel according to their divisions". With the details of the whole land now recorded, Joshua obtained direction from the Lord for dividing it by casting lots. In so doing he finished the task of assigning the inheritance of every tribe of Israel. A description of the territory apportioned to each of the seven tribes makes up the narrative until the end of ch.19. Thereafter the records of the cities of refuge and the Levitical cities are provided which conclude the detailed land grants and form the title deeds to the inheritance of Israel.

Verses 11-28: Benjamin's Inheritance

Benjamin was the youngest of Jacob's children and had occupied a special place in his affections. With Joseph, he was Rachel's son, and it was as a result of his birth that Rachel had died. The inheritance given to Benjamin had strategic significance within the land in light of the tensions that would develop between the tribes and these were known to the Lord.

Out of the seven tribes who received their inheritance at Shiloh, Benjamin has eighteen verses given to its description, in contrast to an average of eight verses for each of the other six tribes. Calvin comments that "In the lot of Benjamin nothing occurs particularly deserving of notice, unless that a small tribe takes precedence of the others. I admit, indeed, that its limits were narrowed in proportion to the fewness of its numbers, because it obtained only twenty-six cities; but still an honour was bestowed upon it in the mere circumstance of its receiving its inheritance before more distinguished tribes".

Location of the inheritance (v.11)

"And the lot of the tribe of the children of Benjamin came up according to their families: and the coast of their lot came forth between the children of Judah and the children of Joseph". Moses had prophesied concerning Benjamin: "The beloved of the Lord shall dwell in safety by him; and the Lord shall cover him all the day long, and he shall dwell between his shoulders" (Deut 33.12). With Judah on their southern boundary, and Joseph (Ephraim) to the north, their inheritance lay between the two most powerful tribes within the land. They should have been able to rely on the protection of these two tribes in times of crisis. However, a brief look at the subsequent history of the nation (Judg 20.12-14; 2 Sam 2.15-16; 1 Chr 8.40) demonstrates that Benjamin was a warlike tribe displaying the character of which Jacob had spoken: "Benjamin shall ravin as a wolf: in the morning he shall devour the prey, and at night he shall divide the spoil" (Gen 49.27). As a tribe they did not enjoy a peaceful existence. In subsequent years they formed a close alliance with Judah and even shared in the possession of Mount Zion. Originally it had been part of Benjamin's territory, but later it was given to Judah. In the north there was bound to be empathy between Joseph and Benjamin since they were both sons of Jacob and Rachel. The location of Benjamin between Joseph and Judah should have had significance for the unity of the nation. A shared affection for Benjamin on the part of Joseph and Judah had been the catalyst for reconciliation among the sons of Jacob in Egypt. Now Benjamin provided a link between their descendants: two powerful, rival tribes. This ought to have played a major role in binding the nation together, but sadly this was not the case.

Northern boundary (vv.12-13)

"And their border on the north side was from Jordan; and the border went up to the side of Jericho on the north side, and went up through the mountains westward; and the goings out thereof were at the wilderness of Beth-aven. And the border went over from thence toward Luz, to the side of Luz, which is Bethel, southward; and the border descended to Ataroth-adar, near the hill that lieth on the south side of the nether Beth-horon". Little needs to be said about the northern boundary of Benjamin's inheritance because it was the same boundary line that formed part of the southern border of Joseph and is described earlier (16.1-5).

Western boundary (v.14)

The geography of Benjamin's inheritance was such that the western boundary was short, whereas the northern and southern boundaries were comparatively long, thus giving a short north to south distance within their territory but a longer west to east aspect. "And the border was drawn thence, and compassed the corner of the sea southward, from the hill that lieth before Beth-horon southward; and the goings out thereof were at Kirjath-baal, which is Kirjath-jearim, a city of the children of Judah: this was the west quarter".

With the notable exception of Josephus, it is generally accepted that the western border of Benjamin is the eastern boundary of Dan and does not reach to the Mediterranean Sea. The problem occurs with the expression, "the corner of the sea southward". Matthew Henry raises this issue: "The western border is said to compass the corner of the sea southward, whereas no part of the lot of this tribe came near to the great sea. Bishop Patrick thinks the meaning is that it ran along in a parallel line to the great sea, though at a distance. Dr. Fuller suggests that since it is not called the great sea, but only the sea, which often signifies any lake or mere, it may be meant of the pool of Gibeon, which may be called a corner or canton of the sea; it is called the great waters of Gibeon (Jer 41.12), and it is compassed by the western border of this tribe".

The translation given to the verse by the NKJV is interesting: "Then the border extended around the west side to the south, from the hill that lies before Beth Horon southward; and it ended at Kirjath Baal (which is Kirjath Jearim), a city of the children of Judah. This was the west side". The difference between the NKJV and the AV is that the word "sea" (3220) and "west" (3220) in the AV is actually the same original Hebrew word which is translated as "west" on both occasions in the NKJV, thus removing the problem of trying to place Benjamin on the coast of the Mediterranean Sea.

Southern boundary (vv.15-19)

The southern boundary is given the most detailed description and coincides with the northern boundary line of Judah's territory as described in 15.5-9. The only significant difference is that the description traces the border from west to east whereas Judah's runs from east to west.

"And the south quarter was from the end of Kirjath-jearim, and the border went out on the west, and went out to the well of waters of Nephtoah. And the border came down to the end of the mountain that lieth before the valley of the son of Hinnom, and which is in the valley of the giants on the north, and descended to the valley of Hinnom, to the side of Jebusi on the south, and descended to En-rogel, and was drawn from the north, and went forth to En-shemesh, and went forth toward Geliloth, which is over against the going up of Adummim, and descended to the stone of Bohan the son of Reuben, and passed along toward the side over against Arabah northward, and went down unto Arabah: and the border passed along to the side of Beth-hoglah northward: and the outgoings of the border were at the north bay of the salt sea at the south end of Jordan: this was the south coast". The one notable difference between the border description of Judah and Benjamin is the mention of Gilgal (15.7) in Judah, and Geliloth (v.17) in Benjamin. It would appear that the names relate to the same place with Geliloth (1553) meaning circuits or districts. This may have been an alternative name for Gilgal or could refer to the area around Gilgal.

Eastern boundary (v.20)

There is no problem in identifying the eastern boundary of Benjamin's inheritance, it was the River Jordan: "And Jordan was the border of it on the east side".

Eastern cities (vv.21-24)

"Now the cities of the tribe of the children of Benjamin according to their families were Jericho, and Beth-hoglah, and the valley of Keziz, and Beth-arabah, and Zemaraim, and Bethel, and Avim, and Parah, and Ophrah, and Chephar-haammonai, and Ophni, and Gaba; twelve cities with their villages". Jericho was included in the list of cities, for, although the curse placed upon it meant that it should never be rebuilt with walls and gates, it could exist without the means for its own protection and therefore be a place of habitation, but not fortification.

Some of the cities mentioned here also appear in boundary descriptions relating to other tribes, e.g. Jericho (v.21) on the Ephraimite border (16.1,7; 18.12); Beth-hoglah (v.21) on the Judahite border (15.6; 18.19); Bethel (v.22) on the border with Ephraim (16.1-2; 18.13). Beth-arabah is also mentioned in Judah's city list but is assigned to Benjamin for reasons which are not revealed in Scripture. This could have been as an adjustment owing to the later assignation of cities to Benjamin after Judah had received its inheritance earlier at Gilgal.

Western cities (vv.25-28)

The second group consists of fourteen cities which lay within the western area of Benjamin's inheritance: "Gibeon, and Ramah, and Beeroth, and Mizpeh, and Chephirah, and Mozah, and Rekem, and Irpeel, and Taralah, and Zelah, Eleph, and Jebusi (which is Jerusalem), Gibeath, and Kirjath: fourteen cities with their villages".

Thus the inheritance given to Benjamin is concluded. It was a small tribe, even being referred to as "little Benjamin" (Ps 68.27), yet it played a pivotal role in shaping the history of the nation.

JOSHUA 19

Verses 1-9: Simeon's Inheritance

The impact of prophecy upon the division of the land has already been noted (18.11). When Jacob spoke to his sons he linked Simeon and Levi together and, amongst other things, said, "I will divide them in Jacob, and scatter them in Israel" (Gen 49.7). The reason for this harsh prophecy lay in their conduct toward the city of Shechem after their sister Dinah had been defiled. Their father strongly disapproved of their deceit and violence. When the land was divided Simeon and Levi were the only tribes to receive an inheritance that did not include the grant of land. Levi's inheritance was given a threefold description (13.14,33; 18.7) that elevated them to a unique place of privilege among the tribes. The children of Levi were recovered to a sphere of honour and blessing as a result of their response in the matter of the golden calf (Ex 32.27-29). There was no such blessing for the tribe of Simeon which ceased to be closely linked with their brother, following Levi's elevation to the priesthood. Two brothers who had a bad start and were the subject of censure from their father had very different futures. The key issue was their commitment to the Lord, as demonstrated by Levi's conduct at Mount Sinai. Levi was recovered, whereas Simeon was not. Brothers are often seen in this way in Scripture from Cain and Abel, Jacob and Esau, Isaac and Ishmael down to the parable of the lost son.

Location of the inheritance (v.1)

Jacob's prophecy concerning Simeon can be seen in the character of their inheritance which consisted of cities located within the borders of Judah: "And the second lot came forth to Simeon, even for the tribe of the children of Simeon according to their families: and their inheritance was within the inheritance of the children of Judah". They had no land; therefore they had no borders nor territorial integrity.

Cities (vv.2-8)

The cities are divided into groups by reference to villages: "And they had in their inheritance Beer-sheba, or Sheba, and Moladah, and Hazar-shual, and Balah, and Azem, and Eltolad, and Bethul, and Hormah, and Ziklag, and Beth-marcaboth, and Hazar-susah, and Beth-lebaoth, and Sharuhen; thirteen cities and their villages" (vv.2-6). All of these cities are mentioned in Judah's city list and are placed within the south-land (15.21-32).

"Ain, Remmon, and Ether, and Ashan; four cities and their villages" (v.7). The first two cities within this group also appear in the south-land portion of Judah's city list. Ether and Ashan appear in the section of Judah's city list dealing with the lowland (15.42).

"And all the villages that were round about these cities to Baalath-beer,

Ramath of the south" (v.8). Commentators are divided as to whether Baalath-beer and Ramah of the south are two distinct places or are the description of one place. Keil & Delitzsch take the view that the names ought to be rendered as "Baalath-beer, the Ramah of the south".

Explanatory verse (v.9)

There is a simple reason for Simeon receiving cities within Judah's territory: "The part of the children of Judah was too much for them: therefore the children of Simeon had their inheritance within the inheritance of them". For reasons which are not revealed, Judah had found that their inheritance was too much for them to occupy and therefore more than they required. It is apt that the tribe from which the Lord Jesus would come could accommodate the needs of Simeon and their landless state. They had an abundance within their inheritance that overflowed to meet the needs of others.

Verses 10-16: Zebulun's Inheritance

The descriptions of the portions divided to the remaining five tribes are succinct and contain references to cities and land features whose whereabouts are unknown. Therefore, the precise location of the land given to these tribes is difficult to determine. It is interesting that the information recorded is sufficient to see the fulfilment of Old Testament prophecies given about the tribes through Jacob and Moses.

Jacob said of Zebulun, his sixth and youngest son by Leah, "Zebulun shall dwell at the haven of the sea; and he shall be for an haven of ships; and his border shall be unto Zidon" (Gen 49.13). Moses said, "Rejoice, Zebulun, in thy going out; and, Issachar, in thy tents. They shall call the people unto the mountain; there they shall offer sacrifices of righteousness: for they shall suck of the abundance of the seas, and of treasures hid in the sand" (Deut 33.18-19). Not much is said of Zebulun throughout Scripture, but what is said is of the greatest significance since it relates to the Lord Jesus Christ. When He left Nazareth, following the imprisonment of John the Baptist, "he came and dwelt in Capernaum, which is upon the sea coast, in the borders of Zabulon and Nephthalim: that it might be fulfilled which was spoken by Esaias the prophet, saying, the land of Zabulon, and the land of Nephthalim, by the way of the sea, beyond Jordan, Galilee of the Gentiles; the people which sat in darkness saw great light; and to them which sat in the region and shadow of death light is sprung up" (Mt 4.13-16).

"The boundaries of the possession assigned to them extended from the Lake of Chinnereth (Sea of Galilee) on the east, to the Mediterranean on the west. Although they do not seem at first to have touched on the western shore – a part of Manasseh running north into Asher (17.10) – they afterwards did" (Jamieson, Fausset and Brown). They were placed between the plain of Jezreel and the mountains of Naphtali and, according to Keil &

Delitzsch, "bounded by Asher on the west and north-west (19.27), by Naphtali on the north and north-east (19.34), and by Issachar on the south-east and south". Evidently from Matthew 4.13 the inheritance of Zebulun did ultimately extend to the sea in fulfilment of the Old Testament prophecies regarding their location and character as a trading tribe.

Southern boundary (vv.10-12)

"The border of their inheritance was unto Sarid: and their border went up toward the sea, and Maralah, and reached to Dabbasheth, and reached to the river that is before Jokneam; and turned from Sarid eastward toward the sunrising unto the border of Chisloth-tabor, and then goeth out to Daberath, and goeth up to Japhia" (vv.10-12). The details of the southern boundary commences at Sarid, which appears to be a central location, and proceeds westwards to the river, or ravine, near Jokneam, a city associated with Mount Carmel (12.22) and assigned to the Levitical family of Merari (21.34). Thereafter the boundary is traced from Sarid eastward as far as Japhia, which is a place of uncertain location.

Eastern boundary (v.13)

"And from thence passeth on along on the east to Gittah-hepher, to Ittah-kazin, and goeth out to Remmon-methoar to Neah" (v.13). The hometown of the prophet Jonah was Gittah-hepher, rendered as Gath-hepher (2 Kings 14.25), and it was one of the two notable landmarks on the eastern boundary. Most translations render Remmon-methoar as "Rimmon" and relate it to another city given to the Levitical family of Merari (1 Chr 6.77).

Northern boundary (v.14)

"And the border compasseth it on the north side to Hannathon: and the outgoings thereof are in the valley of Jiphthah-el" (v.14). The boundary line which formed the northern border is not readily identified since Hannathon has never been located and, like many of the place names within the description of Zebulun's inheritance, does not occur again in Scripture. Keil & Delitzsch speculate that it is Cana of Galilee, the home of Nathanael (Jn 21.2). Jiphthah-el was the point where the territory of Zebulun and Asher touched.

Cities (vv.15-16)

"And Kattath, and Nahallal, and Shimron, and Idalah, and Bethlehem: twelve cities with their villages" (v.16). From the twelve cities that are recorded as belonging to Zebulun, only five are named. Two of the five are not mentioned again in Scripture, Kattath and Idalah,s and one – Nahallal – occurs once again in a list of Levitical cities (21.35). It may appear that it was a mistake to say that there were twelve cities when only five names are provided; it is evident that Zebulun was granted other cities which brought the total to twelve: "And unto the families of the children of Merari, the rest of the Levites, out of the tribe of Zebulun, Jokneam with her suburbs, and Kartah with her suburbs" (21.34). This Bethlehem is not the place where the Lord Jesus was born; that was precisely identified in prophecy as Bethlehem Ephratah (Mic 5.2). The Bethlehem that lay within Zebulun was the place where Ibzan the judge was buried (Judg 12.8-10).

Verses 17-23: Issachar's Inheritance

Located in the region of Galilee, Issachar was north of Manasseh, east and south of Zebulun and south of Naphtali. The precise location of its territory is not clear since the inheritance is described primarily by the use of city names without reference to a complete boundary line.

"The thirteen cities appear to be arranged in four groups, based on the Masoretic accents (i.e. verse divisions)" (*The New American Commentary*, David M. Howard Jnr.). The cities do not appear to have significance within Scripture beyond their mention as belonging to Isaachar. Some of their names do not appear again and two are mentioned only within the lists of cities given to the Levites (21.28-29).

West (vv.17-19)

"And their border was toward Jezreel, and Chesulloth, and Shunem" (v.18). Jezreel was a fertile plain and gave its name to the residence of many kings of Israel in years to come (1 Kings 18.45; 2 Kings 9.30). It should be distinguished from the town in Judah (15.56) from which Ahinoam, one of David's wives, very probably came (1 Sam 27.3).

"And Hapharaim, and Shion, and Anaharath" (v.19).

These cities are thought by commentators to have been in the western portion of Issachar, but lying in a north – south line slightly to the east of the first group.

North (v.20)

"And Rabbith, and Kishion, and Abez" (v.20).

East (v.21)

"And Remeth, and En-gannim, and En-haddah, and Beth-pazzez" (v.21).

Boundary Description (vv.22-23)

The boundaries of Issachar are not extensively described with three cities of uncertain location mentioned providing a limited northern boundary. The eastern border was the River Jordan and the western boundary is not specified. The southern boundary of Issachar was the eastern portion of Manasseh's northern boundary (17.10).

"The coast reacheth to Tabor, and Shahazimah, and Beth-shemesh; and the outgoings of their border were at Jordan: sixteen cities with their villages" (v.22). Tabor was a city close to the mountain which bore the same name (1 Chr 6.77), Shahazimah is not mentioned anywhere else in Scripture and Beth-shemesh is probably the city mentioned as also belonging to Naphtali (19.38).

"This is the inheritance of the tribe of the children of Issachar according to their families, the cities and their villages" (v.23).

Verses 24-31: Asher's Inheritance

The eighth son of Jacob and the second son of Zilpah, Leah's handmaid, is unremarkable in Scripture. Apart from Anna, the prophetess (Lk 2.36), no judge nor notable person arose from this tribe. The fifth lot provided them with an inheritance in the northwest consisting of a narrow strip of land with the Mediterranean Sea on the west and the lands of Zebulun and Manasseh on the east.

The description of Asher's inheritance differs from the others, consisting of a mixture of cities and boundaries with no clear delineation.

South (vv.24-27)

"Their border was Helkath, and Hali, and Beten, and Achshaph, and Alammelech, and Amad, and Misheal; and reacheth to Carmel westward, and to Shihor-libnath " (vv.25-26). The border ran first to the west from its starting point at Helkath, where it proceeded toward Mount Carmel and included the seven cities mentioned in these verses, most of which are of uncertain location and do not feature again in Scripture.

"And turneth toward the sunrising to Beth-dagon, and reacheth to Zebulun, and to the valley of Jiphthah-el toward the north side of Beth-emek, and Neiel, and goeth out to Cabul on the left hand" (v.27). From the same starting point at Helkath, the border ran eastward to Beth-dagon and then turned northward.

North (vv.28-31)

On the east side of Asher's territory, the border ran northward, parallel to the Mediterranean Sea, toward the territory of Zebulun and the valley of Jiphthah-el, again incorporating cities which are not mentioned again in Scripture and are of uncertain location: "Hebron, and Rehob, and Hammon, and Kanah, even unto great Zidon; and then the coast turneth to Ramah, and to the strong city Tyre; and the coast turneth to Hosah; and the outgoings thereof are at the sea from the coast to Achzib: Ummah also, and Aphek, and Rehob: twenty and two cities with their villages" (vv.28-30).

It is worth noting that "the language in the verses uses…a verb which indicates a 180-degree reversal in direction. Sometimes, as in vv.27 and 34, what this means is that the boundary description moves out from a fixed point in one direction and then returns to that same point to go out in the other direction. However, here in v.29a it appears to indicate that the boundary line reversed itself from its previously northward direction culminating in great Zidon (v.28) and came south to Ramah and the other cities. Then, to include the fortress of Tyre, the line would have to go out to the island city, then reverse itself to come back to Hosah" (*The New American Commentary,* David M. Howard Jnr.). The list of cities concludes with the mention of three cities on the southwest of Asher's territory in the coastal region.

Verses 32-39: Naphtali's Inheritance

Naphtali, the sixth son of Jacob, whose mother was Bilhah, Rachel's handmaid, is like Asher in that he is unremarkable and does not significantly feature in the history of the children of Israel. As a tribe they received land in the north of Canaan with Asher to the west, Zebulun and Issachar to the south and the eastern half of Manasseh to the east, beyond the Sea of Galilee and the River Jordan.

Boundary (vv.32-34)

"Their coast was from Heleph, from Allon to Zaanannim, and Adami, Nekeb, and Jabneel, unto Lakum; and the outgoings thereof were at Jordan: and then the coast turneth westward to Aznoth-tabor, and goeth out from thence to Hukkok, and reacheth to Zebulun on the south side, and reacheth to Asher on the west side, and to Judah upon Jordan toward the sunrising" (vv.33-34). The southern border is described in some detail, commencing at Heleph and running eastward to the Jordan and then commencing again at Heleph and Hukkok, which is of uncertain location but presumed to be at the western extremity of Naphtali's territory. Seven cities are named with only one of them, Zaanannim, appearing again in Scripture.

Cities (vv.35-39)

"And the fenced cities are Ziddim, Zer, and Hammath, Rakkath, and Chinnereth, and Adamah, and Ramah, and Hazor, and Kedesh, and Edrei, and Enhazor, and Iron, and Migdal-el, Horem, and Beth-anath, and Beth-shemesh; nineteen cities with their villages" (vv.35-38). It is interesting that the city list for Naphtali differs from that of the other tribes. The cities are described as "fenced" (4013); this word which only occurs on three occasions in the book of Joshua (10.20; 19.29, where it is translated "strong", and, 19.35) emphasises the fortifications of the cities.

Verses 40-48: Dan's Inheritance

Dan was the elder brother of Naphtali being the fifth son of Jacob and son of Bilhah, Rachel's maid. The blessing pronounced on him by his father was, "Dan shall judge his people" (Gen 49.16), the reference probably being to Samson, who was of the tribe of Dan. This tribe brought up the rear of the nation when journeying through the wilderness and so it is appropriate that it was the last of the tribes to receive its inheritance.

The territory given to Dan was in the south of the land, yet they are given a place among the northern tribes in the lot, since that is where they finally settled. Their south land was never fully conquered and they were pressed by the Amorites and Philistines to such an extent that they sent out five spies who discovered land in the north at the foot of Mount Hermon. This they occupied having conquered the Sidonians (Judg 18), and they settled in the renamed town of Dan, which place became synonymous with the northern extremity of the land of Israel (Judg 20.1).

The significance of their failure to settle in their territory is reflected in the lack of any stated boundaries. The territorial descriptions of the other tribes, together with the list of Dan's cities, place their territory north of Judah, west of Benjamin, south and west of Ephraim and Manasseh, with the Mediterranean Sea as their western boundary.

Cities (vv.41-46)

"And the coast of their inheritance was Zorah, and Eshtaol, and Ir-shemesh, and Shaalabbin, and Ajalon, and Jethlah, and Elon, and Thimnathah, and Ekron, and Eltekeh, and Gibbethon, and Baalath, and Jehud, and Bene-berak, and Gath-rimmon, and Me-jarkon, and Rakkon, with the border before Japho" (vv.41-46). The city list contains eighteen names, seven of which are not mentioned again in Scripture, although some of these cities may reappear with an alternative spelling, e.g. Shaalabbin may be the same city as Shaalbim (Judg 1.35).

Migration north (vv.47-48)

The circumstances, which precipitated the move northward, are described as, "the coast of the children of Dan went out too little for them" (v.47). This is translated in the RSV as, "When the territory of the Danites was lost to them". The inability of the Danites to drive out the Amorites from several of their towns (Judg 1.34-35) had the effect of making their territory too small for them, resulting in their move into the northern area of the land. "Therefore the children of Dan went up to fight against Leshem, and took it, and smote it with the edge of the sword, and possessed it, and dwelt therein, and called Leshem, Dan, after the name of Dan their father" (v.47). Unfortunately, the history of their conquest of Leshem and their subsequent settlement in that area is a sad tale of idolatry involving Micah's image (Judg 18.27-31).

The experience of Dan is yet another cautionary tale involving the failure of the people of God to possess the land given as an inheritance. On this occasion the people found it too hard and responded by moving to another location. The "grass seemed greener" to the north of the land and indeed the conquest and occupation was easier there than in the portion which they had received from the Lord. However, the movement from one location to the other brought sin in amongst them, which was a heavy price to pay for their new land.

Running away to an easier location can be a tempting prospect when the going becomes hard in the Christian pathway. Some move location in the hope that they will find the way easier, forgetting that it was their own failure that had made the way hard in the last place. Unless the root cause of the failure is addressed, it will travel with those who move. Such withdrawal on the part of the tribe of Dan brought them into spiritual decline.

Verses 49-50: Joshua's Inheritance

It was appropriate that when the land was divided among the tribes which settled on the west of the Jordan, it began with Caleb (14.6-15) and finished with Joshua. The two faithful spies had brought their good report to Moses and then had suffered thirty-eight years of wilderness conditions owing to the failure of the rest of the nation. The Lord's promise to both of them (Num 14.30) was exceeded in them receiving special portions within the land. They had been promised that among those who had turned back from the border of Canaan, they would be the only ones to enter the land. As is so often the case when considering the promises of the Lord to His people, they received much more than they had anticipated. The fulfilment of God's promises always exceed expectation. Paul often expressed this in his epistles when he employed the word "exceeding" in relation to the attributes or promises of the Lord, e.g. "Now unto him that is able to do exceeding abundantly above all that we ask or think, according to the power that worketh in us" (Eph 3.20).

"The children of Israel gave an inheritance to Joshua the son of Nun among them" (v.49). It would have been inappropriate for Joshua to have given himself an inheritance and so it fell to the children of Israel to give him his portion among them. He was the only individual in the nation to be given a city. Caleb had requested Hebron and was granted his desire, but the city of Hebron belonged to Judah and not to Caleb (15.13,54) and it became both a Levitical city (21.11,13) and a city of refuge (20.7). Joshua received a rich recompense for his faithful leadership of the people of God; to this day that has never been an easy task. Scripture recognises this special responsibility, and those fulfilling that function can look forward to a recompense from their Lord, commensurate with their responsibility. "When the chief Shepherd shall appear, ye shall receive a crown of glory that fadeth not away" (1 Pet 5.4).

"According to the word of the Lord they gave him the city which he asked, even Timnath-serah in mount Ephraim: and he built the city, and dwelt therein" (v.50). Joshua sought a city within the territory of his own tribe (Num 13.8) and was settled there until he died (24.29). The greatest man among the children of Israel waited until the whole nation had received its portion before he requested his own. His example points to the Lord Jesus who always put the things of others before his own things (Phil 2.3-4). It is the mark of true greatness in a leader that he will consider himself only when the needs of those whom he leads have been met. Joshua neither demanded nor dictated, but "asked", and received his request from a grateful nation.

Verse 51: Completion of the Land Distribution

"These are the inheritances, which Eleazar the priest, and Joshua the son of Nun, and the heads of the fathers of the tribes of the children of Israel, divided for an inheritance by lot in Shiloh before the Lord, at the door of the tabernacle of the congregation. So they made an end of dividing the country" (v.51). The process, which has been the subject of the book from the beginning of ch.14, is now brought to a conclusion. The immediate reference is to the division of the land which took place when the remaining seven tribes received their portion at Shiloh and to the main characters involved in that process. The only work left to was to name cities for the tribe of Levi and to allocate the cities of refuge.

JOSHUA 20

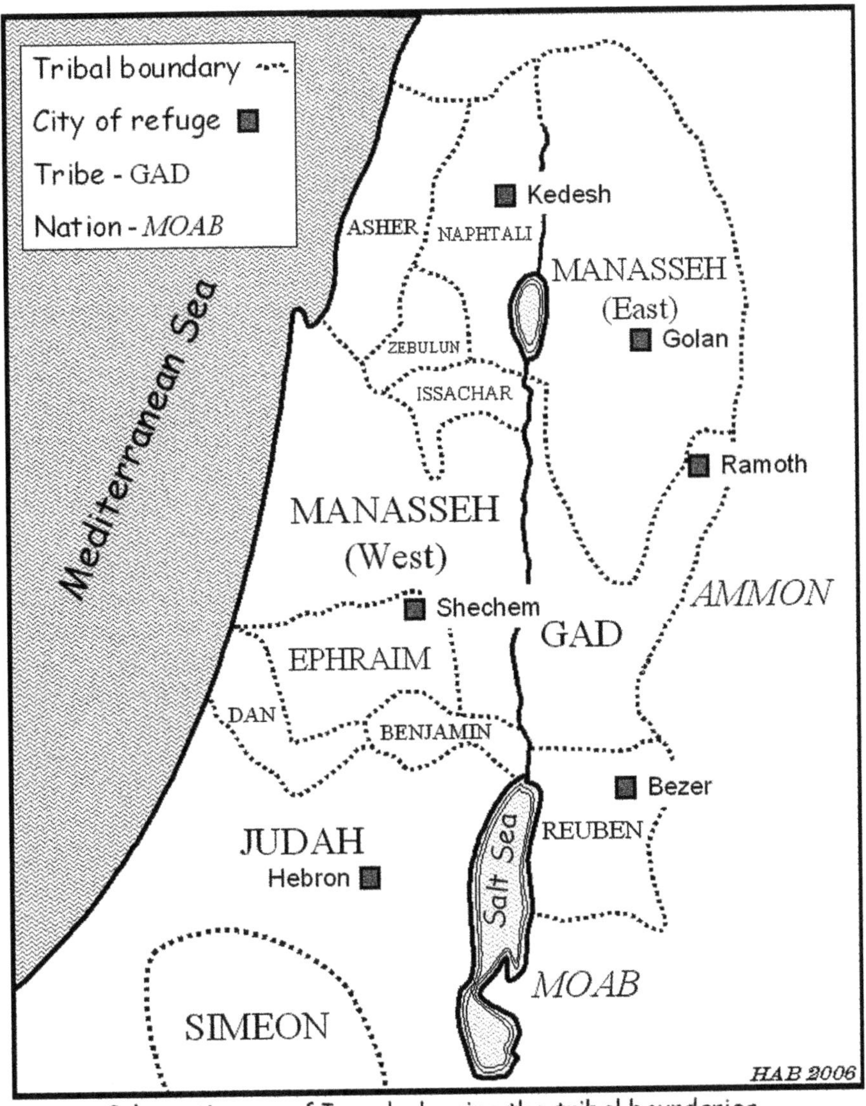

Schematic map of Israel, showing the tribal boundaries and the Cities of Refuge.

JOSHUA 20

Cities of Refuge

Historical background

The Old Testament is often under attack because of the perceived harshness of the justice system provided by God for the nation of Israel. Modern critics point to the severe penalties for what are, by today's standards, seemingly trivial offences. They take the view that a system of justice based upon the Law of the Old Testament would be primitive, unjust and inadequate compared to the sophisticated judicial systems of the modern world.

However, a close examination of the Law of the Old Testament reveals that both the criminal and civil systems were sophisticated and equitable. They incorporated concepts of justice, structures of governance, and laws, which have been the hallmarks of flourishing societies and empires throughout history. Equally, they have been abandoned or disregarded by decadent and failing governments.

One of the central issues in God's Law is the sanctity of life. Prior to the Mosaic Law, God gave precepts which were for all mankind, for all time, making this declaration following the flood: "Whoso sheddeth man's blood, by man shall his blood be shed: for in the image of God made he man" (Gen 9.6). Thus, at the beginning of the post-flood age God made clear that the penalty for murder was the death of the murderer.

When the Law was given by Moses, this precept had to be amplified and set in the context of a national legal framework which could be implemented equitably. This would take into account the issues of motive and intent, thus drawing a distinction between murder and what is now referred to as culpable homicide or manslaughter. God's declaration regarding the sanctity of life and the severity of punishment for those who took it was not repealed: "He that smiteth a man, so that he die, shall be surely put to death. And if a man lie not in wait, but God deliver him into his hand; then I will appoint thee a place whither he shall flee. But if a man come presumptuously upon his neighbour to slay him with guile; thou shalt take him from mine altar, that he may die." (Ex 21.12-14). Accidental killing was distinguished from premeditated murder and, interestingly, was attributed to the actions of God in delivering the victim into the hand of the slayer. A victim's death was never seen as an accident; it was either murder or circumstances within the providential control of God. For murder the penalty remained death. In other cases there was the provision of a place of refuge. The altar evidently served as such a refuge but it did not guarantee safety for any who fled there. The character of the crime determined whether the altar would serve as a sanctuary, and if the crime was murder then the man would be removed and put to death. The implementation of such laws can be seen when Benaiah slew Joab, who had fled to the altar for refuge (1 Kings 2.29-31).

When the children of Israel were approaching Canaan, the Lord gave further instruction concerning the places of refuge (Num 35.9-15). Six cities were to be appointed within the land with three on each side of the Jordan, thus providing refuge for the tribes which had settled on the east of the Jordan as well as those on the west. In addition, the Lord gave specific details regarding the definition of murder and provided a system whereby the accused, after entering the city of refuge, had to stand trial before the congregation. Refuge within the city could only be maintained when it was established that the death had not been the result of murder. The Lord gave further details regarding the burden of proof and the determination of motive, thus demonstrating a mature and complex approach to justice surrounding the sanctity of life. The importance of motive and the subsequent distinction between the crimes of murder and manslaughter have become an integral part of most established justice systems today.

Further information regarding the provision of refuge for any person guilty of manslaughter is contained in Deuteronomy 4.41-43 where the three cities on the east side of Jordan were selected by Moses, and in Deuteronomy 19.1-13 where Moses gave instructions regarding the three cities on the west of Jordan.

Verses 1-6: Instructions Restated

The instructions to Moses concerning the cities of refuge are restated to Joshua for their full implementation. It was the appropriate time for the cities to be designated, since all six were selected from the cities assigned to the tribe of Levi, the details of which are recorded in the following chapter.

Action required (vv.1-2)

"The Lord also spake unto Joshua, saying, Speak to the children of Israel, saying, Appoint out for you cities of refuge, whereof I spake unto you by the hand of Moses". In keeping with most of the Lord's instructions to Moses for the land, it would appear that the Lord required Joshua to remind the children of Israel to implement His words now that they were in Canaan.

General purpose of the cities of refuge (v.3)

"That the slayer that killeth any person unawares and unwittingly may flee thither: and they shall be your refuge from the avenger of blood". Two words are used to qualify the circumstances in which a person who had killed another could flee for refuge. "Unawares" (7684), is also translated as "accidentally" (NKJV) and, "inadvertently" (YLT). "Unwittingly" (1847) carries the idea of a lack of knowledge or a lack of intent. The circumstances covered by the provision of refuge included deaths caused accidentally, unintentionally, or even unknowingly. Notwithstanding the provision of refuge in such circumstances, the person who killed was guilty of taking life. He had violated the principle stated by the Lord to Noah: "Whoso sheddeth man's blood, by man shall his blood be shed: for in the image of God made he man" (Gen 9.6). The righteousness of God is seen in these verses. In his trial by the congregation, the slayer's motive was a material factor. It is important to note that the avenger of blood was not at liberty to take matters into his own hands and he had to abide by the judgment of the congregation within the city of refuge. He could not act outside the boundary of the Law or he would himself be guilty of murder. If, however, the perpetrator of the killing came out of the city of refuge, the avenger of blood had the legal right to kill him. Unrestrained vengeance does not belong to man; the Lord has reserved vengeance to himself. "For we know him that hath said, Vengeance belongeth unto me, I will recompense, saith the Lord. And again, The Lord shall judge his people" (Heb 10.30).

Judicial procedure (vv.4-6)

a) Presumption of innocence (v.4)

"And when he that doth flee unto one of those cities shall stand at the entering of the gate of the city, and shall declare his cause in the ears of the elders of that city, they shall take him into the city unto them, and give him a place, that he may dwell among them". The earlier instructions in Exodus, Numbers and Deuteronomy did not provide the detail that is presented in this verse. Moses had told the people that the congregation would decide each case with the emphasis being upon their right to return the guilty party to his home thereby giving the blood avenger the opportunity to take his life. In this section the presumption is that of innocence in relation to a murder charge, with no mention of the return of the guilty party. He was to state his case before the judicial authorities within the city of refuge, which would then provide him with a dwelling place. Someone seeking refuge was guilty of taking a life and by seeking refuge in one these cities had accepted his guilt. He was not pleading his innocence in relation to the loss of life, but was rather seeking to establish that he had not committed murder. The presumption of innocence is generally recognised as yet another central aspect of any equitable criminal justice system.

b) Pre-trial protection (v.5)

Having declared to the elders of the city that he was fleeing for refuge "because he smote his neighbour unwittingly, and hated him not beforetime", the person was to be given the protection of the city from the avenger of blood. This was not the final determination of the man's case and equates to the modern day remand procedure pending trial.

c) Trial (v.6a)

The man who had fled into a city of refuge and had been accepted by the elders of the city into their protection, remained there "until he stand before the congregation for judgment". The instructions given to Moses (Num 35.9-34) provided for a trial of the case before the congregation and also set out the criteria for qualifying for refuge. If the congregation came to the conclusion that "he thrust him suddenly without enmity, or have cast upon him any thing without laying of wait, or with any stone, wherewith a man may die, seeing him not, and cast it upon him, that he die, and was not his enemy, neither sought his harm: then the congregation shall judge between the slayer and the revenger of blood according to these judgments: and the congregation shall deliver the slayer out of the hand of the revenger of blood, and the congregation shall restore him to the city of his refuge, whither he was fled" (Num 35.22-25).

d) Duration of confinement (v.6b)

The establishment of his case before the congregation did not mean that he went free. The Law still provided for consequences following the accidental or unintentional taking of life, which are to a certain extent reflected in the modern prison systems throughout the world. Although the guilty party did not lose his life, he did lose his liberty for a defined period of time. He had to remain within the city of refuge "until the death of the high priest that shall be in those days".

e) Freedom (v.6c)

Should the high priest die within his lifetime, the guilty party was at liberty to "come unto his own city, and unto his own house, unto the city from whence he fled". There were no further consequences for him to bear and he was set free. Anyone seeking his life then, or while he was within the protection of the city of refuge, would be doing so outside the system of justice and would be guilty of murder themselves.

Verses 7-8: Cities of Refuge

"They were all Levites' cities, which put an honour upon God's tribe, making them judges in those cases wherein divine providence was so nearly concerned, and protectors to oppressed innocency. It was also a kindness to the poor refugee, that when he might not go up to the house of the Lord, nor tread his courts, yet he had the servants of God's house with him, to instruct him, and pray for him, and help to make up the want of public ordinances. If he must be confined, it shall be to a Levite city, where he may, if he will, improve his time" (Matthew Henry).

West of the Jordan (v.7)

"And they appointed Kedesh in Galilee in mount Naphtali, and Shechem in mount Ephraim, and Kirjath-arba, which is Hebron, in the mountain of Judah". Three cities were named on the west side of the Jordan. The first point of note is that each of these cities was located on high ground and is linked with a mountain. They were visible from a distance and would be easily accessible by the roads that were to be built (Deut 19.3). The division of the land into three portions and the location of a city in each of the three sections of the land enhanced the accessibility of the cities. It would appear that one was never more than a day's journey from a city which was set high and was clearly visible with a marked way towards it.

The names of the cities are also instructive as they speak of the Lord Jesus and His work. Kedesh (6943) is defined as "holy place", Shechem (7927) means "shoulder", and Hebron (2275) signifies "fellowship". The Lord Jesus is able to provide refuge for the sinner because He is holy and His holiness was undiminished throughout His sojourn in the world: "And ye know that he was manifested to take away our sins; and in him is no sin" (1 Jn 3.5). The shoulder in Scripture often speaks of strength and safety (Is 9.6; Lk 15.5). How appropriate it is for the second city to point to the safety and security that the Lord Jesus is able to provide in all His strength and capability. Hebron speaks of the fellowship into which the Lord Jesus brings the sinner. He not only saves from the consequences of sin but positively brings the sinner into a wonderful relationship with God which was impossible to obtain apart from being in Christ.

East of the Jordan (v.8)

Moses had already specified the three cities of refuge on the east of the Jordan (Deut 4.43) and the names are now repeated: "And on the other side Jordan by Jericho eastward, they assigned Bezer in the wilderness upon the plain out of the tribe of Reuben, and Ramoth in Gilead out of the tribe of Gad, and Golan in Bashan out of the tribe of Manasseh". There was one city in the territory of each tribe, giving the same accessibility to refuge as was enjoyed on the west of the Jordan.

The names of these cities also speak of the Lord Jesus Christ. Bezer (1221) means "fortress", Ramoth (7216) is defined as "heights", and Golan (1474) signifies "rejoicing", or "joy". The Lord Jesus is a stronghold against the foes that beset the believer. He elevates the sinner above the world in heavenly places (Eph 2.6) and finally, and appropriately, in Christ there is fulness of joy (Ps 16.11).

Verse 9: Summary

The summary of the provision of refuge within the land is succinctly set out with one important addition to that which has gone before: "These were the cities appointed for all the children of Israel, and for the stranger that sojourneth among them, that whosoever killeth any person at unawares might flee thither, and not die by the hand of the avenger of blood, until he stood before the congregation". Any strangers living within the land, and among the children of Israel, could avail themselves of the provision of refuge. The issues of murder and manslaughter were not peculiar to the children of Israel and were an expression of God's righteousness for all mankind. Therefore the provision of refuge was not limited to the people of God. It is also an important aspect of the picture of the Lord Jesus as the only refuge for sinners; He is a refuge for Jew and Gentile.

Illustration of the Grace of God

The provision of refuge for the manslayer is a wonderful picture of the grace of God and a tremendous illustration of the truth of the gospel. There was a safe haven available to the man who recognised that he was guilty of the death of another, but he had to flee for refuge in order to be saved from the consequences of his actions. His old life was left behind and there was a great urgency about the whole matter. In the Lord Jesus Christ, God has provided shelter from the consequences of sin. For the benefits of the safety and refuge which are offered in Christ to be enjoyed, action is required. It cannot be experienced without rejecting the old life of sin. Abandoning every other hope or plea, the manslayer fled, not worrying about his pride or any other person. The sinner who is convicted of sin should flee to Christ with no thought of his pride or concerns for anyone else until he is safe within the refuge that God has provided in His Son.

Picture of the Lord Jesus

There are other aspects of the provision of refuge, which also point to the Lord Jesus Christ and the refuge he provides for the guilty sinner:-

1. The cities were appointed by the Lord and were established before the need arose. In this they are a reminder of New Testament truth concerning the Lord Jesus. His sacrificial death, which created the basis for safety for the repentant sinner, was planned in the counsels of God before time began: "Him, being delivered by the determinate counsel and foreknowledge of God, ye have taken, and by wicked hands have crucified and slain" (Acts 2.23).
2. It has already been noted that the cities were a refuge from an avenger who would pursue and kill the guilty person. Fleeing to the city was the only hope of safety. The New Testament record is, "Neither is there salvation in any other: for there is none other name under heaven given among men, whereby we must be saved" (Acts 4.12).
3. It is interesting that the cities were positioned in locations which made them accessible to anyone (Deut 19.2-3). Refuge was nearby whether one lived in the north or south of the land, or on the east or west of Jordan. No one was excluded from the opportunity of finding refuge. Again, this is one of the great themes of the gospel: "Whosoever shall call on the name of the Lord shall be saved" (Acts 2.21).
4. Refuge was available "for the children of Israel, and for the stranger, and for the sojourner among them" (Num 35.15). Initially the preaching

of the Lord Jesus Christ as the Saviour for sinners was to the nation of Israel alone. However, the Lord Himself gave instruction: "Ye shall be witnesses unto me both in Jerusalem, and in all Judaea, and in Samaria, and unto the uttermost part of the earth" (Acts 1.8). The apostle Paul wrote, "For he is our peace, who hath made both one, and hath broken down the middle wall of partition…having abolished in his flesh the enmity, even the law of commandments contained in ordinances; for to make in himself of twain one new man, so making peace…and came and preached peace to you which were afar off, and to them that were nigh" (Eph 2.14-17).

5. The death of the high priest brought about the liberty of the guilty party. Until the high priest died there was safety in the city but no liberty. In this can be seen another aspect work of the Lord Jesus, who is the believers' Great High Priest. Before He died upon the cross, Old Testament saints were saved; however, it was not until the Lord Jesus had died that He brought true liberty in the gospel (Gal 4.1-7). There is also the thought of the removal of guilt by the death of the high priest. There was, after all, no ransom that could liberate the guilty party from the city of refuge (Num 35.32). As Greenberg states in the *The Biblical Conception of Asylum*, "the sole personage whose religious-cultic importance might endow his death with expiatory value for the people at large is the high priest". It was only on the death of the high priest, that the consequences of the man's sin were removed. The picture does point to the Lord Jesus and His once for all sacrifice at Calvary. It is contrasted to the frequently offered sacrifices of the old covenant which could never take away sins: "In those sacrifices there is a remembrance again made of sins every year. For it is not possible that the blood of bulls and of goats should take away sins…But this man, after he had offered one sacrifice for sins for ever, sat down on the right hand of God" (Heb 10.3-4,12).

JOSHUA 21

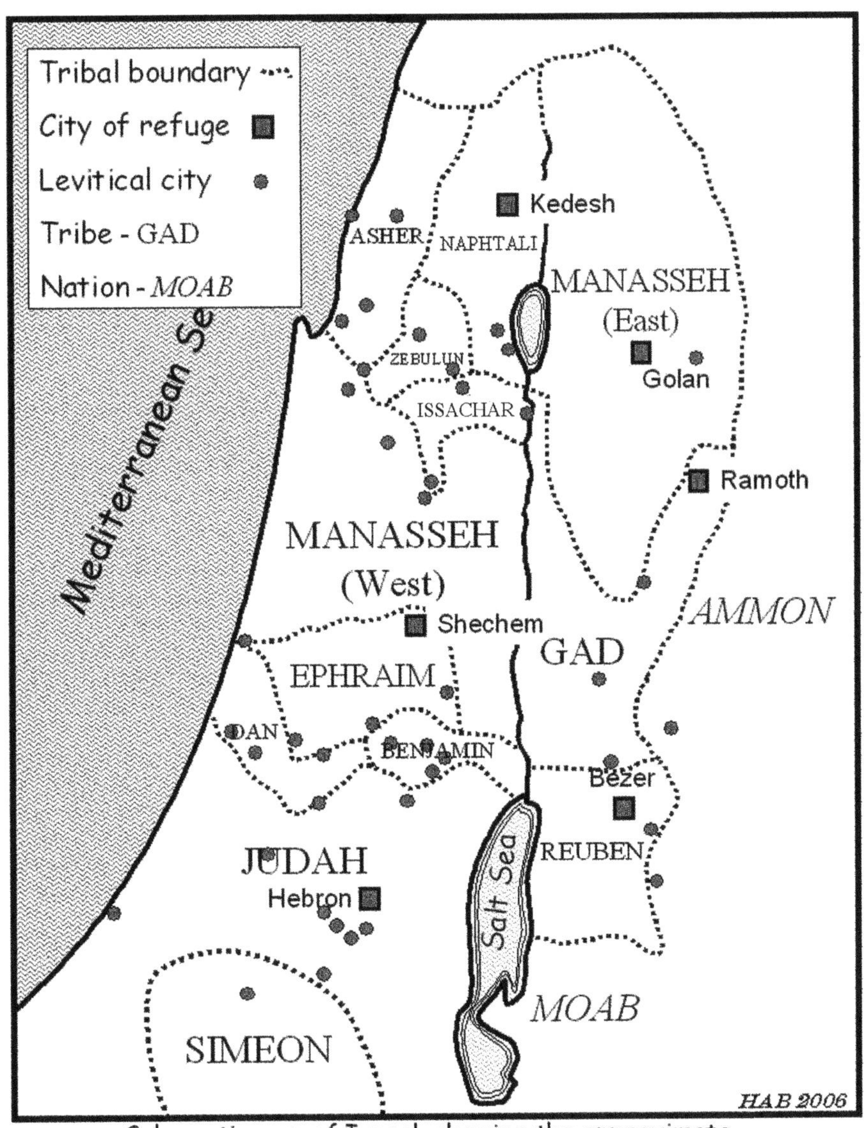

Schematic map of Israel, showing the approximate location of the Cities of Refuge and the Levitical cities.

JOSHUA 21

Levitical Cities

The tribe of Levi was the last to be provided for during the land distribution at Shiloh. It has already been noted in relation to Simeon (19.1-9), that Levi and Simeon were the only tribes who did not receive an inheritance of land (Gen 49.7). However, the tribe of Levi were declared to be set apart to the Lord following their stand at Sinai in the matter of the golden calf (Ex 32.27-29), and thereafter were devoted to the service of the sanctuary (Num 3-4). All three of Levi's sons, Gershon, Kohath, and Merari, and their descendants constituted the Levites among the children of Israel; Aaron and his descendants were the priests, Aaron being a grandson of Kohath.

The Levites were excluded from military service (Num 1.45-47) and were given responsibility to assist the priests in the daily functioning of the tabernacle and its transportation (Num 8.19; 18.2-7). Their place of privilege and service was also reflected in the provision that the Lord made for them, which was in keeping with their landless state. They received their portion from the sacrifices and tithes which were brought to the tabernacle and offered before the Lord (Num 18.9-19,24), and were thus fed from the altar they served. In addition to the produce of the land, the Levities were also given cities from the inheritances of the tribes and, as a result, were sustained by the Lord, through His people.

When Paul wrote to the assembly in Corinth he taught them that, as an apostle, he had the right to forbear working. He was ministering to their spiritual needs and therefore they ought to have been ministering to his material needs (1 Cor 9.11). Paul never insisted upon his right when he was in Corinth, but he did take the opportunity to establish the scriptural basis for his assertion. In his argument he used the example of the Lord's provision for those of His people who had served the altar in the Old Testament. "Do ye not know that they which minister about holy things live of the things of the temple? and they which wait at the altar are partakers with the altar?" (1 Cor 9.13). Having established the principle from the Old Testament, he then made the application: "Even so hath the Lord ordained that they which preach the gospel should live of the gospel" (1 Cor 9.14). Therefore the provision of the Lord for the tribe of Levi established principles which apply to those who spend their time preaching the gospel.

Response to the Word of God

The Lord had spoken to Moses and commanded that cities be given to the Levites for them to dwell in (Num 35.2-8). Now that the children of Israel had received their inheritance, they were in a position to obey His command. It is interesting that the commandment of the Lord is referred to twice in the opening verses of the chapter (vv.2-3), directing the attention of the people away from the need of the Levites to the Lord Himself.

It is important to point out that when the New Testament deals with the subject of giving, the emphasis is upon the Lord and not upon the recipients of the gifts. Paul stressed this when he wrote to the saints in Philippi and acknowledged their sacrificial giving: "But I have all, and abound: I am full, having received of Epaphroditus the things which were sent from you, an odour of a sweet smell, a sacrifice acceptable, wellpleasing to God. But my God shall supply all your need according to his riches in glory by Christ Jesus" (Phil 4.18-19). Although he was the grateful beneficiary of their kindness, he pointed out that the gift was actually a sacrifice to the Lord. When he wrote to the Corinthian assembly regarding their gift to needy saints, he reminded them that their motivation was not only the need of others, but also the example of the Saviour. He thus fixed their attention upon the Lord Jesus, putting their giving into a proper perspective: "For ye know the grace of our Lord Jesus Christ, that, though he was rich, yet for your sakes he became poor, that ye through his poverty might be rich" (2 Cor 8.9).

When the children of Israel gave cities out of their inheritance to the tribe of Levi, it was an obedient response to the commandment of the Lord, as well as an evidence of fellowship in the work to which the Levites had been called.

Contribution from each Tribe

It will be noted, when the detail of the chapter is considered, that each tribe gave cities to the tribe of Levi. There was almost an equality of giving in respect of the number of cities from each tribe. Four cities were provided from each tribe, the only difference being that Naphtali gave three and Judah and Simeon between them gave nine. This was entirely appropriate since each of the tribes benefited from the work that the Levites performed, and therefore had a responsibility to share in providing for them. In the sight of the Lord they shared the burden, although there is no doubt that some of the cities would be larger than others and some would have better pasture land. That information is not recorded, since it is not relevant in the assessment of their sacrificial giving. The principle was made clear to Moses: "And the cities which ye shall give shall be of the possession of the children of Israel: from them that have many ye shall give many; but from them that have few ye shall give few: every one shall give of his cities unto the Levites according to his inheritance which he inheriteth" (Num 35.8). The value of their giving did not lie in the size of the city or land, but rather in the relationship between what they gave and the extent to which the Lord had prospered them. This principle is illustrated by the value that the Lord placed on the two mites given into the treasury by the widow, in contrast to the large sums of money given by the rich men (Mk 12.41-44). Paul applied this principle when writing to the Corinthians: "Upon the first day of the week let every one of you lay by him in store, as God hath prospered him" (1 Cor 16.2).

National Presence

One of the duties of the Levities was to teach the Law to the people (Deut 33.10; 2 Chr 17.7-9; Mal 2.7). Accessibility to those who had the responsibility of teaching was an important issue if the people were going to have a continuing understanding of the Law that governed them. The Law set out the parameters for every aspect of their life and society, with the preservation of their relationship with the Lord as the central theme. By giving them cities in each tribe's portion of the land, the Lord ensured that there was no excuse for ignorance.

Assigned by Lot

The word "lot" is employed on eight occasions in this chapter. Through this means, which had been used extensively in the division of the land, the Lord directly assigned cities to the Levites. Some critics have seen this chapter as a late insertion to the book owing to the number of cities mentioned and the seeming discrepancies in some of the names and associated tribes. One of the chief criticisms relates to the small number of Levites and the large number of cities. It is said by some that there would have been insufficient Levites to occupy the forty-eight cities named in the chapter and that this is evidence that the chapter must have been written much later and inserted into the text when the Levites had grown considerably in number and had taken possession of these cities. Keil & Delitzsch point out that "if the 23,000 males, the number of the Levites at the second census which was taken in the steppes of Moab, were distributed among the 35 towns, it would give 657 males, or 1,300 male and female Levites for every town". This does not deal with the thirteen cities given to the priests, which are perhaps more problematic for those who would criticise the chapter. It must be remembered that the cities were given by lot and there is no indication as to whether they were under the control of the children of Israel or remained unconquered at the time of assignation. The provision for the Levites was also for the future and anticipated the natural growth in population. Keil & Delitzsch estimate that, by the time the cities were assigned, the descendants of Aaron could have numbered 200 families. Therefore the number of cities in relation to the number of Levites is not a problem unless the size of the cities is overestimated and the number of the Levites is underestimated.

Verses 1-3: Levites' Petition

When the Levites made their approach, they did do so in a manner, and at a time, which was in keeping with their unique place among the children of Israel. At the end of the process of land allocation at Shiloh, after all the land had been divided and the cities of refuge named: "Then came near the heads of the fathers of the Levites unto Eleazar the priest, and unto Joshua the son of Nun, and unto the heads of the fathers of the tribes of the children of Israel" (v.1). They waited until last and made their approach to the appropriate persons, without rancour or impatience. It was in keeping with their association with the altar and the sanctuary that they were the last to be granted their portion. In the same way as Joshua waited until the other tribes had received their land before his portion was assigned, so the Levites stood aside for the rest of the nation before they stepped forward with their petition. It is worth repeating that the Lord Jesus taught His disciples that greatness and blessing in His kingdom is not manifested in elevation above others, but in lowliness and humility.

It has already been noted that there were five recorded occasions when individuals or groups petitioned for land. Caleb (14.6-15) and the daughters of Zelophehad (17.3-6) petitioned for the implementation of the the word of the Lord, which they had received through Moses. Achsah (15.18-19) made a spiritual plea to her father for the means to produce fruit from her land and her request was granted. The tribe of Joseph (17.14-18) was dissatisfied with its inheritance and had no basis of spiritual ambition or promise from the Lord upon which to base the claim; as a result they were refused their request. When the Levites brought their claim, it was based upon the firm foundation of the word of the Lord:, "And they spake unto them at Shiloh in the land of Canaan, saying, The Lord commanded by the hand of Moses to give us cities to dwell in, with the suburbs thereof for our cattle" (v.2). They did not appeal to their own merit or to the favour that they might have had with the people. Instead they relied upon the commandment of the Lord which established their claim. It was not a plea for charity or for benign toleration; it was the equitable provision of the Lord for those who would serve Him by serving His people.

The response of the children of Israel to the word of the Lord has often been the subject of adverse comment, and rightly so. However, on this occasion they did what the Lord commanded without delay: "And the children of Israel gave unto the Levites out of their inheritance, at the commandment of the Lord, these cities and their suburbs" (v.3). It was not always so in the subsequent history of Israel and the extent to which the tribe of Levi was provided for was often a direct measure of the devotion of the children of Israel to the Lord.

Verses 4-8: Overview of the Levitical Cities

Levi had three sons, Kohath, Gershon, and Merari and the cities were divided among them.

Kohath (vv.4-5)

The cities given to the families of Kohath were subdivided to reflect the special status given to the sons of Aaron, the grandson of Kohath, as the priestly family, who were granted cities in close proximity to Jerusalem, where they would later serve in the temple. "And the lot came out for the families of the Kohathites: and the children of Aaron the priest, which were of the Levites, had by lot out of the tribe of Judah, and out of the tribe of Simeon, and out of the tribe of Benjamin, thirteen cities" (v.4).

The rest of the descendants of Kohath were Levites and as such were not marked out for special status and received their cities in the same way as the other families of Levi: "And the rest of the children of Kohath had by lot out of the families of the tribe of Ephraim, and out of the tribe of Dan, and out of the half tribe of Manasseh, ten cities" (v.5).

Gershon (v.6)

"And the children of Gershon had by lot out of the families of the tribe of Issachar, and out of the tribe of Asher, and out of the tribe of Naphtali, and out of the half tribe of Manasseh in Bashan, thirteen cities".

Merari (v.7)

"The children of Merari by their families had out of the tribe of Reuben, and out of the tribe of Gad, and out of the tribe of Zebulun, twelve cities".

The overview of the allocation of cities to the Levites concludes as it began in v.3: "And the children of Israel gave by lot unto the Levites these cities with their suburbs, as the Lord commanded by the hand of Moses" (v.8). The additional information provided in v.8 is that the commandment which the children of Israel obeyed was given "by the hand of Moses". This expression appears twenty-seven times in the Old Testament and describes the process whereby the Lord moved among His people through Moses.

Verses 9-26: Kohathites' Cities

Children of Aaron (vv.9-19)

It has already been noted that the Aaronic priesthood came from the descendants of Kohath and as such received a special inheritance of thirteen cities, given to them out of the portions of Judah, Simeon and Benjamin (vv.9,17). The significance of this lay in their close association with the sanctuary which ultimately would be the temple at Jerusalem. Throughout the history of Israel, even when the nation divided into Israel and Judah, the priests were not separated from the sanctuary. Jerusalem remained within the territory of Judah and, as a result, the Lord ensured that the sanctuary would be served. It was only when Judah was delivered into captivity that the cities of the priests were taken from them.

From Judah and Simeon they received nine cities (vv.11-16):

- Hebron
- Libnah

- Jattir
- Eshtemoa
- Holon
- Debir
- Ain
- Juttah
- Beth-shemesh.

From Benjamin they received four cities (vv.17-19):
- Gibeon
- Geba
- Anathoth
- Almon.

With regard to Hebron, the city was designated as a city of refuge (v.13) and, although it was given to the priests, "the fields of the city, and the villages thereof, gave they to Caleb the son of Jephunneh for his possession" (v.12) in fulfilment of Joshua's response to Caleb's request (14.13-15).

"All the cities of the children of Aaron, the priests, were thirteen cities with their suburbs" (v.19).

Remaining Kohathites (vv.20-26)

From Ephraim they received four cities (vv.20-22):
- Shechem
- Gezer
- Kibzaim
- Beth-horon.

From Dan they received four cities (vv.23-24):
- Eltekeh
- Gibbethon
- Aijalon
- Gathrimmon.

From Manasseh on the west of the Jordan they received two cities (v.25):
- Tanach
- Gathrimmon.

Shechem was designated a city of refuge. The repctition of Gathrimmon from Dan and Manasseh should be noted. These were different cities, with the one in Manasseh also known by the name of Bileam (1 Chr 6.70).

"All the cities were ten with their suburbs for the families of the children of Kohath that remained" (v.26).

Verses 27-33: Gershonites' Cities

From Manasseh on the east side of the Jordan they received two cities (v.27):

- Golan in Bashan
- Beesh-terah.

From Issachar they received four cities (vv.28-29):

- Kishon
- Dabareh
- Jarmuth
- En-gannim.

From Asher they received four cities (vv.30-31):

- Mishal
- Abdon
- Helkath
- Rehob.

From Naphtali they received three cities (v.32):

- Kedesh in Galilee
- Hammoth-dor
- Kartan.

The Gershonites had two of their cities allocated as cities of refuge - Golan in Bashan and Kedesh in Galilee.

"All the cities of the Gershonites according to their families were thirteen cities with their suburbs" (v.33).

Verses 34-40: Merarites' Cities

From Zebulun they received four cities (vv.34-35):

- Jokneam
- Kartah
- Dimnah
- Nahalal.

From Reuben they received four cities (vv.36-37):

- Bezer
- Jahazah
- Kedemoth
- Mephaath.

From Gad they received four cities (vv.38-39):

- Ramoth in Gilead
- Mahanaim
- Heshbon
- Jazer.

Bezer and Ramoth in Gilead were the two remaining cities of refuge.

"So all the cities for the children of Merari by their families, which were remaining of the families of the Levites, were by their lot twelve cities" (v.40).

Verses 41-42: Summary of the Allocation of the Levitical Cities

The allocation of the cities to the tribe of Levi concludes with a brief summary: "All the cities of the Levites within the possession of the children of Israel were forty and eight cities with their suburbs. These cities were every one with their suburbs round about them: thus were all these cities" (vv.41-42). "This may appear too great a proportion compared with those of the other tribes. But it must be borne in mind that the list given here contains the name of every Levitical city; whereas only those cities of the other tribes are mentioned which lay on the frontier or along the boundary line" (Jamieson, Faussett and Brown). The other issue to bear in mind is that the Levites were granted only the suburbs of their cities, which would have been the immediate area of land around the city, whereas the other tribes received the cities, villages, and land, thus constituting a far larger inheritance.

Verses 43-45: Summary of the Allocation of the Inheritance

The record of the process commenced in ch.13 is brought to a conclusion by a wonderful summary of the distribution of Israel's promised inheritance from the Lord. In these verses the emphasis is upon the Lord and what He gave the children of Israel in fulfilment of His promises to their forefathers.

Land (v.43)

"And the Lord gave unto Israel all the land which he sware to give unto their fathers; and they possessed it, and dwelt therein". The division of the land was a comprehensive allocation of all the territory which the Lord had promised to the fathers of the children of Israel. There is seeming inconsistency between the previous accounts of partial possession of the land and this statement of complete occupation. It must be borne in mind that this summary is stating the position immediately following Joshua's campaigns. Insofar as they could, the tribes possessed what they had been given. It was the Lord's intention that they would not take possession of all of their land before they were numerous enough to cultivate it and prevent it going into wasteland (Ex 23.29-30). The years that followed were a sad history of their failure to progressively drive out the remaining nations and enjoy full possession of their inheritance.

Rest (v.44)

"And the Lord gave them rest round about, according to all that he sware unto their fathers: and there stood not a man of all their enemies before them; the Lord delivered all their enemies into their hand". The Lord had promised Moses that He would give them rest in the land of Canaan (Deut 12.9-10) and had promised Joshua that "There shall not any man be able to stand before thee all the days of thy life" (1.5). As long as Joshua and the elders who had been with him at the commencement of the conquest of Canaan lived (24.31), the people experienced the benefit of peace inasmuch as they were obedient to the Lord. The nations which had opposed the children of Israel had been subdued, and had been rendered powerless by the Lord, and they would have remained so if the people had continued in a pathway of obedience to His word.

Promises fulfilled (v.45)

"There failed not ought of any good thing which the Lord had spoken unto the house of Israel; all came to pass".

It is fitting that the distribution of the land of Canaan to the children of Israel is concluded with a declaration of the Lord's faithfulness and the complete fulfilment of His promises. When the Israelites groaned under the bondage of Egypt, the Lord promised Moses at the bush, "I am come down to deliver them out of the hand of the Egyptians, and to bring them up out of that land unto a good land and a large, unto a land flowing with milk and honey; unto the place of the Canaanites, and the Hittites, and the Amorites, and the Perizzites, and the Hivites, and the Jebusites" (Ex 3.8). He had expanded upon that initial promise and throughout the wilderness journey had spoken to the people of their responsibilities to observe His commandments in order to remain and enjoy the blessing of the land (Lev 20.22; 26.14-45). Their ongoing possession of the inheritance of Canaan was not unconditional, although their entrance and initial rest was. With the land divided among the tribes and their enemies overcome in battle and subdued, the words of the Lord were fulfilled. In the days of Solomon the people acknowledged His faithfulness in this matter and declared, "Blessed be the Lord, that hath given rest unto his people Israel, according to all that he promised: there hath not failed one word of all his good promise, which he promised by the hand of Moses his servant" (1 Kings 8.56).

JOSHUA 22

Departure of Trans-Jordan Tribes

Verses 1-8: Commendation, Exhortation and Blessing

Commendation (vv.1-3)

The conquest was completed; the land was subdued, and it was time for demobilisation. The children of Israel were not instructed to maintain a standing army, or to conquer beyond their borders, therefore the people were sent to their land to cultivate it and to live in peace. The background to Joshua's speech to the two and a half tribes was noted earlier (1.12-18).

"Then Joshua called the Reubenites, and the Gadites, and the half tribe of Manasseh" (v.1). The use of the word "Then" does not necessarily place the events of this chapter after those recorded in the previous chapter. It does have the meaning of "then, at that time" and is "to be thought of as having taken place before the completion of the preceding action" (*Introduction to Biblical Hebrew Syntax,* 31.6.3b, by B K Waltke and M O O'Connor). Some scholars translate the word as "this was when". The placing of the account of Joshua's summons of the trans-Jordan tribes after the division of the land provides important spiritual lessons, even though the chronology is not easily determined.

a) Fidelity to their leaders (v.2)

"Ye have kept all that Moses the servant of the Lord commanded you, and have obeyed my voice in all that I commanded you". Moses had received their initial request to settle on the east side of the Jordan and had granted it under certain conditions (Num 32). The stipulations had been adhered to by the tribes crossing the Jordan armed and prepared to fight. They had also accepted Joshua's leadership and been obedient to his commands during the conflict. It was commendable that they had demonstrated such fidelity to Moses and Joshua and had willingly acknowledged their authority.

b) Fidelity to their brethren (v.3a)

"Ye have not left your brethren these many days unto this day". It had not been a brief venture into the land and then a swift return to their families and cattle. Three military campaigns of conquest had been undertaken, which had taken them away from their inheritance into the south and north of Canaan for a period of approximately seven years (11.18). Despite the length of time, they had not forsaken their brethren in battle and had remained with them until the mission was accomplished. If it took seven years to subdue the land, it would have taken further time to divide. Some commentators take the view that this process could have lasted up to another seven years. Bearing in mind the comments regarding the timing of Joshua's commendation of the trans-Jordan tribes (v.1), it is difficult to determine the period during which these tribes were separated from their families. If it was for at least seven years, and possibly up to fourteen years, then it is no wonder that Joshua commended them for their faithfulness to their brethren.

c) Fidelity to their Lord (v.3b)

"Ye...have kept the charge of the commandment of the Lord your God". A greater proof of fidelity was that they remained true and obedient to the Lord. It is possible to remain faithful to leaders and brethren and yet to stray from the path of obedience to the Lord. Thus it was not only their involvement in the conquest that was commended by Joshua: "Ye have carefully and circumspectly kept the commandment of the Lord your God: not only in this particular instance of continuing in the service of Israel to the end of the war" (Matthew Henry).

This would be a worthy commendation for any soldier to receive, and much more so for a believer. To be commended by the Lord for fidelity to leaders, to brethren, and to the Lord Himself, would be an abundant entrance into the kingdom. Failure in any one of these aspects can all too easily characterise the Christian, with sad consequences. To rebel against elders and spiritual leaders or to abandon the battlefield and fellowship of saints for an easier life in the mire of mediocrity is bad enough, but to demonstrate infidelity toward the Lord and His commandments is surely the ultimate failure.

Exhortation (vv.4-5)

"And now the Lord your God hath given rest unto your brethren, as he promised them: therefore now return ye, and get you unto your tents, and unto the land of your possession, which Moses the servant of the Lord gave you on the other side Jordan" (v.4).

With their brethren enjoying rest, Joshua commanded them to return over the Jordan to their inheritance. The language employed by Joshua is important. He did not instruct them to get to the cities. There is no doubt that the tribes dwelt in fortified towns (Num 32.17), but the word used is "tents" and not cities. It was a reminder of their pilgrim character, for they had come through a wilderness journey in dependence upon the Lord. Joshua is careful to emphasise that the rest enjoyed by the people was attributed to the "Lord your God", and that their inheritance had been granted to them by Moses who was "the servant of the Lord". Rest had been given and the land of their possession had also been given. There was no room for complacency or pride as they returned home. It was all of God.

"But take diligent heed to do the commandment and the law, which Moses the servant of the Lord charged you" (v.5). "No instructions were furnished for the fortifying of their cities or for the cultivation of their land, the whole emphasis being placed upon the regulating of their spiritual lives" (A. W. Pink). The exhortation was to "do" what they had received from Moses, to be careful to practise and observe the Law, which was for all of Israel, and in particular what was relevant to them in their unique circumstances. Knowledge of the word of God was not always accompanied by obedience. The same problem was addressed by James in his epistle when he wrote, "Be ye doers of the word, and not hearers only, deceiving your own selves" (James 1.22).

In his comprehensive expansion of the charge, Joshua employed verbs that summarise the duties of the people of God in any generation. He addressed the people regarding their affections, obedience, dependence, and labour:

- "to love the Lord your God"
- "to walk in all his ways"
- "to keep his commandments"
- "to cleave unto him"
- "to serve him with all your heart and with all your soul".

The expectation was that these tribes would be as committed and devoted to the Lord as the other tribes on the west side of the Jordan. Although a river would separate them from the other tribes, there was to be no separation from the Lord and no lowering of standards.

Throughout Scripture the Holy Spirit focuses the reader's attention beyond the immediate circumstances of their particular age, toward the underlying theme of God's dealings with man. Whether in the Old or New Testaments, the Lord's desire is to bring men into a relationship of love, devotion, and wholeheartedness, which would affect every aspect of their lives. Solomon ended his search for meaning in life with the conclusion, "Fear God, and keep his commandments: for this is the whole duty of man" (Eccl 12.13). The Lord Jesus Himself stated that the first and greatest commandment is, "Thou shalt love the Lord thy God with all thy heart, and with all thy soul, and with all thy mind" (Mt 22.37). God's desire is for the whole person: spirit, soul and body.

Blessing (vv.6-8)

The time had arrived for the two and a half tribes to depart from their brethren. As they left, Joshua blessed them; on such occasions this was customary (Gen 31.55; 2 Sam 19.39). The account of his blessing is interrupted with a parenthetical verse, dealing again with the division within the tribe of Manasseh. In effect, two partings were taking place at the same time; Israel and Manasseh were both divided: "Now to the one half of the tribe of Manasseh Moses had given possession in Bashan: but unto the other half thereof gave Joshua among their brethren on this side Jordan westward. And when Joshua sent them away also unto their tents, then he blessed them" (v.7).

Joshua's blessing was marked by equity. He made no difference between the two parts of Manasseh and blessed them both. He also instructed the tribes to share the spoils of war with their brethren who had remained on the east of the Jordan: "And he spake unto them, saying, Return with much riches unto your tents, and with very much cattle, with silver, and with gold, and with brass, and with iron, and with very much raiment: divide the spoil of your enemies with your brethren" (v.8). About 40,000 men from these tribes had passed over Jordan to fight in Canaan (4.13), whereas the record of the men above the age of twenty capable of going to war was over 110,000, allowance being made for the half tribe of Manasseh which came over Jordan (Num 26.7,18,34). This left 70,000 men, together with women and children, on the east of the Jordan. Evidently the campaign to conquer Canaan had brought great wealth to the 40,000 men, and with it the possibility of problems when they returned home. Jealousy, pride and all of the sinful thoughts and deeds which can be provoked by wealth, both in those who possess it, and in others who desire it, could have undermined the commencement of life in their new land. In order to avoid such problems and to reflect the value of the work of the whole tribe, whether in battle or at home, Joshua instructed them to share the spoil.

There was a precedent for such instructions. Following the defeat of the Midianites, the Lord had commanded Moses, "Take the sum of the prey that was taken, both of man and of beast, thou, and Eleazar the priest, and the chief fathers of the congregation: and divide the prey into two parts; between them that took the war upon them, who went out to battle, and between all the congregation" (Num 31.26-27). David applied the same principle and made it a statute in Israel that "as his part is that goeth down to the battle, so shall his part be that tarrieth by the stuff: they shall part alike" (1 Sam 30.24).

Verses 9-12: A Great Altar

Having received the farewell blessing of Joshua, "the children of Reuben and the children of Gad and the half tribe of Manasseh returned, and departed from the children of Israel out of Shiloh, which is in the land of Canaan, to go unto the country of Gilead, to the land of their possession, whereof they were possessed, according to the word of the Lord by the hand of Moses" (v.9). There is finality about the description of their journey, which has all the character of the concluding statement regarding the involvement of these tribes in the conquest of Canaan.

The language indicates a geographical separation, but beyond the geography, a distinction in the way in which these tribes are described is maintained throughout the chapter. The nine and a half tribes which occupied Canaan are described as the "children of Israel" (vv.9,33); "the whole congregation of the children of Israel" (v.12); "the whole congregation of the Lord" (v.16); "the whole congregation of Israel" (v.18). By way of contrast, the two and a half tribes are always referred to as "the children of Reuben, and the children of Gad, and the half tribe of Manasseh". The departure of these tribes brought a threat of disunity which ought to have exercised their hearts.

It is worth pointing out again that they had been given the land of Gilead as an inheritance from the Lord. Some commentators take the view that this area of land was part of the inheritance of the children of Israel and that it was always God's purpose for the two and a half tribes to settle there. There is no doubt that the Lord gave them the land, but this was done only in response to their premature request to settle outside Canaan for reasons which have been the subject of previous comment (1.12-18). They did adhere to the conditions laid down by the Lord, but their initial intention was to remain on the east of Jordan.

This chapter serves as a warning to those who are not willing to settle down within the inheritance of the Lord and who seek to separate themselves in some way and for some reason. The Lord granted them their request; this should not be a surprise to the person who is acquainted with God's dealings. He never compels His people to enjoy His blessings, neither does He withdraw from them when they move away from Him. Placing three of the six cities of refuge within their territory is an indication that the Lord still cared for His people, despite their location on the east of the Jordan.

They were nearly home: "And when they came unto the borders of Jordan, that are in the land of Canaan" (v.10). For reasons that are not revealed at this point in the narrative, "the children of Reuben and the children of Gad and the half tribe of Manasseh built there an altar by Jordan, a great altar to see to" (v.10). When they had passed over Jordan to come into the land, they had assisted in the construction of a memorial of twelve stones taken from the river bed and placed at Gilgal (ch.4). There are striking differences between the erection of the altar and that of the memorial.

• *Instruction from the Lord.*

When Israel passed over Jordan to conquer Canaan, the Lord instructed them to build a memorial. The two and a half tribes received no such instruction for an altar.

• *Altar and memorial*

Although the stone memorial may have looked like an altar, it is never described as such. However, the altar is always referred to as an altar. This is significant, since the Lord instructed Moses that when the people came into the land they had to ensure that there was only one altar as the focus of national worship. The hearts of the people had not to be distracted. Their attention was to be centred in one place where the Lord would have them approach and worship Him.

• *Size of altar*

The altar is described as "a great altar to see to". Other translations have "a great, impressive altar" (NKJV) and "an altar of great size" (RSV). It was an impressive sight and of imposing size. This is in contrast to the memorial of twelve stones, which consisted of stones each of which a man could lift on his shoulder and, when constructed, must have been less than the height of a man. It was not the Lord's intention for the people to worship the memorial, but rather to use the memorial to remember and worship the Lord.

"And the children of Israel heard say, Behold, the children of Reuben and the children of Gad and the half tribe of Manasseh have built an altar over against the land of Canaan, in the borders of Jordan, at the passage of the children of Israel" (v.11). The altar was built near the River Jordan. There is some disagreement among commentators as to whether the altar was built on the east or west side of the river. The uncertainty arises from the two descriptions given in the verse, "over against Canaan" and, "at the passage of the children of Israel", which would appear to indicate that the altar was built on the east of the Jordan, facing the land of Canaan and at the place where they crossed the Jordan dry shod. Some translations have the last clause of the verse as "on the children of Israel's side" (NKJV) or, "on the side that belongs to the people of Israel" (RSV), pointing to the altar being built on the west of the Jordan, but the language is ambiguous and cannot be the sole basis for determining the location of the altar. When the response of the children of Israel is considered, and the explanation given by the two and half tribes is taken into account, it is clear that the altar would not have caused the problem that it did, if it had been built on the land of Benjamin, Judah or western Manasseh.

1. For it to be mistaken as an altar for sacrifice, it must have been built in a place where the two and half tribes would have had unrestricted access, without crossing the Jordan into another tribe's territory.
2. To serve as a memorial it would be required to be seen as belonging to the two and half tribes, in order for the generation growing up to enquire about it, and not regard it as a distant object on the other side of the Jordan.
3. If it were on the west of the Jordan, the children of Israel could have destroyed it without reference to the two and half tribes, since it was built on their land without their consent.

"It is more likely that they built it on their own side of the water, for what had they to do to build on another man's land without his consent? And it is said to be over-against the land of Canaan; nor would there have been any cause of suspecting it designed for sacrifice if they had not built it among themselves" (Matthew Henry).

The immediate response of the children of Israel was hostile: "And when the children of Israel heard of it, the whole congregation of the children of Israel gathered themselves together at Shiloh, to go up to war against them" (v.12). Having previously experienced the consequences of idolatry, out of devotion to the Lord or fear of His judgment they were quick to respond to this perceived threat. The gathering of the whole congregation at Shiloh indicates that there was a central consideration of the matter, in accordance with the Law. Shiloh was the seat of government in the land and the Law stated, "If thou shalt hear say in one of thy cities, which the Lord thy God hath given thee to dwell there, saying, Certain men, the children of Belial, are gone out from among you, and have withdrawn the inhabitants of their city, saying, Let us go and serve other gods, which ye have not known; then shalt thou inquire, and make search, and ask diligently; and, behold, if it be truth, and the thing certain, that such abomination is wrought among you; thou shalt surely smite the inhabitants of that city with the edge of the sword, destroying it utterly, and all that is therein, and the cattle thereof, with the edge of the sword (Deut 13.12-15). In accordance with the Law, they did not send an army to engage the two and half tribes in war until they had made enquiry as to the veracity of the report.

Verses 13-20: Confrontation

The zeal of the children of Israel was matched by their wisdom. They sent a delegation that was small, yet representative of the whole congregation, and led by a man whose presence would have reinforced the seriousness of the situation.

United response (vv.13-14)

"And the children of Israel sent unto the children of Reuben, and to the children of Gad, and to the half tribe of Manasseh, into the land of Gilead, Phinehas the son of Eleazar the priest" (v.13). It is interesting that Joshua's name is not mentioned in connection with the response of the children of Israel to the building of the altar. The head of the delegation, sent to the two and a half tribes, was Phinehas, the son of Eleazar the priest. The problem related to the worship of God, and therefore it was fitting that a priest should lead the delegation. In addition to being a priest, Phinehas was a man who had a reputation for dealing with idolatry (Num 25.7-13). He was the right man for the job.

"And with him ten princes, of each chief house a prince throughout all the tribes of Israel; and each one was an head of the house of their fathers among the thousands of Israel" (v.14). The men who accompanied Phinehas represented each of the tribes who dwelt on the west of the Jordan. They were senior men within the tribes who had authority to speak for the congregation.

The united response of the children of Israel to perceived sin within the nation was proportionate to the problem, and is an example of wise action in difficult circumstances.

- They acted in unity, the priesthood and each tribe being represented.
- They acted scripturally, seeking to enquire, search and ask diligently.
- They were ready to implement judgment, preparing for war.
- They carefully chose the right men for the job.

When reports of difficulties arise within an assembly, it would be good if elders were to adopt the same approach.

Accusation (vv.15-16)

"And they came unto the children of Reuben, and to the children of Gad, and to the half tribe of Manasseh, unto the land of Gilead, and they spake with them" (v.15). They did not summon representatives from the two and a half tribes to come and meet them in Shiloh. Time was of the essence and they took the initiative. It was a proactive response. So often when problems arise in an assembly they are the subject of discussion, which is more gossip than genuine enquiry or debate, but no effort is made to speak to the relevant people. This can lead to misunderstandings and inappropriate action.

"Thus saith the whole congregation of the Lord, What trespass is this that ye have committed against the God of Israel, to turn away this day from following the Lord, in that ye have builded you an altar, that ye might rebel this day against the Lord?" (v.16). The accusation was clear and direct. The key issue of an altar being constructed was raised and placed within its correct context. They had not sinned against the trans-Jordan tribes by building this altar, this was a transgression against the Lord. Two words are employed within the verse to describe their actions - "trespass" (4604) and "rebel" (4775) - indicating infidelity in a relationship and rebellion against authority.

Precedent (v.17-18a)

Having made the accusation, they illustrated the seriousness of the problem by reference to the circumstances surrounding the iniquity of Peor, and the lasting effects among the children of Israel: "Is the iniquity of Peor too little for us, from which we are not cleansed until this day, although there was a plague in the congregation of the Lord, but that ye must turn away this day from following the Lord?".

During the wilderness journey, the children of Israel had committed whoredom with the daughters of Moab; this led them into idolatry and the worship of Baal-peor. The Lord brought a plague into the camp, resulting in the death of 24,000 people before Phinehas killed Zimri and Cozbi, a Midianitish woman: "And the Lord spake unto Moses, saying, Phinehas, the son of Eleazar, the son of Aaron the priest, hath turned my wrath away from the children of Israel, while he was zealous for my sake among them, that I consumed not the children of Israel in my jealousy. Wherefore say, Behold, I give unto him my covenant of peace: and he shall have it, and his seed after him, even the covenant of an everlasting priesthood; because he was zealous for his God, and made an atonement for the children of Israel" (Num 25.10-13).

The plague that came upon the children of Israel had been stopped, but they had not been completely cleansed from the defilement of idolatry, hence the instructions of Joshua: "Now therefore put away, said he, the strange gods which are among you, and incline your heart unto the Lord God of Israel"

(24.23). Even the plague, which came from the Lord, had not wiped out the effects of that idolatry and there was the fear among the children of Israel that the actions of the two and a half tribes could add further idolatry to what was already present.

Warning (v.18b)

"And it will be, seeing ye rebel to day against the Lord, that to morrow he will be wroth with the whole congregation of Israel". The experience of the iniquity of Peor had taught them about collective responsibility. The consequent judgment of the Lord would fall upon the whole congregation of Israel, notwithstanding that it was only the two and a half tribes which had erected the altar and rebelled against the Lord. They were right to be concerned about the perceived sin of their brethren.

Solution (v.19)

It is good to identify a problem, or even a sin, then to proceed to face the people involved having a genuine concern about the collective welfare of the people of God. It is much better to do so having prepared a solution to the problem. The children of Israel had given some thought to the issue of what would cause their brethren to build an altar. They had come to the conclusion that it may have been that the land on the east of the Jordan was unclean and, therefore, they were trying to sanctify it in some way through this altar: "Notwithstanding if the land of your possession be unclean, then pass ye over unto the land of the possession of the Lord, wherein the Lord's tabernacle dwelleth, and take possession among us". The answer to the problem was provided at some cost to themselves. If the land was unclean then they were invited to come back across the Jordan and take land which would have to be given up by the rest of the tribes. It was a self-sacrificial solution that placed obedience to the Lord above their own interests.

It is interesting that they describe the land on the west of the Jordan as "the inheritance of the Lord", confirming again that the land on the east of the Jordan was not the land that the Lord would have given to these tribes had they not made their request.

Even if they refused the offer to relocate to the west of the Jordan, they were exhorted to "rebel not against the Lord, nor rebel against us, in building you an altar beside the altar of the Lord our God".

Another precedent (v.20)

Their right to be concerned about the altar was reinforced by reference to another page of their history: "Did not Achan the son of Zerah commit a trespass in the accursed thing, and wrath fell on all the congregation of Israel? and that man perished not alone in his iniquity". The emphasis in this reference is upon the recent example of collective responsibility involving Achan. His trespass was attributed to the children of Israel (7.1) and thirty-six men died at Ai as a result. In addition to the men who perished in the debacle at Ai, Achan's family was killed in the judgment of his sin. The tribes from the west of the Jordan did not want to pay a similar price for the perceived idolatry of their brethren.

Verses 21-29: The Explanation

God is witness (vv.21-22a)

Before answering the accusation of their brethren, the two and a half tribes called upon God as their witness: "The Lord God of gods, the Lord God of gods, he knoweth, and Israel he shall know" (v.22).

"The combination of the three names of God – El, the strong one; Elohim, the Supreme Being to be feared, and Jehovah, the truly existing One, the covenant God – serves to strengthen the invocation of God, as in Psalm 50.1; and this is strengthened still further by the repetition of these names" (Keil & Delitzsch).

The calling upon God in such terms indicates earnestness on the part of the two and a half tribes, and a belief that Israel would accept their explanation when they came to know what God already knew.

Denial of idolatry (vv.22b-23)

The seriousness of the accusation was acknowledged and the legitimacy of any judgment, should the accusation prove correct, was accepted. In fact, they state that there could be no other outcome should they be found guilty of idolatry.

The declaration from the two and a half tribes took the form of a challenge: "If it be in rebellion, or if in transgression against the Lord, (save us not this day)" (v.22b). They had no expectation of preservation should they be found to be committing idolatry and agreed that it would be right for the children of Israel to take military action against them.

They went further: "That we have built us an altar to turn from following the Lord, or if to offer thereon burnt offering or meat offering, or if to offer peace offerings thereon, let the Lord himself require it" (v.23). They appealed directly to the Lord, who knows the hearts of His people, to take action if they were guilty of building an altar to offer sacrifices to the Lord.

Reason for the altar (vv.24-25)

There is no doubt that the answer was transparent and genuine. However, it displayed strange thinking on the part of those making a deliberate decision, namely to distance themselves from the children of Israel and settle beyond the Jordan.

They realised that the Jordan would have the effect of creating a barrier between their children and the children of Israel and this would become more than a geographical problem: "And if we have not rather done it for fear of this thing, saying, In time to come your children might speak unto our children, saying, What have ye to do with the Lord God of Israel? For the Lord hath made Jordan a border between us and you, ye children of Reuben and children of Gad; ye have no part in the Lord: so shall your children make our children cease from fearing the Lord".

It was their decision to settle on the east of the Jordan which was the cause of any potential difficulty. They had made that choice and therefore were directly responsible for its consequences. Instead, they identified the problem as the responsibility of the children of Israel. They spoke of two issues:

- Future generations of the children of Israel would consider the Jordan as the eastern border of Israel and the children of Reuben and Gad as no longer part of the nation.
- The children of Reuben and Gad would be hindered from following the Lord, for they would be required to cross the Jordan to gain access to the house of the Lord.

The decision to settle on the east of Jordan did have a detrimental effect upon their children in the years that followed. They took them away from the Lord's inheritance, and then worried that they would lose touch with Him and the children of Israel. They were worrying about a problem of their own creation. It is a scenario that is often repeated in local assemblies if parents who are in fellowship distance themselves from the other saints in the assembly and, by their lifestyle and choices, demonstrate that they do not value the assembly. This is manifested in criticism of the saints, a lack of attendance at the gatherings, associations with the world, or an evident admiration for denominational systems. Such parents should understand that their actions will have a detrimental effect upon their children and usually results in them leaving the assembly. The sad part of the scenario is that the parents often remain in the assembly that they have soured for their children, clinging on to some aspects of fellowship and bitter that their children were neglected, or that someone failed them, when really the failure has been on the parents' part.

There is no mention of the half tribe of Manasseh having concerns about being separated from the children of Israel. This was due to the location of their inheritance in the north of Gilead where the Jordan was not such a barrier. Reuben's territory lay on the east of the Dead Sea and Gad's border ran along the banks of the Jordan from the Dead Sea in the south to the Sea of Galilee in the north. They also had tribal ties with the other half of Manasseh which would not be lightly severed.

Purpose of the altar (vv.26-29)

Before positively declaring the purpose of the altar, they reiterated that "we said, let us now prepare to build us an altar, not for burnt offering, nor for sacrifice" (v.26). This strong denial permeates the answer of the two and a half tribes and demonstrates an appreciation of the serious predicament that they faced.

The purpose of the altar was "that it may be a witness between us, and you, and our generations after us, that we might do the service of the Lord before him with our burnt offerings, and with our sacrifices, and with our peace offerings; that your children may not say to our children in time to come, Ye have no part in the Lord" (v.27). The altar was for a witness to deal with the two-fold problem which they had anticipated. It seems that it was intended to act as a reminder of the relationship that existed between the tribes on either side of the Jordan. The word "witness" (5707) means more than an observation or reminder; it has the implication of a legal testimony and was often used of people bearing witness in a legal or solemn context. There are examples in the Old Testament of a heap of stones (Gen 31.48), a song composed (Deut 31.19), the book of the Law (Deut 31.26), and a stone (Josh 24.27) which were all described as acting as "a witness".

"Therefore said we, that it shall be, when they should so say to us or to our generations in time to come, that we may say again, Behold the pattern of the altar of the Lord, which our fathers made, not for burnt offerings, nor for sacrifices; but it is a witness between us and you" (v.28). The children of Gad and Reuben had anticipated the situation unfolding and had built the altar as a replica of the altar of the Lord to confirm their relationship within the nation, and not as strangers. The whole situation was based upon the premise that the children of Israel would react in a certain way in years to come and took no account of the true problem, which proved to be their complacency (1 Chr 5.25-26).

The altar was modelled on the real thing, but was just a pale imitation. It would never be warmed with fire or stained with blood; it sat in an unremarkable place without the presence of the Lord. As an altar, it was large and useless. Anything which has been set up with no warrant from God may seem a good idea at the time, but when time passes and the original men are no longer there, the object or organisation can change. To build something that is an imitation of the real thing, even for noble reasons, is a danger for the generations that follow.

The answer concludes with a restatement of their passionate denial of idolatry. "God forbid that we should rebel against the Lord, and turn this day from following the Lord, to build an altar for burnt offerings, for meat offerings, or for sacrifices, beside the altar of the Lord our God that is before his tabernacle" (v.29).

Verses 30-34: Crisis Averted

Response of the delegation (vv.30-31)

Phinehas, and the men with him, accepted the explanation without demur. They did not doubt nor dispute the answer and accepted it at face value. It was perhaps with some relief that they had listened to the passionate appeal of the two and a half tribes: "When Phinehas the priest, and the princes of the congregation and heads of the thousands of Israel which were with him, heard the words that the children of Reuben and the children of Gad and the children of Manasseh spake, it pleased them" (v.30).

Phinehas concluded that two important matters had marked that day:

1. "This day we perceive that the Lord is among us, because ye have not committed this trespass against the Lord" (v.31).
2. "Now ye have delivered the children of Israel out of the hand of the Lord" (v.31).

They had experienced the presence of the Lord among them and had been spared His judgment. It is no wonder that Phinehas and the men that were with him were pleased. It was a successful outcome to a difficult situation. Their approach and wisdom in the circumstances had averted a war based upon a misunderstanding; the problem had been resolved through dialogue.

Report of the delegation (vv.32-33)

"And Phinehas the son of Eleazar the priest, and the princes, returned from the children of Reuben, and from the children of Gad, out of the land of Gilead, unto the land of Canaan, to the children of Israel, and brought them word again. And the thing pleased the children of Israel; and the children of Israel blessed God, and did not intend to go up against them in battle, to destroy the land wherein the children of Reuben and Gad dwelt" (vv.32-33). The congregation of the children of Israel was pleased at the outcome. God's judgment had been averted and civil war was not now necessary. It is always a matter for rejoicing amongst the people of God when misunderstandings are cleared up through wise counsel and scriptural decisions. Unwise counsel, resulting in hasty action, often based upon false reports, can cause unnecessary conflict.

The altar named (v.34)

As if to reinforce their intention for the altar "the children of Reuben and the children of Gad called the altar Ed: for it shall be a witness between us that the Lord is God". The word "Ed" is translated as "witness" (NKJV). Easton's *Revised Bible Dictionary* has the following comment:, "Witness - a word not found in the original Hebrew, nor in the LXX. and Vulgate, but added by the translators in the Authorized Version, also in the Revised Version. The words are literally rendered: 'And the children of Reuben and the children of Gad named the altar. It is a witness between us that Jehovah is God' ".

JOSHUA 23

Joshua's First Farewell Discourse

Verses 1-2: Leaders Summoned

Toward the end of their lives, some of the great leaders of Israel concluded their service for the Lord with notable discourses containing warnings and exhortations (Gen 49; Deut 32-33; 2 Sam 23.1-7). The apostle Paul also gave such an address to the elders from the assembly at Ephesus as he was about to leave them for the last time (Acts 20.17-38). Joshua gave two such discourses towards the end of his life.

"And it came to pass a long time after that the Lord had given rest unto Israel from all their enemies round about, that Joshua waxed old and stricken in age" (v.1). The Lord had promised them rest before they entered the land (1.15) and, on four occasions within the book, it is recorded that the Lord fulfilled His promise (11.23; 14.15; 21.44; 22.4). A long time had passed since He had given them rest and Joshua himself was now an old man. He had been described as "old and stricken in years" (13.1) following the campaigns of conquest, and prior to his division of the land. Now he was nearing the end of life (v.14) and, in a manner similar to the apostle Paul (2 Tim 4.6), he anticipated the end of his days.

David M. Howard Jnr. (*New American Commentary*) estimates that Joshua's discourses came some 25 years after the main events of the book. This is based upon the assumption that Joshua was of similar age to Caleb and that they were eighty-five years of age when the land was distributed. Joshua was 110 years old when he died (24.29) and therefore, if he died soon after his discourses, twenty-five years or so must have elapsed from the commencement of the land distribution until his death.

"And Joshua called for all Israel, and for their elders, and for their heads, and for their judges, and for their officers, and said unto them, I am old and stricken in age" (v.2). It is unclear whether Joshua called the men to assemble at his inheritance at Timnath-serah (19.50), or had gathered them at Shiloh. When he spoke at Shechem in his final discourse, he addressed all the tribes of Israel (24.1), but some commentators take the view that, on this occasion, he did not call the whole congregation together for this shorter message.

Verses 3-5: The Work of "the Lord your God"

The repetition of the title "the Lord your God" is significant, occurring thirteen times in the chapter. In addition, "Lord" occurs a further four times on its own. The overriding emphasis of the chapter is upon what the Lord God had done, what He promised to do in the future and upon their resultant responsibility.

"Lord" (3068) is the Hebrew word "Jehovah" and according to Strong means "the existing one". The name had special significance to the children of Israel since it was the name by which God made himself known to them and covenanted with them (Ex 6.2-8). "God" (430) is "Elohim" in Hebrew and, again, according to Strong, is a plural form of a word meaning "God" and is associated with the tri-unity of God. It is first used in connection with creation, occurring thirty times in Genesis 1. By using the title "the Lord your God", Joshua diverted the attention of the listeners away from himself to the eternal, covenant keeping, all-powerful God. His parting addresses were not memorials to himself; they were a powerful plea to the people to fix their gaze upon the Lord and, by remembering Him and His works, to face up to the responsibilities that lay before them as His people.

The past (vv.3-4)

"And ye have seen all that the Lord your God hath done unto all these nations because of you; for the Lord your God is he that hath fought for you" (v.3). Joshua called the people to bear witness to the work of the Lord their God in subduing the nations and he provided them with a reason as to why the Lord had done it; it was "because of you". They were the reason for the Lord God having defeated those nations. There are two aspects to the subjugation of the nations which had occupied Canaan. Firstly, the promise of the Lord to Abraham was that the land would be given to him and his descendants, only when the iniquity of the Amorites was full (Gen 15.16). The annihilation of the nations in Canaan was commanded by the Lord in order to judge their sin and to prevent the children of Israel from being affected by their idolatry (Deut 7.1-5). Secondly, Israel was the nation that the Lord had chosen for blessing, and His grace was manifested toward them in the giving of the land as a promised inheritance.

"Behold, I have divided unto you by lot these nations that remain, to be an inheritance for your tribes, from Jordan, with all the nations that I have cut off, even unto the great sea westward" (v.4). The nations had been defeated and their land distributed by Joshua. He described it as reaching from the Jordan to the Mediterranean Sea and, by so doing, confirmed that he was addressing the nine and a half tribes. It is interesting that Joshua referred to the "nations that remain" and not to the land. As has been previously noted, some of the nations that had been subdued in battle remained in the land that had been distributed to the children of Israel.

The future (v.5)

Joshua was careful to encourage the leaders of the tribes that the same Lord God who had kept His promises thus far would continue to fulfil them: "He shall expel them from before you, and drive them from out of your sight: and ye shall possess their land as the Lord your God hath promised you". He had made promises to both Moses (Deut 6.19) and Joshua, and Joshua expressed his faith in the Lord to fulfil His word.

Verses 6-13: Threefold Exhortation

The passage of time had not altered the exhortations which Moses had given to Joshua (Deut 31.7) and which were subsequently received by Joshua directly from the Lord (Josh 1.6-9). He took what had been committed to him and passed it on to those who would lead the people when he was gone. The apostle Paul gave similar instruction to Timothy, "the things that thou hast heard of me among many witnesses, the same commit thou to faithful men, who shall be able to teach others also" (2 Tim 2.2).

"Be ye therefore very courageous" (vv.6-7)

"Be ye therefore very courageous to keep and to do all that is written in the book of the law of Moses" (v.6). The Law had to be obeyed and it was placed at the centre of national life; this required courage. The leaders of the people had to be strong and courageous in the preservation and implementation of the Law. Leaders among God's people must always keep the Word of God at the centre of assembly life and this still requires courage. There are many who would prefer that the teaching of the Word of God should be less prominent or not be applied in certain circumstances. In situations where applying the Word is not the most popular course of action, courage is required on the part of those who lead. The implications of this exhortation were twofold:

• "That ye turn not aside therefrom to the right hand or to the left"*(v.6)*. Obedience meant absolute compliance. Legalism, which goes beyond and adds to the Word of God, is as unacceptable as liberalism, which falls short of the revealed truth of God. The warning of the apostle John as he concluded the book of Revelation, and which the Spirit of God has placed at the end of the canon of Scripture, is pertinent in this context: "For I testify unto every man that heareth the words of the prophecy of this book, If any man shall add unto these things, God shall add unto him the plagues that are written in this book: and if any man shall take away from the words of the book of this prophecy, God shall take away his part out of the book of life, and out of the holy city, and from the things which are written in this book" (Rev 22.18-19).

• "That ye come not among these nations, these that remain among you" (v.7). No social intimacy with the nations of Canaan was to be permitted, for that would be the first step on the road to idolatry. It is interesting that Joshua links preservation from idolatry with obedience to the Law. The extent to which they had to remain separate from these nations is stated in four prohibitions:

1. "neither make mention of the name of their gods"
2. "nor cause to swear by them"
3. "neither serve them"
4. "nor bow yourselves unto them" (v.7).

Their separation was to be their preservative from idolatry. They were not even to talk about the gods which were venerated by the nations of Canaan. Familiarity with these gods was to be avoided and the best way to accomplish this was not even to mention them. The apostle Paul warned about the danger of talking about matters which were unprofitable and sinful: "But fornication, and all uncleanness, or covetousness, let it not be once named among you, as becometh saints; neither filthiness, nor foolish talking, nor jesting, which are not convenient. but rather giving of thanks…have no fellowship with the unfruitful works of darkness, but rather reprove them. For it is a shame even to speak of those things which are done of them in secret" (Eph 5.3-4, 11-12).

There was now an exhortation regarding oaths. In business dealings with the nations there was to be no value placed upon an oath that was sworn by any pagan deity. On the basis that these gods were idols and had no power, any oath sworn by them was worthless as it relied upon a powerless idol for its authority. Any insistence upon such an oath by the children of Israel was a tacit acknowledgment of the existence of these gods and amounted to idolatry.

"Cleave unto the Lord your God" (vv.8-10)

Having warned them of the perils of association with the nations and the need for vigilance lest they become involved in idolatry, Joshua exhorted them positively to "cleave unto the Lord your God, as ye have done unto this day" (v.8). From the commencement of the conquest of Canaan the children of Israel had followed the Lord and remained faithful to Him. Joshua encouraged them to continue on this pathway. They had experienced the blessing of obedience, "For the Lord hath driven out from before you great nations and strong: but as for you, no man hath been able to stand before you unto this day" (v.9). Their knowledge of the faithfulness of the Lord in keeping His promises (Deut 4.38; 7.1,24; 9.1; 11.23,25) ought to have been a compelling reason for their continuance in cleaving to the Lord their God.

Past blessing was combined with the promise of blessing in the future: "One man of you shall chase a thousand: for the Lord your God, he it is that fighteth for you, as he hath promised you" (v.10). If the Lord had kept His promises during the war to conquer Canaan, then He ought to be trusted to keep His promises for the completion of the occupation (Lev 26.7-8). How little of the lessons of the past are learned in the present and form the basis for encouragement for the future !

"Love the Lord your God" (vv.11-13)

The greatest commandment of the Law, according to the Lord Jesus, was, "Thou shalt love the Lord thy God with all thy heart, and with all thy soul, and with all thy mind" (Mt 22.37). This exhortation lies at the heart of Joshua's address to the leadership of Israel and, no doubt, was intended to be communicated to the people. If their separation from the nations around them was to be maintained, it could not be done by sterile religiosity; it required deep affection for the Lord. And so Joshua exhorted them to "Take good heed therefore unto yourselves, that ye love the Lord your God" (v.11). "Now it requires more watchfulness and diligence than it did in the wilderness, because your temptations are now more and stronger; partly from the examples and insinuations of your bad neighbours, the remainders of this wicked people; and partly from your own peace and prosperity, and the pride, security, forgetfulness of God, and luxury which usually attend upon that condition, as God had warned them, (Deut 6.10-12)" (Matthew Poole's Commentary of the Bible). It is true that their love for the Lord would be the means of preservation from idolatry, but it was much more than that, it was the end in itself. There is no greater aim, or accomplishment, than to "love the Lord your God".

Should their affections be taken up with other gods, there were consequences to be borne, for God is a jealous God (Ex 20.5): "Else if ye do in any wise go back, and cleave unto the remnant of these nations, even these that remain among you, and shall make marriages with them, and go in unto them, and they to you: know for a certainty that the Lord your God will no more drive out any of these nations from before you; but they shall be snares and traps unto you, and scourges in your sides, and thorns in your eyes, until ye perish from off this good land which the Lord your God hath given you" (vv.12-13).

The sad history of Israel unfolds in the book of Judges when they neglected the warnings of Joshua and became embroiled with the nations which remained in Canaan (Judg 3.5-7). The children of Israel experienced only trouble and difficulty as a result of their association with them and ultimately idolatry led to captivity, in fulfilment of Joshua's warnings.

The lessons of the faithfulness of the Lord must be learned. He is faithful to His Word when He blesses the obedience of His people, but He is also faithful when He disciplines His people in accordance with His Word. Time and again the Scriptures warn that idolatry brings disaster to the children of God.

Verses 14-16: The Faithfulness of the Lord

As his address drew to a conclusion, Joshua lingered upon the theme of the faithfulness of the Lord and the double implication of this for the children of Israel. He urged them to take heed to this, drawing again upon their knowledge of the past and reminding them of his impending death. "And, behold, this day I am going the way of all the earth: and ye know in all your hearts and in all your souls, that not one thing hath failed of all the good things which the Lord your God spake concerning you; all are come to pass unto you, and not one thing hath failed thereof" (v.14). It was not a broad sweep of vague promises to which Joshua referred. He appealed to their genuine understanding of the detailed and comprehensive fulfilment of God's promises towards them. Not one had been overlooked or had failed.

If the Lord fulfilled His word to the letter when it came to blessing, He would be as diligent when it came to judgment. This was a concern for Joshua as he anticipated the dangers of idolatry for the children of Israel in years to come: "Therefore it shall come to pass, that as all good things are come upon you, which the Lord your God promised you; so shall the Lord bring upon you all evil things, until he have destroyed you from off this good land which the Lord your God hath given you" (v.15).

There is an element of prophecy about the admonition which Joshua gave in his discourse. He described their future conduct in relation to the nations of Canaan and their gods in a threefold way:

- "When ye have transgressed the covenant of the Lord your God, which he commanded you..."
- "...and have gone and served other gods ..."
- "...and bowed yourselves to them" (v.16a).

Joshua closed his address with the stark and uncompromising warning to a people who had begun a long-awaited occupation of their inheritance: "Then shall the anger of the Lord be kindled against you, and ye shall perish quickly from off the good land which he hath given unto you" (v.16b). In the complacency that follows conquest, the presence of the enemy was tolerated, then slowly accepted, and ultimately desired by the children of Israel. The faithfulness of the Lord who had given them the land was forgotten, as were the words of warning in relation to idolatry, sowing the seeds of disaster and discipline.

JOSHUA 24

Joshua's Second Farewell Discourse

Verse 1: Gathering at Shechem

For this second discourse "Joshua gathered all the tribes of Israel to Shechem". It was the last service that he would render to the Lord, and His people. "All the tribes of Israel" gathered at Shechem to hear Joshua reaffirm the covenant between the Lord and the people.

Shechem had appeared in the lists of cities and land distribution (17.2,7; 20.7; 21.21), but apart from that, nothing of note had taken place there for some time. For an Israelite, the city was a place of great historical significance. It was at Shechem, called Sichem, where Abraham received his first promise from the Lord and built an altar (Gen 12.6-7). Jacob built an altar there, which he named El-elohe-Israel, and later buried the idols of his household under the oak which was by Shechem (Gen 33.18-20; 35.2,4). These two events in the history of Israel meant that Shechem was associated with the presence of the Lord and the renunciation of idolatry; these being two of the main issues Joshua dealt with in his discourse.

Joshua "called for the elders of Israel, and for their heads, and for their judges, and for their officers", taking the same group of leaders that he had previously addressed, expecting them to represent the people and to communicate his words to them.

The statement, "They presented themselves before God", indicates that this assembly was more formal than the gathering at Timnath-serah or Shiloh. According to Keil & Delitzsch, "From the expression 'before God' it by no means follows that the ark had been brought to Shechem...for...'before God' (Elohim) is not to be identified with 'before Jehovah', which is used in 18.6 and 19.51 to denote the presence of the Lord above the ark of the covenant". As the people gathered, they did so in the conscious knowledge that "they came together in a solemn religious manner, as into the special presence of God, and with an eye to His speaking to them by Joshua" (Matthew Henry).

Verses 2-13: Brief Review of Israel's History

Joshua began his second discourse in a different way from his first: "And Joshua said unto all the people, Thus saith the Lord God of Israel" (v.2). Chapter 23 records his own last words to the people, but when he spoke at Shechem it was as the mouthpiece of the Lord. This was a direct communication from the Lord with Joshua acting as His prophet.

The "other side of the flood" (vv.2-4)

"Your fathers dwelt on the other side of the flood in old time, even Terah, the father of Abraham, and the father of Nachor: and they served other gods" (v.2). The Lord commenced His review of their history by taking them back to the days before Abraham had left Ur, with the emphasis upon their idolatrous background. Their ancestors had dwelt "of old beyond the Euphrates" (RSV). "The flood" (5104) is usually translated as "the river" and is the word used of the River Euphrates elsewhere in Scripture (Gen 31.21; Ex 23.31; Num 22.5; Josh 1.4). It is only here that Abraham's family is revealed to have been idolaters with the implication that Abraham was also an idolater, having been raised in a family where his father worshipped other gods.

It is interesting that although Terah had three sons (Gen 11.27), yet only Abraham and Nachor (Nahor) are named, and Haran is omitted. Keil & Delitzsch state that "Nahor is mentioned as well as Abraham, because Rebekah, and her nieces Leah and Rachel, the tribe-mothers of Israel, were descended from him (Gen 22.23; 29.10)".

"And I took your father Abraham from the other side of the flood, and led him throughout all the land of Canaan, and multiplied his seed, and gave him Isaac" (v.3). The Lord reminded them that it was He, and not Terah (Gen 11.31), who was responsible for Abraham's departure from Ur. In a demonstration of sovereign grace, Abraham was plucked from the obscurity of an idolatrous family and brought into the sphere of God's blessing. The verbs employed in the verse are instructive. He "took", "led", "multiplied", and "gave" to Abraham. The children of Israel are reminded, not only of their inglorious past, but also of the Lord's hand in the life of Abraham.

"And I gave unto Isaac Jacob and Esau: and I gave unto Esau mount Seir, to possess it; but Jacob and his children went down into Egypt" (v.4). The Lord continued to be with Abraham and his family. Esau and Jacob are presented in contrast to each other. Esau was given his inheritance, which was Mount Seir, whereas Jacob went down to Egypt with his family. The time for Canaan to be His people's possession had not come since the iniquity of the Amorites was not yet full (Gen 15.16).

Deliverance from Egypt (vv.5-7)

In the previous section, the Lord had referred to "your fathers" (v.2) and "your father Abraham" (v.3). A subtle progression in the language occurs through vv.5-7:

- "I brought you out" (v.5)
- "I brought your fathers out" (v.6)
- "ye came unto" (v.6)

- "after your fathers" (v.6)
- "when they cried" (v.7)
- "between you and the Egyptians" (v.7)
- "and your eyes have seen" (v.7)
- "and ye dwelt in the wilderness" (v.7).

By progressing to speak of "you" and "your", rather than "your fathers" and "they", the Lord linked the past with the present generation. The exodus from Egypt provided the bridge between the generations. Apart from Joshua and Caleb, all of the adults who had left Egypt had perished in the wilderness. However, there would have been some who were children during the exodus and who grew into adulthood in the wilderness.

"I sent Moses also and Aaron, and I plagued Egypt, according to that which I did among them: and afterward I brought you out" (v.5). He reminded them that He did three things when they were in Egypt. He provided leadership, plagued the Egyptians, and in so doing paved the way for their exodus from Egypt, which He also accomplished. As a nation they owed their leadership and liberty to the Lord. Only those who were aged twenty or over at the time of the exodus fell in the wilderness. Therefore, He said, "I brought you out", which was true of them as a nation but would have had a particular meaning for those who were now the leaders of the people and had probably been small children during the exodus.

"And I brought your fathers out of Egypt: and ye came unto the sea; and the Egyptians pursued after your fathers with chariots and horsemen unto the Red sea" (v.6). As he recounts their deliverance out of Egypt to the shore of the Red Sea, He uses "your fathers" and "ye" to speak of their journey toward the Red Sea and the pursuit by the Egyptian chariots and horsemen.

"And when they cried unto the Lord, he put darkness between you and the Egyptians, and brought the sea upon them, and covered them; and your eyes have seen what I have done in Egypt: and ye dwelt in the wilderness a long season" (v.7). The crossing of the Red Sea and the subsequent forty years in the wilderness are summarised succinctly. The Lord delivered them from Egypt and preserved them as they crossed the Red Sea (Ex 14.24-28), destroying the Egyptian chariots in the process. He calls them as witnesses to what he had done for them in Egypt. It was their disobedience which took them into the wilderness for forty years, although here He does not dwell on the fruit of that disobedience. "He protected them in the wilderness, where they are here said, not to wander, but to dwell for a long season. So wisely were all their motions directed, and so safely were they kept, that even there they had as certain a dwelling-place as if they had been in a walled city" (Matthew Henry).

Before the Jordan (vv.8-10)

The third aspect of the actions of the Lord on behalf of His people Israel is divided into two parts and relate to the conquest of the Amorites and the frustration of Balak and Balaam.

"And I brought you into the land of the Amorites, which dwelt on the other side Jordan; and they fought with you: and I gave them into your hand, that ye might possess their land; and I destroyed them from before you" (v.8). Although the names of Sihon and Og are not mentioned, their armies were defeated, and their land was conquered before the children of Israel passed over the Jordan (Num 21.21-35). The victory gained over the Amorites was one of the reasons that Rahab had given for her belief that the Lord had given the land of Canaan to Israel.

"Then Balak the son of Zippor, king of Moab, arose and warred against Israel, and sent and called Balaam the son of Beor to curse you: but I would not hearken unto Balaam; therefore he blessed you still: so I delivered you out of his hand" (vv.9-10). Balak sought to destroy the children of Israel by using subtle methods which did not involve him leading an army into the field of battle (Judg 11.25). The Lord thwarted his plan to have a curse pronounced upon the children of Israel and Balaam pronounced a blessing rather than a curse.

Warfare against the people of God does not always take the form of blatant hostility and is often conducted in a subtle and devious manner. In the beginning, the serpent gave notice of his methods when he approached Eve in the garden (Gen 3.1), tempting her with subtlety. The opposition of Sanballat and Tobiah to the rebuilding of the walls of Jerusalem, in the days of Nehemiah (Neh 2.19), is another example of the variety of methods which are used against the people of God.

Conquest of Canaan (vv.11-13)

"And ye went over Jordan, and came unto Jericho: and the men of Jericho fought against you, the Amorites, and the Perizzites, and the Canaanites, and the Hittites, and the Girgashites, the Hivites, and the Jebusites; and I delivered them into your hand" (v.11). The fourth aspect of the Lord's dealings with His people relates to the defeat of the nations which occupied the land. Jericho is specifically mentioned and then seven nations, of which Joshua had spoken prior to the crossing of the Jordan (3.10), are listed as being delivered by the Lord into the hand of the Israelites. It is interesting that the Lord states that the men of Jericho fought against the children of Israel. The earlier account (ch.6) gave no indication of active opposition apart from the city being "straitly shut up because of the children of Israel: none went out, and none came in" (6.1).

"And I sent the hornet before you, which drave them out from before you, even the two kings of the Amorites; but not with thy sword, nor with thy bow" (v.12). The conquest of Jericho, together with the defeat of the seven nations within Canaan and the two kings of the Amorites on the east of the Jordan, were all accomplished by the Lord and not as a result of military power.

Commentators are divided as to the meaning of "the hornet". It is possible that the Lord actually sent swarms of hornets before the children of Israel when they went into battle, bringing terror and confusion to the enemy. He had promised, "I will send my fear before thee, and will destroy all the people to whom thou shalt come, and I will make all thine enemies turn their backs unto thee. And I will send hornets before thee, which shall drive out the Hivite, the Canaanite, and the Hittite, from before thee" (Ex 23.27-28). However, it is worth pointing out that there is no mention of hornets in any of the battle accounts and it is probable that the mention of "the hornet" is metaphorical, indicating the effect upon Israel's foes of the Lord's intervention. There is no doubt that, whether or not the hornet is to be understood in a literal sense, the point is that the Lord went before the children of Israel and was responsible for the victories which they accomplished on the battlefield.

"And I have given you a land for which ye did not labour, and cities which ye built not, and ye dwell in them; of the vineyards and oliveyards which ye planted not do ye eat" (v.13). Finally, the Lord reminds them that His provision for them went beyond the minimum. He gave them victory and possession of the land, but it was not vacant possession, the bounty of the land was included. It was a complete inheritance. When settlers advance into new land they often have to start a process of clearing ground, planting crops and building houses. The children of Israel moved into a land which already had cities and cultivated fields. Yet again, the Lord had fulfilled His promises (Deut 6.10-11).

Verses 14-28: Covenant

Challenge (v.14)

With the Lord's words ringing in their ears, Joshua challenged the people to respond. "Now therefore", is a compelling form of argument when set against the backdrop of divine grace and mercy. Paul wrote in a similar way to the Romans: "I beseech you therefore, brethren, by the mercies of God, that ye present your bodies a living sacrifice, holy, acceptable unto God, which is your reasonable service" (Rom 12.1).

Joshua's challenge was threefold:

a) "Fear the Lord"

Having seen and experienced the Lord's character manifested in great works of power, grace and judgment, Joshua challenged the people to fear Him. The fear of the Lord in Scripture is a large subject and is worthy of study, particularly the occurrences in the book of Proverbs. John Gill wrote in his *Expositor* that "Since He has done such great and good things, fear the Lord and His goodness, fear Him for His goodness' sake; nothing so influences fear, or a reverential affection for God, as a sense of His goodness; this engages men sensible of it to fear the Lord, that is, to worship Him both internally and externally in the exercise of every grace, and in the performance of every duty".

b) "Serve him in sincerity and in truth"

The fear of the Lord is consistent with activity. Their attitude of heart toward the Lord ought to have produced a willingness to serve Him. The character of such service must be in accordance with the character of the Lord, whom they fear. Therefore, Joshua challenged them to serve the Lord "in sincerity and truth"; this would determine not only what they did for the Lord, but how and why they did it, without hypocrisy and in keeping with His revealed will.

c) "Put away the gods which your fathers served on the other side of the flood, and in Egypt"

Moses and Joshua had often warned the people of the importance of their fidelity to the Lord. Joshua was aware that as a family and, subsequently, as a nation, they had never fully divested themselves of the idolatry which characterised them in Ur (v.2). He referred to the "gods which your fathers served...in Egypt". This is the first direct indication in Scripture that the children of Israel were idolaters when they resided in Goshen, although there is reference to the practice of idolatry in the Law (Lev 17.7).

Joshua's challenge was balanced. They had to put the Lord in His rightful place and serve Him, whilst rejecting the various forms of idolatry that abounded in the nations around them. The verse ends with repetition of the exhortation, "...and serve ye the Lord". The NKJV translates the expression as, "Serve the Lord!".

Choice (v.15)

Joshua clearly expressed the decision which the people faced: "And if it seem evil unto you to serve the Lord, choose you this day whom ye will serve; whether the gods which your fathers served that were on the other side of the flood, or the gods of the Amorites, in whose land ye dwell". The choice was to serve the Lord or return to the gods which their fathers had known in Ur of the Chaldees, or to those of the Canaanites.

There are two ways in which Joshua sought to point the children of

Israel in the right direction. He categorised a rejection of the Lord as a completely illogical response to what He had done for them by using the expression, "if it seem evil unto you". Here the idea is that serving the Lord would be "unjust, unreasonable, or inconvenient" (Matthew Poole Commentary), which, under any interpretation of the Lord's dealings with them, was unreasonable. Joshua declared his own position, as any good leader should when seeking to direct the people of God: "But as for me and my house, we will serve the Lord". It was an unambiguous statement of intent, which was independent of the decision reached by the children of Israel. The statement was bold, incisive, exemplary and courageous.

There are times when elders and spiritual leaders have to bring the people of God to a point of decision regarding their service for the Lord. Such moments are crucial in determining the direction of an individual, or an assembly, and are often crossroad experiences where vital decisions are made. In the early days of new life experiences, such as leaving home for further study, looking forward to marriage, establishing a home, or moving location, a decision has to be made regarding the service of the Lord. What will be the main factor in the decision? Will it be the service of the Lord or the gods of materialism, pleasure, or success? When making such a decision, the believer ought to remember what the Lord has done for him and take into account the example of godly elders and spiritual leaders. The Christian has no logical or legitimate alternative to serving the Lord.

Response (vv.16-18)

"And the people answered and said, God forbid that we should forsake the Lord, to serve other gods" (v.16). It was the right response, articulated in strong and definite language. "They speak with the utmost abhorrence of idolatry, as a thing far from their hearts and thoughts, as the most abominable and execrable that could be thought or spoken of" (John Gill's Expositor). They appeared to understand that they could not go after other gods and serve the Lord. To serve one is to forsake the other. The basis for their decision summarised what they had heard from the Lord (vv.2-13).

"For the Lord our God, he it is that brought us up and our fathers out of the land of Egypt, from the house of bondage, and which did those great signs in our sight, and preserved us in all the way wherein we went, and among all the people through whom we passed" (v.17). This was the first time in the book of Joshua that they had used the title "the Lord our God". The two and a half tribes had invoked it when they were pleading their case with the children of Israel, in the matter of the altar Ed (22.29). It is covenant language and was an appropriate title to use in the circumstances. When challenged to decide about the service of the Lord they begin by stating that the Lord (3068 - Jehovah) is their God (430 - (Elohim).

They assented to all that the Lord had said to them and gladly attributed their deliverance from Egypt and their preservation throughout the wilderness journey to the Lord. This preservation was through difficult terrain and hostile nations. It is interesting that they described Egypt as "the house of bondage". This is one of the ten occasions within Scripture when Egypt is referred to in this way, this being the penultimate reference, the final one being in Judges 6.8. This is the only time that the children of Israel use the expression, the other nine references are reminders to them of the true character of their latter years in Egypt.

"And the Lord drave out from before us all the people, even the Amorites which dwelt in the land: therefore will we also serve the Lord; for he is our God". They also agreed that it was the Lord who had driven out the seven nations of Canaan, "all the people" even the strongest of the nations, "even the Amorites" (v.18; Amos 2.9). In conclusion, they joined with Joshua and committed themselves to the service of the Lord and summarised what had gone before with their declaration that they have one God and He is Jehovah.

Warning (vv.19-20)

Joshua responded by setting before them the solemnity of their undertaking and the seriousness of the consequences should they fail. It was essential that they clearly understood what they were doing when they declared that they would serve the Lord. If they relied on their own strength and resources, it was an impossible task. "And Joshua said unto the people, Ye cannot serve the Lord" (v.19), "by your own resolution only, and without the assistance of divine grace, without solid and serious conversion from all idols and without true repentance and faith" (J. H. Michaelis, quoted by Keil & Delitzsch).

a) Character of the Lord

Serving the Lord was not like serving other gods: "He is an holy God; he is a jealous God" (v.19). His holiness meant that those who serve Him must be holy (Lev 19.2). As a jealous God, He would not accommodate any rival for their devotion (Ex 20.4-6). In the New Testament the character of the Lord brings the same demands upon the Christian for exclusive and holy service (James 4.4-5; 1 Pet 1.16).

b) Reaction of the Lord to failure

The Lord's character meant "he will not forgive your transgressions nor your sins" (v.19). Herein lay the problem for the children of Israel; they were willing to serve the Lord, but the demands of His service were such that transgressions and sins would not be tolerated. Provision for atonement for sins had been made in the offerings and therefore, although it is an absolute statement, it does require to be read in conjunction with the verse that follows, which sets out the transgressions and sins to which Joshua referred.

"If ye forsake the Lord, and serve strange gods" (v.20). There was the possibility that they could presume upon the goodness of the Lord. Joshua warned that if they served other gods and became an idolatrous nation, they would experience judgment at the hand of the Lord. The Lord's response to idolatry would be threefold:

- "then he will turn"

He would assume a different attitude to them from that which they had enjoyed.

- "and do you hurt"

The contrast is with the good which He had done to them. In the past they had received "good" from the Lord and, although there were notable exceptions owing to their sin in the wilderness, this had been their general experience.

- "and consume you"

It was not only a change of attitude, He would actively move in judgment against them.

Response (v.21)

"And the people said unto Joshua, Nay; but we will serve the Lord". There is no record of a dissenting voice among the people. They spoke as one and re-affirmed their undertaking to serve the Lord, notwithstanding Joshua's warning. The reader who knows the subsequent history would want to intervene at this point in the narrative and ask them to take time to consider their own weakness and propensity to sin, before entering into such a covenant with the Lord. They were confident of their own ability to meet the demands of such an undertaking, without placing a caveat in their response. It would have been more realistic for them to declare that with the help of the Lord, and despite their own failings, they would seek to serve Him. It appears that they had not learned the lesson of Mount Sinai when they stated, "All that the Lord hath spoken we will do" (Ex 19.8).

Witness (vv.22-24)

The undertaking was a voluntary decision which they had made with all of the facts before them: "And Joshua said unto the people, Ye are witnesses against yourselves that ye have chosen you the Lord, to serve him. And they said, We are witnesses" (v.22). Their repeated affirmation served to place them in a position of not only being a party to the covenant, but also serving as a witness to what had been stated. In effect, if they transgressed, their words would condemn them. Comment has previously been made (22.27) on the subject of "witness".

It is interesting that Joshua did not let the people make such a declaration without insisting on immediate implementation: "Now therefore put away, said he, the strange gods which are among you, and incline your heart unto the Lord God of Israel" (v.23). It is unlikely that the people carried about with them idols of wood and stone. Keil & Delitzsch comment that "the grosser forms of idolatry had disappeared from Israel with the dying out of the generation that was condemned at Kadesh. The new generation, which had been received afresh into covenant with the Lord by circumcision at Gilgal, and had set up the covenant at Ebal...had no idols of wood, stone, or metal but only...the idols of the heart". This is confirmed by Joshua's demand to "incline your heart". There were no statues abandoned or groves destroyed following Joshua's command, which does seem to indicate that Joshua was referring to their hearts when he told them to put away the strange gods. On other occasions when similar requests were made (Gen 35.4; 1 Sam 7.4), idols were destroyed. All idolatry is essentially rooted in an attitude of heart which eventually finds an external expression. Solomon's example ought to serve as a warning (1 Kings 11.2,4,9).

In a final response, the people make their third declaration of fealty and obedience: "And the people said unto Joshua, The Lord our God will we serve, and his voice will we obey" (v.24).

Ratification of the covenant (vv.25-28)

The word "covenant" does not appear in the chapter until this point; this has caused some discussion among commentators. For a covenant to exist there must be an agreement between a minimum of two parties. On this occasion it appears that there is only a unilateral declaration by the people. However, the Lord's part in the covenant is implicit in Joshua's warning regarding His character and the response He would make to any failure by the people. Joshua was reminding them of the covenant which had been established at Mount Sinai and renewed on the plains of Moab (Deut 28-30) and binding them to their obligation. It was no longer their fathers and forefathers who had made the commitment. They were now directly accountable for their own declaration.

"So Joshua made a covenant with the people that day, and set them a statute and an ordinance in Shechem" (v.25). The formal nature of the covenant is seen by the ceremony associated with its ratification. In its singular form, the expression "a statute and an ordinance" is used to describe the covenant which the Lord made with Israel at Marah, after He made the waters sweet (Ex 15.25). It is also used of the principle that David established at the brook Besor: "As his part is that goeth down to the battle, so shall his part be that tarrieth by the stuff: they shall part alike" (1 Sam 30.24). On this occasion, Joshua was principally concerned with the possibility of the people seeking after other gods and committing idolatry. This was the specific context of the statute and ordinance and does not mean that the Lord altered the Law which had been given to Moses on Sinai.

"And Joshua wrote these words in the book of the law of God, and took a great stone, and set it up there under an oak, that was by the sanctuary of the Lord" (v.26). He did not add the words to the Law, since they do not appear in the Pentateuch, and therefore must have placed them with the Law. Moses had delivered the written form of the Law as a book to the priests with the instruction, "Put it in the side of the ark of the covenant of the Lord your God, that it may be there for a witness against thee" (Deut 31.26). The recorded words of this covenant must have been placed with Moses' book. The only other mention of the book of the Law of God is when Ezra "read in the book of the law of God. And they kept the feast seven days; and on the eighth day was a solemn assembly, according unto the manner" (Neh 8.18). It is interesting that this was part of the re-establishment of the Feast of Tabernacles when "all the congregation of them that were come again out of the captivity made booths, and sat under the booths: for since the days of Jeshua the son of Nun unto that day had not the children of Israel done so" (Neh 8.17).

"As it often happens, that that which is written remains concealed in unopened books, another aid is given to the memory, one which should always be exposed to the eye, namely, the stone under the ark, near the sanctuary" (Calvin). Keil & Delitzsch translate "under the oak that was in the sanctuary of Jehovah". They take the view that the reference is not to the tabernacle, nor any temporary altar erected for the renewal of the covenant, but rather to the "holy place under the oak, where Abraham had formerly built an altar and worshipped the Lord, and where Jacob had purified his house from the strange gods, which he buried under this oak, or rather terebinth tree (Gen 12.6,7; 35.2,4)". Most commentators link the "book of the law of God" and the "sanctuary of the Lord" and conclude that the tabernacle, or at least the ark, was present at Shechem (see comments on v.1).

"And Joshua said unto all the people, Behold, this stone shall be a witness unto us; for it hath heard all the words of the Lord which he spake unto us: it shall be therefore a witness unto you, lest ye deny your God" (v.27). There were now two witnesses to the covenant. The people had heard and the great stone set up under the oak at Shechem was also a witness, metaphorically listening to all that had been said and it now stood as a silent testimony to the covenant. The covenant had been witnessed in accordance with the general principle that "in the mouth of two or three witnesses every word may be established" (Mt 18.16).

"So Joshua let the people depart, every man unto his inheritance" (v.28). It was the last recorded occasion that the people saw him. His work was complete.

Verses 29-33: Three Burials

Joshua (vv.29-31)

"And it came to pass after these things, that Joshua the son of Nun, the servant of the Lord, died, being an hundred and ten years old" (v.29). For the last time Joshua is given his full name and for the first time is called "the servant of the Lord". It is a title which Moses received after he had died. With his labours over and service rendered, Joshua received this high accolade and is no longer referred to as Moses' minister (1.1). When Moses died, Joshua was there to assume responsibility, but there was no successor to Joshua. The nation was established in the land with a civil structure of governance which did not require a central leader. "The elders of Israel, and...their heads, and...their judges, and...their officers" (24.1), who had presented themselves before the Lord in Shechem, together with the Levitical system of priesthood, meant that no judge, king, or prophet was required in Israel. There was no need for a standing army and if the people had adhered to the covenant, they would have experienced undisturbed peace and prosperity.

"And they buried him in the border of his inheritance in Timnath-serah, which is in mount Ephraim, on the north side of the hill of Gaash" (v.30). He was buried in his own land (19.50). There is no record of national mourning; this is appropriate when the typology is considered. Joshua had finished his life with the land opened and the inheritance divided. This was a cause for rejoicing rather than mourning.

"And Israel served the Lord all the days of Joshua, and all the days of the elders that overlived Joshua, and which had known all the works of the Lord, that he had done for Israel" (v.31). There are occasions when the good influence of a godly man diminishes after his death, e.g. the influence of Jehoiada upon king Joash (2 Chr 24.17-18). It was not so with Joshua. The people observed the covenant while Joshua lived, and continued to do so after his death and while the elders, who had been with him, remained among them.

Joseph (v.32)

"And the bones of Joseph, which the children of Israel brought up out of Egypt, buried they in Shechem, in a parcel of ground which Jacob bought of the sons of Hamor the father of Shechem for an hundred pieces of silver: and it became the inheritance of the children of Joseph". As the book draws to a close, the immediate links with Egypt are drawn together. Joseph's bones, which had been brought out of Egypt (Gen 50.25-26), were buried in fulfilment of their fathers' promise in Egypt. It is likely that the burial took place at the same time as the gathering of the people at Shechem but is only incorporated in the narrative at this point.

Eleazar (v.33)

"And Eleazar the son of Aaron died; and they buried him in a hill that pertained to Phinehas his son, which was given him in mount Ephraim". Like Joshua, Eleazar, his contemporary, was buried on his own land.

JUDGES

C. T. Lacey

CONTENTS

BIBLIOGRAPHY

Barber, Cyril J. *Judges - A Narrative of God's Power.* Loizeaux Brothers, 1990.

The author brings out the parallels between the times of the judges and our modern difficulties and challenges. He highlights the problems and draws out the path to recovery.

Coates, C.A. *An Outline of the Books of Joshua, Judges and Ruth.* Kingston Bible Trust, undated.

A very brief outline of the book, based on notes taken at a series of Bible Readings. It contains many useful applications of the text to believers and local assemblies today.

Cundall, Arthur E. *Judges – An Introduction and Commentary.* Tyndale Old Testament Commentaries: Inter-Varsity Press, 1968.

This is a very helpful commentary that takes the book section-by-section and draws out the main themes. It comments on the individual verses, including the difficult ones. It is both scholarly and readable.

Davis, Dale R. *Judges – Such Great Salvation.* Christian Focus Publications, 2000, reprinted 2003.

This is a lively and practical exposition of Judges in which the author analyses the major literary and theological themes of each section of the book. Some readers may find the author's use of humour inappropriate in the setting of such dark days for Israel.

Fausset, A.R. *A Critical and Expository Commentary on the Book of Judges.* The Banner of Truth Trust, 1999.

A very comprehensive commentary in which the author examines the original Hebrew, gives a great deal of interesting background to the book, and seeks to draw out the spiritual lessons. The "Synopsis of Contents" at the beginning of the book is essential to access easily the amount of material available.

Kelly, William. *Lectures on The Book of Judges.* Bible Truth Publishers, 1945.

A very brief book based on two lectures delivered by the author to stimulate further study of the book of Judges.

Gooding, A.M.S. *The 13 Judges.* Gospel Tract Publications, 1986.

This book is based on tapes of addresses given in various parts of the world. The judges are dealt with in a practical way and it contains many valuable lessons for the present time.

Goslinga, C.J. *Joshua, Judges, Ruth.* Zondervan Publishing House, 1986 (translated from Dutch).

A comprehensive introduction to, and verse-by-verse exposition of, Judges. It contains numerous footnotes which are worth taking the time to access.

Jennings, F.C. *Judges and Ruth.* Believers Bookshelf Inc., 1905.
In the writer's own words, this book makes "no pretension to be anything more than an endeavour to discern the practical application to the present day of the incidents recorded in the book of Judges".

Marshall, F. *The Book of Judges* (Oxford and Cambridge Edition). George Gill & Sons, undated.
It contains helpful background notes, maps and brief comments on the text.

Mawson, J.T. *How to Overcome: Being Talks on the Judges.* R.Besley, Patternoster Row, undated.
A series of talks given by the author on Judges, covering the themes of overcoming the world, the flesh, the devil, earthly things, and carnal religion.

Meyer, F.B. – *The Christian Bible Readings.* London: Morgan & Scott.
The author refers to this book as "jottings on the books of the Old Testament". The brief section on Judges inspires the reader to meditation and further study.

Paisley, Ian R.K. *Divine Intervention in Days of Declension – Studies in the Book of Judges.* Ambassador Publications, 2002.
Based on a series of messages preached by the author. He argues powerfully that the God of the judges is our God, and that His desire is to stir up to dedication and prayer to thirst for and expect divine intervention today.

Ridout, S. *Overcoming in Days of Ruin – Lectures on the Book of Judges.* Loizeaux Brothers, undated.
The author submits that his book is not intended to be "a manual for study". Produced in the form of lectures he delivered, it has a familiar and colloquial style, easy to be understood. It makes many thought-provoking applications that challenge the reader to be among the overcomers in days of ruin.

Rossier, H.L. *Meditations on the Book of Judges.* Bible Truth Publishers, undated.
A series of short meditations on Judges, which show that, in a day of ruin, God can be fully glorified as in the church's brightest days.

Unger, Merrill F. *Commentary on the Old Testament.* AMG Publishers, 2002.
A very useful commentary, providing a section by-section-section exposition that makes the characters and stories come alive. It abounds with very helpful scriptural cross-references that are worth taking the time to explore.

Wiersbe Warren W. *Be Available.* Chariot Victor Publishing, 1979.
A readable and practical survey of Judges that emphasises, no matter how dark the day, God can still work through people who will trust His Word, yield to His Spirit, and do His bidding. It challenges believers to "be available".

Willcock, Michael. *The Message of Judges.* The Bible Speaks Today Series – Inter-Varsity Press, 1992.

A helpful exposition of the text that relates it to contemporary life. The author shows that God never abandons His people, and that the book of Judges is the story of God's grace.

Wiseman, Luke H. *Practical Truths from Judges.* Kregel Publications, 1985. *The author gives a general overview of the period of the judges and then provides an in-depth study of just four of them – Barak, Gideon, Jephthah, and Samson. As the title suggests, he brings out many practical lessons.*

INTRODUCTION

Setting the Scene

"The Lord our God will we serve, and his voice will we obey" (Josh 24.24) - this was the boast of the children of Israel in response to Joshua's final words to them before his death: "Choose you this day whom ye will serve" (Josh 24.15). He had given them a solemn warning as to the consequences of departure from God in order to serve strange gods. He had brought them into "a land that floweth with milk and honey" (Josh 5.6), the land the Lord had promised to them, and each tribe had been allotted an inheritance within it. They faced the challenge to move forward and possess what belonged to them. That same challenge faces believers today. Paul wrote to the Ephesians, "Blessed be the God and Father of our Lord Jesus Christ, who hath blessed us with all spiritual blessings in heavenly places in Christ" (Eph 1.3). Our blessings are spiritual, but they are just as real and we need to lay claim to them. A. Leckie writes, "No earthly or temporal blessing could exceed these...God does not dole out His blessings piecemeal; there are no first, second or third blessings; they are all ours. The enjoyment of them is another matter" (*Ephesians – Ritchie New Testament Commentaries*).

The book of Judges opens on an optimistic note as the children of Israel turned to the Lord and asked, "Who shall go up for us against the Canaanites first, to fight against them?" (1.1). They recognised that there was a battle to be fought and enemies to be expelled if they were to lay hold of and enjoy their blessings. Joshua had been the clear successor to Moses, but at this time they faced a very different situation. There was no obvious leader to act as a central unifying focus for them. The book draws towards its conclusion with similar words, "Which of us shall go up first to the battle against the children of Benjamin?" (20.18). However, the context had changed and an ominous note was struck. The battle was no longer against the enemy, but against their brethren! The book of Judges charts the course of events that resulted in this dramatic deterioration. F.C.Jennings remarks, "How serious must have been the declension between the two incidents! The question of chronology is of small importance; it is not an easy one to determine; but morally these two incidents evidently begin and end the book" (*Judges and Ruth*).

The early promise could have been maintained and developed if the children of Israel had, in obedience to the Lord, driven out the Canaanites and possessed the inheritance He had given them in the land of Canaan. The major threat posed by the Canaanites was not so much a military one, but a spiritual. Their corrupt religion was destined to undermine the children of Israel's covenant relationship with God, their worship, their relationships with each other and God's call for them to be holy (Lev 11.44). However, they failed to recognise the danger and the days of the judges were marked by an ever-increasing decline into disobedience, apostasy and anarchy. Indeed, military success over their enemies did not go hand-in-hand with spiritual progress. They did not succeed in driving out the Canaanites and therefore what appeared to be success was, in fact, failure in the eyes of God. Both individuals and tribes pursued their own personal agendas, so that any sense of direction and unity was lost. S.Ridout writes, "The key thought of the Book of Judges is this – the failure to make progress ... failure to make progress is the root of all the failure and departure from God of His people" (*Lectures on the book of Judges*).

The children of Israel ought to have acknowledged God as King, but the book draws to its close with a sad testimony: "In those days there was no king in Israel: every man did that which was right in his own eyes" (21.25). Gideon responded to the men of Israel's request for him to lead them by saying, "I will not rule over you, neither shall my son rule over you: the Lord shall rule over you" (8.23). If the people had accepted and embraced this truth, there would have been no need for God to raise up judges. Later on He declared to Samuel, "for they have not rejected thee, but they have rejected me, that I should not reign over them" (1 Sam 8.7). It was at that point that the monarchy was introduced and God said to Samuel, "Hearken unto their voice, and make them a king" (1 Sam 8.22). Indeed, it may well be that the Book of Judges was written during the early years of the monarchy in Israel. Its author is unknown, although Hebrew tradition maintains that it was the work of Samuel.

However, there is a danger in dwelling exclusively on the failures of the day. It could lead to the justifiable charge of giving a one-sided picture, both of the Lord and of His people. The divine record is frequently punctuated with the phrase, "the land had rest". Indeed, it should be observed that the total recorded years of rest during the period of the judges outnumbered those spent under the servitude and oppression of their enemies. Again, F.C.Jennings' comments are appropriate here. He pictured the downward path of the children of Israel as "like that from 'Jerusalem to Jericho', not uninterrupted, but crossing many a healthy mountain range, as, by the Lord's sovereign mercy, it rises above the low mists and swamps of unbelief, and goes over some fair upland of faith where a 'worthy one' has his dwelling place: a Gideon, a Barak, a Jephthah" (*Judges and Ruth*). His words reflect the truth expressed in the New Testament's great gallery of faith: "And what shall I more say? for the time would fail me to tell of Gedeon, and of Barak, and of Samson, and of Jephthae; of David also, and Samuel, and of the prophets: who through faith subdued kingdoms, wrought righteousness, obtained promises, stopped the mouths of lions, quenched the violence of fire, escaped the edge of the sword, out of weakness were made strong, waxed valiant in fight, turned to flight the armies of the aliens" (Heb11.32-34). It is interesting to note that the inspired writer included four characters from the times of the judges in his gallery of only six named people. Clearly, a significant faithful remnant was to be found in the land. The names of

Gideon, Samson and Samuel bear testimony to this. It reminds us that, even in the darkest of days, the Lord has found men and women of faith who, whatever the personal cost, have experienced the truth of His words to the apostle Paul: "My grace is sufficient for thee: for my strength is made perfect in weakness" (2 Cor 12.9).

The book of Judges bears testimony time and time again to the truth that God is sovereign and in total control of the affairs of His people and the nations surrounding them. In spite of the anarchy of the day, He was still on the throne! His faithfulness shone out against the dark backdrop of Israel's infidelity. As well as using the nations to discipline and chasten the children of Israel (2.14), the Lord also "raised up judges, which delivered them out of the hand of those that spoiled them" (2.16). The word for "judge" (SHAPAT – 8199) has the thought of pronouncing judgment (for or against), to vindicate or punish, to govern, to save, to rescue. Their influence therefore went beyond that of the legal sphere of administering justice and arbitrating in disputes between the people. Clearly, they were looked upon as leaders and saviours from the power of Israel's enemies and therefore their actions were given greater prominence than their words. However, it would be doing them an injustice to limit their contribution to success in battle alone. The people also valued their wisdom and judgments. For example, it is said of Deborah, "the children of Israel came up to her for judgment" (4.5).

The message of the book of Judges is timeless. It is impossible to read it and feel divorced from it. It is not difficult to see the strong parallels between then and now. Spiritual anarchy, disobedience to God's word, idolatry, an increasing tolerance of immorality, a lack of unity among believers and their unwillingness to walk a pathway of separation to God are features of this present day, as they were in the times of the judges. Believers will do well to heed the warnings and recognise the downward spiral awaiting those who pursue such a course. However, it is the present writer's prayerful desire that believers will capture something of the exciting rewards open to those who bow to the sovereignty of God, obey His word and allow His strength to work through their weakness. S.Ridout expresses the same desire when he writes, "Faith shines brightest in the dark, and the book before us gives many examples of a faith that brightens by contrast with its surroundings. May we learn not to be disheartened by the ruin about us, but be rightly exercised. May we see God's purpose in leaving the evil about us, not that we should be engulfed by it, but conquer it" (*Lectures on the book of Judges*).

The author of the book of Judges increasingly confronts his readers with the weaknesses and failures of the various judges (saviours) presented to them. However, this ought to encourage believers to consider the perfections of their Saviour, the Lord Jesus Christ. The deliverance the judges brought was partial and often tainted by their own shortcomings. They led the people into victory and a period of peace, but they could not keep them there. Indeed, there is the distressing sight of Samson ending his days in the Philistines' prison house, bound with fetters of brass (16.21). The writer to the Hebrews says, "For such an high priest became us, who is holy, harmless, undefiled, separate from sinners" (Heb 7.26). Long before He came, Isaiah prophesied of Him, "He shall not fail nor be discouraged, till he have set judgment in the earth: and the isles shall wait for his law" (Is 42.4). There is nothing incomplete about the salvation He brings: "But this man, because he continueth ever, hath an unchangeable priesthood. Wherefore he is able also to save them to the uttermost that come unto God by him, seeing he ever liveth to make intercession for them" (Heb 7.24-25). He not only saves from the penalty of sin, but daily from the power of sin. His intercession keeps His people and sustains them as they travel through this corrupt and immoral world. J.Flanigan writes, "But this ability to save completely is based upon the fact that He continues for ever. He will not carry us through the wilderness for part of the journey, only to hand us over at some stage to the care of another. He will carry us all the way. He will save completely and to the end" (*Hebrews – Ritchie New Testament Commentaries*). The Lord's people ought to respond in thankfulness and praise, "Hallelujah, what a Saviour!".

OUTLINE

The SEEDS of failure 1.1 – 3.6

The SAVIOURS who delivered 3.7 – 16.31

Othniel and the Syrians 3.7-11

Ehud and the Moabites 3.12-30

Shamgar and the Philistines 3.31

Deborah, Barak and the Canaanites 4.1-5.31

Gideon and the Midianites 6.1-8.35 (internal discord following his death – Abimelech, his son, seizes kingship 9.1-57)

Tola and Jair 10.1-5

Jephthah and the Ammonites 10.6-12.7

Ibzan, Elon and Abdon 12.8-15

Samson and the Philistines 13.1-16.31

The SUMMIT of the nation's sin 17.1 – 21.25

Religious Corruption - idolatry 17.1-18.31

Moral Corruption - immorality 19.1-30

Anarchy 20.1-21.25

THE SEEDS OF FAILURE (1.1–3.6)

JUDGES 1

Verses 1-15: The Potential for Possession of the Land

Joshua's time as leader of the children of Israel was drawing to a close when the Lord said to him, "Thou art old and stricken in years, and there remaineth yet very much land to be possessed" (Josh 13.1). Each tribe had been allotted its particular inheritance in the land, but the commencement of the book of Judges reveals that they had not yet possessed all of it. It serves as a reminder to believers today that the Person and work of Christ has opened up to them innumerable blessings for the enrichment of their spiritual lives, but they must possess them by faith if they are to enjoy them. Sadly, like the children of Israel, many are content to live as spiritual paupers.

Initially, it appeared as if the potential for possessing Canaan, the "land which floweth with milk and honey" (Num 14.8), would be turned into reality.

Firstly, in v.1 the people of Israel turned to the Lord for guidance as to who should go up against the Canaanites first. This request was in itself an indication that the quest to possess the land was not as far advanced as it ought to have been. If the people had been living in the good of all that Joshua had achieved, such a request would not have been necessary. For example, Judah and Simeon did not seek to take possession of territory that was new to them. Joshua had conquered "all the country of the hills, and of the south, and of the vale, and of the springs, and all their kings" (Josh 10.40) and they had settled there (Josh 15 & 19), but the Canaanites began to regain a foothold in the land. The term "Canaanites" is a general designation of the enemies of Israel that inhabited the promised land and includes the Jebusites, Amorites, Girgashites and Hivites. They worshipped Baal, a male fertility god, and his female consort, Asherah. However, on a positive note, at least the children of Israel displayed a commendable desire to do the right thing here and sought the Lord's direction. A vital ingredient for success in spiritual warfare is for Christians to know what the Lord's will is, so that they tread His pathway, not their own.

Secondly, in v.2 the Lord responded to their exercise and indicated that Judah should go up. Judah was the largest, most powerful and kingly tribe. Jacob said of him, "Thou art he whom thy brethren shall praise: thy hand shall be in the neck of thine enemies" (Gen 49.8). Clearly, God marked him out as the one upon whom the leadership mantle, left by the departures of Moses and Joshua, should fall. When the Lord answers, it will be accompanied by the promise of guaranteed success: "Judah shall go up: behold, I have delivered the land into his hand." Judah could, therefore, set out against the might of the enemy with confidence and without fear.

Thirdly, in v.3 there was a display of unity at the outset that progressively deteriorated during the period of the judges. Judah invited Simeon, his brother, to go up and fight against the Canaanites; this received a positive response. Some commentators regard this as an act of disobedience, a sign of weakness and a lack of faith on the part of Judah. They point out that there was no need to depend on his brother when God had given such positive assurances of success and, therefore, it is no surprise that Simeon's name was not included in the record of the victory. It may well be that there is more than a grain of truth in this observation. However, it should be noted that they were blood brothers (Gen 35.23) and Simeon's inheritance was within that of the tribe of Judah (Josh 19.1). It is a legitimate argument, therefore, that it was a strength, not a weakness, to see them working in harmony during such exacting times, even though Judah could claim to be a far more prominent tribe than Simeon. David, who had seen much disunity in his personal and national life, highlighted the importance of unity among the Lord's people: "Behold, how good and how pleasant it is for brethren to dwell together in unity!" (Ps 133.1). There must be an atmosphere of mutual help and support among the Lord's people if they are to function effectively in their spiritual warfare. Paul encouraged the assembly at Corinth to appreciate that "those members of the body, which seem to be more feeble, are necessary ... there should be no schism in the body; but that the members should have the same care one for another" (I Cor 12.22,25). C.A.Coates remarked, "We must not move without our brethren. While it remains true that we can get everything from God – in an abstract sense everything comes from God, even help from the brethren – but we not only get help from God, but from our brethren" (*An Outline of the Book of Judges*).

Fourthly, in vv.4-7 the outcome of this unity was victory over the Canaanites and Perizzites at Bezek and the capture of one of their kings, Adoni-bezek (137), which means "lord of Bezek". They cut off his thumbs and great toes, thus rendering him unstable and incapable of holding a weapon or running. Some have questioned the morality of these actions and, indeed, of the conquest of the Canaanites in general. However, it must be remembered that the Canaanites, typified here by Adoni-bezek, were wicked in the extreme (Deut 9.4-6) and therefore the judgment was just. Indeed, God had displayed infinite patience towards them and it was of His mercy that they had not been consumed already. They had seen God's judgment of other nations, but they had failed to heed the warnings and repent. Interestingly, Adoni-bezek did not have a difficulty about the treatment he received. He acknowledged the justice of his fate, having meted out the same punishment on seventy kings that he had captured, humiliated and treated like dogs. He accepted that "as I have done, so God hath requited me" (v.7). God's judgments are always in accord with the nature of the transgression and are a vindication of His glory and majesty. Adoni-bezek was eventually taken to Jerusalem and died there (v.7); this was a powerful message to the Jebusites, the inhabitants of the city, of the final outcome for all who rebel against God.

Fifthly, in vv.10-15, we are introduced to three remarkable characters of faith from the same family, namely Caleb, Othniel and Achsah. They shone like beacons in the midst of the darkness. If their contemporaries had displayed the same faith, things would have turned out differently. The territory to be possessed varied considerably in its nature, consisting of mountains, the south lands (Negev) and valleys or, more correctly, foothills (v.9).

Caleb led the attack in the mountainous region of Hebron (2275), which means "fellowship; companionship", formerly Kirjath-arba (7153), which means "city of the giants". It may have been an unattractive place to the natural eye, but, through its links with the patriarchs, it was rich in its spiritual history. Moses had promised it to Caleb (v.20; Josh 14.9) and the desire to possess it lived in his heart throughout the wilderness years. He could not rest until he had taken it out of the control of the three tribes that ultimately emanated from Sheshai, Ahiman and Talmai, descendants of the giant Anak (v.10).

Not surprisingly, such a whole-hearted act of faith inspired his nephew, Othniel, to reach similar spiritual heights (vv.11-15). Like Caleb, his genealogy linked him to the Kenezites, who came from Eliphaz, Esau's eldest son (Gen 36.15). At some point in their history, the grace of God linked the Kenezites to the tribe of Judah and brought them into the sphere of blessing. It was Esau "who for one morsel of meat sold his birthright" and "afterward, when he would have inherited the blessing, he was rejected" (Heb 12.16-17). Othniel's exploits ensured that such a sad testimony would never be attached to his name. He rose to Caleb's challenge to smite Kirjath-sepher (7158), which means, "city of books", that was in the Negev or south land (v.9). It was probably a centre of Canaanite learning and reminds us therefore of the corrupting influence of the wisdom of this world. Othniel's victory brought about a dramatic transformation and it became known as Debir (1688), which means "oracle". W.E.Vine defines the New Testament word "oracle (*logion*)" as denoting "a Divine response or utterance; it is used of (a) the contents of the Mosaic Law, Acts 7.38: (b) all the written utterances of God through Old Testament writers, Rom 3.2; (c) the substance of Christian doctrine, Heb 5.12; (d) the utterances of God through Christian teachers, 1 Pet 4.11". It is a word, therefore, that clearly equates in the New Testament to the living Word of God. It serves as a powerful reminder of the need to be guided and directed by the Word of God rather than by the wisdom of men. Paul emphasised to the Corinthians that God "will destroy the wisdom of the wise, and will bring to nothing the understanding of the prudent" (1 Cor 1.19). Othniel's (6274) name means "lion or force of God" and the secret of his strength was found in his desire to listen to and be obedient to God's word.

God is no man's debtor and Othniel was rewarded for his labours. He received Achsah, Caleb's daughter, as his wife. The reward, the very best that Caleb could give, far outweighed the cost! In Rev 22.12 the Lord says, "And, behold, I come (am coming) quickly; and my reward is with me, to give every man according as his work shall be". This is a great encouragement to believers to give the very best for Him, even if the days are difficult and the cost of commitment is high. When He returns He will reward His people directly, immediately, individually and justly. The rewards for believers at the Judgment Seat of Christ will be commensurate with what has been gained (2 Cor 5.10). Achsah was, indeed, a "help meet (suitable) for him" (Gen 2.18). Solomon wrote of such a woman, "her price is far above rubies ... The heart of her husband doth safely trust in her ... She will do him good" (Prov 31.10-12). She was not satisfied with anything less than the best. Caleb had taught her well and she had been swift to learn. The man who had said to Joshua, "Give me this mountain" (Josh 14.12), must have been deeply moved and impressed by the spiritual exercise of his daughter. While Othniel hesitated, she "lighted (leaped forth, indicating an eager impulse - 6795) from off her ass" (v.14) and seized the opportunity to ask even more of the man she knew would give liberally: "Give me a blessing: for thou hast given me a south land; give me also springs of water" (v.15). She was intelligent in her asking. She appreciated that a south land could be a dry land without water. She received over and above what she could have expected: "And Caleb gave her the upper springs and the nether springs" (v.15). She secured an ample supply of water for all conditions and times of year. If the upper springs dried up in the summer, they would still have access to the lower springs for their livestock. God had promised to bring His people into "a good land, a land of brooks of water, of fountains and depths that spring out of valleys and hills" (Deut 8.7). Achsah claimed that promise and challenges believers to learn the value and power of laying hold in prayer on a God who "giveth to all men liberally, and upbraideth not" (James 1.5). Just as she approached a loving and generous father who was longing to bless her, so can they. The refreshing streams of the Spirit of God are available to them as they travel through a dry and barren world.

Sadly, these rays of light that pierced the darkness in the early days of the book of Judges were not replicated in general across the children of Israel and the potential for possessing and enjoying the land did not materialise.

Verses16-36: The Progressive Failure to Possess the Land

A cursory glance at this section might lead the readers to the conclusion that they are in the midst of a success story. Truly, it does give an account of Israel's military successes, including the subjection of her enemies to forced labour and the payment of tribute. However, this would be to misjudge the situation. Contrary to the word of God, they failed to drive the Canaanites out and allowed them to remain within the land, a policy that would soon reap disastrous spiritual consequences for them. They had the power to drive them out, but they made the deliberate choice not to do so. Indeed, it is clear that two of the tribes made a positive decision not to make any attempt to expel their enemies, but they were content to dwell among them (vv.30,33). Their victories were, at best, partial and incomplete. It was not long before they intermarried and imbibed their corrupt religion. The skills their captives had to offer, the fleshly appeal of their worship and the prospect of drawing upon their wealth proved a far more attractive proposition to the children of Israel than obedience to the word of God. In the early days it appeared as if no real harm was being done and, indeed, there were short-term gains. However, the long-term consequences were severe. Their actions serve as a warning to believers today to be careful how they judge success. What appears to be success may well be failure as far as God is concerned.

The partial success of Judah (vv.16-20)

In spite of earlier victories, even Judah fell short of what God required. The Kenites (v.16) were a nomadic group who had originally settled in Jericho, the city of palm trees, after the Israelites had defeated it. There was a curse upon any connected with Jericho and yet they were found living within Judah's possession. They were the natural descendants of Jethro, Moses' father-in-law. Clearly, they kept a close eye on the political scene and eventually linked themselves to Judah. However, when they came up out of Jericho, instead of driving the inhabitants out, they went and dwelt among the people on the southwest edge of the wilderness of Judah. They had no concept of the impact that this course of action would have on Israel's future attempts to possess the land. Jael, the wife of Heber the Kenite, stood out as an exception to the rest when she slew Sisera, the captain of the king of Canaan's army (4.21,22).

Judah, fulfilling his promise to Simeon (1.3), moved on with him to destroy Zephath, in the south, which was called, Hormah (2767), meaning "devoted to destruction" (1.17). This fulfilled the Israelites' earlier vow to destroy completely the cities of the king of Arad (Num 21.1-30), a course of action that they ought to have taken with the rest of their enemies.

From there, Judah, without Simeon, took the Philistine cities of Gaza, Askelon and Ekron (v.18). However, the victories were incomplete. Their successes against their enemies in the mountains and the south (v.9) were not matched by their achievements in the foothills. They stopped short of driving the inhabitants out from there, reaching the decision that they could not combat their chariots of iron. They lacked faith and confidence in the God who had already promised to be with them in such circumstances: "When thou goest out to battle against thine enemies, and seest horses, and chariots, and a people more than thou, be not afraid of them: for the Lord thy God is with thee, which brought thee up out of the land of Egypt" (Deut 20.1). They failed to take Him at His word and, therefore, contented themselves with partial success. There is a danger that believers, like the children of Israel, measure God against their own inadequacies and, therefore, set limits on what they believe He can do through them.

Later on, once the men of Judah and Simeon had left, the remaining Philistines re-established themselves and re-gained a measure of control (2.3). It was God's intention that Judah should take the lead, set the example and inspire others. However, their failure to secure complete victories was soon mirrored in the experience of the other tribes. The quality of leadership is vital among God's people, since they rarely rise above it. Benjamin, Ephraim, Manasseh, Zebulun, Asher, Naphtali, and Dan all failed to drive out the enemies and allowed them to live alongside the children of Israel. The outcomes for Dan were particularly disastrous.

The partial success of Benjamin (v.21)

Although Jerusalem bordered on to Judah's inheritance, it was allotted to Benjamin (Josh 18.28). Earlier on in the chapter it is recorded that, "the children of Judah had fought against Jerusalem, and had taken it, and smitten it with the edge of the sword, and set the city on fire" (v.8). Clearly, this early success had not been sealed and for some reason they did not occupy the city. The Jebusites, the Canaanite inhabitants of Jerusalem, had been allowed to re-enter and rebuild the city and live alongside the children of Benjamin, who never succeeded in driving them out. Jacob had said, "Benjamin shall ravin as a wolf: in the morning he shall devour the prey, and at night he shall divide the spoil" (Gen 49.27). However, the tribe at this stage failed to live up to this prediction and did not drive the enemy out of Jerusalem, the place where God was later to set His name. Indeed, it remained out of Israel's control until the time of David (2 Sam 5.6-7). Its subsequent troubled history, leading to its fall, stands as a lasting testimony as to how damaging this co-existence became.

The partial success of the house of Joseph (vv.22-29)

The house of Joseph directed the first campaign in the central hill country against Bethel (1008), which means "house of God". It was called Luz (3870) at the first, which means "separation". It had strong links with the patriarchs, Abram (Gen 12.8) and Jacob (Gen 28.19), and became one of the principal sanctuaries in the northern kingdom. Joshua had already conquered it (Josh 12.16), but it had passed back into the possession of the Canaanites. Victory was assured, because "the LORD was with them" (v.22), but this did not satisfy them. They felt the need to rely on the use of spies and an informant coming out of the city before they moved against it.

They smote it, but the victory was incomplete. They failed to obey God's command to destroy the Canaanites and allowed their informant and his family to flee to the land of the Hittites and build another city, which he called by the same name of Luz! He had no appreciation of anything that spoke of the house of God. He departed and built a replica of what ought to have been utterly defeated by the house of Joseph. Again, they would reap the results of this strategy in the future. Both the tribes of Manasseh and Ephraim gained only partial victories in their territories. The Canaanites were prepared to accept forced labour and the payment of tribute, in exchange for an agreement by the children of Israel to allow them to continue living in the land (vv.27-28). Sadly, Manasseh and Ephraim agreed to the compromise. M.F.Unger observes that Manasseh failed to gain control of the "strongly fortified towns guarding access through the Plain of Esdraelon, separating the tribes of Joseph from the northern tribes" (*Commentary on the Old Testament*). This would have effectively led to a divided country. Ephraim failed to take control of Gezer, the most important commercial city on the coastal plain, preferring, no doubt, to secure financial gain from its tribute money rather than driving its people out. The ultimate end of such folly was emphasised many years later in the words of the prophet Hosea: "Ephraim is joined to idols: let him alone" (Hos 4.17).

The partial success of Zebulun, Asher and Naphtali (vv.30-33)

If the more powerful and prominent tribes failed to trust God to give them complete victories over their enemies and therefore contented themselves with living among the Canaanites, it is not surprising to see a similar lack of success among the smaller tribes in the north of the country. Indeed, the tribe of Asher sank to new depths when, as a deliberately disobedient act, they "dwelt among" them (v.32). They made no apparent effort to expel the Canaanites and allowed them to control what God had promised to give them for their inheritance. The tribe of whom Jacob said, "his bread shall be fat, and he shall yield royal dainties" (Gen 49.20), exchanged possession of some of the most beautiful land in Canaan for short-term gain, which in turn left them spiritually bankrupt. Naphtali followed an almost identical track to Asher, although they did ensure that some of their enemies became tributaries. However, although Naphtali (5321) means "wrestler", they had ceased to wrestle with the enemy and capitulated to their power. They dwelt among their various forms of idolatrous worship, which ultimately became a deadly snare to Israel.

The partial success of Dan (vv.34-36)

Here we reach the lowest point of all. Dan had the smallest part allotted to any tribe, but the powerful tribes of Ephraim, Benjamin and Judah bordered their land. Their territory between the hill country and the sea was extremely fertile and therefore it was clear that the Amorites would not give it up easily. It was not simply that Dan failed to drive the enemy out, but "the Amorites forced the children of Dan into the mountain" (v.34).

They were driven out of the fruitful valleys, where most of their inheritance was to be found, into the hill country. They could not even subject the Amorites to the payment of tribute and it was left to the house of Joseph to do so (v.35), a clear indication that unity between the tribes had broken down. They possessed Heres, in Aijalon, where Joshua had once been victorious and caused the sun and moon to stand still (Josh 10.12-14). However, that mighty victory when "the Lord hearkened unto the voice of a man: for the Lord fought for Israel" (Josh 10.14), was but a distant memory. The extent of the Amorites' domination was reflected in their control over a wide area (v.36). They confined the Danites to an extremely small territory, which would explain their later move north to capture the city of Laish (18.1-31).

This catalogue of incomplete victories does not, of course, give the complete picture. The tribe of Issachar and the tribes of Reuben, Gad and the half-tribe of Mannesseh, on the east of Jordan, are not mentioned. However, a clear picture has emerged of the outcomes of disobedience, revealing the existence of an immoral and idolatrous people within the inheritance that Israel should have possessed and enjoyed. What had appeared to be innocuous to begin with, led to nation-wide apostasy!

JUDGES 2

Verses 1-5: God's Perspective

The Psalmist gives a succinct commentary on the events of the previous chapter: "They did not destroy the nations, concerning whom the Lord commanded them: but were mingled among the heathen, and learned their works. And they served their idols: which were a snare unto them" (Ps 106.34-36). However, this chapter moves on from describing the failures of the children of Israel and focuses on the divine perspective of events. Once again, the Psalmist states clearly how the Lord viewed and dealt with the disobedience of Israel: "Therefore was the wrath of the Lord kindled against his people, insomuch that he abhorred his own inheritance. And he gave them into the hand of the heathen; and they that hated them ruled over them. Their enemies also oppressed them, and they were brought into subjection under their hand" (Ps 106.40-42). The children of Israel would, no doubt, have given a very different interpretation of events!

God's "journey" (v.1a)

The chapter opens with "an (the) angel of the Lord" coming up "from Gilgal to Bochim" (v.1). Although this should not be understood in terms of a literal journey, the fact that it is described in such a way implies that the children of Israel were not where God intended them to be and therefore in a state of spiritual decline. The term "angel of the Lord" is never used in the Old Testament to signify a messenger or a prophet, as some commentators have suggested. The prophets would not have identified themselves as closely as this with the Lord and they always prefaced their messages with, "Thus saith the Lord". The angel was undoubtedly Jehovah Himself (a theophany) or, more precisely, a pre-incarnation appearance of Christ (a Christophany). The Jehovah of the Old Testament is, indeed, the Jesus of the New Testament. This is the first of three appearances of the angel of the Lord in the book of Judges (6.11 and 13.3).

The angel of the Lord's journey started at Gilgal. He was waiting for the people to return there, but they had failed to do so. Gilgal had been an important and significant place throughout the book of Joshua. It was there that the Lord had told Joshua to make sharp knives and the new generation, born in the wilderness, were circumcised (Josh 5.2). This was, indeed, a great act of faith on their part. If their enemies had attacked them at that precise moment in time, they would have been physically incapable of resisting them. However, the Lord was in control and when their enemies heard what He had done for them in drying up the waters of the Jordan, "their heart melted, neither was there spirit in them any more, because of the children of Israel" (Josh 5.1). It was at Gilgal therefore that the Lord was able to say to Joshua, "This day have I rolled away the reproach of

Egypt from off you" (Josh 5.9). It was the place that spoke of an end to any confidence in the flesh and the need to move, by faith, in total dependence upon the Lord.

The outcome of this experience was positive and rewarding. The children of Israel kept the Passover (Josh 5.10) and the Lord assured Joshua of His presence with him as he led the people into battle against the seemingly impregnable city of Jericho (Josh 5.13-15). Their return to the land that had been promised to Abraham and his descendants led them to renew their covenant relationship with the Lord. It is not surprising therefore to discover that Gilgal assumed such significance in the days of Joshua. They set out from there to fight their enemies and returned there following their victories.

Paul took up the theme of circumcision, as it applies spiritually to believers, when he taught the Philippians, "For we are the circumcision, which worship God in the spirit, and rejoice in Christ Jesus, and have no confidence in the flesh" (Phil 3.3). He wrote in similar vein to the Colossian Christians: "In whom also ye are circumcised ("were circumcised", RV) with the circumcision made without hands, in putting off the body of the sins of the flesh by the circumcision of Christ" (Col 2.11). Paul took them back to their conversion, when spiritual circumcision took place.

Union with Christ brings about a circumcision that goes beyond that which the children of Israel knew in the days of Abraham and Moses. Man has no part in this circumcision. Paul had in view positional circumcision, not physical. "The circumcision of Christ" does not point back to His circumcision in infancy (Lk 2.21), but to His death. When a person trusts Christ, all the value of His death is made good to him. It can truly be said of him, "But ye are not in the flesh, but in the Spirit, if so be that the Sprit of God dwell in you" (Rom 8.9). The old sinful nature is not eradicated, but its power is stripped away and therefore the believer does not need to obey its dictates any longer. H.L.Rossier puts it succinctly: "At the cross of Christ, in His death, the flesh was absolutely condemned and made an end of for the believer … but continual returning to Gilgal was a necessity. There must be for the believer the constant realisation before God, what the cross of Christ teaches, that 'the flesh profiteth nothing'. True self-judgment must be maintained if we would know wherein lies the secret of spiritual power by which we mortify our members, which are upon the earth. We may learn this from the victories in the book of Joshua. The Israelites always returned to Gilgal, except in one case (Josh 7.2), where they were defeated" (*Meditations on the Book of Judges*).

Sadly, Gilgal appears only twice in the book of Judges (2.1 and 3.19) and therein is the reason for the spiritual weakness of those days. It held no position of importance or significance in the children of Israel's thinking and therefore the angel of the Lord had to undertake the journey to Bochim (1066), which means "weepers", to meet them there. Its location is uncertain, but it was probably situated somewhere between Bethel and

Shiloh. W.Kelly remarks, "But the angel of Jehovah now finds Himself in a place as characteristic of the Book of Judges as Gilgal was of Joshua. It is the place of tears. Not to know sorrow when the people of God have slighted Him and declined is not to know where His Spirit dwells" (*Lectures on the Book of Judges*).

God's judgment (vv.1b-5)

He reminded the people of His *deliverance* of them out of Egypt and His *declaration* to them, "I will never break my covenant with you" (v. 1). However, such faithfulness made demands upon them to live a life of separation to Him. The covenant that He had made with them was not unconditional. They had failed and therefore He confronted them with their *disobedience*: "but ye have not obeyed my voice: why have ye done this?" (v.2). They stood condemned and had no answer to give. The present generation cannot escape from the same challenge. In the light of God's unfailing faithfulness, it is a tragedy to see such widespread disobedience to, and disregard for, His Word. Many Christians have settled down in this world and made a league with the inhabitants of this land" (v.2). The Lord's *decision* was clear as far as Israel was concerned (v. 3). They had departed from Him, so He would depart from them. If they would not drive out the inhabitants of the land, neither would He! They would become thorns in their sides (the Hebrew text reads, "they shall be as sides to you") to afflict them and their gods would be snares to entrap them. Thorns are painful irritants that fester if they are not removed, whereas snares catch their unsuspecting targets unawares. The children of Israel thought they could have the best of both worlds, but God taught them otherwise.

Such a course of action could only lead to pain, weakness and bondage. Confronted with their sin, the *distress* of the people was evident and they "lifted up their voice, and wept ... and they sacrificed there unto the Lord" (vv.4-5). C.A.Coates remarks, "They had not yet lost all spiritual feeling, or sense of what was *due* to the Lord" (*An Outline of the book of Judges*). There is a place for tears as an expression of true repentance, but God is looking for more than just tears. If they are shed, only out of concern for self and fear of the judgment pronounced, as appears to be the case here with Israel, little of lasting value will be accomplished. God looks for tears that stem from the heart. Later on in their history, He challenged His people through Joel, the prophet, saying, "Therefore also now, saith the Lord, turn ye even to me with all your heart, and with fasting, and with weeping, and with mourning: and rend your heart, and not your garments, and turn unto the Lord your God" (Joel 2.12-13). Israel's subsequent behaviour as recorded in the book of Judges suggests that their repentance was only on the surface and did not touch their hearts. L.H.Wiseman writes, "The evening twilight soon fades into total darkness; so their negative evil soon degenerated into positive revolt ... for a time, perhaps the worship of God and the worship of idols were observed together, but a further step in the downward course – their abandonment of Jehovah and open adoration of the Canaanitish idols – was not long in being taken" (*Practical Truths from Judges*).

Paul wrote to the Corinthian believers, "For godly sorrow worketh repentance to salvation not to be repented of ("never to be regretted", JND): but the sorrow of the world worketh death" (2 Cor 7.10). He acknowledged that they had "sorrowed to repentance" (2 Cor 7.9) and commended them, because they "sorrowed after a godly sort" (2 Cor 7.11) when putting right the error that they had allowed to come in among them. He concluded, "In all things ye have approved yourselves to be clear in this matter" (2 Cor 7.11). A genuine change had been brought about in the hearts of those in the assembly at Corinth, but no such transformation was in evidence among the children of Israel. They simply continued to do as they pleased, in disobedience to God's word. They went through the motions of sacrificing (ZABACH - 2076) unto the Lord, but they displayed no real appreciation of what He required of them. They would have to face many more painful experiences before learning the truth of Samuel's words, "Behold, to obey is better than sacrifice, and to hearken than the fat of rams" (1 Sam 15.22). David, the penitent Psalmist, wrote, "The sacrifices (ZEBACH - 2077) of God are a broken spirit: a broken and a contrite heart, O God, thou wilt not despise" (Ps 51.17). He wept (2 Sam 12.22) but his tears found their source in a penitent heart (2 Sam 12.13).

Verses 6-23: God's Preview

This section gives a preview of, and lays the foundation for an understanding of, the remainder of the book of Judges. There could be a danger of the readers getting caught up solely with the exploits of men but this panorama of events at the outset gives an important insight into what God was doing. Firstly, however, a clear picture emerges of the character of the children of Israel.

Their dependence

They were totally dependent on strong leadership. Following their tears at Bochim, Joshua gathered them together at Shechem to renew the covenant and their commitment to the Lord (Josh 24.1-28). Judges 2.6 is, indeed, a summary of Joshua 24. They returned from there with fresh vigour and determination (v.6) to possess their inheritance in the land. They maintained that high level of commitment and "served the Lord all the days of Joshua, and all the days of the elders that outlived Joshua" (v.7). Clearly, Joshua had gained their loyalty and respect. He knew the Lord in a personal way and had seen His great works at first hand (v.7). He received the simple, but moving, epitaph at the close of his days, "Joshua the son of Nun, the servant of the Lord" (v.8). God set a similar seal of approval on Moses, his predecessor (Deut 34.5). Joshua died and was buried in Timnath-heres (v.9), referred to as Timnath-serah in Joshua 19.50, where his inheritance was. A.McShane draws attention to the fact that this city was "one of no importance nor of any fertile qualities. In accepting this as his portion he displayed the humility of his mind, and the unselfishness of his heart. Joshua began as the servant of Moses, and he was content to end in humble circumstances; in this he is typical of the One who began His life on earth in a manger and ended it on a cross" (*Joshua – Possessing the Land*). Believers in this present day ought to seek to live in a manner that will earn the final commendation from the Lord, "Well done, good and faithful servant" (Mt 25.23). There can be no higher praise than that!

Their divergence

Sadly, the new generation of the children of Israel lacked the personal experience and knowledge of God enjoyed by Joshua and the elders that outlived him. It was a generation "which knew not the Lord, nor yet the works which he had done for Israel" (v.10). It was not a matter of ignorance on their part. They knew a great deal about God, but they did not know Him as a personal living reality in their lives. There is always a danger that the "next generation" will not live up to the high standards of the previous one. Paul demonstrated his awareness of this when he wrote to Timothy, "And the things that thou hast heard of me among many witnesses, the same commit thou to faithful men, who shall be able to teach others also" (2 Tim 2.2). He covered four generations in this verse and stressed that each one had a responsibility to the next. Only then would truth be preserved and succeeding generations have the opportunity to know God. Clearly, the young man Timothy had already experienced something of the truth of this in his own family upbringing. Paul spoke of "the unfeigned (sincere, genuine) faith that is in thee, which dwelt first in thy grandmother Lois, and thy mother Eunice; and I am persuaded that in thee also" (2 Tim 1.5). Timothy did not simply rest on the spiritual strength of others. He applied what they had taught him and therefore he was in a strong position to continue the work when they had passed on.

The same could not be said of the children of Israel. They rested heavily on the spiritual strengths of Joshua and the elders that outlived him. However, when they were no longer present, they soon forgot them and began on the slippery slope towards idolatry and apostasy. They replicated this behaviour throughout the days of the judges. Following the death of each judge, "they returned, and corrupted themselves more than their fathers" (v.19). F.C.Jennings sounds the warning to all "next generation" believers when he writes, "Does it not add a kind of extra solemnity to our lot if we are living after a 'first generation' has passed away? Does it not give stronger grounds for heart searching; for strong crying to God; for increased watchfulness; for clustering together in mutual love and exhortation?" (*Judges and Ruth*). If the present generation of believers do not heed this warning, the outlook is bleak for the next generation, if the Lord does not return in the meantime.

Their desertion

Gradually, almost imperceptibly, the children of Israel abandoned the Lord. They "did evil in the sight of the Lord ... provoked the Lord ... forsook the Lord" (vv.11-13). They faced the charge of going "a-whoring after other gods" (v.17). This is strong language and it seems almost unthinkable that such things should characterise the Lord's people. However, it was the inevitable consequence of not knowing God and being content to live alongside the Canaanites, instead of driving them out. They were prepared to abandon the God who had "brought them out of the land of Egypt" (v.12). The book of Judges records, on no less than seven occasions, that they "did evil in the sight of the Lord" (2.11; 3.7; 3.12; 4.1; 6.1; 10.6; 13.1) and each one introduces a period of apostasy. As far as they were concerned, they still honoured God, but they no longer acknowledged Him as the only God. They broke the first commandment and "served Baal and Ashtaroth" (v.13). Baal (1168) means, "lord, master, owner". He was the god of the storm and the rains and therefore the controller of all vegetation, including the harvests. He was worshipped widely throughout the ancient Near East. There were various forms of Baal worship, hence the appearance of the plural form, "Baalim" (v.11). His female consort was Ashtaroth (6252) (v.13), which means "increase". She was worshipped as the goddess of war and fertility. The worship of these gods was accompanied by numerous sexual and immoral practices. It was a sign of how far the children of Israel had departed that they were prepared to forsake the one true Lord and acknowledge the lordship of one who had not, and could not, do anything for them. They forsook the Lord who had given them their inheritance for a goddess who could never give them any material or spiritual increase. It was not surprising therefore that they locked themselves into a cycle of rebellion, discipline from the Lord, distress, crying to the Lord and deliverance by the Lord. At the end of each cycle they showed that there had been no real change of heart: "they ceased not from their own doings, nor from their stubborn way" (v.19). Believers today need to take care that they do not end up with the same testimony!

As well as revealing the character of the children of Israel, this chapter also gives an insight into the character of the Lord and therefore throws valuable light on His ways with His people throughout the book.

His demands

He is a jealous God. This ought not to have come as a surprise to them. He had already made it clear to them, following their deliverance from Egypt: "For thou shalt worship no other god: for the Lord, whose name is Jealous (7067), is a jealous God" (Ex 34.14). Joshua reminded them of this truth when he gathered them together at Shechem and they boldly declared, "therefore will we also serve the Lord; for he is our God" (Josh 24.18). Joshua responded, "Ye cannot serve the Lord: for he is an holy God; he is a jealous God; he will not forgive your transgressions nor your sins" (Josh 24.19). God's character never changes and therefore believers of all generations need to be aware of the danger of allowing idolatry of any kind to come in and mar their testimony. Anything that displaces God is an idol and John's words are as relevant in this present day as they were in the first century: "Little children, keep yourselves from idols" (1 Jn 5.21).

His displeasure

He is a God who can be provoked to anger. Joshua announced to the children of Israel the inevitable consequence of any failure on their part to live up to their boast to be loyal to the Lord: "If ye forsake the Lord, and serve strange gods, then he will turn and do you hurt, and consume you, after that he hath done you good" (Josh 24.20). Commenting on the parting words of Joshua (Josh 24.19-20), A.McShane writes: "What apparently he had in mind was, that His character is such that for a people to serve Him they must be holy as He is, and if they deviate from Him, as they were likely to do, then, because He is a jealous God He will not tolerate any rival, and so will fall upon them in His wrath. The strong language used here is meant to give them some idea of the seriousness of what they were promising" (*Joshua – Possessing the Land*). The next generation after Joshua and the elders that outlived him grieved the Lord by allowing idolatry to come in (v.12) and therefore "the anger of the LORD was hot against Israel" (vv. 14,20). "Anger" ('APH – 639) has the thought of breathing hard, being enraged. God keeps to His promises in blessing, but He is also faithful to them in discipline and judgment. The children of Israel discovered that the God who gave them their inheritance was also able, if their infidelity demanded it, to deliver them "into the hands of spoilers that spoiled them" (v.14) and set His hand "against them for evil" (v.15).

His devotion

He is a longsuffering, faithful, merciful and gracious God. Although the children of Israel would have found it difficult to believe it at the time, the fact that the Lord was behind the actions that led to them being "greatly distressed" (v.15), proved His love for them and gave them hope. The writer to the Hebrews reminded his readers that "whom the Lord loveth he chasteneth, and scourgeth every son whom he receiveth" (Heb 12.6). The Lord's anger towards the children of Israel was not a loss of temper by a vindictive God. It was a clear demonstration of His love, compassion and care for them. If He is a loving God, it follows that He is a jealous God, who demands the total loyalty of His people and will bring them under discipline in order to achieve it. The children of Israel failed to appreciate that, through their disobedience, they were robbing and grieving God. S.Ridout brings home the challenge to believers of all generations, when he writes, "You say perhaps in your inmost heart, if I am not enjoying the highest kind of spiritual life, it is my own fault, it is my own loss. No, my brother, it is God's loss. He is the loser. What He craves from you is the obedience and worship of a heart, which is so full of His blessing that it has got to express itself in worship and service. No, you are not the chief loser. Our blessed God is the loser" (*Lectures on the Book of Judges*).

It was love and compassion for His people that also led Him to raise up judges (8199) or saviours, "which delivered them out of the hand of those that spoiled them" (v.16), even though they showed no apparent sign of repentance (the Introduction to this commentary gives a brief outline of the work of the judges). They may have been "greatly distressed" (v.15) and groaned (v.18), but their subsequent actions proved that their repentance was not genuine. The true strength of feeling came from the Lord, not from His people. His love for them moved Him to act: "it repented the Lord because of their groanings by reason of them that oppressed them and vexed them" (v.18). The word "repented" (NACHAM - 5162) is not meant to imply that God had taken a wrong course of action that required Him to change. It also has the thought of sighing, pitying, and consoling. The Lord showed the same compassion for His distressed people as He had displayed towards them when they were in Egypt (Ex 2.23-25; 3.7-9). Their love for Him might have ebbed and flowed since those days but His love remained constant. Sadly, they did not reciprocate this love and consistently returned to their rebellious ways. During a judge's lifetime there were external signs of recovery but when the judge died it became clear that these were only superficial (vv.17-19). Indeed, there was progressive deterioration, until such time as God could no longer refer to them as "my people" but "this people" (v.20). The word used for "people" (GOY – 1471) denotes a foreign or Gentile nation that is outside of God's covenant and therefore its use here emphasises how far Israel had drifted away from Him. As each judge died, "they … corrupted themselves more than their fathers" (v.19) and therefore the chastening from the hand of a loving God became more intense. The judges only held back the tide of corruption for a short while but they failed to touch the people's hearts.

His designs

He is the all-wise God. His actions in relation to His people and their enemies in the Book of Judges are somewhat bewildering to the natural mind. A.E.Cundall sums it up when he writes, "To the modern reader it seems somewhat incongruous that God should leave the foreign elements within Israel's borders as a punishment for apostasy, and to test the future faithfulness of the nation, when the very reason for the nation's defection is attributed to the failure to drive out this alien population" (*Judges – An Introduction and Commentary*). However, this presents no problem to those who bow to the sovereignty of God. Abraham's assessment of the Lord remains true: "Shall not the Judge of all the earth do right?" (Gen 18.25). Although the nations did not appreciate it, they were not in control of the situation. God, in His sovereignty, did not drive them out but left them to "prove (test) Israel, whether they will keep the way of the Lord to walk therein" (v.22). It was the positive act of a wise and sovereign God that defied the logic of man.

It is easy to be critical of the children of Israel and to forget that "whatsoever things were written aforetime were written for our learning" (Rom 15.4). F.E.Stallan, commenting on this verse, writes, "The amazing statement of 15.4 implies that the inspired writers of the past were not only writing for their own generations, but in the wisdom of God and under the guidance of the Holy Spirit were writing for future generations also. Not only so, but it infers that in every age following the completion and circulation of the sacred writings, the recipients of them would be responsible to read them, hear them, consider them and apply them to daily living" (*Romans – Ritchie New Testament Commentaries*). To read this preview of God's dealings with Israel during the period of the judges and simply assign it to the archives of biblical history would be to fail in this responsibility. Israel's departure was, to a large extent, the result of not learning the lessons of their past and therefore they kept repeating their shortcomings. Believers of this present day need to be constantly aware of the danger of presuming on God's grace and thereby gradually slipping away from total loyalty to Him. It will lead inevitably to mingling with unbelievers and turning to their "gods". A personal knowledge of God and His works (v.10) will keep them from such disastrous consequences. There is a daily spiritual warfare in which they should be engaged (Eph 6.12). Any failure to do so will lead to defeat at the hands of the enemies, over whom they ought to be victorious, and discipline from a loving God. The enemies that seek to rob believers of a rich spiritual life should be viewed positively. God may, on occasions, use them to chastise His disobedient people but they are also there to give them the opportunity to show their willingness and resolve "to keep the way of the Lord to walk therein" (v.22). How much better to pass the tests than to keep losing the battles!

JUDGES 3

Verses 1-6: God Teaches and Tests His People

God teaches His people

As well as providing a fitting summary to the initial outline of Israel's spiritual condition in chs.1 and 2, this section extends the theme of how God used the nations in order to bring blessing to His people, as well as to discipline them. Although they had to learn that God was sovereign, and therefore in total control of the nations, knowledge of this did not exempt them from the responsibility to engage in warfare against them.

Unlike the nations dealt with in the opening chapter, "the nations which the Lord left" (v.1) were the ones that had been unconquered. They lived in their own territories, rather than among the Israelites, and refused to acknowledge any claim of Israel to the land. It explains the words of God to Joshua: "There remaineth yet very much land to be possessed" (Josh 13.1). There was a marked difference between the territory that had been promised to Moses, and that which the people actually possessed. M.F.Unger identifies the nations referred to (v.3) as, "the five lords of the Philistines, who about 1190 BC invaded Palestine from Caphtor … all the Canaanites are included in the list of enemies in Jud 1.27-33 … the Sidonians were Phoenicians on the coast … the Hivites were likely a branch of the Horites (Hurrians)" (*Commentary on the Old Testament*).

The new generation that followed on from Joshua and the elders that outlived him, referred to in the previous chapter (2.10), had not engaged in warfare. Life in the land had become too comfortable as they mingled with the inhabitants. They needed to be taught the meaning of war and the necessary skills required to engage in it successfully. "Only that the generations of the children of Israel might know, to teach them war, at the least such as before knew nothing thereof" (v.2). Surrounded, as they were, by so many hostile nations, they would not have survived without the will and ability to fight. F.C.Jennings remarks, "But all works for good. The nations are not left in Israel to enslave Israel; the flesh is not left in us that we should serve its lusts, nay, but to learn by war, the love of His heart, the strength of His arm, and that He can make our enemies work His purposes of grace" (*Judges and Ruth*).

God tests His people

Any success for the children of Israel in warfare against their enemies, rested on them passing the test of listening to and obeying the commandments of the Lord that He had given through Moses (v.4). Those commandments emphasised that there had to be a clear line of demarcation between them and the inhabitants of the land. Indeed, they had to be driven out. Sadly, they failed the test consistently. Instead of driving the nations out, they "dwelt among" them (v.5). Far from being distinct from them, they became "unequally yoked" (2 Cor 6.14) with them. "And they took their daughters to be their wives, and gave their daughters to their sons, and served their gods" (v.6). The tragic outcome was that they descended from serving the Lord (2.7), to serving their gods (vv.6-7). Once they married outside of God's will, it was not long before they embraced the worship of their partners and abandoned devotion to the Lord. When marriage takes place outside of the will of God, it will always lead to compromise. The ensuing catalogue of disasters for the children of Israel serves as a constant reminder to believers today of the importance of marrying "only in the Lord" (1 Cor 7.39).

THE SAVIOURS WHO DELIVERED (3.7–16.31)

Othniel and the Syrians

Verses 7-11: God sells His People into the Hand of the Enemy

This is the second of four occasions in the Book of Judges when the spiritual condition of the children of Israel was such that God sold them into the hands of their enemies (cf. 2.14, 4.2 & 10.7). The word "sold" (MAKAR - 4376) has the thought of being sold as slaves. They did evil, forgot the Lord and became slaves to the idolatry that surrounded them. God therefore dealt with them like slaves. It is an abiding principle of Scripture that "whatsoever a man soweth, that shall he also reap" (Gal 6.7).

God's anger

Although the children of Israel did not appreciate it at the time, the intensity of the Lord's anger towards them, as a result of their unfaithfulness to Him, was an evidence of His love for them. They deserved to be chastised, abandoned and left to suffer the disastrous consequences of their own actions. However, the Lord could not remain indifferent to their condition and He began the process that would lead to their recovery and deliverance. If His anger had not been "hot against Israel" (v.8), there would have been no hope for them.

God's actions

Firstly, "he sold them into the hand of Chushan-rishathaim king of Mesopotamia" (v.8). Mesopotamia (763) was Aram-naharaim, which means, "Aram of the two rivers (Euphrates and Tigris)". The tragedy of this situation is heightened when it is remembered that this was the very country out of which the Lord had called Abram. C.A.Coates gives a warning to believers of all generations when he writes, "if we give up in heart the heavenly calling, we shall fall under the influence of the place out of which we are called" (*An Outline of the Book of Judges*). Chushan-rishathaim (3573) means, "Chushan of double wickedness", which may well have been an epithet assigned to him by those he oppressed. It highlights the depth of the depravity and wickedness into which the children of Israel had sunk. The fact that he came from the far north and Othniel, the deliverer God raised up, came from Judah in the south, indicates that he made swift and deep inroads into the land. He represents the enemy from without, rather than from within. The children of Israel became so complacent in their disobedience that they failed to see the danger approaching and were rapidly engulfed by it. It was the inevitable outcome of taking their eyes off God.

Secondly, God responded immediately to the people's cries. "And when the children of Israel cried ... the Lord raised up a deliverer to the children of Israel" (v.9). What a contrast to the slowness of their response! They were content to serve Chushan-rishathaim for eight years before they were stirred to seek release from his bondage. It can take believers a long time to appreciate, and respond to, the spiritual poverty into which their infidelity to God brings them. It is not God's desire to see His people in bondage a moment longer than is necessary. Even though the cry of the children of Israel was probably out of distress at the bitterness of the circumstances in which they found themselves, rather than an indication of true repentance of heart, the Lord responded in grace and mercy. The feeblest and faintest cry from His people will always bring His deliverance.

Thirdly, God raised up precisely the right man for the occasion. The king of "double wickedness" needed the strength of Othniel (6274), whose name means "force or lion of God", to subdue him. God, in His sovereignty, used Chushan-rishathaim as an instrument of wrath against His people, but He cut off his power the moment he had accomplished His purposes. The source of Othniel's strength is best expressed in the words of Zechariah, the prophet: "Not by might, nor by power, but by my spirit, saith the Lord of hosts" (Zech 4.6). Clearly, Othniel had been waiting patiently in the background following his exploits in defeating Kirjath-sepher, described in the opening chapter (1.12-13). Indeed, it must have been difficult for him and his wife, Achsah, to endure the conditions imposed by Chushan-rishathaim. However, he appreciated the need to wait on the Lord and, at precisely the right moment, "the Spirit of the Lord came upon him" (v.10) for the task in hand. Indeed, it was the Lord who raised him up (v.9) and empowered him to defeat Chushan-rishathaim (v.10). Unlike those around him, Othniel had kept himself free from idolatry and, when he was called upon to do so, he "went out to war" (v.10). He had not lost the will nor the ability to fight!

Fourthly, the outcome of the Lord's actions was that the land had rest from war for forty years (v.11). Othniel not only delivered Israel from the bondage of Chushan-rishathaim but he judged Israel throughout those forty years. Clearly, he was instrumental in bringing about the conditions of peace. It is important to observe that it was the land that had rest; this challenges believers today to pray, "that we may lead a quiet and peaceable life in all godliness and honesty" (1 Tim 2.2). If one spiritual man could have such a positive influence in the troubled days of the judges, the same possibility exists for godly believers today.

EHUD AND THE MOABITES

Verses 12-30: God Strengthens the Enemy against His People

All the Lord's people know what it is to be engaged in the battle encountered by the children of Israel in this period of their history. The enemy was Eglon, king of Moab, who represents the power of the flesh in the life of the believer. It is not surprising therefore to discover that he is described as "a very fat man" (v.17). There was nothing spiritual about the origins of the Moabites. They came from the natural and fleshly union of Lot with the older of his two daughters (Gen 19.30-38). They were therefore related to the Israelites and had established themselves in the territory to the south east of Canaan before the time of the exodus. However, it was a carnal and fleshly relationship. God decreed, "An Ammonite or Moabite shall not enter into the congregation of the Lord; even to their tenth generation shall they not enter into the congregation of the Lord for ever: because they met you not with bread and water in the way, when ye came forth out of Egypt" (Deut 23.3-4). They were a nation who had no interest in the welfare of a people redeemed out of Egypt but preferred to see them dead in the wilderness.

Paul confessed, "For I know that in me (that is, in my flesh,) dwelleth no good thing" (Rom 7.18). The flesh is our fallen and sinful nature inherited from Adam and therefore it is incapable of change or improvement. The Lord told Nicodemus, "That which is born of the flesh is flesh" (Jn 3.6). It is a constant enemy of believers throughout their lives. Paul described his personal experience of the battle when he wrote, "For the good that I would I do not: but the evil which I would not, that I do" (Rom 7.19). The fact that the battle takes place in a person's life is a sign of spiritual life; an unbeliever knows nothing of the struggle.

Many commentators have experienced great difficulty understanding this particular incident and find little to commend in Ehud's actions. However, the inspired Word of God records, "the Lord raised them up a deliverer, Ehud" (v.15). God did not depict him as a deceiver or a murderer but as a saviour in Israel. He was involved in a physical battle, with a cruel and oppressive earthly enemy. His experiences have valuable practical lessons to teach believers today as they engage in the daily spiritual battle against the flesh in their lives.

How to lose the battle!

Firstly, by continually committing sin. The children of Israel not only sinned but they "did evil *again* in the sight of the LORD" (v.12). It became a habit for them to do so. They had been in the land for a comparatively short period (less than one hundred years) and yet, during that time, there had been two great spiritual declines. No matter how much pain they suffered, they never learned the lessons of their discipline. As soon as their pain disappeared, they returned to their evil ways. It is easy to condemn them and fail to see that believers in this present day are guilty of the same failure.

On this occasion, the Lord strengthened Eglon against them, the enemy over whom they ought to have been victorious. God was evidently in control of the nations. Eglon did not appreciate, of course, that the Lord had strengthened him and therefore his first move was to gather others of the same nature, Ammon and Amalek, to join him against Israel (v.13). The Ammonites, like the Moabites, were also descendants of Lot (Gen 19.30-38). The Amalekites, one of the bitterest of Israel's enemies, traced their origins back to Esau's children (Gen 36.12) and God commanded their extinction as a nation. He instructed the children of Israel to "blot out the remembrance of Amalek from under heaven" (Deut 25.19). Both Lot and Esau were men who acted according to the dictates of the flesh and therefore moved outside of God's will. The sins of the past had, indeed, come to visit the children of Israel in the present.

God delights in strengthening His people against their enemies. When all had turned away from Paul, and left him isolated, he wrote, "Notwithstanding the Lord stood with me, and strengthened me" (2 Tim 4.17). It is a tragedy when rebellion and disobedience to the Lord's commandments reaches such a level that He has to take enemies and strengthen them against His people.

Secondly, by serving the flesh. "So the children of Israel served Eglon the king of Moab eighteen years" (v.14). They were prepared to serve him for eighteen years before they made any move to be released from his bondage. They did not want to serve the Lord, so they ended up serving Eglon, who was a hard master. They lived and served as if they owed him something, when all he had given them was bondage. The apostle Paul, who, like Ehud (v.15), came from the tribe of Benjamin (Phil 3.5), reminded his readers, "Therefore, brethren, we are debtors, not to the flesh, to live after the flesh. For if ye live after the flesh, ye shall die" (Rom 8.12-13). Serving the flesh will not lead to a loss of salvation, but it will damage the testimony of believers. It is significant that Eglon possessed "the city of palm trees", Jericho (v.13). This was the first city that they defeated by faith when they entered the land. It may well be that Israel had re-occupied the city after its destruction, but had not fortified it because of the curse upon it (Josh 6.26). The Scriptures link the palm tree with rejoicing, flourishing, uprightness, praise and victory (Lev 23.40; Ps 92.12; Jer 10.5; Jn 12.13; Rev 7.9-10). Sadly, all these positive aspects disappear from believers' lives when they give themselves over to serve the flesh.

Thirdly, by pandering to the flesh. Eglon was a living example of the fact that the flesh loves to be pampered. When Ehud came to him, "he was sitting in a summer parlour, which he had for himself alone" (v.20). The children of Israel sent a present, probably tribute money or produce from the land, to him (v.15), and they had the audacity to put it in the hand of the man God had equipped to be their saviour! They failed to appreciate that the flesh is never satisfied, and the more they pandered to Eglon, the more he would want. A.R.Fausset writes, "The Hebrew word for 'present' (*Minchah*) here is the same as elsewhere is used of the thank-offering presented to Jehovah by pious worshippers according to the Law. They had neglected to render to God the tribute due to a loving God; so now, in retributive judgment, they must render to a heathen oppressor the offering which through their sin had become his due" (*A Critical and Expository Commentary on the Book of Judges*). However, God, in His sovereignty, was able to use this to bring deliverance and accomplish His purposes. Ehud's leadership of "the people that bare the present" enabled him to gain entrance into the presence of the king on two separate occasions (vv.17-19).

Fourthly, by living lives that are a contradiction. Ehud traced his origins back to Benjamin (1144), which means, "son of the right hand", and yet he was "a man lefthanded" (v.15). "Lefthanded" (ITTER YAD YAMIYN - 334, 3027, 3225) is made up of three Hebrew words and means, "shut up of the right hand". The right hand in Scripture is linked with power and favour (Eph 1.20; Heb 1.3; 1 Pet 3.22). Ehud was, indeed, a picture of the spiritual condition of the children of Israel. They had lost divine power and favour through continually serving the flesh and disobeying God's word. Their lives were a total contradiction of their rich spiritual heritage. Believers in this present day owe their spiritual life to the Son, who is at God's right hand (Rom 8.34). Like Benjamin (Gen 35.18), they have received life out of the death of another. It behoves them therefore to live up to their heritage and to respond to the words of Scripture, "Walk in the Spirit, and ye shall not fulfil the lust of the flesh" (Gal 5.16).

How to win the battle!

Firstly, by turning to the Lord. It had taken the children of Israel eight years to turn to the Lord during the days of Chushan-rishathaim. They served Eglon for eighteen years before they "cried unto the LORD" (v.15). Each time they sinned, the discipline became more protracted or more painful. However, the moment they turned to the Lord, He had the answer to their need and raised up a deliverer. The only way back to God in days of declension is to cry to the Lord in prayer.

Secondly, by applying the Word of God. The people gave Ehud a present to take to Eglon (v.15) to appease him but he was only interested in taking "a dagger which had two edges" (v.16). It does not stretch the application of the text to equate this dagger with the Word of God. When Ehud confronted Eglon he declared, "I have a message from God (ELOHIM – the general Word for God - 430) unto thee" (v.20), and that "message" was, indeed, the dagger. It was "of a cubit length" (v.16), which may indicate the completeness of the word of God. When writing about the "whole armour of God", Paul referred to "the sword of the Spirit, which is the word of God" (Eph 6.17). In the Epistle to the Hebrews it is described as "quick, and powerful, and sharper than any two-edged sword" (Heb 4.12). It is important to observe that Ehud did not borrow the dagger but fashioned it himself (v.16). It is only as believers read, meditate upon and apply the Word of God that it will have the desired effect upon their lives. It will judge the flesh and do a work in them that they could never accomplish through their own efforts. Again, the Epistle to the Hebrews speaks of it as "piercing even to the dividing asunder of soul and spirit, and of the joints and marrow, and is a discerner of the thoughts and intents of the heart" (Heb 4.12). It will search into the deepest recesses of their beings, judging the inner motives of their hearts. When Ehud thrust the dagger into Eglon, "the haft also went in after the blade; and the fat closed upon the blade, so that he could not draw the dagger out of his belly; and the dirt came out" (v.22). The dagger did a work that reached into the deepest parts of Eglon's flesh and could not be undone. Such will be the impact of the word of God on believers' lives, once they apply it to their hearts and consciences. C.A.Coates writes, "We have to kill the Moabite in ourselves … We need to use the sword, so as not to allow ourselves to be robbed of the enjoyment of the inheritance by our acquaintances, or our relatives, or anything on the line of the natural" (*An Outline of the Book of Judges*).

Thirdly, by recognising the weakness of the human vessel and depending upon God for success. All of the saviours God used to deliver His people in the Book of Judges were marked by weakness. As well as being left-handed, Ehud came from the smallest of the tribes. He was the last one the children of Israel would have chosen to deliver them. However, he did not pretend to be anything different from what he was. His brethren, from the tribe of Benjamin, were noted for the fact that "they … could use both the right hand and the left in hurling stones and shooting arrows out of a bow" (1 Chr 12.2). Ehud acknowledged his weakness and "did gird it (*the dagger*) under his raiment upon his right thigh" (v.16) and, when the time came to use it, he "put forth his left hand, and took the dagger from his right thigh" (v.21). He moved by faith, in the light of his limitations, and allowed God's strength to work through him. Eglon would have expected Ehud to draw any weapon that he had with his right hand and therefore he was taken by surprise. God has, indeed, "chosen the weak things of the world to confound the things which are mighty … that no flesh should glory in his presence" (1 Cor 1.27, 29). Paul, recognising his own weakness in the battle against the flesh, cried out, "O wretched man that I am! who shall deliver me from the body of this death? I thank God through Jesus Christ our Lord" (Rom 7.24-25).

Fourthly, by separating from those who will be of no help in the battle. Ehud knew that pandering to Eglon, the man of the flesh, would not bring deliverance. The time came therefore when he disassociated himself from those who would have led him down that track. Once the tribute had been delivered to Eglon, "he sent away the people that bare the present. But he himself turned again from the quarries that were by Gilgal" (vv.18-19). Gilgal was the place where the twelve stones, taken out of Jordan, stood to commemorate the Lord taking them through the river on dry land (Josh 4.20-24). It was there that the new generation, born in the wilderness, had been circumcised (Josh 5.2). These momentous events in their history, that marked an end to any confidence in the flesh, had ceased to have any practical impact on the children of Israel's lives. The word "quarries" (PASIL - 6456), which means idols or carved images, suggests that Eglon may well have erected stone images to his own gods in the vicinity to emphasise his supremacy over Israel's God. However, when Ehud reached that spot, it had the effect of turning him back to deal with Eglon, the man of the flesh, in his summer parlour. J.T.Mawson writes, "The man who had been to Gilgal could not tolerate the presence and domination of Eglon; nor shall we tolerate the flesh and its workings if we have truly learnt the lessons which Gilgal teaches; instead; we shall be most unsparing in our judgment of its slightest movements" (*How to Overcome*).

Fifthly, by gaining the personal victory, in secret, first. It is not possible for believers to achieve anything for God publicly, unless they have first been alone with Him and His Word, and won the private battle against the flesh. Some of the greatest works have been done in people's lives when they were alone with God, e.g. Jacob (Gen 32.24). Having sent the people away that were a hindrance to him, Ehud said to Eglon, "I have a secret errand unto thee, O king: who said, Keep silence. And all that stood by him went out from him" (v.19). It was only after the private and personal victory that Ehud was in a position to unite the children of Israel and say, "Follow after me" (v.28). F.B.Meyer writes, "every saint must have a closet of which he can shut the door, and in which he can pray to the Father which is in secret ... pitiable is the man who cannot, miserable is the man who dare not, meet God face to face" (*Abraham, Friend of God*).

Sixthly, by escaping! As far as the world is concerned, this would be the coward's way but it is God's way for the believer. Having gained the victory over the man of the flesh, Ehud "went forth through the porch, and shut the doors of the parlour upon him, and locked them" (v.23). His victory was complete and he had no desire to return. Eglon's servants were altogether different. They could not restrain themselves from unlocking the doors and entering into the parlour. The distressing discovery for them was that "their lord was fallen down dead on the earth" (v.25). What a contrast this was to the victory that awaited the man who "escaped while they tarried" (v.26). Ehud came to Seirath, "blew a trumpet in the mountain of Ephraim" (v.27) (where Joshua's inheritance was), gathered the people together and called on them to follow him, "for the Lord hath delivered your enemies the Moabites into your hand" (v.28). His personal victory now gave him the moral right to invite others to follow him, and allowed him to unite a people that had been in total disarray. Indeed, Ehud's (261) name means, "united". The outcome was that they "took the fords of Jordan toward Moab" (v.28) and "they slew of Moab at that time about ten thousand men, all lusty, and all men of valour; and there escaped not a man" (v.29). Moab was therefore subdued and "the land had rest fourscore years" (v.30). The Book of Judges will reveal that, as time progressed, the numbers responding to the call to battle against the enemies grew less and less, until no one responded! Such conditions are all too prevalent in this day of grace.

Paul's words to the young man, Timothy, warn of the dangers of the flesh: "Flee (keep on fleeing) also youthful lusts: but follow (keep on following) righteousness, faith, charity, peace, with them that call on the Lord out of a pure heart" (2 Tim 2.22). There are occasions when Christians must stand and fight but they must also learn to discern when it is right to flee.

Ehud may have brought deliverance to the people, and a measure of rest to the land, but he was an imperfect saviour. The deliverance was, at best, only temporary. He was unable to change the hearts of the people or release them from the bondage of sin. Following his death, "the children of Israel again did evil in the sight of the Lord" (4.1). God's deliverances in the Book of Judges had little lasting impact on the generations that followed. A similar pathway can be traced in the history of the Christian church.

However, Paul wrote of the perfect Saviour, "For what the law could not do, in that it was weak through the flesh, God sending his own Son in the likeness of sinful flesh, and for sin, condemned sin in the flesh: that the righteousness of the law might be fulfilled in us, who walk not after the flesh, but after the Spirit" (Rom 8.3-4). The salvation He gives is perfect, complete and eternal.

Shamgar and the Philistines

Verse 31: God Strengthens His Servant against the Enemy

Some commentators refer to Shamgar as a "minor judge" or view him as an insertion into the text by a later editor. Others conclude that he was not a judge at all. It is as well that the assessment of a believer's service does not rest in the distorted and ill-informed opinions of men, but in the righteous estimate of the Lord! Whatever unjustified conclusions men might have reached in relation to Shamgar, the record of Scripture remains, "he also delivered Israel" (v.31). His achievements for the Lord have an abiding message of encouragement for all servants of the Lord.

His origins. He was "the son of Anath", a Gentile name, which suggests that he may have come from a pagan background. As far as his employment was concerned, he was a simple ploughman. However, the grace and mercy of God gave him a place among His people. It is not the vessel but what God puts into the vessel that counts!

His exploits. The book of Judges has already revealed the great achievements of Caleb, Othniel and Ehud. It will unfold, in succeeding chapters, the stirring deeds of men such as Gideon, Jephthah and Samson. Shamgar only slew 600 Philistines, and it may well be asked what difference this made in the great scheme of things. However, the Scriptures record, "he also delivered Israel". The Lord considers no victory, achieved in His name, as insignificant or unimportant. The service of the humblest believer is recognised, recorded and rewarded in heaven. Shamgar recognised the threat posed by the Philistines, the enemy from within the land. They were descended from Ham, whose son, Canaan, was cursed by Noah (Gen 9.25). They came up out of Egypt at the same time as the Israelites and settled on the west coast of Canaan. However, they did not come out, as Israel had done, by way of the shed blood of the lamb, the Red Sea and the river Jordan. They proved to be a constant thorn in the side of the children of Israel. They could be described as, "Having a form of godliness, but denying the power thereof". Paul's instruction to Timothy was, "from such turn away" (2 Tim 3.5).

His power. All Shamgar had at his disposal was an ox goad, which was a pole, six to eight feet in length, with a sharp metal point at one end for prodding stubborn oxen. It was a powerful instrument in the hands of a skilled farmer but men would have treated it with derision in the context of a battle. Indeed, it would have failed to make any impact on six hundred Philistines, unless the Lord had been with Shamgar. He did for God what he could, with what he had, and God honoured him for that.

JUDGES 4

Deborah, Barak and The Canaanites

Deborah's challenge to Barak, "Up; for this is the day in which the Lord hath delivered Sisera into thine hand: is not the Lord gone out before thee?" (v.14), is a pivotal statement in this chapter. Against the dark background of the rebellion of His people and the fearsome might of the king of Canaan, the sovereignty of the Lord shone through. The children of Israel and their oppressors might have felt, in very different ways, that they were in control of their own destinies. However, they soon discovered that they were not; the Lord was.

The Lord's discipline - "The Lord sold them" (v.2)

As they had done in the days following the death of Othniel (3.12), "the children of Israel again did evil in the sight of the LORD, when Ehud was dead" (v.1). Yet again, "it came to pass, when the judge was dead, that they returned, and corrupted themselves more than their fathers" 2.19). Their loyalty to the Lord was superficial and depended entirely on the restraining influence of the judges. Once their positive presence was removed, they returned to their evil ways and demonstrated that their hearts had not changed. They were delivered from the yoke of their enemies but they failed in the all-important requirement to depart from evil. A true repentance of heart, that would have guaranteed lasting recovery, was always lacking.

The children of Israel had enjoyed eighty years of peace under the leadership of Ehud (3.30), the longest period of peace recorded in the days of the judges. However, after his death, they proceeded to act as if they could do as they pleased and escape the consequences. The Lord taught them otherwise and "sold them into the hand of Jabin king of Canaan" (v.2). The sadness that this must have brought to His heart is captured in the words of the Psalmist: "Thou sellest thy people for nought, and dost not increase thy wealth by their price" (Ps 44.12). He sold them for nought and had not been enriched Himself by doing so.

The tragedy of the situation was heightened by the fact that Joshua had comprehensively defeated this enemy a century before. "Jabin" was probably a hereditary title adopted by the successive, powerful kings of the region. Hazor, their capital city, was a strategically positioned northern town about four miles south west of Lake Huleh in Galilee, in the territory allotted to the tribe of Naphtali. An earlier Jabin and his hosts had come against Israel, but "they smote them, until they left them none remaining" (Josh 11.8). Joshua "houghed (hamstrung - 6131) their horses, and burnt their chariots with fire" (Josh 11.9). He then proceeded to destroy Hazor, with the intention that it should not be inhabited again. The victory was so comprehensive that, "there was not any left to breathe: and he burnt

Hazor with fire" (Josh 11.11). However, the complacency and wickedness of the children of Israel led to the Canaanites regaining a foothold in the land. They rebuilt Hazor and replaced the chariots of iron. Like the Philistines, they proved to be a dangerous and powerful enemy within the land. S.Ridout writes, "Satan knows what resurrection is just as well as we do. Satan knows what the resurrection of the power of evil is that can overthrow the believer, and bring him into captivity to that same power which he had once mastered" (*Lectures on the Book of Judges*). M.F.Unger expresses the same thought when he writes, "He (Jabin) illustrates the fact that old foes can be resurrected in new forms to vex and enslave the Lord's people who lapse into former sinful ways" (*Commentary on the Old Testament*).

Jabin (2985) means, "intelligence, understanding", and Hazor (2674) means, "an enclosure, a fortress, a place surrounded by a wall". He represents the wisdom of the world, which is totally opposed to divine revelation and will do all it can to exclude it. He does not play a prominent role in the events recorded in this chapter (v.23), which would suggest that the real power rested in the hands of Sisera, the captain of his army, who "dwelt in Harosheth of the Gentiles (so named because of the mixed races that inhabited it)" (v.2). The wisdom of this world will frequently turn to aggression and oppression in order to achieve its ends, and therefore for "twenty years he mightily oppressed the children of Israel" (v.3). His 900 chariots of iron (v.3) gave him total control of the plains and valleys and left Israel powerless. Unnoticed by the complacent and rebellious children of Israel, the Canaanites had learned to smelt iron and build the chariots that led to them regaining the territory that Joshua had once so decisively conquered. Whenever human wisdom and understanding gains the ascendancy over divine things, it spells weakness and spiritual decline for the Lord's people.

The Lord's word - "Hath not the LORD God of Israel commanded?" (v.6)

Nothing short of the Lord's intervention could bring deliverance to the children of Israel. If the mighty oppression and worldly wisdom of Jabin and Sisera were to be overcome, His voice had to be heard and obeyed. The vessel through whom He chose to speak, in response to the people's cry for deliverance from their suffering (v.3), underlined the extent of their failure and was an indictment of the spiritual condition of the men of the day. There was no man deemed fit to convey His message of deliverance and therefore He entrusted the responsibility to a woman. Deborah was the only woman among the judges but this should not lead to her being viewed as an unworthy, or lesser, vessel. She was, indeed, a remarkable person and displayed the necessary features that led God to use her in bringing about the release of His people from bondage.

Her name. Deborah (1683) means "a bee". She was industrious and busy in the Lord's work. There was nothing half-hearted about her. It is such people that the Lord can use at a moment's notice to do His work. It is recorded that, "she judged (was judging) Israel at that time" (v.4). The implication is that she judged permanently. She had gained great respect and credibility among the children of Israel over a lengthy period of time and therefore she was qualified to be the Lord's mouthpiece. In the midst of a society oppressed by the worldly wisdom of Jabin and his captain, she was used by God to communicate the divine wisdom that would bring deliverance.

Her gift. Deborah was a prophetess. The idea of a prophetess is not foreign to the Scriptures. She stands alongside other women who were similarly gifted: Miriam (Ex 15.20), Huldah (2 Kings 22.14), Anna (Lk 2.36), and Philip's four daughters (Acts 21.9). However, on almost all occasions when a prophetess was used, the nation was in spiritual decline. As a prophetess, Deborah communicated the mind of God to others and foretold what was to come. Her prophetic voice was heard when she foretold the final outcome of the battle against the Canaanites: "the Lord shall sell Sisera into the hand of a woman"(v.9).

Her service. Deborah did not move outside the God-given sphere for the service of women. She did not force herself into the public arena. She did not sit at the gate of the city, but simply made herself available, "and the children of Israel came up to her for judgment" (v.5). It would appear, from the influence she exerted on this particular occasion, that people came from some distance to seek her counsel. When communicating the mind of the Lord to a somewhat reluctant Barak, "she sent and called" (v.6) for him privately. She did not seek to usurp his position or humiliate him publicly. When she agreed to accompany him to the battle against Sisera (v.9), she did not attempt to take over his leadership role or gain any of the glory. She spoke readily of the Lord delivering Sisera into the hands of a woman, knowing that the honour would go to another.

Her testimony. Deborah set a good example in her family life. During the times of the judges, when every man was doing what was right in his own eyes, village and family life broke down altogether (5.7). However, this was not the case with Deborah. She may have been a judge, a prophetess and more spiritual than her husband, but she was still known as "the wife of Lapidoth" (v.4). Lapidoth (3941), which means "a bright and shining torch", provides a fitting description of the testimony of this couple during such a dark period in the history of Israel. Whatever spiritual heights she may have reached, she would not have wished to be separated from the name of her husband. She would have been entirely comfortable with the New Testament teaching of headship: "the head of every man is Christ; and the head of the woman is the man; and the head of Christ is God" (1 Cor 11.3). C.A.Coates writes, "God could not raise up a prophetess to traverse His own order. If the Lord gives prominence to a woman, she will be prominent in a way suitable to the position, and will recognise headship" (*An Outline of the Book of Judges*). Deborah and Lapidoth were, indeed, a shining testimony to God's creatorial order, when these principles were being overturned among the Lord's people at large. She reminds believers in the present day of the importance of reflecting the divine order in the way they conduct themselves, both in the home and the local assembly.

Her dwelling. Deborah could be found in a spiritually attractive place. The people knew precisely where to find her when they came to her for judgment. "And she dwelt under the palm tree of Deborah between Ramah and Bethel in mount Ephraim" (v.5), which was situated some fifty miles from the scene of the final battle against Sisera. It has already been observed in the commentary on ch.3 that the Scriptures link the palm tree with rejoicing, flourishing, uprightness, praise and victory. Unlike the children of Israel during the days of Ehud, Deborah displayed these features. There was a particular palm tree in Israel that was known as "the palm tree of Deborah" (v.5), which conveys that she was a personal overcomer and did not simply depend on the strengths of others. On one side of her dwelling stood Ramah (7414), which means "heights", and on the other stood Bethel (1008), which means "house of God". Mount Ephraim was the place where Joshua's inheritance was to be found (Josh 19.50). It is no surprise that a woman like Deborah should want to be surrounded by places so rich in their spiritual associations. She encourages believers to value the "house of God" and to desire to live on the spiritual heights opened up to them through the Person and work of Christ. If they do, they too will overcome the wisdom of this world and be marked by the features associated with the palm tree.

The Lord's salvation - "I will deliver him into thine hand" (v.7)

Deborah communicated the Lord's assurances to Barak, the son of Abinoam (v.6): "I will draw unto thee to the river Kishon Sisera … I will deliver him into thine hand" (v.7). Barak greeted these promises of certain victory with a mixture of faith and doubt. H.L.Rossier writes, "We must not expect in a day of ruin to see all the divine resources displayed in the instruments employed of God" (*Meditations on the Book of Judges*).

His name. Barak (1301) means, "lightning", and Abinoam (42) means "father of pleasantness or graciousness". Lightning has to do with the heavens and speaks of light moving in the form of storm and judgment. As far as the wisdom of this world is concerned, these two thoughts are incompatible. The unbelieving mind has no appreciation of the character of God and therefore cannot understand that the God of grace is also the God who "doth judge and make war" (Rev 19.11). When the time came, Barak moved as lightning to deliver the children of Israel from the oppression of the enemy.

His home. Deborah called Barak "out of Kedesh-naphtali" (v.6). Naphtali was one of the tribes most severely oppressed by Jabin. Barak had experienced the suffering at first-hand and would therefore have been anxious to see the people released from bondage. Kedesh (6943) means "sanctuary", and Naphtali (5321) means "to wrestle". A.M.S.Gooding brings these thoughts together when he writes, "This man pictures a man of the sanctuary and in the sanctuary he is praying and, as a result of his praying, divine power is exerted against the enemies of God's people, against principalities and powers" (*The 13 Judges*). Barak's actions remind the Lord's people of the need to be men and women of prayer if they wish to engage in successful warfare against the wisdom of this world.

His commission. The instruction that Deborah gave to him was unequivocal: "Hath not the Lord God of Israel commanded, saying, Go and draw toward mount Tabor, and take with thee ten thousand men of the children of Naphtali and of the children of Zebulun? And I will draw unto thee to the river Kishon Sisera, the captain of Jabin's army, with his chariots and his multitude; and I will deliver him into thine hand" (vv.6-7). A.E.Cundall writes, "Mount Tabor ... was a conical shaped mountain rising a little over 1300 feet from the north-eastern corner of the Esdraelon valley, and was such a prominent landmark that any confusion on the part of the assembling Israelites would be avoided" (*Judges – An Introduction and Commentary*). It would have been safe from Sisera's chariots and an ideal place from which to launch a surprise attack. All Barak had to do was to obey the command and the Lord would do the rest. The enemy was not in control of the situation; the Lord was.

His faith. The wisdom of this world would mock at the Lord's command to Barak. To take the Israelite forces into the territory through which the river Kishon flowed was to play right into Sisera's hands. His chariots would very quickly gain the ascendancy over the children of Israel in the plain and they would be subject to even greater oppression than before. However, there is no indication that Barak questioned the command or doubted that the Lord could accomplish what He said He would do. What he did was an act of faith and the Lord acknowledged this by including him in the great gallery of faith in Hebrews (Heb 11.32). Even though there were very few weapons in Israel (5.8), and no established army, he trusted the Lord to gain the victory. He enlisted 10,000 men from his own tribe, Naphtali, and the neighbouring tribe of Zebulun. The song of Deborah and Barak, following the victory, indicates that others joined them later from the tribes of Benjamin, Ephraim, Manasseh (referred to as Machir) and Issachar (5.14-15). However, even with the increase in numbers, they could not have hoped to contend successfully against the might of Jabin and Sisera. Salvation would have to come from the Lord, and Deborah and Barak believed that it would.

His reticence. Some commentators state that vv.8 and 9 should not be viewed as a rebuke for Barak's lack of faith. They believe that he was humbly acknowledging his weakness and therefore his total dependence on God's guidance through the voice of the prophetess. The fact that he moved by faith, and ultimately gained the victory over Jabin and Sisera, is not in doubt. Indeed, to question this would be to deny God's verdict on him in Hebrews 11. It would also be unjust, in the light of his stirring exploits against Sisera (vv.14-16), to brand him as a coward. However, it is difficult not to hear the reticence in his voice as he said to Deborah, "If thou wilt go with me, then I will go: but if thou wilt not go with me, then I will not go" (v.8). He listened to God's word but supplemented it with his own conditions. God had said, "I will", but his response was, "If thou wilt". It is equally difficult not to detect a measure of disappointment in Deborah's reply, "I will surely go with thee: notwithstanding the journey that thou takest shall not be for thine honour; for the Lord shall sell Sisera into the hand of a woman" (v.9). C.A.Coates writes, "The word of Jehovah should have been enough. There was an element of weakness, along with the faith that is mentioned in Hebrews. He lost some of the glory, some of the honour God would have put on him" (*An Outline of the Book of Judges*). Indeed, Deborah's initial message to him, "Hath not the Lord God of Israel commanded" (v.6), indicated that God had already spoken and he had not responded. There must also have been some regret and shame in Barak's heart as he pursued Sisera, only to be met by Jael's invitation at the end of his journey to, "Come, and I will shew thee the man whom thou seekest" (v.22).

The Lord's victory - "And the Lord discomfited Sisera" (v.15)

The means by which the victory was achieved defied all human logic and bore testimony to the fact that, "Salvation belongeth unto the Lord" (Ps 3.8). Deborah reflected this in her confident call to Barak, "Up; for this is the day in which the Lord hath delivered Sisera into thine hand: is not the Lord gone out before thee?" (v.14). The Lord controlled the movements of men and women in order to accomplish His purposes.

The Lord used Barak. "So Barak went down from mount Tabor, and ten thousand men after him" (v.14). Against all human reason, he led his infantry down mount Tabor for a surprise attack in the Plain of Esdraelon against the host of Sisera and his chariots. L.H.Wiseman describes the scene when he writes, "Not a chariot is among them; scarcely a weapon of war. But there is a prophet amongst them, the appointed representative of Him who has 'chosen the foolish things of the world to confound the wise; and … the weak things of the world to confound the things which are mighty' (1 Cor 1.27). And at their head there is a man of faith, believing in the covenant, and therefore undismayed by the nine hundred chariots of iron; knowing that 'with God all things are possible' (Mt 19.26)" *(Practical Truths from Judges)*. The outcome was that the Canaanite army was "discomfited" (put in commotion, crushed, destroyed - 2000) and its commander "lighted down off his chariot, and fled away on his feet" (v.15). The scene is one of a complete and utter rout of the enemy. The song of Deborah and Barak throws further light on this remarkable scene. They refer to the fact that "the earth trembled, and the heavens dropped, the clouds also dropped water" (5.4), and "The river of Kishon swept them away" (5.21). Clearly, there was a violent rainstorm and the river burst its banks, flooding the area. Any advantage that Sisera had was lost as his chariots stuck fast in the ground. The Lord had caused his strength to become his weakness. All this took place in the traditional dry season in Canaan, when the river Kishon would have been little more than a wadi, and therefore it is easy to understand why Sisera and his host fled before Barak. Their god, Baal, was the god of storms and they must have deduced that he had forsaken them. Knowledge of how the battle was won does not detract from, but rather enhances, the belief that it was the Lord who gained the victory. Only He could have controlled the elements with such precise timing and devastating effect.

The Lord used Heber. A seemingly irrelevant statement is made before the account of the battle. "Now Heber the Kenite, which was of the children of Hobab the father in law of Moses, had severed himself from the Kenites, and pitched his tent unto the plain of Zaanaim, which is by Kedesh" (v.11). Human wisdom would discount this fact as of little importance in the context of God's great plan for the deliverance of His people. It has already been observed, earlier on in the book, that the Kenites were a nomadic group who had settled in Judah's territory in the south of the country (1.16). However, Heber had, for some reason, separated himself from the rest of the Kenites and moved north. It is interesting to observe that Zaanaim (6815) means "to remove, and to take down". He might have felt that he was in control of his relocation but little did he know that the Lord would use his movements to deliver His people. Heber (2268) means "joining, company", and has the thought of companionship and fellowship associated with it. Sadly, his separation from the Kenites had led him away from his links with Judah and into companionship with the Canaanites. This led to "peace between Jabin the king of Hazor and the house of Heber the Kenite" (v.17), and therefore he lost his pilgrim character. Indeed, it appears as if it were Heber who turned informer and told Sisera "that

Barak the son of Abinoam was gone up to mount Tabor" (v.12). However, the Lord, in His sovereignty, over-ruled and turned the seemingly unimportant actions of Heber into blessing for the children of Israel. Believers can look back to what appeared to be insignificant and unrelated events in their lives and see the Lord's over-ruling.

The Lord used Jael. Once again, He used a woman to bring about His purposes, thus highlighting the failure of the male leadership of the day. Jael, Heber's wife, was of a very different character from that of her husband.

Her name. Jael (3278) means, "a wild goat" - this is associated with the thought of climbing and ascending. Unlike her husband, she was not prepared to lower her standards by forging a friendship with Jabin. She had her sight set on a path of ascent that would lead to re-establishing links with the children of Israel.

Her home. Even though Heber had lost his pilgrim character and abandoned the associations that would have been of spiritual help to him, Jael had not. She had retained the features of a tent-dweller, bearing testimony to the fact that she had no permanent dwelling place on earth. Among the tents of the Kenites there was one that was known as "the tent of Jael the wife of Heber the Kenite" (v.17). She may have given Sisera the impression that he was safe in a woman's tent by serving him milk instead of water and covering him with a blanket but nothing could have been further from the truth. He made a wise move as far as the wisdom of the world was concerned and his deep sleep (v.21) was evidence of how secure he felt. However, he was totally ignorant of the fact that a God-given prophecy would be fulfilled in Jael's tent that day, when the Lord sold him into the hand of a woman. For the commander of the army to die when fleeing from the battle would have been disastrous enough but to be slain by a woman was total humiliation.

Her actions. Heber, her husband, was at peace with Jabin but Jael was not. The very fact that Sisera was fleeing to her dwelling in Kedesh when she met him, and his command that no one should be told of his whereabouts (v.20), must have confirmed to her that Barak's army had gained a resounding victory. Kedesh (to be distinguished from the Kedesh in Naphtali, which was thirty miles [48 kilometres] away) was probably only a few miles from the battlefield and thus Sisera was able to reach it in spite of his exhausted and demoralised condition. She had the insight to see how dangerous he was and her one aim therefore was to slay him. She did so by taking a nail of the tent and a hammer (v.21). It was the women who put up and took down the tents, so she was skilled at using both. The tent peg would speak of her pilgrim character, and reminds believers today that they have here "no continuing city, but we seek one to come" (Heb

13.14). However, the nail would have been of little use without the hammer, which represents the power of the Word of God. The Lord spoke through Jeremiah, "Is not my word like as a fire? saith the Lord; and like a hammer that breaketh the rock in pieces?" (Jer 23.29). It is only the Word of God that can silence and defeat the wisdom of this world. Jael "went softly unto him, and smote the nail into his temples, and fastened it into the ground" (v.21). She targeted the very seat of his wisdom and understanding. Paul reminded the Corinthians of God's word through the prophet, Isaiah, "I will destroy the wisdom of the wise, and will bring to nothing the understanding of the prudent (1 Cor 1.19).

Some commentators find it difficult to support the actions of Jael and are critical of the way in which she deceived and slew Sisera. However, the ruthless nature of the enemy has to be borne in mind. Had Sisera been allowed to live, he would have continued with acts of great brutality towards the children of Israel, which would have included heinous sexual crimes against the women. She was not prepared to compromise with a man like this, as her husband had done. The Word of God does not condemn her actions. Indeed, Deborah and Barak sang, "Blessed above women shall Jael the wife of Heber the Kenite be, blessed shall she be above women in the tent" (5.24).

The verdict of Scripture, following the death of Sisera, is, "So God (ELOHIM - 430, as opposed to Jehovah throughout the rest of the chapter) subdued on that day Jabin the king of Canaan before the children of Israel. And the hand of the children of Israel prospered, and prevailed against Jabin the king of Canaan, until they had destroyed Jabin king of Canaan" (vv.23,24). The victory was so complete that the Canaanites did not regain their power over Israel again.

JUDGES 5

The Lord's deliverance of the children of Israel out of the hand of the Egyptians prompted an immediate response from their hearts: "Then sang Moses and the children of Israel this song unto the Lord" (Ex 15.1). They were united in their praise to the Lord, who had "triumphed gloriously". However, His deliverance of them from the oppression of Jabin and Sisera led to a song from just Deborah and Barak. It is the only song recorded in the book of Judges. Drawing out the contrast between the two songs, C.A.Coates writes, "I trust that we have all learned to sing the song of Moses but in the last days we have to learn to sing the song of Deborah and Barak. I suppose one would hardly be a Christian at all if one could not sing with Moses but it is only overcomers who can sing with Deborah and Barak. The song of Moses is the common property of all: it is the song of the redeemed; but the song of Deborah and Barak is a song sung in difficult times, a song which celebrates how God comes in for His people, and how He provides what is needed for their deliverance in a very dark day. One is as important as the other" (*An Outline of the book of Judges*). Overcomers will always find something for which to praise God, no matter how dark and difficult the days may be.

Clearly, the setting for the song was bleak as far as the children of Israel were concerned. There was nothing about their situation that would have led to a song. It might have been the days of Shamgar, the son of Anath, and Jael (v.6) but few matched their exploits for, or devotion to, the Lord and His people. Conditions had deteriorated to such a degree that "the highways (well-trodden roads - 734) were unoccupied, and the travellers walked through byways (crooked ways - 6128)" (v.6). The dangerous state of the country meant that travellers had to abandon the use of the main highways for fear of attack. They were forced therefore to seek out their own routes, through the byways, in order to escape detection by their Canaanite enemies. Any meaningful form of travel, trade and commerce had ground to a halt.

A further tragic outcome was that "The inhabitants of the villages ceased" (v.7). In such uncertain and lawless conditions, the villages were no longer safe places to be and therefore the people deserted them in order to live in the walled cities. It appears that the family unit, which was at the heart of village life, had all but come to an end in Israel, the very place where it ought to have been seen at its strongest. However, the initial feeling of safety engendered by dwelling in the cities was soon replaced by "war in the gates" (v.8). Such was the domination of the Canaanites that they oppressed the children of Israel wherever they found them, even in the gates of the fortified cities where their judges and magistrates sat. They were so impoverished that there was not "a shield (to defend with) or spear (to attack with) seen among forty thousand in Israel" (v.8). Even if there had been, they would not have had the confidence to use them against the might of Jabin and Sisera. The Philistines and the Canaanites had secured the smelting rights and therefore Israel was totally dependent on them for the possession of any weapons.

If the children of Israel had been asked why they had reached such a deplorable state, the majority of them may well have pointed the finger of blame at the Canaanites. However, Deborah and Barak reminded them in their song of the real reason: "They chose new gods; then was war in the gates" (v.8). If they had remained loyal to the Lord, they would not have been under the yoke of the Canaanites. Their deliberate abandonment of the Lord and experimentation with the gods of their enemies, led Him to chastise them and sell them into the hand of Jabin, king of Canaan. The disastrous consequences of their actions stand as a constant reminder to believers not to forsake "the highways" of divine truth and "walk through byways" of their own wisdom and choosing, which are contrary to the Word of God.

However, it is encouraging to observe that this chapter is not dominated by doom and gloom. Indeed, the darkness was lifted "on that day" (v.1) i.e. the day when "Sisera lay dead, and the nail was in his temples" (4.22). The song of the overcomers filled the air in the aftermath of a mighty victory. Clearly, the frequent use of the first person pronoun throughout indicates that Deborah was the author of the song (vv.3,7,9,13,21). However, Barak joined her in the singing and, together, they gave expression to the feelings of the liberated children of Israel.

Praise for the Lord

The Lord may have worked through human agencies to bring about the victory over Jabin and Sisera but the song acknowledged that the praise and glory primarily belonged to Him. It opened with the words, "Praise ye the Lord for the avenging of Israel" (v.2). As well as being a call to Israel to praise the Lord, Israel's enemies were also addressed: "Hear, O ye kings; give ear, O ye princes; I, even I, will sing unto the Lord; I will sing praise to the Lord God of Israel" (v.3). God's deliverance of Israel was a challenge to the kings and princes of the nations to fear and to marvel. The psalmist echoed the same thought when he wrote, "Be wise now therefore, O ye kings: be instructed, ye judges of the earth. Serve the Lord with fear, and rejoice with trembling" (Ps 2.10-11).

The song celebrated the unchanging nature of the Lord. The One who brought deliverance from the oppression of the Canaanites was none other than the God of Sinai. "Lord, when thou wentest out of Seir, when thou marchedst out of the field of Edom, the earth trembled, and the heavens dropped, the clouds also dropped water. The mountains melted from before the Lord, even that Sinai from before the Lord God of Israel" (vv.4-5). The voice of the covenant-making God at Sinai had been accompanied with thunder and lightning and "the whole mount quaked greatly" (Ex 19.18). The children of Israel might have changed but He had not. He was not simply a God of the past but also of the present. The One who appeared at Sinai, had also brought them present deliverance, and was therefore worthy of their praise. The God who brought them through the Red Sea saved them "by the waters of Megiddo" (5.19); the God who appeared at Mount Sinai was also with them at Mount Tabor (4.6). He was, indeed, the living and unchanging God.

When He moved to deliver His people, creation moved in accordance with His will. Sisera found this out to his great cost. Although he did not know it, he was not simply fighting against a feeble band of demoralised Israelites but against the Lord Himself. The song declared, "They fought from heaven; the stars in their courses fought against Sisera. The river of Kishon swept them away, that ancient river, the river Kishon. O my soul, thou hast trodden down strength" (vv.20-21). As well as using human agents, the sovereign Lord also marshalled the forces of nature (probably a reference to a violent rainstorm that engulfed Sisera and his chariots) to deliver His people. All Deborah and Barak could do was to praise Him!

In the light of what God has done for them, every child of God ought to desire to sing the words of the hymn writer:

How good is the God we adore,
Our faithful, unchangeable Friend,
Whose love is as great as His power,
And knows neither measure nor end.

'Tis Jesus, the First and the Last,
Whose Spirit shall guide us safe home;
We'll praise Him for all that is past,
And trust Him for all that's to come.
(Joseph Hart)

It is so easy for the Lord's people to forget to praise Him in the aftermath of deliverance. They are happy to enjoy the blessings but they forget the One who has blessed them. Deborah and Barak recognised this danger and therefore they made an appeal to different classes of people: "Speak (ponder, reflect, meditate - 7878), ye that ride on white asses, ye that sit in judgment (things which are measured or stretched out, such as carpets or coverings - 4055), and walk by the way" (v.10). White asses were rare and would have been owned by the wealthy nobles. Those who sat on carpets may be a further reference to the owners of the white asses, who placed expensive saddle-cloths on the backs of their animals before sitting on them, or it may refer to those who remained at home, living in luxury. Those who walked by the way depicted the ordinary travellers, including the merchants, who were now able to leave the walled cities and travel in safety on the highways. Whichever class was being addressed, the change in their circumstances, following the death of Sisera, was dramatic. It was a far cry from the conditions experienced in the days of Shamgar and Jael (vv.6-8). The enemies who had oppressed and impoverished them had been defeated. "The noise of archers" (v.11) had been silenced and therefore they were now able to go to the wells and draw water, without fear of attack. As they pondered and reflected upon this, they were encouraged to "go down to the gates" (v.11), where there had previously been war (v.8), to "rehearse (ascribe, celebrate, commemorate - 8567) the righteous acts of the Lord, even the righteous acts towards the inhabitants of his villages in Israel" (v.11). The Lord's deliverance had been so complete that they were able to leave the walled cities and return to their former village life, ascribing all the praise to Him and celebrating His righteous acts towards them.

Praise for the People

The song opens with praise for those who, "willingly offered themselves" (v.2). As well as praising the Lord for the victory over the Canaanites, the song also acknowledged the involvement of His people in that victory. Deborah and Barak reviewed and assessed the contributions of individuals and tribes. It reminds believers of Paul's message to the Corinthians, "For we must all appear before the judgment seat of Christ; that every one may receive the things done in his body, according to that he hath done, whether it be good or bad" (2 Cor 5.10). It is humbling to remember that, although it is the Lord who gives the victory, He will graciously reward His people for what He accomplishes through them.

The leaders were singled out for praise

The quality of the leadership given is key to the success of any group engaged in warfare, and the children of Israel were no exception to this. Before the people, in general, would stir themselves to action, it was necessary for the leaders to set the example. Indeed, Deborah and Barak recognised that it had to begin with them. They understood that they would not be morally qualified to call on others to take action, unless they were prepared to make the first move. Deborah therefore issued the personal challenge, "Awake, awake, Deborah: awake, awake, utter a song: arise, Barak, and lead thy captivity captive, thou son of Abinoam" (v.12). Her words concerning Barak foreshadow Christ, although Barak was but a pale reflection of Him. The same theme is taken up in the Messianic Psalm: "Thou hast ascended on high, thou hast led captivity captive: thou hast received gifts for men" (Ps 68.18). Paul went on to apply these words to the Lord Jesus when he wrote, "Wherefore he saith, When he ascended up on high, he led captivity captive, and gave gifts unto men" (Eph 4.8). Unlike Barak, He was not the reluctant leader, who needed to be prompted into action. His triumph was complete as He led captive those He had defeated at the cross: "And having spoiled principalities and powers, he made a shew of them openly, triumphing over them in it" (Col 2.15).

Deborah had already described herself as "a mother in Israel" (v.7). She displayed genuine care and concern for the welfare of the Lord's people, qualities that were absolutely vital to effective leadership. If leaders do not have an interest in the people they lead, they will act from selfish motives. Paul reminded the Thessalonian believers of how he, and his fellow-workers, "were gentle among you, even as a nurse (nursing mother) cherisheth her children" (1 Thess 2.7). He introduced Timothy to the assembly at Philippi as a man, "who will naturally (genuinely) care for your state" (Phil 2.20).

Deborah looked for and praised the Lord when she found these same caring qualities in other leaders in Israel. "My heart is toward the governors of Israel, that offered themselves willingly among the people. Bless ye the Lord" (v.9). There was no half-heartedness or reluctance about their involvement but a willing surrender to the cause. Particular mention was also made of the governors of Machir (v.14) and the princes of Issachar (v.15). Such willing and sacrificial giving has always been at the heart of effective leadership among the Lord's people. In the New Testament Peter encourages elders to, "Feed the flock of God which is among you, taking the oversight thereof, not by constraint, but willingly; not for filthy lucre, but of a ready mind; neither as being lords over God's heritage, but being ensamples to the flock" (1 Pet 5.2-3). It is this positive and constructive leadership that encourages similar responses from "the flock".

The contributions of particular tribes were noted and praised

Only a remnant of Israel participated in the victory but they were remembered. Six tribes are mentioned, namely Ephraim (who had settled in the mount (hill country) of the Amalekites, cf. 12.15), Benjamin, the western half of Manasseh (here referred to as Machir), Issachar, Zebulun and Naphtali (vv.14-18). Two of them, Zebulun and Naphtali, received particular recognition, because they "jeoparded (exposed, despised, disdained - 2778) their lives unto the death in the high places of the field (probably a reference to Mount Tabor from whence they attacked the Canaanites)" (v.18). The previous chapter indicates that they formed the main part of Barak's army (4.10). They willingly exposed themselves to reproach and were prepared for the ultimate cost of laying down their lives for the Lord and their brethren. Also from Zebulun came "they that handle the pen of the writer (scorer, recorder – in a military sense, denotes the officer who kept the muster roll - 5608) " (v.14). The name of every soldier recruited to the battle was recorded. It is comforting, and challenging, to know that the name and actions of each believer are recorded in heaven.

The non-participants were condemned

Sadly there were those tribes, living on the other side of Jordan, who put personal interests above those of the Lord and their brethren, and they lost out on the reward. They responded in different ways. Some gave the call to battle serious consideration, while others remained totally indifferent to it. There were those who may have concluded that the scene of the conflict was some way from them and therefore of little relevance to their daily lives. It is so easy for believers to distance themselves from the needs of their brethren if they do not appear to be directly affected by events. However, the failure of certain tribes to do anything positive, for whatever reason, did not absolve them from censure. God views sins of omission as seriously as sins of commission. Some of the greatest denunciations in the Scriptures were against those who did nothing. It was no credit to these tribes that the Canaanite kings "took no gain of money" from the battle (v.19) but departed from the scene defeated and empty handed. If it had been left to their interest and endeavours, the enemy would have won the battle and carried away the spoils of victory.

As far as the Reubenites were concerned, they reflected the words of Jacob, "Unstable as water, thou shalt not excel" (Gen 49.4). The song testified of them, "For the divisions of Reuben there were great thoughts of heart. Why abodest thou among the sheepfolds, to hear the bleatings of the flocks? For the divisions of Reuben there were great searchings of heart" (vv.15-16). They knew that they had a responsibility to respond to the call to battle and they agonised about it. However, following great deliberations, they decided to stay where they were. Their home comforts and business interests won the day. It does not reflect well on believers if they are intent on looking after their own comforts, while fellow-believers suffer affliction and reproach. As he neared the end of his life, Paul wrote to Timothy, "At my first answer no man stood with me, but all men forsook me" (2 Tim 4.16). J.T.Mawson brings home the challenge, when he writes, "Oh! Why did Reuben abide by the sheepfold while the great conflict waged? Why, oh, why do Christians today, loving ease and comfort, abide in the safety of the sheepfolds, when God's glorious gospel is going forth, and is opposed by all the power and ingenuity of Satan? Surely where such indifference holds sway the devices of Satan have been successful, and he has got the advantage" (*How to Overcome*).

Gilead, which probably refers to the tribes of Gad and the eastern part of Manasseh, also failed to respond to the call to battle and "abode beyond Jordan" (v.17). The tribes of Dan and Asher, both of whom were situated on the coast, also remained in their comfortable positions, while their brethren were being prepared to lay down their lives for the cause. The song records of them, "and why did Dan remain in ships? Asher continued on the sea shore, and abode in his breaches (havens - 4664)" (v.17), Clearly, both were more interested in engaging in profitable maritime trade with their neighbours than in supporting their oppressed brethren.

The most severe censure of all was reserved for the city of Meroz and its inhabitants. "Curse ye Meroz, said the angel of the Lord, curse ye bitterly the inhabitants thereof; because they came not to the help of the Lord, to the help of the Lord against the mighty" (v.23). Their indifference was so serious that it was none other than the Lord Himself, in the form of the angel of the Lord, who cursed them through the mouths of Deborah and Barak. Their sin was a failure to help the Lord in His cause, not simply a failure to assist Israel. They chose to remain in a neutral position and therefore missed out on the greatest privilege of all, helping the Lord "against the mighty". S.Ridout writes, "Of course, He does not need our help for Himself; He can, and one day will, overthrow all His and our enemies with the sword that proceedeth out of His mouth. But as our Lord identifies Himself with His poor brethren who are afflicted and imprisoned, and regards help afforded to them as though done to Himself personally, so it is here" (*Lectures on the Book of Judges*). It is not precisely clear where Meroz was situated but it is probable that it was so close to the scene of the conflict that its inhabitants had the greatest opportunity, and therefore responsibility, of all the tribes to become involved. Some commentators have suggested that they were strategically well placed to cut off any retreat by Sisera and his army. The curse was so complete that, following its announcement, Meroz is not heard of again.

It is important to observe that some of the tribes were not included in the review by Deborah and Barak, either for praise or condemnation, e.g. Judah and Simeon. Clearly, they had other issues to address and therefore they were not held accountable for what they had not been called to do. The Lord's people are called upon to serve Him in many different ways and circumstances. They are not all expected to have the same exercises or to do precisely the same things. However, the review of the tribes who were called provides a timely reminder to present day believers that, at the judgment seat of Christ, "Every man's work shall be made manifest: for the day shall declare it, because it shall be revealed by fire; and the fire shall try every man's work of what sort it is. If any man's work abide which he hath built thereupon, he shall receive a reward. If any man's work shall be burned, he shall suffer loss; but he himself shall be saved; yet so as by fire" (1 Cor 3.13-15).

Praise for Jael

Jael's contribution to the battle condemned the selfishness and indifference of the inhabitants of Meroz and the other non-participative tribes. They received censure from the Lord, whereas she received praise: "Blessed above women shall Jael the wife of Heber the Kenite be, blessed shall she be above women in the tent" (v.24). Deborah and Barak gave the divine verdict on the deeds of Jael, which does not contain one word of condemnation. It is significant that a stranger, who was a tent-dweller, put those tribes who had settled down in Canaan and lost their pilgrim character to shame. Even though she belonged to the Kenites, who did not originally have a place among the children of Israel, she had more feelings for the welfare of the people of God than they did. Whereas they were content for the enemy to live, as long as he did not disturb their comfortable lifestyle, she recognised the danger. She lulled Sisera into a false sense of security: "He asked water, and she gave him milk; she brought forth butter in a lordly dish" (v.25). Having achieved this, she proceeded to "put her hand to the nail, and her right hand to the workmen's hammer; and with the hammer she smote Sisera, she smote off his head, when she had pierced and stricken through his temples" (v.26). With the nail and the hammer, instruments associated with a tent-dweller (commented upon at the conclusion of the previous chapter), she humbled and slew the one who represented the wisdom of this world. "At her feet he bowed, he fell, he lay down: at her feet he bowed, he fell; where he bowed, there he fell down dead" (v.27). Ehud (3.15) was left-handed (shut up of the right hand) but Jael took the hammer in her right hand, which speaks of divine power and favour. She allowed God's strength to work through her and therefore the enemy's humiliation was total and complete.

The scene in Jael's tent was a direct contrast to the one revealed in Sisera's household. The song that began by highlighting "a mother in Israel" (v.7), closed with an ungodly Canaanite mother. Deborah and Barak gave a vivid and dramatic portrayal of the anxiety of Sisera's mother as she awaited the return of her son from the battle. Little did she appreciate, as she looked expectantly out of the window, that there was no hope. She, along with the wisest of the women that waited on her (v.29), sought to provide answers to her questions, "Why is his chariot so long in coming? why tarry the wheels of his chariots?" (v.28). Their knowledge of Sisera's character convinced them that he must have been gathering the spoils of victory, which would have included abusing the women. They went on to envisage the colourful and embroidered garments that he would return with to adorn their necks. "Have they not sped (found, attained, acquired - 4672)? have they not divided the prey; to every man a damsel or two; to Sisera a prey of divers colours, a prey of divers colours of needlework, of divers colours of needlework on both sides, meet for the necks of them that take the spoil?" (v.30) It underlines the evil of their hearts that they were longing for the return of a depraved man, who was capable of such atrocities towards their own sex. The ungodly have always spent their lives looking out of the window of man's wisdom, hoping for the best that all will be well, when only disappointment and destruction await them.

The Final Note of Praise

It would have sounded strange if this song of praise had ended in Sisera's palace, with the false hopes and ambitions of his mother and her wise women. However, Deborah and Barak passed on from that scene of desolation and expressed an absolute certainty: "So let all thine enemies perish, O Lord" (v.31). They saw the destruction of Sisera as a foreshadowing of the time when all the enemies of the Lord would be destroyed. It is thrilling to remember that believers today are near to that time, "when the Lord Jesus shall be revealed from heaven with his mighty angels, in flaming fire taking vengeance on them that know not God, and that obey not the gospel of our Lord Jesus Christ: who shall be punished with everlasting destruction from the presence of the Lord, and from the glory of his power" (2 Thess 1.7-9).

Deborah and Barak linked the glorious prospect of the demise of all the Lord's enemies with a stirring challenge that is applicable to the Lord's people in all generations: "but let them that love him be as the sun when he goeth forth in his might" (v.31). There will, of course, be a time when this hope is fully realised. However, it had an immediate relevance for Israel and, indeed, for the Lord's people today. The Lord Jesus said to His disciples, "If ye love me, keep my commandments" (Jn 14.15). It was the path of loyalty and obedience to the Lord that brought rest to the land for forty years in the days of Deborah and Barak (v.31), and will bring rest to believers' lives at this present time as they travel on to an eternal rest.

JUDGES 6

Gideon and The Midianites

The previous chapter ended with Deborah and Barak singing and anticipating the time when all the enemies of the Lord would perish. Sadly, the period of rest that ensued was not destined to last. After forty years, the triumphant strain of the song was forgotten as a new generation arrived on the scene. Years of prosperity often lead the Lord's people to forget Him. The short span of time that it took for the deterioration to set in stands as a warning to believers of all generations of the daily need for them to be watchful (1 Cor 16.13; 1 Thess 5.6). The children of Israel ought to have been enjoying communion with the Lord, but sadly they found themselves under the control of the enemy.

The Lord Chastened Israel (vv.1-6)

Israel had suffered much at the hands of their previous oppressors, but now they experienced greater depths as "the Lord delivered them into the hand of Midian seven years" (v.1). The Midianites, a semi-nomadic group from the desert areas east and southeast of Canaan, were related to the Israelites through Abraham's relationship with his concubine, Keturah (Gen 25.1-2; 1 Chr 1.32); this relationship lasted for thirty- eight years and proved unfruitful for God. C.A.Coates warns believers about the dangers of natural relationships: "Nothing impoverishes more than the influence of people with whom we have something naturally in common, so that one's own relatives may be a greater snare than any others" (*An Outline of the Book of Judges*).

The Midianites had displayed their true colours during Israel's past. They acted as the intermediary between Israel and the world when they took Joseph from his brothers' hands and sold him into bondage in Egypt (Gen 37.23-28). They also joined Moab in seeking to persuade Balaam to curse Israel (Num 22.1-7), and later tempted Israel to whoredom and idolatry (Num 25.1-15). Following these encounters, the Lord commanded Moses, "Vex the Midianites and smite them: for they vex you with their wiles" (Num 25.17-18). However, by the days of Gideon they had regrouped and renewed their strength. They speak of the influence of the world and earthly things upon the lives of the Lord's people. They were joined in their incursions into Israel by the Amalekites and the children of the east, who were probably a nomadic group from the Syrian desert (v.3). It has already been noted in the commentary on ch.3 that the Moabites and Amalekites speak of the power of the flesh in the life of the Lord's people. S.Ridout writes, "The world and the flesh are close allies, and constantly act together, while with these come in a flood of evil principles and practices which, while not classified, are confederate" (*Lectures on the Book of Judges*).

Midian (4080) means "strife, division, contention", which serves as a powerful warning of the inevitable outcome to the Lord's people when they allow the world and the flesh to infiltrate and overrun their lives. Strife is, indeed, a characteristic of the world. James warned his readers about the dangers of strife when he wrote, "But if ye have bitter envying and strife in your hearts, glory not, and lie not against the truth. This wisdom descendeth not from above, but is earthly, sensual, devilish. For where envying and strife is, there is confusion and every evil work" (James 3.14-16). A.M.S. Gooding warns believers today, "There is nothing that will impoverish the saints like strife. It will bring the choicest gathering of the saints into bitterness and despondency" (*The 13 Judges*). Solomon, in the Book of Proverbs, described a man who stirs up strife as wrathful (15.18), froward (perverse – 16.28 - 8419), a talebearer (26.20), contentious (26.21), proud (28.25), and angry (29.22). The Lord's people today would do well to meditate upon his words if they wish to avoid strife. As the events of this chapter unfold, it will be evident that the influence of the Midianites brought strife into the lives of individuals, families and the nation as a whole.

The reference to the Midianites as "grasshoppers (locusts - 697)" (v.5), accurately describes both their numerical strength and the devastating effect they had upon the land: "they entered into the land to destroy it" (v.5). They were not content to remain in the borders of the country, but their influence spread westward "till thou come unto Gaza" (v.4), which stood on the shores of the Mediterranean Sea, at the southern end of Philistia. Their use of camels (v.5) gave a new dimension to warfare, increasing their ability to attack swiftly and from a distance. Camels were capable of making long journeys without water, which asses were unable to do. Indeed, the Midianites' might and dominance was such that there do not appear to have been any battles fought between them and the Israelites. They moved at will around the area, striking fear into the inhabitants of the land. Israel's response to them was simply to escape and make "dens which are in the mountains, and caves, and strong holds" (v.2). As soon as harvest time arrived (v.3), they descended on the land and "destroyed the increase of the earth ... and left no sustenance for Israel, neither sheep, nor ox, nor ass ... And Israel was greatly impoverished" (vv.4,6). They robbed the children of Israel of their security, freedom, productivity and source of nourishment. Israel's only hope of deliverance was to turn to the Lord, which ultimately they did: "the children of Israel cried unto the Lord" (v.6).

The Lord Rebuked Israel (vv.7-10)

The Israelites had already shown in the past that their cries to the Lord had not come from truly penitent hearts, but simply from a self-centred desire to be released from the suffering they were enduring at the hands of their enemies (cf. 3.9 & 4.3). This occasion was no exception, since they "cried unto the Lord because of the Midianites" (v.7). The Lord knew their motives and therefore He responded to their cry in a way they would not have been expecting. They could not see any further than the circumstances in which they found themselves and therefore they longed only for immediate deliverance from the oppression of the Midianites. However, the Lord sent a prophet to them to cause them to think more deeply and honestly about their condition (v.8). The prophet is unnamed, emphasising that it was the message, rather than the messenger, that was important. He made no mention of a deliverer in his words to them. F.C.Jennings observes, "The people need to have their sin brought home to their consciences. The distress has made them cry, but what is at the back of the distress? This is what the prophet comes for. God's chastening hand is never upon us, merely that it may be withdrawn again; there is some other object in His mind" (*Judges and Ruth*). The children of Israel would, no doubt, have preferred to have avoided the searching message they received, but it was the first step on the road to repentance and restoration.

The Lord reminded them, through the prophet, of His gracious and merciful acts towards them: "I brought you up ... and brought you forth ... I delivered you... and gave you" (vv.8-9). Indeed, He emphasised that they had already experienced release from bondage (v.8) and oppression (v.9). However, He also reminded them of the solemn responsibility He had placed upon them in the light of His care for them: "I am the Lord your God: fear not the gods of the Amorites, in whose land ye dwell" (v.10). How miserably they failed to live up to this responsibility is evidenced by the brief, yet powerful, rebuke, "but ye have not obeyed my voice" (v.10). This message was a direct appeal to their consciences and challenged them as to the real reason why they found themselves in such a low physical and spiritual condition. It was the outcome of their own unfaithfulness and disobedience to the Lord's word, rather than any strength possessed by the Midianites. It was therefore only obedience to His voice that would bring them deliverance.

H.L.Rossier applies the message to believers today when he writes, "God has a means by which to bless us: His word, which meets every requirement and ought to be quite sufficient for us. Psalm 119 shows us the marvellous part the word plays in the life of the faithful. This psalm exceeds all others in length. The word of God ought to occupy a corresponding place in our lives" (*Meditations on the Book of Judges*).

The Lord Came...the Lord Appeared to Gideon (vv.11-16)

The Lord's denouncement of the disobedience of the children of Israel was not followed, as they deserved, by immediate judgment. Suddenly, and unexpectedly, He came and appeared among them.

He came in Person "And there came an angel of the Lord" (v.11)

As has already been noted in the commentary on ch.2, this term is never used in the Old Testament to signify a messenger or a prophet, but denotes a pre-incarnation appearance of Christ (a Christophany).

He sat "under an oak which was in Ophrah, that pertained unto Joash the Abi-ezrite" (v.11)

Ophrah (6084) means, "dust" and speaks of Israel's weakness. Clearly, Joash had imbibed the religion of the land (v.25), which was the reason for the weakness. Indeed, the presence of the oak tree suggests that he was the local leader of Baal worship at that particular spot. However, the Lord was now sitting under the oak. The word "oak" comes from a root Hebrew word meaning "strength". Strength can, indeed, be found in weakness, but only through the Lord. Although spoken in a very different context, the Lord's words to Paul are applicable here: "My grace is sufficient for thee: for my strength is made perfect in weakness" (2 Cor 12.9). One man in Israel, Gideon, was about to discover the truth of these words in a very practical way.

He appeared "unto him (Gideon)" (v.12)

Among the rebellious people, the Lord found an individual who, though weak in his own estimation, stood out from the rest and through whom He could bring deliverance. Clearly, the message of the prophet had made an impact upon Gideon.

He promised – He made precious promises to Gideon that ought to have filled him with immense strength and confidence: "The Lord is with thee ... have not I sent thee? ... Surely I will be with thee " (vv.12,14,16).

Whenever God sends a man out in service for Him, He equips him for the task and promises to be with him. However, Gideon needed a great deal of reassuring. Initially, he was not fully aware of the identity of the angel who had appeared to him and therefore he was filled with doubt.

Firstly, he struggled with the Lord's estimation of him as a "mighty man of valour" (v.12). He only saw himself as he was at that time, whereas God saw his potential and knew what he would accomplish for Him. As far as Gideon was concerned, his current activity hardly warranted the description of a "mighty man of valour", but God saw it differently. He "threshed (knocked out - 2251) wheat by the winepress, to hide it from the Midianites" (v.11). Naturally speaking, this was a most inappropriate place and manner in which to thresh wheat. It would have been a lengthy process that yielded little. A.R.Fausset writes, "Usually they threshed on an area of hard earth, a 'threshing floor' in the open field, with threshing carriages armed with teeth, or else oxen which trod out the grain. Only the very poor knocked out the grain of their gleanings with a stick. That Gideon was obliged to knock out his little grain in the winepress, a pit sunk in the ground or hewn in the rock, implies the soreness of the Midianite oppression" (*A Critical and Expository Commentary on the Book of Judges*).

Secondly, he doubted the Lord's presence, even though he had heard the angel's words of assurance, "The Lord is with thee (singular)" (v.12). No servant could wish for a greater confidence-boost than this. Primarily, this is what believers need to know as they venture out to serve the Lord. They may not know precisely how He will work things out, but they can be confident of the outcome when He is with them. However, Gideon could not see beyond the immediate circumstances and responded, "Oh my Lord (Adoni – master, lord - 113), if the Lord (Jehovah - 3068) be with *us*, why then is all this befallen *us*? and where be all his miracles which our fathers told *us* of, saying, Did not the Lord bring *us* up from Egypt?" (v.13). Such questioning led him to conclude, "the Lord hath forsaken *us*, and delivered *us* into the hands of the Midianites" (v.13). The Lord had spoken to him personally, but he was preoccupied with the condition of the people. He used the word *"us"* on six occasions, whereas the Lord had used *"thee"* (singular). In one sense it was commendable, and necessary, that he identified himself with the condition of the people (cf. Neh 1.6-7). Any servant of God who stands aloof from the condition and need of the people he seeks to reach will be of little use to the Lord. However, on this occasion, Gideon missed the key point that the Lord was promising His presence with him, personally, to deliver the people from all that had befallen them. He was also slow to realise that the Lord's deliverance of them into the hands of the Midianites was, indeed, proof that He had not forsaken them. The Scriptures teach that discipline from the Lord, when it is viewed aright, "yieldeth the peaceable fruit of righteousness unto them which are exercised thereby" (Heb 12.11).

Thirdly, he questioned the Lord's choice. He is not alone in the Scriptures in challenging the Lord's wisdom in choosing him for service (cf. Ex 3.11-17 & Jer 1.6). God's commission to him was clear: "Go in this thy might, and thou shalt save Israel from the hand of the Midianites: have not I sent thee?" (v.14). However, he could not grasp how one whose family was "poor (weak - 1800) in Manasseh", and who was "least in my father's house" (v.15), could ever be used to save Israel. His family's weakness and his personal position as the youngest son robbed him of any sense of the power and authority that was at his disposal to bring about a change in the nation's condition. Indeed, he may well have felt that his position was weakened still further through his personal stand against the worship of Baal. However, the Lord assured him, "Surely I will be with thee, and thou shalt smite the Midianites as one man" (v.16). By encouraging him to see them as "one man", He was revealing to him that he would not be involved in a lengthy military campaign against them, but he would defeat them at a single stroke.

There is a sense, of course, in which each servant of God ought to be characterised by the humility displayed by Gideon if he is to achieve anything for Him. Paul reminded the Corinthian believers, that God has "chosen the weak things of the world to confound the things which are mighty ... that no flesh should glory in his presence" (1 Cor 1.27,29). However, such humility must not become a barrier to service. The Lord Jesus sent His disciples out with a sense of their total dependence upon Him, but also with the assurance that they could achieve great things through His power and presence with them: "All power is given unto me in heaven and in earth. Go ye therefore, and teach all nations, baptizing them in the name of the Father, and of the Son, and of the Holy Ghost: teaching them to observe all things whatsoever I have commanded you: and lo, I am with you alway, even unto the end of the world. Amen" (Mt 28.18-20).

The Lord Waited for Gideon (vv.17-24)

Although Gideon continued to display a lack of confidence, he also had a genuine desire to be absolutely sure as to who it was that was speaking to him. It would be easy to criticise his request for a sign that it was the Lord speaking to him (v.17), but it must be viewed in the context of Israel's spiritual poverty and lack of confidence at this time. The angel of the Lord uttered no such criticism and was not impatient as Gideon pleaded, "Depart not hence, I pray thee, until I come unto thee, and bring forth my present, and set it before thee" (v.18). It would have taken some time, possibly up to an hour or more, for Gideon to prepare the kid, the unleavened cakes and the broth, but the angel of the Lord graciously responded, "I will tarry until thou come again" (v.18). The hurried and impatient manner in which the Lord's people often respond towards each other stands in marked contrast to the calm and measured way in which He addresses their doubts and fears. He waited patiently for Abraham (Gen 18.1-8), and He did the same here for Gideon. He did not expect him to move beyond his experience and therefore revealed Himself to him a step at a time.

Gideon's present for the angel of the Lord was of a very different nature from the one sent earlier by the children of Israel to Eglon, king of Moab. As has already been noted in the commentary on ch.3, the latter was probably in the form of tribute money or produce of the land, and was designed to pander to a man of the flesh, whereas Gideon's offering was made with a spiritual desire to get to know more about the divine visitor. The word "present" (MINCHA - 4503) has the thought of "a voluntary sacrificial gift to God" associated with it, and it may well have been that he brought his offering in the light of his knowledge of the teaching of the Scriptures relating to the offerings and the altar. The flesh would point to the burnt offering (Lev 1.1-17), the unleavened cakes to the meal offering

(Lev 2.1-16) and the broth to the drink offering (Lev 23.13,18,37). Clearly, his sacrifice was costly during a time of such great poverty and need. An ephah of flour would have made a considerable amount of bread for his family, and the precious kid must have been one of the few in Israel that had been hidden from the marauding Midianites. Worship is, indeed, a costly business.

The angel of the Lord proceeded to give clear instructions to Gideon concerning his offering as he brought it to him under the oak, and presented it (v.19). He said to him, "Take the flesh and the unleavened cakes, and lay them upon this rock, and pour out the broth" (v.20). There was no room for Gideon to use his own discretion as to where to place the offering; it had to be on "this rock". It must have delighted the Lord, in the midst of a disobedient people, to speak with a man of whom it was recorded, "And he did so" (v.20). The angel of the Lord responded and "put forth the end of the staff that was in his hand, and touched (struck or smote - 5060) the flesh and the unleavened cakes" (v.21). As Gideon looked on, the result of this action was dramatic: "and there rose up fire out of the rock, and consumed the flesh and the unleavened cakes" (v.21).

Retrospectively, believers today can see Christ and His sacrifice at Calvary reflected in Gideon's offering. They have come to know Him as the Rock, who is the only true ground for lasting peace. The flesh reminds them that He "hath given himself for us an offering and a sacrifice to God for a sweet smelling savour" (Eph 5.2). The unleavened cakes point to His holy, spotless and pure life; and the broth testifies to the fact that "he hath poured out his soul unto death" (Is 53.12). The staff that touched the flesh and the bread prefigures the solemn truth expressed through Isaiah, "Yet it pleased the Lord to bruise him" (Is 53.10). The fire consumed Gideon's offering, but Christ consumed the fire of divine judgment at Calvary.

The appearance of the fire and the sudden disappearance of the angel finally persuaded Gideon that he had been speaking with the Lord (vv.21-22). His immediate response was fear of death, "because I have seen an angel of the Lord face to face" (v.22). He had requested a sign (v.17) and yet, after being granted it, he feared that the God who gave it to him would slay him. However, such a response was understandable when viewed in the context of the belief that no man could see God's face and live (cf. 13.22 & Ex 33.20). The Lord graciously addressed His troubled servant with words of calm assurance, "Peace be unto thee; fear not: thou shalt not die" (v.23). Through this experience he came to know the Lord as Jehovah-shalom (Jehovah is peace - 3073), which led him to build an altar and to worship. M.F.Unger points out that, "shalom denotes welfare in its broadest connotation, including peace of mind, health of body, salvation of soul, comfort in distress, and success in life" (*Commentary on the Old Testament*). It is also associated with the thought of reconciliation, based on the completion of a contract or the payment of a debt. S.Ridout sums it up when he writes, "In the midst of all the tumult that raged about him, in spite of the dread conflicts that were soon to take place, there was one place where all was perfect peace, one Person with whom there was no conflict – Jehovah Himself ... how beautiful and quiet is all this in the midst of utter ruin and confusion ... Gideon has found the God of peace, and we see him, the accepted worshipper" (*Lectures on the Book of Judges*).

This same God is to be found in the pages of the New Testament. Paul, the apostle, spoke of Him as the God of peace (Rom 15.33, 16.20; Phil 4.9) and the Lord of peace (2 Thess 3.16). He directed his readers' attention to Christ as the One who "made peace through the blood of his cross" (Col 1.20) and through whom they had "peace with God " (Rom 5.1). He revealed to the believers at Ephesus, who had once been without hope and without God in the world, that Christ "is our peace" and that He "came and preached peace to you which were afar off, and to them that are nigh" (Eph 2.14,17). Believers therefore come to know the God of peace at conversion, but Paul also reminded the saints at Phillipi of His continuing ministry throughout their lives: "Be careful for nothing; but in everything by prayer and supplication with thanksgiving let your requests be made known unto God. And the peace of God, which passeth all understanding, shall keep your hearts and minds through Christ Jesus" (Phil 4.6-7). He went on to stress the importance of obedience if this peace were to be experienced: "Those things, which ye have both learned, and received, and heard, and seen in me, do: and the God of peace shall be with you" (Phil 4.9). The children of Israel had sacrificed the enjoyment of peace and rest, because of their disobedience. Believers today must take care that they do not do the same.

The Lord Commanded Gideon (vv 25-32)

The requirement (vv.25-26)

The Lord had already told Gideon that he would save Israel (v.14), but before he moved on to the public stage he was commanded to deal with matters at home. The Lord's servants will not command credibility publicly if things are not right in their personal lives. No time was lost following his meeting with the angel of the Lord; the thrill of the day was succeeded by a challenging night for Gideon. The Lord spoke to him again and instructed him to, "Take thy father's young bullock, even the second bullock of seven years old, and throw down the altar of Baal that thy father hath, and cut down the grove (image - the wooden representation of the goddess Asherah (842), the consort of Baal) that is by it: and build an altar unto the Lord thy God upon the top of this rock, in the ordered place, and take the second bullock, and offer a burnt sacrifice with the wood of the grove which thou shalt cut down" (vv.25-26). It may well have been that Joash's bullock had been preserved for sacrifice on the altar to Baal. However, the fact that it was the "second" points to Christ as, "the second man ... the Lord from heaven" (1 Cor 15.47). It is also written of Him, "He taketh away the first, that he may establish the second" (Heb 10.9). The bullock was seven years old, corresponding to the seven years of Midianite oppression for which it was to make atonement. God cannot tolerate any rivals and therefore the two altars could not possibly exist side by side. Before ever the Spirit of the Lord could come upon Gideon (v.34), the idols had to be destroyed. He had to live up to the name of Gideon (1438, 1439), which means "to cut or hew down". This was an occasion when obedience to parents had to be set on one side, because what his father was doing was completely contrary to the Word of God (Deut 16.21-22).

The hymn writer challenges believers today to deal with the idols in their lives:

The dearest idol I have known,
Whate'er that idol be,
Help me to tear it from Thy throne,
And worship only Thee.
(William Cowper)

The response (v.27)

The children of Israel, including Gideon's father, wanted the best of both worlds. However, the man who had come to know the God of peace, "did as the Lord had said unto him" (v.27). It says a great deal about the effectiveness of his quiet and consistent testimony at home that there were ten trustworthy servants who were prepared to accompany him on his dangerous and demanding mission. The prophet's message had also made an impact upon them and emboldened them for action. It would be easy to be critical of the lack of trust that led Gideon to fear his father's household, but the Lord was not. He had not given him any instructions as to when, and with whom, to carry out the task. Although he decided to take others with him, and to do it at night, the important thing is that He obeyed the command.

The repercussions (vv.28-30)

Before the Midianites and Amalekites ranged themselves against him, Gideon had to face the hostility of the men of the city. The altar of Baal cast down and the grove that was by it cut down were disturbing enough for them. However, the appearance of an altar unto the Lord, Joash's precious bullock offered upon it as a burnt offering, and the wood of the Asherah pole used to kindle the fire raised their anger to even greater heights (v.28). The intensity of their opposition explains why Gideon had been so fearful of them. As far as they were concerned, such audacity demanded nothing short of death (v.30) and it did not take them long to track down the culprit. Indeed, they were probably already aware of Gideon's opposition to the worship of Baal and therefore they sensed immediately that this act had his mark upon it. Once others had confirmed it, they moved against him. Any stand taken by a believer against idolatry will call forth the hostility of the world and, sadly, the opposition of those among the Lord's people who prefer to "halt ... between two opinions" (1 Kings 18.21).

The reward (vv.31-32)

However, the Lord was in control and Gideon was rewarded for his faithfulness. Protection came from a totally unexpected source. He discovered that his testimony had not only made an impression upon his ten servants, but his father also came out in his support. He had already lost two of his sons to the Midianites (8.18-19) and he was not prepared to lose the youngest. The men of the city found it impossible to reject his logical and skilful argument. He suggested that if Baal were really a god, he would be well able to deal with Gideon without help from the people. Indeed, it would be folly for them to enter into his affairs (v.32). Far from punishing his son, Joash called him Jerubbaal (let Baal contend - 3378) - a name of honour that witnessed to the powerlessness and emptiness of Baal worship. Gideon's first victory was therefore a sign from the Lord, even though he had not asked for it, to assure him that He had sent him and was with him.

Verses 33-35: The Lord Empowered Gideon

The victory at home had been won and therefore Gideon was now ready to lead the children of Israel against the Midianites as they embarked upon their annual invasion of the land (v.33). It was at this point that "the Spirit of the Lord came upon (wrapped around or clothed Himself with - 3847) Gideon" (v.34). Thus the implication is that the Spirit of the Lord clothed Himself with Gideon. It was not simply an external experience, but one that empowered him within. Gideon learned that nothing would be achieved for the Lord in his own strength. The New Testament challenges believers today to "be filled with the Spirit" (Eph 5.18), and it is only if this is so that their labours will bear fruit. The Lord's words, through the prophet Zechariah, are relevant at all times: "Not by might, nor by power, but by my spirit, saith the Lord of hosts" (Zech 4.6).

A man empowered by the Spirit of the Lord is qualified to lead others and has the potential to unite them. Gideon therefore blew the trumpet with a view to gathering the people together. It must have encouraged him to see the response from his home town: "and Abi-ezer was gathered after him" (v.34). Clearly, his exploits and testimony in the town had made a great impression. The next port of call was his own tribe of Manasseh, followed by Asher, Zebulun and Napthtali (v.35). His influence was such among these northern tribes that 32,000 men responded to the call (7.3). It is interesting to observe that he did not send messengers to Ephraim. It was the largest tribe, full of a sense of its own importance and referred to as "the children of Joseph" (Josh 17.14). Some commentators have suggested that Gideon was afraid of them, but it may well be that their arrogance did not sit easily alongside his true humility and therefore he saw them as a hindrance, rather than a help, in the fight of faith against the enemy. Indeed, they showed themselves in their true colours after the victorious battle (8.1).

Verses 36-40: The Lord Reassured Gideon

It would probably have taken some considerable time to gather 32,000 men together to confront the Midianites. As Gideon waited therefore for the messengers to visit the various tribes, his constant need for reassurance surfaced again. On this occasion, he not only asked for a sign, but he suggested to God what it should be. "If thou wilt save Israel by mine hand, as thou hast said, behold, I will put a fleece of wool in the floor; and if the dew be on the fleece only, and it be dry upon all the earth beside, then shall I know that thou wilt save Israel by mine hand, as thou hast said", (vv.36-37). Gideon was not "putting out the fleece", as it is often referred to, so that he might discover what the will of God was or to suggest that He might have got things wrong. He knew clearly what that will was and he had no doubts that He would accomplish it, but he lacked the faith and the assurance that He would save Israel through him. L.H.Wiseman summarises succinctly Gideon's genuine inner struggle: "And who was he that he should be a captain of thirty thousand soldiers? He had been accustomed to the flail and the plough, not to the spear and the sword; he knew nothing of the manoeuvring of troops, and probably had never seen a battle … No wonder that, in the extremity of his conscious weakness, he appealed once more to a merciful God to give him an assuring sign that he was still in the path of duty" (*Practical Truths from Judges*). The Lord, once more, dealt graciously and patiently with him and granted the sign of the dew on the fleece and the dry ground.

Not content with this sign, Gideon then asked for it to be reversed, so that there was a dry fleece and wet ground (v.39). The ground of the threshing floor would have been hard and therefore largely unaffected by the dew. In the first sign, it was in the nature of wool to absorb moisture, but the second sign would have meant going against nature and demonstrating God's power to do what is impossible to men.

Dew is a picture in the Scriptures of God's blessing (Gen 27.28; Deut 33.28; Hos 14.5). The fleece therefore may be viewed as representing Israel as the nation that was being constantly "sheared or fleeced" by the surrounding nations. The hard ground of the threshing floor, where the grain was separated from the chaff, points towards the nations being used by God to discipline His people. If He decreed that the fleece should be wet and the ground dry, it was so. If He decided to bless Israel and judge the nations, He did so. However, if it were His will for the fleece to be dry and the ground wet, it was so. If it pleased Him therefore to bless the nations and chastise Israel, He did so. The "fleece" today is dry. Israel is scattered throughout the nations and spiritually barren. However, the Lord has not abandoned His people and the time will come when, in the words of the prophet, "The remnant of Jacob shall be in the midst of many people as a dew from the Lord, as the showers upon the grass, that tarrieth not for man, nor waiteth for the sons of men" (Micah 5.7).

The fact that God granted Gideon's additional request does not mean that believers should seek to emulate his actions. His plea for the sign to be reversed demonstrates that signs do not increase faith; they only lead to the desire for more. Following this, Gideon moved forward in faith and did not ask for further signs. The time had arrived when he had to trust God and take Him at His word.

JUDGES 7

Later on in the history of the children of Israel, when Jonathan, the son of king Saul, approached the mighty Philistines' garrison, he said to his young armour-bearer, "it may be that the Lord will work for us: for there is no restraint to the Lord to save by many or by few" (1 Sam 14.6). These two men were prepared to cast themselves wholly on the Lord for His support and therefore "the Lord saved Israel that day" (1 Sam 14.23). It is only as the Lord's people recognise their weakness that He can fully display His power through them (cf. 2 Cor 12.9).

Gideon and the children of Israel were about to discover how the Lord would save "by few". The various experiences through which they passed, before ultimately breaking the hold of the Midianites upon them, testified to their weakness and the Lord's strength. Indeed, the New Testament commentary on Gideon, and other men of like faith, is, "out of weakness were made strong, waxed valiant in fight, turned to flight the armies of the aliens" (Heb 11.34).

Verses 1-8: Bewildering Commands

Deborah had previously expressed her disappointment that more had not presented themselves for battle against Jabin and Sisera (5.15-17), but here the Lord twice told Gideon that the people offering themselves for battle against the Midianites were too many (vv.2,4). Naturally speaking, this was a bewildering command. Gideon and 32,000 men were "pitched beside the well of Harod" (v.1). Most commentators identify this spot with the modern 'Ain Jalud, at the foot of Mount Gilboa. Harod (5878) means, "fountain of trembling", and they might well have been excused for trembling in the face of about 135,000 Midianites (8.10) who were camped in the valley, some five miles to the north, "by the hill of Moreh".

Human reasoning would have decreed that Gideon needed more men for the conflict, not less. However, the Lord challenged this obvious conclusion and said, "The people that are with thee are too many for me to give the Midianites into their hands" (v.2). He knew their propensity for arrogance and pride and therefore gave the reason for His statement by adding, "lest Israel vaunt themselves against me, saying, Mine own hand hath saved me" (v.2). Thus the first sifting took place when He commanded, "Whosoever is fearful and afraid, let him return and depart early from mount Gilead" (v.3). Such a challenge should not have come as a surprise to the children of Israel, because it was in total accord with His instructions to those who went out to battle: "What man is there that is fearful and fainthearted? let him go and return unto his house, lest his brethren's heart faint as well as his heart" (Deut 20.8). Fear is contagious and soon undermines morale. The result of the challenge testified as to how well the Lord knew the hearts of His people: "And there returned of the people twenty and two thousand; and there remained ten thousand" (v.3). As they assembled, no one would have believed that so many of them were "fearful and afraid" (lit. downright afraid), to the extent of being prepared to desert the cause. How many believers today would turn back if they were given the opportunity so to do? Paul challenged Timothy's natural tendency to timidity when he wrote in one of his letters to him, "God hath not given us the spirit of fear; but of power, and of love, and of a sound mind" (2 Tim 1.7).

A further command was given to Gideon that was even more bewildering than the first: "The people are yet too many; bring them down unto the water, and I will try (refine - 6884) them for thee there" (v.4). The Lord went on to test them in the way in which they drank water. He often tests His people, unbeknown to them, in the ordinary circumstances of life. The outcome was that Gideon's fighting force was reduced to 300 men. Commentators have provided a variety of explanations as to why those who "lapped, putting their hand to their mouth" were chosen, as opposed to those who "bowed down upon their knees to drink water" (v.6). M.F.Unger brings a number of these explanations together when he writes, "Lapping water like a dog, however it was done, separated the vigilant and watchful from the less alert and those who were concerned about natural comforts and less fired by faith to spot the enemy and press on to victory. The Lord selected the three hundred who lapped water. Evidently they bent over, but kept their heads erect to see any possible movement of the enemy" (*Commentary on the Old Testament*). It has been suggested by some commentators that they used their hands to scoop up the water, while they remained on their feet, ready for any sign of attack by the enemy.

Whatever the correct interpretation of the men's actions might be, Gideon did not receive any explanation from the Lord. If the reader becomes too engrossed in what the Scriptures do not reveal, the simplicity of the lesson can be missed. The Lord chose this straightforward test for His people to teach them truth about their total dependence upon Him. Any virtue found, even in the three hundred, was not going to bring them deliverance; salvation would come from His strength working through their weakness. If the 32,000, or the 10,000, had gone forth to gain the victory, inadequate though they might have appeared at the time, they would have claimed the honour. However, the victory of 300 over the might of the Midianites was, humanly speaking, absolutely impossible and could only lead to one conclusion: "Salvation is of the Lord" (Jonah 2.9). The 9,700 were sent "every man unto his tent" (v.8); they would be used later in the pursuit of the Midianites.

Verses 9-15: Barley Bread

Having brought the people into a position of weakness and dependence on Him, the spotlight was then turned on the leader. The Lord said to Gideon that same night, "Arise, get thee down unto the host" (v.9). After three assurances of victory (6.14,16; 7.7) and three signs (6.17,37,39) from the Lord, Gideon ought to have been brimming with confidence at this stage. However, nothing could have been further from the truth. Once again, the power of the Lord and the weakness of the vessel run like a thread throughout this section of the book.

Firstly, Gideon was afraid. The promise to him was unequivocal: "I have delivered it (the host) into thine hand" (v.9). The victory was absolutely assured, but it would belong to the Lord. Gideon's fear was not like that of the men who turned back from the battle (v.3), otherwise he would have done the same. It was fear, mingled with faith; faith that the Lord was well able to win the battle, but fear as to whether he was the right vessel for the task. He continued to need a great deal of reassurance. The Lord knew the frailties of His servant and, once again, acted with great patience towards him. He did not ignore or condemn his fear, but graciously gave him the means by which he could overcome it: "But if thou fear to go down, go thou with Phurah thy servant down to the host" (v.10). He knew the strength that can come to His servants through fellowship in the work (cf. Lk 10.1; Acts 3.1; 13.2). Gideon did not pretend to be anything other than afraid and therefore he went down with his servant. Phurah, who was probably a young man, must have grown in wisdom and strength through his close associations with his master. What he was about to witness would have made lasting impressions on him. It will always prove spiritually beneficial to younger believers if they seek to "rub shoulders with" men and women of faith. However, Phurah also illustrates that the benefits are not all one way; his loyalty, commitment and courage were an immense support to Gideon.

Secondly, Gideon discovered that the Lord was in total control of the enemy, even though their numerical strength was such that they "lay along in the valley like grasshoppers for multitude; and their camels were without number, as the sand by the sea side for multitude" (v.12). However, when Gideon with Phurah came "unto the outside (extremity - 7097) of the armed men that were in the host" (v.11), he learned where the true power was to be found. The Lord had promised him that he would be reassured through the lips of his enemies: "And thou shalt hear what they say; and afterward shall thine hands be strengthened to go down unto the host" (v.11). Sure enough, He was true to His word and the promise came to fruition. He caused one of the armed men from this select group of soldiers guarding the Midianite camp to have a dream. Furthermore, he related it to a colleague at the precise moment when Gideon arrived and began to listen in. Only the sovereign Lord could have ordered events with such precision. It would not be the last time that He would use ungodly men to declare His truth (cf. Jn 11.49-52; 19.19-22; Acts 5.34-39), even though they would be unaware that He was doing so.

For some men, the message that Gideon and Phurah heard would have been disappointing. The Midianite soldier's opening words were not promising: "Behold, I dreamed a dream, and, lo, a cake (round or flattened - 6742) of barley bread tumbled into the host of Midian" (v.13). Barley was the grain grown, and used, by the poor in Israel. Some commentators have suggested that the word "cake", used only here in the Old Testament, has the thought of stale and hard bread, which would be commensurate with it rolling down a hill without breaking. If Gideon had ceased listening at this point, he might well have gone away feeling depressed and humiliated. Being likened to a cake of barley bread rolling into the host of Midian would have further stimulated his fear and confirmed his initial estimate that he was "the least in my father's house" (6.15). However, he learned that a cake of barley bread in the hands of Jehovah was a force to be reckoned with. As he listened further, he heard how it "came unto a tent (representing the nomadic life of the Midianite), and smote it that it fell, and overturned it, that the tent lay along" (v.13); the destruction was comprehensive and complete. The Lord did not even leave him to make the application. The soldier's colleague confirmed, "This is nothing else save the sword of Gideon the son of Joash, a man of Israel: for into his hand hath God delivered Midian, and all the host" (v.14). To hear his own name linked with the name of God, and coming from the mouth of a godless man, removed his fear immediately and led him to worship (v.15). He observed the divine order of worship before successful service (cf. Josh 5.13-15).

Gideon no longer possessed the spirit of fear, but confidently declared to Israel, "Arise; for the Lord hath delivered into your hand the host of Midian" (v.15). He was, indeed, a changed man from the one who went down to the camp of the Midianites. He stands as an encouragement to servants of all ages that God can take the most unlikely and fearful of believers and enable them to achieve great things for him. S.Ridout provides a helpful application of this stirring episode in Gideon's life when he writes, "Barley bread is the poorest of all the foods – the food of paupers. It suggested thus poverty and feebleness – the very lessons emphasised all along. The fact, too, that it was food and not a sword that was to overthrow Midian is significant. When the people of God are feeding upon Christ, they are getting a sword for the enemy. God can use even our feeble and partial apprehensions of Christ as a most effective weapon. The lad had but five barley loaves of bread, yet these were enough in the Lord's hand to feed the multitude. So it is ever. Will we not learn the simple lesson? Weakness, helplessness, nothingness - in Christ's hands will win the day against all the power of the world. The Lord grant that we may know more of this practically, for the sake of Christ our Lord, and the help of His Church" (*Lectures on the Book of Judges*).

Verses 16-25: Broken Vessels, Blown Trumpets and Burning Lamps

The fact that victory was assured did not mean that Gideon and the 300 men could abandon the Lord, trust in their own abilities and use carnal methods to gain success. The features of this victory were:

Firstly, order – "And he divided the three hundred men into three companies" (v.16)

This strategy, used at other times in Israel's history (cf. 1 Sam 11.11; 2

Sam 18.2), allowed him to surround the camp (vv.18,21) and therefore to employ the small number of men to maximum effect. The Lord delights in order and expects to see it in the activities of His people. Paul exhorted the believers at Corinth, "Let all things be done decently and in order" (1 Cor 14.40).

Secondly, full hands – "So the people took victuals in their hand … and he put a trumpet in every man's hand, with empty pitchers, and lamps within the pitchers … the lamps in their left hands, and the trumpets in their right hands" (vv.8,16,20)

David, the Psalmist, wrote, "Blessed be the Lord my strength, which teacheth my hands to war, and my fingers to fight" (Ps 144.1). He acknowledged that it was the Lord's strength that enabled him to be victorious in battle. Gideon and his men had full hands as they went forth to fight the Midianites, but they were totally dependent on the Lord's help for success.

Thirdly, obedience – "And he said unto them, Look on me, and do likewise: and, behold, when I come to the outside of the camp, it shall be that, as I do, so shall ye do" (v.17)

If the enemy that had caused so much strife and division was to be overcome, there was no place for independent action within the ranks; the commands of Gideon had to be obeyed if they were to move forward in harmony. The writer to the Hebrews, when instructing readers who were seeking to defeat the divisive elements among them, said, "Obey them that have the rule over you, and submit yourselves: for they watch for your souls, as they that must give account, that they may do it with joy, and not with grief: for that is unprofitable for you" (Heb 13.17).

Fourthly, appropriate 'weapons' for the warfare

If Gideon and the three hundred men were to be successful in the battle against the Midianites, their hands had to be full of the right weapons. As well as having sufficient food for his need, each man had a trumpet (SHOPAR - ram's horn – used by Joshua at the defeat of Jericho - 7782), an empty pitcher (earthenware jar - 3537), and a lamp (a flambeau, lamp or flame - 3940). Trumpets were used in Israel as a signal to gather, to move camp, to battle and to worship. They were the audible way of communicating God's mind to the people and therefore point to the authority of the Word of God in believers' lives. The purpose of the earthenware jars was to contain the lamp, and ultimately to be broken to reveal the light. F.C.Jennings writes, "Man as such is but a poor pitcher, an earthen vessel, and what can God do with such? Break him, that is all. As long as the pitchers were unbroken they were worse than useless. They only hid the light within them, and prevented its outshining. The pitcher must be smashed, and now the hand that held it – the confidence that is still lingeringly attached to the earthen vessel – changes its hold to the lamp or torch – in absolute dependence, it is true, for it is the left hand which speaks of realised weakness; but the light shines out unhindered" (*Judges and Ruth*).

Paul may have had this incident in mind when he wrote, "For God, who commanded the light to shine out of darkness, hath shined in our hearts, to give the light of the knowledge of the glory of God in the face of Jesus Christ. But we have this treasure in earthen vessels, that the excellency of the power may be of God, and not of us" (2 Cor 4.6-7). He challenged the saints at Philippi, by exhorting them to, "Do all things without murmurings and disputings … shine as lights in the world; holding forth the word of life" (Phil 2.14-16). The "murmurings and disputings" are a reminder of the Midianitish spirit of strife and contention that can mar the testimony of a local church. It is only by shining as lights (being broken vessels) and giving attention to the word of God (blowing the trumpets) that such a destructive spirit can be overcome.

H.L.Rossier brings home the challenge of the three 'weapons' to believers involved in spiritual warfare today when he writes, "There is not a single Christian in the world who cannot be the bearer of these three elements of testimony for God. How is it then that so few are found? It is because these three principles that God requires are lacking. The trumpet must be sounded, the pitchers must be broken, the lamp must not be put under a bushel" (*Meditations on the Book of Judges*).

Fifthly, a united voice – "and they cried, The sword of the Lord, and of Gideon" (v.20)

Gideon and his men "came unto the outside of the camp in the beginning of the middle watch" (v.19). Based on the assumption that both the Israelites and the Midianites divided the hours of darkness into three watches, the attack probably took place at 10 pm. or thereabouts. The Midianite soldiers involved in the first watch of the night had reached the end of their period of duty and had settled down to rest. The second guard "had but newly set the watch" (v.19) when the peace of the night was shattered by trumpets being blown, vessels broken and lights shining from all sides of the camp. This was followed by the cry, "The sword of the Lord, and of Gideon" (v.20). The three hundred men did not move or raise a single literal sword against the Midianites. There had been a lengthy build-up in preparation for this battle, but it was accomplished in a moment by a simple shout of the name of Jehovah. John, as he wrote of "things which must be hereafter" (Rev 4.1), described the Lord as going forth to "judge and make war … and he was clothed with a vesture dipped in blood: and his name is called The Word of God … and out of his mouth goeth a sharp sword, that with it he should smite the nations" (Rev 19.11,13,15). Believers today "wrestle not against flesh and blood", but their warfare is just as real; it is "against principalities, against powers, against the rulers of the darkness of this world, against spiritual wickedness in high places" (Eph 6.12). They are encouraged in the New Testament to take the armour God has provided for the battle, part of which is "the sword of the Spirit, which is the word of God" (Eph 6.17). It is the Word of God, used in the power of the Spirit, which will overcome the might of their enemies.

Clearly, the surprise attack spread total panic throughout the camp of Midian, because "all the host ran, and cried, and fled" (v.21). The strategy employed led them to believe that the Israelites must already have been in the camp and in their confusion they struck out in the darkness at everything that moved. The result was that "the Lord set every man's sword against his fellow" (v.22), and ultimately they fled eastwards, from where they had come.

Sixthly, a united people – "And the men of Israel gathered themselves together out of Naphtali, and out of Asher, and out of all Manasseh" (v.23)

Although the battle had been won with three hundred men, more were needed to pursue the Midianites. Gideon was not content with a partial victory; he wanted to see the enemy destroyed totally. It may well be that most of the additional forces came from those who had responded to his original call.

Ephraim was also called into action at this point. They were in a prime position to take the fords "unto Beth-barah and Jordan" (v.24) and therefore cut off the flight of the remaining Midianite army. At this stage they acted immediately and, seemingly, without complaint, although later events suggest otherwise. They captured two Midianite princes (v.25) called Oreb (raven - 6158) and Zeeb (wolf - 2062). Their names reveal the unclean, corrupt and cruel nature of the world that must be overcome in the lives of the Lord's people if they are to be an effective testimony for Him. Gideon's journey to victory began with him threshing wheat by the winepress in order to hide it from the Midianites (6.11), but it ended with Oreb slain "upon the rock Oreb" and Zeeb slain "at the winepress of Zeeb" (v.25). Although their deaths appeared to be only a minor part of the greater success, they remained in Israel's history as a vivid picture of the awesomeness of the Lord's judgment, both in the past and in the future (Ps 83.11; Is 10.26). A.R.Fausset writes, "The places of their shelter became the places of their slaughter. They were punished in kind, the instrument of their sin being made the instrument of their punishment. So shall it be in the final award" (*A Critical and Expository Commentary on the Book of Judges*). F.C.Jennings reminds the believer of the place where deliverance can be found, when he writes, "The 'rock' and the 'winepress' are both found at the cross of our Lord Jesus Christ. There is the sharp rock and the winepress of judgment, and there all corruption and violence must make their end. They cannot live there" (*Judges and Ruth*).

JUDGES 8

The Scriptures illustrate time and again that the Lord's people are at their most vulnerable following periods of victory. It is then that they are tested as to the reality of their faith. The flesh often raises its head and seeks to rob them of all that has been gained by faith. Gideon and the children of Israel were about to learn this painful lesson. A chapter that begins positively with them "faint, yet pursuing" (v.4), ends with them failing to remember the Lord, who delivered them, and Gideon, who led them: they "remembered not the Lord their God, who had delivered them out of the hands of all their enemies on every side: neither shewed they kindness to the house of Jerubbaal, namely, Gideon, according to all the goodness which he had shewed unto Israel" (vv.34-35). Sadly, as is so often the case, the divisive influences that undermined the victory over the Midianites came from within. Paul warned the elders of the church at Ephesus, "Also of your own selves shall men arise, speaking perverse things, to draw away disciples after them" (Acts 20.30).

The Dissatisfaction of Ephraim (vv.1-3)

It has already been noted in the commentary on ch.6 that Ephraim was one of the largest tribes and full of a sense of its own importance. Its position in the central highlands cushioned it from many of the attacks by Israel's enemies. The two important religious centres, Bethel and Shiloh, were also situated within its territory. Clearly, the men of Ephraim found it difficult to give credit to others when it was merited. They refused to accept that anything could take place in Israel without their approval and involvement. Their response to Gideon's achievements was to express their dissatisfaction with the way in which he had handled things. Their anger, pride and jealousy led them to "chide with him sharply" (v.1). Their words revealed their total preoccupation with self: "Why hast thou served us thus, that thou calledst us not, when thou wentest to fight with the Midianites?" (v.1). They displayed the spirit of Diotrephes, of whom the apostle John wrote, "who loveth to have the pre-eminence among them ... prating against us with malicious words" (3 Jn vv.9-10). The external strife brought about by the Midianites had been overcome, but the men of Ephraim were stirring up strife from within.

Paul exhorted the saints at Philippi, "Let nothing be done through strife or vainglory; but in lowliness of mind let each esteem other better than themselves" (Phil 2.3). This was the very spirit that Gideon displayed to diffuse the potentially damaging attitude of Ephraim. He resisted any temptation to be critical or vindictive. Some commentators have suggested that he resorted to flattery to win them over, but this does him a grave injustice. Solomon wrote, "a flattering mouth worketh ruin" (Prov 26.28): a charge that can hardly be levelled at Gideon here. Far from resorting to this tactic, his genuine humility shone through as he praised Ephraim's contribution in comparison with his own: "What have I done now in comparison of you? Is not the gleaning of the grapes of Ephraim better than the vintage of Abiezer? God hath delivered into your hands the princes of Midian, Oreb and Zeeb: and what was I able to do in comparison of you?" (vv.2-3). The outcome was positive: "Then their anger was abated toward him, when he had said that" (v.3). His wise response serves as a reminder to the Lord's people that, "A soft (tender - 7390) answer turneth away wrath: but grievous words stir up anger" (Prov 15.1).

Verses 4-12: The Disdain of the Princes of Succoth and the Men of Penuel

If the attitude displayed by Ephraim was disappointing and damaging, the response of the princes of Succoth and the men of Penuel was reprehensible. As Gideon and the three hundred men pursued after Zebah and Zalmunna, two of the Midianitish kings, they crossed Jordan and reached Succoth in Gad. Gad was one of the two and a half tribes that lived on the east of Jordan; this gave them a detached feeling from the rest of the tribes. It has already been observed in the commentary on ch.5 that they "abode beyond Jordan" (5.17 – they are referred to as Gilead) when called to battle against Jabin, king of Canaan, and Sisera, the captain of his host. Gideon's request of them was perfectly reasonable and therefore he might have expected a positive response: "Give, I pray you, loaves of bread unto the people that follow me; for they be faint" (v.5). Sadly, the princes of Succoth not only refused to minister to the needs of their brethren, but they treated Gideon with the utmost contempt: "Are the hands of Zebah and Zalmunna now in thine hand, that we should give bread unto thine army?" (v.6). They were more interested in preserving their own safety than in sustaining their brethren. Indeed, they displayed a total lack of faith by preferring to place their confidence in the power of the Midianites. They were dismissive of the ability of Gideon's three hundred men to overcome fifteen thousand Midianites. There are few things more demoralising for believers than to be engaged in the Lord's battles and yet to be confronted with the disinterest and disdain of those who profess to belong to Him. Peter, writing to saints who were scattered and suffering, stressed the importance of hospitality: "Use hospitality one of another without grudging" (1 Pet 4.9).

Gideon was not deflected from his pathway by the princes of Succoth, but the severity of his response underlines how seriously the Lord views, and will deal with, such a negative spirit: "Therefore when the Lord hath delivered Zebah and Zalmunna into mine hand, then I will tear your flesh with the thorns of the wilderness and with briers" (v.7). Their disdain for God's leader and his men was tantamount to rejecting God; it was far more serious than the pride and jealousy of the men of Ephraim.

Penuel lay a short distance to the east of Succoth. It was the place Jacob named "Peniel: for I have seen God face to face, and my life is preserved"

(Gen 32.30). There was a tower there, which was probably used to provide the men of Penuel with security from any marauding enemies and therefore stood as a symbol of their strength. However, their refusal to help Gideon meant that, even if they were safe from their enemies, they would not escape judgment on his return. He promised them swift recompense for their lack of support: "When I come again in peace, I will break down this tower" (v.9).

Once again, Gideon refused to become sidetracked or disillusioned by their disgraceful response and, even though his men were faint, he continued to pursue the two Midianitish kings and the 15,000 men that remained of "all the hosts of the children of the east" (v.10). This may have been a small number in comparison with their original army of one hundred and thirty five thousand, but they still heavily outnumbered Gideon's men. They had fled to Karkor, a remote city far to the east of Jordan. They were lulled into a sense of false security: "for the host was secure" (v.11), comforted, no doubt, by the thought that Gideon would not pursue them so far. However, he "went up by the way of them that dwelt in tents on the east of Nobah and Jogbehah" (v.11); this is probably a reference to the caravan routes in the area. He surprised them by night, smote them and scattered them. They do not appear to have put up any significant resistance. Indeed, Zebah and Zalmunna deserted their men, but Gideon overtook and captured them: "And when Zeba and Zalmunna fled, he pursued after them, and took the two kings of Midian ... and discomfited all the host" (v.12). The victory was swift and comprehensive.

Verses 13-21: The Discipline Enforced

Firstly, Gideon dealt with Succoth (vv.13-16)

The men of Succoth had been given every opportunity to share in the victory, but their indifference to the cause meant that they reaped their just reward. The discipline administered by Gideon was not rash, random and vindictive. As he "returned from battle" (v.13), he "caught a young man of the men of Succoth" (v.14) and discovered from him the names of the seventy-seven princes (head persons - 8269) of Succoth. It was a testimony to the young man's knowledge of the city that he was able to supply him with all of their names. It was these men who had upbraided (defamed - 2778) Gideon (v.15) and therefore he held them responsible. He paraded the spoils of the victory before them, namely Zebah and Zalmunna, and reminded them of their failure to give bread to their weary brethren: ""Behold Zebah and Zalmunna, with whom ye did upbraid me, saying, Are the hands of Zebah and Zalmunna now in thine hand, that we should give bread unto thy men that are weary?" (v.15). He taught them a painful lesson, as he had promised, by chastising them with the "thorns of the wilderness and briers" (v.16). The precise nature of this discipline is uncertain, but it was an experience they would not quickly forget.

Secondly, he "beat down the tower of Penuel, and slew the men of the city" (v.17)

The outcome for the men of Penuel was more severe than for those of Succoth. It may well be that they used the tower to resist Gideon and, in the process of defending it, they were slain.

Some commentators regard Gideon's actions as disturbingly ruthless and argue that they cast a shadow over his previous victories, particularly as they were directed against his fellow-Israelites. However, presenting an alternative view, M.F.Unger writes, "He was carrying out the divine will against weak, vacillating Israelites who were compromising with the Midianites, the oppressors of God's people who illustrate the enslavement that the world and the flesh impose and with which there must be no compromise on the part of a victorious warrior like Gideon" (*Commentary on the Old Testament*). There is, indeed, a danger of minimising the seriousness of what these men did; by siding with the enemy they were guilty of nothing less than treason against God and His people. Great privilege always brings with it great responsibility; and any failure to live up to the responsibility will bring appropriate chastisement from the Lord. Paul wrote in strong terms to erring Corinthian believers, "being absent now I write to them which heretofore have sinned, and to all other, that, if I come again, I will not spare" (2 Cor 13.2). Peter wrote, "For the time is come that judgment must begin at the house of God: and if it first begin at us, what shall the end be of them that obey not the gospel of God?" (1 Pet 4.17).

Thirdly, Gideon turned his attention to the two Midianitish kings, Zebah and Zalmunna (vv.18-21)

It is possible that he had returned to Ophrah by this time. Initially, he confronted them with a crime that they might have thought had gone by unnoticed or had been forgotten: "What manner of men were they whom ye slew at Tabor?" (v.18). The exact details are not recorded, but at some time, probably during one of the Midianites' annual incursions, they had displayed excessive and unnecessary violence by slaying Gideon's brothers. Confronted with their evil deed, the two kings admitted, "As thou art, so were they; each one resembled the children of a king" (v.18). However, Gideon was unmoved by their flattery. His simple, yet poignant, response to their wickedness emphasised the depth of his feeling: "They were my brethren, even the sons of my mother: as the Lord liveth, if ye had saved them alive, I would not slay you" (v.19). Even though his gracious spirit was reflected in these words, he knew that judgment had to fall upon such men. Once again, some commentators have charged him with unbridled personal revenge, instead of seeing him as acting in accord with the Word of God as he took the position of "the avenger of blood" (Deut 19.12).

Sadly, at this point, Gideon displayed a lack of wisdom. He turned to

Jether, his firstborn, and said, "Up, and slay them" (v.20). If he had obeyed, it would have meant total humiliation for the two seasoned warriors to be slain at the hands of such a young man, as well as bringing great kudos for him. Indeed, the kings recognised this and pleaded with Gideon that they might be saved from the shame of such an undignified end. They were realistic about the fact that their end was in sight and therefore they said to him, "Rise thou, and fall upon us" (v.21). The outcome was that Jether "drew not his sword: for he feared, because he was yet a youth" (v.20). H.L.Rossier writes, "Here Gideon, committing to a child the destruction of the enemy he despised, did not act in keeping with the ways of God, who does not call those who are but children in the faith to perform publicly brilliant actions; a child goes to school and not to war" (*Meditations on the Book of Judges*). Zebah and Zalmunna remained arrogant and disdainful to the end. They may even have been taunting Gideon when they said, "Rise thou, and fall upon us: for as the man is, so is his strength" (v.21) Gideon responded by slaying them; he also "took away the ornaments that were on their camels' necks" (v.21). These "ornaments" were probably shaped like a crescent or half moon and were added to the considerable spoils of war that were gathered following the victories over the Midianites. The events that follow show that Gideon's misuse of these spoils damaged his testimony and led the people back to idolatry.

Verses 22-35: The Desire of Gideon

Clearly, the relief for the children of Israel at being released from seven years of impoverishment at the hands of the Midianites was enormous. It led to them offering Gideon the opportunity to establish a hereditary dynasty: "Rule thou over us, both thou, and thy son, and thy son's son also: for thou hast delivered us from the hand of Midian" (v.22). This offer almost certainly came only from the tribes that had joined him in the battle against the Midianites (6.35) and not from all the tribes in Israel. It is also unlikely that Ephraim would have joined in the general acclaim. However, seeds were sown, which led later on to the more widespread request made to Samuel, "Give us a king to judge us … that we also may be like all the nations" (1 Sam 8.6,20). Gideon's response was unequivocal: "I will not rule over you, neither shall my son rule over you: the Lord shall rule over you" (v.23). His words reveal that the request came from a people who had forgotten the Lord and who were doing precisely what He had warned against: "lest Israel vaunt themselves against me, saying, Mine own hand hath saved me" (7.2). Later on, when the desire for a king reached its crescendo, the Lord told Samuel, "they have not rejected thee, but they have rejected me, that I should not reign over them" (1 Sam 8.7).

Some commentators believe that Gideon's response was not as sincere as it might appear to be at first sight. They believe that his refusal was superficial and that subsequent events showed that it was really a veiled acceptance of kingship. They point out that, even if he did not directly accept kingship, he went on to live the lavish lifestyle of a king: he had great wealth (v.26); he had many wives and a concubine (vv.30-31); he called his concubine's son, Abimelech, which means, "my father is king" (v.31). However, this is to attribute motives to him that are not recorded in the text. It would appear that his outright rejection of kingship was sincere and that he genuinely saw it as removing the Lord from His rightful position.

If Gideon did not covet kingship, the same could not be said of him when it came to priesthood. In one breath he said to the men of Israel, "I will not rule over you" (v.23), but in the next he said, "I would desire a request of you, that ye would give me every man the earrings of his prey (For they had golden earrings, because they were Ishmaelites)" (v.24). "Ishmaelites" was an inclusive term for Israel's nomadic cousins that included the Midianites, and their great love of jewellery meant that they usually wore numerous rings. All of Gideon's men would undoubtedly have seized one or more of these earrings. This test came from within and it centred entirely on self. He exploited his popularity, knowing that the people would "willingly give" what he asked (v.25). They surrendered to him the considerable spoils that they had amassed from the victory over the Midianites: "And they spread a garment, and did cast therein every man the earrings of his prey. And the weight of the golden earrings that he requested was a thousand and seven hundred shekels of gold; beside ornaments, and collars, and purple raiment that was on the kings of Midian, and beside the chains that were about their camels' necks" (vv.25-26). It is not surprising therefore to discover that Gideon was able to sustain and enjoy a comfortable lifestyle when he left the public sphere of service and "dwelt in his own house" (v.29).

However, the greatest tragedy was that he used the materials to make an ephod (v.27). Some scholars believe that this was an idol erected by Gideon, but there are no compelling reasons to believe that it was anything other than an imitation of the high priestly ephod described in Exodus 28 and 39. This was the outer garment worn by the high priest over his other garments. It was made of costly materials – gold, blue, purple, scarlet, and fine-twined linen. It consisted of front and back pieces, which were joined by two shoulder pieces, and by a band at the bottom. Two onyx stones, set in gold and engraved with the names of the twelve tribes of Israel, were on the shoulders. Attached to the ephod was a breastplate in which twelve precious stones, representing the twelve tribes, were set. Inside the pocket formed by the ephod there was placed the Urim and Thummim (Ex 28.30). The precise nature of these two objects is unknown, but they were used to seek the Lord's guidance and direction (cf. Num 27.21; 1 Sam 23.9-12; 30.7-8).

The ephod became synonymous with priesthood during Israel's history and the priests wore "a linen ephod", a light, outer garment, even though the word of God did not instruct them to do so (1 Sam 22.18). There were occasions when those who were not priests also wore a linen ephod, e.g. Samuel and David (1 Sam 2.18; 2 Sam 6.14). Sadly, however, this holy garment also became linked with idolatry. Gideon placed the ephod he made "in his city, even in Ophrah" (v.27). Clearly, he coveted priesthood and may have felt he had the necessary credentials to fulfil the role. It was true that he had been privileged to experience close communion with God in the past: the appearance of the angel of the Lord (6.12); the acceptance of his sacrifice (6.21); the building of an altar and the offering of a burnt sacrifice upon it (6.26); the Lord's direct guidance to him concerning the overthrow of the Midianites (7.2-4). However, this did not give him the right to parade as a priest and to believe that he could place himself in the position of conveying the Lord's guidance to His people in addition to, or as an alternative to, the true priesthood and the ephod in the sanctuary at Shiloh. This humble man, who started out by doubting his credentials to lead Israel, allowed pride and fleshly desires to grip his heart and dictate his movements. His actions meant that Ophrah became the gathering point for the children of Israel, which drew them away from Shiloh: "and all Israel went thither a whoring (committing adultery - 2181) after it: which thing became a snare (noose - 4170) unto Gideon, and to his house" (v.27).

Tragically, therefore, Gideon's ephod led the people back to the pathway of idolatry. Midian was "subdued before the children of Israel, so that they lifted up their heads no more. And the country was in quietness forty years" (v.28). However, this was the last period of rest that Israel was to experience in the days of the judges. They so often abused the rest that God gave them that this occasion proved to be a step too far, so much so that He did not grant it to them again. It is dangerous for the Lord's people to trifle with His grace and mercy and to believe that they can escape unscathed.

Gideon, referred to again as "Jerubbaal (let Baal contend - 3378), the son of Joash", returned home and "dwelt in his own house" (v.29). This name, given to him by his father, was a reminder of his former exploit in throwing down the altar of Baal (6.32) that proved to be the basis for the peace secured. However, it was not long before the "snare" began to tighten its grip on both Gideon and Israel. His personal standards began to slip; contrary to the will of God "he had many wives" and a "concubine that was in Shechem" (vv.30-31). The relationships with his wives resulted in "threescore and ten sons of his body begotten" (v.30). The birth of Abimelech to his concubine was later to lead to the raising of the question of kingship again. The outcome of these relationships was to prove disastrous. The differing backgrounds of the seventy sons and Abimelech led to tensions between them that ultimately came to a head when Abimelech "slew his brethren the sons of Jerubbaal" (9.5).

The children of Israel's standards also plummeted and they drifted back to the idolatry from which Gideon had sought to deliver them: "And it came to pass, as soon as Gideon was dead, that the children of Israel turned again, and went a whoring after Baalim, and made Baal-berith (Baal of the covenant - 1170) their god" (v.33). Once they had entered into a covenant with Baal, it was not surprising that they "remembered not the Lord their God, who had delivered them out of the hands of all their enemies on every side: neither shewed they kindness to the house of Jerubbaal, namely, Gideon, according to all the goodness which he had shewed unto Israel" (vv.34-35).

C.A.Coates sounds a solemn warning note from the life of Gideon to the Lord's people today: "Gideon is like many of those who have been much used for the deliverance of the people of God all through the history of the church. Many who have been extraordinarily used have failed in what is priestly; they have brought worldly elements into the service of God … it is a very solemn thing to make an ephod; it represented the priestly thought in Israel. The ephod as an object was nothing; the value of the ephod was dependent on the person who wore it. An ephod without a priest was simply the form of godliness without the power of it, and that is what Christendom has fallen into, and largely under the influence of men who have been wonderfully blessed and used of God" (*An Outline of the Book of Judges*).

JUDGES 9

Abimelech Seizes Kingship

The failures of the children of Israel immediately prior to, and following, the death of Gideon brought a new dimension to the way in which the Lord dealt with them. Prior to this, He had chastised them when they did evil in His sight by delivering them into the hands of non-Israelite oppressors. However, this familiar pattern was interrupted following the death of Gideon. Judgment took the form of internal strife, which was instigated by "Abimelech the son of Jerubbaal" (v.1). Gideon is referred to as "Jerubbaal (let Baal contend - 3378)" throughout this chapter (vv.1,2,5,16,19,24,28,57); this serves to emphasise the tragedy of what followed. This name of honour, given to him after he had destroyed the altar of Baal (6.32), serves as a reminder of how far removed the people were from those early days when Gideon's actions had declared the weakness and powerlessness of Baal. As has been noted in the commentary on ch.8, the internal strife and bloodshed that marked the days of Abimelech arose as a result of the decline in Gideon's personal standards and the failure of the children of Israel to remember both the Lord their God and the goodness of Gideon towards them (8.34-35).

Verses 1-5a: The Pre-eminence of Abimelech

His ambition

Gideon had grasped after priesthood, but this was of no interest to Abimelech, particularly during a time when the people had returned to the worship of Baal. His name, Abimelech (40 – my father is king), points to his motives. He was driven by a passion for kingship, the very position that Gideon had refused. However, he paraded as if his father had been king and therefore he sought succession to the position. It is interesting to observe that Philistine kings bore the title "Abimelech", and their kingship was handed down from father to son. Abimelech had no right to claim the position of king and there is no sense in which he may be referred to as a judge; indeed, he is never spoken of as such. Unlike those who were judges, there was absolutely nothing spiritual about him and therefore it is no surprise to discover that the Lord's name was never upon his lips.

There is nothing wrong with ambition or with the desire for leadership among the Lord's people. Paul wrote, "If a man desire the office of a bishop (overseer), he desireth a good work" (1 Tim 3.1). However, these two things become a dangerous combination when they are driven by a selfish lust for power and position. Gamaliel, a Pharisee and a doctor of the law in New Testament days, warned the men of Israel of the disastrous outcomes of such a spirit: "For before these days rose up Theudas, boasting himself to be somebody; to whom a number of men, about four hundred, joined themselves: who was slain; and all, as many as obeyed (or believed) him, were scattered, and brought to nought. After this man rose up Judas of Galilee in the days of the taxing, and drew away much people after him: he also perished; and all, even as many as obeyed (or believed) him, were dispersed" (Acts 5.36-37). These were wise words, albeit from the lips of an unbeliever, to men who were intent upon slaying the apostles. At a later date, one of the apostles, John, warned his readers of men like "Diotrephes, who loveth to have the pre-eminence" (3 Jn v.9). Peter, another of the apostles, exhorted elders in the local church to "Feed the flock of God which is among you, taking the oversight thereof, not by constraint, but willingly; not for filthy lucre, but of a ready mind; neither as being lords over God's heritage, but being ensamples to the flock" (1 Pet 5.2-3). The desire to display high quality spiritual leadership of this nature was far removed from the mind of Abimelech. His burning ambition was to lord it over his people.

His associates

Abimelech's desire for kingship led him back to Shechem, the place of his origins. His first move was to approach "his mother's brethren" and "all the family of the house of his mother's father" (v.1). It appears that, although he had been born in Shechem, he had been brought up in Ophrah, along with his half-brothers. Shechem was within the boundaries of Ephraim, a tribe that had already displayed a desire for position and power (Josh 17.14 – referred to here as "the children of Joseph"). It was a city of some strategic importance that was situated in the very fertile valley between Mount Ebal and Mount Gerizim. Many of the important trade routes of the day converged on the city. It was captured early on in Joshua's campaigns and experienced a chequered 'spiritual' history in its relationship with Israel. It was the place where the Lord first revealed himself to Abraham (Gen 12.6-7), Jacob buried the false gods of his household (Gen 35.4), Joshua renewed the covenant with the children of Israel (Josh 24.1,25), and the bones of Joseph were buried (Josh 24.32). Sadly, the place that had seen a renunciation of all that was associated with idol-worship also became the spot where Gideon entered into a fleshly relationship with a concubine (8.31), Abimelech grasped after kingship (v.2), and "the house of Baal-berith (Baal of the covenant - 1170)" was set up (v.4). There is no reason to believe that it was in Canaanite hands at this time, although there was undoubtedly a strong Canaanite influence within it. Abimelech was therefore able to exploit the tensions that existed within the city to his own advantage. It is significant that his allies are referred to throughout the chapter as "the men (baals, lords, owners - 1167) of Shechem" (vv.2-3,6-7,18,20,23-26,39,57). F.C.Jennings writes of them, "They are all 'lords' now, everyone aims to be uppermost. They have a moral character consistent with the object of their worship (cf. Ps 115.8), and are thus named according to that character. They are 'baalim' filled with the same spirit of self-exaltation as ruined him who is called the devil (1 Tim 3.6)" (*Judges and Ruth*).

His appeal

Abimelech understood the character of the men he was dealing with and therefore he knew precisely how to appeal to them. He made no attempt to promote any of the positive spiritual links between Shechem and Israel. Through the brothers of his mother (v.1), he appealed to the self-interest of the men of Shechem: "Whether is better for you, either that all the sons of Jerubbaal, which are threescore and ten persons, reign over you, or that one reign over you?" (v.2). He knew that by referring to his father as "Jerubbaal" he would be inflaming the prejudices of those who worshipped Baal. There was no indication that the seventy sons of Gideon had aspirations for rule of any kind. Indeed, their continuance in Ophrah indicated that they were contented with their lot. As a final seal to his appeal, Abimelech reminded the men of Shechem, "I am your bone and your flesh" (v.2). His subtle and devious approach won the day: "and their hearts inclined to follow Abimelech; for they said, He is our brother" (v.3).

His actions

Abimelech's plan to remove his half-brothers required financing. Joseph's brethren sold him to the Ishmeelites for twenty pieces of silver (Gen 37.28) and Judas agreed to deliver the Lord Jesus to the chief priests for thirty pieces of silver (Mt 26.14-15). By so doing, both showed how little they valued the person they sold. Abimelech placed such a low estimate on the value of his seventy brethren that he was content to receive "threescore and ten pieces of silver out of the house of Baal-berith" (v.4) from the men of Shechem to finance their murder: one piece of silver for each brother, acquired from the temple treasury of a false god!

Abimelech sank to even greater depths when he used the tainted silver to hire "vain (empty, worthless - 7386) and light (frothy, unimportant - 6348) persons" (v.4). Accompanied by this worthless and wicked band of criminals he "went unto his father's house at Ophrah, and slew his brethren the sons of Jerubbaal ... upon one stone" (v.5). The fact that the place of execution was "upon one stone" seems to indicate that it must have been some kind of ritual slaughter. It may have been that they were slain one-by-one upon an altar-like rock in order to ensure that they did not escape. A.R.Fausset, commenting on the method used, suggests that the sons slain "were intended to be expiatory victims to Baal for the sacrilege done to him by Jerubbaal their father. As Jerubbaal had sacrificed to Jehovah upon the altar rock, using the sacred bullock and the Asherah grove associated with Baal worship to consume his burnt offering; so the Baal worshippers, who had been offended at his act ... offer them all together upon an altar-like stone" (*A Critical and Expository Commentary on the Book of Judges*).

Abimelech's carefully devised plan to eliminate all seventy of his father's sons lacked perfection in its execution and one of them, "Jotham (Jehovah is perfect - 3147) the youngest son of Jerubbaal was left; for he hid himself" (v.5). It is an encouragement to the Lord's people to know that God is sovereign, even when it may appear that the evil of men is running unchecked. However, Abimelech was blind to such spiritual insights and therefore he was not prepared to allow one small setback to frustrate his ambitions. He returned to Shechem and "all the men of Shechem gathered together, and all the house of Millo, and went, and made Abimelech king" (v.6). "The house of Millo" is probably a reference to Beth-millo, which may well have been an independent part of the city of Shechem. A.E.Cundall writes, "The word *millo* derives from a verb meaning 'to be filled', and originally referred to a rampart or earthwork; but its association with fortifications may have developed into a reference to a fortress generally. Thus *Beth-millo* may be identical with *the tower of Shechem* (vv.46-49)" (*Judges – An Introduction and Commentary*). Although Abimelech was proclaimed king, his sphere of influence was not vast: in addition to Shechem and Beth-millo, only Arumah (v.41) and Thebez (v.50) are specifically mentioned as having come under his control.

Abimelech's plans eventually led to him being crowned king "by the plain of the pillar that was in Shechem" (v.6). This was undoubtedly the stone that Joshua had set up to mark the spot where the covenant had been renewed and the people had pledged their loyalty to the Lord (Josh 24.1,25-27). The contrast between the two occasions could not be more marked. Joshua said of this stone, "for it hath heard all the words of the Lord which he spake unto us: it shall be therefore a witness unto you, lest ye deny your God" (Josh 24.27). Abimelech displayed total disdain for all that this high point in Israel's history stood. He deliberately denied God and served Baal-berith, thereby fulfilling his own lusts for position and power.

Verse 5b: The Preservation of Jotham

God never leaves Himself without a witness, even in the darkest of days of men's depravity. Later on in Israel's history, "one of the sons of Ahimelech the son of Ahitub, named Abiathar, escaped, and fled after David" (1 Sam 22.20): he was the sole survivor following the slaughter of all the priests at Nob at the hand of Doeg the Edomite. Similarly, when Athaliah, the mother of Ahaziah the king, destroyed all the royal seed of the house of Judah, one of them, Joash, was preserved and was "hid in the house of God six years" (2 Chr 22.12). On this occasion, it was Jotham who was watched over, preserved and delivered by God from Abimelech's evil act.

Verses 6-21: The Parable of Jotham

The place

The news of Abimelech's coronation brought Jotham out of hiding, and "he went and stood in the top of mount Gerizim" (v.7). The acoustics of this vantage point made it the perfect place for his message to carry to all his hearers. Moses had commanded that six of the tribes should stand on mount Gerizim to declare the blessings of the law, and six of them on mount Ebal to declare the cursings on those who disobeyed the law (Deut 27.12-13). Joshua had fulfilled this command when the children of Israel entered the land (Josh 8.33-35). It was particularly poignant therefore that Jotham stood on mount Gerizim, the mount of blessing, to condemn the wickedness of the men of Shechem towards his brethren. Sadly, their actions meant that the place of blessing became the place of condemnation. They had forfeited any right to the blessings that had formerly been proclaimed from that mount. The tribe of Joseph (Ephraim and Manasseh) was one of the tribes that stood on it to pronounce the blessings. Gideon was from the tribe of Manasseh (6.15) but the rebellion of Abimelech, his son, and the men of Shechem, a city that was within the borders of Ephraim, brought no blessing to the tribe.

The parable

Jotham's simple, yet powerful, parable is the first to be recorded in the Scriptures. He pictured the trees going forth "to anoint a king over them" (v.8). Trees were a particularly appropriate illustration as they speak of men in the Bible. Indeed, Daniel linked a tree, a man and kingship together when he imparted to Nebuchadnezzar, king of Babylon, the interpretation of his dream: "The tree that thou sawest, which grew, and was strong, whose height reached unto the heaven, and the sight thereof to all the earth ... it is thou, O king, that art grown and become strong" (Dan 4.20,22). The blind man at Bethsaida, responding to Jesus' enquiry as to whether he saw anything, said, "I see men as trees, walking" (Mk 8.24). The Psalmist likened the man who delights in the law of the Lord to "a tree planted by the rivers of water" (Ps 1.3).

Three prominent and productive trees were approached to become king. Firstly, the olive tree stood in prime position in the estimation of the other trees. They came to it with more of a statement than a request: "Reign thou over us" (v.8). It did not appear to have crossed their minds that such an opportunity would be refused. Much to their surprise, no doubt, the olive tree refused: "Should I leave my fatness, wherewith by me they honour God and man, and go to be promoted (wave, hover - 5128) over the trees?" (v.9). Its oil, which is a picture of the Holy Spirit, was one of the ingredients in the holy anointing oil (Ex 30.24). Such oil was also used to feed the golden candlestick, the only light in the holy place of the tabernacle (Lev 24.2), and it was mingled with the offerings. It was therefore used to honour God. However, it was also used to honour man, pictured in the Samaritan who came to the man on the Jerusalem to Jericho road and "bound up his wounds, pouring in oil and wine" (Lk 10.34). Indeed, olive oil was used for a range of medicinal purposes. It was also used to anoint the kings of Israel (1 Sam 10.1; 16.13). Such a fruitful tree was never going to sacrifice its position of fatness and blessing for the short-term gain of being "promoted over the trees".

Secondly, the trees approached the fig tree. They had learned the lesson from their first attempt and, on this occasion, there was an invitation: "Come thou, and reign over us" (v.10). However, they met with a similar response: "Should I forsake my sweetness, and my good fruit, and go to be promoted over the trees?" (v.11). The fig tree provided the staple food of the land and it was highly valued for its sweetness and wholesome fruit. When the Lord Jesus was hungry, He looked to a fig tree for fruit (Mk 11.12-13). If the fig tree had embraced the desire of the trees for it to be king, it would have lost its sweetness and ceased to produce good fruit. It would have brought forth bitterness and evil figs (cf. Jer 24.2-3).

Thirdly, the trees attempted to attract the vine: "Come thou, and reign over us" (v.12). The vine declined and drew attention to the prime purpose for its existence: to produce wine, "which cheereth God and man" (v.13). Wine was used as the drink offering, which was poured out in association with the sweet savour burnt offering, meal offering and peace offering (Num 15.5,7,10,24; 28.7,14). J.J.Stubbs writes, "Wine, of which this offering is composed, speaks of joy. It would set forth the pleasure that God has received from the lovely life of the Lord Jesus, from His devotion unto death, and from a completed sacrifice upon which God with pleasure can feast with His people (*Numbers – Ritchie Old Testament Commentaries*). The Psalmist spoke of "wine that maketh glad the heart of man" (Ps 104.15). It was therefore the privilege and responsibility of the vine to bring joy to the heart of God and man. This was displayed to perfection in the Lord Jesus, who said, "I am the true vine … These things have I spoken unto you, that my joy might remain in you, and that your joy might be full" (Jn 15.1,11). If the vine had grasped after the power and position offered by kingship there would have been no joy, only sadness, for God and man. The truth of this was seen at a later date when Samuel told the children of Israel, "And ye shall cry out in that day because of your king which ye shall have chosen you; and the Lord will not hear you in that day" (1 Sam 8.18). Sorrow came to both the Lord and His people as a result of their rejection of His rule over them.

Finally, "all the trees" made the disastrous decision to turn to the bramble and said, "Come thou, and reign over us" (v.14). This is the first time that the words "all the trees" appear. Up until this point there had been an absence of harmony among the trees as they approached the olive, fig and vine trees. The bramble would most certainly not have joined with them in their desires for these trees to reign. It had its own selfish hidden agenda for power that would have brought it into direct conflict with their wishes. It was waiting for the appropriate time for that agenda to come out into the open and, even when it did, it would be cloaked with deception and threats. It displayed its true colours when it said, "If in truth ye anoint me king over you" (v.15): the desire to rule was not far beneath the surface. However, it was the worst possible candidate to reign. Unlike the other three trees it had nothing of value to leave, if it were to embrace kingship.

It produced no fruit and its wood was worthless. It was easily set on fire in the heat of the summer and therefore threatened the safety of other trees, including the mighty cedars of Lebanon (v.15). It was not part of God's original creation and only appeared as a result of Adam's sin: "And unto Adam he said ... cursed is the ground for thy sake ... thorns also and thistles shall it bring forth to thee" (Gen 3.17-18). It was nothing more than a low-lying thorn bush over which the other trees towered. It was absurd therefore that it should offer its protection to them: "come and put your trust in my shadow" (v.15). It was so close to the ground that it hardly cast a shadow and its sharp thorns would have wounded any who sought shelter under it. Its vicious and vindictive nature was displayed in its response to those who dared not to place their trust in it: "and if not, let fire come out of the bramble, and devour the cedars of Lebanon" (v.15). Destruction would be swift and decisive for any who stood in its pathway to power.

The purpose

It almost defies belief that the trees should have turned to a tree like the bramble and made it king; and yet they did! It would be easy to direct all the criticism towards the bramble, but the desire for a king came from them in the first place. They must take their share of the blame for what unfolded. Instead of discerning the lessons from the responses of the olive, fig and vine trees, they persisted in their quest for one to reign over them and therefore they ended up with the king they deserved. Likewise, it was the men of Israel who first approached Gideon and said, "Rule thou over us" (8.22). This set in motion the chain of events that ultimately led to Abimelech seizing power. Later on it was the elders of Israel who requested Samuel to "make us a king to judge us like all the nations" (1 Sam 8.5); and the Lord gave them Saul.

Jotham was not condemning leadership among the people of God, or even kingship. The parable is not primarily about the three trees that refused to reign, but about the folly of the other trees in choosing the bramble as king and its total unsuitability for such a position. His overriding purpose was to highlight to his hearers the dangers and folly of the self-exalting and unscrupulous leadership that was displayed by Abimelech and others like him (cf. 1 Kings 1.5). In a skilful and non-vindictive manner he brought home the application of his parable. Firstly, he challenged them as to their truth and sincerity both in relation to Abimelech and Jerubbaal: "Now therefore, if ye have done truly and sincerely, in that ye have made Abimelech king, and if ye have dealt well with Jerubbaal and his house, and have done unto him according to the deserving of his hands" (v.16). Secondly, in order for them to reach an honest conclusion as to their integrity, he invited them to remember all that his father had done for them: "For my father fought for you, and adventured his life far, and delivered you out of the hand of Midian" (v.17). Thirdly, he confronted them with how they had responded to such a high level commitment to their welfare: "And ye are risen up against my father's house this day, and have slain his sons, threescore and ten persons, upon one stone" (v.18). Fourthly, he declared plainly the nature of the man they had proclaimed king. He referred to Abimelech as "the son of his maidservant (female slave, bondmaid - 519) ... your brother" (v.18), which provided a powerful contrast to the affectionate terms, "my father" (v.17) and "his sons" (v.18). The reference to "maidservant" would undoubtedly have been regarded as an insult, since Abimelech's mother would have been a free-woman of Shechem. Fifthly, he picked up the theme of truth and sincerity again, and mockingly wished them joy: "If ye then have dealt truly and sincerely with Jerubbaal and with his house this day, then rejoice ye in Abimelech, and let him also rejoice in you" (v.19).

The clear message was that they had acted without integrity and therefore he left them in no doubt as to tragic outcome for both Abimelech and themselves: "But if not, let fire come out from Abimelech, and devour the men of Shechem, and the house of Millo; and let fire come out from the men of Shechem, and from the house of Millo, and devour Abimelech" (v.20). Such a fleshly relationship could only end in the mutual destruction of both.

With this powerful message still ringing in the people's ears, Jotham "ran away, and fled, and went to Beer (a well - 876), and dwelt there, for fear of Abimelech his brother" (v.21). S.Ridout comments, "He cannot join in all this conflict and strife, so he flees to Beer and dwells there. Beer is 'a well', and he dwells by the well, while the people of God are in their unseemly strife over authority. He drinks of the authority of the fountain of the word of God, from whence alone come sustenance and refreshing" (*Lectures on the Book of Judges*).

The Prophecy of Jotham Fulfilled (vv.22-55)

Two phrases sum up the events that followed Jotham's departure from the scene: they are, "God sent" and "men ... dealt treacherously" (v.23). The treachery of men appeared to run rampant and unchecked throughout the remainder of Abimelech's life. However, nothing could have been further from the truth. God is sovereign and therefore He was in control of the drama that unfolded.

The Treachery of the Men of Shechem (vv.22-25)

Abimelech "reigned (was prince over - 7786) three years over Israel" (v.22). The word used for "reign" is not the usual word employed for the rule of a king, indicating that his sphere of influence was only local and confined to a comparatively small area in the north of the country. However, all was not well and his three years of relative success eventually came to an end at the hands of the men of Shechem. They had already shown themselves to be unstable by following him in the first place and therefore it should not have come as a surprise that they "dealt treacherously" (v.23) with him when it suited them to do so. However, the divine record makes it absolutely clear that it was neither Abimelech, nor the men of Shechem who were in control of their destinies: "God (ELOHIM - 430) sent an evil spirit between Abimelech and the men of Shechem" (v.23). Such a course of action highlighted the depths to which Israel had sunk at this time. It also explains why the more general word for God, *Elohim*, is employed, rather than "the Lord (*Jehovah*)" that emphasised their special covenant relationship with Him. It is not clear what reasons the men of Shechem would have given for dealing so treacherously with the one they had acclaimed as king, but it is abundantly clear that the divine hand was behind their actions: "That the cruelty done to the threescore and ten sons of Jerubbaal might come, and their blood be laid upon Abimelech their brother, which slew them; and upon the men of Shechem, which aided him in the killing of his brethren" (v.24).

The men of Shechem knew how to damage Abimelech and therefore they "set liers in wait for him in the top of the mountains, and they robbed all that came along that way by them" (v.25). They stationed bandits along the various trade routes into Shechem with the object of ambushing both Abimelech and his men, if they should pass that way, and any other travellers bringing trade into the city. Their strategy would have undermined the security of the area and therefore discouraged traders from passing through. Abimelech's ability to control his territory would have been brought into question and he would also have suffered financially. The ability of the men to put their plan into action before news reached Abimelech (v.25) suggests that he was almost certainly not living in Shechem at the time. Indeed, it became clear later that he had a representative in the city to relay messages to him (vv.30-31).

Verses 26-41: The Treachery of Gaal

Abimelech did not appear to take any immediate action against the activities of the men of Shechem in the mountains, but he became more concerned when "Gaal the son of Ebed came with his brethren, and went over to Shechem" (v.26). Nothing is known about Gaal apart from what is recorded in this chapter. He probably roamed the area, along with his brethren, seeking to exploit the kind of politically unstable situations he found in Shechem. Once he had exploited them, he would move on. Clearly, he was a man of some ability and, above all, a smooth talker. It appeared to take him only a short time to get the easily influenced men of Shechem to "put their confidence in him" (v.26).

Gaal seized his opportunity to gain their allegiance when the men were at their most vulnerable: "And they went out into the fields, and gathered their vineyards, and trode the grapes, and made merry, and went into the house of their god, and did eat and drink, and cursed Abimelech" (v.27). It was the season of harvest when the summer fruits were being gathered in.

For Israel this would have been the Feast of Tabernacles (Lev 23.34,39), but this commemoration of the end of the summer harvest in Shechem was a far cry from the rejoicing before the Lord (Lev 23.40) associated with the Feast of Tabernacles. Here, within the context of Baal worship, the merriment arose from over-indulgence and drunkenness, rather than pure joy. In such a condition they were ripe for Gaal to sway with his smooth talk. He addressed his own men, but through them he was very skilfully inciting the men of Shechem to overthrow Abimelech: "Who is Abimelech, and who is Shechem, that we should serve him? is not he the son of Jerubbaal? and Zebul his officer? serve the men of Hamor the father of Shechem: for why should we serve him?" (v.28). In order to encourage division, he deliberately highlighted Abimelech's links with his father, Jerubbaal, but reminded them of their heritage as descendants of Hamor, the father of Shechem (Gen 33.19; 34.2). He was challenging them as to their wisdom in being linked to one whose father was opposed to the worship of Baal and who himself was only half-Shechemite, whereas they were pure Shechemites. He then, very subtly, suggested that they might consider him as their leader: "And would to God this people were under my hand! then would I remove Abimelech" (v.29). Finally, he threw out the challenge to Abimelech, "Increase thine army, and come out" (v.29); words that he would soon regret.

Treachery begets treachery, and "when Zebul the ruler of the city heard the words of Gaal the son of Ebed, his anger was kindled" (v.30). His anger probably stemmed from injured pride as a result of Gaal's derogatory and humiliating remark about him being only Abimelech's "officer" (superintendent - 6496), rather than out of a concern or love for his master (v.28). Indeed, as subsequent events unfolded, it was clear that his plans did not include bringing Abimelech back to the city. However, at this stage, he "sent messengers unto Abimelech privily (deceitfully - 8649)" (v.31) to warn him of the danger and even gave him a strategy as to how he could defeat the planned attack. He suggested to him that during the night he and his men should "lie in wait in the field ... rise early, and set upon the city ... when he and the people that is with him come out against thee, then mayest thou do to them as thou shalt find occasion" (vv.32-33). Carnal men can appeal to their own kind and therefore Abimelech heeded Zebul's advice. He "rose up, and all the people that were with him, by night, and they laid wait against Shechem in four companies" (v.34). Unlike Gaal, Zebul had clearly thought out his plan to the last detail. His capacity for deceit grew as he convinced Gaal that the people he saw in the half-light of the morning in the mountains was really "the shadow of the mountains as if they were men" (v.36). By the time Gaal realised that they really were people, and not shadows, it was too late. The strategy employed by Abimelech of dividing his army into four companies gave Gaal the impression that it was larger than it was: "See there come people down by the middle of the land, and another company come along by the plain of

Meonenim" (v.37). His natural inclination was to abandon the cause, but Zebul's final challenge shamed him into action: "Where is now thy mouth, wherewith thou saidst, Who is Abimelech, that we should serve him? is not this the people that thou hast despised? go out, I pray now, and fight with them" (v.38). He had to live up to his proud boasts if he were not to face total humiliation. He was left with no alternative and therefore "Gaal went out before the men of Shechem, and fought with Abimelech" (v.39). In spite of the numbers that he had with him, he was ill prepared for such a confrontation and Abimelech easily overcame his forces: "And Abimelech chased him, and he fled before him, and many were overthrown and wounded, even unto the entering of the gate" (v.40).

Clearly, it was Zebul who continued to hold the power in Shechem and Abimelech was not welcome there. He did not therefore enter the city to pursue after and slay Gaal. Following the victory, he "dwelt at Arumah" (v.41), which was probably in the near vicinity of Shechem. It was left to Zebul to "thrust out Gaal and his brethren, that they should not dwell in Shechem" (v.41). He managed immediately to restore a measure of stability to the troubled city. However, all that he achieved was about to be undone. If his anger had been abated with the overthrow and expulsion of Gaal, the same could not be said of Abimelech.

Verses 42-55: The Treachery of Abimelech

Abimelech's vindictive spirit led him to sink to alarming depths as he vented his anger against the place and the people he ruled over. Jotham had predicted that fire would come out from Abimelech, and devour the men of Shechem, and the house of Millo (v.20). His words were about to be fulfilled. Following the defeat of Gaal, the inhabitants of Shechem must have felt that things had returned to normality and therefore "it came to pass on the morrow, that the people went out into the field" (v.42). They had no sense of the fire of Abimelech's anger that was about to engulf them. He was set on vengeance against Shechem, because of their treachery towards him. He was informed about their movements (v.42) and he divided his men into three companies in order to deal with them (vv.42-43). Two of the companies surprised those who were working in the fields and slew them (v.44). He took the other company and "stood in the entering of the gate of the city" (v.44). He was intent on the total destruction of the city and therefore he "fought against the city all that day; and he took the city, and slew the people that was therein, and beat down the city, and sowed it with salt" (v.45). Sowing it with salt was a symbolic act that condemned Shechem to desolation (cf. Deut 29.23; Ps 107.34; Jer 17.6), although it was built again during the reign of Jeroboam 1 (1 Kings 12.25).

Abimelech's trail of destruction continued unabated. He was told that the men of "the tower of Shechem", which was probably the stronghold of the city, had "entered into an hold of the house of the god Berith (identical with Baal-berith in v.4)" (v.46). It appears that these two buildings were in close proximity to each other. Whether the "hold" refers to an underground vault in the house of the god or to the tower itself is not certain. However, one thing was abundantly clear: their god was powerless to protect them from Abimelech's fury. It was ironical that they were hiding in the very place in which they had "cursed Abimelech" a short while before (v.27). Abimelech, with an axe in his hand, led his men up to mount Zalmon and instructed them to follow his example. He "cut down a bough from the trees, and took it, and laid it on his shoulder ... And all the people likewise cut down every man his bough, and followed Abimelech" (vv.48-49). What ensued literally fulfilled the first part of Jotham's prophecy. Abimelech and his men took the boughs and "put them to the hold, and set the hold on fire upon them; so that all the men of the tower of Shechem died also, about a thousand men and women" (v.49). The fact that they "set the hold on fire upon them" suggests that they may well have been in a vault or cellar beneath the building.

However, Abimelech's work was still not complete. He marched on a city, approximately ten miles (16 kilometres) to the north of Shechem, and "encamped against Thebez, and took it" (v.50). Clearly, he suspected the inhabitants of having been involved in the rebellion against him and therefore they had to be punished. There was "a strong tower within the city" and all the men and women of the city fled to the top of it for refuge from the wrath of Abimelech (v.51). It is significant that, unlike the tower of Shechem, the women are specifically mentioned, because one of them was to play a prominent role in the demise of Abimelech. When he came to the tower he "went hard unto the door of the tower to burn it with fire" (v.52). Clearly, he became careless and came too near the tower and "a certain woman cast a piece of millstone upon Abimelech's head, and all to brake his skull" (v.53). The word employed for "millstone" (7393) suggests that this was an upper millstone, between one and two feet (30-60 cms) in diameter and two to four inches (5-10 cms) thick. Justice was done when the man who had slain his brethren "upon one stone" (v.5) was himself crushed by a single stone. He was "the son of Jerubbaal", but he had embarked on his trail of destruction by appealing to "his mother's brethren" (v.1). It was fitting therefore that his journey should end at the hands of a woman. His head that had "worn the crown" was ultimately crushed.

To avoid the double shame of not perishing in battle and being slain by a woman, "he called hastily unto the young man his armourbearer, and said unto him, Draw thy sword, and slay me" (v.54). The young man obeyed and the days of Abimelech came to an undignified and inglorious end. The "men of Israel" who had supported him against Shechem, "departed every man unto his place" (v.55). Thus the second part of Jotham's prophecy had been fulfilled: "and let fire come out from the men of Shechem, and from the house of Millo, and devour Abimelech" (v.20). The "bramble" that had lusted after being "promoted over the trees" departed as violently as he had appeared on the scene.

Verses 56-57: The Primary Lesson

It is easy to become caught up in the dramatic and rapid course of events that surrounded Abimelech's life and thereby miss the primary lesson that God was teaching His people through it. Indeed, it is possible to lose sight of God completely; the participants in this drama were guilty of this. It is not surprising that in the midst of so much carnality He was never referred to as "the Lord (Jehovah)" or even spoken of as "God" by His people between vv.24 and 56. However, as the final act in the drama closes, the divine record brings the reader back to the key message: "Thus God rendered the wickedness of Abimelech, which he did unto his father, in slaying his seventy brethren: and all the evil of the men of Shechem did God render upon their heads: and upon them came the curse of Jotham the son of Jerubbaal" (vv.56-57). The evil of men appeared to be running rampant during this stage of Israel's history, but God was in control and working behind the scenes throughout. As the sovereign God, He entered into the affairs of men and "sent an evil spirit between Abimelech and the men of Shechem" (v.23), but that did not absolve them from responsibility for their own actions. Each of the protagonists brought about his own destruction and reaped what he had sown. God cannot be charged with unrighteousness; His judgment is always just and falls only upon the guilty. It is interesting to observe that He removed Abimelech before he could execute the final judgment on those within the tower at Thebez. Although they may have been guilty of undermining his position, they had not joined him in the slaughter of the seventy sons of Jerubbaal. However, Abimelech and the Shechemites did have the blood of the sons upon their hands and therefore justice was done as, under the hand of God, they consumed each other. The words of Paul are applicable here: "But we are sure that the judgment of God is according to truth against them which commit such things … who will render to every man according to his deeds" (Rom 2.2,6).

The record of Abimelech's life is also a powerful reminder that leadership and government among the Lord's people are vital, but they must be of the right nature if they are to be a blessing. "The curse of Jotham the son of Jerubbaal" (v.57) came upon those who abused the position of leadership by using it to promote their own selfish lusts. When commenting on rule among God's people, F.C.Jennings writes, "Most surely there is rule; but it is the rule of love and nothing else. Love that seeks no authority, no exaltation; love that recognises the greatest place in him that serves and that ever, in some way, according to the measure of the gift of Christ, addicts itself to the service of the saints. Love, whom I find, not above my head, but at my feet – here may Christians find their rulers still, and may freely, in responsive affection, submit themselves unto such, and to everyone who is a co-helper and true labourer" (*Judges and Ruth*). Paul warned the churches of Galatia about the dangers of displaying the kind of spirit seen in Abimelech and the men of Shechem: "For, brethren, ye have been called unto liberty; only use not liberty for an occasion to the flesh, but by love serve one another … But if ye bite and devour one another, take heed that ye be not consumed one of another. This I say then, Walk in the Spirit, and ye shall not fulfil the lust of the flesh" (Gal 5.13,15-16).

JUDGES 10

Tola and Jair

The previous chapter concluded with a curse: "upon them came the curse of Jotham the son of Jerubbaal" (9.57). It took a lengthy chapter of fifty-seven verses to describe "the wickedness of Abimelech" (9.56) and "the evil of the men of Shechem" (9.57) that led to the curse coming upon them. It was not surprising therefore that, at the conclusion of this tragic chapter in their history, "the men of Israel ... departed every man unto his place" (9.55); their hopes and dreams had died with Abimelech. However, the present chapter opens on an optimistic note: "And after Abimelech ..." (v.1). It would have been a totally demoralising scene if there had not been anything positive to follow his disastrous leadership. However, God had an "after" in store for His people and fresh hope dawned following the darkness. G.Campbell Morgan observes, "God's 'afters' are worth the waiting for. However dark the 'now' is, there will be light enough in God's 'after' to explain the darkness" (*The Crises of the Christ*).

Verses 1-5: The Lord's Deliverers

Two seemingly insignificant judges rose up following the death of Abimelech. The record of their involvement in the course of Israel's history spans just five verses. Some commentators have been dismissive of their contributions by referring to them as "minor judges". However, to treat Tola and Jair in this manner is to do them a grave injustice. The very fact that their service spanned a combined total of forty-five years is enough in itself to raise them above the level of being termed, "minor men of God". No service for the Lord, how ever small it might appear to be, should be devalued or dishonoured by referring to it as "minor".

They arrived on the scene immediately "after Abimelech" (v.1) and addressed the void left by his wickedness. They brought back a time of peace and security for the children of Israel following those turbulent days. The record of their lives may be brief, but their contributions were immense. Indeed, they are unique in the record of the judges in that the familiar pattern of deliverance by a judge, followed by the people doing evil again before the next judge arose, was broken. Tola and Jair maintained the stability and peace for forty-five continuous years, which bears testimony to the positive impact they made. Idolatry did not raise its head again until after they had both died (v.6); this suggests that they were successful in keeping the people from it.

Tola

Tola came from the tribe of Issachar, although "he dwelt (sat, presided - 3427) in Shamir in mount Ephraim" (v.1). The exact location of Shamir is unknown, but Tola probably felt that he could judge more effectively from this strategic position in Ephraim. Shamir (8069) means, "a thorn", which is particularly appropriate in the light of the fact that Tola's service followed on from Abimelech, the "bramble king".

He is introduced as "Tola the son of Puah, the son of Dodo" (v.1). His name, and that of his father, linked them back to the original founders of their families in Issachar (Gen 46.13; Num 26.23). All that is said about Issachar indicates that it was a tribe that preferred quietness and peace to warfare. Jacob spoke of him as "a strong ass couching (crouching, reclining, reposing - 7257) down between two burdens: and he saw that rest was good, and the land that it was pleasant; and bowed his shoulder to bear, and became a servant unto tribute" (Gen 49.14-15). The picture is that of one who ought to have been enjoying his inheritance, but he preferred to live comfortably alongside the world, thereby avoiding conflict. Ultimately this approach led him into servitude and bearing burdens for his masters. However, this criticism could not be directed at Tola. His role was most certainly not a passive one that simply sought the easy life. Although there do not appear to have been any battles or spectacular victories during the time that "he judged Israel" (v.2), he undertook the vital and demanding work of actively promoting and maintaining conditions that were conducive to peace. Such believers are important in the Lord's work today. There are always those who are intent on stirring up strife, but few who work for peace among His people.

Over a period of time the men of Issachar built up a reputation for wisdom. At a later date, when they were with those who gathered in Hebron to make David king, it was said of them, "And of the children of Issachar, which were men that had understanding of the times, to know what Israel ought to do; the heads of them were two hundred; and all their brethren were at their commandment" (1 Chr 12.32). There were those at that time, like Joab, who were expending their energies fighting against the remnant of Saul's house, but the children of Issachar appreciated that the time had come to promote harmony and to unite around David. Clearly, Tola could have stood alongside these men: he displayed wisdom and an "understanding of the times" in which he lived. He appreciated the quiet and consistent testimony that was required following the turbulent days of Abimelech.

Tola's name means, "worm", which is suggestive of his lowly character. It was absolutely vital that a leader who was "clothed with humility" (1 Pet 5.5) should succeed the arrogant and proud Abimelech. It was only a man with a gentle and lowly nature who would be able to heal the deep wounds inflicted by him and the men of Shechem. As such, Tola points to the Lord Jesus, whose voice is heard through the words of the Psalmist: "But I am a worm (TOLAAT - 8438), and no man; a reproach of men, and despised of the people" (Ps 22.6). Paul wrote of Him, "And being found in fashion as a man, he humbled himself, and became obedient unto death, even the death of the cross" (Phil 2.8). Paul encouraged the believers at Philippi to display that same spirit of lowliness in order to overcome the division that was creeping in to ruin the local assembly: "in lowliness of mind let each esteem other better than themselves … Let this mind be in you, which was also in Christ Jesus" (Phil 2.3,5). It is interesting to note that Tola lived out his quiet and humble testimony in the territory of Ephraim, the tribe that was noted for its lack of humility (8.1-2). The fact that he judged there for twenty-three years, and they did not drive him out, suggests that his quiet testimony must have made a favourable impression upon them and may even have produced a softer spirit within them.

Tola departed from the scene as quietly and unassumingly as he appeared on it: he "died, and was buried in Shamir" (v.2). However, the testimony that he left spoke volumes about the valuable service he had rendered: he "arose to defend (save or liberate) Israel … he judged Israel twenty and three years" (vv.1-2). He left behind conditions of unity and peace among the people of God, a testimony that any servant of the Lord should covet.

Jair

"And after him (Tola) arose Jair" (v.3). Jair (2971) means "enlightener", which is suggestive of one who brought light during what were often dark days for the children of Israel. Unlike Tola, he inherited conditions of peace, rather than turmoil and strife. However, it was an equally challenging task to maintain the peace following such settled conditions. The Lord's people are particularly vulnerable following times of stability. It is then that the enemy attacks and seeks to destroy all that has been built up.

Jair came from the land of Gilead that was east of the river Jordan, whereas Tola's judgeship had been in western Canaan. Only one thing is recorded of him: "he had thirty sons that rode on thirty ass colts, and they had thirty cities, which are called Havoth-jair unto this day, which are in the land of Gilead" (v.4). The sons' possession of thirty cities and thirty colt asses suggests that the family was rich and influential. However, this wealth did not hinder Jair from serving the Lord by judging Israel for twenty-two years (v.3).

The little that is said of him suggests that his judgeship was marked by harmonious relationships. Firstly, he appears to have been at one with his thirty sons. Secondly, the sons were all involved in the same pursuit: they "rode on thirty ass colts, and they had thirty cities" (v.4). Ass colts were a symbol of peace, whereas horses were a symbol of war. It is possible that they rode on them from city to city to assist their father in imparting wisdom, administering justice and promoting peace. Thirdly, the cities were called "Havoth-jair (cities of Jair)" (v.4). Each one was undoubtedly different but there was a unity about them in that they reflected the character of the man whose name they bore.

Jair and his sons provide a foreshadowing of Christ. As the "enlightener", Jair is a reminder of Christ's words, "I am the light of the world: he that followeth me shall not walk in darkness, but shall have the light of life" (Jn 8.12). Matthew saw His triumphal entry into the city of Jerusalem as the fulfilment of Zechariah's prophecy: "All this was done, that it might be fulfilled which was spoken by the prophet, saying, Tell ye the daughter of Sion, Behold, thy King cometh unto thee, meek, and sitting upon an ass, and a colt the foal of an ass" (Mt 21.4-5). His entry was with dignity and authority, but it was also with meekness. He came to the city as King, as the bringer of peace and righteous judgment. Sadly, they rejected Him and therefore in a coming day He will appear upon "a white horse ... and in righteousness he doth judge and make war" (Rev 19.11). He promised those servants who were faithful to Him during the days of His rejection that they would rule over cities in His coming kingdom (Lk 19.17,19). Indeed, He promised His disciples that they would "sit on thrones judging the twelve tribes of Israel" (Lk 22.30).

Jair's death and burial in Camon (v.5) brought forty-five years of peace to an end. It was alarming how quickly conditions deteriorated following this, but it was even more distressing to see the wholesale apostasy that set in. Clearly, the influence of judges like Tola and Jair had not fundamentally changed the condition of the hearts of the people.

Jephthah and The Ammonites

Verses 6-9: The Lord's Anger

Never before had there been such a catalogue of idolatry recorded in the history of the children of Israel. They "did evil again in the sight of the Lord, and served Baalim, and Ashtaroth, and the gods of Syria, and the gods of Zidon, and the gods of Moab, and the gods of the children of Ammon, and the gods of the Philistines, and forsook the Lord, and served not him" (v.6). They immersed themselves in a sevenfold idolatry that reflected the foreign gods from across the entire land of Canaan. The number seven speaks of completeness in the Scriptures. Some commentators believe that this is a general statement reflecting the entire period of the judges, but there is no real ground for this. It is perhaps significant that it stands at the midpoint of the book of Judges. The judges that God raised up to deliver the children of Israel had not produced any lasting changes and therefore conditions would deteriorate still further as the future unfolded.

It was serious enough that the children of Israel served these foreign gods, but they compounded the issue by deliberately excluding the Lord from their worship and their service. Such extreme departure called for a severe response from Him: "And the anger of the Lord was hot against Israel, and he sold them into the hands of the Philistines, and into the hands of the children of Ammon" (v.7). Although their oppression of Israel almost certainly overlapped at this time, the threat of the Ammonites, who feature strongly in the life of Jephthah as recorded in chs.11 and 12, is dealt with first. The story of the Philistines is picked up again in the exploits of Samson in ch.13.

As has already been noted in the commentary on ch.3, the Ammonites, like the Moabites, were the descendants of Lot (Gen 19.30-38). There was nothing spiritual about their origins: they came out of the fleshly union of Lot with his two daughters. God had decreed that they "shall not enter into the congregation of the Lord; even to their tenth generation shall they not enter into the congregation of the Lord for ever: because they met you not with bread and with water in the way, when ye came forth out of Egypt; and because they hired against thee Balaam the son of Beor of Pethor of Mesopotamia, to curse thee" (Deut 23.3-4). They were a nation that had no interest in the welfare of a people redeemed out of Egypt, but preferred to see them die in the wilderness. They were undoubtedly delighted to have Israel at their mercy again. Like Moab, they represent the power of the flesh in the life of the believer. It was the fleshly lusts of the children of Israel that had led them to forsake the Lord and to serve the gods of the land and therefore it was appropriate that the Lord, in His anger, should use the Ammonites to chasten them. The Lord's anger is always just. He simply gave the people over to them to reap what their rebellion had sown.

Although the Ammonites' influence was felt for eighteen years (v.8), the impact on the children of Israel was both immediate and severe: "And that year (the year the oppression began) they vexed (harassed, dashed in pieces - 7492) and oppressed (cracked in pieces, bruised, crushed - 7533) the children of Israel" (v.8). The language employed reveals how serious things had become. The Ammonites not only made their presence felt "on the other side (the east) Jordan in the land of the Amorites, which is Gilead", i.e. in the Israelite territory in Transjordan, close by their own kingdom, but they also encroached into the west and "passed over Jordan to fight also against Judah, and against Benjamin, and against the house of Ephraim" (v.9). The oppression was widespread, humiliating and extremely painful for Israel: "Israel was sore distressed" (v.9). At the same time, the Philistines would also have been putting pressure on them from the west.

Verses 10-16a: The Lord's Test

The children of Israel reverted to a formula that had been successful in the past: they "cried unto the Lord" (v.10). They had shown prior to this that their cries did not come from truly repentant hearts, but from a purely selfish desire to be released from further suffering. However, they went a step further on this occasion and added, "We have sinned against thee, both because we have forsaken our God (Elohim - 430), and also served Baalim" (v.10). After eighteen years of idolatry, they were not morally qualified to refer to him as "the Lord (Jehovah)": they had lost all sense of their covenant relationship with Him.

The Lord's response shook them to the core and showed that their words did not demonstrate true repentance. They announced what they had done wrong, but they gave no evidence of what they intended to do about it. He responded to their sevenfold idolatry by reminding them of His sevenfold deliverance of them: "Did not I deliver you from the Egyptians, and from the Amorites, from the children of Ammon, and from the Philistines? The Zidonians also, and the Amalekites, and the Maonites, did oppress you; and ye cried to me, and I delivered you out of their hand" (vv.11-12). The identity of the Maonites is uncertain, but it may well be a reference to the Midianites. The response of the children of Israel to His mercy in the past had been consistently to trample it underfoot. They became so accustomed to it that they presumed upon it. They convinced themselves that all they had to do when the going became tough was to cry to Him and He would respond. His reply underlined that they had reached the end point as far as He was concerned: "Yet ye have forsaken me, and served other gods: wherefore I will deliver you no more. Go and cry unto the gods which ye have chosen; let them deliver you in the time of your tribulation" (vv.13-14). They had forsaken the Lord and He was about to abandon them. They had chosen other gods and therefore He suggested that they should now turn to them for deliverance. Their position was now critical; for them to forsake the Lord was one thing, but for Him to forsake them and give them up to their enemies would have been disastrous. None of this would have come as a surprise to them if they had remembered the words that the Lord had spoken to them through Moses: "this people will rise up, and go a whoring after the gods of the strangers of the land … Then my anger shall be kindled against them in that day, and I will forsake them, and I will hide my face from them, and they shall be devoured, and many evils and troubles shall befall them; so that they will say in that day, Are not these evils come upon us, because our God is not among us?" (Deut 31.16-17). The Lord had told Moses to put these words into a song and to teach it to the children of Israel. Clearly, that song had been forgotten by the current generation.

The Lord's strong words to them at this time were a test and a challenge as to the sincerity of their hearts. He wanted more than a cry for His help or even a recognition that they had erred if He were to grant them deliverance. He demanded both words and actions that demonstrated a true change of heart. It had the desired effect: "And the children of Israel said unto the Lord, We have sinned: do unto us whatsoever seemeth good unto thee; deliver us only, we pray thee, this day" (v.15). The words were backed up by positive actions: "And they put away the strange gods from among them, and served the Lord" (v.16).

Verses 16b-18: The Lord's Grief

There is a danger of dwelling on how the children of Israel felt at this time under the yoke of the Ammonites and to forget how the Lord felt. It was not a cold and heartless God who was chastising His people. It is "whom the Lord loveth he chasteneth" (Heb 12.6). If the children of Israel had lost all feelings for Him, the same charge could not be levelled against Him. He felt their sufferings to a depth they would never know: "and his soul was grieved for the misery of Israel" (v.16). It was not their repentance, genuine as it might have been, that led to their deliverance. Any hope of restoration for them rested in His feelings for them, not in any words or actions on their part. The words of Isaiah provide an appropriate commentary on this moving scene: "I will mention the lovingkindnesses of the Lord ... the multitude of his lovingkindnesses ... in all their affliction he was afflicted, and the angel of his presence saved them: in his love and in his pity he redeemed them; and he bare them, and carried them all the days of old" (Is 63.7,9). It was the sight of their misery that grieved Him and led Him to reach out and meet their need. The word translated "grieved" (QATSAR - 7114) can also mean, "curtailed, shortened", thus suggesting His desire to bring their sufferings to an end. Although His holiness means that He must judge the sin and rebellion of His people, His heart is always towards them to deliver them from the misery that they have brought upon themselves. "It is of the Lord's mercies that we are not consumed, because his compassions fail not" (Lam 3.22).

Fortified and refreshed by the Lord's compassion towards them and their subsequent restoration, the children of Israel were able to go out and face the might of the Ammonites, instead of succumbing to their cruel oppression: "Then the children of Ammon were gathered together, and encamped in Gilead. And the children of Israel assembled themselves together, and encamped in Mizpeh" (v.17). The exact location of Mizpeh, which means "watchtower", is uncertain. However, the years of idolatry and oppression had not been conducive to the development of leaders and therefore there was no one to lead the army against the Ammonites: "And the people and princes of Gilead said one to another, What man is he that will begin to fight against the children of Ammon?" (v.18). This was the first time they had been in the position of not having a divinely appointed judge, which was once again a sign of their low spiritual condition. They did not seek the Lord's guidance in the matter, but in order to attract a suitable candidate they promised that he would become "head over all the inhabitants of Gilead" (v.18). It was this response that paved the way for the arrival of Jephthah on the scene.

JUDGES 11

At the close of the previous chapter the children of Israel and leaders in Gilead had asked a pressing question to which there seemed no immediate answer: "What man is he that will begin to fight against the children of Ammon?" (10.18). For the first time they were faced with the situation when there was no identified leader who had been raised up by God to deliver them from their oppressors. Perhaps this in itself was designed by the Lord to test them as to their spiritual exercises after their being immersed in idolatry for so many years. Some commentators believe that they may have sought divine counsel from the high priest or that the Spirit of God secretly led them in their quest for a leader. However, there is no indication of this in the Word of God. Having forsaken God for so long, it is not surprising to discover that the leaders in Gilead appear to have had no inclination to seek the Lord's guidance as to who their captain should be. Nevertheless, they responded to the urgent need of the hour and chose Jephthah (vv.4-6).

However, it would be incorrect to reach the conclusion that the elders made the wrong choice of Jephthah as leader. The parenthetical section in vv.1-3 confirms that the Lord is sovereign and He is always in control of the affairs of men. Clearly, the Lord had His man to meet the need of the day and therefore Jephthah is introduced before it is recorded that the leaders turned to him for help. Commentators who wish to prove that Jephthah was the people's choice, and not God's, point to the numerous flaws in his character and actions that were revealed as events unfolded; and it has to be conceded that he was far from perfect. However, this would be to ignore the Lord's verdict, which placed him in the great "gallery of faith" of Hebrews 11: "And what shall I more say? for the time would fail me to tell of Gedeon, and of Barak, and of Samson, and of Jephthae; of David also, and Samuel, and of the prophets ... these all, having obtained a good report though faith" (Heb 11.32,39). There is a natural tendency to be preoccupied with Jephthah's shortcomings, but the Lord honoured his faith.

Verses 1-3: The Leader's Rejection

Paul's words to the Corinthian believers are particularly appropriate in relation to this parenthetical section introducing Jephthah: "For ye see your calling, brethren, how that not many wise men after the flesh, not many mighty, not many noble, are called: but God hath chosen the foolish things of the world to confound the wise; and God hath chosen the weak things of the world to confound the things which are mighty; and base things of the world, and things which are despised, hath God chosen, yea, and things which are not, to bring to nought things that are: that no flesh should glory in his presence" (1 Cor 1.26-29). The pen-picture that is given of Jephthah in this opening section reflects the truth of these words. He may be described as "a mighty man of valour" (v.1), but he would appear to have been the most inappropriate choice as leader that the elders could have found. He most certainly had nothing in the flesh of which to glory.

His birth (v.1)

Jephthah's origins were less than desirable and hardly designed to inspire confidence in others that he was suitable material for leadership of the children of Israel: "Now Jephthah the Gileadite … was the son of a harlot: and Gilead begat Jephthah" (v.1). His father bore the name of the founder of "the family of the Gileadites" (Num 26.29). Although he appears to have had only one wife, he had a relationship with a harlot, which led to the birth of Jephthah. It is possible that his mother was not an Israelite, but from one of the surrounding nations.

His worth (v.2)

Clearly, in spite of his illegitimate birth, Jephthah's father had allowed him to grow up in the family home. However, when Gilead's legitimate sons had grown to maturity, "they thrust out Jephthah". Their words revealed that they considered him to be the worthless "son of a strange woman". He was considered to be an outsider and therefore deserving of their contempt. They were content to thrust him out to find his own way in life. Little did they realise that they had the potential leader of the people in their midst! Jephthah was in an even more difficult position than Abimelech, who was the son of Gideon's concubine (8.31). The word of God was clear about the son of a harlot: "A bastard shall not enter into the congregation of the Lord; even to his tenth generation shall he not enter into the congregation of the Lord" (Deut 23.2). However, it is highly unlikely that this was the reason for the actions of Jephthah's half-brothers. Their words revealed their true motives: "Thou shalt not inherit in our father's house". They were more concerned about their own financial security than they were about upholding the truth of God's word. Such a hostile and heartless rejection must have wounded Jephthah. There is evidence as the chapter progresses that their actions rankled with him and, unlike Joseph before him, he never truly forgave them.

His work (v.3)

The hatred towards Jephthah was so intense that he "fled from his brethren, and dwelt in the land of Tob". A.E.Cundall writes, "Tob has been identified with the modern el-Taiyibeh, about fifteen miles (24 kilometres) east-north-east of Ramoth-gilead, in the desolate area which lay just outside the eastern boundary of Israel and the northern frontier of Ammon" (*Judges – An Introduction and Commentary*). Some commentators have suggested that it may have been in the land of his mother's kindred. Wherever it was, it was there, in strange and unusual circumstances, that God prepared him for the leadership of His people. He had already proved himself to be "a mighty man of valour" (v.1) and therefore it did not take him long to attract others: "and there were gathered vain (empty, worthless - 7386) men to Jephthah, and went out with him". He became the brigand-leader of this group of worthless, idle and unprincipled men. He gathered around him those with whom he had some empathy; those who like him were despised and rejected. It is possible that they carried out successful raids against the Ammonites, news of which may have spread to the elders of Gilead. However, there is no evidence in the text to substantiate this.

It would be possible at the outset to take a negative stance in relation to Jephthah's character and actions. However, it is important to remember that he was the man whom God was going to use to deliver His people. He was more offended against than offending in the early stages of his life. He cannot be blamed for being the son of a harlot or for the jealousy and hatred of his brothers that drove him to Tob. Indeed, a consideration of some striking parallels with other events and people in the Scriptures would guard against any hasty judgments regarding him.

Firstly, there is a remarkable similarity between the way in which the children of Israel had treated the Lord in the previous chapter and the way in which the Gileadites treated Jephthah. The children of Israel both used and abused the Lord as it suited them. If that was how they treated Him, it was no surprise that they treated Jephthah, His servant, in the same way. The Lord Jesus told his disciples, "If the world hate you, ye know that it hated me before it hated you. If ye were of the world, the world would love his own: but because ye are not of the world, but I have chosen you out of the world, therefore the world hateth you" (Jn 15.18-19).

Secondly, there is a parallel with the experiences of David. Hated and hunted down by the jealousy of Saul, he sought refuge in the cave of Adullam. It was there that "every one that was in distress, and every one that was in debt, and every one that was discontented, gathered themselves unto him: and he became a captain over them" (1 Sam 22.2). Like Jephthah, David felt the rejection: "I cried … I poured out my complaint … my spirit was overwhelmed … there was no man that would know me: refuge failed me; no man cared for my soul" (Ps 142.1-4). Saul's hostility later increased to such an extent that he decided, "there is nothing better for me than that I should speedily escape into the land of the Philistines (1 Sam 27.1), and it was there that he led a band of men into battle against the enemies around.

Thirdly, the fact that Jephthah was despised and rejected by his brethren inevitably points to Christ, of whom Isaiah wrote, "He is despised and rejected of men; a man of sorrows, and acquainted with grief" (Is 53.3). John said of Him, "He came unto his own, and his own received him not" (Jn 1.11). Jephthah can, of course, only be a very faint picture of Christ – the fact that he was "the son of harlot" means that great caution must be exercised in making the application. S.Ridout expresses it well: "It is a despised and rejected one who can effect a deliverance ... the only deliverer, then, of the people of God from the power of evil and evil doctrine is one who himself has been rejected by his brethren. So it points us in this way to Christ as the only One who can deliver" (*Lectures on the Book of Judges*).

Verses 4-11: The Leader's Return

The course of events, left at the conclusion of ch.10, is now picked up. "The children of Ammon made war against Israel" (v.4) and this sharpened the resolve of the elders of Gilead to call the leader who could meet the need: "And it was so, that when the children of Ammon made war against Israel, the elders of Gilead went to fetch Jephthah out of the land of Tob: and they said unto Jephthah, Come, and be our captain, that we may fight with the children of Ammon" (vv.5-6). Clearly, news of his exploits in leading his band of "vain men" must have reached their ears. Although not all of the people would have shared in the elders' enthusiasm for Jephthah's return, as far as they were concerned he was the only one qualified to lead them.

Jephthah's response implied that the elders had been involved in his expulsion from the country: "Did not ye hate me, and expel me out of my father's house? and why are ye come unto me now when ye are in distress?" (v.7). They would undoubtedly have been in agreement with, if not personally involved in, the harsh treatment meted out to him by his brethren. Clearly, a forgiving spirit did not feature very highly in Jephthah's make-up: there was too much emphasis on self about him for that to be so. He could not have joined Joseph and said to his brethren, "So now it was not you that sent me hither, but God": neither would he have "kissed all his brethren, and wept upon them" (Gen 45.8,15) as Joseph had done. Both he and the elders were guilty of less than spiritual responses at this stage. Unlike Joseph, he would not let go the past and, unlike Joseph's brethren, they stopped short of expressing any remorse for what they had done. They did not respond to Jephthah's questions, but were driven solely by a political desire for deliverance from the Ammonites: "Therefore we turn again to thee now, that thou mayest go with us, and fight against the children of Ammon, and be our head over all the inhabitants of Gilead" (v.8). At least they were prepared to swallow their pride, although self-interest was the over-riding motive for their actions. It has to be acknowledged that there is a sense in which Jephthah's anger towards them was justified in the light of what they had done and that they reaped what they had sown. Indeed, his response mirrored the Lord's response to the children of Israel in the previous chapter (cf. 10.11-14). The difference, of course, was that there was no vindictiveness on the Lord's part towards His people as there was with Jephthah. The Lord chastened them out of genuine love for them.

There was a strange mixture of the spiritual and unspiritual in the hard bargain that Jephthah drove with the elders: "If ye bring me home again to fight against the children of Ammon, and the Lord deliver them before me, shall I be your head?" (v.9). He did not trust them and therefore pressed them on the offer they had made. He not only wanted to lead them into battle, but he coveted headship over them following the victory. He was not going to let the moment slip by without gaining the maximum from it in return for what they had done in rejecting him. He could not have entered into the spirit of Peter's words to elders, "taking the oversight thereof, not by constraint, but willingly; not for filthy lucre, but of a ready mind" (1 Pet 5.2). However, it would be unfair to condemn him as a mere unprincipled opportunist who was seeking only to look after his own interests. Clear indications of his spirituality shone through when he mentioned "the Lord", testifying to his dependence on Him for any success in the battle. He introduced therefore a dimension that was totally absent from the words of the elders. It is harmful to the welfare of the Lord's people if those who lead them do not know God and seek purely political solutions to spiritual problems. Clearly, Jephthah knew God and he displayed this throughout the remainder of his exploits. He spoke of "the Lord" (vv.9,31,35), "the Lord God of Israel" (vv.21,23), "the Lord our God" (v.24) and "the Lord the Judge" (v.27). He knew Him as Jehovah, the eternal, covenant-keeping God. The clear message is that, in spite of the scheming of men, the Lord was in control of all that took place.

True to form, the elders accepted the demands of Jephthah and, for once, decided to bring the Lord's name into their deliberations by calling upon Him as a witness to the agreement: "The Lord be witness between us, if we do not so according to thy words" (v.10). At this point, "Jephthah went with the elders of Gilead, and the people made him head and captain over them: and Jephthah uttered all his words before the Lord in Mizpeh" (v.11). A.R.Fausset writes, "The high priest with an ephod may have been summoned to Mizpeh or Ramoth Gilead, as being a Levitical city (Josh 21.34,38), but there is no clear proof that the words 'before the Lord' express more than that he solemnly confirmed his engagement as before the omnipresent God of Israel" (*A Critical and Expository Commentary on the Book of Judges*). This must have been an amazing scene when the rejected and despised servant returned as head and captain. The "son of a strange woman" (v.2) was finally vindicated before all. It can only be a matter of conjecture as to how his brothers must have felt when he returned. The Lord always vindicates His servants before the eyes of those who cast them out. He did so with Joseph, David and Jephthah. He will do so for His Perfect Servant, the Lord Jesus Christ, in a coming day: "Behold he cometh with clouds; and every eye shall see him, and they also which pierced him: and all kindreds of the earth shall wail because of him. Even so, Amen" (Rev 1.7).

Verses 12-28: The Leader's Negotiation

Jephthah soon dispelled any doubts some might have had that he was no more than a bloodthirsty brigand-leader who was bent solely on warfare and destruction. His first move as leader was to enter into patient negotiations with the enemy: "And Jephthah sent messengers unto the king of the children of Ammon" (v.12). Some commentators have criticised the length of time he took in seeking to make peace with the Ammonites. They complain that he spent more time negotiating with the enemy than he did with the people of God, and there may be an element of truth in this. However, it can be argued that he was simply being obedient to the Word of God: "When thou comest nigh unto a city to fight against it, then proclaim peace unto it" (Deut 20.10).

In many ways, Jephthah's handling of the Ammonites provides believers with a sound example as to how to handle false teachers. Firstly, his manner was right. He did not display hostility, anger or vindictiveness. He revealed a meekness of spirit that ensured the listening ear of the Ammonites. Secondly, his method was right. He did not rush in to destroy them, but he gave them every opportunity to reach a peaceable agreement. However, it is important to note that he took the initiative and sent messengers to them. He was never on the defensive: he did not sit and wait for them to attack him. Thirdly, his material was right. He confronted their challenge with the Scriptures. The name Jephthah (3316) means, "he will open". His desire was to open up the truth of God's Word to the gainsayers. His lengthy message to them revealed that he was well acquainted with the content of the Pentateuch. The Lord's people are at their weakest in the face of false teaching when they do not know what God's Word says. The fact that he based his arguments on the Scriptures ensured that there was no compromise on his part with the enemy; if what they were saying and doing was contrary to what God said, they were wrong and stood condemned.

In these early stages Jephthah reflected the words of Paul to Timothy, "And the servant of the Lord must not strive; but be gentle unto all men, apt to teach, patient, in meekness instructing those that oppose themselves; if God peradventure will give them repentance to the acknowledging of the truth; and that they may recover themselves out of the snare of the devil, who are taken captive by him at his will" (2 Tim 2.24-26).

Jephthah's approach would no doubt have surprised the Ammonites. They were not accustomed to being called upon to give reasons for their actions or to entering into negotiations of this nature. Jephthah's initial question to them through the messengers, "What hast thou to do with me, that thou art come against me to fight in my land?" (v.12), was met with a swift and curt response from the king of the children of Ammon: "Because Israel took away my land, when they came up out of Egypt, from Arnon even unto Jabbok, and unto Jordan: now therefore restore those lands again peaceably" (v.13). He argued that he was only claiming land that Israel had stolen from the Ammonites in the first place. However, he was not going to shake off Jephthah that easily: he proceeded to draw on Scripture to combat the king's distortion of the truth.

Firstly, through the mouth of his messengers (v.14), Jephthah reminded the king of the true course of events that proved "Israel took not away the land of Moab, nor the land of the children of Ammon" (v.15). He took him back to the point when Moses and the children of Israel came up out of Egypt by way of "the wilderness unto the Red sea" (v.16). When they reached Kadesh, they had sent messengers to both the king of Ammon and the king of Moab. Their simple request, "Let me, I pray thee, pass through thy land", was rejected by both kings (v.17). The result was that they had "compassed the land of Edom, and the land of Moab, and came by the east side of the land of Moab, and pitched on the other side of Arnon, but came not within the border of Moab: for Arnon was the border of Moab" (v.18). For Israel to have done otherwise would have meant disobedience to the word of God: "Distress not the Moabites, neither contend with them in battle: for I will not give thee of their land for a possession...and when thou comest nigh over against the children of Ammon, distress them not, nor meddle with them: for I will not give thee of the land of the children of Ammon any possession" (Deut 2.9,19). However, they had occupied the land north of Arnon, which was in the hands of Sihon, king of the Amorites. He had refused the children of Israel entry through his territory (v.19) and, indeed, had "gathered all his people together, and pitched in Jahaz, and fought against Israel" (v.20). Jephthah emphasised that "the Lord God of Israel" gave the children of Israel the victory and they "possessed all the land of the Amorites, the inhabitants of that country. And they possessed all the coasts of the Amorites, from Arnon even unto Jabbok, and from the wilderness even unto Jordan" (vv.21,22). This was the very territory that the king of the Ammonites was disputing with Jephthah.

The message from the Scriptures was clear; the king of the Ammonites was distorting the truth in claiming, "Israel took away my land" (v.13). The land did not belong to the Ammonites or the Moabites when Israel had taken possession of it. It was "the land of the Amorites ... the coasts of the Amorites" (vv.21,22) and the children of Israel had possessed it by right of conquest. Jephthah simply stated the facts of Scripture and let them speak for themselves. It is a useful exercise from time-to-time to take stock of the Lord's dealings with His people as revealed in the Scriptures. Peter and Stephen did so to great effect in the Acts of the Apostles. It not only condemns and stops the mouths of the false teachers, but it also encourages the Lord's people to see His hand at work throughout history. He is, indeed, the sovereign Lord.

Secondly, Jephthah strengthened his argument still further by grounding Israel's possession of the land in what the Lord had done for them. He made it clear that they only possessed it, because the Lord had dispossessed the Amorites: "So now the Lord God of Israel hath dispossessed the Amorites from before his people Israel, and shouldest thou possess it?" (v.23). He challenged them on the grounds of their own beliefs: ""Wilt thou not possess that which Chemosh thy god giveth thee to possess? So whomsoever the Lord our God shall drive out from before us, them will we possess" (v.24). It would be wrong, of course, to deduce from this that Jephthah believed in the existence of Chemosh. He was simply referring to it in his line of argument to substantiate that their case for possession of the land was spurious. They should be satisfied with what they believed their god had given them and not seek to take what the Lord had given Israel.

Jephthah's mention of Chemosh has caused difficulties for some commentators, since Chemosh was the god of the Moabites, not the Ammonites. Their god was Milcom or Molech (I Kings 11.5,7). Some believe that Jephthah simply got it wrong here. However, the close links between the Moabites and the Ammonites may have meant that the Ammonites also worshipped Chemosh. It is perhaps significant that Jephthah linked both Moab and Ammon together throughout his review of Israel's history. Others have suggested that the Ammonites conquered the land of the Moabites south of Arnon before they marched on Israel, and by the time they marched against Israel from that direction, they had taken on the worship of Chemosh.

Thirdly, Jephthah took the king of the Ammonites back to the actions of a past king of the Moabites: "And now art thou any thing better than Balak the son of Zippor, king of Moab? did he ever strive against Israel, or did he ever fight against them?" (v.25). Balak's concern was not that the children of Israel had taken his land, but that their presence and strength posed a threat to the Moabites. He had said to Balaam, "Come now therefore, I pray thee, curse me this people; for they are too mighty for me" (Num 22.6). He would love to have driven them out, but he did not do so. He recognised their rights and refrained from entering into warfare against them. Jephthah's appeal to the king of the Ammonites was that he should learn from Balak and act wisely in relation to Israel.

Fourthly, Jephthah concluded his argument by casting doubt upon the sincerity of the king's actions in raising the matter after such a long time. Israel had been living in the area for three hundred years and the Ammonites had made no claim upon the territory before: "While Israel dwelt in Heshbon and her towns, and in Aroer and her towns, and in all the cities that be along by the coasts of Arnon, three hundred years? why therefore did ye not recover them within that time?" (v.26). If this was their land and they felt so passionately about it, it was strange that it had taken so long for it to become a major point of contention! Jephthah's mention of three hundred years testifies to the accuracy of his facts. The period of the judges had run for three hundred and nineteen years up to that point, but if the eighteen years of Ammonite oppression (10.8) are subtracted it can be seen how precise he was in his negotiations.

Although Jephthah displayed great patience in laying out the truth of Scripture before the king of the Ammonites, there was no doubt as to where he stood. There was absolute conviction and assurance in his message as he placed the responsibility firmly in the court of the Ammonites: "Wherefore I have not sinned against thee, but thou doest me wrong to war against me: the Lord the Judge be judge this day between the children of Israel and the children of Ammon" (v.27). Jephthah was totally confident that the Lord would prove in the events that followed that the children of Israel were in the right. However, it was no surprise that the Ammonites remained unmoved by any reasoning from Scripture: "the king of the children of Ammon hearkened not unto the words of Jephthah which he sent him" (v.28)

Verses 29-31: The Leader's Vow

Following Jephthah's painstaking negotiations with the Ammonites from the Scriptures, the Lord placed His seal of approval on His servant: "Then the Spirit of the Lord came upon Jephthah" (v.29). The words "came upon" (exist, come to pass - 1961) do not have the same force as those used of Gideon. In the commentary on ch.6 it was noted, "the Spirit of God came upon (wrapped around or clothed Himself with - 3847) Gideon" (6.34). However, Jephthah was nonetheless empowered by God to deliver His people. It is only a man who is empowered by the Spirit of God who is qualified to lead others and to accomplish the Lord's work. Jephthah may have gained success in his own strength in leading his band of "vain men" (v.3) when he was in exile, but any success against the Ammonites had to be, "Not by might, nor by power, but my spirit, saith the Lord of hosts" (Zech 4.6). Further to this confirmation that the Lord was with him, he went out in person to recruit his army: "and he passed over Gilead, and Manasseh, and passed over Mizpeh of Gilead, and from Mizpeh of Gilead he passed over unto the children of Ammon" (v.29).

However, in spite of his evident knowledge of the Scriptures and the Spirit's power available to him, Jephthah's lack of knowledge of God and failure to depend totally upon the Spirit's power, cast a dark cloud over events that would haunt him for the remainder of his days and cost him dear. He had shown great patience in his initial dealings with the Ammonites, but at this point he acted rashly in making a vow to the Lord: "If thou shalt without fail deliver the children of Ammon into mine hands, then it shall be, that whatsoever cometh forth of the doors of my house to meet me, when I return in peace from the children of Ammon, shall surely be the Lord's, and I will offer it up for a burnt offering" (vv.30-31). It is dangerous to attribute motives to Jephthah that are not stated in the text, but his vow was probably made out of devotion to and zeal for the Lord.

Some commentators submit that he was bargaining with the Lord. Vows were permissible in Old Testament times and were always made voluntarily. J.J.Stubbs makes some helpful observations concerning Old Testament vows: "There they are generally in reference to God, and may be made to perform something (Gen 28.20-22), to abstain from something (Ps 132.2-5), or be an act in return for God's favour (Num 21.1-3), or an expression of devotion to God (Ps 22.25). No sin was committed whether a vow were made or not made, but if it were made or actually uttered it became solemnly binding as far as God was concerned. This is clear from Deuteronomy 23.21-23 where the principle is stressed that vows must be discharged as soon as possible. Vows were not to be made rashly (Prov 20.25) ... In this age of grace then, the believer is not under any oath, nor required to make promises of something to God ... The child of God in the Christian dispensation can live a life of devotion to Christ and to God, but it is only by the power of the indwelling Holy Spirit that he or she is able to fulfil any spiritual obligations" (*Numbers – Ritchie Old Testament Commentaries*).

Clearly, Jephthah's vow involved a "burnt offering" (ascending, going up in smoke - 5930). It is true that the word "whatsoever" in Hebrew does not specify either species or gender, but the language that follows makes it difficult to believe that he had anything other than a human sacrifice in view. "Then it shall be, that whatsoever cometh forth of the doors of my house to meet me" is hardly the language that would be appropriate in relation to an animal. Jephthah may have had an impressive knowledge of the history of the children of Israel from the Scriptures, but he was selective in what he chose to know. If it were to be a human sacrifice that he had in view, a more intimate knowledge of the Scriptures would have led him to the conclusion that his vow was totally unacceptable and abhorrent to God (Lev 18.21; 20.1-5; Deut 12.29-31; 18.9-14) and therefore he would not have made it. Whether he actually sacrificed his daughter or not will be considered at the close of the chapter.

Verses 32-33: The Leader's Victory

Jephthah's victory over the Ammonites is dealt with swiftly and succinctly in the divine record: "So Jephthah passed over unto the children of Ammon to fight against them; and the Lord delivered them into his hands." (v.32). He was not content with anything less than a comprehensive victory and therefore his pursuit of the Ammonites went beyond the immediate battle and embraced their cities: "And he smote them from Aroer, even till thou come to Minnith, even twenty cities, and unto the plain of the vineyards with a very great slaughter. Thus the children of Ammon were subdued before the children of Israel" (v.33). It is probable that Aroer was their capital city, but the location of Minnith is uncertain. The brevity of the account seems to suggest that the divinely inspired writer was anxious to bring his readers back to the outcome of Jephthah's vow and his actions towards the men of Ephraim (12.1-6).

Verses 34-40: The Leader's Anguish

Such a resounding victory ought to have been the highlight of Jephthah's life and his homecoming should have been joyous. Indeed, it started out in that way: "And Jephthah came to Mizpeh unto his house, and, behold, his daughter came out to meet him with timbrels and with dances: and she was his only child; beside her he had neither son nor daughter" (v.34). To the unknowing eye there were few scenes of domestic bliss and harmony that could have compared with this. This erstwhile brigand leader, unlike many of his day, had been content with one wife and one daughter. She had, no doubt, experienced with him the hardships of exile as he led his band of men, but now she saw him returning victorious as the leader of his people. Little did she know how short-lived the excitement of the occasion would be. It was not the first time, and it would certainly not be the last, when the joy of victory for the Lord's people would be marred by sorrow and tragedy through the rash actions of men.

Jephthah was confronted with the folly of his vow in a way that he could never have imagined: "And it came to pass, when he saw her, that he rent his clothes, and said, Alas, my daughter! thou hast brought me very low, and thou art one of them that trouble me: for I have opened my mouth unto the Lord, and I cannot go back" (v.35). Like Ahab with Elijah (cf. 1 Kings 18.17), Jephthah failed to see that he was the source of the "trouble", not his daughter. His vow had not only come back on him, but it had impacted on her more than on himself. He stands as a constant reminder to the Lord's servants to set a guard on what they say, since the Lord will often test them on their boasts.

His daughter's gentle and gracious resignation to the consequences of what her father had done was the only ray of light in this darkest of scenes: "My father, if thou hast opened thy mouth unto the Lord, do to me according to that which hath proceeded out of thy mouth; forasmuch as the Lord hath taken vengeance for thee of thine enemies, even of the children of Ammon" (v.36). Her commitment, loyalty and unquestioning submission to both the Lord and her father stand as an amazing testimony to believers of all generations. She was prepared to pay the ultimate price in order for the vow unto the Lord to be met. This is not to say, of course, that she did not feel the cost to the depth of her being. The emphasis in the closing verses of the chapter on her virginity bears testimony to the pain she felt: "Let this thing be done for me: let me alone two months, that I may go up and down upon the mountains, and bewail (weep, bemoan - 1058) my virginity, I and my fellows" (v.37). The greatest heartache for her was the fact that she would be barren, which was a cause of great distress for any woman of the day (cf. 1 Sam 1.5-7). The fact that she was Jephthah's only daughter also meant that his family line would cease. What should have been a scene of great rejoicing and hope had, indeed, become a place of tears!

Jephthah granted her wish and said, "Go. And he sent her away for two months: and she went with her companions, and bewailed her virginity upon the mountains" (v.39). Again, the surrender of this woman to her father's will was touching: "And it came to pass at the end of two months, that she returned unto her father" (v.39). There was no question of her not returning at the conclusion of the two months: she promised she would, and she did, in spite of the prospect of sacrifice. The moment of truth, however, had to come and Jephthah "did with her according to his vow which he had vowed: and she knew no man" (v.39). Her remarkable act of submission became "a custom in Israel ... the daughters of Israel went yearly to lament (celebrate, ascribe praise, attribute honour, commemorate - 8567) the daughter of Jephthah the Gileadite four days in a year" (v.40).

The statement that Jephthah "did with her according to his vow which he had vowed" (v.39) has caused much debate among, and divided, commentators over the years: does it mean that he literally offered his daughter as a burnt offering or not? It may be helpful to survey some the arguments for and against and the reader will then have to come to his or her own prayerful conclusion.

Arguments in favour of the belief that Jephthah sacrificed his daughter

1. It is difficult to ignore the clear statement, "who did with her according to his vow which he had vowed: and she knew no man (*i.e. she had never known a man*)" (v.39).

2. The Hebrew word for "burnt offering" (OLAH - 5930) usually indicates a sacrificial offering. There is no indication that Jephthah intended the offering to be anything other than a literal burnt offering.

3. It is clear from the language employed that Jephthah expected to offer a human sacrifice – "whatever cometh forth of the doors of my house to meet me" (v.31) is not the language that he would have used if he was expecting an animal to meet him. Indeed, he did not express any surprise when a person confronted him on his return: the tragedy for him was that it was his only daughter. He probably expected to be confronted by a lowly slave.

4. Jephthah's action in slaying 42,000 Ephraimites (12.6) demonstrates that he was perfectly capable of committing such an act. He was inconsistent in the ways in which he acted. He could exercise patience with the enemy and then be harsh in the treatment of his brethren.

5. Jephthah was not a man who would go back on this word – "I have opened my mouth unto the Lord, and I cannot go back (v.35).

6. The promise of a life of perpetual virginity for his daughter, which some commentators believe was the final outcome (referred to in point 3 below), did not feature in Jephthah's vow. His distress (v.35), the two-

month reprieve granted to her (v.38) and an annual four-day feast to lament her (v.40) would appear to be somewhat excessive and unnecessary if perpetual virginity was the final outcome of his vow. There is no indication in the text that she joined a special group of holy women attached to the sanctuary in Shiloh (Ex 38.8; 1 Sam 2.22) as others have suggested. Indeed, there is no justification for believing that those women were virgins.

7. The tabernacle at Shiloh, where his daughter would have gone to live her celibate life, was in Ephraim, which was hostile territory for Jephthah (12.2). It would have been unlikely therefore that they would have received her there.

8. God often takes His people up on their boasts and that is precisely what He did with Jephthah.

9. "To lament" (v.40), means that the daughters of Israel came each year to rehearse the story and to bewail her virginity. It does not indicate in v.40 that they came to meet her: they simply came "to lament the daughter of Jephthah".

10. Jephthah was a legal man who could not bear to lose face, even if he knew God's law of the redemption price that could be paid for his daughter (Ex 13.11-13; Lev 27.2-5). He was prepared to sacrifice another if it was to his own advantage so to do.

11. The brevity of the text gives a clear impression that something tragic took place that the writer did not wish to dwell upon or to over dramatise.

Arguments against the belief that Jephthah sacrificed his daughter

1. If Jephthah did sacrifice her, the Lord would have condemned it, because it would have been abhorrent to Him and against His law.

2. A man upon whom "the Spirit of the Lord came" (v.29) would not have committed such an act. It does not sit easily with a man who had his knowledge of the Scriptures and who had given the Lord such a prominent place in his words and actions (vv.9,11,27,30,35). In spite of the low spiritual conditions of the day, it is inconceivable to think that, as a judge, he would have approved of human sacrifice.

3. The meaning of the first part of v.39 comes out in the phrase "and she knew no man *(i.e. after that)*". This indicates that the vow was fulfilled in her life of perpetual virginity. It was a spiritual burnt offering on the part of Jephthah. It may be that he sent her to join the holy women that "assembled at the door of the tabernacle of the congregation" (Ex 38.8; 1 Sam 2.22) in Shiloh. These women had renounced worldly ties and therefore in a very real sense were "dead to the world".

4. There was little point in her bewailing her virginity (v.37) for two months if she were to be sacrificed immediately on her return. She would have wanted to spend her final days with her family. The two months would have given Jephthah time to reflect on his vow and to consider how he could fulfil it without sacrificing her.

5. If Jephthah did sacrifice her, it is inconceivable that he should have been included in the great gallery of faith of Hebrews 11 or that Samuel would have spoken of him so positively shortly after the event (1 Sam 12.11).

6. The Mosaic law imposed the death penalty on those who sacrificed one of their children to Molech (Lev 20.2). If Jephthah had sacrificed his daughter, even though it was to the Lord, it is hard to believe that divine record and the children of Israel would not have condemned him. Indeed, the men of Ephraim did not mention it when they criticised him (12.1), and it appears that he continued to be accepted as a judge until his death (12.7).

7. It is difficult to see where Jephthah would have sacrificed her and who would have been prepared to do it.

8. The text allows two alternatives to his vow: the word "and" in the phrase, "and I will offer it up" (v.31) can be translated "or". Jephthah would either dedicate whoever met him to Jehovah (if it were a person) or offer it as a burnt offering (if it were an animal). As it was a person, albeit his daughter, he dedicated her to perpetual virginity.

9. It is not stated explicitly in the text that Jephthah sacrificed her.

10. "To lament" (v.40) can have the thought of celebrating and praising. It is not likely that the daughters of Israel would have come each year to celebrate a human sacrifice. It is more likely that they came each year to the tabernacle in Shiloh to commemorate her act of devotion that had allowed her father to fulfil his vow.

11. The hostility of Ephraim (12.2) would not have allowed Jephthah to sacrifice his daughter in Shiloh, where the tabernacle and the altar stood.

The various arguments expressed above serve to emphasise how difficult it is to reach a decision as to whether Jephthah did literally carry out his vow or not. C.J.Goslinga sums up the dilemma facing the reader when he writes, "The view that Jephthah's daughter was indeed sacrificed finds its strongest support in the literal words of vv.30-40; but the picture of Jephthah given elsewhere in Scripture (11.1-29; 12.1-7; 1 Sam 12.11; Heb 11.32) makes it hard to believe that he actually stooped to offer a human sacrifice. It is difficult to make a definite decision, and the dearth of evidence compels us to exercise caution. Although the former view may seem the most likely on first consideration, the latter remains possible. Indeed the mere fact that Jephthah retained his office of judge after v.39 speaks in its favour" (*Joshua, Judges, Ruth*). It is therefore the responsibility of each reader prayerfully to examine the divine record and to reach his or her own conclusions.

It is the present writer's belief that the statement, "who did with her according to his vow which he had vowed" (v.39), makes it difficult to reach any other conclusion than that he offered his daughter up as a burnt offering to the Lord. However, this conclusion is held humbly before the

Lord, acknowledging that the sincerely held views of others may well be correct. Committing his daughter to perpetual virginity was never part of Jephthah's vow. His later ill-treatment of the Ephraimites (12.1-6) reveals the inconsistencies in his character and demonstrates that he would have been capable of such an act. Alternative views often appear to involve taking the text and making it fit a preferred image of Jephthah, rather than allowing the text to speak for itself. W.Kelly writes, "Scripture does not in any way vouch for the immaculateness of those even who wrought in faith. It does not throw a veil, as man loves to do, over that which is uncomely and distressing in those that bear the name of the Lord; especially as the very object the Spirit of God has here in view is to show the frightful results of a vow so little weighed before God, not at all drawn from His guidance … We can easily therefore comprehend how the holy wisdom of Scripture avoids details on a fact so contrary to the mind of God, as a man dealing thus with a human being, yea, with his own daughter. It seems to me then that the reserve of the Holy Spirit is as strikingly according to God as the rashness of Jephthah is a solemn warning to man" (*Lectures on the Book of Judges*).

JUDGES 12

Verses 1-6: The Leader's Severity

It is always an encouragement to see believers living together in harmony. The Psalmist wrote, "Behold, how good and how pleasant it is for brethren to dwell together in unity!" (Ps 133.1). It was the strength of the early believers in Jerusalem: "And all that believed were together, and had all things common … And the multitude of them that believed were of one heart and of one soul" (Acts 2.44; 4.32). However, it is not a pleasant sight for Satan; he recognises the potential in it for good and he will always seek to break it down. It is therefore sad to see believers 'at war' with each other and the unity shattered. It is one thing to contend with those who seek to threaten the harmony from without, but it quite another thing when the danger comes from within. The former is to be expected, but the latter ought to be anathema to believers.

Sadly, Gideon experienced disunity from within at the hands of the princes of Succoth and the men of Penuel (8.4-9). There was still further disunity after he died (8.33-35), which paved the way for the destructiveness of Abimelech. It was a sign of the increasingly dark days of the period of the judges that this lack of harmony appeared once more during Jephthah's days. Christians today would do well to heed the exhortation of Paul to the Thessalonians: "And be at peace among yourselves" (1 Thess 5.13).

As is so often the case during times of strife, blame rested on both sides in this sad incident. The men of Ephraim have to shoulder a major share of the responsibility for what ensued. If it had not been for their pride, the tragedy would not have occurred. However, they ran true to form: "And the men of Ephraim gathered themselves together, and went northward, and said unto Jephthah, Wherefore passedst thou over to fight against the children of Ammon, and didst not call us to go with thee? we will burn thine house upon thee with fire" (v.1). Clearly, they had not learned from their previous experiences to control their arrogant and aggressive spirit. They had witnessed the wise manner in which Gideon had dealt with their petulant behaviour in the past (8.1-3), and they had also been privileged to live through twenty-three years of the humble Tola's judgeship (10.1-2). However, their response to Jephthah gave clear evidence that there had been no inward change of heart on their part. Indeed, their confrontational stance had intensified in that not only had their words become more aggressive and malicious, but also they had gathered together an army with the intention of fighting against Jephthah. C.A.Coates describes them as, "touchy brethren; they are always ready to complain if they are left out" (*An Outline of the Book of Judges*). It was no surprise that they left their complaints until the battle was over. Once again, they were eaten up with pride and jealousy, traits they had already displayed in their dealings with Gideon. As soon as they discovered that threats did not work with Jephthah, they showed a total lack of wisdom by taunting him with the accusation that the Gileadites were traitors and deserters: "Ye Gileadites are fugitives (refugees that have escaped - 6412) of Ephraim among the Ephraimites, and among the Manassites" (v.4). The tribes of Reuben, Gad and half of the tribe of Manasseh had been allotted their land east of the Jordan by Moses (Num 32.29,33) and therefore their accusation was totally without foundation. Indeed, the Gileadites came partly from the half tribe of Manasseh and partly from Gad and therefore the reasons behind the charge that they were "fugitives of Ephraim" are unclear.

The Ephraimites soon discovered that they had picked on the wrong man to insult in this aggressive manner and they reaped the results of their folly. It has already been observed in the commentary on ch.8 that Gideon met their aggression towards him with humility and meekness. He needed their support and he appreciated that "a soft answer turneth away wrath" (Prov 15.1). However, they met their match in Jephthah: he had a much more combative style than Gideon. He began by rehearsing to them the truth as to what had really happened. Firstly, he pointed out how serious the situation had been: "I and my people were at great strife with the children of Ammon" (v.2). The implication was that the immediate danger he and his people were in had been of paramount importance to him, not the sensitivities of his brethren. Secondly, he reminded them that he had appealed to them for their help: "and when I called you, ye delivered me not out of their hands" (v.2.). Although there is no record of this call, there is no reason to doubt that it took place; they did not dispute the claim with him. Thirdly, with a mixture of self-aggrandisement and giving the glory to the Lord, he informed them, "when I saw that ye delivered me not, I put my life in my hands, and passed over against the children of Ammon, and the Lord delivered them into my hand" (v.3). Fourthly, he threw the challenge back to them: "wherefore then are ye come up unto me this day, to fight against me?" (v.3). The message was clear: by opposing him the men of Ephraim were, in fact, opposing God, and there could only be one loser in that battle. Unlike the language Gideon had used with them (8.2), Jephthah's message was not designed to make them feel good and it would certainly not feed their already oversized egos

The scene that developed was yet another dark blot on Israel's history in those days. Clearly, the attitude, words and actions of the men of Ephraim were reprehensible. A different response was called for from the one seen in Gideon's handling of them. Judgment on them needed to be swift and firm. The time had come when they had to learn that their proud, divisive, selfish, demoralising and destructive spirit would not be tolerated any longer. However, Jephthah's approach, although administered with his usual thoroughness and zeal, was harsh in the extreme. There was too much of self in his response to his brethren; he used the pronoun "I" or "me" on eleven occasions (vv.2-3). He had dealt severely with the Ammonite threat, and rightly so, but he responded with equal severity towards his brethren. Jude, in the New Testament, urged his readers to make "a difference (distinction, separation)" (v.22) in the way in which they dealt with those who were caught up in false teaching. Jephthah made no distinction in the way in which he dealt with the enemy and his own people; he was equally severe on both.

The tragic and disgraceful spectacle of brethren fighting with brethren followed on inevitably from the bitter war of words: "Then Jephthah gathered together all the men of Gilead, and fought with Ephraim: and the men of Gilead smote Ephraim" (v.4). Jephthah was ruthless in his pursuit of them: he was not prepared for any of them to escape punishment. He took and manned "the passages of Jordan" and devised a scheme to deal with any who sought to escape from judgment by that route (v.5). The Ephraimites' dialect distinguished them from others, which was just one sign of the gradual breakdown of the unity among the tribes. This one, seemingly insignificant, difference was used by Jephthah to cause even greater disunity. They had a peculiar way of pronouncing the word, "Shibboleth" (a flowing stream, ear or head of grain - 7641). They were unable to pronounce the sound of "sh", and therefore they called the word, "Sibboleth". Any Ephraimite who escaped, and then sought to conceal his identity (v.5), faced a simple test: "Then said they unto him, Say now Shibboleth: and he said Sibboleth: for he could not frame to pronounce it right" (v.6). The consequences of failing the test were severe: "Then they took him, and slew him at the passages of Jordan" (v.6). The outcome was that "there fell at that time of the Ephraimites forty and two thousand" (v.6).

It was ironical that the Ephraimites died at the same spot where they had cut off and slain the fleeing Midianites in the days of Gideon (7.24). Jordan was, of course, the river through which a united Israel had passed as Joshua led them into Canaan (Josh 3.14-17). F. C. Jennings writes, "This is certainly a strange place to slay his brethren. The ford of Jordan is the one spot which, we may say, alone united them; for here alone could Jordan, the river of death, be safely crossed and Gileadite and Ephraimite, be as one … but the one precious uniting place of all that is of God; it is just here that Jephthah cuts off his brethren!" (*Judges and Ruth*). Believers today need to stand uncompromisingly for the truth of God's word, but they must also take care not to introduce their own "shibboleths" and unreasonably cut off others who differ from themselves. Such a spirit is divisive and destroys the testimony. A.M.S.Gooding comments, "They slew a man because he couldn't pronounce one letter right – that's legality! And legality among the saints thousands of times since has slain fellow brethren and sisters because they couldn't say one word right" (*The 13 Judges*). Ephraim's defeat led to them losing their leading position among the tribes, a status that they never regained.

Verse 7: The Leader's Departure

The remainder of Jephthah's judgeship, following the slaughter of the Ammonites, may well have been carried out east of the Jordan. His treatment of the Ephraimites would probably have alienated him from those tribes immediately west of the river. However, as he passed from the scene, he was credited with the fact that he "judged Israel six years" (v.7), although this was the shortest period recorded for a judge. There can be no doubt that he had many noteworthy characteristics and he brought the Lord's deliverance to Israel. He was a decisive leader, who was good with words and skilled in battle. His knowledge of the Scriptures and acknowledgement of the Lord's hand in his life and that of the people are undeniable. Clearly, Samuel recognised his contribution (1 Sam 12.11) and the Lord honoured his faith (Heb 11.32). He nullified the considerable threat of the Ammonites and confronted the pride of the Ephraimites. He was not a man who sought to evade the issues that needed to be addressed. As has been pointed out in the commentary on ch.11, his rejection and links with the outcasts of society, and subsequent return as head over his people, point towards the Lord Jesus. However, his shortcomings meant that the deliverance he brought fell well short of perfection. His rash vow concerning his daughter and drastic treatment of the Ephraimites cast dark shadows over his achievements in bringing deliverance to the children of Israel. It is only the Lord Jesus who is "the author of eternal salvation unto all them that obey him" (Heb 5.9), and who has "obtained eternal redemption for us" (Heb 9.12). His work was perfect and complete. Jephthah "died … and was buried in one of the cities of Gilead", but sadly, he left no family to continue his name. Of the Lord Jesus it is said, "when thou shalt make his soul an offering for sin, he shall see his seed, he shall prolong his days, and the pleasure of the Lord shall prosper in his hand. He shall see of the travail of his soul, and shall be satisfied: by his knowledge shall my righteous servant justify many; for he shall bear their iniquities" (Is 53.10-11).

Ibzan, Elon and Abdon

Verses 8-15: The Leader's Successors – "and after him"

It was noted in the commentary on ch.8 that Gideon's defeat of the Midianites marked the last occasion in the book of Judges when it was recorded that God granted peace to the land: "And the country was in quietness forty years" (8.28). Up until that point it had been a recurring feature following his deliverance of the children of Israel from their enemies. Sadly, the people's rebellion and departure into idolatry had forfeited that peace. The best that they could hope for was periods of stability and relative peace brought by the various judges. Jephthah appears to have handed over stable conditions to his successors. The tranquil conditions were fragile and they were soon to be shattered at the hands of the Philistines, but for a combined total of twenty-five years, three judges maintained a measure of stability. As was the case with Tola and Jair (10.1-5), very little is recorded about them. There is no mention of stirring battles fought or victories won. However, this must not lead the reader to the conclusion that their impact was either minimal or unimportant. It would also be easy to put a negative slant on some of the things that are said of them, but the divine record does not.

Ibzan

He came from Bethlehem (v.8). However, this is very unlikely to have been Bethlehem in Judah, the birthplace of the Lord, but Bethlehem in Zebulun, some seven miles (11 kilometres) west-northwest of Nazareth (Josh 19.15; Judg 12.10). He came therefore from a good stock. Zebulun had already assisted in the defeat of Jabin and Sisera (4.10) and had received unqualified praise from Deborah and Barak for being among those who "jeoparded (exposed, despised, disdained - 2778) their lives unto the death in the high places of the field" (5.18). Reference to his "thirty sons, and thirty daughters" (v.9) suggests that he must have had a number of wives, but no comment is made on this. He "sent abroad *(gave in marriage to husbands from another clan)*" his daughters and "took in thirty daughters from abroad *(from another clan*) for his sons" (v.9). He stands in marked contrast to Jephthah whose one daughter was either assigned to perpetual virginity or sacrificed as a burnt offering, according to whichever view the reader holds to (the various views on this have been considered in the commentary on ch.11). If it were assumed that Ibzan, like Jair before him (10.4), brought his family up in the fear of the Lord, the spiritual influence of that family would have been considerable. A christian family today can also have a wide impact on many lives over a number of generations, particularly in days, like those of the judges, when there is a breakdown in family life (cf. 5.7).

Ibzan "judged Israel seven years" before he "died ... and was buried at Bethlehem" (vv.9-10). He was introduced as "Ibzan of Bethlehem" (v.8) and he died there. Although his family must have been spread far and wide, his sphere of service, including his seven years as judge, was entirely local. It is not easy for a believer to bear a consistent testimony throughout his life in the one place, but Ibzan achieved it.

Elon

Very little is known about Elon. He too was a Zebulonite and "he judged Israel ten years" (v.11). He died and "was buried in Aijalon in the country of Zebulun" (v.12). It has been suggested that there is a play on words here with the names Elon (ELOWN - 356), meaning "strength", and Aijalon (AYAL - 354) meaning, "a stag", coming from the same Hebrew root word (AYIL - 352). The stag is strong, yet graceful in its movements and perhaps this is suggestive of the quiet strength of Elon's judgship over the course of ten years. It would have taken great strength of character in such volatile times to bear a consistent testimony over such a period.

Abdon

Abdon (5658) means, "service" and " he judged Israel eight years" (v.14). He was "the son of Hillel (praising - 1985)" (v.13), suggestive of the fact that productive service springs out of a heart that is full of praise for the Lord. Unlike Ibzan and Elon, he did not come from Zebulun, but from "Pirathon in the land of Ephraim, in the mount of the Amalekites" (v.15). Although it is not stated, his presence must have given Ephraim back some dignity following their total humiliation at the hands of Jephthah. They had been privileged to have Tola in their company for twenty-three years and now they experienced eight years of faithful service from Abdon. Later on, Benaiah, one of David's mighty men, was a native of Pirathon (2 Sam 23.30).

Clearly, the size of his family meant that, like Gideon, Jair and Ibzan, he must have had several wives: "And he had forty sons and thirty nephews (grandsons - 1121)" (v.14). He was also a man of wealth; his sons and grandsons "rode on threescore and ten ass colts" (v.14). It was noted in the commentary on ch.10 that riding on ass colts was a symbol of peace and dignity, whereas the horse is a symbol of war. It suggests therefore that the service of Abdon, his sons and his grandsons (three generations) was directed towards the promotion and maintenance of peace and unity among the children of Israel.

The reference to "the mount of the Amalekites" (v.15) suggests that there was an Amalekite presence in Ephraim (cf. 5.14). However, Abdon appears to have overcome their influence and claimed their territory, because he was buried in "Pirathon … in the mount of the Amalekites" (v.15). Like Ibzan and Elon before him, his service for God and the children of Israel was local; he was born, lived and died in Pirathon.

JUDGES 13

Samson and the Philistines

The Evil of the Children of Israel - "But where sin abounded ..." (Rom 5.20)

"And the children of Israel did evil again in the sight of the Lord" (v.1). Although there is a familiar ring to this statement (cf. 2.11; 3.7,12; 4.1; 6.1; 10.6), the evidence of the following four chapters suggests that the children of Israel had reached a lower point than ever before in their downward spiritual spiral.

Firstly, Samson was the last of the saviours in the book of Judges and therefore there were no further deliverances recorded following his death. These were, indeed, "last days" and "perilous times" for the children of Israel (cf. 2 Tim 3.1).

Secondly, the spotlight fell on Samson as an individual to bring deliverance. He never led an army against his enemies as his predecessors had done, but faced them alone. S. Ridout observes, "National faithfulness is gone; you have scarcely anything but the individual. And in corporate things when you come down to the individual, mark my words, you come down to failure" (*Lectures on the Book of Judges*). One of the seven churches addressed in Revelation 2 and 3, the church of the Laodiceans, had lost its corporate testimony and therefore the Lord had to appeal to individuals within it: "Behold, I stand at the door and knock: if any man hear my voice, and open the door, I will come in to him, and will sup with him, and he with me" (Rev 3.20).

Thirdly, for the first time in the history of the judges, the deliverer ended up in the hands of the enemy and in need of deliverance himself. Samson's days as a judge drew to a close when, "the Philistines took him, and put out his eyes, and brought him down to Gaza, and bound him with fetters of brass; and he did grind in the prison house" (16.21).

Fourthly, "the Lord delivered them into the hand of the Philistines forty years" (v.1). The story now focuses upon the second of the enemies mentioned in 10.7; the "forty years" proved to be the longest period of servitude for the children of Israel under the hand of any enemy. Jephthah dealt with the oppression of Ammon, but the more serious threat of the Philistines was to last into the reign of David. The commentary on Shamgar (ch.3) has already pointed to their great danger as the enemy from within the land. They descended from Mizraim, one of the sons of Ham (Gen 10.6); he "begat ... Casluhim, (out of whom came Philistim)" (Gen 10.13-14). They arrived in Canaan, as the children of Israel had done, from the direction of Egypt. However, they came out in a very different way: they knew nothing of the Passover, the crossing of the Red Sea, life in the wilderness and the crossing of the river Jordan.

They settled on the west coast of Canaan, in territory that the Israelites had been unable to secure for themselves (Josh 13.1-2). They were therefore intruders in the land that Israel ought to have possessed. They controlled only a small area, but their influence was felt much more widely. They established a strong base in the five major cities of Gaza, Ashkelon, Ashdod, Ekron and Gath. They were a very religious people, "having a form of godliness, but denying the power thereof" (2 Tim 3.5). Their principal god was Dagon (1 Sam 5.2), but they also worshipped Ashtaroth, a goddess of fertility (1 Sam 31.10). Initially, they did not employ the aggressive tactics used by Israel's other oppressors but they were content to permeate the whole fabric of Israelite society with their ways and beliefs. It was only individuals, like Shamgar (3.31), who recognised the danger and opposed them. It is possible that the exploits of Shamgar and Samson led the Philistines to adopt a much more confrontational approach towards Israel.

Fifthly, the silence of Scripture confirms that the children of Israel had reached a new low. Previously, the oppression of their enemies had led them to cry to the Lord for deliverance (3.9,15; 4.3; 6.7; 10.10). Although their cries had not been a sign of true repentance, at least they had turned to the Lord, if only for relief from suffering. However, their cries were now a thing of the past and had been replaced by a complacent attitude. They appear to have had no desire to strive against the Philistines as the Lord had intended them to do (cf. 3.2) but they preferred to settle down to a comfortable existence under their influence. The simple truth was that they did not wish to be delivered. Indeed, they were unhappy and uncomfortable with Samson's aggression towards the Philistines and challenged him when he disturbed the peace: "Knowest thou not that the Philistines are rulers over us? what is it that thou hast done unto us?" (15.11).

Sixthly, conditions were so poor that there was no man suitable for the Lord to raise up to deliver His people as He had been able to do in the past. The one, who would bring deliverance, Samson, was yet to be born. After he was born, there had to be a period of waiting until he grew to maturity.

The Grace of God – "grace did much more abound" (Rom 5.20)

If the children of Israel had been left to themselves at this lowest point of their history in the days of the judges, they would never have risen out of the ashes. They were so blind that they could not see the danger they were in. However, "where sin abounded, grace did much more abound" (Rom 5.20). It was as well for them that God had not lost interest in them and abandoned them to face the inevitable outcome of their sin.

The setting for God's grace

The Lord does not need the dramatic backdrops of men against which to work the wonders of His grace. A.McShane writes, "He delights in doing wonders that commence in the shade of obscurity. Often the thought steals into our minds that if only we were in some more prominent position or some vast city we could do wonders for God ... God chooses His workmen from despised places...may we be preserved from blaming our surroundings for a lack of usefulness" (*Lessons for Leaders*).

Firstly, the display of God's grace began in a humble family setting: "a certain man of Zorah, of the family of the Danites, whose name was Manoah" (v.2). Naturally speaking, this was the last place to have looked for hope of deliverance. Zorah was a small town about fourteen miles (22 kilometres) west of Jerusalem in the territory of Dan. Dan occupied the smallest landmass of all the tribes and was the last to receive its inheritance. The more powerful tribes of Ephraim, Benjamin and Judah bordered its land. Indeed, the Danites had not been very successful in possessing their part of the land. It was a rich and fertile area and therefore the Amorites had been reluctant to give it up. They forced the children of Dan from the fruitful valleys into the less productive hill country (1.34-35). Many of them eventually decided to move north to capture the city of Laish and to live there (18.1-31). Dan was not therefore one of the more prominent or glamorous tribes. However, it was from this tribe that the deliverer was to come. It points forward to the humble setting for the birth of the perfect Saviour: "But thou, Bethlehem Ephratah, though thou be little among the thousands of Judah, yet out of thee shall he come forth unto me that is to be ruler in Israel; whose goings forth have been from of old, from everlasting" (Mic 5.2).

Secondly, the setting was one that spoke of barrenness: "and his wife was barren, and bare not" (v.2). Manoah's name (4495) means, "a quiet and settled place". However, in all likelihood, there would have been a lack of rest in Manoah's home on account of the barrenness. The grace of God always works in the context of man's weakness and helplessness. Indeed, the first words to the woman confirmed her condition: "Behold now, thou art barren, and bearest not" (v.3). Manoah and his wife were, humanly speaking, in an impossible situation and only God could answer the need. The fact that she is not even named emphasises that what followed was all to do with God and His sovereign grace. Her emptiness provided the setting for His grace to be displayed. Sadly, the children of Israel were unconcerned about their own spiritual barrenness at this time.

The declarer of God's grace

The darkness was lifted when "the angel of the Lord appeared unto the woman" with a stirring message of grace: "but thou shalt conceive, and bear a son" (v.3). It has already been substantiated in this commentary that the three appearances of "the angel of the Lord (JEHOVAH - 3068)" in the book of Judges were pre-incarnation appearances of Christ (cf. 2.1; 6.11). The Jehovah of the Old Testament is, indeed, the Jesus of the New Testament. Manoah and his wife also referred to Him as "a (or the) man of God (ELOHIM - 430)" (vv.6,8), "an angel of God (ELOHIM - 430)" (v.6), "the man" (vv.10,11). Clearly, the emphasis is on the appearance of the Lord in human form; their appreciation of Him developed as He revealed Himself to them. The occasion and the declaration were of such importance that none less than the Lord Himself appeared to communicate the message. It demonstrated therefore His deep concern for the condition of the children of Israel.

The recipients of God's grace

Manoah and his wife are typical of the faithful remnant that the Lord preserves for Himself even in the darkest of days. The Lord knew that He could communicate His message of grace to this couple and that they would receive it. They may have sought further light on the situation (vv.11-12) but they never once questioned the possibility of what He revealed to them. They were not indifferent to barrenness as the children of Israel were. Indeed, there was no adverse reaction from Manoah's wife when the angel of the Lord said, "Behold now, thou art barren, and bearest not" (v.3). She recognised and accepted His words as a true statement of her condition.

There was a harmony about their marriage that was not a general feature in Israel. They communicated with each other concerning the revelation (vv.6,10,22-23), and they showed no desire to move independently of each other. There are clear evidences throughout that Manoah's wife had greater spiritual insights than he did. The angel of the Lord appeared to her on two occasions (vv.3,9) before He spoke with Manoah (v.11). She also displayed a greater understanding of the Lord's ways after the angel left them (vv.22-23). She may have been "the weaker vessel" (1 Pet 3.7) constitutionally, but this was not the case spiritually. However, she ever moved with grace towards her husband and was subject to him. The fact that the Lord appeared to her first, rather than to Manoah, reflected the spiritual state of the children of Israel. The Lord chose to work through "the weaker vessel" to emphasise that it was only His strength, working through His people's weakness, that would bring deliverance.

During barren and rebellious days the Lord was able, and pleased, to enter such a spiritual family atmosphere to declare His message of grace. The influence of a godly home should never be underestimated. The woman, both as a wife and a mother, has a privileged place and a special influence there. She leaves that position to the detriment of her family. The special impact that Manoah's wife was to have on Samson was revealed in the angel's words, "Now therefore beware, I pray thee, and drink not wine nor strong drink, and eat not any unclean thing" (v.4). She was also given a further instruction later on not to "eat of anything that cometh of the vine (v.14). By so doing, she was declaring that she was not dependent upon earthly stimulation or seeking wordly joy. She had to be a fit vessel through whom God could bring in His deliverer. She had to reflect the nature of the child she was to bare so that she would not distract him from the pathway he was to tread. It is so easy for parents to bring things into the home that are detrimental to the spiritual growth of their children. Manoah's wife did not place a stumbling block in Samson's path during his formative years. Samuel also benefited greatly from a godly mother, Hannah, who "weaned him" before she "brought him unto the house of the Lord in Shiloh" (1 Sam 1.24). In "last days" conditions (2 Tim 3.1), Paul reminded Timothy that he owed a great debt to "the unfeigned faith … which dwelt first in thy grandmother Lois, and thy mother Eunice" (2 Tim 1.5).

The experience of Manoah and his wife foreshadows the announcement of the greatest expression of God's grace when, "the angel Gabriel was sent from God unto a city of Galilee, named Nazareth, to a virgin espoused to a man whose name was Joseph, of the house of David; and the virgin's name was Mary" (Lk 1.26-27).

The deliverer provided by God's grace

Firstly, Samson's uniqueness among the judges was shown in the fact that he was promised from before his birth (v.3), whereas the Lord had raised up the former judges in their mature years to deliver Israel. God's deliverer on this occasion therefore was to be marked out in a special way from conception. Again, it is a reminder of the visit and the message of the angel Gabriel to Mary, "and the angel said unto her, Fear not, Mary: for thou hast found favour with God. And, behold, thou shalt conceive in thy womb, and bring forth a son, and shalt call his name JESUS" (Lk 1.30-31).

Secondly, Samson was unique among the judges in that he was to be a Nazarite from the womb: "For, lo, thou shalt conceive, and bear a son; and no rasor shall come on his head: for the child shall be a Nazarite unto God from the womb" (v.5). Nazarite (5139) means, "to separate, to consecrate". The law and the vow of the Nazarite are presented in Numbers 6. Nazariteship was open on a purely voluntary basis to any person, male or female, in Israel. It involved such in making a vow "to separate themselves unto the Lord" (6.2) for a specified period of time. Samson's Nazariteship differed in that it was not voluntary (he was designated a Nazarite "from the womb") and it was for life. For a full and helpful survey of Nazariteship in the Old Testament the reader is encouraged to consult the companion volume in this series on *Numbers* (pp.79-93).

The children of Israel had lost any inclination to live a separated life. They had imbibed the Philistine religion and manner of life to such a degree that they had abandoned their distinctive features. Although they did not appreciate it, the desperate need of the day was for a deliverer who was distinct and different. Samson's exploits, including his failures, would teach them that their strength rested in consecration to God; this would lead to separation from idols. Nazarites had three distinguishing features: "When either man or woman shall separate (distinguish - 6381) themselves to vow a vow of a Nazarite" (Num 6.2). They were distinguishable by their abstinence from wine and strong drink, their uncut hair and their avoidance of contact with any dead body (Num 6.4-7). As far as Samson was concerned, particular emphasis was placed upon the fact that "no rasor shall come on his head" (v.5). However, the fact that he was described as "a Nazarite unto God from the womb" (v.5) indicates that he would not have been exempt from other aspects of the Nazarite vow. Nevertheless, the long hair was the secret of his strength and was of particular importance in his life. Nature taught that long hair was a shame to a man (1 Cor 11.14) and was a sign that he was in subjection to another's authority. However, in the case of the Nazarite, it was a visible sign of his separation from the world and his willingness to bear the shame, rejection and reproach out of devotion to the Lord.

Once again, Samson points towards Christ. Although He was not a literal Nazarite, He was the only true Nazarite to walk this earth. He did not need the external features that marked out the Nazarite. His life was one of complete devotion to His Father and obedience to His will. He challenged His accusers who were heaping reproach and shame upon Him: "Which of you convinceth (rebukes, admonishes) me of sin?" (Jn 8.46). They failed to bring a successful accusation against him of defilement or rebellion to His Father's will. They resorted therefore to accusing Him of having a devil and casting stones at Him (Jn 8.52,59). He, indeed, bore shame and reproach: "Because for thy sake I have borne reproach; shame hath covered my face" (Ps 69.7).

Although the law and vows of the Nazarite are not directly applicable to believers today, the principle of separation most certainly is. The moment someone is born again, they are called to a life of separation. It is not, of course, something that can be forced upon them but it is absolutely essential if they are to be of use in the Lord's service. There will be something distinctive about the appearance and actions of those who devote themselves fully to Him. The Focus Booklet on *Separation* (published by John Ritchie) expresses clearly and succinctly what separation means in practical terms: "To be separate is to be different; to live among people, yet to be distinct from them; to get close to them without being identified with them in aims, habits, partnerships or fellowships".

Thirdly, Samson was unique among the judges in that he was the first of them of whom it was said, "he shall begin to deliver Israel out of the hand of the Philistines" (v.5). He began a work that others would finish. However, this should not necessarily be viewed, as some commentators have done, as a veiled criticism of him. It must always be remembered that the word of God does name him among those, "who through faith subdued kingdoms, wrought righteousness, obtained promises, stopped the mouth of lions, quenched the violence of fire, escaped the edge of the sword, out of weakness were made strong, waxed valiant in fight, turned to flight the armies of the aliens" (Heb 11.33-34). The Lord knew that the Philistines' hold on Israel was so great that it would not be broken by one man and therefore there would still be much to do following Samson's death. Indeed, that work was not completed until the reign of David.

Samson stands in marked contrast to the Lord Jesus. He completed the work of salvation that He came to do. He prayed to His Father, "I have glorified thee on the earth: I have finished the work which thou gavest me to do" (Jn 17.4). He is, indeed, the "author and finisher of [our] faith" (Heb 12.2).

The response to God's grace

Manoah and his wife grew in their understanding of the Lord and their appreciation of His message of grace deepened as He progressively revealed Himself to them. The Lord did not expect them to move beyond the level of their knowledge and experience of Him and therefore He led them on gently.

Manoah's wife knew that she had seen a man of God: "A man of God came unto me, and his countenance was like the countenance of an angel of God, very terrible (fearful, frightful - 3372)" (v.6). However, it was not a fear that drove her away but one that led her to want to know more. She appeared to regret that she had only been taken up with what she saw and that her fear prevented her from finding out more: "but I asked him not whence he was, neither told he me his name" (v.6). She repeated to Manoah the message that the angel had given her (v.7), except for the prediction that the son born to her would "begin to deliver Israel out of the hand of the Philistines". Perhaps she felt that it was beyond the bounds of possibility that she should be considered worthy of such a high honour and therefore she dared not to express it.

Manoah's response to God's grace was to pray: "Then Manoah intreated (interceded, burned incense in worship - 6279) the Lord, and said, O my Lord (Adonai), let the man of God which thou didst send come again unto us, and teach us what we shall do unto the child that shall be born" (v.8). The use of the word "us" reveals that there was nothing selfish about his prayer and there was an unwavering belief that God could do this great thing. Husband and wife were sharing in this experience together. Clearly, there was also a spirit of worship about it that ascended and gave pleasure to the Lord, because He graciously heard and answered his prayer: "And God hearkened to the voice of Manoah; and the angel of God came again unto the woman as she sat in the field" (v.9). Manoah "was not with her" and therefore she "made haste, and ran, and shewed her husband, and said unto him, Behold, the man hath appeared unto me, that came unto me the other day" (v.10). She longed for him to share in her spiritual experience.

Manoah sought confirmation as to whether He was the man who had spoken to his wife: "Art thou the man that spakest unto the woman?" He received the simple response, "I am" (v.11), which should have sufficed to convince him that this was the angel of the Lord. However, Manoah pressed their divine visitor further: "Now let thy words come to pass. How shall we order the child, and how shall we do unto him?" (v.12). Total trust that what the angel had said would come to pass was mingled with the desire to know still more. The angel made it clear that He had nothing to add to what He had already said: "Of all that I said unto the woman let her beware. She may not eat of anything that cometh of the vine, neither let her drink wine or strong drink, nor eat any unclean thing: all that I commanded her let her observe" (vv.13-14). However, although the requirements for bringing up the child remained the same as those revealed to his wife, by repeating them to Manoah the angel of the Lord brought home to him that he had a personal responsibility in relation to the matter. He had to provide her with the necessary support and conditions for her to be able to fulfil His commands. It is vital for Christian husbands and wives to provide mutual support for each other as they seek to live in obedience to God's word. Manoah also had a headship role to ensure that the Lord's commands were adhered to in the home. Paul taught the Corinthian believers that, "the head of every man is Christ; and the head of every woman is the man; and the head of Christ is God" (1 Cor 11.3).

Manoah did not want to let this divine guest go and therefore he sought to detain him with the offer of a meal: "until we shall have made ready a kid for thee" (v.15). The angel of the Lord declined the offer but graciously suggested to Manoah that a more appropriate response to mark the occasion would be to "offer a burnt offering...unto the Lord" (v.16). Manoah still failed to grasp that this was the angel of the Lord and that it was only such an offering that would detain Him. He went on therefore to press Him, "What is thy name, that when thy sayings come to pass we may do thee honour?" (v.17). His wife had shown greater discernment. She had said, "neither told he me his name" (v.6), suggesting that this was not something she would have dared to ask. Manoah received a response that both rebuked and taught him: "Why askest thou thus after my name, seeing it is secret (PILI - remarkable, wonderful - 6383)?" (v.18). The word "secret" is the same word "wonderful", which was used by the psalmist as he contemplated the Lord's intimate knowledge of him: "Such knowledge is too wonderful for me; it is high, I cannot attain unto it" (Ps 139.6). The Lord was therefore telling Manoah that His name was beyond his knowledge and understanding. Isaiah wrote of the coming Messiah, "and his name shall be called Wonderful" (Is 9.6). Paul wrote to the believers in Rome, "O the depth of the riches both of the wisdom and knowledge of God! how unsearchable are his judgments, and his ways past finding out! For who hath known the mind of the Lord? or who hath been his counsellor?" (Rom 11.33-34).

The response of the angel of the Lord silenced Manoah's questions, and he "took a kid with a meat (meal) offering, and offered it upon a rock unto the Lord" (v.19). He and his wife looked on as "the angel did wondrously" (v.19). "Wondrously" (PALA - wonderfully, marvellously, miraculously - 6381) is the root word from which "secret" (PILI – 6383) is derived in the previous verse. The Lord was, indeed, acting in accordance with His name. All Manoah and his wife could do was to stand back and watch as the Lord revealed Himself to them: "and Manoah and his wife looked on" (v.19). They "fell on their faces to the ground" in response to the amazing scene that unfolded before them: "For it came to pass, when the flame went up toward heaven from off the altar, that the angel of the LORD ascended in the flame of the altar" (v.20).

The outcome convinced Manoah that he had met an angel of the Lord (v.21) and therefore they had "seen God" (v.22). His conclusion was, "We shall surely die" (v.22). Such a response was understandable in the light of the prevailing belief that no man could see God's face and live (cf. 6.22; Ex 33.20). However, it was Manoah's wife who spoke words of wisdom and comfort to calm the fears: "If the Lord were pleased to kill us, he would not have received a burnt offering and a meat offering at our hands, neither would he have shewed us all these things, nor would as at this time have told us such things as these" (v.23). She had the insight to appreciate that the grace of God would never bring His people to such a point to slay them! The purpose of His grace was to bring deliverance.

Retrospectively, believers today can look back to Manoah's sacrifice on the rock and see Christ. The burnt offering, speaking of His death for the glory of God, and the meat (meal) offering, speaking of the fragrance and preciousness of His life, point towards Calvary. It was there that the Lord "did wondrously". His life and death were offered as a sacrifice to God. The Scriptures declare that, "by his own blood he entered in once into the holy place, having obtained eternal redemption for us...who through the eternal Spirit offered himself without spot to God" (Heb 9.12,14). F.C.Jennings writes of Manoah's sacrifice, "The flame of the offering ascends from that holy altar, and with it ascends the angel of Jehovah...here He adds Himself to the offering; and this we may safely say, is the only value it possesses; but who can estimate its worth now? He to whom it ascends, and only He" (*Judges and Ruth*). Having "ascended in the flame of the altar...the angel of the Lord did no more appear to Manoah and to his wife" (vv.20-21), symbolising that the sacrifice had been accepted and the angel therefore returned from whence He had come. God set His seal upon the work of Calvary by raising Christ from the dead and receiving Him into heaven. Like Manoah and his wife, the disciples could only stand and witness the amazing scene on the Mount of Olives as "he was taken up; and a cloud received him out of their sight" (Acts 1.9). They would not see Him again but He promised them that they would be "endued with power from on high" (Lk 24.49). From that spot therefore they returned to Jerusalem, where ultimately they were indwelt by the Holy Spirit and witnessed to the death and resurrection of Christ. S.Ridout writes, "All true Nazariteship, all true separation to God, and thus victory over unreality, must come through our identification with that Wonderful Person, who is none other than Christ, the blessed Christ of God" (*Lectures on the Book of Judges*).

The appearance of God's grace

The Lord was true to His word: "And the woman bare a son" (v.24). If the Lord had promised a deliverer, the point would come when that promise would be fulfilled and the deliverer would step into time. It was not conditional upon men's state or acceptance of His grace. The same was true of the sending of His only Son. Peter wrote of Him, "Who verily was foreordained before the foundation of the world, but was manifest in these last times for you" (1 Pet 1.20). Paul reminded Titus, "For the grace of God that bringeth salvation hath appeared to all men" (Tit 2.11).

His name. Samson's (8123) name means, "sunlight, sunny, bright", suggesting possibly the light that he brought into the lives of Manoah and his wife and that it was intended he should bring the same into the darkness of Israel. Sadly, the light was to dim in Samson's life and he ended it in darkness when the Philistines "put out his eyes" (16.21). He stands in direct contrast to the Lord's words through Malachi concerning Christ: "But unto you that fear my name shall the Sun (the root Hebrew word from whence the name 'Samson' is derived - 8121) of righteousness arise with healing in his wings" (Mal 4.2). There will be no dimming of Christ's brilliance and beauty when He returns to reign. His enemies will never be able to extinguish the light that He brings. Deborah and Barak had already looked forward to that day in their song following the defeat of Jabin and Sisera: "So let all thine enemies perish, O Lord: but let them that love him be as the sun when he goeth forth in his might" (5.31). In the meantime, in the days of His rejection, believers are called upon to "shine as lights in the world" (Phil 2.15).

His growth. If the detail surrounding the birth of Samson is unique in the Book of Judges, the glimpse into his childhood is too. In the so-called "hidden years" it is recorded that "the child grew, and the Lord blessed him" (v.24). The Lord took a special interest in the growth of Samson throughout his childhood and growth to maturity. Clearly, the care of his godly parents would have had an impact on him. Before he appeared on the public scene there was therefore a period of spiritual growth before the Lord. Curiosity may lead the reader to want to know more but the Lord does not reveal it. All that needs to be known is encapsulated within the one statement.

Once again, Samson is a reminder of Christ. Only one incident is recorded in the Word of God about His childhood (Lk 2.41-51) and therefore it can be concluded that all God desires to say about the "hidden thirty years" is to be found within the account of His visit to Jerusalem at the age of twelve for the Feast of the Passover. Luke succinctly records of those years, "the grace of God was upon him" (Lk 2.40) and He "increased in wisdom and stature, and in favour with God and man" (Lk 2.52).

His movements. "And the Spirit of the LORD began to move him at times" (v.25). The word "move" (PAAM - 6470) has the thought of impelling, tapping, i.e. beating regularly. Although the precise details of what Samson did are not given, it is clear that during the years of relative obscurity the Spirit of the Lord enabled him to perform mighty deeds. It is possible that some of these deeds would have involved actions against the Philistines. However, whatever the outcomes were of these occasional, although regular, movements of Spirit of the Lord, they took place in his home territory: "in the camp of Dan between Zorah and Eshtaol" (v.25). The Lord was confirming to the people where he lived and grew up that he was being marked out for special service for Him. It was necessary for him to gain acceptance and credibility there first if he were to gain wider support later. It was in His home town of Nazareth that the Lord Jesus went into the synagogue and read from the prophet Isaiah concerning Himself, "The Spirit of the Lord is upon me, because he has anointed me to preach the gospel to the poor; he hath sent me to heal the brokenhearted, to preach deliverance to the captives, and recovering of sight to the blind, to set at liberty them that are bruised, to preach the acceptable year of the Lord" (Lk 4.18-19). Samson can therefore be but a pale reflection of Him.

Many commentators believe that "the camp of Dan" could refer to a temporary dwelling place that the Danites had been forced to set up as a result of the hostilities of both the Amorites and the Philistines. Samson may therefore have travelled there with his father on a regular, even daily, basis. Zorah was, of course, his birthplace and Eshtaol was a short distance to the northeast. The scene was now set for Samson to move out in more public service for the Lord on behalf of His people.

JUDGES 14

There is a very real danger that the reader of this chapter may become so engrossed in the exploits of Samson as to lose sight of the Lord. It is as well therefore that the author reveals at the outset a truth that was hidden from Samson's parents but which is key to an understanding of the events that followed: "But his father and his mother knew not that it was of the Lord, that he sought an occasion (opportunity - 8385) against the Philistines: for at that time the Philistines had dominion over Israel" (v.4). Some commentators believe that the "he" in the statement, "he sought an occasion", refers to the Lord rather than to Samson. It is possible to interpret it in this way, but it can justifiably be held that Samson is in view. Whichever line is taken, the major thought of the verse is that the perplexing events of Samson's life can only be understood in the light of the truth that the Lord is sovereign. He was therefore in control of all that unfolded. This does not, of course, imply that He approved of Samson's actions in relation to the Philistines or that He was the author of them. However, He did overrule in the events of his life and turned his folly into opportunities for him (or Him, i.e. the Lord, depending on the line of interpretation taken) to oppose the Philistines. L. H. Wiseman writes, "The sin of Samson was not of the Lord, though the deliverance wrought thereby was. Not the evil, but the good elicited from it, was of the Lord" (*Practical Truths from Judges*).

It is a comfort and an encouragement for believers to know that the Lord's purposes will never be thwarted by the failures and weaknesses of men. They can rest assured that He is able to bring good out of even the most unpromising of circumstances. This chapter traces five downward journeys which, without the Lord's overruling, would have resulted in total disaster. The activities of Samson must never be allowed to obscure the divine hand that permitted events to run their course and used them to fulfil His will.

Verses 1-4: "And Samson went down to Timnath"

The commentary on ch.13 has already noted that the Philistines employed different tactics from those used by Israel's former oppressors. Initially, they avoided direct confrontation and they were content to permeate the whole of the Israelites' way of life with their customs and beliefs. The opening of the chapter confirms the ease with which the children of Israel lived alongside them. Timnath was only about four miles from Samson's home in Zorah. It had once been in the hands of the children of Israel and was allotted to the tribe of Dan (Josh 19.40,43 – called Thimnathah here). However, they had failed to possess their inheritance in the fertile valleys (1.34) and the Philistines eventually controlled the city. Clearly, Samson's freedom of movement between his home and Timnath, as well as his desire to marry a Philistine, underlines the comparative peace that existed between both parties.

This was the first of Samson's downward steps and it set the scene for what was to follow later on in his life. He was probably in his late teens or early twenties at this stage. His journey down to Timnath resulted in him seeing "a woman" (v.1), and he was drawn away by "the lust of the eyes" (1 Jn 2.16). If believers find themselves where they ought not to be, they will soon discover things attractive to the eyes that will lead to their downfall. Once he had seen the woman, Samson was "drawn away of his own lust, and enticed" (James 1.14). There was nothing spiritual about his request to his father: "Get her for me; for she pleaseth me well" (v.3). Although it is possible to commend him for the fact that "he came up, and told his father and his mother" (v.2), it was clear that his mind was made up and nothing they could say to him would dissuade him. His attitude towards his parents stands in marked contrast to the Lord Jesus who, in spite of His parents' lack of understanding about the purpose of His life, "went down with them, and came to Nazareth, and was subject unto them" (Lk 2.51). Samson's pathway was marked by self-will rather than subjection. Clearly, he had little regard for the teaching that he must have received in the home concerning his Nazariteship and his mission in life. It was not surprising therefore that he ignored his parents' concerns in the daily circumstances of life. Paul reminds children to "obey your parents in all things: for this is well pleasing unto the Lord" (Col 3.20).

Everything about the proposed relationship was wrong, and therefore it would be incorrect to suggest that the Lord sanctioned this fleshly union. Mixed marriages were contrary to His word: "Neither shalt thou make marriages with them (the nations); thy daughter thou shalt not give unto his son, nor his daughter shalt thou take unto thy son" (Deut 7.3). The language of his parents also emphasised to Samson that the two of them were incompatible: "Is there never a woman among the daughters of thy brethren, or among all my people, that thou goest to take a wife of the uncircumcised Philistines?" (v.3). However, if a child of God is being driven by fleshly desires, his ears will be deaf to any spiritual appeals. What Samson did was, of course, a reflection of the unholy union that the children of Israel had forged with the Philistines. The Word of God is equally clear to believers today as far as their relationships, including marriage, are concerned: "Be ye not unequally yoked together with unbelievers: for what fellowship hath righteousness with unrighteousness? and what communion hath light with darkness?" (2 Cor 6.14). Many have disregarded this to their spiritual detriment.

As has already been noted in the opening paragraph, it was as well for Samson and his parents that the Lord was in control and used Samson's folly as a means for him (or Him) to seek "an occasion (opportunity - 8385) against the Philistines" (v.4).

Verses 5-6: "Then went Samson down, and his father and his mother"

This was Samson's second downward step. There is a double tragedy about the journey. On this occasion his parents accompanied him down to Timnath, presumably to make arrangements for the marriage. They must have thought back to the amazing events prior to his birth and the words of the angel of the Lord concerning his Nazariteship. They had, no doubt, sought to bring him up in a godly atmosphere, but all their hopes now appeared to be evaporating before their eyes. Clearly, a suitable bride-to-be among the women in Israel had not been found for Samson and he was insistent on getting his own way. It would be unfair to be overly critical of them but, apart from expressing their initial misgivings, they appear to have gone along with his movements.

When Samson and his parents reached Timnath and "came to the vineyards of Timnath" (v.5), he became separated from them. Clearly, they did not witness the event that followed (v.6). The vineyards were, of course, the last place that a Nazarite should have been in the light of the requirement to abstain from wine and strong drink, and anything connected with the vine (Num 6.3-4). It was there that "a young lion roared against him" (v.5). If he had not been on the pathway of disobedience he would not have met the lion. The word of God and his parents had already told him he was on the wrong road, and now the young lion was giving him the same message. Samson resisted the lion but not in his own strength: "And the Spirit of the Lord came mightily upon him, and he rent him as he would have rent a kid, and he had nothing in his hand" (v.6).

There may be a tendency for the reader to become preoccupied with Samson's indubitable great size and superhuman strength. However, to do so would be to miss the primary point of the record of his life. If size and natural strength were the basis for his successes, the Philistines would not have been anxious to know "wherein his great strength lieth" (16.5), and Hebrews 11.34 would not have included him among those who "out of weakness were made strong". Even the Philistines appreciated that there was something extraordinary about his power that could not be explained naturally. Anything of worth he achieved for the Lord against them was the result of his being empowered by the Spirit of the Lord. Thus, in "the vineyards of Timnath", the Lord enabled him to see what he could achieve if he allowed His strength to work through him. He would never have been able to face the lion without a weapon in his hand and to rend "him as he would have rent a kid" (v.6) in his own natural strength, no matter how great and strong he was naturally. Peter exhorted his readers, and believers of all generations, to "Be sober, be vigilant; because your adversary the devil, as a roaring lion, walketh about, seeking whom he may devour: whom resist stedfast in the faith" (1 Pet 5.8-9).

Thus, three clear indications to Samson that he was on a downward spiral were totally ignored by him and showed how lightly he regarded his Nazarite vow. It is not surprising that "he told not his father or his mother what he had done" (v.6). Some commentators argue that this was an evidence of his humility about his achievement. However, it is far more likely that it was a sense of guilt that led to his silence. He did not want to confess to his parents that he had compromised his Nazariteship by going into the vineyards. M. F. Unger writes, "But while the Nazarite did exploits and conquered Satan, as it were (cf. 1 Pet 5.8) on one front, he was falling a victim to the stratagems of Satan on another front in becoming infatuated with the Timnite woman" (*Commentary on the Old Testament*).

Samson's pathway of disobedience that led to his encounter with the lion means that he could never be regarded as a type of the Lord Jesus. However, he does, by way of contrast, point towards Him. He came down from heaven in complete obedience to His Father's will. The writer to the Hebrews reminded his readers of the manner and purpose of His coming: "Forasmuch then as the children are partakers of flesh and blood, he also himself likewise took part of the same; that through death he might destroy him that had the power of death, that is, the devil; and deliver them who through fear of death were all their lifetime subject to bondage" (Heb 2.14-15). Unlike Samson He did not come to embrace the enemy, but to destroy him.

Verses 7-9: "And he went down, and talked with the woman"

This was undoubtedly a continuation of the journey that Samson took with his parents (vv.5-6) but it presents a third downward step. If he had heeded the lesson the Lord had taught him in the vineyards, his footsteps would have been arrested and he would have avoided entering still further into the danger zone. However, he rejoined his parents and continued his descent to Timnath, where he "talked with the woman" (v.7). Prior to this he had simply seen her (v.2) but by talking to her he came to know her better. This only served to excite his fleshly interests still further, and "she pleased Samson well" (v.7). In all likelihood, the betrothal took place at this time.

Clearly, the conversations Samson had had with the woman remained with him and it was only a matter of time before "he returned to take her" (v.8). At some point, either on the way down or, possibly, on the way back, "he turned aside to see the carcase of the lion" (v.8). Whether it was curiosity, pride or a genuine desire to revisit the scene of his victory in the Lord's strength is not clear. However, whatever the motive might have been, the outcome was disastrous both for him and his parents. The intense heat had dried up the carcase of the lion "and, behold, there was a swarm of bees and honey" (v.8) within it. It took just a moment of time for Samson to disregard and break his Nazarite vow by touching a dead body. "And he took thereof in his hands" (v.9) implies that he scraped the honey out with his hands and thereby became defiled. It was distressing enough that he had wilfully defiled himself but he returned from that scene, "and went on eating, and came to his father and mother, and he gave them, and they did eat" (v.9). If it is not entirely clear as to why he did not tell them about his initial encounter with the lion (v.6), there can be no real mystery about why "he told not them that he had taken the honey out of the carcase of the lion" (v.9). A guilty conscience and a sense of shame would have prevented him from confessing what he had done. He had, indeed, something to hide and was prepared therefore to stoop to the depths of compromising and defiling his parents to protect his own standing.

There is a sense in which honey speaks of sweetness that is good and spiritual. Canaan was "an exceeding good land…a land which floweth with milk and honey" (Num 14.7-8), and the children of Israel were encouraged to go into it and possess it. On the shore of the lake of Galilee, they gave the resurrected Lord, "a piece of a broiled fish, and of an honeycomb. And he took it and did eat before them" (Lk 24.42-43). S.Ridout writes, "The very fact of Satan's mastery over us, gave the occasion for Christ to overthrow Him. That very occasion becomes the means of our spiritual food, the richest sustenance of heaven; honey out of the carcase. Surely from the cross of Christ all sweetness and all food have come … We eat and drink abundantly because of that slaughter of the lion that was in the way" (*Lectures on the Book of Judges*). However, honey can also speak of natural sweetness and attractiveness and, as such, God decreed that there should not be "any honey, in any offering of the Lord made by fire" (Lev 2.11). Samson's taking of the honey from the carcase resulted in his defilement. How unlike the Lord Jesus he was, who could touch the unclean thing and not be defiled (cf. Mk 1.41; Lk 7.14). He could, indeed, "bring a clean thing out of an unclean" (Job 14.4).

Verses 10-18: "So his father went down unto the woman"

Manoah would never have been in this position if Samson had not led the way. The downward spiritual path of any believer will invariably have an adverse effect on others. From this point onwards, Manoah and his wife fade from the scene. Indeed, his mother is not even mentioned here. "Samson made there (in Timnath) a feast; for so used the young men (bridegrooms) to do" (v.10). However, his father was probably there in a formal capacity to claim the woman as his son's bride. No doubt he fulfilled this role with a heavy heart, because he was as yet unable to see that the Lord would bring good out of the sadness (v.4).

The fact that the celebrations took place in the bride's house indicates that events were being driven by Philistine beliefs and customs, not those of the children of Israel. Samson had come down alone and therefore, "it came to pass, when they saw him, that they brought thirty companions to be with him" (v.11). These were "the children (sons) of the bride-chamber" (Mt 9.15) and the bridegroom's family would normally have provided them. It was tragic that Samson should have found himself in the position where his close companions for the occasion were drawn from among the Philistines. They would have provided protection for Samson, but it is possible that the Philistines were somewhat wary of Samson and also had in mind their own safety.

Although Samson was at the centre of the celebrations, and appeared to be at ease, it has already been noted, "he sought an occasion against the Philistines" (v.4). He did not miss this particular opportunity therefore to place them in an impossible situation when he could score a victory over them. He challenged the "thirty companions" with a riddle: "I will now put forth a riddle unto you: if ye can certainly declare it me within the seven days of the feast, and find it out, then I will give you thirty sheets (linen shirts - 5466) and thirty change of garments: but if ye cannot declare it me, then shall ye give me thirty sheets and thirty change of garments" (vv.12-13). Samson was offering expensive garments and therefore the rewards were great. They readily accepted the challenge: "Put forth thy riddle, that we may hear it" (v.13).

Sadly, Samson based the riddle on his encounter with the lion in the vineyards of Timnath: "Out of the eater came forth meat, and out of the strong came forth sweetness" (v.14). It was disappointing enough that he had gone into the vineyards in the first place but to use his failure as the basis for sport with uncircumcised Philistines at a wedding feast was indicative of the low regard he had for his Nazariteship. It was no surprise that "they could not in three days expound the riddle" (v.14). Only Samson had the key to unlock that door, because only he had encountered the lion, the bees and the honey.

It was not long therefore before the thirty men and the woman displayed the true nature of the Philistines. They were happy to adopt a non-confrontational approach until they realised that they were in a no-win situation that was going to cost them dear. The men were prepared to turn on their own in order to gain the ascendancy: "And it came to pass on the seventh day (the Septuagint says the fourth day), that they said unto Samson's wife, Entice thy husband, that he may declare unto us the riddle, lest we burn thee and thy father's house with fire: have ye called us to take that we have? is it not so?" (v.15). They encouraged her to be subtle in her dealings with Samson but they showed little subtlety in spelling out the consequences of failure on her part! They implied by their words that she was involved in Samson's plan to impoverish them. It is hardly surprising therefore that she was afraid in the face of such threats and that she resorted to tactics that have been successfully employed over the years by her sex to bring about the downfall of even stronger men spiritually than Samson. She "wept before him, and said, Thou dost but hate me, and lovest me not: thou hast put forth a riddle unto the children of my people, and hast not told it me" (v.16).

Samson may have slain the young lion in the vineyards but at that time "the Spirit of the Lord came mightily upon him" (v.6). However, he was moving on his own here in enemy territory. He sought to exonerate himself by saying, "Behold, I have not told it my father nor my mother, and shall I tell it thee?" (v.16). However, this was not going to pacify a woman whose life was at stake, and "she wept before him the seven days, while their feast lasted" (v.17). Although the thirty companions did not approach her until the "seventh (Septuagint – fourth) day" (v.15), it appears that she wept throughout the seven days of the feast in order to pressure Samson into telling her the secret. It is unlikely that he would have given in to her as a result of a single day of tears. However, whatever the correct interpretation is of the exact sequence of events in the chapter, the final outcome was that a woman's tears wore down the man who had slain a lion, and therefore "it came to pass on the seventh day, that he told her, because she lay sore upon him" (v.17). His decision to do so may also have been driven by the fact that the marriage was to be consummated on the seventh day. Not surprisingly, her next act was one of betrayal: he told her, "and she told the riddle to the children of her people" (v.17). Any loyalty or feelings she might have had towards Samson counted for nothing when it came down to saving her own life and that of her family. These events in Timnath preceded an even greater enticement and betrayal by Delilah in ch.16 that was to lead to Samson's imprisonment and death.

The "men of the city" met Samson's deadline and approached him "on the seventh day before the sun went down" with the answer to his riddle: "What is sweeter than honey? and what is stronger than a lion?" (v.18). He knew that there was no possibility of them having worked out the answer by their own wisdom and that he had therefore been betrayed by his wife. However, far from acknowledging his own failings that led to the betrayal, he turned on them and accused them, in the form of proverb, of having gained the answer through deceit: "If ye had not plowed (to fabricate, or devise in secret - 2790) with my heifer, ye had not found out my riddle" (v.18). He failed to appreciate that he had done precisely the same thing that he was accusing them of by becoming unequally yoked with a Philistine woman. He had, indeed, "plowed with my heifer" and therefore he reaped the bitter harvest.

Verse 19: "And he went down to Ashkelon"

This marks Samson's final path of descent in this chapter. Some commentators condemn his actions and claim that the flesh motivated him. However, such a view is not supported by the text. It is clearly stated that, "the Spirit of the Lord came upon him" (v.19). It would be wrong therefore to suggest that he was driven by personal anger and revenge. The Lord overruled in the circumstances that he found himself and graciously gave him an opportunity to "begin to deliver Israel out of the hands of the Philistines" (13.5) Although the thirty men had acted deceitfully in claiming to have solved the riddle, he honoured his side of the bargain with them. However, they received their reward in a manner that they would not have expected. They might have thought that they had gained the upper hand but the Lord was about to teach them that they were not going to have the final say.

Samson travelled to Ashkelon, one of the five key Philistine cities, which was approximately twenty-five miles away from Timnath. It was there that he "slew thirty men of them, and took their spoil, and gave change of garments unto them which expounded the riddle" (v.19). They gained their reward at the expense of their own brethren. It is not clear why he travelled so far but it is possible that this was not an act of indiscriminate slaughter, but that he pursued particular Philistines in that city who had troubled Israel. Some commentators have suggested that he did not carry out the act close to home, as this would have put those close to him in danger. However, whatever the reason, it was a small beginning and, once again, the Lord displayed to Samson the power that was available to him, if he sought to please Him rather than himself.

On his return to Timnath with the spoils of victory from Ashkelon, Samson was clearly unhappy with the scene that greeted him. In his absence, his wife was "given to his companion, whom he had used as his friend" (v.20). No longer was he moving in the power of the Spirit of the Lord, because "anger was kindled" in his heart (v.19). He was no doubt angry with his wife, her father and his companion. It would have been more fitting if he had been angry with himself for taking the downward path to Timnath in the first place. However, the Lord was in control and used the circumstances to extricate him from his unequal yoke, and for the first time in the chapter he "went up" (v.19) rather than down. He ought to have taken up with him the clear knowledge from his experiences that he would only be able to seek "an occasion (opportunity) against the Philistines" (v.4) by living a life of separation and opposing them, not by fraternising with them. However, subsequent events will reveal that his dealings with the Philistines were very much on a personal level and that he never really grasped the bigger picture that his mission was "to begin to deliver Israel out of the hand of the Philistines" (13.5). It was only the grace of God that gave him a place in the history of Israel as one who "judged Israel in the days of the Philistines twenty years" (15.20).

JUDGES 15

F.C.Jennings writes, "Samson was a Nazarite, but a Nazarite apart from the Spirit of the Lord can do ten times more mischief than another man" (*Judges and Ruth*). The truth of this statement is well illustrated in this chapter. Samson is seen in action when he was motivated by the desire for personal revenge, and this resulted in disaster for him and those associated with him. However, he is also portrayed in situations when "the Spirit of the Lord came mightily upon him" (v.14), and when he "called on the Lord" (v.18). The outcome on these two occasions was both positive and fruitful.

Samson in Timnath (vv.1-8a)

Samson was last seen when "his anger was kindled, and he went up to his father's house" (14.19). Clearly, his anger had now abated and he could not get the Philistine woman out of his mind. The sovereign Lord had extricated him from the circumstances in which he had found himself, but "it came to pass within a while after, in the time of wheat harvest (probably late May or early June according to Gregorian calendar), that Samson visited his wife with a kid" (v.1). Some commentators believe that Samson had entered into a form of marriage, known as "sidîqâ", where the wife remained in her parents' home and received visits from her husband from time to time. However, there are no compelling arguments for believing that this was the case. Indeed, the Philistines do not appear to have practised such a custom and it was certainly not acceptable in Israel.

Samson had left Timnath without consummating the marriage to his wife. However, armed with a kid as a gift, he sought to return and continue the relationship: "I will go in to my wife into the chamber" (v.1). Her father's response was swift and decisive: "But her father would not suffer him to go in. And her father said, I verily thought that thou hadst utterly hated her; therefore I gave her to thy companion" (v.2). Although his actions revealed the true character of the Philistines, Samson had no real grounds for complaint at the treatment he received from his father-in-law who showed that the Philistines had no respect for the marriage bond or any sense of loyalty. He wasted little time therefore in giving his daughter to the best man. Samson should not have entered into the relationship in the first place, and he did leave Timnath abruptly, giving the impression that he "utterly hated her".

There may be a hint in his father-in-law's response of an acceptance that he had acted hastily: "is not her younger sister fairer than she? take her, I pray thee, instead of her" (v.2). However, the offer may also have been made out of fear of what Samson might do. Indeed, the events that followed indicate that such fear, if it existed, would have been well founded. It would, of course, have been contrary to the word of God if Samson had accepted the offer (Lev 18.18). Yet, even though he did not fall into this error, there was nothing spiritual about his response. He was personally affronted by the suggestion and therefore believed that he was totally justified in the action that he was to take: "And Samson said concerning them, Now shall I be more blameless than the Philistines, though I do them a displeasure" (v.3). The havoc that he went on to cause could never be cloaked with respectability by referring to it as "righteous indignation". His actions were extreme, inappropriate and vindictive.

Firstly, he "went and caught three hundred foxes" (v.4). Many commentators have pointed out that the word used for "foxes" (SHUAL - 7776) can also be used to refer to "jackals", which, they say, is more likely to be the case in this context. They point out that, whereas foxes are solitary creatures, jackals are much more gregarious and hunt in packs. They would therefore be easier to capture. They are unclean beasts and they prey on dead bodies. However, there is no reason why they should not have been foxes. Certainly, their long, bushy tails would have made them ideal for the purpose Samson had in mind for them. Solomon described them as, "the foxes, the little foxes, that spoil the vines" (Song 2.15), which certainly proved to be the case here. Whether they were foxes or jackals, Samson used unclean things to gain the victory. Paul reminded the Corinthian believers that, "though we walk in the flesh, we do not war after the flesh: (for the weapons of our warfare are not carnal, but mighty through God to the pulling down of strong holds)" (2 Cor 10.3-4).

Secondly, Samson "took firebrands (a flambeau, flame - 3940), and turned tail to tail, and put a firebrand in the midst between two tails. And … set the brands on fire" (vv.4-5). Previously, in the book of Judges, the angel of the Lord had kindled fire (6.21; 13.20) and Gideon's men had lamps (the same word as used for "firebrand", v.4) in their empty pitchers (7.16). However, the fire in Samson's hands was kindled for carnal purposes.

Thirdly, "he let them (the foxes) go into the standing corn of the Philistines, and burnt up both the shocks (stacks of sheaves - 1430), and also the standing corn, with the vineyards and olives" (v.5). His argument was with the Philistines, and yet not one Philistine was slain by his hand in this encounter. The Lord had brought the children of Israel unto the land (2.1), and He had described it as "a good land and a large … a land flowing with milk and honey" (Ex 3.8). Instead of Samson dealing with the Philistines who were robbing the children of Israel of its richness, his vindictive act destroyed the produce of the land.

The impact of his scheme was far-reaching and catastrophic for the Philistines. The fire devastated their grain harvest and engulfed their vineyards and their olive groves. If Samson believed that this would put an end to the matter, he could not have been more wrong. The Philistines did not take long to come up with an answer to their question, "Who hath done this?" (v.6). They immediately identified the culprit and what they believed to be the reason: "And they answered, Samson, the son in law of the Timnite, because he had taken his wife, and given her to his companion" (v.6). They were quite capable of kindling their own fire but it fell in a place where Samson might least have expected it to: "And the Philistines came up, and burnt her and her father with fire" (v.6). True to character, rather than take on the real culprit, they used two of their own people as scapegoats and exacted vengeance on them. Samson's carnal actions had not only affected him but they were costly to others. It was ironical that his wife, who betrayed him in order to avoid being burned with fire, ultimately suffered that same fate as a consequence of his actions. However, the fact that the Philistines deserved the judgment of God does not excuse the manner in which Samson went about things.

Once a chain of revenge is set in motion, it is difficult for either side to bring it to an end. Samson's reaction to what the Philistines had done was an indication of the depth of his feelings for the Philistine woman. He made it clear therefore that he would not cease until he had exacted his revenge: "And Samson said unto them, Though ye have done this, yet will I be avenged of you, and after that I will cease" (v.7). He seemed to believe that his action would bring the conflict to an end but it continued long beyond his death. Nevertheless, once again, he "sought an occasion (opportunity) against the Philistines" (14.4). No indication is given as to how he gained his victory but "he smote them hip and thigh with a great slaughter" (v.8). Although it is not entirely clear what is meant by the expression "hip and thigh", commentators are generally agreed that the implication is that the slaughter was ruthless and cruel.

Verses 8b-13: Samson in the Top of the Rock Etam

Following his great slaughter of the Philistines and the devastation of their land, Samson "went down and dwelt in the top of the rock (lofty rock, stronghold - 5553) Etam" (v.8). Although this was a downward path topographically, it was, in contrast to the past, an upward path spiritually. The exact location of Etam is uncertain but it is unlikely that it was the place mentioned in 2 Chronicles 11.6, which would have been too far away. Subsequent events make it clear that it was somewhere in the territory of Judah. A.E.Cundall writes, "A site in the vicinity of Samson's home is much more likely and there is much to support the view that it was a cave in the cliffs above the Wady Isma'in, which was accessible only by descending through a fissure in the cliff-face, wide enough for one person to pass through at a time. This strongpoint, in an area well known to Samson, lay about two and a half miles south-east of Zorah" (*Judges - An Introduction and Commentary*). Wherever it was situated, it proved to be a place in the cleft of a rock where he could dwell. Moses was found in such a place when the Lord's glory passed by (Ex 33.21-22).

The ease with which the men of Judah found him (v.11) indicates that Samson had not gone to hide in the rock through fear. It is possible that he wished to protect the children of Israel from any possible reprisals against him as a result of his slaughter of the Philistines. Notwithstanding, it may also have been that he went there out of a spiritual exercise for solitude. It was, indeed, an appropriate place for a Nazarite to be found and therefore he touched spiritual heights at this period of time that he had not reached before. There was a different atmosphere at "the top of the rock Etam" from that which he had experienced when he "went down to Timnath" (14.1). That rock reminds believers of Christ as their only true abiding place of refuge and security.

> O safe to the rock that is higher than I
> My soul in its conflicts and sorrows would fly;
> So sinful, so weary, Thine, Thine would I be;
> Thou blest Rock of Ages I'm hiding in Thee.
> (William Cushing)

At least 1,000 Philistines (vv.15-16), and probably more, also took a journey. They "went up, and pitched in Judah, and spread themselves in Lehi" (v.9). Samson's slaughter of them had not put an end to the chain of revenge. Clearly, they were not looking for a fight, neither with Samson nor the men of Judah. The men of Judah were understandably surprised that such a considerable band of Philistines should come against them and therefore asked, "Why are ye come up against us?" (v.10). They were mystified that the people they lived alongside in comparative peace should suddenly be in contention with them. They had lost sight of the true nature of the Philistines. If they had turned on their own in Timnath and burned them with fire, they were more than capable of doing the same, and more, to the children of Israel when it suited them. The professing religious world is dangerous and not to be trusted. The men of Judah must have been greatly relieved by the response, "To bind Samson are we come up, to do to him as he hath done to us" (v.10). The Philistines had no argument with them but with Samson. Nevertheless, their fear of his great strength led them to pressurise and to threaten the men of Judah into doing their work for them.

The ease with which the men of Judah acquiesced was symptomatic of their low spiritual condition and the loss of any sense of their distinctiveness as the Lord's people. Firstly, they were prepared to muster 3,000 men together (v.11). This was the first time such a thing had happened during the days of Samson. They had previously shown no desire to gather such an array of strength against their enemy. The large number gathered to bind one man reflects the fear they had of the might of both Samson and the Philistines.

Secondly, their words displayed that they were content to live under the yoke of the Philistines and therefore they lacked sympathy for any individual who wanted to disturb the peace: "Knowest thou not that the Philistines are rulers over us? what is this that thou hast done to us?" (v.11). They might have deluded themselves into believing that the lack of conflict meant that there was a peaceful co-existence between them but the reality was that the Philistines ruled and they were subservient to them.

Thirdly, instead of opposing the Philistines, they were prepared to bind God's deliverer and hand him over to them. They were not prepared to listen to any arguments that Samson put before them: "And he said unto them, As they did unto me, so have I done unto them" (v.11). Their agenda was clear and straightforward: "We are come down to bind thee, that we may deliver thee into the hand of the Philistines" (v.12). Their only concession was in their response to Samson's request, "Swear unto me, that ye will not fall upon me yourselves" (v.12). They had no desire to have his blood on their hands. They were more than willing for someone else to bear the responsibility for that: "No; but we will bind thee fast, and deliver thee into their hand: but surely we will not kill thee" (v.13). His meek submission to their will stood in direct contrast to their lack of loyalty to him. Graciously, he spared them from the fate that was about to come upon the Philistines, and would also have come upon them if they had sought to slay him. They might be prepared to betray him, but he had no desire to use his power and strength against them, even though they were deserving of it. In addition, if he had refused their request and escaped, he would have left them to face the wrath of the unscrupulous Philistines.

Fourthly, the sequence of words and actions reached its crescendo when, "they bound him with two new cords, and brought him up from the rock" (v.13). Tragically, those who needed deliverance led the deliverer and handed him over to the enemy. The fact that they bound him with "new (fresh - 2319) cords" suggests that they made them specially for the occasion. It was therefore a premeditated act on their part. They were not confident that a single cord would hold him and therefore they made two.

Lest the reader is tempted to believe that those among the Lord's people could never sink any lower than they did in their treatment of Samson, such events point forward to an even more tragic scene where they reached even greater depths: "And while he yet spake, lo, Judas, one of the twelve, came, and with him a great multitude with swords and staves, from the chief priests and elders of the people ... Then came they, and laid hands on Jesus, and took him...Then did they spit in his face, and buffeted him; and others smote him with the palms of their hands...And when they had bound him, they led him away, and delivered him to Pontius Pilate the governor...Then answered all the people, and said, His blood be on us, and on our children...And they crucified him" (Mt 26.47,50,67; 27.2,25,35). However, in the face of such treatment, He "did no sin, neither was guile found in his mouth: who, when he was reviled, reviled not again; when he suffered, he threatened not: but committed himself to him that judgeth righteously" (1 Pet 2.22-23).

Verses 14-20: Samson "came unto Lehi"

The exact location of Lehi (jawbone - 3896 from 3895) is uncertain but it must have been somewhere in Judah. The man who had been in the cleft of the rock of Etam did not need foxes to bring about deliverance now. When "the Philistines shouted against him…the Spirit of the Lord came mightily upon him, and the cords that were upon his arms became as flax that was burnt with fire, and his bands loosed from off his hands" (v.14). As the Philistines saw him bound and led in apparent weakness into Lehi by his own people, they must have felt that the victory belonged to them. However, they had not reckoned with the God of Samson. The bonds of men could not restrain a man who was empowered by the Spirit of the Lord. Once again, the Lord did not abandon him in his hour of need and gave him a further "occasion (opportunity) against the Philistines" (14.4). He was among those of whom the Psalmist said, "Our fathers trusted in thee: they trusted, and thou didst deliver them" (Ps 22.4).

If Samson is a faint picture of the Christ being bound and led away to Calvary, his breaking of the cords foreshadows His resurrection. Men thought that they had gained the victory at the cross and mocked Him: "He trusted in God; let him deliver now, if he will have him" (Mt 27.43). Unlike Samson, He endured the fires of Calvary and experienced the abandonment that led Him to say, "O my God, I cry in the daytime but thou hearest not; and in the night season, and am not silent" (Ps 22.2). However, speaking of Him on the day of Pentecost, Peter declared, "Whom God hath raised up, having loosed the pains of death: because it was not possible that he should be holden of it" (Acts 2.24).

Yet again, in the ensuing events, Samson exhibited a strange mixture of that which was spiritual and that which was fleshly. Clearly, the bursting of the bonds had nothing to do with his natural strength but was achieved by the power of the Spirit. His desire to seize the opportunity to slay the Philistines was in accord with the purpose of his life to "begin to deliver Israel out of the hand of the Philistines" (13.5). Sadly, his next act revealed the ease with which he compromised his Nazarite vow: "And he found a new jawbone of an ass, and put forth his hand, and took it" (v.15). The word "new" (TSARI - 2961) means, "moist, dripping, fresh", the implication being that it was recently made as such. It was not a dry and brittle jawbone from a skeleton but one that was taken from a recently slain animal. Thus the Nazarite deliverer picked up an unclean instrument to bring about deliverance. Once again, the Lord overruled and he "slew a thousand men therewith" (v.15). Initially, the success was all about him. His victory song focused upon his role in the slaying of the Philistines and he failed to give God the glory. It was a clever play on the similarity between the sounds of the Hebrew words for "ass" and "heap", which is difficult to capture in the English translation: "With the jawbone of an ass, heaps upon heaps, with the jaw of an ass have I slain a thousand men" (v.16). Following his song, he "called that place Ramath-lehi (height of a jawbone - 7437)" (v.17), thereby directing attention to the way in which he had gained the victory. However, to his credit "he cast away the jawbone out of his hand" (v.17), perhaps recognising the potential for it to become an object of worship as Gideon's ephod had become (8.27).

Samson was exhausted by his exploits and therefore he was brought face to face with the need for dependence upon the Lord: "and he was sore athirst" (v.18). His response on this occasion was spiritual and one that would be expected from a Nazarite (v.18). Firstly, he "called on the Lord". This is the first recorded occasion when he was shown turning to the Lord in weakness and dependence upon Him. Secondly, he gave the glory to the Lord for the victory over the Philistines: "Thou hast given this great deliverance". Thirdly, he acknowledged that he was simply the Lord's "servant" in the victory: "into the hand of thy servant". Fourthly, he recognised the distinction between himself and the Philistines by referring to them as "the uncircumcised". Fifthly, he confessed that his need was great and that he was not sufficient in himself to meet it: "and now shall I die for thirst?". There is perhaps a hint here that he may also have been concerned about the damage that it would do to the Lord's name if he were to perish as a direct result of his conflict with the uncircumcised Philistines.

The Lord not only heard but He answered the prayer of His dependent servant in a remarkable way. Samson experienced the truth of the words of the psalmist: "The Lord is nigh unto all them that call upon him, to all that call upon him in truth" (Ps 145.18). The Lord answered in the form of a miracle: "But God clave (rent, broke, opened - 1234) an hollow place (a mortar, a socket of a tooth - 4388) that was in the jaw (LECHI - jawbone – the same word used for Lehi in v.14 - 3895), and there came water thereout" (v.19). The use of the word "God" (ELOHIM - 430) indicates that it was the Creator God (cf. Gen 1.1) who exercised control over the forces of nature to meet the needs of His thirsty servant. Some commentators believe that the word "jaw" implies that the water came out of the jawbone of the ass but the context makes it much more likely that it refers to the particular place where Samson was in Lehi (jawbone). Indeed, he had already "cast away the jawbone" of the ass (v.17). It was therefore in some rocky place in Lehi that God created a hollow in the rock out of which the water flowed. The naming of the specific place where this took place suggests that this interpretation is the more likely: "wherefore he called the name thereof En-hakkore, which is Lehi unto this day" (v.19). The name Ramath-lehi recalled the weapon that Samson had used to destroy the Philistines but En-hakkorc (thc fountain of one calling, the caller's spring - 5875) was a constant reminder of man's weakness, and the power and the grace of God to provide spiritual refreshment for His people (cf. Ex 17.6; Is 41.17). When Samson "had drunk, his spirit came again, and he revived" (v.19). H.L.Rossier, making the application to believers today, writes, "If we do not wish to lose the results of conflict, we must use the Word of God for our refreshment, and not only for combat...The rock everywhere and always is Christ. 'If any man thirst, let him come unto me, and drink' (Jn 7.37). Let us get back into Christ's presence after conflict. His word will refresh us" (*Meditations on the Book of Judges*).

It is significant that the author of the Book of Judges, under the guidance of the Holy Spirit, records of Samson at this point, "And he judged Israel in the days of the Philistines twenty years" (v.20). It is fitting that this statement should appear immediately following one of the brighter spiritual periods in his life. It would have been inappropriate to record it at the end of the following chapter after he loses his Nazariteship, his sight, his freedom and ultimately, his life. Clearly, nothing is recorded of many of the twenty years but God took cognisance of them. Indeed, Samson's impact was only felt within a comparatively small area of the land, but the grace of God recognises and honours his contribution to judging "Israel".

JUDGES 16

One of the saddest statements in the Old Testament is to be found in this final stage of Samson's life: "And he wist not that the Lord was departed (turned off, removed, withdrawn - 5493) from him" (v.20). There can be no more parlous position for a man to be found in than this. It was serious enough that the Lord had departed from him but for him to be ignorant of this fact emphasises his low spiritual condition. It was a far cry from his beginnings: "and the child grew, and the Lord blessed him. And the Spirit of the Lord began to move him at times in the camp of Dan" (13.24-25). There had been so much hope for the child who was to "be a Nazarite unto God from the womb" (13.5). The writer of Lamentations graphically describes Nazarites as those who are "purer than snow ... whiter than milk ... more ruddy in body than rubies, their polishing ... of sapphire" (Lam 4.7). However, he describes a time to come in the city of Jerusalem when, sadly, "Their visage is blacker than a coal; they are not known in the streets: their skin cleaveth to their bones; it is withered, it is become like a stick" (Lam 4.8). Samson descended into a similar condition as his days drew to a close. The events that follow reveal the journeys that he took in reaching the lowest point of his life, when the Lord departed from him.

Verses 1-3: A Journey of Lust – "Then went Samson to Gaza"

The words that introduce Samson's next journey, "And it came to pass afterward" (v.4), suggest that his first journey when he "went to Gaza" (v.1), set the scene for the even more disastrous events that were to unfold. When he "went down to Timnath, and saw a woman", at least he "told his father and his mother" on his return (14.1-2). However, the journey to Gaza (strong place - 5804) was taken alone and the outcomes shared with no one. He should not have taken the journey in the first place and, once again, it was only the grace of the sovereign Lord that brought him out of the city alive.

Gaza was the southern-most of the five key Philistine cities. It had once been in the possession of Judah (1.18) but they ultimately lost control of it to the Philistines. It may have been a stronghold to the Philistines but it was a place that exposed the weakness of a Nazarite. It is not stated why Samson went to Gaza, which was about forty miles from his home town of Zorah. The distance he travelled suggests that it was a deliberate and planned journey. If there were any pure motives, such as seeking another "occasion (opportunity) against the Philistines" (14.4), they were soon lost as, once again, "the lust of the flesh, and the lust of the eyes" (1 Jn 2.16) proved to be his downfall. He was not there long before he "saw there an harlot, and went in unto her" (v.1). It seems almost unthinkable that a Nazarite, upon whom the Spirit of the Lord had come mightily, should be found in the house of a prostitute. Nevertheless, it was so, and it therefore serves to remind believers that no child of God is immune from facing the temptations that could lead to such a fall. If they are found in wrong places, they will see forbidden things. Some commentators have sought to put a positive gloss on Samson's actions by suggesting that he was not driven by lust. They suggest that by visiting the prostitute he was signalling his complete power over the enemy to do with them as he willed. However, there is no justification for turning such a deplorable act into one that is respectable. Clearly, once Samson saw the woman, he was unable to control his inner lusts and he "went in unto her". It was tragic that a Nazarite, who should have stood out as a result of his separated life unto God, attracted the attention of the ungodly through his immorality: "And it was told the Gazites, saying, Samson is come hither" (v.2). They were, no doubt, surprised that he was to be found in their city, emphasising how inappropriate it was for him to be there.

Clearly, Samson's reputation had gone before him and the Gazites displayed some reluctance in confronting him: "And they compassed him in, and laid wait for him all night in the gate of the city, and were quiet all the night, saying, In the morning, when it is day, we shall kill him" (v.2). However, their plans were thwarted and they were caught off their guard: "And Samson lay till midnight, and arose at midnight" (v.3). Whether it was a guilty conscience that caused him to stir or the fact that he had simply gratified his lust is not stated. What is clear is that the Lord had not yet departed from him and therefore He delivered him out of the dangerous territory in which he found himself. At least he arose at midnight, which was better than remaining in the woman's house and not rising at all. In an amazing display of strength, Samson "took the doors of the gate of the city, and the two posts, and went away with them, bar and all, and put them upon his shoulders, and carried them up to the top of an hill that is before Hebron" (v.3). As well as being an impressive physical act that would have caused the enemy to tremble, it was also a highly symbolic act. The "gate of a city" spoke of its power and security. It was also the place where business took place (Ruth 4.1-2) and where justice was administered (2 Sam 15.2). The angel of the Lord promised Abraham, "thy seed shall possess the gate of his enemies" (Gen 22.17). It was therefore a sign of his dominance over the power of the Philistines that Samson tore up by his great strength the doors, the posts and the bars and carried them off, leaving the city defenceless and exposed. He, indeed, possessed "the gate of his enemies".

Commentators are divided as to how far Samson carried the gates. If he carried them as far as Hebron, as the text suggests, it would have involved a journey of almost forty miles (64 kilometres). However, some believe that "before Hebron" means, "facing or in the direction of Hebron", which suggests that he may have taken them to a hill outside of Gaza that was facing Hebron. It is the present writer's view that it is preferable to take the text as it stands. If Samson's victory was to be complete, he needed to carry the gates out of Philistine territory and not to leave them in the close vicinity of Gaza, thus allowing them to be recovered and re-erected. There would seem to be little point in mentioning Hebron if it is not to be taken literally. It would have been an appropriate spot for him to take the spoils of his victory. It has already been noted in the commentary on ch.1 that Hebron means, "fellowship, companionship", and that it was rich in its spiritual history. It was perhaps fitting therefore that Samson, who had sought companionship in the wrong place and with the wrong woman, should travel towards such a place. The Lord would always have His people to seek fellowship in the right spiritual atmosphere. It is also interesting that a man displaying such superhuman strength should reach the place that had formerly been called Kirjath-arba, which means, "city of the giants". The Lord was still showing him, even in the latter days of his life, that he still had the power to break the might of the Philistines if he were to live the separated life.

It is encouraging for believers to know that a greater and mightier than Samson has gained the victory over Satan, sin and death. If the Philistines thought they had made Samson secure in order for them to gain the victory, Christ's enemies believed they had done the same to Him. They had to surround a harlot's house to keep watch over Samson but Christ's enemies set a watch and sealed the stone of a new sepulchre in which He had been laid (Mt 27.66). The hymn writer expresses the futility of their efforts in the face of His might:

Death cannot keep his prey,
Jesus, my Saviour,
He tore the bars away,
Jesus, my Lord

Up from the grave He arose
With a mighty triumph o'er His foes;
He arose a victor from the dark domain,
And He lives forever with His saints to reign;
He arose! He arose!
Hallelujah! Christ arose.

(Robert Lowry)

Verses 4-20: A Journey of Love – "he loved a woman in the valley of Sorek"

Although Samson came out of Gaza with the gates of the city upon his shoulders, his victory was not complete. He did not display any sign of repentance for the actions that had led to a need for deliverance in the first place and it was therefore only a matter of time before he fell again: "it came to pass afterward, that he loved a woman in the valley of Sorek, whose name was Delilah" (v.4). This lapse was to be his last with women and the outcomes were catastrophic. Lust in Gaza now became love in "the valley of Sorek" (vines - 7796). This woman was more than in his sight; she was in his heart's affection. For a Nazarite, with a vow to be separate from wine and strong drink, to be found in the Philistine "valley of vines" promised nothing but heartache and ruin. Delilah (1809) means, "languishing", and she was the only one of the three women with whom Samson was associated to be named. Yet again, his eyes strayed into forbidden territory and danger is ever "languishing" in such a place to engulf the vulnerable child of God. Delilah's name is Semitic, which has led some commentators to believe that she was an Hebrew. However, intermarriage with surrounding peoples was a known feature of the Philistine way of life and it is much more likely that she was a Philistine. M.F.Unger describes her as, "an excellent illustration of the world, the fair, alluring, pleasure-loving religious world, which aims, as she did, to rob the true Nazarite of his separation as the real power of the spiritual life (*Commentary on the Old Testament*).

Clearly, news of what Samson had done at Gaza placed him in the number one position of the Philistines' most wanted men. The "lords of the Philistines" (cf. 3.3), undoubtedly the five rulers of the five principal cities, saw his love for Delilah as an opportunity not to be missed: "Entice him, and see wherein his great strength lieth, and by what means we may prevail against him, that we may bind him to afflict (look down on, browbeat, depress, abase - 6031) him" (v.5). They do not appear to have wanted to kill him but their ambition was to humiliate him and to abuse him at their leisure. Prior to this, Philistines in Timnath had issued threats of death to a woman if she failed to entice Samson to tell her the answer to his riddle but here the influential and wealthy lords attracted Delilah with the promise of money to betray him: "we will give thee every one of us eleven hundred pieces of silver" (v.5). Such a considerable sum of money would have set her up financially for life and therefore she displayed no scruples in pursuing the reward. As far as the lords were concerned Samson, the Nazarite, was a prize worth the payment.

Delilah's strategy was to play a none-too-subtle game with Samson in order to gain the desired secret from him: "Tell me, I pray thee, wherein thy great strength lieth, and wherewith thou mightest be bound to afflict thee" (v.6). This was hardly the language of one who had any love or affection for him but Samson was too consumed by his passion for her to discern what she was doing. Sadly, he was prepared to go along with her and to use his Nazariteship as a matter for sport. He had a secret that could not be shared with ungodly and uncircumcised Philistines and he well knew that. The Lord Jesus warned His disciples, "Give not that which is holy unto the dogs, neither cast ye your pearls before swine, lest they trample them under their feet, and turn again and rend you" (Mt 7.6). Samson embarked on a dangerous course of action by sailing as close to the wind as he could without divulging the secret. He found himself telling downright lies in order to enter into the spirit of the game. He appears to have made frequent visits to Delilah and each step of the journey led him into increased danger.

Firstly, he told her, "If they bind me with seven green (new, fresh, unused - 3892) withs (bowstrings) that were never dried, then shall I be weak, and be as another man" (v.7). The lords of the Philistines were happy to supply her with the "seven green withs which had not been dried" (v.8). Yet, unbeknown to her, this was not the secret of his strength. "She bound him with them" but when she said, "The Philistines be upon thee, Samson ... he brake the withs, as a thread of tow is broken when it toucheth the fire" (vv.8-9). The men who were "lying in wait, abiding with her in the chamber" (v.9) to seize Samson, suddenly found themselves redundant. The Lord graciously preserved the secret of his strength: "So his strength was not known" (v.9).

Secondly, in response to Delilah's complaint, "thou hast mocked me, and told me lies" (v.10), Samson said, "If they bind me fast with new ropes that never were occupied, then shall I be weak, and be as another man" (v.11). Clearly, the Philistines seem to have been unaware that this had been attempted without success at Lehi (15.13-14), and therefore the outcome was the same as it had been previously. She bound him with the new ropes but when she repeated the words, "The Philistines be upon thee, Samson...he brake them from off his arms like a thread" (v.12). Yet again, the "liers in wait abiding in the chamber" (v.12) were surplus to requirements!

Thirdly, Samson came as near as it was possible to divulging the secret of his strength. He used his hair, the symbol of his Nazariteship, to prolong the game. In response to Delilah's further complaint that he had mocked her and told her lies, he said, "If thou weavest the seven locks of my head with the web" (v.13). She was undaunted by her previous failures and, while he slept she did as he had suggested and then, "she fastened it with a pin (peg, stake – probably a flat piece of wood - 3489)" (v.14). By this time the Philistines appear to have lost faith in her ability to accomplish the task, because they are not recorded as being present. It is not precisely clear from the text what Delilah did, but it appears that she wove his hair into the warp (the threads stretched lengthwise in a loom) and then beat it into the web with the pin. His hair therefore would have been intertwined with the woven material. For the third time she was deceived, and at her words, "The Philistines be upon thee, Samson ... he awaked out of his sleep, and went away with the pin of the beam, and with the web" (v.14). It was a feat that would have called for remarkable strength. It is hard to imagine how his hair would have been disentangled afterwards!

If Samson had thought that this would mark the end of the game, he could not have been more wrong. Delilah's desire for the reward led her to keep up the pressure. She now played upon his affections and love for her. She did not reciprocate that love but she was happy to use it to achieve her own selfish ends. "And she said unto him, How canst thou say, I love thee, when thine heart is not with me? thou hast mocked me these three times, and hast not told me wherein thy great strength lieth" (v.15). It was love that had led him down into the valley of Sorek, and therefore he should not have been surprised that it was now being used against him.

Such was his love for her, that Samson clearly made frequent visits to Delilah. On these occasions, "she pressed him daily with her words, and urged him, so that his soul was vexed to death" (v.16). The pressure was so intense that it was beginning to take the pleasure out of his visits, and so the sad day arrived when, "he told her all his heart, and said unto her, There hath not come a rasor upon mine head; for I have been a Nazarite unto God from my mother's womb: if I be shaven, then my strength will go from me, and I shall become weak, and be like any other man" (v.17). His heart was so blinded by passion that he appears to have trusted her implicitly with his secret. He regarded his Nazariteship so lightly that he was now prepared to go beyond using it as part of a game and divulged it to a scheming and unscrupulous woman. After three failed attempts, she would, no doubt, have recognised a further lie but this had a ring of truth about it. She again called the lords of the Philistines, saying, "Come up this once, for he hath shewed me all his heart" (v.18). They responded and "brought money in their hand" (v.18). They, along with Delilah, were about to witness to the truth that, "the love of money is the root of all evil" (1 Tim 6.10).

To see the Nazarite who had slain the young lion (14.6), slain Philistines (14.19; 15.15), and carried away the gates of Gaza (16.3), asleep upon the knees of a godless woman to whom he had divulged the secret of his strength was a scene of abject weakness that could only degenerate still further. She seized the moment and "called for a man, and she caused him to shave off (make bald, lay waste - 1548) the seven locks of his head" (v.19). She was not simply content for the man to cut off his locks but she insisted that he was shaved so that every appearance of his Nazariteship was removed. As a Philistine, she would have had no appreciation of the fact that his strength was not really in his long hair, as such, but in his devotion and separation to the Lord, of which the long hair was a sign. It was not Delilah therefore that had deprived him of his strength but he brought himself to that position by breaking his vow.

From that point onwards, "she began to afflict him, and his strength went from him" (v.19). It is unlikely that the word "afflict" is meant to convey the meaning that she physically abused him in any way, because, after all, he was still asleep on her lap at the time. It is the same word as used in v.5 and probably means that she was in a position to abase and subdue him now that he had been deprived of his strength. On the three previous occasions when she had said, "The Philistines be upon thee, Samson", he had broken his bonds but this time it was different. The moment he awoke, he must have realised that all was not well, but he still went through the motions as normal: "I will go out as at other times before, and shake myself" (v.20). The word "shake" (NAAR - 5287) has the thought of "the rustling of the mane that accompanies a lion's roar". It conjures up a picture of fearsome strength and power. Sadly, Samson's breaking of his vow had left him powerless, and he no longer possessed the potential to deliver Israel. Nevertheless, like many of the Lord's people since, he continued to give the outward impression that he could still do all the things he had done previously. He had sunk so low that he failed to discern that "the Lord was departed (turned off - 5493) from him" (v.20). He had no appreciation of the seriousness of his actions in breaking all three aspects of his Nazarite vow and therefore he had no sense of how the Lord felt about it. Separation unto the Lord was a serious business and yet he had treated it as a matter of sport in Timnath and now in the valley of Sorek. Although it gave the Lord no pleasure to do so, He had reached the point with Samson where His Spirit could no longer come "mightily upon him" as in the past.

Verse 21: A Journey of Loss

The sight of Samson failing to "shake" himself as he had done "at other times before" (v.20) was tragic enough but the next step on his journey was even more tragic. "But the Philistines took him, and put out his eyes, and brought him down to Gaza, and bound him with fetters of brass; and he did grind in the prison house" (v.21). On his previous visit to the city he had carried away the gates on his shoulders (v.3) but now he was in the prison house grinding corn, a menial and humiliating task that was usually assigned to women and slaves. Taking up the imagery suggested by the word "shake", the "lion" that had struck fear into the Philistines had lost his roar and the mane no longer rustled. The chapter that began with Samson taking a journey to Gaza of his own free will (v.1), draws towards its conclusion with him being taken back there by the Philistines against his will. There would have been some dignity in the account if the once mighty man had "fallen in the midst of the battle" (2 Sam 1.25). Sadly, the Philistines took him when he was doing anything but carrying the battle to them. He was on their soil, loving a woman he had no right to love.

He presented a sad and wretched figure as he was taken down to Gaza. Not only did the Lord, in His sovereignty, chastise Samson by taking away his strength but he also lost his sight. His eyes had lusted after Philistine women (14.1; 16.1) and had been the cause of his downfall. It was therefore fitting that the Philistines were the instruments used by the Lord to discipline His wayward servant. Blindness is a feature of "last days" (2 Tim 3.1) conditions. Eli, the last priest in the tabernacle at Shiloh before the Lord removed the testimony from there (1 Sam 3.2), Zedekiah, the last king of Judah (2 Kings 25.7), and the church of the Laodiceans, the last of the seven churches in Asia Minor to be addressed (Rev 3.17), were blind. And now, Samson, the last judge in the book of Judges ends his days in darkness. The Lord Jesus said to His disciples, "And if thine eye offend thee, pluck it out: it is better for thee to enter into the kingdom of God with one eye, than having two eyes to be cast into hell fire" (Mk 9.47). If only Samson had exercised self-discipline throughout his life he would not have experienced the chastening hand of the Lord.

Verses 22-30: The Last Journey

The sad scene in the prison house might lead the reader to the conclusion that the purposes of the Lord had been thwarted. When Manoah's wife reported to her husband the message of the angel of the Lord to her, she said, "For the child shall be a Nazarite to God from the womb to the day of his death" (13.7). Whilst these were not the exact words of the angel (13.5), they certainly conveyed the sense of what was said to her. The pathetic figure of a man who had lost his Nazariteship, his sight and his freedom would appear to be a far cry from the fulfilment of these hopes. From a human standpoint there was no possibility of a way back. The actions of the Philistines gave the impression that they, and their god, had gained the victory: "Then the lords of the Philistines gathered them together for to offer a great sacrifice unto Dagon their god, and to rejoice: for they said, Our god hath delivered Samson our enemy into our hand" (v.23). The sight of Samson led the people to the same conclusion as their leaders: "And when the people saw him, they praised their god: for they said, Our god hath delivered into our hands our enemy, and the destroyer of our country, which slew many of us" (v.24). There was a real sense of relief in their voices that Israel's deliverer, who had caused them so much distress, was now seemingly in their power. There was no disputing the fact that he had been delivered into their hands but their blindness meant that they were attributing the praise to the wrong god. The sight of "the daughters of the Philistines" rejoicing and "the daughters of the uncircumcised" triumphing (2 Sam 1.20) over the fall of the deliverer did not go by unnoticed by the Lord and they would ultimately feel the force of His wrath.

The chastening of the Lord is never intended to be an end in itself. He is always looking for restoration. His promise is that "afterward it yieldeth the peaceable fruit of righteousness unto them which are exercised thereby" (Heb 12.11). Godless and uncircumcised Philistines failed to see what was happening in the prison house. A work of grace and recovery was taking place in the darkness that would mean the purposes of the Lord would be fulfilled. The Philistines might have restricted the movements of Samson but they could not control the stirrings within his heart. Clearly, although unable to see what was going on around him, and facing countless hours of boring labour, he began to recover his devotion to the Lord: "Howbeit the hair of his head began to grow again after he was shaven" (v.22).

It was from this point that Samson began the last stage of his journey. The Philistines rejoicing at their success had reached fever pitch and it was "when their hearts were merry, that they said, Call for Samson, that he may make us sport" (v.25). Sad as it was to see Israel's deliverer used as an object of sport, the Philistines failed to grasp that he was also the Lord's chosen deliverer and that they could not treat him as they willed and escape unscathed. By setting him "between the pillars" (v.25) of their temple, they were in fact setting the stage for their own destruction. As far as they were concerned, Samson no longer posed a threat to them. The sight of "the destroyer of our country" (v.24) being led by a "lad that held him by the hand" (v.26) filled them with a sense of false security. His request of the lad would only have confirmed to them his weakness: "Suffer me that I may feel the pillars whereupon the house standeth, that I may lean upon them" (v.26). They were so confident that his strength had gone forever that "the house was full of men and women; and all the lords of the Philistines were there; and there were upon the roof about three thousand men and women, that beheld while Samson made sport" (v.27). In his former days, before the Lord had departed from him, they would not have displayed such complacency in his presence. They had seen what he had done to the gates of their city but all that was in the past. However, they had not reckoned on Samson's God.

The proof that a genuine work of recovery had taken place in Samson's heart was shown by his final prayer in which he used three different titles for God: he "called unto the Lord (Jehovah), and said, O Lord (Adonai) God (Jehovah), remember me, I pray thee, and strengthen me, I pray thee, only this once, O God (Elohim), that I may be at once avenged of the Philistines for my two eyes" (v.28). This was only the second recorded time that he had called upon the Lord. In his first prayer (15.18) he asked for his life to be sustained but in the second he asks for death. Some commentators view this second request as one that was primarily prompted by a selfish desire for vengeance. Clearly, the Lord did not regard it as such, otherwise He would not have heard and answered. It is much more likely that it was the prayer of a penitent man who viewed what the Philistines had done to him personally as an affront to the Lord Himself. He recognised his total dependence upon the Lord as, for the last time, "he sought an occasion (opportunity) against the Philistines" (14.4). As "Samson took hold of (clasped, grasped - 3943) the two middle pillars upon which the house stood, and on which it was borne up, of the one with his right hand, and of the other with his left" (v.29), he said, "Let me die with the Philistines" (v.30). He voluntarily chose death as the means of removing his shame and restoring the Lord's honour among the Philistines. The Lord graciously responded: "And he bowed himself with all his might; and the house fell upon the lords, and upon all the people that were therein" (v.30).

The magnitude of his victory is captured in a simple statement: "So the dead which he slew at his death were more than they which he slew in his life" (v.30). Viewed negatively, this statement might appear to be a sad commentary on the unrealised potential of his life. However, viewed positively, as it should be, it speaks of the grace of God that allowed His restored servant to fulfil the promise that he would "begin to deliver Israel out of the hand of the Philistines" (13.5) and thus earn his place in the New Testament gallery of faith (Heb 11.32). In spite of Samson's failures, the purposes of God had not been thwarted. C.A.Coates brings out the positive aspect of his death, and applies it to the believer today, when he writes, "When Samson, the blind prisoner, grinding in the prison house, and making sport for the Philistines, called on the Lord, he was a greater man than he had ever been before. He could do more than he ever did before, but he did it by death. He had to learn that his own death was the secret of power. We have all to face these lessons…When Samson had learnt the secret of death, he was ready to be taken away. He had reached the climax; he slew more in his death than ever in his life. When I come to accept my death, the great secret of the power of God works in me, and I become an efficient instrument for the use of God" (*An Outline of the Book of Judges*).

Verse 31: The Journey's End

It is touching to note that after Samson had taken the final step on his eventful journey there were those who cared enough to come to Gaza and recover his mutilated body from the midst of the ruined temple: "Then his brethren and all of the house of his father came down, and took him, and brought him up, and buried him between Zorah and Eshtaol in the buryingplace of Manoah his father" (v.31). It would have taken a great deal of courage for them to venture into enemy territory after the Philistines had suffered such a humiliating and crushing defeat. They would have been far from welcome visitors once they declared their link with Samson. However, the grace of God allowed the body of the man whose journey had so often taken him downwards to be taken up out of the land of the Philistines and buried with dignity where his father was buried. His journey had taken him full circle and he was back "between Zorah and Eshtaol", where the Spirit of the Lord first "began to move him at times" (13.25). There had been many twists and turns along the way but as the sun finally set on his life the Word of God reaffirms that "he judged twenty years" (15.20; 16.31).

Although Samson's shortcomings mean that it would be inappropriate to refer to him as a type of Christ, these closing scenes of his life point towards the time of the Lord's death, burial and resurrection. The love of money on the part of Judas Iscariot was the motivating factor in His betrayal by one who never truly loved Him (Mt 26.15). During the time of His arrest He became the object of sport in the hands of His enemies: "And when they had platted a crown of thorns, they put it upon his head, and a reed in his right hand: and they bowed the knee before him, and mocked him, saying, Hail, King of the Jews! And they spit upon him, and took the reed, and smote him on the head" (Mt 27.29-30). Willingly and voluntarily, "he humbled himself, and became obedient unto death, even the death of the cross" (Phil 2.8).

The destruction and deliverance that Christ brought about by His death was far greater than that accomplished by Samson: "Forasmuch then as the children are partakers of flesh and blood, he also himself likewise took part of the same; that through death he might destroy him that had the power of death, that is, the devil; and deliver them who through fear of death were all their lifetime subject to bondage" (Heb 2.14-15). Paul writes, "And having spoiled principalities and powers, he made a shew of them openly, triumphing over them in it" (Col 2.15). John writes, "For this purpose the Son of God was manifested, that he might destroy the works of the devil" (1 Jn 3.8). At the time of His death, "the veil of the temple was rent in twain from the top to the bottom; and the earth did quake, and the rocks rent; and the graves were opened; and many bodies of the saints which slept arose, and came out of the graves after his resurrection" (Mt 27.51-53). A secret disciple, Joseph of Arimathæa, ignored the risk to his own life and "begged the body of Jesus", and with loving hands "took it down, and wrapped it in linen, and laid it in a sepulchre" (Lk 23.52-53). As they lifted Samson's body out of the rubble of the temple at Gaza they knew that there was no hope that the voice of their deliverer would be heard again. At best, he had only begun to bring deliverance, but Paul writes of Christ, "But now is Christ risen from the dead...For as in Adam all die, even so in Christ shall all be made alive...For he must reign, till he hath put all enemies under his feet" (1 Cor 15.20,22,25).

Samson's death brought to a close the history of the judges as recorded in the book of Judges. The true value of his life will be lost if it is viewed simply as that of an individual who struggled throughout his life with the principle of separation and the need for him to be distinctive among the nations. The Lord intended that the children of Israel and, indeed, believers of all generations, should see their own struggle reflected in that of Samson and learn the lessons. The problem was that the children of Israel were too blind to see, let alone heed, the warning. They too had been chosen by God to be distinctive among the nations and they had the great potential for His power to be displayed through their weakness. From time to time, like Samson, they experienced the liberating nature of that power. However, in general, instead of allowing the potential to be realised, they struggled to retain their identity until eventually, they lost it altogether. Instead of subduing their enemies, they courted favour with them and willingly became subservient to them. Peter urges believers to appreciate that they are "a chosen generation, a royal priesthood, an holy nation, a peculiar people; that ye should shew forth the praises of him who hath called you out of darkness into his marvellous light" (1 Pet 2.9). Although Samson's life sounds out a warning of the dangers that await those who leave the path of separation to God, it also serves as an encouragement. The Lord may discipline His erring servants but He longs for them to call upon Him so that He can recover them and deliver them. They only have to come to an end of themselves, cry to Him in true repentance and He will answer.

A. T. Pierson brings home the challenge of the final episode in Samson's life when he writes, "I believe that you will often find that a Christian never gets to the end of himself until he gets to his deathbed. Really, his whole life has been spent in temporising with the world, until he gets face to face with eternal issues, and there is an end of self as there is an end of life … We ought to reach our deathbed long before that. We ought to reach the end of self long before that; surely so. The end of self should be reached at the cross, and there we should abide, always counting ourselves dead unto sin, but alive unto God in Christ Jesus" (*Lectures on the Book of Judges*).

THE SUMMIT OF THE NATION'S SIN (17.1-21.25)

JUDGES 17

The final five chapters of the book of Judges stand in marked contrast to those that have gone before. The familiar occurrences of Israel doing evil in the sight of the Lord, the presence of foreign oppressors and the provision of judges by the Lord are absent. Some commentators have suggested that this concluding section must have come from the pen of a different author and that it was added at a later date. However, such a view fails to appreciate the distinctive contribution that it makes to the completeness and harmony of the divine record of the period. Clearly, the two events recorded in chs.18-19 and chs.20-21 respectively, take the reader back to the early days of the judges, immediately following the death of Joshua and the elders that outlived him (2.7-8). The reference to the fact that "in those days the tribe of the Danites sought them an inheritance to dwell in; for unto that day all their inheritance had not fallen unto them among the tribes of Israel" (18.1), reflects an earlier statement that "the Amorites forced the children of Dan into the mountain: for they would not suffer them to come down to the valley" (1.34). It was this opposition that eventually led to the movement northwards of part of the tribe of Dan in order to seek an inheritance.

Under the guidance of the Holy Spirit, the author of the book of Judges used the final two stories to provide a fitting summary to the whole. He was therefore more concerned with moral rather than chronological order. He began his record with the words, "Now after the death of Joshua" (1.1) and, in the opening section of the book (1.1-3.6), he revealed the seeds of Israel's failure as seen in their relationships with the Canaanites who were left in the land following Joshua's death. By returning to those earlier days, and recording two representative incidents from them to close his account, he gave a deeper insight into what took place in the people's hearts from the outset and, indeed, throughout the entire period. It would appear, at first glance, that the two events are recorded without him expressing either approval or disapproval of what happened. Nevertheless, it soon becomes clear in his recurrent statement, "In those days there was no king in Israel" (17.6; 18.1; 19.1; 21.25) that he saw the lawlessness of the day as the major cause of Israel's problems. It is possible that he was writing in the early days of the monarchy and that he was comparing the more settled form of central government then with the moral, religious and social chaos during the time of the judges. However, it is more probable that he was identifying Israel's rejection of Jehovah as their rightful king (cf. 1 Sam 8.6-7) as the major reason for the state of anarchy that existed, when "every man did that which was right in his own eyes"

(17.6; 21.25). Such conditions became a fertile breeding ground for all kinds of idolatry and immorality.

Religious Corruption - Idolatry (17.1-18.31)

Verses 1-6: The Man of Mount Ephraim

Micah's (4319) name means, "who is like Jehovah?" but this was as far as any similarity went. There was no one more unlike the Lord than Micah. He came from "mount Ephraim (669)" (v.1), which means "double fruit", but there was no fruit for the Lord in his life. It was barren of anything that would have given pleasure to the Lord. Indeed, both he and his mother contrived to break many of the Ten Commandments.

Firstly, he appeared on the scene as a thief. He confessed to his mother, "The eleven hundred shekels of silver that were taken from thee, about which thou cursedst, and spakest of also in mine ears, behold, the silver is with me; I took it" (v.2). In direct disobedience to the fifth, eighth and tenth of the Ten Commandments, "Honour thy father and thy mother...Thou shalt not steal...Thou shalt not covet" (Ex 20.12,15,17), he coveted that which belonged to his mother and eventually took it. This was the same sum of money that each of the lords of the Philistines had given Delilah to bring about Samson's downfall (16.5). Paul reminded the Colossian believers, "covetousness ...is idolatry" (Col 3.5). Secondly, it is unlikely that his confession arose out of any sense of remorse or genuine repentance. It was born out of fear for the suffering he would have to endure as a consequence of his mother's curse. He was therefore more concerned about his personal welfare than he was with any wrong that he had done. There is little doubt that she suspected him, because she made sure that he heard the curse loud and clear! Thirdly, he already had a "house of gods" (v.5) before the events recorded here unfolded, and yet God had instructed the people in the first of the Ten Commandments, "Thou shalt have no other gods before me" (Ex 20.3). The house of God that stood in Shiloh (18.31), in the territory of Ephraim, was not sufficient for him. He had the audacity to set up a system of worship in his own house that rivalled what was at Shiloh. He "made an ephod, and teraphim (household gods, cf. Gen 31.19,34,35 – referred to as 'the images'; 1 Sam 19.13 – referred to as 'an image'), and consecrated (4390, 3027- filled the hand of, cf. Ex 29.24) one of his sons, who became his priest" (v.5). False religion always seeks to imitate what is true. His later appointment of a Levite to be his priest (v.12), even though this was contrary to the word of God, suggests that he knew he was doing wrong in consecrating his son. Nevertheless, this did not hinder him from doing so.

Micah's mother set a poor example to him and must shoulder a major share of the blame for leading him into idol worship. Clearly, she was an inconsistent woman. James, when teaching concerning the power of the tongue, writes, "Therewith bless we God, even the Father; and therewith curse we men, which are made after the similitude of God. Out of the same mouth proceedeth blessing and cursing" (James 3.9-10). This certainly proved to be the case with Micah's mother. Her immediate response to the loss of her 1,100 shekels of silver was to curse the one who had taken it (v.2). This curse must have been issued with some venom for it to draw such a swift confession from her son. Yet, once he had owned up to his misdemeanour, she blessed him in the Lord's name: "Blessed be thou of the Lord, my son" (v.2). Her words revealed a total disregard for the third of the Ten Commandments, "Thou shalt not take the name of the Lord thy God in vain" (Ex 20.7). The Lord values His name, and therefore it should never be used for ungodly causes. She did not issue one word of rebuke for Micah's actions. If she had done so, she might have brought home to him the seriousness of what he had done.

Her lack of sincerity and consistency was revealed by her subsequent actions. In one breath she claimed, "I had wholly dedicated the silver unto the Lord from my hand for my son", but in the very next breath she revealed that she would use it "to make a graven image (PESEL - a sculpture or carving - 6459) and a molten image (MASSA – liquefy, pour out, project - 4551)" (v.3). Such an action was, of course, directly contrary to the second of the Ten Commandments, "Thou shalt not make unto thee any graven image … Thou shalt not bow down thyself to them, nor serve them" (Ex 20.4-5). Initially, Micah was reluctant to accept the offer, and "he restored the money unto his mother" (v.4). However, she would not be deflected from her wicked intentions and it would appear from her words that she ordered "the founder (refiner, silversmith - 6884)" to make two images (v.4). The first, the "graven image", would have been made out of carved wood, and the second, the "molten image", would have been cast from silver. Some commentators believe that there was only one image, and that "graven" is a generic term, whereas "molten" refers to the method by which it was made. They point out that only one image is mentioned in the next chapter (18.20,30).

Clearly, Micah's covetous spirit had been learned from his mother. When she visited the silversmith she parted with only "two hundred shekels of silver" (v.4), less than one fifth of the 1,100 shekels she had saved for the purpose. Like Ananias and Sapphira in the days of the early church, she "kept back part of the price" (Acts 5.2), no doubt seeking to create the impression that she had given the whole. Her deceitful action serves to remind believers of the importance of giving their very best to the Lord. It is so easy to cultivate a covetous spirit, which holds back more than is given, and yet seeks to give the impression to others that there has been a total surrender of, for example, time or money.

The book of Judges reveals the extent to which the children of Israel became immersed in the religion of the nations that surrounded them (10.6). The author's early comment that "they went a whoring after other gods, and bowed themselves unto them" (2.17) was illustrated repeatedly throughout the time of the judges. However, in the story of Micah and his mother, no mention is made of foreign gods, which indicates that idolatry was in the hearts of the people long before they became immersed in worshipping the gods of the nations. The blame for the rapid deterioration in their spiritual condition rested fairly and squarely on their own shoulders, not on the nations around them. Indeed, earlier on in their history, it was the people, not Aaron, who had said in the wilderness, "Up, make us gods, which shall go before us" (Ex 32.1).

A.R.Fausset issues an important warning to all believers, when he writes, "The root of idolatry and priestcraft is in the human heart; and it will put forth its noxious shoots...even among those favoured with the greatest spiritual privileges, such as we Christians enjoy. It is natural to our sensuous cravings...the sure and only antidote to it is to 'worship God in the spirit, and rejoice in Christ Jesus, and have no confidence in the flesh' (Phil 3.3)" (*A Critical and Expository Commentary on the Book of Judges*).

Verses 7-13: The Young Man out of Bethlehem-judah

As has already been observed, Micah would have been well aware of the fact that he had no authority to consecrate one of his sons as priest. Nevertheless, it answered a need at the time until a more fitting person could be found to fill the role. The perfect solution, as far as he was concerned, was found with the arrival of "a young man out of Bethlehem-judah of the family of Judah, who was a Levite" (v.7). A Levite could not, of course, be a descendant of Judah, which has led some commentators to suggest that he was not a member of the tribe of Levi. However, the reference to "the family of Judah" probably means that he was linked with the tribe of Judah by virtue of his residency among them, albeit only as a sojourner. The fact that he "sojourned (lodged as a guest - 1481)" in Bethlehem-judah says much about his spiritual condition. Levites had responsibilities in relation to the service of the tabernacle, not least of which were to guard the tabernacle and to convey it through the wilderness. The nature of their service meant that they were not given any part of the land as an inheritance. Nevertheless, the Lord graciously provided for their needs: "So all the cities which ye shall give to the Levites shall be forty and eight cities: them shall ye give with their suburbs (4054 – open area around the city)" (Num 35.7). Bethlehem-judah was not one of those cities and therefore the young man would have known that he should not have been there in the first place, and that he could not remain there. His predicament may have been partly to do with the failure of the children of Israel to live up to their responsibilities in relation to the Levites. The Lord had commanded that the Levites should receive tithes from the various tribes (Num 18.21,24,26) but it is probable that there were periods, such as in the days of the judges, when this requirement was ignored; this would have left the Levites in great need.

However, whatever the reasons were for this young man being in Bethlehem-judah, his motives for moving on were not of a spiritual nature. Instead of depending on the Lord to lead him and to provide for him, his eventual departure from the city was for purely materialistic reasons. It is not surprising that the journey of such a man, devoid as it was of any spiritual exercise, should end in the house of Micah, an idolater (v.8). His response to Micah's question, "Whence comest thou?", summed up the contradictions and compromises in his life: "I am a Levite of Bethlehem-judah, and I go to sojourn where I may find a place" (v.9). A true Levite would not have been pursuing such an aimless journey. Indeed, he ought to have been horrified at what he found when he reached Micah's house. He should have condemned the idolatry and shunned the offer, "Dwell with me, and be unto me a father and a priest, and I will give thee ten shekels of silver by the year, and a suit of apparel, and thy victuals" (v.10).

Sadly, the statement, "So the Levite went in. And the Levite was content to dwell with the man" (vv.10-11), confirms that he was prepared to sacrifice everything that a Levite stood for in order to acquire material security. There is no doubt that the invitation to be a priest attracted him, even though he had no right to the position. All Old Testament priests were Levites but not all Levites were priests; this was reserved for Aaron's sons (Num 3.10). Yet, dissatisfied with his own lot, he coveted the position to the extent of allowing an unauthorised person to consecrate him: "And Micah consecrated the Levite; and the young man became his priest, and was in the house of Micah" (v.12). Indeed, he felt so at home in Micah's "house of gods" (v.5) that he "was unto him as one of his sons" (v.11). It is significant that he is not named until 18.30, which suggests that the author was more concerned with focusing on what he did, rather than on who he was. Thus, with no pangs of conscience, Micah and the young man corrupted the priesthood. There are those who are engaged in such a pursuit today, and have instituted a priesthood that is of man's appointing with a "suit of apparel" and in "shekels of silver by the year" – a fixed stipend (v.10). The Lord's people need to hold on tenaciously to the New Testament teaching of priesthood. There is but one High Priest, which is Christ (Heb 5.5-6), and through His death and resurrection all believers have been constituted priests (1 Pet 2.5,9; Rev 1.6).

Micah's interpretation of events stand as a clear warning to believers of the danger of using circumstances alone to determine whether or not they are moving in the will of God. Circumstances have their place in determining that will but it is only the obedient and submissive believer who can hope to interpret them aright. The ease with which everything had fallen into place following his confession to his mother led Micah to declare, "Now know I that the Lord will do me good, seeing I have a Levite to my priest" (v.13). He was so spiritually blind that he convinced himself he was on the right track, believing that the Lord would bless him, even though he was an idolater who had polluted the priesthood. It was not long before he discovered how imperfect his knowledge was. What he thought he knew to be right could not have been further from the truth. The day would come when the Lord would take from him the gods and the priest that he believed were a sign of His blessing, and leave him with nothing (18.24).

JUDGES 18

Verses 1-31: The Children of Dan

Their dissatisfaction (vv.1-6)

The chapter opens with the author commenting for the second occasion in these closing sections, "In those days there was no king in Israel" (v.1). Clearly, he intended the statement to provide the setting for what was to follow. It has already been noted in the commentary on ch.17 that the lawlessness of the day, when the children of Israel failed to acknowledge God as their rightful king, provided a fertile breeding ground for idolatry. Such conditions also encouraged a spirit of dissatisfaction to blossom among the children of Dan. They had received an inheritance in the land of Canaan in the days of Joshua (Josh 19.40-48) but they had failed to possess it: "and in those days the tribe of the Danites sought them an inheritance to dwell in: for unto that day all their inheritance had not fallen unto them among the tribes of Israel" (v.1). They would, no doubt, have pointed to the pressure from the Amorites (1.34) and the Philistines (10.7) as the reason for them being forced to live in a confined area of the hill country. However, they showed no desire to fight for what had been given to them.

A significant proportion of the Danites soon became dissatisfied with their lot and decided to seek an easier place to possess: "And the children of Dan sent of their family five men from their coasts, men of valour, from Zorah, and from Eshtaol, to spy out the land, and to search it; and they said unto them, Go, search the land" (v.2). This discontentment led the five men to travel northwards, approximately one hundred miles away from the inheritance the Lord had allotted to them. Not surprisingly, their journey led them away from the Lord and into the house of an idolater: "who when they came to mount Ephraim, to the house of Micah, they lodged there" (v.2). S.Ridout sounds a warning note to the Lord's people of all generations, when he writes, "The people of God who are not satisfied with the full enjoyment of their own inheritance surely are just ready for the enemy to come in and lead them astray. It is an unfilled heart, a heart that has failed to enter upon its own portion, which is open to these assaults" (*Lectures on the Book of Judges*).

It is interesting to observe that the five men, who were representatives of a dissatisfied people, came under the influence of a priest who had himself been discontented with his position. They were surprised, and so they should have been, to find a Levite in the home of a man in Ephraim. Clearly, his southern accent betrayed him: "they knew the voice of the young man the Levite" (v.3). They may well have overheard him reciting prayers and other rituals. The tribes of Dan and Judah had close links and therefore it is possible that they might even have known him from the days when he sojourned in Bethlehem-judah (17.7). Their questions were searching: "Who brought thee hither? and what makest thou in this place? and what hast thou here?" (v.3). The only thing that can be said in the young Levite's favour is that he did not seek to hide the truth. Apparently, without a pang of conscience, he declared, "Thus and thus dealeth Micah with me, and hath hired me, and I am his priest" (v.4).

The fact that he claimed to be a priest aroused the interest of the spies still further. The Danites could, and should, have consulted the Lord through the tabernacle and the high priest at Shiloh (v.31) but they had failed to do so. The spies turned instead to a wayward Levite and said, "Ask counsel, we pray thee, of God (ELOHIM - 430), that we may know whether our way which we go shall be prosperous" (v.5). Their use of the general word, "Elohim", for God, rather than "the Lord (JEHOVAH - 3068)" reflected the low spiritual condition of the children of Dan at the time, as well as that of the Levite. They had lost sight of Jehovah as the covenant-keeping God, and they had little confidence that the Levite would know Him either. The latter's swift response to their enquiry confirmed that he was a sham: "And the priest said unto them, Go in peace: before the Lord (JEHOVAH -3068) is your way wherein ye go" (v.6). There is no indication that he made any attempt to seek the Lord's guidance. He simply told the men what they wanted to hear and, without any moral right to do so, he took the name of "Jehovah" upon his lips.

Their decision (vv.7-10)

The ease with which everything fell into place might well have led the five spies to believe that the Levite's words could be trusted. They "departed, and came to Laish, and saw the people that were therein, how they dwelt careless (safely - 983), after the manner of the Zidonians, quiet (reposing - 8252) and secure (confident - 982); and there was no magistrate (restraint - 6114) in the land, that might put them to shame in any thing; and they were far from the Zidonians, and had no business with any man" (v.7). As far as the spies were concerned, the ease with which they could possess this territory stood in marked contrast to the difficulties they were facing in occupying the area allotted to them by the Lord in the south of the land. The vulnerability of the inhabitants of Laish was a different proposition to the might of the Amorites and Philistines. Laish, or Leshem (Josh 19.47), appears to have been a Sidonian settlement but its geographical location meant that it was isolated from the Phoenecian city of Sidon by Mount Lebanon, and from other territories around it by Mount Hermon. This isolation gave its inhabitants a false sense of security, which made them apathetic and complacent. Interestingly, like the children of Israel, they lived without restraint and did what was right in their own eyes (cf. 21.25). The absence of magistrates meant that it was a lawless society, and therefore there was no sense of shame about anything they did. They had made their city, in the words of the spies, into "a place where there is no want of any thing that is in the earth" (v.10). They believed that there were no immediate enemies to threaten their selfish existence. However, they failed to see how vulnerable they were and therefore they were defenceless when the moment of reckoning came.

Sadly, the five spies, and ultimately, the children of Dan, could see the weakness of the inhabitants of Laish, but they failed to see their own vulnerability mirrored in them. Instead of perceiving and heeding the warning, the spies returned "unto their brethren to Zorah and Eshtaol" (v.8) with great enthusiasm for what they had seen. In response to their brethren's request for advice as to what they should do (v.8), they said, "Arise, that we may go up against them: for we have seen the land, and, behold, it is very good: and are ye still? be not slothful to go, and to enter to possess the land. When ye go, ye shall come unto a people secure, and to a large land: for God (ELOHIM - 430) hath given it into your hands" (vv.9-10). It was tragic that they were unable to speak so positively and enthusiastically about their true inheritance in the land. Such was their spiritual state that they even claimed that God's hand was with them in this matter. Their decision was based purely on what they had seen, rather than on any inward desires or promptings of the heart. They were prepared to fight what they perceived to be the 'easy' battles but they had no desire to engage in the fight of faith against their enemies, which called for total dependence on the Lord.

Their disregard for Micah (vv.11-18a)

"Six hundred men appointed with weapons of war" moved "out of Zorah and out of Eshtaol" (v.11) in response to the encouragement of the spies to go and possess Laish. It is clear that they were accompanied by their children (v.21 – referred to as "little ones") and also, by inference, their women; this would have slowed down their journey. This group represented only a proportion of the tribe: there were many who would have remained in Zorah and Eshtaol, including Samson's forebears. The initial stage of the journey took them to Kirjath-jearim, a city of Judah, some eight miles from Jerusalem. They called this place, "Mahaneh-dan (camp of Dan - 4265) unto this day: behold it is behind (beside - 310) Kirjath-jearim" (v.12). The reference to it as a "camp" appears to confirm that it was a partial migration of the tribe that took place. It was in this camp that, at a later date, "the Spirit of the Lord began to move" Samson (13.25).

The second stage of the journey saw the 600 men and those accompanying them reach "mount Ephraim", and it was there that they "came unto the house of Micah" (v.13). It was a further indictment of Micah's spiritual condition that the five spies said, "Do ye know that there is in these houses an ephod, and teraphim, and a graven image, and a molten image?" (v.14). The reference to "houses" (plural) suggests that a small village may have built up around Micah's house to share in the worship instituted by him. The young Levite was so closely identified with Micah that his house was synonymous with the house of Micah: "And they turned thitherward, and came to the house of the young man the Levite, even unto the house of Micah, and saluted him" (v.15). The spies, no doubt, were still enthused with the apparent guidance they had received on their earlier visit to the house, and therefore their challenge to the 600 men to "consider what ye have to do" (v.14) was designed to encourage them to secure for themselves the contents of the house linked to that guidance. In spite of the previous friendly reception and help given, they displayed no respect for, or loyalty towards, Micah. The 600 men "stood by the entering of the gate" (v.16); this may refer to the gate of the city or to the entrance to the group of houses that surrounded Micah's dwelling. The five spies took on the task of entering the house and stole "the carved image, the ephod, and the teraphim, and the molten image" (v.18). Micah's idolatry had begun with him stealing from his mother, and now he reaped what he had sown.

Their deal with the Levite (vv.18b-20)

While the five men were plundering Micah's house, "the priest stood in the entering in of the gate with the six hundred men" (v.17), ignorant of what was taking place. Clearly, the children of Dan had succeeded in distracting him from his priestly activities in the house and their actions took him by surprise. As they brought out the spoils he asked, "What do ye?" (v.18). His enquiry was no doubt prompted by anxiety at the sight of his position and livelihood disappearing before his eyes.

However, any concern that he might have had was short-lived. His covetous and ambitious spirit was more than satisfied with the offer that they made to him in exchange for his silence and co-operation: "And they said unto him, Hold thy peace, lay thine hand upon thy mouth, and go with us, and be to us a father and a priest: is it better for thee to be a priest unto the house of one man, or that thou be a priest unto a tribe and a family in Israel?" (v.19). His thin veneer of spirituality and loyalty was easily pierced, and he grasped after the prospect of greater position and power. Instead of being concerned at the treatment that was meted out to Micah, the man who had been good enough to employ him, his "heart was glad, and he took the ephod, and the teraphim, and the graven image, and went in the midst of the people" (v.20). Without any scruples, he took the idolatry he had promoted in a household and introduced it into a tribe, which, as the Book of Judges reveals, proved disastrous to the future spiritual health of the nation of Israel.

The word of the Lord, through the prophet Ezekiel, to the false shepherds of Israel provides a fitting commentary on the Levite's self-centred actions: "Thus saith the Lord God unto the shepherds; Woe be to the shepherds of Israel that do feed themselves! should not the shepherds feed the flocks? Ye eat the fat, and ye clothe you with the wool, ye kill them that are fed: but ye feed not the flock" (Ezek 34.2-3). Once self-interest and self-advancement dictate the movements of those who claim to be spiritual shepherds, the Lord's people will suffer (cf. 1 Pet 5.2).

Their dismissal of Micah (vv.21-26)

The actions of the Danites as they departed from Micah's house testified to men who knew that they had done wrong and who expected repercussions. They "put the little ones and the cattle and the carriage (weightiness, wealth they were carrying - 3520) before them" (v.21). They expected Micah to pursue and therefore they put the six hundred armed men at the rear, both to intimidate him and to protect the weaker members of their party. Although they had stolen Micah's gods and the ephod, they displayed no confidence in the ability of these things to guide and protect them.

When Micah discovered what had happened, his reaction betrayed the inward condition of his heart. The fact that the children of Dan were some distance from his house did not prevent him from gathering together "the men that were in the houses near to" his own house in order to pursue after them (v.22). If he had been truly exercised about the matter, he would have perceived that the Lord's hand was in the events. He would have realised that the Danites had done him a favour in removing the things that were displacing the Lord. However, his thoughts were dominated by what he had lost, rather than by any good that could have come out of it. His passionate desire to recover what had been lost, and the slow progress made by their mixed company meant that it was only a matter of time before Micah "overtook the children of Dan" (v.22).

True to character, the Danites feigned surprise at the presence of Micah and his men: "What aileth thee, that thou comest with such a company?" (v.23). Micah's reply betrayed a man who was so steeped in idolatry that he had lost sight of, and confidence in, the Lord: "And he said, Ye have taken away my gods which I made, and the priest, and ye are gone away: and what have I more? and what is this that ye say unto me, What aileth thee?" (v.24). His gods were of his own creation but they were powerless to help him in time of need. Nevertheless, he still felt bereft without them! His response stands in marked contrast to the words of the Psalmist, "God is our refuge and strength, a very present help in trouble" (Ps 46.1). The threats of the children of Dan proved enough to dissuade him from pursuing the matter any further: "And the children of Dan said unto him, Let not thy voice be heard among us, lest angry fellows run upon thee, and thou lose thy life, with the lives of thy household" (v.25). Stripped of any confidence in the power of his own gods to help him, and with no thoughts of Jehovah, "when Micah saw that they were too strong for him, he turned and went back unto his house" (v.26).

Their destruction of Laish (vv.27-28a)

Armed with "the things which Micah had made, and the priest which he had", the children of Dan approached Laish (v.27). The city was located "in the valley that lieth by Beth-rehob (cf. Num 13.21)" (v.28). Its precise location is uncertain but it became the northernmost city in Israel, hence the expression to describe the extent of Israel's territory, "from Dan even to Beer-sheba" (20.1; 1 Sam 3.20). Although the lawless living of the inhabitants of Laish cannot be condoned, their wanton destruction of "a people that were at quiet and secure" (v.27) was extreme. Their destruction of the city was comprehensive: "and they smote them with the edge of the sword, and burnt the city with fire" (v.27). The inhabitants, who had felt secure in their isolation, discovered that they had no one to support them in their hour of need: "And there was no deliverer, because it was far from Zidon, and they had no business with any man" (v.28).

Their disobedience to God's word in setting up a rival sanctuary (vv.28b-31)

Instead of fighting for their rightful inheritance, the children of Dan had taken the easier route and possessed the territory where Laish stood. Once they had destroyed it, "they built a city (Heb., 'the city'), and dwelt therein" (v.28); this city was far removed from the place where the Lord would have had them to dwell. They sought to eradicate its past and therefore "they called the name of the city Dan, after the name of Dan their father, who was born unto Israel" (v.29). However, the author, perhaps underlining their disobedience, reminds his readers, "howbeit the name of the city was Laish at the first" (v.29).

The Danites may have changed the name of the city but they did not make a fresh start themselves. They could trace their origins back to "Israel" (Gen 35.10 - the changed name of Jacob) but there was no radical transformation in their manner of life, as there had been in that of Jacob. Contrary to the word of God (Deut 12.10-14), they "set up the graven image" (v.30) and proceeded to establish their own sanctuary and ritual in Dan. This required the institution of priesthood, and they had the ready-made solution to this problem in the form of the Levite who, for the first time, is named: "and Jonathan, the son of Gershom, the son of Manasseh, he and his sons were priests to the tribe of Dan" (v.30). Jonathan (3083, 5414) means, "the gift of Jehovah" (3068, 5414), but such was the character of his life that the Lord used him to chastise His rebellious people. Many commentators believe that "the son of Manasseh" should read, "the son of Moses". M.F.Unger expresses the reasoning behind this view when he writes, "A line of priests whose genealogy went back to Gershon (Gershom in the AV), the son of Moses, officiated at the Danite sanctuary. The reading of 'Gershon, the son of Manasseh', is based on a scribal notation in which the raised letter *nun* was inserted in *môshìh* (Moses) to make it read Manasseh in order to remove the name of Moses from this idolatrous association" (*Commentary on the Old Testament*). A. R. Fausset brings the two thoughts together when he writes, "He was a child of Moses by descent, but of the idolatrous Manasseh by imitation" (*A Critical and Expository Commentary on the Book of Judges*).

The priesthood that was introduced had far-reaching consequences for Israel. It lasted "until the day of the captivity of the land" (v.30). Commentators are divided as to the precise time referred to in this statement. Some believe that it is a later addition and relates to the defeat of the northern kingdom of Israel at the hands of Tiglath-pileser king of Assyria in 733-732 BC (2 Kings 15.29). However, others consider that such a view conflicts with the statement in the next verse, "And they set them up Micah's graven image, which he made, all the time that the house of God was in Shiloh" (v.31). They point out that, by Saul's time, the tabernacle was no longer in Shiloh, but Nob (1 Sam 21.1), and in David's reign it was at Gibeon (1 Chr 16.39). They further suggest that it is unlikely that such an evil and idolatrous system would have been tolerated in the days of David and therefore it is more probable that "the captivity of the land" refers to Israel's defeat at the hands of the Philistines, which resulted in the capture of the ark of the covenant and the slaying of Eli's two sons (1 Sam 4.10-11). Whichever view is taken, the most tragic feature of this period of time was that a man-made god became the centre of the people's worship at the very time when the Lord was dwelling in the midst of them in the tabernacle at Shiloh. Later on, the wicked king of Israel, Jeroboam, set up a rival centre to Jerusalem, when he "made two calves of gold ... and he set the one in Bethel, and the other put he in Dan. And this thing became a sin: for the people went to worship before the one, even unto Dan" (1 Kings 12.28-30).

It is significant that the tribe of Dan, along with Ephraim, is not named among the "hundred and forty and four thousand of all the tribes of the children of Israel" who will be sealed before the beginning of the tribulation period (Rev 7.4-8). W.Scott writes, "In the Apocalyptic enumeration Dan and Ephraim are omitted. Both of these tribes are remarkable as being connected with idolatry in Israel – the probable reason for the blotting out of their names here (Deut 29.18-21). But in the end grace triumphs and Dan is named first in the future distribution of the land amongst the tribes (Ezek 48.1), but, while first named, it is the farthest removed from the temple, being situated in the extreme north" (*Exposition of the Revelation*). Commenting on this view, J.Allen writes, "A more realistic reason is that the tribe of Dan was the first to abandon their God-given heritage in Canaan and carve out with the sword a new inheritance which God had not given (Judges 18). This may have led to their scattering and eventual absorption by the other tribes. In the later years of the monarchy their numbers were considerably smaller than the numbers of Levi" (*Revelation – Ritchie New Testament Commentaries*).

Covetousness, discontent and lawlessness were rampant in the midst of the children of Israel in the days of Micah; this led to wholesale apostasy from God and the worship of idols to flourish. Sadly, history has often repeated itself among the Lord's people and it would be unwise for believers of any generation to feel that they are immune from the dangers. The warning given by John is as needful as ever: "Little children, keep yourselves from idols. Amen" (1 Jn 5.21). Anything that displaces God in the heart of a believer is an idol.

Moral Corruption (19.1-21.25)

JUDGES 19

The Depravity of Gibeah

It has already been observed in the commentary on ch.17 that the author was more concerned with moral than chronological order in the final section of the book. Clearly, the events described in the closing three chapters occurred very early on in the period of the judges. Phinehas, a grandson of Aaron, who appears in the latter stages of the book of Joshua (Josh 22.10-34), is identified as being a priest in the house of God at the time (20.26-28) and therefore the events predate those of chs.17 and 18. However, the author dealt first with the error brought in by Micah, Jonathan and the tribe of Dan in order to highlight that idolatry was the root of Israel's departure. Once the Lord had been displaced, the inevitable outcome was that moral corruption set in.

There is an ominous ring to the opening of the chapter, "And it came to pass in those days, when there was no king in Israel ..." (v.1), which sets the tone for what is to follow. Idolatry and immorality have always gone hand-in-hand throughout the history of mankind. Moral corruption is to be expected among the ungodly but the depths of depravity that unfold in this chapter among the children of Israel almost defy belief. It even led them to say, "There was no such deed done nor seen from the day that the children of Israel came up out of the land of Egypt unto this day" (v.30). It is not surprising therefore to discover that what took place left a dark blot on Israel's history that was never forgotten. Later on, when speaking of Israel's sins, the prophet Hosea recalled these terrible events and used them as an example of moral depravity: "They have deeply corrupted themselves, as in the days of Gibeah…O Israel, thou hast sinned from the days of Gibeah" (Hos 9.9; 10.9).

The Moral Corruption of the Levite (vv.1-9)

The religious corruption brought in by Jonathan, the Levite, according to chs.17 and 18, resulted in idolatry spreading throughout an entire tribe. Here an unnamed Levite introduced moral corruption that had some of the most heart-rending and distressing outcomes imaginable. As a Levite, he should have set a high standard for others to follow. His task was to be a minister of the sanctuary but he was motivated by corrupt and fleshly desires. Although he was "sojourning on the side of mount Ephraim" (v.1), like Jonathan, he strayed into Bethlehem-judah, which was not among the forty-eight cities marked out by God in which the Levites could find safety and provision (Num 35.7). There was nothing of spiritual value that came out of this journey. Contrary to the word of God, he "took to him a concubine of Bethlehem-judah" (v.1) to gratify his own lusts; and little did he realise the chain of moral corruption that he was setting in motion! It is encouraging to note that, whereas the two Levites in the final chapters of the book of Judges brought evil and corruption up out of Bethlehem-judah, the prophet Micah prophesied of that same place, "out of thee shall he come forth unto me that is to be ruler in Israel; whose goings forth have been from of old, from everlasting" (Mic 5.2).

The Levite's concubine "played the whore against him, and went away from him unto her father's house to Bethlehem-judah, and was there four whole months" (v.2). Some commentators believe that it is more likely that she returned home, because she was angry with him, and that this would explain why he "arose, and went after her" (v.3). They argue that if she had "played the whore against him", the law would have demanded her death (Lev 20.10), and therefore it would have been unlikely that he would have sought to bring her home. However, such arguments do not take into account the lawlessness of a time when God's rule was not acknowledged and His word ignored. The Levite's subsequent actions betrayed him as a man who had little regard for either. His ears were closed to the voice of God and his conscience deadened. After "four whole months (marg. a year and four months)" (v.2), his fleshly desires drove him back to Bethlehem-judah, not to bring the judgment of the law to bear upon her but "to speak friendly unto her (to her heart), and to bring her again" (v.3). The fact that he had "his servant with him, and a couple of asses", gave every indication that his intention and desire were to bring her back. Indeed, there appears to have been no hostility between them, because "she brought him into her father's house: and when the father of the damsel saw him, he rejoiced to meet him" (v.3).

The ease with which "his father in law, the damsel's father, retained him" (v.4) indicates how quickly the Levite found himself at home in an environment that ought to have held no attractions for him. Three days of eating and drinking (v.4) were followed by a fourth. Even rising "early in the morning" (v.5) on the fourth day, with the intention of departing, did not achieve its objective, and the attraction of further lavish hospitality won the day (vv.5-7). The Levite knew nothing of communion with the Lord and yet, when it came to the father of his concubine, they "did eat and drink both of them together: for the damsel's father had said unto the man, Be content, I pray thee, and tarry all night, and let thine heart be merry" (v.6). The outcome was that "when the man rose up to depart, his father in law urged him: therefore he lodged there again" (v.7). A further rising "early in the morning on the fifth day to depart" (v.8) was partially thwarted by pressure from the damsel's father: "And they tarried until afternoon, and they did eat both of them" (v.8). However, the host's words, unbeknown to him, were particularly fitting for the occasion: "Behold, now the day draweth toward evening, I pray you tarry all night: behold, the day groweth to an end, lodge here, that thine heart may be merry; and tomorrow get you early on your way, that thou mayest go home" (v.9). S.Ridout makes a very poignant comment on this scene: "Then, as evening shades begin to fall, he leaves suddenly...in spite of all the requests of the father-in-law to remain another day, he goes off, the shades already falling. Surely evening it was indeed, for her, for him, and for the nation too. Evening was closing in" (*Lectures on Judges*). A dark night was about to descend that was unparalleled in Israel's history. The Levite would live to regret waiting "until afternoon" (v.8) before he departed!

Verses 10-30: The Moral Corruption of Gibeah

Once the Levite had taken the decision that he "would not tarry that night, ... he rose up and departed, and came over against Jebus, which is Jerusalem" (v.10). The tragic outcome of his delay in departing from Bethlehem-judah was about to unfold. "Jebus" (2982) means, "the place trodden down or threshing place"; this was an apt description of it during the days when the Levite came upon it. It ought to have been in Israelite hands but it was "trodden down" by Gentile Jebusites. The children of Benjamin had failed to take possession of it and therefore it was known as Jebus; "And the children of Benjamin did not drive out the Jebusites that inhabited Jerusalem; but the Jebusites dwell with the children of Benjamin in Jerusalem unto this day" (1.21). It was left to David to conquer it and to free it from foreign domination: "And the king and his men went to Jerusalem unto the Jebusites...David took the stronghold of Zion: the same is the city of David" (2 Sam 5.6-7).

It was a six-mile (9.5 kilometre) journey northwards from Bethlehem-judah to Jerusalem and, as it would have been late in the afternoon, it was the obvious place for the Levite, his servant, his concubine and the two asses to rest for the night. The inconsistencies in the life of the Levite are illustrated by his response. He would happily enjoy the hospitality of his father-in-law for almost five days in a city where a Levite ought not to have been found, but he would refuse the suggestion of his servant, "Come, I pray thee, and let us turn in into this city of the Jebusites, and lodge in it" (v.11). He referred to it as, "the city of a stranger, that is not of the children of Israel" (v.12). He was not confident about entering such a place and preferred to journey either to Gibeah or Ramah, which were four miles and six miles (6.5 and 9.5 kilometres) further north respectively, in order to be among his own people. His confident words to his servant, "Come, and let us draw near to one of these places to lodge all night, in Gibeah, or in Ramah" (v.13) were about to be tested in a way that he could never have imagined. It is a terrible indictment of the condition of the children of Israel that, as things turned out, he would have been more secure among the strangers of Jebus than he was among the Benjamites in Gibeah.

The author's words seem to underline the vulnerability of the three travellers: "the sun went down upon them when they were by Gibeah, which belongeth to Benjamin" (v.14). They were left with no alternative but to terminate their journey and to turn "aside thither, to go in and to lodge in Gibeah" (v.15). Little did the Levite realise that the inhabitants of the city, even though they were Benjamites, were as morally corrupt as he was, if not more so. The sun, indeed, "went down upon them" in more ways than one! It was no surprise therefore that the hospitality he might have expected was not forthcoming. A love of hospitality ought to be at the heart of the belief and behaviour of the Lord's people: "Let brotherly love continue. Be not forgetful to entertain strangers: for thereby some have entertained angels unawares" (Heb 13.1-2). However, the Levite discovered that the inhabitants of Gibeah were so depraved that there was a total absence of brotherly love amongst them: "and when he went in, he sat him down in a street of the city: for there was no man that took them into his house to lodging" (v.15). It was left to an old man, who was coming in "from his work out of the field at even" (v.16), to approach them. Ironically, like the Levite, he was also an Ephraimite and therefore he was a "stranger" in the town: "he sojourned (lodged as a guest - 1481) in Gibeah" (v.16). His heart had not been hardened to the needs of others and therefore when "he saw a wayfaring man in the street of the city", he enquired of him, "Whither goest thou? and whence comest thou?" (v.17).

The response of the Levite was less than honest and emphasised, once again, the depth of his own moral corruption: "We are passing from Bethlehem-judah toward the side of mount Ephraim; from thence am I: and I went to Bethlehem-judah, but I am now going to the house of the Lord; and there is no man that receiveth me to house" (v.18). This was the first time the Lord's name had been upon his lips and he had not honoured Him by his actions. Some scholars believe that the text should read, "my house" instead of, "the house of the Lord". However, the past and future actions of the Levite show that there is no reason not to believe that he would have said such a thing to gain acceptance and credibility with the old man. He highlighted his preoccupation with, and confidence in, material possessions when he added, "Yet there is both straw and provender for our asses; and there is bread and wine also for me, and for thy handmaid, and for the young man which is with thy servants: there is no want of any thing" (v.19). This might have been true materially, but spiritually and morally he was bankrupt.

The Benjamites had not been attracted by the Levite's possessions and he would soon discover why. If he had not seen the warning signs by now, the response of the old man ought to have alerted him: "Peace be with thee; howsoever, let all thy wants lie upon me; only lodge not in the street" (v.20). He had been in the city long enough to know the character of the inhabitants and therefore "he brought him into his house, and gave provender unto the asses: and they washed their feet, and did eat and drink" (v.21). What was about to happen may have caught the Levite off-guard but it was not a surprise to the old man.

As they "were making their hearts merry" (v.22), the men of Gibeah displayed their evil brand of hospitality: "behold, the men of the city, certain sons of Belial (base and worthless men), beset the house round about, and beat at the door, and spake to the master of the house, the old man, saying, Bring forth the man that came into thine house, that we may know him" (v.22). The nature of their lust for homosexual relations with the Levite is summed up by Paul in his letter to the Romans: "And likewise also the men, leaving the natural use of the woman, burned in their lust one toward another; men with men working that which is unseemly" (Rom 1.27). Such behaviour was to be expected in a Gentile city like Sodom (Gen 19.4-5) but not in Gibeah, an Israelite city. The features of Sodom within an Israelite city were a grave commentary upon how morally corrupt Israel had become. Mercifully, Lot was led out of Sodom by angels (Gen 19.15-16) but there was no such ministry present to deliver the Levite and his companions.

The old man was desperate to maintain the safety of his visitors and therefore he appealed to the men of Gibeah not to break all the rules of hospitality. He "went out unto them, and said unto them, Nay, my brethren, nay, I pray you, do not so wickedly; seeing that this man is come into mine house, do not this folly" (v.23). However, he knew that words alone would not be enough to pacify them. He had to offer them an attractive alternative to keep them from violating the Levite. This offer came in the form of his virgin daughter and, seemingly without his permission, the Levite's concubine: "Behold, here is my daughter a maiden, and his concubine; them I will bring out now, and humble ye them, and do with them what seemeth good unto you: but unto this man do not so vile a thing" (v.24). To his credit, he wanted to protect his visitor but he was prepared to do so by sacrificing the honour of the women. The Word of God affords women a place of dignity and honour but both the old man and the Levite treated them with a singular lack of respect and used them to bargain with corrupt men. The old man's pleadings fell on deaf and rebellious ears: "But the men would not hearken to him" (v.25).

Any lingering thoughts that the reader might have that the Levite genuinely cared for his concubine ought to be dispelled as the story unfolds. Even if there had been any such feelings for her when he went after her to bring her back, they did not run very deep and true. Self-preservation soon took over and dictated his actions. His treatment of her was cold, callous and uncaring in the extreme. Once he had seen the old man's lack of success in negotiating with the Benjamites, he "took his concubine, and brought her forth unto them" (v.25). He must have known what would happen to her and yet he retired for the night, seemingly, without a pang of conscience. She suffered a night of painful and humiliating sexual abuse, which defies detailed description. The author summed up her horrific experience in a simple statement: "and they knew her, and abused her all the night until the morning: and when the day began to spring, they let her go" (v.25). She may have "played the whore against him" but the Levite's treatment of her was utterly reprehensible.

She must have presented a tragic and pathetic figure as she came "in the dawning of the day, and fell down at the door of the man's house where her lord (ruler, master, sovereign, controller – 113) was, till it was light" (v.26). The sight of her ought to have stirred sympathetic feelings even in the hardest heart but this was not so in "her lord's" case. The Levite's mastery over her was driven by self-interest. As he "rose up in the morning, and opened the doors of the house, and went out to go his way ... the woman his concubine was fallen down at the door of the house, and her hands were upon the threshold" (v.27). Her pose suggests that she was reaching out for acceptance and protection from those within the house in her hour of need. However, there was no hope of that from such unprincipled men and she died there, a lonely, abused and broken woman. It can be argued that she received the due reward for her unfaithfulness but only the most morally corrupt and unfeeling of men could have reacted as the Levite did. Her pitiful condition did not strike any chord of concern in his heart and his only words to her were, "Up, and let us be going" (v.28). When she failed to obey this harsh command, he realised that she was dead.

The Levite's immediate response was to put her upon an ass and to take her back "unto his place" (v.28). If the story had ceased there, the events would have been distressing enough and without parallel in Israel's previous history. If, on his way home, he had sought counsel at "the house of the Lord", to which he had claimed he was travelling (v.18), the final outcome would have been different. However, he took the law into his own hands and, by so doing, reached even greater depths of depravity. He was set on revenge against the men of Gibeah and to achieve this he needed to stir up the feelings of the tribes of Israel against them. He did so by treating his concubine's body like that of an animal being prepared for sacrifice. When he entered his house, "he took a knife, and laid hold on his concubine, and divided her (cf. Ex 29.17; Lev 8.20), together with her bones, into twelve pieces, and sent her into all the coasts of Israel" (v.29). Sadly, but not surprisingly, he did not acknowledge any failure on his own part for the atrocities that had been committed. If he had not entered Bethlehem-judah in the first place and taken a concubine, none of this would have happened. Both he and the children of Israel were outraged at the evil committed by the men of Gibeah and recognised that it outstripped any evil that had been seen "from the day the children of Israel came up out of the land of Egypt" (v.30). Nevertheless, they failed to apply the lesson to their own hearts and to appreciate that the moral corruption sprang from the root of lawlessness that was abroad. Israel had never been in the condition before where such a deed could have been committed but she was now! The tribes were challenged as to how they should respond to the disturbing and gruesome "package" that the Levite distributed throughout the land: "consider of it, take advice, and speak your minds" (v.30). The outcome of their deliberations is the subject of the following chapter.

JUDGES 20

Anarchy (20.1 - 21.25)

The Destruction of the Benjamites

Verses 1-7: The Report of the Levite

The strategy of the Levite in sending the divided body of his concubine (19.29) throughout the twelve tribes of Israel had the desired effect: "Then all the children of Israel went out, and the congregation was gathered together as one man, from Dan even to Beersheba, with the land of Gilead, unto the Lord in Mizpeh" (v.1). Most commentators agree that Mizpeh (Mizpah - 4708) is probably Tell en-Nasbeh, which is about eight miles north of Jerusalem and close to Gibeah. It was therefore a convenient place for the assembly to gather. There was a sense of revulsion at what had happened in Gibeah; this led to an impressive display of unity by the tribes. On three occasions the author uses the phrase, "as one man" (vv.1,8,11), to emphasise the harmony that existed among them. It has already been noted in the commentary on ch.18 that the expression "from Dan even to Beersheba" became a term to describe the extent of Israel's territory. Even the tribes east of the river Jordan, referred to here as "the land of Gilead", supported the cause. However, it would be wrong to infer that all the men of Israel were present. Indeed, there would not have been room for all, and therefore the "chief (leaders) of all the people, even of all the tribes of Israel, presented themselves in the assembly of the people of God, four hundred thousand footmen that drew sword" (v.2).

The Levite was in a strong position to be able to appeal to the assembly as representative of all the people: "Behold, ye are all children of Israel; give here your advice and counsel" (v.7). Corporate identity was intact to such an extent that he could expect his suffering and loss to be felt by all (cf. 1 Cor 12.26). It was disappointing that this same unity was not experienced throughout the period of the judges. For many of them, what took place at Gibeah was only hearsay and therefore they asked the question, "Tell us, how was this wickedness?" (v.3). He gave them an account of what had happened (vv.4-6) but, true to form, he put his spin upon it, no doubt to gain their sympathy and support. There had been no indication that the men of Gibeah had "thought to have slain" (v.5) him, although he might be excused for assuming this in the light of what they did to his concubine. He omitted, not surprisingly, to tell them that it was he who had thrust her out the house into the arms of these unscrupulous men. He was swift to judge them and charge them with committing "lewdness and folly in Israel" (v.6) but he displayed no evidence of self-judgment.

This display of unity among the tribes during these early days of the judges was fragile and when it was later put to the test it was found wanting.

The signs of weakness and a lack of reality were already there. Firstly, both the Levite and the children of Israel were simply taken up with the evil as it affected them. They had no concept of the damage that had been done to God's honour and glory.

Secondly, they were quick to judge others but blind to their guilt before God for precisely the same things that they were condemning. C.A.Coates writes, "They used right terms about it…but we often say right things without feeling them at all. They did not feel it as the sin of Israel but as the sin of Gibeah. If they had felt it as the sin of Israel, they would all have been on their faces before God, confessing it as their own sin…There was a natural indignation about what was manifestly wicked, which was not the fruit of communion with God at all. There was no sign of their being humbled before God" (*An Outline of Judges*).

Thirdly, there were notable absentees from the assembly: "Now the children of Benjamin heard that the children of Israel were gone up to Mizpeh" (v.3). They heard about it but for obvious reasons they did not go. It transpired later on that none of the inhabitants of Jabesh-gilead (21.8-9), who had close ties with Benjamin, went either.

Fourthly, and tragically, it was a unity against their brethren. The joy and hope that arose from the three times that the children of Israel were seen gathering (v.1), rising up (v.8) and acting (v.11) as "one man" were cancelled out by the three times when the author observes that they were the brethren of the children of Benjamin (vv.13,23,28). Brethren fighting against brethren can only end in disaster for all concerned. The Lord Jesus said, "Every kingdom divided against itself is brought to desolation; and a house divided against a house falleth" (Lk 11.17). Clearly, the dreadful sin of the men of Gibeah had to be dealt with, but it was sad that the children of Israel did not show this same unity when confronting their enemies in the land. Sadly, when it came to facing the Canaanites, Midianites, Ammonites and Philistines, the judges found a singular lack of unity among the people. There has been a sad history of internal strife and division among the Lord's people that has often left them spiritually impoverished and weakened.

The Resolve of the People (vv.8-11)

Not only were the people united in their coming together but they were "as one man" in their resolve to address the issue concerning Gibeah: "We will not any of us go to his tent, neither will we any of us turn into his house. But now this shall be the thing which we will do to Gibeah; we will go up by lot against it" (vv.8-9). The mention of "tent" and "house" confirms the early setting of this story. Clearly, some of the children of Israel were still living in tents and had not as yet become more permanent house-dwellers. Commentators are divided as to what is meant by going "up by lot against it". Some of them believe that the lot would determine who should go up first against the men of Gibeah and therefore they link it in with the question put to God by the children of Israel: "Which of us shall go up first to the battle against the children of Benjamin?" (v.18). Others suggest that it refers to the subsequent dividing of land by lot once the men of Gibeah had been defeated, just as they had done with the Canaanites when they entered the land. The people also made the decision to give one-tenth of their men the task of finding provisions for the army: "And we will take ten men of a hundred throughout all the tribes of Israel, and an hundred of a thousand, and a thousand out of ten thousand, to fetch victual for the people" (v.10). This ensured that the remainder of the men were released and in the right physical condition when they reached Gibeah to do "according to all the folly (vileness, wantonness – 5038) that they (the Benjamites) have wrought in Israel" (v.10). The status of the resolution was further enhanced by the unity of purpose that underpinned it: "So all the men of Israel were gathered against the city, knit together as one man" (v.11).

Verses 12-13a: The Request of the Tribes

It would appear as if there may well have been some wise men among "the chief of all the people" (v.2) who recognised the importance of not rushing headlong into executing ther decision. They realised the need to give the tribe of Benjamin the opportunity to put their house in order and therefore "the tribes of Israel sent men through all the tribe of Benjamin, saying, What wickedness is this that is done among you?" (v.12). They appreciated that if the specific men who had committed the appalling act against the Levite were dealt with, evil could be removed from Israel and the rest of the inhabitants of the city would be spared. So they appealed to the Benjamites, "Now therefore deliver us the men, the children of Belial, which are in Gibeah, that we may put them to death, and put away evil from Israel" (v.13). Spiritual leaders should always take care not to mar the entire testimony of a local church when dealing with a specific issue. The wise woman of Abel (2 Sam 20.14-22) set an excellent example in this respect when she prevented the rampant and vindictive Joab from indiscriminately destroying the entire city of Abel in his desire to deal with one errant man, Sheba. Her question to Joab stands as a challenge to spiritual leaders of all generations to exercise great caution when seeking to deal with error: "I am one of them that are peaceable and faithful in Israel: thou seekest to destroy a city and a mother in Israel: why wilt thou swallow up the inheritance of the Lord?" (2 Sam 20.19).

Verses 13b-17: The Refusal of Benjamin

Sadly, the children of Benjamin failed to grasp the opportunity offered to them: "But the children of Benjamin would not hearken to the voice of their brethren the children of Israel" (v.13b). They promoted their own misguided form of unity and allowed their relationship with the men of

Gibeah to cloud their judgment. Instead of arriving at a peaceful solution to the problem, they precipitated a civil war in Israel. Sadly, the history of the Lord's people is littered with examples of close relationships preventing sound judgment when discipline was required.

The Benjamites therefore "gathered themselves together out of the cities unto Gibeah, to go out to battle against the children of Israel" (v.14). Although, naturally speaking, they were facing a hopeless task in ranging their forces against those of the other eleven tribes, they must have been supremely confident in their own prowess to defeat their opponents. They amassed "out of the cities twenty and six thousand men that drew sword", and these were supplemented by "seven hundred chosen men" from among "the inhabitants of Gibeah" (v.15). There were "among all this people ... seven hundred chosen men left-handed (shut up of the right hand - 334, 3027, 3225); every one could sling stones at an hair breadth, and not miss" (v.16). It is probable that this elite group of warriors were the same seven hundred men from Gibeah referred to in v.15. Clearly, they were regarded by the Benjamites as a "secret and surprise" weapon in the battle. The majority of their opponents would have been right-handed and therefore they would have carried their shields on their left arms. As left-handed slingers, they would have had the advantage of being able to propel their missiles at a different angle from right-handed men and thus attack their opponents' unguarded side. This fact, combined with their unerring accuracy, made them a force to be reckoned with. A sling was no mean weapon, and a large rock could be propelled from it with considerable velocity.

The Benjamites therefore must have set out with a considerable degree of optimism, even though the men of Israel, beside Benjamin, "numbered four hundred thousand men that drew sword: all these were men of war" (v.17). However, they had failed to consider that they would be fighting against God. A. R. Fausset writes, "Self-conceit, relying on that skill, and especially on the expertness of their slingers, tempted them to such a presumptuous venture. Sinners, instead of counting the awful cost of meeting God in battle, rush blindly against Him who is infinitely stronger than they. Clever as the Benjamites' marksmen were to sling stones at an hair breadth and not miss, they utterly missed their mark in defending an unrighteous cause. The Hebrew for 'sin' (*chata*) is the same as that for 'missing the mark'. The glory of God is man's true aim." (*A Critical and Expository Commentary on the Book of Judges*).

Verses 18-23: The Request of the Children of Israel – the First Battle

As far as the children of Israel were concerned, their cause was right and just. It did not even occur to them as to whether it was correct, or not, for them to go into battle against the children of Benjamin. Their just cause and strength of numbers led them to believe, no doubt, that success would be automatic. They failed to take into account that the Benjamites would be fighting on "home territory" with which they were familiar with and that they had a great deal to lose if they were defeated: they would, indeed, fight to the death. However, more importantly, they did not reckon with the chastening hand of the Lord in their own lives. The only uncertainty in their minds was related to a matter of procedure, and therefore they "went up to the house of God (BETH-EL - 1008), and asked counsel of God (ELOHIM - 430), and said, Which of us shall go up first to the battle against the children of Benjamin?" (v.18). The use of the general word, "Elohim", for God, rather than "the Lord (JEHOVAH - 3068)", indicates that they were moving in their own strength and that they had no real sense of their relationship with the covenant-keeping God. Some commentators believe that "Beth-el" should be read in place of "house of God" throughout this section (vv.18,26,31; 21.2). They argue that when the "house of God" is referred to the word "Elohim" is used (18.31), rather than the shorter form of "El". They also point out that the central sanctuary was almost certainly at Beth-el during the early days of the judges, which was very close to Mizpeh.

The Lord's reply, "Judah shall go up first" (v.18), expressed neither approval nor disapproval of their intended actions. It certainly did not guarantee them success in their mission. He was to teach them the painful lesson that, although their cause was just, they were in the wrong condition to execute it. It has already been observed in the commentary on the opening verses of ch.1 that Judah was the largest and most kingly tribe upon whom the leadership mantle fell following the departures of Moses and Joshua. At that time the children of Israel had asked a similar question of the Lord (Jehovah, not Elohim), "Who shall go up for us against the Canaanites first, to fight against them?" (1.1). The Lord not only said, "Judah shall go up", but he included in His answer the promise of guaranteed success: "behold, I have delivered the land into his hand" (1.2). However, this initial battle had been against one of Israel's enemies, whereas the current request was made in the sad context of fighting their own brethren.

It is probable that the children of Israel, "rose up in the morning, and encamped against Gibeah" (v.19) and subsequently, "went out to battle against Benjamin" (v.20), in the belief that the battle would be short-lived and the outcome would be in their favour. What ensued must have been a huge shock to them: "And the children of Benjamin came forth out of Gibeah, and destroyed down to the ground of the Israelites that day twenty and two thousand men" (v.21). It dented their pride and challenged their complacency. If they had been perceptive enough to learn the lessons that the Lord was teaching them through this unexpected defeat, all would have been well.

The following two verses (vv.22-23) can appear to be somewhat ambiguous if they are not viewed together as two things that happened at virtually the same time. To the credit of the children of Israel, their defeat led them back to the house of the Lord and produced tears: "the children of Israel went up and wept before the Lord (Jehovah, not Elohim) until even" (v.23). They would not make the automatic assumption again that they were embarking on the right course of action, therefore they "asked counsel of the Lord, saying, Shall I go up again to battle against the children of Benjamin my brother?" (v.23). There were signs of increasing dependency on the Lord and sensitivity to the tragedy that this battle was against "my brother". However, as yet, there was no indication that they were seeing beyond the immediate issue of dealing with the crime committed by their brethren, to the deeper matter of their own personal guilt for the conditions that led up to it. There was no evidence that their tears were an expression of humble repentance. Once again, the Lord's response, "Go up against him" (v.23), carried with it no promise of success. The Lord had still further lessons to teach them before they could claim the victory. They "encouraged themselves" (v.22), but not "in the Lord" as David later did at Ziklag (1 Sam 30.6). Nevertheless, they were sufficiently self-confident to "set their battle again in array in the place where they put themselves in array the first day" (v.22). They refused to display any weakness in the face of the opposing army and therefore declined to change their tactics.

Verses 24-28: The Repentance of the Children of Israel - the Second Battle

Clearly, the children of Israel were anxious to get straight back into the battle prior to their initial setback: they "came near against the children of Benjamin the second day" (v.24). However, the outcome was the same as before: "And Benjamin…destroyed down to the ground of the children of Israel again eighteen thousand men; all these drew the sword" (v.25). Forty thousand men had been destroyed in two days of battle! The experience must have been both devastating and humiliating for them but the result demonstrated that the Lord was in it.

Yet again, they made their way to the house of God but this time it was different. Firstly, "all the children of Israel, and all the people, went up" (v.26). There was total unity in their quest. Secondly, the complete company "wept, and sat there before the Lord" (v.26). As the tears flowed they were deeply conscious of being in the presence of the Lord. Thirdly, they "fasted that day until even" (v.26). All natural desires were set aside and there was an atmosphere of repentance that day. Fourthly, they "offered burnt offerings and peace offerings before the Lord" (v.26) as signs of their genuine desire for reconciliation and restoration, and to honour God (Lev 1.4; 3.6). Fifthly, it was on the basis of this repentance and restoration to communion with the Lord that they "inquired of the Lord…Shall I yet again go out to battle against the children of Benjamin my brother, or shall I cease?" (vv.27-28). Self-will had been broken down to such an extent that they were even prepared for the Lord to say, "Cease", and to acknowledge that His will was best. At this point the Lord was able to tell them, "Go up; for tomorrow I will deliver them into thine hand" (v.28). He not only gave them the authority to go but He revealed to them when they should go, and He guaranteed them a successful outcome. It had been a painful pathway for them to reach this stage but the Lord, in His infinite grace and mercy, had brought them to it.

The author observes that "the ark of the covenant of God was there in those days, and Phinehas, the son of Eleazar, the son of Aaron, stood before it in those days" (v.27-28). As well as confirming an early date in the period of the judges for this story, the mention of Phinehas is particularly appropriate in the context. He had stood in the days of Moses as a shining testimony of faithfulness to God during a time of great moral corruption, when Israel "began to commit whoredom with the daughters of Moab" (Num 25.1). He dealt decisively and swiftly with one of the children of Israel who brought a Midianitish woman into the camp and thereby earned a glowing commendation from the Lord: "Behold, I give unto him my covenant of peace: and he shall have it, and his seed after him, even the covenant of an everlasting priesthood; because he was zealous for his God, and made an atonement for the children of Israel" (Num 25.12-13). He was equally active during the days of Joshua in combating the error introduced by the tribes east of the river Jordan (Josh 22.13-34) and thus averted division and bloodshed. C.A.Coates writes, "No man in Scripture was more noticed than Phinehas for judgment of evil; he judged it unsparingly...he was entirely apart from any human motives; he took the javelin in his hand in jealousy for God; there was no natural indignation with him at all, but holy, priestly and spiritual indignation" (*An Outline of the Book of Judges*). If there had been more men of his spiritual calibre in Israel during the days of the judges, the religious and moral corruption that abounded would have been avoided. This is the only mention of "the ark of the covenant of God" in the book of Judges, and Phinehas was morally qualified to have it recorded of him that he "stood before it in those days" (v.28). The ark spoke of the Lord dwelling in the midst of His people, and a greater sense of this would have resulted in holy living.

Verses 29-35: The Reward of Victory for the Children of Israel – the Third Battle

In the second battle, the children of Israel used the same tactics as they had employed in the first. However, although they had been assured of success by the Lord for the third battle, they decided to employ a different strategy. At least this showed a lack of complacency on their part. The Lord may have promised to bless them, but they had responsibilities in the matter. There are a number of difficulties in piecing together the precise details and order of events in this third battle. However, the main outline is comparatively clear.

Before they marched on the city, the children of Israel "set liers in wait round about Gibeah" (v.29), who were to be employed later to ambush the city. The main army then "went up against the children of Benjamin on the third day, and put themselves in array against Gibeah, as at other times" (v.30). The Benjamites were, no doubt, lulled into a sense of false security and could not believe that the children of Israel were using the same tactic that had so spectacularly failed in the past. Their early successes would have further increased their confidence that they would be victorious again: "and they began to smite of the people, and kill, as at other times, in the highways, of which one goeth up to the house of God, and the other to Gibeah in the field, about thirty men of Israel" (v.31). Their understandable conclusion was that "They (the children of Israel) are smitten down before us, as at the first" (v.32). They displayed the same over-confidence that had led to their brethren's downfall in the two previous battles. They were oblivious to the fact that they were being "drawn away from the city" (v.31). This was precisely what the children of Israel intended, and they were prepared for initial losses in order to achieve their long-term goal.

At this point the Israelites feigned retreat: "But the children of Israel said, Let us flee, and draw them from the city unto the highways" (v.32); this had the desired effect. However, suddenly, they halted their retreat and confronted the Benjamites at Baal-tamar (v.33), a place of unknown location. This signalled the point at which "the liers in wait of Israel came forth out of their places, even out of the meadows of Gibeah" (v.33) to ambush the defenceless city of Gibeah. The strategy of the children of Israel had drawn the Benjamites so far away from their city that they were powerless to act. The remaining inhabitants of Gibeah, "knew not that evil was near them", and they were taken by surprise as "ten thousand chosen men out of all Israel" came against them (v.34). It would be tempting to stand back and applaud the tactics used by the children of Israel as they outwitted and outmanoeuvred the children of Benjamin but the divine record says, "And the Lord smote Benjamin before Israel: and the children of Israel destroyed of the Benjamites that day twenty and five thousand and an hundred men: all these drew the sword" (v.35). It was, indeed, the Lord who had gained the victory, and yet graciously He acknowledged the part played by the children of Israel.

Verses 36-48: The Realisation of Defeat by the Benjamites

Having stated the outcome of the battle as far as the Lord and the children of Israel were concerned (v.35), the author proceeds to view it from the standpoint of the Benjamites: "So the children of Benjamin saw that they were smitten" (v.36). He revisits the battle recorded in the earlier verses and supplies further details as to how they came to the realisation of their defeat. He began by focusing on the contribution of the "liers in wait". He reveals that "the men of Israel gave place to the Benjamites, because they trusted unto the liers in wait which they had set beside Gibeah" (v.36). Their confidence in these men was not misplaced, because when the opportune time arrived they "hasted, and rushed upon Gibeah … and smote all the city with the edge of the sword" (v.37). There was "an appointed sign (cf. Jer 6.1 – translated here as, 'a sign of fire') between the men of Israel and the liers in wait, that they should make a great flame with smoke rise up out of the city" (v.38). It had been agreed between them that the setting on fire of the city so that the smoke ascended skywards would be the sign that indicated to the main army that they could halt their retreat.

The author returns to events he has already covered in the earlier account of the battle: "And when the men of Israel retired in the battle (referred to in vv.32-33), Benjamin began to smite and kill of the men of Israel about thirty persons (referred to in v.31): for they said, Surely they are smitten down before us, as in the first battle" (v.39). However, he then gives the reader an insight into the events that led to a dramatic turnaround in the fortunes of the two armies. The early optimism of the Benjamites was short-lived as they turned their gaze towards their smitten city: "But when the flame began to arise up out of the city with a pillar of smoke, the Benjamites looked behind them, and, behold, the flame of the city ascended up to heaven" (v.40). This awesome sight, coupled with the fact that "the men of Israel turned again" (v.41) and confronted them, led the men of Benjamin to be "amazed: for they saw that evil was come upon them" (v.41).

Over-confidence turned to fear, and "they turned their backs before the men of Israel unto the way of the wilderness: but the battle overtook them" (v.42). Their escape route was cut off when they were confronted by "them which came out of the cities (singular, 'city', in many manuscripts)" (v.42), which probably refers to the men who overcame and destroyed Gibeah. They were surrounded by this highly effective pincers movement: "Thus they inclosed the Benjamites round about, and chased them, and trode them down with ease over against Gibeah toward the sunrising" (v.43). Some commentators believe that it is unlikely that they would have fled towards their stricken city and therefore they submit that the reference is to Geba, rather than Gibeah. However, there is no compelling reason to change the text and they may well have ended up in the vicinity of Gibeah. Whichever view is correct, by the time they reached this point they had lost "eighteen thousand men; all these were men of valour" (v.44).

A number of Benjamites managed to escape out of the clutches of the children of Israel. They "turned and fled toward the wilderness unto the rock of Rimmon" (v.45), which was situated northeast of Geba, which itself lay northeast of Gibeah. However, although the children of Israel had gained the victory, they were ruthless in the final stages of the battle. They overtook and slew 5,000 of the escapees on the highways. They then slew a further 2,000 of them as they "pursued hard after them unto Gidom (of unknown location)" (v.45). 25,000 Benjamites lost their lives that day, and "all these were men of valour" (v.46). Only 600 men managed to flee into "the wilderness unto the rock Rimmon" (v.47). The men of Israel did not continue with the pursuit of such a small number and therefore they "abode in the rock Rimmon for four months" (v.47). Instead, they turned their attention to the other Benjamite cities. As far as they were concerned, the entire tribe was associated with the guilt of the inhabitants of Gibeah and had to be judged. The execution of this judgment was comprehensive, swift, ruthless, without partiality and without mercy: "And the men of Israel turned again upon the children of Benjamin, and smote them with the edge of the sword, as well the men of every city, as the beast, and all that came to hand: also they set on fire all the cities they came to" (v.48). A.R.Fausset, in seeking to summarise the various numbers, writes, "18,000 in the battle (v.44); 5,000 gleaned in the highways (v.45); 2,000 near Gidom (v.45). The whole number was 26,700 (v.15); 600 escaped to Rimmon (v.47); 100 more are mentioned (v.35), as slain in the battle on the third day. The 1,000 still unaccounted for, probably fell in the battles of the former two days" (*A Critical and Expository Commentary on the Book of Judges*).

This final indiscriminate slaughter, in addition to the thousands of Benjamites slain on the battlefield, marked a sad day, indeed, for the children of Israel. There was no song of triumph following victory as there had been in the time of Deborah (5.1). Those slain were their brethren, not their enemies, and it could have been so easily avoided. A Levite's movement outside of his allotted sphere of service, his taking of a concubine and his inability to break away from the hospitality of a father-in-law he should never have had, reaped a bitter harvest that could lead only to sorrow and regret.

JUDGES 21

Verses 1-9: The Reflection and Regret of the Men of Israel

Any feelings of euphoria following the victory over the Benjamites were quickly dampened as it dawned upon the men of Israel that there was, in their words, "one tribe lacking in Israel…one tribe cut off from Israel this day" (vv.3,6). It was rather late in the day for them to be concerned and it was a pity that they had not considered the possible outcomes of their campaign against their brethren before it began. However, at least they were exercised about it and began to appreciate the implications of what had happened. C.A.Coates writes, "What a dreadful thing it would have been if one stone had to be torn out of the (high priest's) breastplate … when they came to look at things according to God they could not bear to think of Benjamin being lost. It should be more of a real sorrow to have to part company with anyone we can recognise as a true saint" (*An Outline of the Book of Judges*). It was not surprising therefore that the victory was 'celebrated' in a very unusual way: "And the people came to the house of God (BETH-EL - 1008), and abode there till even before God, and lifted up their voices, and wept sore" (v.2). Tears replaced the song that would have accompanied their victory had it been over a foreign enemy. Indeed, the only people who would have been truly celebrating were their foreign enemies, who probably looked on with pleasurable amazement as they saw brother fighting against brother and thousands of the children of Israel left dead, either on the battlefield or in the cities. Satan is delighted when the Lord's people destroy themselves from within. It was only the sovereign mercy of God that preserved 600 Benjamites in the rock Rimmon (20.47) until such time as the men of Israel had reflected upon their actions and sought, albeit in their own way, to put things right.

Although the children of Israel were beginning to have serious concerns about what had happened to their brethren, they would, no doubt, have claimed that their personal actions throughout this unhappy episode of their history were totally justified. They would have pointed out that the reprehensible behaviour of the men of Gibeah demanded the severest judgment and that they had faithfully executed it. They would also have justified the oath they "had sworn in Mizpeh, saying, There shall not any of us give his daughter unto Benjamin to wife" (v.1), even though that oath was now proving to be a major barrier in ensuring that the tribe of Benjamin continued. They did not want to play any part in promoting the growth of such a tribe, or to see their daughters linked with depraved men.

Their initial response was to turn to the Lord: "O Lord God of Israel, why is this come to pass in Israel, that there should be today one tribe lacking in Israel?" (v.3). Sadly, they had not even considered that the answer to their question rested largely in the part they had played. Their actions may have been right in their own eyes, and they could have justified them, but they had been carried out in such a vindictive, selfish and legalistic manner that they found themselves with no room for manoeuvre when they wished to move more graciously. They had made their oath and, as far as they were concerned, they could not go back on it.

Following what may well have been a night of restless contemplation, "it came to pass on the morrow, that the people rose early, and built there an altar, and offered burnt offerings and peace offerings" (v.4). If, as has already been suggested in the commentary on ch.20, this took place at Beth-el, there would already have been an altar there. However, it is unlikely that they intended to build a "rival" altar. It is probable that they offered so many sacrifices that day to consecrate themselves to God and to seek His help in the difficult issue confronting them that a larger, rather than an alternative, altar had to be built to accommodate them. C.J.Goslinga, commenting on these offerings, writes, "Their burnt offerings and fellowship offerings show that they thought their relationship to the Lord was normal and proper, but the offerings were also motivated by the Israelites' desire to propitiate Him and move Him to heal the wound in their nation. They had yet to learn that obedience is better than sacrifice" (*Joshua, Judges, Ruth*).

The children of Israel finished making their offerings and then acted in a manner that denied all that they spoke of. True to character, they proceeded to devise their own plan to solve their dilemma as to how to restore the tribe of Benjamin. They decided to turn to another oath that they had made, which would allow them to circumvent the one that was giving such great difficulty. They asked, "Who is there among all the tribes of Israel that came not up with the congregation unto the Lord?" The reason for the question was that "they had made a great oath concerning him that came not up to the Lord to Mizpeh, saying, He shall surely be put to death" (v.5). Even though they "repented them for Benjamin their brother" (v.6), turning to one rash vow to solve the problems created by another was destined to produce an unhappy outcome. It would have been preferable for them to have confessed to the Lord the folly of that initial vow, and then to have sought His forgiveness, rather than to have embarked on a course of action that caused further unnecessary bloodshed.

The answer to the seemingly impossible question, "How shall we do for wives for them that remain?" (v.7) was therefore found in the inhabitants of Jabesh-gilead: "And, behold, there came none to the camp from Jabesh-gilead to the assembly. For the people were numbered, and, behold, there were none of the inhabitants of Jabesh-gilead there" (vv.8-9). Jabesh-gilead was the chief city of Gilead and was located to the east side of the river Jordan, twenty miles south of the sea of Galilee. They descended from Manasseh, one of Joseph's sons (Num 26.29), which meant therefore that they had family links with the tribe of Benjamin. Rachel, Benjamin's mother, was Manasseh's grandmother. This explains why, when "the people were numbered" who joined the battle against the Benjamites, "there were none of the inhabitants of Jabesh-gilead there" (v.9).

Verses 10-24: The Restoration of Benjamin as a Tribe

The men of Israel put their plan into action: "And the congregation sent thither twelve thousand men of the valiantest, and commanded them, saying, Go and smite the inhabitants of Jabesh-gilead with the edge of the sword, with the women and the children" (v.10). Once again, they may well have pointed to the failure of the Gileadites to join the rest of the people in dealing with the Benjamites as the justification for their actions but their response was excessive and carried out from the wrong motives. They betrayed those motives when they commanded the twelve thousand men, "Ye shall utterly destroy every male, and every woman that hath lain by man" (v.11). If they had believed their cause was just, they would have commanded the slaughter of all the inhabitants of the city but their very specific command ensured that any virgins within the city would be spared: "And they found among the inhabitants of Jabesh-gilead four hundred young virgins, that had known no man by lying with any male: and they brought them unto the camp to Shiloh, which is in the land of Canaan" (v.12). The way in which Shiloh is referred to means that it was almost certainly not the central sanctuary in Israel at this time that it had been for a brief period Joshua's day (Josh 18.1) and that it would again become in the future.

Even though this story must be viewed in the context of the times in which it was set, the slaughter of almost an entire city with the edge of the sword, including defenceless women and children, so that "four hundred young virgins" could be provided as wives for the Benjamites and thereby extricate the children of Israel from the consequences of their rash vow, was excessive and cruel in the extreme.

Clearly, they did not appreciate that they had only partly solved the problem. The next move was that "the whole congregation sent some to speak to the children of Benjamin that were in the rock Rimmon, and to call peaceably unto them" (v.13). Benjamin responded and "came again at that time" (v.14). However, when "they gave them wives which they had saved alive of the women of Jabesh-gilead", they discovered that the four hundred virgins, "sufficed them not" (v.14). Six hundred men had fled to the rock Rimmon for refuge (20.47), and therefore an additional two hundred maidens were still needed.

Once again, the people "repented them for Benjamin, because the Lord had made a breach (break - 6556) in the tribes of Israel" (v.15) but "the elders of the congregation" were left with the question, "How shall we do for wives for them that remain, seeing the women are destroyed out of Benjamin?" (v.16). Yet again, there was no recognition of their personal guilt in the matter. They were clear about the fact that, "There must be an inheritance for them that be escaped of Benjamin, that a tribe be not destroyed out of Israel" (v.17). Yet, nothing that had happened had removed their oath and the consequences of breaking it: "Howbeit we may not give them wives of our daughters: for the children of Israel have sworn, saying, Cursed be he that giveth a wife to Benjamin" (v.18).

A second plan was therefore devised and implemented: "Behold, there is a feast of the Lord in Shiloh yearly in a place which is on the north side of Beth-el, on the east side of the highway that goeth up from Beth-el to Shechem, and on the south of Lebonah" (v.19). The Benjamites were told the precise spot where the feast was taking place. Some commentators have suggested that the "feast of the Lord" referred to was the Passover, and that the dancing (v.21) looked back to that of Miriam and her companions after the children of Israel crossed the Red Sea (Ex 15.20). Others believe that mention of "the vineyards" (v.20) means that it was the Feast of Tabernacles (Lev 23.33-44). The latter suggestion is probably the more likely. It says a great deal about the true spiritual condition of the children of Israel that they were prepared to use the occasion of one of the Lord's "holy convocations" (Lev 23.2) to execute their own fleshly plan. In addition, in order to avoid soiling their own hands, they made the Benjamites put the plan into operation for them: "Therefore they commanded the children of Benjamin, saying, Go and lie in wait in the vineyards; and see, and, behold, if the daughters of Shiloh come out to dance in dances, then come ye out of the vineyards, and catch (clutch; seize as a prisoner - 2414) you every man his wife of the daughters of Shiloh, and go to the land of Benjamin" (vv.20-21). It was, of course, nothing short of kidnap and rape. Once again, they dishonoured, shamed and violated the women among them. Nevertheless, as far as the children of Israel were concerned, the end justified the means.

Their scheme was thought through to the extent that they even considered how to handle the inevitable objections they knew would come from the men of Shiloh. The elders assured the Benjamites that, when the protest came, they would support their actions and appeal to the men of Shiloh for forbearance: "And it shall be, when their fathers or their brethren come unto us to complain, that we will say unto them, Be favourable unto them for our sakes: because we reserved not to each man his wife in the war: for ye did not give unto them at this time, that ye should be guilty" (v.22). Clearly, the men of Shiloh had no input into the decision and appear to have decided to take the line of least resistance by complying. The plan ensured that they could not be accused of giving their daughters to the Benjamites, and thereby breaking their oath, but rather they were taken from them. In addition, it did not involve the Benjamites in the kind of violence that had been witnessed at Jabesh-gilead (v.10). Thus the two hundred remaining Benjamites obtained their wives and the eleven tribes kept their vow – a "perfect solution" by human standards! However, they may have kept the letter of the oath, but the means they used totally violated its spirit.

The children of Benjamin must, of course, take their share of the responsibility for going along with the plan without question: "And the children of Benjamin did so, and took them wives, according to their number, of them that danced, whom they caught: and they went and returned unto their inheritance, and repaired the cities, and dwelt in them" (v.23).

Thus the tribe that had been so near to extinction, naturally speaking, was preserved, but at an immense cost. It was the grace and mercy of the sovereign Lord, not the schemes of the children of Israel that allowed it to survive. Indeed, although the children of Israel failed to appreciate it, it was a miracle of God's grace that He had not wiped out all the tribes of Israel by the close of the period of the judges. Nevertheless, content with their work, the assembly broke up and "the children of Israel departed thence at that time, every man to his tribe and to his family, and they went every man to his inheritance" (v.24).

Verse 25: The Reflection of the Author

For the fourth, and final time, in these closing chapters (17.6; 18.1; 19.1), the author writes, "In those days there was no king in Israel: every man did that which was right in his own eyes" (v.25). However, the "right" that they thought they had done was completely unacceptable in the Lord's sight. S.Ridout writes, "What a world of yearning there is in that expression, 'there was no king in Israel'. How it tells of the only hope there could be for God's people. It was to have His king. God Himself surely wanted to be their king, would have been their king, but they refused Him. Later on they desired a king like all the nations, and He gives them a king after their own heart, king Saul; but they find him not a deliverer at all. But at last God gives them, in figure, the man after His own heart, and David in that way is surely a type of the coming King for Israel, the King for whom the nation still waits, though not consciously. He is the King in another sense for whom the people of God everywhere wait, and for whom, all unknown to itself, this poor world is groaning and sighing today" (*Lectures on the Book of Judges*).

It is interesting to observe that the following book of Ruth was set "in the days when the judges ruled" (Ruth 1.1). It is encouraging to know that during the dark and gloomy days of the judges, beautiful characters like Boaz, Naomi and Ruth could be found. They tell a story of redemption, grace and new life, which culminate in the birth of a son, and testify to the fact that, in spite of their rebellion, there is a future for Israel. God's plan of salvation can never be thwarted by the waywardness of His people or by the opposition of mankind in general. C.A.Coates writes, "He has shown us in Judges what failure there was everywhere among His people, but He reserves this beautiful book of Ruth as an appendix to show what was of Himself in the midst of it all" (*An Outline of the Book of Judges*).

RUTH

J. M. Flanigan

CONTENTS

BIBLIOGRAPHY

Atkinson, David. *The Message of Ruth*. Leicester: Inter-Varsity Press, 1983.
After a lengthy Introduction, a commentary written in a rather modern style, based on the RSV and with much emphasis on the providence of God in the story of Ruth.

Boone, Edward. *The Romance of Redemption*. Belfast: Ambassador Productions Ltd., 1993.
A helpful commentary with much practical teaching and exhortation.

Brenton, Sir Lancelot C. L. *The Septuagint with Apocrypha*. Massachusetts: Hendrickson Publishers, 1998.
A most helpful edition of the Septuagint, an early Greek translation of the original Hebrew text, giving the complete Greek text with a parallel English translation.

Coates, C. A. *An Outline of the Book of Ruth*. Kingston-on-Thames: Stow Hill Bible and Tract Depot.
A helpful approach to the book of Ruth in the same form and format as the author's other "Outlines". More devotional and practical than expositional.

Darby, J. N. *Collected Writings, Vol 19. Thoughts on Ruth.* Kingston-on-Thames: Stow Hill Bible and Tract Depot, 1972.
A short summary of the book of Ruth briefly explaining Mr Darby's view of Ruth as a type of the remnant of Israel received back in grace after being "Lo-Ammi".

Darby, J. N. *Synopsis of the Books of the Bible, Vol 1: Ruth.* Kingston-on-Thames: Stow Hill Bible and Tract Depot, 1964.
A brief thought provoking synopsis of the book of Ruth in which the widowed Naomi is viewed as a type of desolate Israel and Ruth a picture of the redeemed remnant.

DeHaan, M. R. *The Romance of Redemption*. Sub-titled *Studies in the Book of Ruth.* Grand Rapids: Kregel Publications, 1996.
A very readable commentary with much emphasis on the application to the nation of Israel in its dispersion and eventual return to the Land.

Delitzsch, F. *Ruth.* Keil & Delitzsch Commentary on the Old Testament, Volume 2. Grand Rapids: Wm. B. Eerdmans Publishing Co., 1973.
In the customary and conservative style of Delitzsch. A scholarly work with much quotation from Hebrew. Not as easy to read as some, but a very valuable commentary.

Edersheim, Alfred. *Israel under Joshua and the Judges*. London: Wm. Clowes & Sons, 1877.
A single chapter at the close of this volume is entitled "The Story of Ruth". It is a brief but thoughtful treatment of Ruth in the usual scholarly manner of Dr Edersheim.

Gaebelein, Arno C. *The Book of Ruth.* The Annotated Bible. New Jersey: Loizeaux Brothers, 1970.
A brief but helpful commentary, more in the form of an analysis, closely following, as the Preface states, "a dispensational foreshadowing".

Grant, F. W. *Ruth.* The Numerical Bible, Volume 2. New Jersey: Loizeaux Brothers, 1932.
Thoughtful and thought provoking, being a revised translation with expository notes with much application to Israel in her exile and unbelief and in her return to the Land.

Henry, Matthew. *Ruth.* Commentary, Volume 2. Massachusetts: Hendrickson Publishers. Reprint, 1971.
In the style of the Puritans. Very wordy but soundly conservative.

Heslop, W. G. *Rubies from Ruth.* Grand Rapids: Kregel Publications, 1976.
A brief commentary, at times in the nature of jottings, but easily read and very helpful with many precious thoughts of Christ and His people.

Kane, D. *Meditations on the Book of Ruth.* Glasgow: Gospel Tract Publications, 2000.
With "Levitical Offerings" and "Song of Songs", the third in a series of "Meditations" by David Kane. A valuable little commentary with a fine blending of devotion and exhortation.

Moorhouse, Henry. *Ruth the Moabitess.* London: Morgan and Scott. 1900.
A delightful little volume, being a short series of addresses on the book of Ruth.

Morris, Leon. *Ruth.* Tyndale Old Testament Commentaries. London: Tyndale Press, 1968.
A careful and scholarly treatment of the book of Ruth with a lengthy Introduction and detailed additional notes on the Divine Title "Shaddai" and the meaning of "go'el".

Moss, H. G. *The Book of Ruth.* Hong Kong: Christian Book Room. Undated.
It is, as stated in its title, "Thoughts and Suggestions", but very helpful.

Paisley, H. S. *This Ruth.* Glastonbury, Connecticut: Olive Press, 1995.
A very thorough devotional treatment of the book of Ruth with perhaps more application than exposition. A comment in the Preface says, "It will stimulate the mind of the reader, but it will also reach the heart".

Ridout, Samuel. *Judges and Ruth.* New Jersey: Loizeaux Brothers, 1958.
A helpful commentary described by the author as being, "Gleanings in a field whose golden grain is offered to us with a largeness of heart of which that of Boaz was but a type".

Slotki, Judah J. *Ruth* London: The Soncino Press Ltd., 1965.
Written by a Jew particularly for Jews but containing much valuable comment for Christian readers. Hebrew Text with the English translation of the Jewish Publication Society.

Spurrell, Helen. *A Translation of the Old Testament Scriptures.* London: James Nisbet & Co. Reprint published by Penfold Book & Bible House, Bicester, 1995.

An interesting translation of the Old Testament Scriptures from the original unpointed Hebrew text.

St John, Harold *Ruth the Moabitess.* The Collected Writings, Volume 1. Glasgow: Gospel Tract Publications, 1989.

In the familiar style of Mr St John. Not so much a commentary as a short series of meditations with particular attention to typical teaching and its relevance to Israel.

Strahan, Jack. *Jottings on the Book of Ruth*. Enniskillen: Private.

A collection of helpful notes and jottings gathered over many months of study, with much devotion to Christ and many references to Israel, both the Land and the people.

Thomson, W. M. *The Land and the Book*. London: T. Nelson & Sons, 1905

An invaluable guide to the customs and culture, the geography and topography of Israel. Almost a commentary, with a most extensive index of names, places, and subjects, and of Scripture texts. The fruit of some thirty years of residence in Syria and Palestine.

Tristram, H. B. *The Natural History of the Bible.* London: S.P.C.K., 1898.

A most useful review of the physical geography, geology, and meteorology of the Holy Land, claiming a description of every animal and plant mentioned in Holy Scripture. A very useful companion in any study of the Word.

Watt, John. *Ruth and the Song of Solomon*. New York: Loizeaux Brothers. Undated.

A very helpful volume, being a series of addresses on what the author calls "Two Neglected Books". Very devotional with much of Christ.

INTRODUCTION

The Moabitess

Many books in the Old Testament bear the names of men in their titles, but only two are named after women – Ruth and Esther. Ruth is the story of a poor Gentile girl who came to live among Hebrews and married a wealthy Hebrew husband. Esther is the story of a poor Hebrew girl who came to live among Gentiles and married a wealthy Gentile husband. In this respect the two books may appear to be almost opposites, but they have this in common that together they are the records of God's providential dealings with His people in difficult times. They tell of His sovereign movements behind human scenes for the care and preservation of that which would fulfil His purpose in grace. Both books demonstrate that the sovereignty of God is concerned not only with empires and emperors, but also with the apparently ordinary affairs of men, women, and families. The hearts of all men are in His hand and He can order all things, whether individual, national, or global, for His own ultimate glory. Of the book of Ruth another has written, "The Book of Ruth tells us also of the days of the judges, when there was no king in Israel; but it shows us the fair side of those days, in the operations of the grace of God, who (blessed be His name!) never failed to work in the midst of the evil, as also in the steady progress of events towards the fulfilment of His promises in the Messiah, whatever may have been the simultaneous progress of the general evil" (J. N. Darby, *Synopsis*).

As yet another comments, "The Book of Ruth opens with no king in Israel; it ends with the bringing in of David, the man after God's own heart, who was God's anointed; it points on to 'great David's greater Son', the Lord's anointed, the King of kings; and the crown shall flourish on His head when He fills the throne. Were this little book omitted from the canon of Scripture, it would be an irreparable loss; a most important link would be missing between the judges and the kings" (John Watt).

Five times in the book which bears her name Ruth is referred to as "Ruth the Moabitess" (1.22; 2.2; 2.21; 4.5; 4.10), and this repeated remembrance of her lowly origin and background in Moab is in itself an evidence of the grace of God. Moab, with Ammon, had had an incestuous beginning. The sad story is told in Genesis 19.30-38, and although Hebrews and Moabites were both descended from Abraham, their histories were so very different. The pure faith of Abraham and his descendants had degenerated in Moab into wickedness and idolatry so that the law had declared that "An Ammonite or Moabite shall not enter into the congregation of the Lord; even to their tenth generation shall they not enter into the congregation of the Lord for ever" (Deut 23.3). Yet even under law Jehovah could exercise grace, and this is well illustrated in the story of Ruth the Moabitess. Ruth's name is mentioned only once in the New Testament, but in what beautiful circumstances (Mt 1.5). As with four other women in that detailed genealogy, grace has lifted the girl from Moab and placed her among princes (1 Sam 2.8). Ruth was to become the great-grandmother of King David, giving her an honoured place in the lineage of the promised Messiah.

The book of Ruth ranks among the shortest books in the Old Testament. Its eighty-five verses in but four chapters can be read easily in twenty minutes, but the small compass of the book is out of all proportion to its immense importance in the history of Israel. It abounds in teaching which is not only historical but doctrinal and typical. There are moral, spiritual, dispensational, devotional, and practical lessons. As Matthew Henry says, "We find in this book excellent examples of faith, piety, patience, humility, industry, and loving-kindness, in the common events of life. Also we see the special care which God's providence takes of our smallest concerns". With its literary beauty it merits a place among the sweetest of love stories, portraying in a beautiful simplicity the triumph of love over racial, national, social, and legal barriers, as will be observed in the commentary.

Summary

A learned Jewish commentator writes, "Ruth is a perfect short historical epic in four chapters. It gives us a glimpse into the everyday life of Bethlehem, in the home and in the field, in its general gossip and its lawsuits, more than three thousand years ago" (Slotki). It is a story set in the times of the judges when there lived in Bethlehem of Judea a man of some standing named Elimelech. Because of famine in the land Elimelech decided to move some fifty miles (80 kilometres) away over the Jordan River to Moab. He was accompanied to Moab by his wife Naomi and their two sons, Mahlon and Chilion, and they would have travelled east through Judean wasteland and rolling hills, passing Jericho in the Jordan Valley at the northern end of the Dead Sea, and over the river to Moab in the vicinity of Mount Nebo.

It may be that Elimelech intended only to sojourn temporarily in Moab, but shortly after the family's emigration he died there. His sons both married Moabitish wives, Mahlon marrying Ruth (4.10), and Chilion marrying Orpah. Sadly, the sons then also died, and the three women were now left widowed. What tragic consequences can follow from a wrong move, and how often do those consequences involve the lives of so many others.

After ten difficult years, Naomi, now three times bereaved, widowed, and childless, decided to return to Judea and to Bethlehem. She had heard, perhaps from travelling merchants, that the famine was past and that there was now bread available in the land. It must have been an emotional day for her when she set out to return to her homeland. Ruth and Orpah decided to accompany their mother-in-law, but as they made their sad way along the road the older woman advised them that perhaps they should return to their own families and their former homes. She reminded them that she would never have any more sons to be their husbands. She wished them well, praying that perhaps they would each find rest with another husband in their own land. As they kissed each other and wept together Orpah was persuaded to return, and left her mother-in-law and sister-in–law somewhere on the road to Bethlehem.

Ruth, however, refused to leave Naomi. She determinedly vowed to go with her all the way. She would lodge where Naomi lodged. Naomi's people would be her people. Naomi's God would be her God. She would die where her mother-in-law died, and there she would be buried. Indeed nothing but death should part them. It was an emotional and immortal entreaty. Ruth would not be dissuaded, and so they travelled on together. It was a big decision for the girl from Moab. It would affect her future, her faith, her family, and her friends, but she was resolute in her choice.

It must have been two weary widows who eventually reached Bethlehem. It was the beginning of the barley harvest, early spring, and this provided employment for Ruth who at once went out into the harvest field to toil as a gleaner among the sheaves. She would by this maintain both herself and her mother-in-law. She found herself in the field of Boaz, a man of some wealth, who was himself a near relative of the deceased Elimelech. Boaz took notice of the stranger in his field, apparently attracted by her modesty and diligence, and on enquiring about her was advised by the steward overseeing the reapers that she was a Moabitish damsel who had come back from Moab with Naomi.

Boaz was kindly disposed toward Ruth and encouraged her to stay in his field for protection and for refreshment, for he had heard, he told her, of her fidelity and kindness to her widowed mother-in-law. He commanded the young men in the field to leave "handfuls of purpose" for her and in no way to molest or embarrass her.

It may have been some three months later, with the harvest gathered in, that Boaz was winnowing corn, and in the evening had gone to rest in his threshing floor. At Naomi's direction, Ruth went to the threshing floor and lay at the feet of Boaz, under the corner of his coverlet. When he awoke she pointed out that he was a near kinsman who could act as redeemer for herself and for Naomi. She asked for his protection as her redeemer. Boaz at once acquiesced but advised Ruth that there was another kinsman, one nearer than he, whose rights had priority. He would approach this other kinsman in the morning and apprise him of the circumstances. This he did, but, as will be considered in detail in the commentary, this kinsman was not willing, or perhaps not able, to redeem the land and marry Ruth.

In the presence of ten chosen men, and witnessed by the elders and other onlookers, Boaz received from the other kinsman the transfer of his redemptive rights in an interesting ceremony. Boaz would redeem the property and would marry Ruth and they would hopefully raise an heir to Mahlon and ensure the perpetuation of Elimelech's line.

In due time a son was born. He was named Obed and was destined to be the grandfather of David the King. It is an instance of the grace of God, even under law, that although Obed was the son of a Moabitess, and the grandson of Rahab a Canaanitess, yet he finds an honoured place in the lineage of the Messiah (Mt 1.5). In the mystery and wonder of the ways of God, Ruth the Moabitess and Rahab the harlot had both been brought as aliens into the knowledge of Jehovah the true God, and destined to become the progenitors of the King of Israel, the Messiah.

Such is the story of this little book of Ruth. Short though it may be it is a story without which, as Edersheim writes, "Our knowledge of that period would be incomplete".

Authenticity

The historical accuracy of the facts recorded in the book of Ruth has rarely been questioned and the little volume has always had a deserved place in the canon of Holy Scripture. Its position in that canon is most interesting. In the Septuagint, an early Greek translation of the Hebrew Scriptures, the book of Ruth is placed between the books of Judges and 1 Samuel, as indeed it is in the AV and RV and other English versions of the Bible. In Hebrew manuscripts it is one of the five *Megilloth*, the five Rolls of Song of Solomon, Ruth, Lamentations, Ecclesiastes, and Esther. It would at one time have been written on parchment preserved in a scroll, and it is known in Hebrew as *Megilloth Ruth*, the Scroll of Ruth.

The book of Ruth has been called a supplement to Judges and an introduction to 1 Samuel, which is really the first book of Kings. It lies, therefore, as a beautiful link between the anarchy of the former and the monarchy of the latter. Judges is a sad history of breakdown and failure, of departure and much distress. It has been said that coming from the book of Judges into the book of Ruth is like coming out of a noisy bustling market-place into a quiet meadow. "After reading Judges 17-21", Graham Scroggie writes, "Ruth is like a lovely lily in a stagnant pool. Here, instead of unfaithfulness is loyalty, and instead of immorality is purity. Here, instead of battlefields are harvest fields, and instead of the warrior's shout is the harvester's song." "It comes upon us with such sweet contrast", says Edersheim, "almost like a summer's morning after a night of wild tempest".

In Jewish Liturgy

In Jewish liturgy, some one of the five *Megilloth* referred to above, is read publicly at one of the annual Feasts. In the order in which they are still celebrated by Jews, these Festivals and readings are as follows.

The Song of Solomon is read at Passover, the first of the Spring Festivals, in the month Nisan, commemorating the Exodus from Egypt. The Song is, for the Jew, the story of the redeeming love of Jehovah for Israel.

Ruth is read at the Feast of Pentecost, which is known also as *Shavuot* or the Feast of Weeks (Ex 34.22). It is observed on the day after seven weeks have been counted from the Feast of Firstfruits. Since Pentecost is primarily a harvest festival it will be obvious that the harvesting scenes in Ruth are so very appropriate for such an occasion.

Lamentations is read at a lesser known Feast known as *Tisha B'Av*, which means literally "the ninth of Av", which is the fifth month in the Jewish Calendar. It is an annual sad remembrance of the destruction of Solomon's Temple in 586 BC, and also the destruction of the Second Temple by the Romans on the same day in AD 70.

Ecclesiastes is read at the Feast of Tabernacles, which is more often now referred to as *Sukkot*. It is an autumn Festival, one of three which are observed in the seventh month of Tishri. During *Sukkot* the people erect booths as temporary shelters as an annual reminder of God's provision during the forty years of sojourn in the wilderness. It is a joyful time, called also the Feast of Ingathering, celebrating the gathering in of the harvest (Ex 23.16; 34.22).

Esther is read at the Feast of Purim, which is sometimes known as the Feast of Esther. It is the last of the Festivals, on the fourteenth day of Adar, the twelfth month in the Jewish Calendar. It is a celebration of the deliverance of the Jews from the wicked Haman, which God wrought through Esther and Mordecai.

Tabernacles is the last of the seven Feasts known as the Feasts of Jehovah as outlined in Leviticus 23. Tisha B'Av and Purim, with several other Festivals, are later additions to the Jewish Liturgy and so are not included with the seven of Leviticus 23.

Date and Authorship

Neither the date nor the authorship of the book of Ruth can be precisely determined. Most Jewish commentators ascribe the authorship to Samuel, and although a few would assign it to a later date, even to post-exilic times, it can be said that the Samuel authorship agrees with Jewish tradition. With this most Christian expositors concur, and while it is indeed very probable, none can be certain. Perhaps in favour of Samuel as the author is his early and close association with David. David's is the last name to be mentioned in the book of Ruth (4.22) and the story of David is then continued in the following book, which is the First Book of Samuel. The connection may be significant.

Two dates then require consideration, but, as with the authorship, so it is with these: neither of them can be positively determined. First there is the date of composition, but this, of course, is essentially linked with the authorship. However, even if Samuel is indeed the author of the book of Ruth, the precise date of writing still remains unknown. Scholars differ widely on the exact years of the prophet Samuel's life and ministry, and all that may be said with any certainty is that he must have ministered sometime during the 11th Century BC.

Second, there is the date of the events which are recorded in the narrative of Ruth. This is mentioned, though but vaguely, in the opening verse of the book. It was, says that verse, "...in the days when the judges ruled". Again it is difficult, if not impossible, to fix a year with any exactitude, for the period of some thirteen or more judges spanned perhaps three or four hundred years. According to the short genealogical account at the close of the book (4.18-22) Ruth and Boaz would have lived several generations before David, and, since Boaz was the son of Rahab who lived in the time of Joshua, this would place him in the early days of the judges. However, as with the authorship, there is great divergence of opinion among scholars as to precise timing. The commentator Adam Clarke acknowledges this, and writes, "When and by whom the book of Ruth was written, are points not agreed on among critics and commentators. As to the transactions recorded in it, they are variously placed. In the book itself there is no other notation of time than merely this, that the things came to pass in the days when the judges ruled; therefore some have placed these transactions under Ehud; others, under Gideon; others, under Barak; others, under Abimelech; and others, under Shamgar. This last is the opinion of Archbishop Usher; and most chronologers adopt it". He later adds, "As to the author, he is as uncertain as the time. It has been attributed to Hezekiah, to Ezra, and to Samuel; and it is most likely that the author of the two books of Samuel was also the writer of this little book, as it seems necessary to complete his plan of the history of David".

The Personalities

Apart from the ten names mentioned in the short genealogy at the close of the book, seven individuals are identified by name throughout the actual narrative, and two persons, though mentioned, remain anonymous. This anonymity may be of symbolic significance, as will be considered in the commentary. So too will be the meanings of the names given. "What is in a name?", is a question discussed in the *Talmud*, the authoritative body of Jewish tradition, which suggests that a name may have had a certain power for good or evil over the person who bore it. The Jewish *Midrash,* however, a Hebrew exposition of the Old Testament, cites cases where the characters of certain individuals did not at all agree with the meanings of their names, and indeed may at times have been quite the opposite. There is though, scriptural precedent for seeing the significance of some names, as when our first parents, Adam and Eve, were so called, in keeping with their origin and their purpose in the creation (Gen 3.20). Significantly, too, was Abram renamed Abraham (Gen 17.5), Sarai became Sarah (Gen 17.15), and Benoni became Benjamin (Gen 35.18). In the New Testament Simon was significantly renamed Cephas (Jn 1.42), and Saul became Paul (Acts 13.9). In the Epistle to the Hebrews also, Melchisedec, King of Salem, is, with inspired significance, "King of righteousness and...King of peace" (Heb 7.2). And is not that most beautiful of all names, "Jesus", itself invested with the utmost significance - "Jehovah-Saviour"?

The two unnamed persons in the book of Ruth are the servant or overseer who was in charge of the reapers (2.5-6), and the other kinsman who was nearer than Boaz (3.12; 4.1-8), but if the meaning of names is important, then the meanings of the names of the persons who are identified by name must be considered. These are, in the order in which they appear in the narrative –

Elimelech: "My God is King"
Naomi: "Pleasant, or Sweet"
Mahlon: "Sickly"
Chilion: "Pining"
Orpah: "Gazelle", or, as some, "Stiff-necked"
Ruth: "Friendship", or "Beauty"
Boaz: "Strength".

It must be said that these meanings of the names, while not universally agreed, are, nevertheless, generally accepted.

Prophetic Pictures

Many commentators have observed in the chief personalities in Ruth symbolic foreshadowings of greater persons and events which were then still future. While "type" is, theologically, perhaps too strong a word to employ in this connection, yet prophetic "pictures" there surely are.

Elimelech and his family leaving the Land of Promise are a sad picture of the breakdown and failure of testimony for God in Israel. Such failure was so very characteristic of the times of the judges but continued throughout the generations until the disobedient nation was eventually carried into captivity and has now been scattered for many centuries.

Naomi in Moab is very generally regarded as an obvious picture of the present condition of the nation of Israel, away from her homeland in her *diaspora*, exiled in unbelief, but destined however, to be restored to her Land in what is called *aliyah*.

Ruth is the Gentile bride, who, because of Naomi's exile and subsequent return, is brought into favour through the mediation of a kinsman-redeemer. She is, in the view of many expositors, such an unmistakeable picture of the Bride of Christ, which is comprised so much of redeemed Gentiles. As Paul writes concerning Israel, "Through their fall salvation is come unto the Gentiles...the diminishing of them the riches of the Gentiles" (Rom 11.11-12). The backsliding of Naomi and her husband results in the blessing of Ruth.

Boaz, mighty man of wealth and valour, who was both able and willing to pay the redemption price and make the poor Gentile his bride, is a fine foreshadowing of Christ, that great Kinsman-Redeemer and Lord of the Harvest.

It must be mentioned, however, that several commentators prefer to see Ruth as a picture of a returning remnant of Israel. Since the unbelieving nation in her exile has been *Lo-ammi*, "Ye are not my people, and I will not be your God" (Hosea 1.9), it is contended that she will be received back in the same manner as Gentiles, through the ministry of the Kinsman-Redeemer, and is prefigured in Ruth. To quote J. N. Darby on this, "She is", he writes, "The type of the remnant (after Lo-Ammi was sentenced and executed on Israel) received back in grace in the last days preparatorily to the kingdom, when the Kinsman-Redeemer espouses their cause".

The unnamed steward, the servant over the reapers, overseeing, directing, and guiding the work in the harvest field, is a fitting picture of the ministry of the Holy Spirit who similarly guides the servants of God in their service today.

The unnamed kinsman, who was not willing, and therefore practically not able, to act as redeemer, may be a suitable representation of the law with its inability to redeem (Rom 8.3-4).

These suggestions will be considered in more detail in the relevant passages throughout the commentary, when their interesting significance will perhaps become more obvious.

Divine Names and Titles

Of the many and varied names and titles of God in the Old Testament, the following are found in the book of Ruth, all teaching the value of intelligent and reverent use of divine titles, as will be noted in due course.

"Jehovah" (3068) is rendered LORD in the AV, and is defined, if definition is possible, as, "Him which is, and which was, and which is to come" (Rev 1.4). He is the Eternally Self-Existent, All-Sufficient One. This is the Jewish national name of God. It is the first divine name to be mentioned in the book of Ruth (1.6) and occurs 17 times throughout the four chapters.

"Elohim" (430) is first used by Ruth (1.16). This is the plural name of the supreme triune God. Had the Moabitess, erstwhile worshipper of the god Chemosh, learned this truth of the true God from Naomi?

"Shaddai" (7706) is rendered "The Almighty" in the AV. A very tender name of God as will be observed in the commentary, it is used twice by Naomi (1.20,21).

"Jehovah Elohim", a combination of 3068 and 430, is rendered "The LORD God" in the AV. It is used by Boaz in his commendation of, and prayer for, Ruth, when he speaks of "The LORD God of Israel" (2.12).

Outline

The predominant personality in the book is, of course, the girl from Moab whose name the book bears in its title. Ruth figures in every chapter and since each chapter is self-contained, any further division of the book is hardly necessary.

Chapter 1

Ruth on the Highway	The Stranger	Her Decision

Chapter 2

Ruth in the Harvest Field	The Gleaner	Her Diligence

Chapter 3

Ruth in the Threshing Floor	The Pleader	Her Duty

Chapter 4

Ruth in the Home	The Mother	Her Devotion

In the commentary however, the chapters are sub-divided as follows.

Chapter 1

Verse 1	Famine in the Land
Verses 1-2	From Bethlehem to Moab
Verses 3-5	Tragedy Strikes
Verses 6-7	From Moab to Bethlehem
Verses 8-15	The Parting of the Ways
Verses 16-18	Ruth's Resolve
Verses 19-22	Bethlehem!

Chapter 2

Verses 1-3	The Field of Boaz
Verses 4-14	Ruth meets Boaz
Verses 15-23	Gleaning in the Field of Boaz

Chapter 3

Verses 1-5	The Kinsman-Redeemer
Verses 6-13	At the Threshing Floor
Verses 14-18	"Until the Morning"

Chapter 4

Verse 1	Levirate Marriage
Verses 1-2	At the Gate
Verses 3-6	The Proposition
Verses 7-8	The Ceremony of the Shoe
Verses 9-12	Marriage
Verses 13-17	A Child is Born
Verses 18-22	The Genealogy

Here then in Ruth is the history of every believer in the Lord Jesus, condemned by the law, helpless and hopeless, but brought by sovereign grace to a knowledge of the Redeemer and into the family of God. "Which in time past were not a people, but are now the people of God: which had not obtained mercy, but now have obtained mercy" (1 Pet 2.10). Well might another Apostle write, "O the depth of the riches both of the wisdom and knowledge of God! how unsearchable are his judgments, and his ways past finding out!" (Rom 11.33).

Here, too, is a prophetic picture of Israel, for two millennia exiled among the nations in bitterness and unbelief, but destined to be restored to the Land of Promise and even now returning to that Land out of their *diaspora*, their dispersion. However, as it was with Naomi and Ruth when they first returned to the Land in their poverty, Jews now in Israel are not yet in the enjoyment of their ultimate redemption. That awaits the coming of the Redeemer, the Blessed Man from Bethlehem, whose Land it is, and whose right alone it is to redeem.

RUTH 1

Verse 1: Famine in the Land

The phrase with which this little narrative begins, "It came to pass", is a familiar one occurring nearly 400 times throughout the Old Testament. There was a Jewish tradition, cited in the *Midrash*, that in every passage where it occurs there is a story of some misfortune. While this may not be true in every instance, it does indeed appear to be generally so, and it is certainly the case here, for "there was a famine in the land".

The scene is in *Eretz Israel*, the Land of Israel, and the timing is so significant. It was "in the days when the judges ruled". "Judges" and "ruled" are the noun and verb form of the same word (SHAPAT - 8199). They were the days when the judges judged. As has been mentioned in the Introduction, there were perhaps thirteen of these judges, raised up at critical times over a period of more than three hundred years to govern and rule in Israel (Judg 2.16). The Scriptures do not specify which judge was ruling at this particular time. For some unknown, but no doubt important reason, he has not been identified and the speculations of commentators are very varied. As Matthew Henry writes, "Under which of the judges these things happened we are not told, and the conjectures of the learned are very uncertain. It must have been towards the beginning of the judges' time, for Boaz, who married Ruth, was born of Rahab, who received the spies in Joshua's time. Some think it was in the days of Ehud, others of Deborah; the learned Bishop Patrick inclines to think it was in the days of Gideon, because in his days only we read of a famine by the Midianites' invasion". Although all admit that it cannot be determined with any certainty, many commentators favour this latter suggestion. The famine of those days must have been extremely serious, extending over a number of years and over the whole land even as far as to Gaza. The Midianites invaded when Israel had planted the grain, and, as the passage in Judges records, "they encamped against them, and destroyed the increase of the earth, till thou come unto Gaza, and left no sustenance for Israel, neither sheep, nor ox, nor ass. For they came up with their cattle and their tents, and they came as grasshoppers for multitude; for both they and their camels were without number: and they entered into the land to destroy it. And Israel was greatly impoverished because of the Midianites" (Judg 6.3-6). This may indeed be the setting of the book of Ruth but perhaps the purpose of the comment, "in the days when the judges ruled", is not really to determine an exact date but probably just to indicate the nature of the times in which the events took place.

Those were dark days. "The children of Israel did evil in the sight of the Lord" (Judg 6.1). They were days of disobedience and declension, of departure from Jehovah to the idolatrous worship of the gods of the heathen. The book of Judges begins with, "Now after the death of Joshua…", and it was indeed soon after this that the decline commenced.

God gave them judges, one after another, for their deliverance from oppression and captivity, but so soon after some deliverance had been granted they were early in rebellion and bondage again. Yet again He would deliver them and yet again they would forsake Him, until, on one occasion, in His grief He had to say to them, "Ye have forsaken me, and served other gods: wherefore I will deliver you no more. Go and cry unto the gods which ye have chosen; let them deliver you in the time of your tribulation" (Judg 10.13-14). Yet even after this He delivered them. Judges ends with the sad comment that "there was no king in Israel: every man did that which was right in his own eyes". It was anarchy.

It is perhaps not to be wondered at that there should be famine in the land, but famine in the land which, twenty times in the Old Testament is called "a land flowing with milk and honey" (Ex 3.8), was tragic in the extreme. Famine was often Jehovah's chosen method of discipline and punishment, but always with the purpose of the restoration and eventual blessing of the people. The same principle of divine chastisement obtains today, as the Epistle to the Hebrews clearly teaches: "Whom the Lord loveth he chasteneth...Now no chastening for the present seemeth to be joyous, but grievous: nevertheless afterward it yieldeth the peaceable fruit of righteousness unto them which are exercised thereby" (Heb 12.6,11). There was a famine in the days of Abram (Gen 12.10) and also in the days of Isaac (Gen 26.1). Again there was a grievous famine in the days of Jacob (Gen 41.27 - 47.20). Later there would be famine in the days of David (2 Sam 21.1). What makes this particular famine in Ruth especially tragic is that it affected Bethlehem, which is *Beyth Lechem* (1035), the House of Bread. That the House of Bread should be impoverished by famine is almost unthinkable, but so it was. As F. W. Grant remarks, "Famine in Bethlehem, mocking it as the House of Bread".

Anarchy in the land! Famine in the House of Bread! Where was the promised milk and honey? It is against this dark and sombre background that the little book of Ruth shines like a precious gem, its lustre relieving the gloom of those sad and dismal days of the judges and brightening the darkness.

Verses 1-2: From Bethlehem to Moab

The first name to be mentioned in the story is that of Elimelech, called, "A certain man of Bethlehem-judah". It should be noted that there are two Bethlehems in Israel and they must not be confused. The other Bethlehem, known as "*Beyth Lechem Ha'Galilit*", Bethlehem in Galilee, is in the territory of Zebulun, near to Nazareth, but with characteristic and inspired accuracy the Scripture states that Elimelech's Bethlehem was Bethlehem-judah, Bethlehem of Judea. "Judah" means "Praise", but there was little praise from the inhabitants of Bethlehem-judah in the circumstances.

Note that the word rendered "man" here is the Hebrew ISH (376). It is suggested by Strong, and Rabbinic exegesis agrees with him, that the word may denote a man of high degree, "not merely a person but a personage, a man of importance, either in learning or in social status, hence the inference that he was a wealthy man, perhaps one of the city's notabilities" (Slotki). He would have been much like his kinsman Boaz.

For reasons which are not clearly defined Elimelech decides to leave Bethlehem for the neighbouring land of Moab. Of course he may simply have been fleeing from the famine conditions which prevailed, but certain Jewish commentators think otherwise. They point out that since he was apparently a wealthy man, like Boaz, he would have had the means to have stored sufficient provision for himself and his family. Did he feel insecure and vulnerable in a famine stricken country where anarchy prevailed? Was there a possible fear of attack on his person and property by crowds of hungry people desperate for food? Whatever the reason, Elimelech has decided. He will rise, with Naomi his wife and his two sons Mahlon and Chilion, and travel to Moab.

As has been mentioned in the Introduction, this was a journey of some fifty miles (eighty kilometres). Although the hills of Moab would have been visible from Bethlehem, it would nevertheless have been a difficult enough journey on foot, across Judean hills, over the River Jordan at the northern end of the Dead Sea, and into Moab somewhere in the vicinity of Mount Nebo. It is a sad reflection to remember that Elimelech's forefathers, the children of Israel of the days of Moses and Joshua, had crossed this same Jordan at the same place, but in the opposite direction, to inherit the Land of Promise. "And the Lord spake unto Moses in the plains of Moab by Jordan near Jericho, saying, Speak unto the children of Israel, and say unto them, When ye are passed over Jordan into the land of Canaan...this shall be your land with the coasts thereof round about" (Num 33.50-51; 34.12). Then later, "Hear, O Israel: Thou art to pass over Jordan this day, to go in to possess nations greater and mightier than thyself, cities great and fenced up to heaven" (Deut 9.1); and, "For ye shall pass over Jordan to go in to possess the land which the Lord your God giveth you, and ye shall possess it, and dwell therein" (Deut 11.31). What a Land it was! "A good land, a land of brooks of water, of fountains and depths that spring out of valleys and hills; A land of wheat, and barley, and vines, and fig trees, and pomegranates; a land of oil olive, and honey; A land wherein thou shalt eat bread without scarceness, thou shalt not lack any thing in it; a land whose stones are iron, and out of whose hills thou mayest dig brass. When thou hast eaten and art full, then thou shalt bless the Lord thy God for the good land which he hath given thee" (Deut 8.7-10; see also 11.9-12; 33.25). It was tragic, that by their disobedience and evil they had forfeited such a land.

Now Elimelech was crossing Jordan going out of that land. Doubtless this is the way they would travel from Bethlehem. It was a momentous decision, a sad decision, a wrong decision, to abandon Immanuel's Land. The Patriarchs could have warned him, from their experience, that running away from famine was often attended by disaster. Elimelech's move was to have disastrous consequences, as will be seen. And did not his kinsman Boaz remain in the Land, and remain wealthy?

Relations between Israel and Moab were varied. At times there was indeed a fragile friendship, and at other times there was bitter enmity. Their peoples were closely related, being descendants respectively of Abraham and of Lot, who was Abraham's nephew, but Moab had long since abandoned the ancestral faith of Abraham. There they worshipped the god Chemosh, called "the abomination of Moab". They had become known as "the people of Chemosh" whose worship consisted of the vilest immoralities and corruptions. "Woe to thee, Moab! thou art undone, O people of Chemosh" (Num 21.29). See also the references in 1 Kings 11.7 and 2 Kings 23.13. They worshipped, too, the Baalim, the gods of Baal, and it was not long after the Exodus from Egypt that Moab became a stumbling block, and Baal a snare, to the redeemed nation of Israel (Judg 2.11; 10.10). Balak, the King of Moab, afraid of the Israelites, engaged Balaam to curse them. This Balaam could not do but he did succeed in seducing Israel to commit fornication and turn to idolatry (Num 22-25; Rev 2.14). There was thereafter, repeated though intermittent, strife between the two nations. It may have been, therefore, and probably was, that at the time of this famine relations were friendly enough between them and Elimelech judged it prudent to move his family to Moab. Did he somehow imagine that he could escape the idolatrous, polluted atmosphere of Moab? Would he be immune to its defiling influence?

They went to sojourn. The word "sojourn" (1481) may suggest that they intended just to lodge for while, to remain only as long as seemed necessary, and then to return to their homeland. As Leon Morris writes, "There was evidently no intention of a permanent migration. The use of the verb *guwr*, 'to sojourn', shows that the man planned to return in due course (Berkeley renders, *to live for a while*). It is the regular word for a resident alien. Such had certain rights in Israel, but we do not know whether this was so in Moab or not". Elimelech never intended to die in Moab. However, "they...continued there", and this seems to indicate that the sojourners had become settlers.

It is stated of the family that they were Ephrathites. Ephratah was an ancient name of Bethlehem which was continued after the occupation of the land by the Hebrews, even down to the time of the prophet Micah (Gen 35.19; Micah 5.2), and Edersheim's explanation of the term is that "the expression is apparently intended to convey that the family had not been later immigrants, but original Jewish settlers – or, as the Jewish commentators have it, patrician burghers of the ancient Ephrath (Gen 35.19; 48.7; 1 Sam 17.12; Micah 5.2)". David the Psalmist remembers his boyhood days in Ephratah (Ps 132.6). There is a sad irony in this, that Ephrath means "fruitfulness". Famine in the land of fruitfulness! Famine in the House of Bread! Ephrath was now no longer "fruitfulness", nor

Bethlehem "the house of bread". There is not much support for an alternative suggestion, that they were Ephraimites.

Why Elimelech, whose name means "my God is King", and Naomi, whose name means "pleasant, or sweet", should have named their two sons "Mahlon" and "Chilion", is difficult, if not impossible, to understand. The two names mean, respectively, "sickly" and "pining". Were the boys born during the famine? Or were their names symbolic of the condition of Israel at that time? Or were these the physical conditions of the children at birth and a possible indicator of future poor health? Would such an actual state of health explain their early deaths and childlessness? We cannot tell, but in accord with Jewish and ancient custom, there must almost certainly have been some reason for their names. Neither Jewish parents, nor parents from among ancient peoples generally, gave their children names just because the chosen names sounded pleasant. There had to be a perceived reason, a meaning in the names.

Verses 3-5: Tragedy Strikes

It seems to have been but a short time after their arrival in Moab that tragedy struck. For exactly how long they had actually been there is not recorded, but Elimelech died, and Naomi was left, and her two sons. She was now widowed and her sons were fatherless in a strange country. They had escaped from the famine, but trouble had pursued them, and many commentators, especially Jewish, think that Elimelech's death was Jehovah's governmental hand in judgment on the family for their abandonment of the Promised Land.

The tragedy deepens when, as recorded in the next verse but one, both sons die also. This, however, was after having taken wives of the women of Moab. The Jewish *Targum* is a free translation of parts of the Old Testament from the original Hebrew language into Aramaic. It is more often a paraphrase, and is interspersed with commentary which has made it the recognised authority on Jewish tradition. The *Targum* is unequivocal in its condemnation of Mahlon and Chilion, stating, as quoted by Adam Clarke, "The *Targum* very properly observes, that they transgressed the decree of the word of the Lord, and took to themselves strange women. The *Targum* adds, And because they transgressed the decree of the word of the Lord, and joined affinity with strange people, therefore their days were cut off". While it is true that the passages in Exodus 34.16 and Deuteronomy 7.3-4 do not specifically prohibit marriage to a Moabite, yet the principle is there and it must be obvious from other Scriptures, as Numbers 25.1-2, that the marriage of the children of Israel with the sons and daughters of idolatrous nations was abhorrent to Jehovah and fraught with danger for the people (cf. Nehemiah 13.23ff).

Those were sad days, especially for Naomi. Her husband and two sons had died outside their inheritance. They had died as strangers in a strange land. As another has put it, "Three graves with three mounds finally marked the spot where the bodies of three Hebrews lay covered with the cold sod of Moab" (Heslop). Naomi was left widowed and childless. Ruth and Orpah were now young widows. There were three vacant chairs in the house that once was home, and three lonely widows were left to grieve. With Naomi, memories would most likely be mingled with regret, and with thoughts of what might have been if they had never left their homeland. If only they had known and obeyed the principle later enshrined in the words of the psalmist: "Trust in the Lord, and do good; so shalt thou dwell in the land, and verily thou shalt be fed" (Ps 37.3). Although there was an obvious bond of affection between the three women, yet, what did Moab now have to offer Naomi, a lonely ageing widow in a foreign country? It was time to return to her native Israel.

Verses 6-7: From Moab to Bethlehem

Like the prodigal in our Lord's parable (Lk 15.11-32), Naomi had doubtless pondered much over her plight and remembered better days in her former home. Just as the prodigal son knew that in his father's house there was bread, enough and to spare, she too had heard that the Lord had visited His people in her homeland in giving them bread. On the word "visited" (6485) Strong says that it may indicate either friendly or hostile intent and indeed it is used in both senses in the several hundred occurrences of it in the Old Testament. Here of course, it is a gracious visitation of Jehovah to His people after the days of famine. Morris writes, "This verb is rarely, if at all, used in our sense of going to see someone briefly. It is often used of the divine activity in the Old Testament. It sometimes carries overtones of punishment (e.g. Jer 25.12, where it is translated 'punish'); sometimes, as here, of blessing". It calls to mind the sad lament of the Lord Jesus over Jerusalem when His ministry was drawing to a close: "They shall not leave in thee one stone upon another; because thou knewest not the time of thy visitation (Lk 19.44).

It may have been from travelling traders that Naomi had heard the news that the famine was over. Doubtless she would often converse with such merchants, anxious always to hear of Israel and of home. More than ten sad and lonely years had passed since the death of Elimelech. There had been much time to think. Impelled then, both by the emptiness of any future in Moab and by the news of plenty in Israel, "she arose". She must certainly have talked the matter over with her daughters-in-law. Would they all have discussed the matter together? Would Ruth and Orpah have conferred privately with each other, discussing and deciding their movements too in view of the pending departure of their beloved mother-in-law?

It must have been with mixed emotions that Naomi "went forth out of the place" on the way that led to *Eretz Judah*, the Land of Judah. Ten years, and more, of sad memories would flood her mind as she walked the road accompanied by her two daughters-in-law. It has been called "the path of repentance" (Boone). It has been the path trodden with tears by many a penitent backslider. Poor Naomi! How she would recall her arrival in Moab with a husband and two sons, with certain plans and prospects for the future of the family. Since then, bereavement, marriages, two more bereavements, a certain feeling of desolation, and now returning empty (v.21). How truly she had learned that "the way of transgressors is hard" (Prov 13.15). Did the women travel in silence? Perhaps they did, until Naomi stops on the way to say what has been in her mind.

Verses 8-15: The Parting of the Ways

Naomi has been both criticised and commended for her attempts to dissuade her daughters-in-law from travelling with her to Judah. Some there are who feel so strongly that she should never have discouraged the two girls from leaving the idolatry of Moab for a new life with the people of God in Judah. Others take the contrary view, that, much as she would have appreciated their companionship and support, Naomi was being realistic and honest with them in making them face the facts and take into account the difficulties and doubtful prospects if they came to Judah with her. It will be remembered that the Lord Jesus did this, of course, when "a certain scribe came, and said unto him, Master, I will follow thee whithersoever thou goest". The Saviour reminded him that the way might be difficult and lonely, saying, "The foxes have holes, and the birds of the air have nests; but the Son of man hath not where to lay his head" (Mt 8.19-20). It is not recorded whether that scribe followed Him or not.

So does Naomi speak to Ruth and Orpah. They had accompanied their mother-in-law along the way, but now it was time to stop, to consider the future, and Naomi says, "Go, return each to her mother's house". In Eastern countries women occupy apartments separate from those of the men, and daughters are most frequently in those of their mothers. Barnes' comment is helpful: "Accompanying their mother-in-law to the borders of their own land would probably be an act of Oriental courtesy. Naomi with no less courtesy presses them to return. The mention of the mother's house, which the separation of the women's house or tent from that of the men facilitates, is natural in her mouth, and has more tenderness in it than 'father's house' would have had; it does not imply the death of their fathers". Indeed it is specifically mentioned that Ruth's father was still alive when they left Moab (2.11). Matthew Henry's comment is characteristically quaint, "Naomi suggests that their own mothers would be more agreeable to them than a mother-in-law, especially when their own mothers had houses and their mother-in-law was not sure she had a place to lay her head in which she could call her own". As Edersheim says, "It was a noble act of self-denial on the part of the aged Hebrew widow by this plain speaking to strip herself of all remaining comfort, and to face the dark future, utterly childless, alone, and helpless".

She wishes them well, praying that Jehovah would deal as kindly with them as they had dealt with the dead, that is, with their deceased husbands and with Elimelech. Perhaps, she prays, the Lord will grant them to be happily married again, and that they may each find rest (4496), meaning comfort and ease, tranquillity and peace, a settled home with future husbands. It was a touching scene on the highway as she kissed them and they wept together. But the two girls remonstrated with Naomi, saying, "Surely we will return with thee unto thy people". Twice she answers them with the same words, "Turn again, my daughters", and gives them what seem to be compelling reasons why they should go back to their own land and to their own people. Were there any more sons in her womb? She did not even have a husband, and if she did, and bore sons again, would they wait in widowhood until such unlikely sons were grown up to a marriageable age? There may be of course, a veiled reference here to that ancient custom in Israel known as the Levirate Law whereby a man was required to marry the widow of his deceased brother and raise a family to perpetuate his brother's name (Deut 25.5,6). This however, would necessitate Naomi's marrying a brother of Elimelech so that the sons born of such a union would be regarded as sons of Elimelech who, in turn, would be required to marry Ruth and Orpah. No, it was all unthinkable! It was purely hypothetical, and highly improbable if not impossible. Naomi was too old now to have a husband and sons. There was no future for her daughters-in-law in coming with her. They should return to Moab where they belonged and find husbands and homes again in their own land and among their own people.

Delitzsch then makes an interesting comment when he says, "One possible case Naomi left without notice, namely, that her daughters-in-law might be able to obtain other husbands in Judah itself. She did not hint at this, in the first place, and perhaps chiefly, from delicacy on account of the Moabitish descent of her daughters-in-law, in which she saw that there would be an obstacle to their being married in the land of Judah". Naomi refers to the bitterness of her own grief for their sakes. The hand of the Lord had gone out against her, not only in taking away her husband but also in taking away her two sons, which left Ruth and Orpah as young widows. The two girls from Moab were suffering because of Jehovah's dealings with their mother-in-law, and this pained her deeply. She was, she felt, responsible for their grief. Again they lifted up their voice and wept. It was no light decision that they were about to make.

While Ruth clung to Naomi, Orpah kissed her again, and then follow those sad words, "Behold, thy sister in law is gone back unto her people, and unto her gods". Several translations, including that of the Jewish Publication Society, render "gods" as a singular "god". If this is so, then Orpah had returned to the worship of the Moabitish god Chemosh (Num 21.29). Orpah is never heard of again. She returned to Moab, to her own kin, to idolatry, and to historical oblivion.

Verses 16-18: Ruth's Resolve

Ruth resolutely refused to follow her sister-in-law, and her words of entreaty to Naomi are enshrined eternally in the narrative. It was a moment of decision which was to have undreamed of consequences. Another has written, "So far she had moved step by step with Orpah. Now Orpah, her sister-in-law, had gone. Behind her, in the sweet light of reminiscence is Moab, the home of her childhood, of her mother and father; the scene of her friendships, the centre of her interests. Before her lies Israel with its dark forbidding hills, its alien faces, its unknown trials. Will Ruth follow her sister-in-law back to Moab?" (Slotki). Ruth's appeal is well known and much loved. It is proverbial among Christians everywhere. It is uniquely beautiful, resolutely calm and yet impassioned, a lovely blending of simplicity and sincerity. She pleads with Naomi, "Intreat me not to leave thee, or to return from following after thee: for whither thou goest, I will go; and where thou lodgest, I will lodge: thy people shall be my people, and thy God my God: Where thou diest, will I die, and there will I be buried: the Lord do so to me, and more also, if ought but death part thee and me". She would go with Naomi and stay with her until death parted them. They would live together, lodge together, share the same people as their mutual friends, and worship the same God. Ruth would die where Naomi died, and be buried with her. The decision affected Ruth's future, her family, her friends, and her faith. It is of interest to note that this girl from idolatrous Moab calls upon "Jehovah", the God of Israel, to witness her resolve when she says "The Lord (3068) do so to me, and more also". It is obvious that she has learned much from her mother-in-law.

On Ruth's brave words to Naomi Adam Clarke paraphrases and comments, "May he inflict any of those punishments on me, and any worse punishment, if I part from thee till death. And it appears that she was true to her engagement; for Naomi was nourished in the house of Boaz in her old age, and became the fosterer and nurse of their son Obed (4.15,16)". Naomi realised that her daughter-in-law was steadfastly minded to go with her. Her choice was made and her mind was fixed. Naomi ceased speaking and they travelled on together toward Bethlehem and "home".

It is tragic to read in 1 Kings 11.7 that Solomon, Ruth's great-great-grandson actually built a high place for the god of the Moabites on the Mount of Olives. "Then did Solomon build an high place for Chemosh, the abomination of Moab, in the hill that is before Jerusalem". What sad departure there can be in the space of but a few generations.

Verses 19-22: Bethlehem!

The quiet village was astir at the sight of the two weary figures approaching from the East. Naomi and Ruth must have been tired and forlorn after the journey from Moab, and with what mixed feelings and emotions did both of them now enter Bethlehem? Naomi would remember happier days. She would recall too, so vividly, the day that she and Elimelech and the boys left the town. Would any of her earlier acquaintances still be here? Would they recognise her after all these years? Would they welcome her? Or would they upbraid her for ever having left Bethlehem? It was a mixture of unknowns. As for Ruth, she would be a stranger, a foreigner, an alien. How would they receive her? What future was there for a Moabitess in Bethlehem?

It was the women of the town who exclaimed "Is this Naomi?" That it was the women who so spoke is indicated by the use of the feminine gender in vv.19-20, and so it is translated by JND, RSV, ASV, and several others, who read, "All the city was moved and the women said, Is this Naomi?". Some, therefore, did indeed recognise her, but what a change there must have been in their former neighbour. Did they ask their question in surprise? Was there compassion? Or was it irony? Can this old lady, weary and worn, with the marks of suffering and sorrow lining her sad face, be the wealthy wife of Elimelech who left Bethlehem more than a decade ago?

Naomi answers their question, saying, "Call me not Naomi", the pleasant one. She had been that in earlier days, but not now. "Call me Mara", she says, in recognition of her bitter experiences, "for the Almighty hath dealt very bitterly with me". Note that "Mara" and "bitterly" are different forms of the same word, and note too the titles of God which Naomi now uses. "Almighty" is the Hebrew *Shaddai* (7706). *Shaddai* occurs some forty-eight times in the Old Testament, more than thirty of them being in the early book of Job. It is usually translated "God Almighty" and first appears in Genesis 17.1. Newberry comments that "*Shaddai* may be derived either from *shaddid*, meaning "strong", or from *shadday*, meaning "the breasts". A combination of these would indicate that *El Shaddai* was a God strong yet tender enough to succour and satisfy every need of His people. Edersheim comments, "Professor Cassel quotes parallel passages from Genesis to show that *Shaddai* means specially the God who gives fruitfulness and increase". *Shaddai* is a God all-powerful and yet compassionate. Leon Morris, who writes extensively on *Shaddai*, cites H. F. Stevenson who thinks that the term denotes "The Breasted One", and he refers also to Campbell Morgan who renders it by "God All-bountiful", or "God All-sufficient". Just as the needs of the infant for succour and comfort are met on the mother's breast, so are the same needs of His people provided by *El Shaddai*.

Another has written of *El Shaddai*, "It is a most beautiful and tender name of God, denoting a God who is big enough and yet tender enough for every human need. The bosom of the Infinite is a refuge for the human heart in every circumstance of life. As on a mother's breast every need of a babe is met, so *El Shaddai* is the Succourer and Satisfier of His people. In *El Shaddai* there is perfect comfort and perfect supply. *El Shaddai* is used by five individuals.

1. Abram learned it (Gen 17.1) – God's compassionate understanding when he had reached the end of all natural resources.

2. Isaac used it (Gen 28.3) – when one of the family was leaving home, '*El Shaddai* bless thee'.

3. Jacob used it (Gen 48.3; 49.25) – on reviewing the path at the close of life. '*El Shaddai* blessed me', and he invokes His blessing on Joseph.

4. Job used it. There are over thirty occurrences in the book of Job. Job knew God as *El Shaddai* though his friends sought to cast doubt. 'Though he slay me, yet will I trust in him' (Job 13.15).

5. Naomi uses it (Ruth 1.20,21) – as she reviewed her path. '*El Shaddai* dealt very bitterly with me…hath afflicted me'. Was she hasty in her words? Did she think hardly of God? Did she know that she would yet prove the truth of *El Shaddai*? Probably Naomi is the only woman in the Bible who uses this lovely title of God" (Strahan).

Naomi confesses, "I went out". There is a certain humility here on the part of Naomi, in that she accepts personal responsibility for having left Bethlehem when she might have argued, perhaps with some justification, that she had been taken to Moab by Elimelech. But no, she had gone out of her own accord, "I went out". She had gone out full, with husband and sons, with health and wealth, now she was home again empty, widowed and childless, poor and lonely. Note the word "empty", and its interesting recurrence in 3.17 which will be observed later in the commentary. Jehovah had testified against her, Naomi says sadly, but, "Jehovah hath brought me home again". His bitter dealings with her were doubtless His judgment of their emigration to Moab, and yet those same bitter dealings were *El Shaddai's* means of bringing her home to Bethlehem and to Israel. If He had not so sorely afflicted them might they not have settled for ever in Moab? In view of her affliction, she asks, "Why then call ye me Naomi?". Does the Lord still afflict His people who stray from Him? "For this cause many are weak and sickly among you", Paul tells the Corinthians (1 Cor 11.30). Jehovah was judging them for their carelessness and their unworthy behaviour, and under His chastening hand many a poor backslider has remembered the better days and returned. *El Shaddai* is the God of recovery.

So Naomi returned, and Ruth the Moabitess, her daughter-in-law, with her. As has been mentioned in the Introduction, this is the first of five references to "Ruth the Moabitess" (1.22; 2.2; 2.21; 4.5; 4.10), and once she is called "the Moabitish damsel" (2.6). Her lowly origin in Moab would never be forgotten. Was this remembrance of humble beginnings to be true also of her great-grandson David, who freely confessed, when greatness was offered to him by the king, "Who am I? and what is my life, or my father's family in Israel, that I should be son in law to the king?" (1 Sam 18.18). "I am a poor man, and lightly esteemed" (1 Sam 18.23), and later Jehovah reminded him, "Thus saith the Lord of hosts, I took thee from the sheepcote, even from following the sheep, that thou shouldest be ruler over my people Israel" (2 Sam 7.8; 1 Chr 17.7). The same spirit of humility is evident in several of David's Psalms.

From the fields of Moab to the fields of Bethlehem Naomi and Ruth had travelled together. Now they had at last arrived, and it was the beginning of barley harvest. As a Hebrew commentator helpfully explains, "The occasion would be the commencement of the general harvesting season, because the first crop to ripen was the barley. This is about April, at the beginning of Passover, when the reaping of the *omer* (Lev 23.10) took place. The chronological detail with which the chapter ends serves as an introduction to the next chapter, which tells how Ruth availed herself of the Mosaic Law providing that a share of the harvest shall be left for the poor" (Slotki).

Believers in the Lord Jesus will of course, be happy to see a typical significance in this. Barley harvest, Passover and Firstfruits! One day both restored Israel and redeemed Gentiles will inherit eternal blessing on the ground of the death and resurrection of Christ. Calvary and an empty tomb have made it all possible for Jew and Gentile alike, and even now many are already enjoying the fruit of the land. The blessings of salvation, forgiveness of sins, peace with God and an assurance of glory forever, are the present portion of every believer in the Lord Jesus because for them He died and rose again.

RUTH 2

Verses 1-3: The Field of Boaz

"Naomi had a kinsman". The word "kinsman" occurs thirteen times in the book of Ruth in the text of the AV, and the plural "kinsmen" occurs once. This is the first occurrence, but it is not the same Hebrew word as the others. Here it is a word taken from the Hebrew root (YADA – 3045, 4129), which simply means an acquaintance, a friend, perhaps a relative, though not necessarily so. In all the other occurrences the word is GA'AL (1350), often written as *go'el*, meaning a near kinsman with the right to redeem, defined by Strong as "a primitive root, to redeem (according to the Oriental law of kinship), i.e. to be the next of kin (and as such to buy back a relative's property, marry his widow, etc.)". Such a kinsman was therefore often known as "a kinsman-redeemer", and such our Lord Jesus was, voluntarily taking part of flesh and blood that He might be so (Heb 2.14). The rights and privileges of the *go'el* will be dealt with more fully in a later chapter when Boaz will indeed accept those rights and responsibilities, but here he is introduced simply as an acquaintance of Naomi. As Delitzsch comments, "That the acquaintance or friend of Naomi through her husband was also a relation, is evident from the fact that he was 'of the family of Elimelech'. According to the Rabbinical tradition, which is not well established however, Boaz was a nephew of Elimelech". Boaz was in some way, the details of which are not known, of the family of Elimelech, belonging to that circle of relatives, a kinsman.

Before his name is actually revealed it is said that Naomi's kinsman was "a mighty man of wealth". He was a man of excellent standing in Bethlehem whose name must have carried a certain weight and authority among the neighbours. "Wealth" (CHAYIL – 2428) may indeed imply riches, in the usual sense of the word, but it has wider implications than this, and Strong explains that it is "probably a force, whether of men, means or other resources; an army, wealth, virtue, valor, strength". Thus Boaz, while obviously a man of means and substance, owning considerable property, was also a man wealthy in virtue, in reputation, and in character, a force and influence for good in his locality and an employer highly respected by those who laboured for him in his harvest field, as subsequent verses will show. In so many ways he becomes a foreshadowing of Christ, the greater Kinsman-Redeemer.

Ruth, identified again as "the Moabitess", said to Naomi, "Let me now go to the field, and glean ears of corn after him in whose sight I shall find grace". Whether the Moabitess was fully aware of it or not, she was about to avail herself of the provision of an ancient Mosaic law which gave certain rights to the poor and to the stranger. Even under law there were instances of grace and this provision was one of them. However, not all landowners were inclined to abide by this decree which gave the poor person the right to gather up the ears of corn which had been dropped by the reapers.

She hoped, therefore, that someone would be gracious enough to allow her so to glean. As Delitzsch explains, "Ruth wished to go to the field and glean among the ears, i.e. whatever ears were left lying upon the harvest field...behind him in whose eyes she should find favour. The Mosaic law (Lev 19.9; 23.22, compared with Deut 24.19) did indeed expressly secure to the poor the right to glean in the harvest fields, and prohibited the owners from gleaning themselves; but hard-hearted farmers and reapers threw obstacles in the way of the poor, and at times even forbade their gleaning altogether. Hence Ruth proposed to glean after him who should generously allow it".

It may be helpful here to record some details of that gracious provision. It expressly stated, "When thou cuttest down thine harvest in thy field, and hast forgot a sheaf in the field, thou shalt not go again to fetch it: it shall be for the stranger, for the fatherless, and for the widow: that the Lord thy God may bless thee in all the work of thine hands. When thou beatest thine olive tree, thou shalt not go over the boughs again: it shall be for the stranger, for the fatherless, and for the widow. When thou gatherest the grapes of thy vineyard, thou shalt not glean it afterward: it shall be for the stranger, for the fatherless, and for the widow" (Deut 24.19-21). Note the threefold reference to the stranger and the widow. Ruth was a stranger and she and Naomi were widows. The provision embraced both of them.

The noble character of Ruth is brought out here in that she consulted with her mother-in-law before going to glean. They were poor, having returned from Moab empty. They needed provision somehow. Naomi was probably too old for the back-breaking task of gleaning, but the younger Ruth would do it willingly. "Let me now go", she says. However, this would really be a rather public, and perhaps humiliating, acknowledgement of the poverty and penury of the two widows. Would it have the approval of her mother-in-law? What would the women of the town think of the widow of the wealthy Elimelech or her daughter-in-law gleaning with the poor in the fields of Bethlehem? Naomi answers simply, "Go, my daughter". Doubtless a request for help from her rich relative Boaz would have been received favourably, but this too would have involved some humiliation and Naomi would not ask for charity.

Ruth accordingly made her way to the harvest field to glean after the reapers, and, in the language of the AV, "her hap was to light upon a part of the field belonging unto Boaz". Although the words "hap" (MIQREH - 4745) and "light" (QARA - 7136) are different Hebrew words, they are in fact from the same root and carry a very similar meaning. Literally, the phrase may be rendered "her chance chanced upon". From the human standpoint it seemed quite accidental that she should be gleaning in that part of the field which belonged to their kinsman Boaz. However, it reveals how Jehovah in sovereignty intervenes in the most trivial events in the affairs of His people so as to order their lives for their good and His own glory.

Who could have imagined the far-reaching effects of Ruth "happening" on the field of Boaz?

In those days, in those parts, harvest fields were not usually divided by fences, but by stone landmarks or simply by the hard-trodden path between them, called "the way side" in the parable of Matthew 13.4. It was a great common grain field at which Ruth arrived, but providentially she came to glean in that part of the field which belonged to Boaz. Then there is yet another reminder that he was of the kindred of Elimelech.

Verses 4-14: Ruth meets Boaz

"And, behold, Boaz came from Bethlehem". He had come from the town to the field to greet the reapers, and the exchange of greetings reveals a delightful harmony between the master and his labourers. "The Lord be with you", he says, desiring that Jehovah would be their Protector and Helper as they laboured. "The Lord bless thee", they reply, in a spirit of respect and goodwill. As another has said, "Courtesy met courtesy. It was a charming scene and it may be reasonably assumed that there was reality in the salutation" (Slotki). Such courtesy of course should always prevail between masters and servants who are believers in the Lord Jesus, as is so often exhorted by the apostles (Eph 6.5-9; Col 3.22; 4.1; Titus 2.9; 1 Pet 2.18).

Now, and it would seem for the first time, Boaz sees Ruth. Was his interest aroused by her appearance, her features, her dress, her modesty, her diligence in the field? Boaz must have been familiar with the gleaners, but this maiden he does not know and so he enquires of the servant who was overseeing the reapers and the reaping, asking, "Whose damsel is this?". The overseer's reply is somewhat vague. Some translations use the indefinite article and read, "It is a Moabitish damsel that came back with Naomi", as if to say, Slotki adds, "A Moabite girl of whom nothing more is known than that she came back from Moab with Naomi". It is evident of course, from the ensuing conversation, that Boaz had heard much about the girl from Moab, but until now had not met her, nor she him. Heslop comments, "What wonderful condescension! The mighty Boaz becomes interested in a poor, penniless, despised, weak, helpless stranger! Marvellous grace! Matchless goodness! Boaz is interested in Ruth!". Those who love the Saviour of course can see here a beautiful picture of His grace toward them. The overseer speaks highly of Ruth's behaviour. She had not boldly intruded into the harvest field, but had requested of him that she might be allowed to glean. Nor had she been idle, but had laboured almost ceaselessly since her arrival in the morning, except for the little while that she had rested in the house. There were, in the harvest fields, sheds, huts, or tents, which provided welcome shelter for the labourers and shade from the heat of the sun, especially during meal times. However, the Septuagint translates concerning Ruth: "She…rested not even a little in the field". She had certainly worked diligently. This unnamed servant of

Boaz, like the unnamed servant of Abraham in Genesis 24, seems to represent the present ministry of the Holy Spirit in the calling out of a Bride for the Redeemer, as well as in the directing of the servants in their particular sphere of ministry in the great harvest field.

For the first time, Boaz now speaks to Ruth. It was a kindly word, almost fatherly, a word of welcome to the modest maiden who had come to nestle like a dove under the sheltering wings of the God of Israel. "Hearest thou not, my daughter?", probably has the sense of, "Now listen, my daughter". He gives her, not only permission, but also encouragement, to continue to glean in his field and not to think of going to another. She should stay by his maidens and glean among them as one of them. Adam Clarke comments, "Abide here fast by my maidens: These were probably employed in making bands, and laying on them enough to form a sheaf, which the binders would tie and form into shocks or thraves. When the maidens had gathered up the scattered handfuls thrown down by the reapers, Ruth picked up any straggling heads or ears which they had left". By the command of Boaz the young men in the field would not molest or embarrass her in any way. Moreover, if and when she was thirsty she should feel free to go to the vessels and drink of the water which the young men had drawn.

Ruth was deeply moved by this cordiality of one whom she had never met before, and she a stranger from Moab. She fell on her face in the harvest field, prostrating herself in the sincerest gratitude before Boaz, and in reverence as before a superior. Her words of thankfulness to him are as immortal as her words of determination to go with Naomi on the day they left Moab (1.16-17). She asks, "Why have I found grace in thine eyes, that thou shouldest take knowledge of me, seeing I am a stranger?". Why should one of such standing in Bethlehem as Boaz take any notice of a girl from Moab, a foreigner, an alien? So many believers in the Lord Jesus have used the same words, bowing in gratitude and worship that the Son of God should deign to love and welcome such poor sinners, and asking, "Why?". Those who, like Ruth, were Gentiles, remember that they had once been "without Christ, being aliens from the commonwealth of Israel, and strangers from the covenants of promise, having no hope, and without God in the world" (Eph 2.12). Wondrous grace indeed, that has reached such.

"And Boaz answered and said unto her…". The word "answered" (6030) is an interesting word, implying that Boaz actually raised his voice and spoke loudly. Others around would hear. Perhaps he intended them to hear. If they knew so little about the girl from Moab, he would enlighten them. Boaz knew much about Ruth. "It hath fully been shewed me", he says, "all that thou hast done unto thy mother in law since the death of thine husband: and how thou hast left thy father and thy mother, and the land of thy nativity, and art come unto a people which thou knewest not heretofore". "Fully" and "shewed" are the same word (5046). He had been given a clear and full report of Ruth. He was aware just what she meant to Naomi and he knew all that she had done for her mother-in-law since the death of Mahlon. She had known the grief of an early widowhood herself but instead of indulging in self-pity she had devoted herself to the care of Naomi. Boaz apparently knew that her father and mother were still alive when she left Moab to accompany her mother-in-law. For Naomi's sake she had left her parents, and had left, too, the land of her birth, to come to a country and a people whom she did not know. How like Abram Ruth had been: "Now the Lord had said unto Abram, Get thee out of thy country, and from thy kindred, and from thy father's house, unto a land that I will shew thee" (Gen 12.1), and "He went out, not knowing whither he went" (Heb 11.8).

The kindly Boaz now pronounces a delightful benediction upon Ruth and says, "The Lord recompense thy work, and a full reward be given thee of the Lord (3068) God (430) of Israel, under whose wings thou art come to trust". The maiden from Moab had come to shelter beneath the wings of Jehovah Elohim just as a defenceless chick might nestle under the protective wings of the mother bird. How often does this same metaphor appear in the Psalms of Ruth's great-grandson David (Ps 17.8; 36.7; 57.1; 61.4; 63.7), and did not the greater Son of David use the same language in His lament over Jerusalem? "How often would I have gathered thy children together, even as a hen gathereth her chickens under her wings, and ye would not! (Mt 23.37; Lk 13.34).

With characteristic and becoming modesty Ruth acknowledges the comfort of the kindness of Boaz. He had spoken to her heart, for such is the meaning of the word "friendly" (3820). "Thou hast spoken friendly unto thine handmaid". As Dr Edersheim comments, "And now for the first time, and when it is past, the secret of her long-hidden sorrow bursts from Ruth, as she tells it to Boaz: 'Thou hast consoled me, and spoken to the heart of thine handmaid'". She humbly entreats that his favour may be continued to her but acknowledges her unworthiness. She calls herself "his handmaid", but in simplicity and humility confesses that she is not to be compared to his other handmaids. She would not look like them, nor speak like them. How like the Shulamite, the spouse, in the Song of Solomon she was. Just like that maiden from Shunem in Solomon's court, Ruth was, after all, an alien in Israel, a stranger indeed, but this only magnified his kindness to her. There is something so morally attractive in humility. Well does Peter speak of "the ornament of a meek and quiet spirit" (1 Pet 3.4).

Boaz continues to encourage Ruth and now invites her to sit with the reapers at mealtime. He would eat with the reapers too, and Ruth must have been seated near to him, as is evidenced by the fact that he was able to reach her parched corn. It is apparently still a custom in Eastern harvest fields that at mealtime grains of corn which as yet are not thoroughly dried or hardened, are roasted in a pan or on a flat plate, and eaten with bread.

Ruth was to feel free to take of the bread and dip her morsel in the vinegar. "Vinegar" is, in Hebrew, CHOMETS (2558), a type of sauce, or "a sour beverage composed of vinegar (wine vinegar or sour wine) mixed with oil; a very refreshing drink, which is still a favourite beverage in the East" (Delitzsch). So did Ruth eat and was not only satisfied herself, but had more than she needed, so that she was able to carry home to Naomi what was left of her own meal (v.18). Yet again the selflessness of the girl appears, in that while she herself was eating, her thoughts were with her mother-in-law at home. Naomi must share also in the bounty of Boaz. There is a delightful picture of Christian fellowship and privilege here. Those who are near to Christ, in the conscious enjoyment of His presence, enjoy good things from His hand and are able to pass something on to others who are less favoured.

Verses 15-23: Gleaning in the Field of Boaz

Ruth appears not to linger over the meal but as soon as is possible and prudent she rises to return to the gleaning. So should it be with the Lord's labourers today. Having spent time with Him and in His Word it is then their responsibility and privilege to go out again into the harvest field to the work. Ruth gleans until the evening. "The night cometh, when no man can work" (Jn 9.4). Her constancy and diligence are exemplary, a lesson to all who labour, to be faithful in their labours, whether indeed it be secular or spiritual. The kindness of Boaz toward her continues as he directs the young men again that they must allow her to glean even among the sheaves. This in itself was a privilege, since gleaners were expected to follow the reapers, gleaning after the harvesters had bound up their sheaves. But the young men of the field were not to insult her, or taunt her, or embarrass her in any way. Neither was the generosity of Boaz to stop here for he now commands the young men to purposely let handfuls of the stalks with their grain fall for Ruth. The JFB Commentary observes, "The gleaners in the East glean with much success; for a great quantity of corn is scattered in the reaping, as well as in their manner of carrying it. One may judge, then, of the large quantity which Ruth would gather in consequence of the liberal orders given to the servants. These extraordinary marks of favour were not only given from a kindly disposition, but from regard to her good character and devoted attachment to her venerable relative".

Ruth gleaned until dusk, after which she beat out the ears, threshing them perhaps with a stick, and was able to carry home to Naomi an ephah (374) of barley. The ephah was believed to be a measure of Egyptian origin, but was in common usage among Hebrews. It was the equivalent of the Hebrew liquid measure "bath" (1324), which was equal to about six or seven gallons (27-32 litres), calculated by Delitzsch to be about twenty or twenty-five pounds weight (9-11 kilos) of grain. This would have been sufficient to support the two women for some five or six days. Ruth therefore must have been well pleased with the results of her diligent gleaning. This she brought home to the city and to her mother-in-law along with that which she had reserved from her own meal after she had eaten at mealtime.

Naomi viewed the quantity of grain which Ruth had carried home and her greeting was three-fold. "Where hast thou gleaned to day? and where wroughtest thou? blessed be he that did take knowledge of thee." There is an element both of surprise and of gratitude in the language of the older woman, and Dr Slotki remarks that "She guessed, from the abundance of the corn brought home and from the joy on Ruth's face, that the gleaning had been done in the field of a particularly friendly owner". Naomi's gratitude is deepened greatly when she learns just where Ruth has gleaned. "The man's name with whom I wrought today is Boaz", Ruth declares, not yet in the full realisation of the implications of this. But Naomi will explain. "Blessed be he of Jehovah", she exclaims. Jehovah had not relinquished His kindness, neither toward the living nor the dead. Naomi and Ruth were the living, and they were the surviving relatives, the widows and representatives of the deceased Elimelech and Mahlon. In order to enlighten Ruth further Naomi explains, "The man is a near kinsman". Literally, she says, "The man is our relative, and one of our redeemers". JFB comments: " 'One of our redeemers,' on whom it devolves to protect us, to purchase our lands, and marry you, the widow of his next kinsman. She said, 'one of them,' not that there were many in the same close relationship, but that he was a very near kinsman, one other individual only having the precedence". Naomi was filled with thankfulness to Jehovah for His gracious ordering of their lives.

But Ruth has yet more to tell, and again she is called "Ruth the Moabitess", as if again to magnify the kindness of Boaz toward such an one as she was. She recalls, "He said unto me also, Thou shalt keep fast by my young men, until they have ended all my harvest". The expression "young men" occurs five times in the book of Ruth and some explanation is necessary. In 2.9 (twice), 2.15, and 2.21, it is the Hebrew word NA'AR (5288), which, although perhaps usually meaning "males", does not always or necessarily have this meaning. As Strong points out, it may mean boy, servant, or girl. In the fifth occurrence of the expression at 3.10 however, "young men" is different, it is the word BACHUR (970), which means, strictly, "young men". Boaz there commends Ruth that she had not selfishly pursued or followed after the young men of the town or the field, whether rich or otherwise. So, when he here encourages Ruth to "keep fast by my young men", this is, as Delitzsch explains, "quite in place as the more comprehensive gender, as a designation of the reapers generally, both male and female". Ruth should stay with the servants of Boaz until all the harvesting was finished, both the barley harvest and the wheat harvest which would follow.

It was good advice Naomi told her. She could not be so sure of the same kindness nor of the same safety if she went to glean in another field. Indeed the word "meet", as in "that they meet thee not in any other field", is the Hebrew word PAGA (6293), which may imply "to encounter, to attack, to fall upon". Ruth could well be faced with danger in another field. A Moabitess among strangers could be subjected to insult and abuse. It was good that she should do as Boaz had said and work only in his field among faithful labourers. How sound is this advice for those who labour in the great harvest field today. Many labourers there are who genuinely acknowledge the Lordship of Christ and the authority of His Word and who labour faithfully and diligently for Him. Sadly, there are those who follow their own opinions and ideas and who disregard some of the clear directions of Scripture. It is well for the young believer to stay fast by those who are true to the guidance of the Lord and His Word. Some others may exercise an influence which is not good and which may result in deflecting the young Christian from a pathway of profitable service for the Lord and His people. Ruth followed the advice of Boaz, which advice was commended by her mother-in-law. She worked closely with the maidens of Boaz until the conclusion of the wheat harvest. This would have been perhaps until the end of May or the beginning of June, a period altogether of some three months, which, as a Jewish commentator interestingly observes, corresponded to the time that had to elapse before a female proselyte was permitted to marry (Slotki).

Of these months, as they passed, Edersheim beautifully comments that they "had given abundant evidence of the utter absence of all self-consciousness on the part of Ruth, of her delicacy and modesty in circumstances of no small difficulty. If these rare qualities must have been observed by Naomi, they could hardly not have remained unnoticed by Boaz, as he daily watched her bearing. Nor yet could Ruth have been insensible to the worth, the piety, and the kindness of him who had been the first in Israel to speak kindness to her heart".

So did the girl from Moab continue gleaning industriously through the months of harvest, all the while dwelling quietly with her mother-in-law, and so was Jehovah providentially preparing the way for what was to follow. Does it not exemplify that oft-quoted word of Proverbs 3.6: "In all thy ways acknowledge him, and he shall direct thy paths"? Ruth was experiencing the truth of a verse which as yet she could not have known since it had not then been written.

RUTH 3

Verses 1-5: The Kinsman-Redeemer

It is touching to notice the affectionate relationship between these two women. One was a mother in Israel and the other a maiden from Moab. Nationally and racially they were very different, but grace had bonded them together in love. How very like assemblies of believers today! From a variety of backgrounds, with different personalities, different temperaments, and different measures of understanding and ability, they are united in love and in purpose. Ruth had given up much to accompany Naomi to Bethlehem, and for these several harvest months she had toiled daily in the fields for their support. She had truly cared for her mother-in-law and had been like a daughter to her. Naomi in turn now feels responsible for Ruth's future welfare and makes known her mind. When she says, "Shall I not seek rest for thee?", by "rest" (4494) she means a settled home, a resting place, where Ruth might enjoy the comforts of home and family life again with a husband and perhaps children too. Naomi had used a very similar word on that earlier day when seeking to encourage her daughters-in-law to return to Moab rather than accompany her to Bethlehem (1.9). Ruth had turned her back on such a prospect in Moab to go with Naomi. Now, in response to the love and faithfulness and dutifulness of her daughter-in-law Naomi is anxious that there should be happy future years for the girl.

The older woman had obviously been musing over the situation and she knew that on certain nights Boaz would be winnowing barley on his threshing floor. Harvesting was completed now, and the stalks of grain would have been gathered to the threshing floor. It would then be beaten out, threshed with a stick until chaff and grain were separated. The chaff however, would have to be removed, and this was known as winnowing (c.f. Ps 1.4). After sunset the cool winds would blow. The chaff and grain would be thrown from a shovel high into the breeze and this would blow away the light chaff while the heavier grain would fall to the floor. As others have explained, "The farmer usually remained all night in harvest-time on the threshing-floor, not only for the protection of his valuable grain, but for the winnowing. That operation was performed in the evening to catch the breezes which blow after the close of a hot day, and which continue for the most part of the night. This duty at so important a season the master undertakes himself; and, accordingly, in the simplicity of ancient manners, Boaz, a person of considerable wealth and high rank, laid himself down to sleep on the barn floor, at the end of the heap of barley he had been winnowing" (JFB).

The threshing floors of Scripture are an interesting study, always associated with the separation of chaff from wheat, when that which is good remains while the worthless thing is blown away. It may be profitable here to mention some of these threshing floors.

In Judges 6 there is the threshing floor of Gideon. Mighty man of valour though he was, threshing wheat in secret and in defiance hiding it from the Midianites, Gideon was filled with doubts and fears. He could not understand why such conditions as then existed should befall Israel. Had Jehovah now forsaken the people whom He had brought out of Egypt? Where were the miracles of former days? Nor could he understand how he, the least in the house of a poor family, could possibly save Israel from the hand of the oppressing Midianites, as the angel said. Jehovah separated the chaff of Gideon's doubts and fears, leaving a fearless man who boldly threw down the altars of Baal and eventually, with a few chosen men, did indeed deliver Israel from the oppressor.

Then there is the threshing floor of Ornan the Jebusite in 1 Chronicles 21.15-28. Here Jehovah winnowed out the chaff of David's pride and sin. On his own confession, David had acted foolishly by numbering the people. It was pride. When he says, however, "I it is that have sinned and done evil indeed" (v.17), then the Lord will acknowledge his repentance, give him the threshing floor of the Jebusite, and allow him to build an altar there and offer burnt offerings and peace offerings. Pride, and the resulting sin, are removed, and worship follows, and this in anticipation of a temple for Jehovah, a house of God on this very threshing floor of Ornan (2 Chr 3.1).

In Matthew 3.12 John Baptist speaks of the threshing floor of the coming Messiah. In that day of His glory Christ "will throughly purge his floor". He will separate the wheat from the chaff, the good from the bad, the true from the false. The chaff is destined for unquenchable fire while the wheat will be gathered into the safety of His garner, for His pleasure.

There is yet another sad reference to the threshing floor in Luke 22.31. There Satan desires to have the little company of the disciples that he may sift them. Sifting was a different process for separating the wheat and chaff. In sifting, a sieve was used when the chaff and the grain were shaken together, the wheat falling through the mesh while the chaff remained. Satan desired to have this little band of the followers of Jesus to sift them. Weak and failing though they were, they were truly faithful to their Lord except for Judas, the son of perdition, who in the records never calls Jesus "Lord". Like chaff in the company he was separated from them and perished in his worthlessness.

This threshing floor of Boaz in Ruth 3.2 is a happier setting. It was to become the place where great issues were to be decided for Ruth and for Boaz. The girl from Moab comes to Boaz as a true daughter of Israel. All traces of her Moabitish idolatrous past have gone. She must come to the threshing floor sweetly prepared for the presence of the man from Bethlehem, probably not fully aware of the far-reaching effects of this meeting with the kinsman-redeemer.

Naomi knows all this and now reveals her plan to her daughter-in-law. Ruth should bathe, anoint herself, and put fresh raiment on her. Some translations and commentators actually render this as "thy best dress"

(NKJV; RSV; Clarke; Delitzsch), while Dr Slotki and Edersheim describe it as "festive". Whether this is the precise meaning of the Hebrew word SIMLA (8071) or not, it is obvious that Naomi desires that Ruth should make herself especially presentable for what she has in mind. So should every believer approach the presence of the Redeemer, the Beloved, with a due and suitable reverence, in the beauty of holiness and in modesty. Ruth is instructed to go down to the threshing floor but not make herself known to Boaz immediately. He would eat and drink, and then, tired and weary, but happy, he would lie down on the grain to sleep. Ruth should then quietly lift the coverlet at his feet and lie down. After that Boaz would tell her what to do. These directions must not be judged by modern or western standards, but rather be understood by the customs and manners of the people of those times and those parts. As the learned Dr Edersheim writes, they "must not be judged by our western notions, although we are prepared to defend its purity and delicacy in every particular. Nor could Naomi have well done otherwise than counsel as she did. For the law which fixed on the next of kin the duty of redeeming a piece of land (Lev 25.25) did *not* connect with it the obligation of marrying the childless widow of the owner, which (strictly speaking) only devolved upon a brother-in-law (Deut 25.5); although such seems to have been the law of custom in Bethlehem, and this, as we believe, in strict accordance with the *spirit* and object, if not with the letter of the Divine commandment. Thus Naomi had no *legal* claim upon Boaz – not to speak of the fact, of which she must have been aware, that there was a nearer kinsman than he of Elimelech in Bethlehem". Ruth's response to Naomi is simple: "And she said unto her, All that thou sayest unto me I will do". There is always, with Ruth, a commendable willingness to be guided by the older woman. How delightful it is when young and old can work harmoniously with one another, when the experience of the older and the energy of the younger can blend together for the blessing and profit of others.

Verses 6-13: At the Threshing Floor

In accordance then with the advice of Naomi, and faithfully following the instructions given to her, Ruth puts off the daily garb of the working widow and now, arrayed festively, almost like a bride, makes her way to the threshing floor where Boaz is winnowing his barley. Initially, however, she remains at a distance, unobserved, watching and waiting until Boaz has eaten and drunk and lain down. Since the threshing floors of the East were generally in the open air it was easy to watch from a short distance, and of course it was dusk and Ruth could remain unseen by Boaz. His heart was merry. This word, in the context, could be misleading. It is important to note that this was not at all a drunken merriment. "Merry" (YATAB - 3190), simply means that he was cheerfully satisfied. He was pleased with his work and with his meal and could now rest contented, with his heart at ease. In the darkness Ruth came softly, covertly, to where

Boaz was lying. She quietly lifted the coverlet at his feet without disturbing him, and there laid herself down.

How much time then elapsed cannot be determined, but at midnight Boaz stirred from his sleep. He awoke in fear, sensing the presence of something or someone at his feet. It was a woman! "Who art thou?", he asked abruptly, obviously not knowing anything of the plan which Naomi had devised. With characteristic and charming simplicity Ruth answers, "I am Ruth thine handmaid". But she adds, "Spread therefore thy skirt over thine handmaid; for thou art a near kinsman". By "skirt" she doubtless just meant the flap or corner of his coverlet or counterpane, but it is interesting to note that the word "skirt" (KANAP - 3671) is on many occasions translated "wing", and it is in fact, the word of 2.12, where Boaz speaks of "The Lord God of Israel, under whose wings thou art come to trust". Ruth therefore is asking for more than a material covering. When she says, "…for thou art a near kinsman", she is really asking for the protection of a redeemer, which, in the circumstances would imply marriage. Adam Clarke enlarges, saying, "Spread therefore thy skirt over thine hand maid, Hebrew, Spread thy wing. The wing is the emblem of protection, and is a metaphor taken from the young of fowls, which run under the wings of their mothers, that they may be saved from birds of prey. The meaning here is, Take me to thee for wife; and so the *Targum* has translated it, Let thy name be called on thy handmaid to take me for wife, because thou art the redeemer; i.e., thou art the *go'el*, the kinsman, to whom the right of redemption belongs. Even to the present day, when a Jew marries a woman, he throws the skirt or end of his *talith* over her, to signify that he has taken her under his protection". Notice that the same metaphor is used for taking in marriage in Ezekiel 16.8.

With his characteristic fatherliness, Boaz pronounces a blessing upon Ruth. "Blessed be thou of the Lord, my daughter." He praises her kindness (2617) and although this is a normal rendering of the word CHESED it does also bear the thought of love, piety, goodness, righteousness (Jer 2.2; Hos 6.4; Is 57.1). Ruth has been consistent in her piety and love. As she had loved the deceased Mahlon and had continued to love and care for Naomi, now she was showing the same goodness in her desire for a kinsman-redeemer. As Boaz says, she had not gone after young men, though there must have been such opportunity in the harvest fields. But whether rich or poor she had ignored them in favour of Boaz who must have been advanced in years. As Adam Clarke writes, "Perhaps *checed*, which we translate kindness, means piety; as if he had said: Thou hast given great proof of thy piety in this latter instance, when thou hast avoided the young, and those of thy own age, to associate thyself with an elderly man, merely for the purpose of having the Divine injunction fulfilled, viz., that the brother, or next akin, might take the wife of the deceased, and raise a family to him who had died childless, that his name might not become extinct in Israel: this latter act is a greater proof of thy piety and sincerity than any thing that could be inferred from thy becoming a proselyte". With this Delitzsch concurs, saying, "The later love she had was shown in the fact, that as a young widow she had not sought to win the affections of young men, as young women generally do, that she might have a youthful husband, but had turned trustfully to the older man, that she might find a successor to her deceased husband, through a marriage with him, in accordance with family custom".

Boaz again addresses her tenderly as "my daughter" and encourages her not to be afraid for he is willing to do all that she requires. Boaz knew that all his townsmen were aware that Ruth was a virtuous woman. It is a fine tribute to the girl from Moab that in such a short time of residence in Bethlehem she should have this testimony, that she was a virtuous woman. He says, "All the city of my people doth know". Some, however, as JND and the JPS and others, render this, "all the gate of my people", or "all the men in the gate of my people do know". "City" (SHA'AR - 8179) may mean "door", or "gate", and the thought appears to be that all who were familiar with those who came and went by the gate of the city would know Ruth. Perhaps it was her piety, as much as any physical beauty that attracted Boaz to Ruth. As a king (some think Solomon their illustrious descendant) was afterward to write, "Who can find a virtuous woman? for her price is far above rubies" (Prov 31.10).

Now Boaz must explain. It was true that he was a near kinsman, as Ruth had said; however, there was another kinsman nearer than he who had prior rights. Although some, as Edersheim quoted above, think otherwise, many have questioned if Naomi knew of this nearer kinsman. As Matthew Henry writes, "We may reasonably suppose Naomi (who had been long abroad, and could not be exact in the pedigree of her husband's family) was ignorant of it, otherwise she would never have sent her daughter to make her claim of Boaz. Yet he does not bid her go herself to this other kinsman; this would have been to put too great a hardship upon her". Jewish tradition suggests that this other kinsman was a surviving older brother of Elimelech, while Boaz was but a nephew, but this is tradition only. The same tradition also makes Boaz at this time an octogenarian and if this latter suggestion is true then there may indeed have been an aged brother of Elimelech still alive, of whom Naomi was not aware, and whose name never appears.

Ruth should wait until the morning, Boaz directs, when he would consult the other kinsman and apprise him of the situation. If he would perform the kinsman's duty, well, so be it, but if not then Boaz certainly would. Meanwhile they would tarry at the threshing floor and they lay down in silence. It says much for the virtue of both, that, alone together on the threshing floor in the night hours, they remained pure. Several commentators, as John Wesley and Matthew Henry, quote Bishop Hall who writes, "Boaz, instead of touching her as a wanton, blesseth her as a father, encourageth her as a friend, promiseth her as a kinsman, rewards her as a patron, and sends her away laden with hopes and gifts, no less chaste, more happy, than she came. O admirable temperance, worthy the progenitor of him in whose lips and heart there was no guile!".

Verses 14-18: "Until the Morning"

Boaz gives Ruth the solemn pledge of his intentions and uses that familiar phrase which occurs some twenty-seven times in the Old Testament, "As the Lord liveth". Dr Slotki observes, "Where the thought of a living God governs the relationship, a man and a woman may meet in the hour of midnight in a lonely threshing floor and part from each other as pure as when they came". At his instruction she lay at his feet until the morning. It is easy to believe that there was little sleep. There would be much to think about, much to anticipate, and perhaps indeed much silent prayer. The thoughts of both would be on the happenings of the morrow. Ruth left before sunrise, before it was light. Though they were themselves conscious of their moral purity, there are evil minds abroad in every town which would speak falsehood and create slander, and the reputation of both must be protected. In such a small town as Bethlehem gossip would spread rapidly. "Let it not be known", said Boaz, "that a woman came into the floor".

"Bring the veil", Boaz now asks her before she leaves. The veil, the MITPACHAT (4304), was a wide cloak or shawl which Ruth now held out like an apron, and into it Boaz measured six measures of barley. It is not clear just what this measure was, the Hebrew text simply reading "six of barley". The Jewish *Targum*, an ancient Chaldee or Aramaic translation of Old Testament Scriptures, renders it "six *seahs* of barley". As Morris comments, "In 2.17 the *ephah* is used, but six *ephahs* seems an impossibly large amount so it is probable that we should take the measure here to be the *seah*, which amounted to a third of the ephah. This was believed to be about two *ephahs,* twice the amount that Ruth had gleaned on that early day in the harvest field (2.17). If this were so it would have been a heavy weight for Ruth to carry and it is likely that when it is said that Boaz 'laid it on her' that he actually placed it on her head, by which means Oriental women still carry heavy loads". Edersheim has an interesting comment, writing, "We mention, without pronouncing any opinion upon it, that some, alike Jews and Christians, have seen a symbolism in the number *six* of the measures of barley which Ruth brought with her, as if days of work and toil were done, and 'rest' about to be granted".

Before dawn, then, they left the threshing floor, but when the common version says, "*she* went into the city" (v.15), several other versions, including JND, JPS, NIV, ASV, read, "*he* went into the city", meaning Boaz. This is the understanding of Delitzsch, Barnes, Slotki, and others, and seems to imply that Boaz was treating the matter in hand as being most urgent. Whether he accompanied Ruth on the way to the town, as some think, is not clear. The accepted Jewish Commentary on the portion, known as the *Midrash,* thinks that he did, for her protection lest she should be molested in that early morning hour.

Ruth arrived home to Naomi, to be greeted by the question, "Who art thou, my daughter?". It may well be, as some suggest, that in the dim twilight of the dawn Naomi did not at first recognise the young woman seeking admittance to the house. Perhaps however, the meaning may well be, "Who are you? Are you still just Ruth the Moabitess, the widow of Mahlon? Or are you now the betrothed wife of Boaz?". Naomi would naturally be anxious to know all that had transpired at the threshing floor. It is likely that she had not had much sleep that night either! Ruth now had such a story to tell the older woman. She rehearsed to her mother-in-law all the happenings of the midnight hour at the threshing floor. She would tell of the reaction of Boaz to her request, and she would relate in detail the conversation between them. "And she said, These six measures of barley gave he me; for he said to me, Go not empty unto thy mother in law" (v.17). "Empty" was Naomi's word to the women of the town on her return to Bethlehem (1.21). Jehovah had brought her home again from Moab empty (7387). Boaz had used exactly the same word, "Go not empty (7387) unto thy mother in law". By the kindness of the kinsman their emptiness was to be a thing of the past. So it is with those who find the Saviour. Hearts that once were empty, and lives that were void of purpose and joy are filled with love and with the fullness of Christ for those who know Him.

Naomi was filled with hope, but knew of course, as Ruth must have explained, that they had yet to wait for the answer of that nearer kinsman whom Boaz had promised to consult in the morning. Delitzsch writes, "Boaz would now certainly carry out the matter to the desired end. 'Sit still, i.e., remain quietly at home, till thou hearest how the affair will turn out'". There was nothing more that could be done just now. They must wait in patience and Naomi's word to Ruth was simple, "Sit still, my daughter". How many sincere and exercised souls have learned the difficulty of being still! "Stand still", was the exhortation of Moses to the children of Israel when, having left Egypt, their way forward was barred by the Red Sea while the chariots of Pharaoh pursued them from behind (Ex 14.13). There was nothing they could do. They must stand still and wait on Jehovah. The exhortation of the Psalmist is the same. "The God of Jacob is our refuge...Be still and know that I am God (Ps 46.7,10). The words may be different in each case, but the meaning is consistent. Stand still, sit still, be still, leaving all with Him who in love orders the lives of His willing people.

The expression, "until thou know how the matter will fall", is apparently based on the ancient custom of casting lots. This custom is referred to some seventy times in the Old Testament and was a way of making decisions when there was little or no specific Scriptural direction about a matter. "Most of the occurrences were in the early period when little of the Bible was available and when God apparently approved of this means for determining His will…In spite of the many references to casting lots in the Old Testament, nothing is known about the actual lots themselves. They could have been sticks of various lengths, flat stones like coins, or some kind of dice; but their exact nature is unknown" (Nelson's Bible Dictionary). Whatever they were, the lots were thrown, or cast, and their fall determined the decision. Who then would be a willing kinsman redeemer for Ruth? Would it be Boaz? Would it be the anonymous nearer kinsman? The two widows must wait and see how the matter would fall.

Notice the interesting contrast now between Ruth and Boaz. Ruth must sit still; she must rest, until she knows the outcome of the morning's business between Boaz and his kinsman. Boaz, on the other hand, would not rest until the matter was accomplished. Ruth must rest while Boaz works! So it is with the believer in the Lord Jesus. In all the vicissitudes of life the saints must rest while the risen Christ their kinsman represents their cause in glory.

Yet it must be, Thy love had not its rest
Were Thy redeemed not with Thee, fully blest;
That love that gives not as the world, but shares
All it possesses with its loved co-heirs.
J N Darby

Some have observed a profitable study in the nine occurrences of the word "until" in the book of Ruth - 1.19; 2.7,17,21; 3.3,13,14,18 (twice). They read almost like a pilgrim's progress from the poverty and sorrow of Moab to marriage with the wealthy kinsman-redeemer from Bethlehem.

The lovely story now hastens to a swift and happy conclusion, told so simply and so delightfully in the twenty-two verses of the closing chapter.

RUTH 4

Levirate Marriage

It may be appropriate at this point to explain that which has become known as "Levirate Marriage". "Levirate" comes from the Latin *levir*, meaning "a husband's brother". It was an ancient custom implying the marriage of a man with the widow of his deceased brother in the event of that brother dying childless, for the purpose that he should raise up seed to his brother so that the name of his near kinsman should not perish out of Israel. This practice prevailed even in patriarchal times and is first mentioned in Genesis 38.8 where Judah calls upon Onan to marry his brother Er's widow. The custom was later incorporated into Mosaic law. Unger states, however, that "The Levirate marriage was not peculiar to the Jews; it has been found to exist in many Eastern countries, particularly in Arabia and among the tribes of the Caucasus".

In the case of Boaz and Ruth, Dr Edersheim, with his Jewish background, must be quoted here at length. He writes, "To understand what passed between Boaz and the unnamed kinsman, we must offer certain explanations of the state of the case and of the law applying to it, different from any hitherto proposed...In general we may here say that the law (Num 27.8,11) does *not* deal with any case precisely similar to that under consideration. It only contemplates one of two things, the death of a childless man, when his next-of-kin (speaking broadly) is *bound* to marry his widow (Deut 25.5); or else a forced sale of property through poverty, when the next-of-kin of the original proprietor may redeem the land (Lev 25.25). It is evident, that the former must be regarded as a *duty*, the latter as a *privilege* attaching to kinship, the object of both being precisely the same, the preservation of the family...Thus it might, for example, be, that a man might marry the widow, but be unable to redeem the property. On the other hand, he never could claim to redeem property without marrying the widow, to whom as the representative of her dead husband the property attached. In any case the property of the deceased husband was vested in a childless widow...In the case before us then, the property still belonged to Naomi, though in reversion to Ruth as potentially representing Elimelech and Mahlon, while the claim to be married to the next-of-kin could, of course, in the circumstances, only devolve upon Ruth. Thus the property still held by Naomi went, in equity and in law, with the hand of Ruth, nor had anyone claim upon the one without also taking the other. No kinsman had performed the kinsman's *duty* to Ruth, and therefore no kinsman could claim the *privilege* of redemption connected with the land...It would have been the grossest injustice to have allowed the privilege of redeeming a property to the kinsman who refused to act as kinsman. Instead of preserving a name in Israel, it would in reality have extinguished it forever". It has seemed profitable to quote Edersheim extensively. His background and knowledge of things Jewish are of immense value in the understanding of a custom with which Western culture is not familiar. But now, to follow Boaz!

Verses 1-2: At the Gate

Boaz lost no time. For him the matter in hand was urgent and he made his way in the morning hour to the gate of the town. Going "up to the gate" does not necessarily imply that the gate was on higher ground than the town, but rather that, as Delitzsch says, "It is to be explained as referring to the place of justice as an ideal eminence to which a man went up". In the same sense, persons travelling to Jerusalem are always regarded as going "up to Jerusalem" from whatever part of the land they come, as in Psalm 122.3-4. The expression "up to Jerusalem" actually occurs twenty-five times throughout the Old and New Testaments. The gate, like Jerusalem, was moral high ground.

The city gate was indeed a most important place, sometimes referred to as the forum of the city. It played a large part in the daily life of the cities of Judaism. It was a roofed portion in the city wall with an open concourse where the judges and elders of the city sat daily to consult about current affairs and to give judgment and make decisions. It is said of the virtuous woman in Proverbs 31 that "Her husband is known in the gates, when he sitteth among the elders of the land" (Prov 31.23). Business transactions were agreed here and disputes were settled. It was the place where one could expect justice and right judgment. As Deuteronomy 16.18 states, "Judges and officers shalt thou make thee in all thy gates, which the Lord thy God giveth thee, throughout thy tribes: and they shall judge the people with just judgment". However, that is a sad comment of the Psalmist David, spoken prophetically of the Messiah in His rejection, "They that sit in the gate speak against me" (Ps 69.12).

The gates were associated too with the commercial life of the city. Markets were often held here, so that the gate at times adopted the name of a particular market, as "The Fish Gate" and "The Sheep Gate". References to "the gate of the city" in the Old Testament are too numerous to mention but it may be remembered that it was at the gate that Absalom won the hearts of the people after casting aspersion on the ability of his father the king to give proper judgment. To quote, "And Absalom rose up early, and stood beside the way of the gate: and it was so, that when any man that had a controversy came to the king for judgment, then Absalom called unto him, and said, Of what city art thou? And he said, Thy servant is of one of the tribes of Israel. And Absalom said unto him, See, thy matters are good and right; but there is no man deputed of the king to hear thee. Absalom said moreover, Oh that I were made judge in the land, that every man which hath any suit or cause might come unto me, and I would do him justice! And it was so, that when any man came nigh to him to do him obeisance, he put forth his hand, and took him, and kissed him. And on this manner did Absalom to all Israel that came to the king for judgment: so Absalom stole the hearts of the men of Israel" (2 Sam 15.2-6).

It was most probable, perhaps almost certain, that the kinsman of whom Boaz had spoken would at some time during the morning pass through the city gate, and soon indeed it was so. As the kinsman in question came by Boaz hailed him, calling out, "Ho, such a one! turn aside, sit down here". It is unthinkable that Boaz did not know the name of his kinsman, but for some reason, not fully known, his name is never given. Various reasons for this have been suggested. Morris writes that "The Hebrew uses two words of address with a meaning rather like our 'so-and-so'". Could it be, some ask, that the author of Ruth did not know the man's identity? Delitzsch comments, "Boaz would certainly call him by his name; but the historian had either not heard the name, or did not think it necessary to give it". Soon it will be revealed that the anonymous kinsman would refuse to play the part of redeemer as far as Ruth was concerned lest it might affect his own inheritance. It may well be that his name is being deliberately withheld, the chronicler concealing the identity of the man because of a reluctance to expose him who refused to redeem the Moabitess. Whatever the reason, it is indeed significant that the unwilling kinsman must now be anonymous for ever. Morris quotes Cassel who says, "It remains an instructive fact that he who was so anxious for the preservation of his own inheritance, is now not even known by name". Perhaps because of his unwillingness to act as redeemer, his identity is concealed by divine decree, as will be considered later.

But, to return to the story, Boaz now summons ten men of the elders of the city, saying to them as he had said to his kinsman, "Sit ye down here". The elders were the heads of leading families in the city, and it is very probable that Boaz himself was reckoned among the elders. Edersheim writes that these elders were to be witnesses or umpires, "the number *ten* being not only symbolical of completeness, but from immemorial custom, and afterwards by law, that which constituted a legal assembly". Another says that it was "the quorum required for the recital of the marriage benedictions. Boaz held them in readiness for the pending ceremony" (Slotki). It was also the minimum number required for a synagogue service, which requirement prevails among Jews even today. Then, as will be considered later, the Commandments of Exodus 20 were ten in number, hence known as the Decalogue.

Verses 3-6: The Proposition

Boaz now explains to his kinsman, in the presence of the elders, the reason for their present assembly. Notice, too, that the gate of the city being an open public place people of the town had gathered with them, probably curious to know what was happening (v.9). There are several difficulties in the verses which follow, particularly for those of other cultures, not conversant with Jewish custom. Perhaps there are textual difficulties also which must be noticed.

There would appear to be reason for believing that Boaz must have had some discussion and agreement with Naomi and Ruth which has not been recorded. The women must both have acquiesced regarding his proposition to the kinsman, and this proposition he now states. "And he said unto the kinsman, Naomi, that is come again out of the country of Moab, selleth a parcel of land, which was our brother Elimelech's: And I thought to advertise thee, saying, Buy it before the inhabitants, and before the elders of my people. If thou wilt redeem it, redeem it: but if thou wilt not redeem it, then tell me, that I may know: for there is none to redeem it beside thee; and I am after thee". Boaz and the other man were therefore the sole surviving kinsmen of the family of Elimelech. The word "brother" (ACH - 251) is not to be understood in any narrow sense. Strong says that this is a primitive word, used in the widest sense of literal relationship as kindred. The Brown-Driver-Briggs Lexicon states that the word implies a relative, kinship, of the same tribe.

A difficulty arises from the fact that the land was Naomi's. In the detailed regulations of Numbers 27.8-11 there is no reference to the rights of the widow. "And thou shalt speak unto the children of Israel, saying, If a man die, and have no son, then ye shall cause his inheritance to pass unto his daughter. And if he have no daughter, then ye shall give his inheritance unto his brethren. And if he have no brethren, then ye shall give his inheritance unto his father's brethren. And if his father have no brethren, then ye shall give his inheritance unto his kinsman that is next to him of his family, and he shall possess it: and it shall be unto the children of Israel a statute of judgment, as the Lord commanded Moses". It may be, of course, that there the wife is presumed dead. If still alive, with no sons, then she might marry the *go'el*, the kinsman-redeemer, and the son of that union would inherit the property. Such however was not a feasible proposition for the aged Naomi. In later years it seems that widows did indeed succeed to land, as in the case of the widow of 2 Kings 8.1-6. Some expositors think that while the law did not provide for a widow to inherit, yet custom in later times allowed it and perhaps this indeed would have been the spirit of the law.

Then there is a textual problem. "Naomi 'selleth', or 'sells', or 'is selling' a parcel of land" is the rendering of the AV and RV and most others. Some, however, as NKJV and YLT, prefer, "Naomi (hath) sold", and with this Delitzsch, F. W. Grant, and Adam Clarke agree. Does the expression then mean that Naomi was now selling the land, or had already sold it and wished it to be redeemed? Slotki, while admitting that, literally, the term means "hath sold", yet says that "The context requires the translation to be either 'intends to sell', or 'is offering for sale'". It may be indeed that Naomi, when she returned from Moab in penury, had, soon after their return, sold the land to support herself and her daughter-in-law as Leviticus 25.25

had prescribed: "If thy brother be waxen poor, and hath sold away some of his possession, and if any of his kin come to redeem it, then shall he redeem that which his brother sold". The "parcel of land" of which Boaz speaks was in fact an allotment in the common grain field. Such fields were not divided by hedges or fences, but, as has been mentioned earlier, by trodden paths or stone landmarks (2.3). Naomi had inherited rights to this allotment as the widow of Elimelech, and if she had in fact sold the land earlier she now wanted it redeemed or bought back. Otherwise she was just now offering it for sale to a next-of-kin. Slotki bases his understanding of the verse, previously mentioned, on the fact that v.5 speaks of buying the field "of the hand of Naomi" and not of some earlier purchaser. Leon Morris also concedes that "the verb 'selleth' is in the perfect tense in Hebrew, a tense which normally describes completed action". But while agreeing that the perfect tense could denote a past sale, and that some others concur with this, he adds, like Slotki, that "it seems to be ruled out, however, by 4.5, which views the sale as future, and by 4.9, where it is imminent".

Whichever is the correct reading, the land was now for sale and Boaz apprises his unnamed kinsman of this fact, he being the true near kinsman. This kinsman replied very quickly, but was apparently not fully aware of all that was involved. His answer is abrupt, "I will redeem it". But Boaz explains. "The day you buy the field from the hand of Naomi, you are also buying Ruth the Moabitess, the widow of the dead, in order to restore the name of the dead to his inheritance". This is the rendering of RSV, NIV, NAS, supported, says Morris, by Moffatt, Knox, and Berkeley, as also by the old Latin Vulgate and Syriac Versions. Perhaps, in relation to Ruth, the preferred word is "acquire", rather than "buy". With the privilege of buying the land there came the duty of acquiring Ruth, to raise up seed to the deceased Mahlon, elder son of Elimelech. No one could have the privilege without accepting the duty.

As Barnes writes, "If there had been no one interested but Naomi, she would have sold the land unclogged by any condition, the law of Levirate having no existence in her case. But there was a young widow upon whom the possession of the land would devolve at Naomi's death, and who already had a right of partnership in it, and the law of Levirate did apply in her case. It was, therefore, the duty of the *go'el* to marry her and raise up seed to his brother, i.e. his kinsman. And he could not exercise his right of redeeming the land, unless he was willing at the same time to fulfil his obligations to the deceased by marrying the widow".

The unnamed kinsman now changes his mind! Perhaps there is a practical lesson here that one should, as far as is possible, be aware of all the implications and probabilities before making hasty decisions. The man who so quickly had said, "I will redeem it", now, knowing all the circumstances, says, "I cannot redeem it". For this kinsman of Boaz things are different now! He says, "I cannot redeem it for myself, lest I mar mine own inheritance: redeem thou my right to thyself; for I cannot redeem it". What does he mean? Most expositors agree that if it had been just a matter of buying the field, with no other implications, then any monies expended on such a purchase would of course have enlarged and augmented his own property. This was not only acceptable but in fact desirable. It would have been shrewd and prudent business to buy. However, marrying Ruth would mean that any son of their marriage would by right inherit the land. Was he then parting with some of his wealth, expending some of his own capital to buy the field in question, only to see a possible succession of the land to a son of Ruth? This would not be an augmentation but rather a diminution of his own inheritance. "I cannot", he says. Does he really mean, "I cannot", or should it rather be, "I will not"? Would he be buying land for the son of a Moabitess?

This raises another suggestion. Notice that Boaz here speaks of Ruth as "the Moabitess". Was this reference to her Moabitish origin a deliberate strategy on the part of Boaz? Did he hope that it might be a deterrent to his kinsman? He did, after all, want Ruth for himself! Would this nearer kinsman be afraid of the stigma of Moab. Many think that this was the real reason for his unwillingness. As another writes, in agreement with this, "The background of Ruth was the obvious hindrance. A childless widow coming from Moab on the far side of the Jordan had nothing attractive about her to the nearer kinsman. She was from Moab and the Scripture was clear, 'An Ammonite or Moabite shall not enter into the congregation of the Lord; even to their tenth generation they shall not enter into the congregation of the Lord for ever' (Deut 23.3). She is called Ruth the Moabitess...and the associated stigma is obvious...It is obvious that the unnamed kinsman only thinks of Moab and all that is associated with it. He seems to completely overlook the fact that Ruth has turned her back upon the land of her nativity forever and thus is now a Jewish proselyte. She has taken refuge under the wings of Jehovah...She is indeed a true daughter of Sarah" (Kane). Delitzsch says, "However it was, this kinsman, when he heard the conditions of the bargain, refused it (v.6): 'I cannot redeem it for myself. I will not meddle with it upon these terms, lest I mar my own inheritance'. The land, he thought, would be an improvement of his inheritance, but not the land with the woman; that would mar it. Perhaps he thought it would be a disparagement to him to marry such a poor widow that had come from a strange country, and almost lived upon alms. He fancied it would be a blemish to his family, it would mar his blood, and disgrace his posterity". So, he says, "I cannot redeem it", and he renounces his rights as redeemer and assigns these to his kinsman Boaz with the ceremony which followed.

What irony is this, that the man who selfishly tried to preserve and protect his inheritance has now gone into oblivion. His name has perished out of Israel. No one, not even the most accurate and meticulous of Jewish archivists, has any knowledge of his identity. He will remain for ever in obscurity and anonymity while the names of Boaz and the Moabitess live on, enshrined in the genealogies of the illustrious King David and of the Messiah Himself (Mt 1.5-6).

Many writers on the book of Ruth have seen in the unnamed kinsman a picture of the law, with its inability to redeem. Some will argue, however, that this cannot be in that the kinsman was able but not willing, whereas the law was just not able to redeem. This is strictly not correct reasoning. The kinsman says, "I cannot", and whatever the reason for it, he was not able. Ten men witness these interesting events in Bethlehem. Samuel Ridout says, "A jury of ten men, witnesses of the law and facts. These ten may well remind us of those 'ten words' or commandments which bear full testimony to the claims of God, the ruin of man, and their own powerlessness to redeem...The law itself witnesses to its own powerlessness to redeem". "So", he adds, "the law transfers its claims to Another. How good it is to know that the law was our schoolmaster till Christ".

Verses 7-8: The Ceremony of the Shoe

It is important to distinguish between the legal requirements detailed in Deuteronomy 25.5-10 and the ceremony in Ruth 4.7-8. The former passage envisages the case of a deceased husband's brother, the widow's brother-in-law (YABAM - 2992), who was legally bound to marry the widow and raise up seed to his brother. In the case of this unnamed kinsman there was no such legal binding. The distant relationship may have excused him, but had he been able and willing to act in the spirit of the law he would have taken Ruth as wife. When, as stated in the Deuteronomy passage, the brother-in-law of the deceased refused to perform the duty required of him, then he was treated with contempt. "Then shall his brother's wife come unto him in the presence of the elders, and loose his shoe from off his foot, and spit in his face, and shall answer and say, So shall it be done unto that man that will not build up his brother's house". It was an ignominious ceremony indeed, but here the deceased brother's wife, Ruth, is apparently not even present. It was the unnamed kinsman himself who voluntarily pulled off his shoe to give to Boaz. There was no need for any further humiliation in the contemptuous spitting in the face prescribed in Deuteronomy 25.9.

Again, some expositors suggest that there is really no connection at all here with the Deuteronomy ceremony. They point out that in Ruth 4.7 it was an accepted custom in Israel, and indeed among other peoples too, for the confirmation of any transaction between neighbours. Drawing off the shoe and handing it to another was a symbolical act signifying the giving up of rights of possession. The shoe is that which treads on the ground and, as Delitzsch writes, "The custom itself, which existed among the Indians and the ancient Germans, arose from the fact that fixed property was taken possession of by treading upon the soil, and hence taking off the shoe and handing it to another was a symbol of the transfer of a possession or right of ownership". Compare the word to Joshua just prior to entering the Promised Land: "Every place that the sole of your foot shall tread upon, that have I given unto you, as I said unto Moses" (Josh 1.3). The unnamed kinsman had conceded his rights to Boaz by giving him his shoe.

Verses 9-12: Marriage

Boaz now turns from his kinsman to address the elders and the people. Twice he says, "Ye are witnesses" and the people reply, "We are witnesses". Everything is legal and orderly. He says, "Ye are witnesses this day, that I have bought all that was Elimelech's, and all that was Chilion's and Mahlon's, of the hand of Naomi". He had redeemed the family possessions. But there was more! "Moreover", he says, "Ruth the Moabitess, the wife of Mahlon, have I purchased to be my wife, to raise up the name of the dead upon his inheritance, that the name of the dead be not cut off from among his brethren, and from the gate of his place: ye are witnesses this day". Slotki, himself a Jewish commentator, has here a nice observation, with practical implications too. He writes, "There is a delicacy in the manner in which Boaz mentions the acquisition of Ruth. He does not refer to it in the same breath as he speaks of his purchase of the property, but gives the act a due weight and importance all its own; as if to stress the distinction between acquiring a wife and acquiring mere chattels. Although the same legal terminology is employed, the analogy ends there and never in Jewish law is the wife regarded as anything but a partner in the sacred duty of building a home". Notice that it is only here that we learn that Ruth was the wife of Mahlon. Boaz pays the redemption price for the land and his bride, and there is a most beautiful foreshadowing of Messiah the Redeemer. What a price He has paid to purchase His Bride and to recover the creation which the first man forfeited by his disobedience. He has endured the suffering of death "so that by the grace of God he should taste death for every thing" (Heb 2.9, JND). One day, when the great Kinsman-Redeemer is manifested in glory with His Bride, the cry will resound throughout the heavens: "The kingdoms of this world are become the kingdoms of our Lord, and of his Christ; and he shall reign for ever and ever" (Rev 11.15). "Thou art worthy…for thou wast slain, and hast redeemed us to God by thy blood out of every kindred, and tongue, and people, and nation" (Rev 5.9).

It is interesting to observe that although every believer in the Lord Jesus rejoices to have a personal knowledge of the Lord Jesus as Saviour, there are only two occasions in Scripture where the expression "My Redeemer" occurs. They are Job 19.25 and Psalm 19.14 - David and Job in their day join in extolling the lovely title. David had been speaking much in that Psalm about sin. There were sins of ignorance. There were presumptuous sins. There were secret sins and great transgressions. Where can he look for help? In the closing verse of his Psalm he lifts his eyes Godward, exclaiming, "O Lord, my strength and my redeemer"! Job has a problem too. He has had more than his share of sorrow. He has lost so much of his family, his wealth, and his health. Those presuming to be his friends were but "miserable comforters", and even his wife had failed to understand. Like David, he looks away from it all, saying, "I know that my redeemer liveth". Whether it is deliverance from sin or release from sorrow, these early saints have found the answer – My Redeemer! The saint today rejoices in the same and sings:

My Redeemer! O what beauties
In that lovely Name appear;
None but Jesus, in His glories,
Shall the honoured title wear.
My Redeemer!
Thou hast my salvation wrought.

By this time, no doubt, a large number of the townspeople had gathered at the gate. What lively conversation there must have been! How the women would comment, and reminisce, and envisage the future. Some of them had known Naomi and Elimelech in their earlier days. They would remember them leaving Bethlehem with their boys, and now they are delighted at the impending marriage of their wealthy and noble neighbour with the young widow of Mahlon. Boaz had proved himself unselfish and honourable in all these dealings and the people pronounce a lovely benediction upon the union: "The Lord make the woman that is come into thine house like Rachel and like Leah, which two did build the house of Israel: and do thou worthily in Ephratah, and be famous in Bethlehem". Ephratah and Bethlehem are of course the same place.

Rachel and Leah were the daughters of Laban and the wives of Jacob. Rachel, although she is mentioned first, and died first, was the younger of the two. She was Jacob's favourite and chosen wife. He had been deceived by Laban their father into marrying Leah first, a deception which Laban justified on the grounds that it was the custom of the country that the older daughter should be the first to marry. Leah bore more children to Jacob than did Rachel. Rachel was the mother of Joseph and Benjamin and died giving birth to the latter (Gen 35.16-18). She was buried on the way to Bethlehem, and her tomb, situated on the Bethlehem Road a little south of Jerusalem, is still revered by Jews, particularly by young Jewish women anxious to bear children and raise a family. Leah, the older sister, bore Jacob six sons and one daughter. She is buried in the family grave in Hebron in the cave of Machpelah where Abraham and Sarah, Isaac and Rebekah are also buried (Gen 49.31).

Rachel and Leah therefore were true mothers in Israel, and from them the twelve tribes were descended. The sons of Bilhah and Zilpah their handmaids, were reckoned to be the sons of Rachel and Leah respectively. The people pray that Ruth may be as fruitful as Rachel and Leah and that Boaz may become as notable and as renowned in Bethlehem as was the patriarch Jacob in his day.

Their benediction and prayer continues, "And let thy house be like the house of Pharez, whom Tamar bare unto Judah, of the seed which the Lord shall give thee of this young woman". This was a most appropriate reference since Tamar's situation was not unlike that of Ruth. The story is told in Genesis 38. Pharez moreover, was one of Boaz's ancestors, and perhaps indeed the ancestor of the Bethlehemites in general. He too is mentioned in the genealogy of the Messiah in Matthew 1.3. The prayer of the people is that the household of Boaz and Ruth may become as honourable and as numerous as that of Pharez.

Verses 13-17: A Child is Born

A period of at least nine months is now embraced in one verse. Boaz and Ruth have consummated their marriage. The girl from Moab is now the wife of the mighty Boaz; she has conceived, and the Lord has given them a son. Was it by divine intervention, that Ruth, who was childless while married to the young Mahlon, should bear a son to the elderly Boaz? Slotki points out that the peculiar construction of the text, "the Lord gave her conception", leads the Jewish *Midrash* to suggest that a miracle had occurred. Ruth the stranger and Ruth the gleaner, is now Ruth the mother in the house of Boaz, and there is general rejoicing in Bethlehem, particularly among the women. It will be remembered that it was the women who had said so sadly, as they looked on the forlorn and weary figure coming out of Moab, "Is this Naomi?" (1.19). Such a change Jehovah had wrought for her. Now it is the same women who say to Naomi, "Blessed be the Lord, which hath not left thee this day without a kinsman, that his name may be famous in Israel". But the kinsman now, the *go'el*, the redeemer, is not Boaz, but the new-born son, born to perpetuate the name of the family in Israel. What a foreshadowing of Messiah! A baby born in Bethlehem! A kinsman to redeem!

The lovely benediction continues with a delightful tribute to the fidelity and faithfulness of Ruth. "And he shall be unto thee a restorer of thy life, and a nourisher of thine old age: for thy daughter in law, which loveth thee, which is better to thee than seven sons, hath born him". Delitzsch comments: "A mother of so many sons was to be congratulated, inasmuch as she not only possessed in these sons a powerful support to her old age, but had the prospect of the permanent continuance of her family. Naomi, however, had a still more valuable treasure in her daughter-in-law, inasmuch as through her the loss of her own sons had been supplied in her old age, and the prospect was now presented to her of becoming in her childless old age the tribe-mother of a numerous and flourishing family". With the birth of her grandson Naomi would live again! The emptiness of the sad years in Moab was gone forever. Now there was something, and someone, to live for. Ruth had been more to her than seven sons, had loved her and borne a son for her, and she would now be sustained and provided for in her "old age", an interesting expression akin to "grey hairs" (7872), and translated "hoar hairs" in Isaiah 46.4.

With what mixed emotions the elderly grandmother must have taken the little one in her arms and held him to her bosom. There must have been times in the past when she had abandoned hope of ever having a grandchild. There had been dark and lonely days in Moab, but now it was different. She was home now, in Bethlehem where she belonged, with people whom she knew and with a loving daughter-in-law and with a kinsman to sustain her into old age. She would nurse this little one as if he were her own son and the neighbour women said, as they looked on and saw her joy and affection, "There is a son born to Naomi". This child would be her kinsman and redeemer, her deliverer from childlessness and reproach.

"And the women her neighbours gave it a name, saying, There is a son born to Naomi; and they called his name Obed." The meaning is that they called out a name, they suggested a name, or, as Adam Clarke writes, "That is, they recommended a name suitable to the circumstances of the case; and the parents and grandmother adopted it". Five men are called Obed in the Old Testament. They are all interesting personalities:

Obed, son of Ruth and Boaz, father of Jesse; grandfather of King David (Ruth 4.17).

Obed, a descendant of Jarha, the Egyptian slave of Sheshan, (1 Chr 2.37,38).

Obed, one of David's mighty men (1 Chr 11.47).

Obed, one of the gate-keepers of the temple; grandson of Obed-edom (1 Chr 26.4,7).

Obed, father of Azariah, a captain in the revolution by which Athaliah fell (2 Chr 23.1).

There are two suggested meanings of the name Obed. Many expositors think it means "servant", while several others prefer "worshipper". Some have combined the two meanings as "servant and worshipper". This is probably acceptable since Obed must have devotedly served his aged grandmother Naomi, and devoted service is in itself a form of worship. As Adam Clarke writes, "They called his name Obed, *`Owbeed* (5744), serving, from *`aabad* (5647), he served. Why was this name given? Because he was to be the nourisher of her (Naomi's) old age. And so he must be by lying in her bosom, even if services in future life were wholly left out of the question". He adds, "Other meanings, of which I am not ignorant, have been derived from these words; those who prefer them have my consent".

Verses 18-22: The Genealogy

The story of Ruth the Moabitess is now all but concluded, but its end is brighter than its beginning. The story which commenced with famine and funerals is ending with a happy family in Bethlehem of Judea. The family genealogy will lead up to David, and so, eventually, to Messiah. The book began in the sad days of the judges when there was no king in Israel but it concludes with David, the illustrious king and sweet psalmist of Israel. As in the genealogy of Matthew 1 some generations may be omitted here, but of this none can be sure. What is certain is that the generations which are mentioned magnify both the grace and the sovereignty of God. Sovereignty has maintained, without question, the lineage of the Coming One. As another writes, "It is evident that our Lord sprang out of Juda" (Heb 7.14). Grace has wrought with sovereignty and has brought into the lineage of Messiah the most unlikely of persons, as Tamar, Rahab, and Ruth from Moab. Bathsheba too is in the genealogy, not mentioned by name in Matthew 1 but nevertheless identified as the wife of Uriah.

Notice the earlier reference to ten men who acted as witnesses to the marriage of Boaz and Ruth (4.2), and notice again the significance of the number ten. Now, again, ten men are witnesses to the ways and purpose of God. Five of these are from the far side of Jordan and five are from Canaan. They are indeed representative men.

The names of these latter ten men are,

Pharez	Gen 38.29
Hezron	Gen 46.12
Ram, also called Aram	Mt 1.3
Amminadab	Ex 6.23
Nahshon	Num 1.7
Salmon, also called Salma	1 Chr 2.11; Mt 1.4-5
Boaz	1 Chr 2.11
Obed	1 Chr 2.12
Jesse	1 Chr 2.12
David	1 Sam 16.19.

Observe that the genealogy begins with Pharez of the tribe of Judah, so establishing David's descent from Judah and the lineage of David's greater Son, the Lion of the tribe of Judah.

John Watt concludes his brief commentary on the book of Ruth with this observation: "Were this little book omitted from the canon of Scripture, it would be an irreparable loss; a most important link would be missing between the judges and the kings; and in Ruth's position in the genealogy of our Lord, in spite of the law expressly levelled to keep the Moabitess out, as another has said, 'We find but another utterance of this selfsame story of grace which, in so many languages, our God so joys to tell'".

So ends this delightful little pastoral. The thoughtful reader is left with the intriguing, but unanswerable question: "Did Ruth live to see and know her great-grandson David?". Could she have seen him on his throne as King David the sweet psalmist of Israel? It is, of course, not beyond the bounds of physical possibility, though if it were indeed so it is perhaps then strange that there is no reference to her in the history of David's life or in his many Psalms. Maybe, if by an earlier decease she was denied seeing him in his days of triumph and glory, she was also preserved from the heartbreak of knowing his sad failings. We cannot tell. Slotki however, writes, "Tradition ascribes to Ruth unusual longevity. She did not die, says a *Midrashic* comment, until after beholding her royal descendant Solomon sitting and judging the case of the two harlots (1 Kings 3.16)". This is though, as Slotki himself admits, tradition only. Since Scripture is silent on the matter of Ruth's death there is no way of knowing, and perhaps we are not intended to know. Everything in the story of Ruth leads up to David, and so the genealogy of the Christ is confirmed. He is, as has been said, "The Lion of the tribe of Juda" (Rev 5.5). To Him be glory!